DERIVATION RULES OF *SD*+

All the Derivation Rules of *SD* and Rules of Inference

Modus Tollens (MT)

$$\begin{array}{l|l} & P \supset Q \\ & \sim Q \\ \rhd & \sim P \end{array}$$

Hypothetical Syllogism (HS)

$$\begin{array}{l|l} & P \supset Q \\ & Q \supset R \\ \rhd & P \supset R \end{array}$$

Disjunctive Syllogism (DS)

$$\begin{array}{l|l} & P \vee Q \\ & \sim P \\ \rhd & Q \end{array} \quad \text{or} \quad \begin{array}{l|l} & P \vee Q \\ & \sim Q \\ \rhd & P \end{array}$$

Rules of Replacement

Commutation (Com)

$P \,\&\, Q \lhd \rhd Q \,\&\, P$
$P \vee Q \lhd \rhd Q \vee P$

Implication (Impl)

$P \supset Q \lhd \rhd \sim P \vee Q$

De Morgan (DeM)

$\sim (P \,\&\, Q) \lhd \rhd \sim P \vee \sim Q$
$\sim (P \vee Q) \lhd \rhd \sim P \,\&\, \sim Q$

Transposition (Trans)

$P \supset Q \lhd \rhd \sim Q \supset \sim P$

Distribution (Dist)

$P \,\&\, (Q \vee R) \lhd \rhd (P \,\&\, Q) \vee (P \,\&\, R)$
$P \vee (Q \,\&\, R) \lhd \rhd (P \vee Q) \,\&\, (P \vee R)$

Association (Assoc)

$P \,\&\, (Q \,\&\, R) \lhd \rhd (P \,\&\, Q) \,\&\, R$
$P \vee (Q \vee R) \lhd \rhd (P \vee Q) \vee R$

Double Negation (DN)

$P \lhd \rhd \sim \sim P$

Idempotence (Idem)

$P \lhd \rhd P \,\&\, P$
$P \lhd \rhd P \vee P$

Exportation (Exp)

$P \supset (Q \supset R) \lhd \rhd (P \,\&\, Q) \supset R$

Equivalence (Equiv)

$P \equiv Q \lhd \rhd (P \supset Q) \,\&\, (Q \supset P)$
$P \equiv Q \lhd \rhd (P \,\&\, Q) \vee (\sim P \,\&\, \sim Q)$

DERIVATION RULES OF *PD*

All the Derivation Rules of *SD* and

Universal Introduction (∀I)

| P(a/x)
▷ | (∀x)P

Provided:

(i) **a** does not occur in an undischarged assumption.

(ii) **a** does not occur in (∀**x**)**P**.

Universal Elimination (∀E)

| (∀x)P
▷ | P(a/x)

Existential Introduction (∃I)

| P(a/x)
▷ | (∃x)P

Existential Elimination (∃E)

| (∃x)P
| | P(a/x)
| | ---
| | Q
▷ | Q

Provided:

(i) **a** does not occur in an undischarged assumption.

(ii) **a** does not occur in (∃**x**)**P**.

(iii) **a** does not occur in **Q**.

DERIVATION RULES OF *PD+*

All the Derivation Rules of *SD*+ and of *PD* and

Quantifier Negation (QN)

~ (∀**x**)**P** ◁ ▷ (∃**x**) ~ **P**

~ (∃**x**)**P** ◁ ▷ (∀**x**) ~ **P**

THE LOGIC BOOK

THE LOGIC BOOK

Fourth Edition

MERRIE BERGMANN *Smith College*
JAMES MOOR *Dartmouth College*
JACK NELSON *University of Washington, Tacoma*

McGraw Hill

Boston Burr Ridge, IL Dubuque, IA Madison, WI New York
San Francisco St. Louis Bangkok Bogotá Caracas Kuala Lumpur
Lisbon London Madrid Mexico City Milan Montreal New Delhi
Santiago Seoul Singapore Sydney Taipei Toronto

The McGraw-Hill Companies

Higher Education

THE LOGIC BOOK, FOURTH EDITION
Published by McGraw-Hill, a business unit of The McGraw-Hill Companies, Inc., 1221 Avenue of the Americas, New York, NY 10020.

6 7 8 9 0 DOC/DOC 0 9 8 7

ISBN: 978-0-07-240189-9
MHID: 0-07-240189-3

Vice president and editor-in-chief: *Thalia Dorwick*
Publisher: *Chris Freitag*
Sponsoring editor: *Jon-David Hague*
Marketing manager: *Lisa Berry*
Production services manager: *Jennifer Mills*
Production service: *Fairplay Publishing Service*
Manuscript editor: *Tom Briggs*
Art director: *Jeanne M. Schreiber*
Design managers: *Sharon Spurlock and Violeta Diaz*
Cover designer: *Clarie Seng-Niemoeller*
Production supervisor: *Tandra Jorgensen*

The text was set in 10/12 New Baskerville by The GTS Companies/York PA Campus and printed on acid-free, 45# New Era Matte by RR Donnelley, Crawfordsville.

Cover image: Jaco BAR-Portrait of *Luca Pacioli and an Unknown Man,* Capodimonte Museum, Naples. Photo SCALA/EPA, Inc.

Library of Congress Cataloging-in-Publication Data

Bergmann, Merrie.
The logic book / Merrie Bergmann, James Moor, Jack Nelson.—4th ed.
p. cm.
Includes bibliographical references and index.
ISBN 0-07-240189-3
1. Logic, Symbolic and mathematical. 2. Predicate (Logic) I. Moor, James II. Nelson, Jack III. Title.
BC135.B435 2003
160—dc21 2003051292

www.mhhe.com

ABOUT THE AUTHORS

MERRIE BERGMANN received her Ph.D. in philosophy from the University of Toronto. She is currently an associate professor of computer science at Smith College. She has published articles in formal semantics and logic, philosophy of logic, philosophy of language, philosophy of humor, and computational linguistics.

JAMES MOOR received his Ph.D. in history and philosophy of science from Indiana University. He is currently a professor of philosophy at Dartmouth College. He has published articles in philosophy of science, philosophy of mind, logic, philosophy of artificial intelligence, and computer ethics. He is currently editor of *Minds and Machines.*

JACK NELSON received his Ph.D. in philosophy from the University of Chicago. He is currently vice chancellor for academic affairs at the University of Washington, Tacoma. He has published articles in epistemology, identity, and the philosophy of science and is co-author, with Lynn Hankinson Nelson, of *On Quine.*

CONTENTS

PREFACE

In this fourth edition of *The Logic Book* we have added new material and rewritten some material from the previous edition, continuing with our overall goal of presenting symbolic logic in an accessible yet formally rigorous manner. This book presupposes no previous training in logic, and because it covers sentential logic through the metatheory of first-order predicate logic, it is suitable for both introductory and intermediate courses in symbolic logic.

The new material appears in Chapters 7–11, where we have augmented our formal systems with complex terms, that is, terms containing functors (the symbols that denote functions). Our treatment of complex terms is more extensive than that available in most other symbolic logic textbooks and includes innovative material in Chapters 8 and 9. Chapter 7 introduces the formal syntax of these complex terms and discusses their role in symbolization. Chapter 8 presents the semantics for complex terms containing functors, both informally and formally, and presents truth-functional expansions for sentences containing complex terms. Chapter 9 extends the tree method by modifying previous rules to accommodate complex terms and adds a new rule for "decomposing" complex terms that occur on a branch. The System is amended to correctly handle sentences with complex terms, guaranteeing open trees for sets of sentences with finite models and closed trees for inconsistent sets. Chapter 10 modifies existing natural deduction rules to cover sentences with complex terms. Finally Chapter 11 extends the metatheoretic results to reflect the new material introduced in previous chapters. Throughout we have been careful to package this new material in a way that allows an instructor to skip it, if desired.

In each chapter of the fourth edition, we have rewritten material where we thought that greater clarity was possible. We have also made the following major changes in addition to the new material on complex terms. In Chapter 2 we have added a table summarizing paraphrases and symbolizations of common English connectives and, thanks to critical analyses by David Sherry, have revised both our discussion of the relative strengths of natural language sentences and their truth-functional paraphrases and our policy governing paraphrases for the non-truth-functional compound sentences that occur in natural languages. In Chapter 3 we have added an explanation of how students can determine the appropriate truth-value assignments to use in shortened truth-tables. In Chapters 4 and 9 the basic tree concepts have been clarified and redefined to improve coherency. In Chapter 5 we have elaborated on the strategies of goal analysis in constructing derivations, with an emphasis on the purpose of auxiliary assumptions. We have also included additional discussion of the negation rules, which are typically the most difficult for students to use.

There is sufficient material in the text for a one- or two-semester course. There are several sequences of chapters that would form good syllabi for courses in symbolic logic. If an instructor has two semesters (or one semester with advanced students), it is possible to work through the entire book. The instructor who does not want to emphasize metatheory can simply omit Chapters 6 and 11. The chapters on truth-trees and the chapters on derivations are independent, so it is possible to cover truth-trees but not derivations, and vice versa. The chapters on truth-trees do depend on the chapters presenting semantics; that is, Chapter 4 depends on Chapter 3, and Chapter 9 depends on Chapter 8. And although most instructors will want to cover semantics before derivations, the opposite order is possible. Finally, in covering predicate logic, the instructor has the option in each chapter of skipping material on identity and functions, as well as the option of including the material on identity but omitting that on functions.

There are plenty of exercises in all of the chapters, including new exercises on material from previous editions and new exercises that have been added for complex terms in Chapters 7–11. Half of the exercises are answered in the *Solutions Manual* for students, and half are answered in the *Instructor's Manual.*

ACKNOWLEDGMENTS

We thank the students, readers, editors, and reviewers who have made insightful and valuable comments that have guided us in developing this fourth edition. Some students who have been especially helpful with suggestions are Joran Elias, Elyse Krantz, Matthew Levine, Alexander Liroff, Nellie McAdams, Raquel Munoz, Brian Pingree, and Daniel Preysman. The reviewers for this edition are:

Robert B. Barrett, *Washington University*
David Griesedieck, *University of Missouri–St. Louis*

Phillip McReynolds, *Pennsylvania State University*
Henry Mendell, *California State University–Los Angeles*
Katherine Shamey, *Santa Monica College*
Cindy Stern, *California State University–Northridge*
James Tappenden, *University of Michigan*
Bangs Tapscott, *University of Utah*
Scott Walden, *New York University*
Mark O. Webb, *Texas Tech University*

We are particularly grateful to Niko Scharer and Raymond Gumb for their suggestions for this edition, David Sherry for his critical analyses of our paraphrase policy in Chapter 2, Austen Clark for his derivation and truth-tree programs Bertie3 and Twootie (http://www.ucc.uconn.edu/~wwwphil/software.html), which provide excellent software supplements for this text, and our editor, Jon-David Hague, for guiding and encouraging us during the preparation of this edition.

M.B.
J.M.
J.N.

Chapter 1

BASIC NOTIONS OF LOGIC

1.1 BACKGROUND

This is a text in deductive logic—more specifically, in symbolic deductive logic. Chapters 1–5 are devoted to sentential logic, that branch of symbolic deductive logic that takes sentences as the fundamental units of logical analysis. Chapters 7–10 are devoted to predicate logic, that branch of symbolic deductive logic that takes predicates and individual terms as the fundamental units of logical analysis. Chapter 6 is devoted to the metatheory of sentential logic; Chapter 11, to the metatheory of predicate logic.

In the following chapters we will explore sentential and predicate logic in considerable detail. Here, we try to place that material in a larger context. Historically two overlapping concerns have driven research in deductive logic and the development of specific formal systems of deductive logic: the desire to formulate canons or principles of good reasoning in everyday life, as well as in science and mathematics, and the desire to formalize and systematize existing and emerging work in mathematics and science. Common to these concerns is the view that what distinguishes good reasoning from bad reasoning, and what makes good deductive reasoning "logical" as opposed to "illogical", is truth preservation.

A method or pattern of reasoning is truth-preserving if it never takes one from truths to a falsehood. The hallmark of good deductive reasoning is that it is truth-preserving. If one starts from truths and uses good deductive reasoning, the results one arrives at will also be true. Because we are all interested, as students and scholars, in everyday life and in our careers, in gaining truths and avoiding falsehoods, we all have reason to be interested in reasoning that is truth-preserving.

Most of the deductive systems of reasoning that have been developed for geometry, mathematics, and selected areas of science have been axiomatic systems. And most of us are familiar with at least one axiomatic system—that of Euclidean plane geometry. Euclid, a Greek scholar of the third century B.C., may have been the first person to develop a reasonably complete axiomatic system. Axiomatic systems start with a relatively small number of basic principles, referred to variously as axioms, definitions, postulates, and assumptions, and provide a way of deducing or deriving from them the rest of the claims or assertions of the discipline being axiomatized (in Euclid's case plane geometry). If the starting principles are significantly altered, a new theory may emerge. For example, when Euclid's fifth postulate (the parallel postulate) is modified, theorems of non-Euclidean geometry can be deduced.

Through the centuries scholars have attempted to produce axiomatic systems for a wide variety of disciplines, ranging from plane and solid geometry, to arithmetic (which was successfully axiomatized by Giuseppe Peano in 1889), to parts of the natural and social sciences. Since successful axiomatic systems use only rules of reasoning that are truth-preserving, that never take one from truths to a falsehood, the advantage of successfully axiomatizing a body of knowledge is that it makes all the claims of that body of knowledge as certain as are the starting principles and the rules of reasoning used.

At about the same time that Euclid was developing his axiomatic treatment of plane geometry, another Greek scholar, Aristotle (384–322 B.C.), was developing a general system of logic intended to incorporate the basic principles of good reasoning and to provide a way of evaluating specific cases of reasoning. The system Aristotle produced is variously known as syllogistic, traditional, or Aristotelian logic. Predecessors of Aristotle, in the Greek world and elsewhere, were interested in reasoning well—in offering cogent arguments for their theses and theories and in identifying flaws and fallacies in their own and others' reasoning. But Aristotle was apparently the first person in the Western world to offer at least the outlines of a comprehensive system for codifying and evaluating a wide range of arguments and reasoning.

The following is an argument that has the form of an Aristotelian syllogism:

All mammals are vertebrates.

Some sea creatures are mammals.

Some sea creatures are vertebrates.

The horizontal line separates the two premises of this syllogistic argument from the conclusion. This syllogism is an example of good reasoning—it constitutes a good argument—because it is truth-preserving. If the first two sentences (the premises) of the syllogism are true, the third sentence (the conclusion) must also be true. Aristotle's achievement was not in identifying this particular argument about vertebrates, mammals, and sea creatures as a good or truth-preserving argument, but rather in providing an explanation of why this and all reasoning of this form are instances of good reasoning. Aristotle would classify the preceding syllogism as being of the form

All As are Bs.
Some Cs are As.

Some Cs are Bs.

And this form or schema produces truth-preserving reasoning whenever 'A', 'B', and 'C' are uniformly replaced by general terms, as in

All cardiologists are wealthy individuals.
Some doctors are cardiologists.

Some doctors are wealthy individuals.

Aristotelian logic is a variety of deductive symbolic logic. It is symbolic because it analyzes reasoning by identifying the form or structure of good reasoning, independent of the specific content of particular instances of such reasoning. It is deductive because the requirement it lays down for good reasoning is full truth-preservation. Argument forms all of whose instances are truth preserving, as well as the arguments that are of those forms, are traditionally termed *valid*. The syllogistic form just displayed is a valid form; that is, no syllogism of this form has true premises and a false conclusion. All actual arguments that can be cast in this syllogistic form are therefore valid arguments.

An example of an *invalid* syllogistic form is

Some As are Bs.
All Cs are As.

All Cs are Bs.

There are, to be sure, actual arguments that are of this form and have true premises and a true conclusion—for example,

Some birds are hawks.
All osprey are birds.

All osprey are hawks.

But there are also arguments of this form that have true premises and a false conclusion—for example,

> Some positive numbers are even numbers.
> All numbers greater than zero are positive numbers.
> ___
> All numbers greater than zero are even numbers.

The two premises of this syllogism are true, but the conclusion, 'All numbers greater than zero are even', is false. The syllogistic form just displayed is an invalid form precisely because there are instances of it that have true premises and a false conclusion.

Aristotelian logic is very powerful. During the centuries following Aristotle, the rules and techniques associated with syllogistic logic were refined, and various test procedures developed, by Roman, Arabic, medieval, and modern logicians. Until the late nineteenth century Aristotelian logic remained the predominant system for formalizing and evaluating reasoning. It is still taught today in many introductory courses.

Nonetheless, there are important drawbacks to Aristotelian logic. Syllogisms are at the heart of Aristotelian logic, and each syllogism must have exactly two premises and a conclusion. Moreover, every sentence of a syllogism must be of one of the four following forms:

> All As are Bs.
> No As are Bs.
> Some As are Bs.
> Some As are not Bs.

Aristotelian logic is thus best suited to reasoning about relations among groups: 'All members of this group are members of that group', 'Some members of this group are members of that group', and so on. Aristotelian logic thus strains to handle reasoning about individuals. For example, 'Socrates is human' must be recast as something like 'All things that are Socrates [there is, we here assume, only one] are things that are human'.

The Aristotelian requirement that every conclusion be drawn from exactly two premises is unduly restrictive and does not mirror the complexity of actual reasoning and argumentation, a single instance of which may make use of a very large number of premises. Consider, for example, the following reasoning:

> Sarah and Hank are the only finalists for a position with Bowles, Blithers, and Blimy, an accounting firm. Whoever is hired will have a baccalaureate degree in accounting. Hank will get his baccalaureate in accounting only if he passes all the business courses he is taking this semester and completes the general education requirements.

> Sarah will get her baccalaureate only if she passes all her courses and raises her grade point average to 2.5. Hank will fail logic and so will not complete the general education requirements. Sarah will pass all her courses, but her grade point average will not reach 2.5. Therefore Bowles, Blithers, and Blimy will hire neither of the finalists.

The above reasoning is truth-preserving. That is, if the premises are all true, then the conclusion, the last sentence of the paragraph, must also be true. But it would be extremely difficult to recast this chain of reasoning in syllogistic terms.

Finally reasoning that relies on relations[1] cannot readily be accommodated within Aristotelian logic. For example, the reasoning 'Sarah is taller than Tom, and Tom is taller than Betty; therefore Sarah is taller than Betty' presupposes the transitivity of the taller-than relation, that is, presupposes the following truth:

> For any three things, if the first is taller than the second, and the second is taller than the third, then the first is taller than the third.

Principles such as the above and arguments relying on them cannot be incorporated within the Aristotelian framework in any intuitive way.

For these and other reasons, logicians in the mid-to-late 1800s looked for alternatives to Aristotelian logic. This work involved the development of systems of sentential logic, that is, systems based on the way sentences of natural languages can be generated from other sentences by the use of such expressions as 'or', 'and', 'if . . . then . . .', and 'not'. Consider this example:

> Karen is either in Paris or in Nairobi. She is not in Nairobi. So Karen is in Paris.

Simple arguments such as this one are not readily represented within syllogistic logic. Yet the argument is clearly an example of good reasoning. Whenever the first two sentences are true, the last sentence is also true. Reasoning of this sort can readily be symbolized in systems of sentential logic.

On the other hand, sentential logic cannot easily deal with reasoning that rests on claims about all, some, or none of this sort of thing being of that sort—the sort of claims Aristotelian logic can often handle. Predicate logic incorporates sentential logic and is also able to handle all the kinds of sentences that are expressible in Aristotelian logic, as well as many of those that pose difficulties for Aristotelian logic.

---

[1]See Chapter 7 for an explication of relations.

1.2 WHY STUDY LOGIC?

There are a variety of reasons for studying logic. It is a well-developed discipline that many find interesting in its own right, a discipline that has a rich history and important current research programs and practical applications. Certainly, anyone who plans to major or do graduate work in areas such as philosophy, mathematics, computer science, or linguistics should have a solid grounding in symbolic logic. In general, the study of formal logic also helps develop the skills needed to present and evaluate arguments in any discipline.

Another reason for studying symbolic logic is that, in learning to symbolize natural language sentences (in our case English sentences) in a formal language, students become more aware and more appreciative of the importance of the structure and complexities of natural languages. Precisely what words are used often has a major bearing on whether an argument is valid or invalid, a piece of reasoning convincing or unconvincing. For example, distinguishing between 'Roberta will pass if she completes all the homework' and 'Roberta will pass only if she completes all the homework' is essential to anyone who wants to reason well about the prospects for Roberta's passing.

However, the focus of this text is not primarily on sharpening the critical and evaluative skills readers bring to bear on everyday discourse, newspaper columns, and the rhetoric of politicians. Inculcating these skills is the goal of texts on "critical thinking" or "informal logic", where the primary emphasis is on nonformal techniques for identifying fallacies, figuring out puzzles, and constructing persuasive arguments. Formal or symbolic logic, which is the domain of this book, is a discipline with its own body of theory and results, just as are mathematics and physics. This text is an introduction to that discipline, a discipline whose principles underlie the techniques presented in informal logic texts. This text will help readers not only identify good and bad arguments but also understand why arguments are good arguments or bad arguments. Even though only the most avid devotees of formal systems will be constructing truth-tables, truth-trees, or derivations after completing this text, mastering these formal techniques is a way of coming to understand the principles underlying reasoning and the relations among sentences and sets of sentences.

There is another, quite practical, reason for studying symbolic logic. In most of the chapters that follow, the discussion will center on seven or fewer central concepts. These concepts are related, from chapter to chapter. For example, the concept of truth-functional validity developed in Chapter 3 is one way of refining the concept of logical validity laid out in this chapter. All these concepts are abstract. They cannot be touched or weighed or examined under a microscope. Mastering these concepts and the relations among them is an exercise in abstract thinking. The skills involved are, we think, important and will be useful in a wide variety of theoretical and applied fields. For these reasons the "theory questions" found at the end of most exercise sets are in many ways the most important part of the exercise sets.

1.3 SENTENCES, TRUTH-VALUES, AND ARGUMENTS

'True' and 'false' are properties of sentences. That is, it is sentences that are either true or false.[2] Throughout this text we will use the notion of a *truth-value.* We will say that true sentences have the truth-value **T**, and false sentences the truth-value **F**. 'Washington, DC, is the capital of the United States' and 'The volume of a gas is directly proportional to its temperature and inversely proportional to its pressure' are both true, and so both have the truth-value **T**. The truth of the first derives from the political organization of the United States, and the truth of the second from the fundamentals of physics and chemistry. 'Toronto is the capital of Canada' and 'Atoms are indivisible' are both false, so both have the truth-value **F**—the first for reasons having to do with the political organization of Canada, and the second for reasons having to do with the existence and behavior of subatomic particles. Although it is only sentences that are either true or false, not every sentence of English is one or the other. Sentences that are obviously neither true nor false include questions ('Where is Kansas City?'), requests ('Please shut the door when you leave'), commands ('Don't darken my door again'), and exclamations ('Ouch!'). The formal systems we develop in this text are intended to deal only with sentences that are either true or false as asserted on a particular occasion in a particular context. To say that the sentences we will be dealing with are those that are either true or false is not, of course, to say that for any given sentence we know which it is, true or false, but only that it is one or the other.

Much of this text is devoted to the study of arguments. Previously, in discussing syllogistic arguments, we presented them by listing the premises following by the conclusion, with a horizontal line separating the premises from the conclusion. Arguments so displayed are presented in *standard form.* Of course, in natural languages, whether in spoken discourse or in writing, arguments are rarely presented in standard form. Indeed, in English and other natural languages, arguments, or bits of reasoning that can be reconstructed as one or more arguments, generally neither occur in what we call standard form nor are set off from preceding and following discourse. Moreover, the premises are not always given first and the conclusion last. Consider

> Michael will not get the job, for whoever gets the job will have strong references, and Michael's references are not strong.

[2]Many philosophical disputes arise about such basic concepts as sentences, meaning, context, and truth. For example, some philosophers argue that propositions are the kinds of entities that are really true or false, propositions being taken to be the meanings of sentences and to exist independently of any particular language. Other philosophers eschew propositions as unnecessary metaphysical baggage. Because we have to adopt some terminology and because all philosophers agree that sentences play some role in language, we shall talk of sentences as being true or false. But we consider such talk to be shorthand for talk of sentences that have certain meanings as used in particular contexts.

This single sentence can be recast as the following explicit argument in standard form:

> Whoever gets the job will have strong references.
>
> Michael's references are not strong.
>
> ---
>
> Michael will not get the job.

As we just saw, in everyday discourse the conclusion is sometimes given before the premises. The conclusion can also come between premises, with the whole argument being buried in an ongoing text:

> I've got more relatives than I know what to do with. I've got relatives in Idaho and in New Jersey, in Ireland and in Israel. Among them are a couple of cousins, Tom and Fred Culverson. Both Tom and Fred are hard working, and Tom is as tenacious as a bulldog. So Tom is sure to be a success, for if there is one thing I have learned in life, it is that everyone who is both hard working and tenacious succeeds. But I'm sure success won't change Tom. He'll work just as hard after he makes his first million as he does now. He is, after all, a Culverson. And no one is as predictable as a Culverson, unless it's a Hutchings. There are lots of Hutchings on my mother's side, but I haven't had much to do with them. . . .

The following explicit argument can be extracted from this passage and placed in standard form:

> Tom and Fred are hard working.
>
> Tom is tenacious.
>
> Everyone who is both hard working and tenacious succeeds.
>
> ---
>
> Tom will succeed.

There is a lot of information in this passage that is not relevant to the specific argument we have extracted. This is frequently the case.

The first step in analyzing arguments is to extract them from the discourse within which they are embedded and present them in standard form. Doing so requires practice. In natural language the presence of an argument is often signaled by the use of premise and/or conclusion indicator words. *Conclusion indicator words*—that is, words indicating that what follows is intended as the conclusion of an argument—include

> therefore
> thus
> it follows that

so
hence
consequently
as a result

Premise indicator words—that is, words whose use signals that what follows is intended as a premise of an argument—include

since
for
because
on account of
inasmuch as
for the reason that

Not every piece of discourse is intended as an argument. Consider

> Our galaxy is made up of our sun and billions of other stars. The galaxy is a huge, flat spiral system that rotates like a wheel, and the myriad of stars move around its center somewhat as the planets revolve around our sun. There are millions of other galaxies in addition to our galaxy.

Each of the sentences in this passage is either true or false, but there is no good reason to treat one of the sentences as a conclusion and the others as premises.

So far we have given examples of arguments, talked about them, and presented several of them in standard form. But we have not defined 'argument', and it is time do so. In our definition we make use, as we frequently will throughout the rest of this text, of the notion of a set of sentences. Sets are abstract objects that have members (no members, one member, two members, . . . an infinite number of members). The identity of a set is determined by its members. That is, if set A and set B have exactly the same members, then they are the same set; if they do not, they are different sets.

> An *argument* is a set of two or more sentences, one of which is designated as the conclusion and the others as the premises.

This is a very broad notion of an argument. For example, it allows us to count the following as an argument:

Herbert is four years old.

The sun will shine tomorrow.

This is, of course, a paradigm of a bad argument. The one premise supplies no support whatsoever for the conclusion. The advantage of this broad definition is that it sidesteps the problem of having to give an account of how plausible a line of reasoning has to be to count as an argument or of how likely it is that a given group of sentences will be taken to support a designated sentence in order for those sentences together to count as an argument.

Given our broad definition, we could recast the passage about our galaxy as an argument for one or another of the constituent claims. But there is no reason to do so except to demonstrate that, by our account, any set of two or more sentences can be taken as an argument and evaluated as such. It is, in fact, our contention that it is the job of the logician, not to set limits on what counts as an argument, but rather to provide means of distinguishing good arguments from bad ones. And this we will do. That said, most (but not all) of the examples of arguments we use in this text will be ones in which someone might think that the premises do support the conclusion.

Sometimes an argument turns out to be a good argument even when the premises do not appear, on first review, to support the conclusion. This is another reason for not appealing to some level of apparent support in the definition of an argument. Consider, for example, this passage:

> Everyone loves a lover. Tom loves Alice. Everyone loves everyone.

If by 'lover' we mean 'someone who loves someone', and if we take the last sentence as the conclusion of an argument of which the first two sentences are premises, we have a valid argument. The conclusion does follow, though not obviously, from the premises. The missing reasoning is this: If Tom loves Alice, then Tom is a lover. It follows from the first premise, 'Everyone loves a lover', that everyone loves Tom. And if a lover is someone who loves someone, it further follows that everyone is a lover (because everyone loves Tom). And if everyone is a lover and everyone loves a lover, it follows, finally, that everyone loves everyone. Of course, this reasoning does not work if 'loves' is not being used in the same way in all its occurrences in the original argument, and it may not be ('Everyone loves a lover' may be being used, for example, in the sense of 'Everyone is fond of a person who is in love').

1.3**E** EXERCISES

(*Note:* The accompanying *Solutions Manual* contains answers to all unstarred exercises.)

1. For each of the following, indicate whether it is the kind of sentence that falls within the scope of this text—that is, is either true or false. If it is not, explain why not.

a. George Washington was the second president of the United States.
*b. The next president of the United States will be a Republican.
c. Turn in your homework on time or not at all.
*d. Would that John Kennedy had not been assassinated.
e. Two is the smallest prime number.

*f. One is the smallest prime number.
g. George Bush senior was the immediate predecessor to George W. as president.
*h. On January 15, 1134, there was a snowstorm in what is now Manhattan, at 3:00 p.m. EST.
i. Sentence m below is true.
*j. May you live long and prosper.
k. Never look a gift horse in the mouth.
*l. Who created these screwy examples?
m. This sentence is false.
*n. Beware of Greeks bearing gifts.

2. For each of the following passages, specify what argument, if any, is being advanced. Where the intent is probably not to express an argument, explain why this is so. Where an argument is probably being expressed, restate the argument in standard form.

a. When Mike, Sharon, Sandy, and Vicky are all out of the office, no important decisions get made. Mike is off skiing, Sharon is in Spokane, Vicky is in Olympia, and Sandy is in Seattle. So no decisions will be made today.
*b. Our press releases are always crisp and upbeat. That's because, though Jack doesn't like sound bytes, Mike does. And Mike is the press officer.
c. Shelby and Noreen are wonderful in dealing with irate students and faculty. Stephanie is wonderful at managing the chancellor's very demanding schedule, and Tina keeps everything moving and cheers everyone up.
*d. This is a great office to work in. Shelby and Noreen are wonderful in dealing with irate students and faculty. Stephanie is wonderful at managing the chancellor's very demanding schedule, and Tina keeps everything moving and cheers everyone up.
e. The galvanized nails, both common and finishing, are in the first drawer. The plain nails are in the second drawer. The third drawer contains Sheetrock screws of various sizes, and the fourth drawer contains wood screws. The bottom drawer contains miscellaneous hardware.
*f. The galvanized nails, both common and finishing, are in the first drawer. The plain nails are in the second drawer. The third drawer contains Sheetrock screws of various sizes, and the fourth drawer contains wood screws. The bottom drawer contains miscellaneous hardware. So we should have everything we need to repair the broken deck chair.
g. The weather is perfect; the view is wonderful; and we're on vacation. So why are you unhappy?
*h. The new kitchen cabinets are done, and the installers are scheduled to come Monday. But there will probably be a delay of at least a week, for the old cabinets haven't been removed, and the carpenter who is to do the removal is off for a week of duck hunting in North Dakota.
i. Wood boats are beautiful, but they require too much maintenance. Fiberglass boats require far less maintenance, but they tend to be more floating bathtubs than real sailing craft. Steel boats are hard to find, and concrete boats never caught on. So there's no boat that will please me.
*j. Sarah, John, Rita, and Bob have all worked hard and all deserve promotion. But the company is having a cash flow problem and is offering those over 55 a $50,000 bonus if they will retire at the end of this year. Sarah, John, and Bob are all over 55 and will take early retirement. So Rita will be promoted.

k. Everyone from anywhere who's anyone knows Barrett. All those who know her respect her and like her. Friedman is from Minneapolis and Barrett is from Duluth. Friedman doesn't like anyone from Duluth. Therefore, either Friedman is a nobody or Minneapolis is a nowhere.

*l. I'm not going to die today. I didn't die yesterday, and I didn't die the day before that, or the day before that, and so on back some fifty years.

m. Having cancer is a good, for whatever is required by something that is a good is itself a good. Being cured of cancer is a good, and being cured of cancer requires having cancer.

*n. The Soviet Union disintegrated because the perceived need for the military security offered by the union disappeared with the end of the cold war and because over 70 years of union had produced few economic benefits. Moreover the Soviet Union never successfully addressed the problem of how to inspire loyalty to a single state by peoples with vastly different cultures and histories.

o. Only the two-party system is compatible both with effective governance and with the presenting and contesting of dissenting views, for when there are more than two political parties, support tends to split among the parties, with no party receiving the support of a majority of voters. And no party can govern effectively without majority support. When there is only one political party, dissenting views are neither presented nor contested. When there are two or more viable parties, dissenting views are presented and contested.

*p. Humpty Dumpty sat on a wall. Humpty Dumpty had a great fall. All the king's horses and all the king's men couldn't put Humpty together again. So they made him into an omelet and had a great lunch.[3]

1.4 DEDUCTIVE VALIDITY AND SOUNDNESS

We have already noted that truth-preservation is what distinguishes good reasoning from bad reasoning. A deductively valid argument is one whose form or structure is fully truth-preserving—that is, whose form or structure is such that instances of it never proceed from true premises to a false conclusion.[4] A deductively invalid argument is one whose form or structure is such that instances of it do, on occasion, proceed from true premises to a false conclusion.

An example of a valid deductive argument is

There are three, and only three, people in the room: Juarez, Sloan, and Wang.

Juarez is left-handed.

Sloan is left-handed.

Wang is left-handed.

All the people in the room are left-handed.

[3]With apologies to Lewis Carroll.

[4]There are good arguments that are not valid deductive arguments. See Section 1.5.

This argument is truth-preserving. That is, if the premises ('There are three, and only three, people in the room: Juarez, Sloan, and Wang', 'Juarez is left-handed', 'Sloan is left-handed', and 'Wang is left-handed') are all true, then the conclusion ('All the people in the room are left-handed') must also be true. Arguments that are truth-preserving in this strong sense, where it is not possible at the same time for all the premises to be true and the conclusion false, are said to be deductively valid. Such arguments never have true premises and a false conclusion.

> An argument is *deductively valid* if and only if it is not possible for the premises to be true and the conclusion false. An argument is *deductively invalid* if and only if it is not deductively valid.

Consider this example of an invalid deductive argument:

Sloan is left-handed.

Wang is left-handed.

Everyone is left-handed.

It is invalid because, whereas the premises may well be true, the conclusion is false. Not everyone is left-handed.

Logic is about the relations among sentences and groups of sentences. For example, if we are told that a given argument is deductively valid, we can conclude that if the premises are true the conclusion must also be true. But we cannot conclude, given only that the argument is valid, that the premises are true or that the conclusion is true. Consider, for example, the following argument:

The corner grocery store was burglarized, and whoever did it both knew the combination to the safe and was in town the night of the burglary.

Carolyn, Albert, and Barbara are the only ones who knew the combination to the safe.

Albert and Barbara were out of town the night of the burglary.

Carolyn committed the burglary.

This argument is deductively valid; that is, if the premises are true, the conclusion must also be true. But it does not follow that the premises are true, and hence it does not follow that the conclusion is true. If we have good reason to believe each of the premises, then we also have good reason to believe the conclusion. But note that it is also the case that, if we have good reason to doubt the conclusion (suppose, for example, that we know Carolyn and also know that burglary is just not her style), then we have good reason to believe that at least one of the premises is false.

The important point to note here is that, given only that an argument is deductively valid, it may still be reasonable to doubt the conclusion or to doubt one or more premises. But what is not reasonable is to accept the premises and doubt or reject the conclusion. One who accepts the premises of a deductively valid argument ought, on pain of irrationality, also accept the conclusion. Correspondingly one who denies the conclusion of a deductively valid argument ought, again on pain of irrationality, reject at least one of the premises of that argument. (In the previous case, no police detective would be impressed by a "defense" of Carolyn that consisted of accepting the premises of the argument but steadfastly denying that Carolyn committed the burglary. If Carolyn did not commit the burglary, then either there was no burglary, or the burglar was not someone who knew the combination, or more people than those mentioned knew the combination, or Carolyn did not know the combination, or Albert and Barbara were not both out of town the night of the burglary, or Carolyn was out of town the night of the burglary, or the person who committed the burglary was not in town the night of the burglary.)

It follows from the definition of deductive validity that if an argument is deductively valid then it does not have all true premises and a false conclusion. But every other combination is possible. For example, a deductively valid argument may have all true premises and a true conclusion. The following is such as argument:

> In 2000 Bush and Gore were the only major party candidates in the presidential election.
>
> A major party candidate won.
>
> Gore did not win.
>
> ---
>
> Bush won the presidential election in 2000.

Deductively valid arguments all of whose premises are true are said to be deductively sound.

> An argument is *deductively sound* if and only if it is deductively valid and its premises are true. An argument is *deductively unsound* if and only if it is not deductively sound.

The foregoing argument concerning Bush and Gore is both deductively valid and deductively sound.

A deductively valid argument may also have one or more false premises and a conclusion that is false. Here is such an argument:

> France and Great Britain were the major powers in the Napoleonic Wars.
>
> France had the largest army, Great Britain the largest navy.

The power with the largest army won in the end.

France won in the end.

The third premise, 'The power with largest army won in the end', is false (and the argument is, for this reason, deductively unsound). The conclusion is also false. (Great Britain won the Napoleonic Wars when Wellington defeated Napoleon at the Battle of Waterloo in 1815.)

Finally a deductively valid argument may have a true conclusion and one or more false premises. An example is

Chicago is the capital of the United States.

The capital of the United States is in Illinois.

Chicago is in Illinois.

Both premises of this argument are false (and the argument is therefore deductively unsound); the conclusion is true. This illustrates that good reasoning can move from one or more false premises to a true conclusion.

A deductively invalid argument may have any combination of truths and falsehoods as premises and conclusion. That is, such an argument may have all true premises and a true conclusion, or all true premises and a false conclusion, or one or more false premises and a true conclusion, or one or more false premises and a false conclusion. Here are some examples:

Albany is the capital of New York State.

Annapolis is the capital of Maryland.

Columbus is the capital of Ohio.

Denver is the capital of Colorado.

The three premises and the conclusion are all true. But the argument is obviously deductively invalid. Were the legislature of Colorado to vote to move the capital to Boulder, the three premises of this argument would be true and the conclusion false. So it is possible for the premises to be true and the conclusion false. Consider

Albany is the capital of New York State.

Annapolis is the capital of Maryland.

Columbus is the capital of Ohio.

Minneapolis is the capital of Minnesota.

This deductively invalid argument has true premises and a false conclusion. (St. Paul, not Minneapolis, is the capital of Minnesota.) It is also easy to produce a deductively invalid argument with at least one false premise (two in the following case) and a true conclusion:

Albany is the capital of New York State.

Minneapolis is the capital of Minnesota.

Annapolis is the capital of Maryland.

Boulder is the capital of Colorado.

Columbus is the capital of Ohio.

The conclusion of this argument is true; the second and fourth premises are false. By changing the conclusion to 'Dayton is the capital of Ohio', we produce a deductively invalid argument with at least one (here two) false premise and a false conclusion.

The point to remember is that the only time we can determine whether an argument is deductively valid, given only the truth-values of the premises and conclusion, is when the premises are all true and the conclusion false. We know, again, that such an argument is deductively invalid. In all other cases, to determine whether an argument is deductively valid, we have to consider not what the actual truth-values of the premises and conclusion are, but whether it is possible for the premises all to be true and the conclusion false. For example, consider this argument:

No sea creatures are mammals.

Dolphins are sea creatures.

Dolphins are not mammals.

It has one false premise (the first), one true premise (the second), and a false conclusion. This information does not determine whether the argument is deductively valid or deductively invalid. Rather, we come to see that the argument is deductively valid when we realize that if both premises were true then the conclusion would have to be true as well—that is, that dolphins, being sea creatures, would have to be nonmammals. This argument is valid because it is not possible for the premises to be true and the conclusion false.

1.4**E** EXERCISES

1. Which of the following are true and which are false? Explain your answers, giving examples as appropriate.

a. If an argument is valid, all the premises of that argument are true.

*b. If all the premises of an argument are true, the argument is valid.

c. All sound arguments are valid.

*d. All valid arguments are sound.

e. No argument with a false conclusion is valid.
*f. Every argument with a true conclusion is valid.
g. If all the premises of an argument are true and the conclusion is true, then the argument is valid.
*h. If all the premises of an argument are true and the conclusion is false, the argument is invalid.
i. There are sound arguments with false conclusions.
*j. There are sound arguments with at least one false premise.

2. Give arguments with the following characteristics:
a. A valid argument with true premises and a true conclusion.
*b. A valid argument with at least one false premise and a true conclusion.
c. A valid argument with a false conclusion.
*d. An invalid argument all of whose premises are true and whose conclusion is true.
e. An invalid argument all of whose premises are true and whose conclusion is false.
*f. An invalid argument with at least one false premise and a false conclusion.

1.5 INDUCTIVE ARGUMENTS

There are good arguments that are not deductively valid—that is, whose use involves some acceptable risk of proceeding from true premises to a false conclusion. Consider the following example:

> Juarez, Sloan, and Wang are all left-handed.
>
> Juarez and Sloan both have trouble using can openers made for right-handed people.
>
> ---
>
> Wang also has trouble using can openers made for right-handed people.

This argument is not deductively valid. But the conclusion, 'Wang has trouble using can openers made for right-handed people', is to some extent probable given the fact that Wang is left-handed and that Juarez and Sloan, who are also left-handed, have trouble using can openers made for right-handed people. Nonetheless, the premises could be true and the conclusion false. This might be the case if, for example, Wang is especially adroit with kitchen implements or if the trouble the other two have derives from their having arthritis rather than from their being left-handed.

An argument that is not deductively valid can still be a useful argument—the premises can, as in the prior case, make the conclusion likely even though not certain. Such arguments are said to have inductive strength, the strength being proportional to the degree of probability the premises lend to the conclusion.

An argument has *inductive strength* to the extent that the conclusion is probable given the premises.

Inductive strength is thus a matter of degree.

Inductive reasoning is extremely common both in science and in everyday life. Walter Reed's hypothesizing that mosquitoes spread yellow fever is an example of inductive reasoning. While serving in Cuba after the Spanish-American War, Reed, a physician, noticed that those stricken with yellow fever always had recent mosquito bites and that those not stricken tended to work in areas not infested by mosquitoes. Based on these observations, Reed hypothesized that mosquitoes spread yellow fever. He then asked volunteers not infected with yellow fever to allow themselves to be bitten by mosquitoes that had recently bitten yellow-fever-infected patients. The volunteers quickly contracted yellow fever. Reed concluded that mosquitoes transmit yellow fever. His reasoning can be represented as follows:

> Individuals stricken with yellow fever have recent mosquito bites.
>
> Individuals not stricken with yellow fever tend to work in areas not infested with mosquitoes.
>
> Most individuals bitten by mosquitoes that have recently bitten yellow fever patients soon contract yellow fever.
>
> ---
>
> Mosquitoes transmit yellow fever.

Reed's observations made his conclusion probable but not certain. The mechanism of transmission might have turned out to be an airborne bacterium that survives only under conditions that also encourage a high density of mosquitoes. It might have been a coincidence that the volunteers contracted yellow fever soon after being bitten by the test mosquitoes. So we can say of this argument that it is inductively strong but deductively invalid.

Deductive logic, which is the province of this text, and inductive logic, which lies beyond the scope of this text, both provide methods for evaluating arguments, and methods of both sorts can be applied to the same argument, as above. Which methods are most appropriately applied depends on the context. If an argument is given with the assumption that if the premises are true the conclusion must also be true, then the argument should be evaluated by the standards of deductive logic. However, if an argument is given with the weaker assumption that if the premises are true the conclusion is probable, then the argument should be evaluated by the standards of inductive logic.

1.5**E** EXERCISES

Evaluate the passages in Exercise 2 in Section 1.3 that contain arguments. In each case say whether deductive or inductive standards are most appropriate. If the former, state whether the argument is deductively valid. If the latter, state to what extent the argument is inductively strong.

1.6 LOGICAL CONSISTENCY, TRUTH, FALSITY, AND EQUIVALENCE

One of the important relations that can hold among a set of sentences is consistency.

> A set of sentences is *logically consistent* if and only if it is possible for all the members of that set to be true. A set of sentences is *logically inconsistent* if and only if it is not logically consistent.

We will indicate that we are talking about a set of sentences by enclosing the component sentences within curly braces— '{' and '}'. The following set is logically consistent:

> {Texas is larger than Oklahoma. The Phlogiston theory of heat has been disproven. The United States Congress consists of the Senate and the House of Representatives.}[5]

Note that there is no requirement that the members of a set have "something to do with each other". The three sentences listed are largely if not entirely unrelated. Together they constitute a consistent set because it is possible that all three are true at the same time. (In fact, all three are true.) We obtain a different but also consistent set by replacing the second sentence, 'The Phlogiston theory of heat has been disproven', with 'The Phlogiston theory of heat has been proven'.

> {Texas is larger than Oklahoma. The Phlogiston theory of heat has been proven. The United States Congress consists of the Senate and the House of Representatives.}

Someone who believes all the members of this new set has, to be sure, at least one false belief ('The Phlogiston theory of heat has been proven'), but this does not make the set inconsistent. There is nothing in the nature of the three sentences and their relations to one another that keeps all three from being true. What keeps the second listed sentence from being true is the nature of heat, that it does not behave the way the Phlogiston theory says it behaves.

The following set of sentences is inconsistent:

> {Michael and Benjamin both applied for positions at the local fast-food outlet, and at least one of them will be hired. No one who applied for a position will get it.}

---

[5]Technically what should be listed between the curly braces are the names of the members of the set—here the names of sentences. These are formed by placing single quotation marks around the sentences. See Chapter 2, Section 2.4.

If the first listed sentence is true, then the second sentence, 'No one who applied for a position will get it', is false. In contrast, if the second sentence is true, then it cannot be (as the first sentence claims it is) that Michael and Benjamin both applied and that at least one of them will be hired. That is, if the second sentence is true, then the first sentence is false. So it is not possible for both members of this set to be true. We are able to figure this out without knowing who Michael and Benjamin are. The relationships between the members of the set make it impossible for all the members to be true.

The following set is also inconsistent:

> {Anyone who takes astrology seriously is foolish. Alice is my sister, and no sister of mine has a husband who is foolish. Horace is Alice's husband, and he reads the horoscope column every morning. Anyone who reads the horoscope column every morning takes astrology seriously.}

A little reflection shows that not all the members of the foregoing set can be true. If the first, third, and fourth sentences are true, the second cannot be. Alternatively, if the second, third, and fourth are true, the first cannot be. And so on.

Logic cannot normally tell us whether a given sentence is true or false, but we can use logic to discover whether a set is consistent or inconsistent. And if a set is inconsistent, we know that at least one member of it is false, and hence that believing all the members of the set would involve believing at least one false sentence, something we don't want to do. Establishing that a set is consistent does not establish that all, or even any, of its members are true; but it does establish that it is possible for all the members to be true.

Although logic cannot normally be used to determine whether a particular sentence is true or false, there are two special cases. Some sentences are true because of their form or structure. For example, 'Either Cynthia will get a job or she will not get a job' is true no matter how Cynthia fares vis-à-vis her job-seeking activities. Indeed, every sentence that is of the form 'either . . . or . . .' and is such that what comes after the 'or' is the denial of what comes after the 'either' is true. Sentences such as these do not give us any new information. They do not "tell us anything about the world". Whoever Cynthia is, we all know that she either will or will not get a job, and so being told this does not convey any new information. Other sentences of this type include 'If Henry gets fired, he gets fired', 'If everyone passes, Denise will pass', and 'If Sarah will go mountain climbing if and only if Marjorie does, then if Marjorie does not go, neither will Sarah'. Sentences of this sort are said to be logically true.

A sentence is *logically true* if and only if it is not possible for the sentence to be false.

Just as some sentences are true by virtue of their form or structure, so too some sentences are false by virtue of their form or structure. These include 'Sarah is an A student and Sarah is not an A student', 'All lions are ferocious but there are lions in zoos that are not ferocious', 'I'm here and nobody is here', and 'Some dollar bills are not dollar bills'. Such sentences are said to be logically false.

A sentence is *logically false* if and only if it is not possible for the sentence to be true.

Logically false sentences, like logically true sentences, give us no information about the world.[6]

Sentences that purport to give us information about the world—and these constitute most of the sentences we encounter outside logic and mathematics—are neither logically true nor logically false. They include 'Ivan is driving from Boston to New Orleans', 'Anyone who takes astrology seriously is foolish', and 'Perkins advocates the relaxation of air pollution standards because he owns a lot of stock in a company producing coal with a high sulfur content'. Such sentences claim that the world, or some part of it, is a certain way, and to determine whether they are true we have to gather information about the world, and not merely about how those sentences are constructed. Such sentences are said to be logically indeterminate.

A sentence is *logically indeterminate* if and only if it is neither logically true nor logically false.

The final concept we introduce in this chapter is that of logical equivalence. Sentences are sometimes related in such a way that, because of their structure or form, if one is true the other is as well, and vice versa. Examples of such pairs of sentences include these:

Henry loves Sarah.
Sarah is loved by Henry.

Both Sarah and Henry will pass.
Both Henry and Sarah will pass.

Not all tumors are cancerous.
Some tumors are not cancerous.

Of course, the members of this pair, perhaps to Henry's dismay, are not logically equivalent:

Henry loves Sarah.
Sarah loves Henry.

[6]But logically true sentences are useful in ways that logically false sentences are not. By some accounts mathematics consists exclusively of logical truths.

The members of a pair of sentences are *logically equivalent* if and only if it is not possible for one of the sentences to be true while the other sentence is false.

Note that we allow a sentence to be equivalent to itself, by counting, for example, 'Sarah is very bright' and 'Sarah as very bright' as constituting a pair of (identical) sentences. On this definition of logical equivalence, it also follows that all logically true sentences are logically equivalent and that all logically false sentences are logically equivalent. But it does not follow that all logically indeterminate sentences are logically equivalent. Clearly, logically indeterminate sentences with different truth-values—for example, 'Philadelphia is in Pennsylvania' (true) and 'Denver is in Wyoming' (false)—are not logically equivalent. Moreover, not all logically indeterminate sentences with the same truth-value are logically equivalent. 'California produces red wine' and 'California produces white wine' are both true, but these claims are not logically equivalent. The test for logical equivalence is not sameness of truth-value, but rather whether the sentences in question *must* have the same truth-value—whether it is impossible for them to have different truth-values. Since it is possible for 'California produces white wine' to be true but 'California produces red wine' to be false (California vintners might decide that all the money is to be made in white wine and stop producing red wine), these sentences are not logically equivalent.

1.6E EXERCISES

1. Where possible, give an example of each of the following. Where not possible, explain why no example can be given.

a. A consistent set all of whose members are true.
*b. A consistent set with at least one true member and at least one false member.
c. An inconsistent set all of whose members are true.
*d. A consistent set all of whose members are false.

2. For each of the following sets of sentences, indicate whether the set is consistent or inconsistent, and why.

a. {Good vegetables are hard to find. The Dodgers are no longer in Brooklyn. Today is hotter than yesterday.}
*b. {Henry likes real ice cream. Real ice cream is a dairy product. There isn't a dairy product Henry likes.}
c. {Washington, D.C., is the capital of the United States. Paris is the capital of France. Ottawa is the capital of Canada.}
*d. {Washington, D.C., is the capital of the United States. Paris is the capital of France. Toronto is the capital of Canada.}
e. {The weather is fine. Tomorrow is Tuesday. Two plus two equals four. We're almost out of gas.}
*f. {Sue is taller than Tom. Tom is taller than Henry. Henry is just as tall as Sue.}
g. {Tom, Sue, and Robin are all bright. No one who fails "Poetry for Scientists" is bright. Tom failed "Poetry for Scientists".}

*h. {The United States does not support dictatorships. In the 1980s the United State supported Iraq. Iraq has been a dictatorship since 1979.}
i. {Roosevelt was a better president than Truman, as was Eisenhower. Eisenhower was also a better president than his successor, Kennedy. Kennedy was the best president we ever had.}
*j. {Jones and his relatives own all the land in Gaylord, Minnesota. Smith is no relation to Jones. Smith owns land in Gaylord, Minnesota.}
k. {Everyone who likes film classics likes *Casablanca.* Everyone who likes Humphrey Bogart likes *Casablanca.* Sarah likes *Casablanca,* but she doesn't like most film classics and she doesn't like Humphrey Bogart.}
*l. {Everyone who likes film classics likes *Casablanca.* Everyone who likes Humphrey Bogart likes *Casablanca.* Sarah likes film classics and she likes Humphrey Bogart, but she can't stand *Casablanca.*}

3. Give an example of each of the following. Explain, in each case, why the given example is of the sort requested.
a. A logically true sentence
*b. A logically false sentence
c. A logically indeterminate sentence

4. For each of the following, indicate whether it is logically true, logically false, or logically indeterminate, and why.
a. Sarah passed the bar exam but she never went to law school.
*b. Helen is a doctor but not an MD.
c. Helen is an MD but not a doctor.
*d. Bob is in London but his heart is in Texas.
e. Robin will either make it to class by starting time or she won't.
*f. Robin will either make it to class by starting time or she will be late.
g. Bob knows everyone in the class, which includes Robin, whom he doesn't know.
*h. Sarah likes all kinds of fish but she doesn't like ocean fish.
i. If Sarah likes all kinds of fish, then she likes ocean fish.
*j. Anyone who likes rare beef likes rare emu.
k. Anyone who loves everyone is lacking in discrimination.
*l. Anyone who loves everyone loves a lot of people.

5. Where possible, give examples of the following. Where not possible, explain why not.
a. A pair of sentences, both of which are logically indeterminate and are logically equivalent.
*b. A pair of sentences that are not logically equivalent but that are both true.
c. A pair of sentences that are logically equivalent, one of which is logically true and one of which is not.
*d. A pair of sentences that are logically equivalent and both false.
e. A pair of sentences, at least one of which is logically true, that are logically equivalent.
*f. A pair of sentences that are logically equivalent, one of which is logically false and the other of which is logically true.

6. For each of the following pairs of sentences, indicate whether the sentences are logically equivalent, and explain why.
a. Henry is in love with Sue.
Sue is in love with Henry.

*b. Sue married Barbara
Barbara married Sue.

c. Tom likes all kinds of fish.
Tom claims to like all kinds of fish.

*d. Bill and Mary were both admitted to the Golden Key Honor Society.
Bill was admitted to the Golden Key Honor Society and Mary was admitted to the Golden Key Honor Society.

e. Neither Bill nor Mary will get into law school.
Bill will not get into law school or Mary will get into law school.

*f. The judge pronounced Bill and Mary husband and wife.
Bill and Mary got married.

g. Only Mariner fans came to the rally.
All Mariner fans came to the rally.

*h. I know there are people who are starving in every large city in America.
In every large city in America I know people who are starving.

i. Every newscast reported that a strike is imminent.
A strike is imminent.

*j. A bad day of sailing is better than a good day at work.
A good day at work isn't as good as a bad day of sailing.

k. Sarah and Anna won't both be elected president of the senior class.
Either Sarah will be elected president of the senior class or Anna will be elected president of the senior class.

*l. Sarah and Anna won't both be elected president of the senior class.
Either Sarah will not be elected president of the senior class or Anna will not be elected president of the senior class.

m. Everyone dislikes someone.
There is someone whom everyone dislikes.

*n. Everyone dislikes someone.
There is no universally liked person.

o. Everyone likes someone.
Someone is liked by everyone.

*p. Not everyone likes someone.
There is someone who doesn't like anyone.

1.7 SPECIAL CASES OF VALIDITY

Having introduced the notions of logical consistency, logical truth, and logical falsity, we are now in a position to consider some special and rather counterintuitive cases of validity. We have defined a deductively valid argument to be one in which it is impossible for the premises to be true and the conclusion false. Such an argument, we have said, is truth-preserving in that it never takes us from true premises to a false conclusion. Here we consider two special cases of validity. Consider first an argument whose conclusion is logically true. An example is

> The Philadelphia Phillies are the best team in the National League.
> ___
> Either the next president will be a woman or the next president will not be a woman.

The conclusion of this argument is clearly logically true. No matter who wins the next presidential election, that person either will or will not be a woman. The premise is, at the moment of this writing, anything but true. Note that the premise is utterly unconnected with the conclusion. For the latter reason one might very well be tempted to say that this is an invalid argument, for surely the premises of a valid argument must be relevant to (have some connection with) the conclusion. But recall our definition of validity: An argument is deductively valid if and only if it is not possible for the premises to be true and the conclusion false. The above argument does satisfy this requirement. It is not possible for the conclusion, a logical truth, to be false. Therefore it is not possible for the premises to be true and the conclusion false—again, because the conclusion cannot be false.[7]

To put the point another way, this argument is truth-preserving. It will never lead us from truths to a falsehood because it will never lead us to a falsehood—because the conclusion is logically true. There is no risk of reaching a false conclusion here precisely because there is no risk that the conclusion is false. All arguments whose conclusions are logically true are deductively valid for this reason.[8]

Consider next arguments whose premises form logically inconsistent sets. This may be because one or more of an argument's premises are logically false (in which case it is impossible for those premises to be true, and hence impossible for all the premises to be true), or it may be because, while no single premise is logically false, the premises taken together are nonetheless logically inconsistent. The following is a case of the latter sort:

Albert is brighter than all his sisters.

Albert and Sally are brother and sister.

Sally is brighter than all her brothers.

Tyrannosaurus rex was the fiercest of all dinosaurs.

In this case, if the first and second premises are both true, the third premise cannot be true. And, if the second and third premises are both true, the first premise cannot be true. So not all the premises can be true. The set consisting of the premises is logically inconsistent. Here, as in the preceding case, there is no obvious connection between the premises and the conclusion. Yet the argument does satisfy our definition of deductive validity because it is impossible for all the premises of this argument to be true and therefore

[7] Arguments whose conclusions are logically true are deductively valid whether or not their conclusions are related to their premises. For example,

> The Philadelphia Phillies are the best team in the National League; therefore the Phillies either will or will not win the National League pennant

is a deductively valid argument, not because the premise and conclusion both concern the Phillies but because the conclusion is logically true and it is therefore impossible for the premise to be true *and* the conclusion false.

[8] One way to think of such an argument is that, since the conclusion is logically true, it requires *no* support. Hence, whatever support the premises provide (even if it is none at all—even if the premises are utterly unrelated to the conclusion) is enough.

impossible for all the premises to be true and the conclusion false. The argument is truth-preserving because it will never take us from truths to a falsehood. It will not do so because the premises cannot all be true, and hence there is no possibility of going from truths to a falsehood. Arguments whose premises are inconsistent, while valid, are of course never sound.

Every argument whose premises constitute a logically inconsistent set is thus deductively valid. As a further example, consider

> Sandra will get an A in the course and Sandra will not get an A in the course.
>
> ---
>
> Sandra will graduate.

The one premise of this argument is logically false. Therefore that premise cannot be true. And so it is impossible for every premise of this argument (there is only one) to be true and the conclusion false. The conclusion may be false, but not while the premise is true.

Arguments of the sort we are discussing here are sometimes dismissed as not being arguments at all, precisely because their validity does not depend on a relation between the premises and conclusion. There are, however, systematic reasons for allowing these cases to constitute arguments and thus for recognizing them as valid deductive arguments. It is important to remember that such arguments are valid because they meet the requirement of truth preservation—they will never take us from truths to a falsehood—not because the premises support the conclusion in any intuitive way.

1.7E EXERCISES

1. Which of the following are true, and which are false? Explain your answers giving examples where appropriate.

a. If at least one member of a set of sentences is logically false, then the set is logically inconsistent.

*b. No two false sentences are logically equivalent.

c. Every argument whose conclusion is logically equivalent to one of its premises is valid.

*d. Any argument that includes among its premises 'Everyone is a scoundrel' and 'I'm no scoundrel' is deductively valid.

e. Every argument that has 'Whatever will be, will be' as a conclusion is deductively valid.

*f. Every argument that has 'Everyone is a scoundrel and I'm no scoundrel' as a conclusion is deductively invalid.

g. Every argument all of whose premises are logically true is deductively valid.

2. Answer each of the following:

a. Does every person who believes that New York City is the capital of the United States have inconsistent beliefs?

*b. Need one be engaged in a disagreement or dispute to have use for an argument as we have been using the term 'argument'? Explain.

c. Explain why logic cannot normally tell us whether a valid argument is sound. Under what conditions could we decide, on logical grounds alone, that a valid argument is sound?

*d. Suppose an argument is valid but has a false conclusion. What can we conclude about the premises? Explain.

e. Explain why an argument with at least one logically false premise must be valid no matter what the other premises are and no matter what the conclusion is.

*f. Suppose an argument has a premise that is logically equivalent to a logical falsehood. Must the argument be valid? Explain.

g. Suppose an argument has a logical truth as its conclusion. Explain why the argument must be valid no matter what its premises are. Explain why some such arguments are sound and some are not.

*h. Suppose the premises of an argument form an inconsistent set of sentences. Explain why the argument must be valid but unsound.

i. Suppose a set of a million sentences is consistent. Now suppose a new set of sentences is constructed so that every sentence in the new set is logically equivalent to at least one of the sentences in the old set. Must the new set be consistent? Explain.

GLOSSARY

ARGUMENT: An argument is a set of two or more sentences, one of which is designated as the conclusion and the others as the premises.

DEDUCTIVE VALIDITY: An argument is *deductively valid* if and only if it is not possible for the premises to be true and the conclusion false. An argument is *deductively invalid* if and only if it is not deductively valid.

DEDUCTIVE SOUNDNESS: An argument is *deductively sound* if and only if it is deductively valid and all its premises are true. An argument is *deductively unsound* if and only if it is not deductively sound.

INDUCTIVE STRENGTH: An argument has *inductive strength* to the extent that the conclusion is probable given the premises.

LOGICAL CONSISTENCY: A set of sentences is *logically consistent* if and only if it is possible for all the members of that set to be true. A set of sentences is *logically inconsistent* if and only if it is not logically consistent.

LOGICAL TRUTH: A sentence is *logically true* if and only if it is not possible for the sentence to be false.

LOGICAL FALSITY: A sentence is *logically false* if and only if it is not possible for the sentence to be true.

LOGICAL INDETERMINACY: A sentence is *logically indeterminate* if and only if it is neither logically true nor logically false.

LOGICAL EQUIVALENCE: The members of a pair of sentences are *logically equivalent* if and only if it is not possible for one of the sentences to be true while the other sentence is false.

Chapter **2**

SENTENTIAL LOGIC: SYMBOLIZATION AND SYNTAX

2.1 SYMBOLIZATION AND TRUTH-FUNCTIONAL CONNECTIVES

Sentential logic, as the name suggests, is a branch of formal logic in which sentences are the basic units. In this chapter we shall introduce *SL*, a symbolic language for sentential logic, which will facilitate our development of formal techniques for assessing the logical relations among sentences and groups of sentences. The sentences of English that can be symbolized in *SL* are those that are either true or false, that is, have truth-values.

In English there are various ways of generating sentences from other sentences. One way is to place a linking term such as 'and' between them. The result, allowing for appropriate adjustments in capitalization and punctuation, will itself be a sentence of English. In this way we can generate

Socrates is wise and Aristotle is crafty

by writing 'and' between 'Socrates is wise' and 'Aristotle is crafty'. Some other linking terms of English are 'or', 'although', 'unless', 'before', and 'if and only if'. As used to generate sentences from other sentences, these terms are called *sentential connectives* (they connect or join sentences to produce further sentences).

Some sentence-generating words and expressions do not join two sentences together but rather work on a single sentence. Examples are 'it is not the case that' and 'it is alleged that'. Prefacing a sentence with either of these expressions generates a further sentence. Since these expressions do not literally connect two sentences, the term "sentential connective" is perhaps a little misleading. Nonetheless, such sentence-generating devices as these are commonly classified as sentential connectives, and we shall follow this usage.

Sentences generated from other sentences by means of sentential connectives are *compound sentences.* All other sentences are *simple sentences.* In developing sentential logic we shall be especially interested in the *truth-functional* use of sentential connectives. Intuitively a compound sentence generated by a truth-functional connective is one in which the truth-value of the compound is a function of, or is fixed by, the truth-values of its components.

> A sentential connective is used *truth-functionally* if and only if it is used to generate a compound sentence from one or more sentences in such a way that the truth-value of the generated compound is wholly determined by the truth-values of those one or more sentences from which the compound is generated, no matter what those truth-values may be.

Few, if any, connectives of English are always used truth-functionally. However, many connectives of English are often so used. We shall call these connectives, as so used, *truth-functional connectives.* A *truth-functionally compound sentence* is a compound sentence generated by a truth-functional connective.

In English 'and' is often used truth-functionally. Consider the compound sentence

Alice is in England and Bertram is in France.

Suppose that Alice is in Belgium, not England. Then 'Alice is in England' is false. The compound sentence is then clearly also false. Similarly, if 'Bertram is in France' is false, the compound 'Alice is in England and Bertram is in France' is false as well. In fact, this compound will be true if and only if both of the sentences from which it is generated are true. Hence the truth-value of this compound is wholly determined by the truth-values of the component sentences from which it is generated. Given their truth-values, whatever they may be, we can always compute the truth-value of the compound in question. This is just what we mean when we say that 'and' functions as a truth-functional connective.

SENTENCES OF SENTENTIAL LOGIC

In *SL* capital Roman letters are used to abbreviate individual sentences of English. Thus

Socrates is wise

can be abbreviated as

W

Of course, we could have chosen any capital letter for the abbreviation, but it is common practice to select a letter that reminds us of the sentence being abbreviated. In this case 'W' reminds us of the word 'wise'. But it is essential to remember that the capital letters of *SL* abbreviate entire sentences and *not* individual words within sentences.

To ensure that we have enough sentences in our symbolic language to represent any number of English sentences, we shall also count capital Roman letters with positive-integer subscripts as sentences of *SL*. Thus all the following are sentences of *SL*:

A, B, Z, T_{25}, Q_6

In *SL* capital letters with or without subscripts are *atomic sentences*. Sentences of *SL* that are made up of one or more atomic sentences and one or more sentential connectives of *SL* are *molecular sentences*.

CONJUNCTION

We could abbreviate

Socrates is wise and Aristotle is crafty

in our symbolic language as 'A', but in doing so we would bury important information about this English sentence. This sentence is a compound made up of two simple sentences: 'Socrates is wise' and 'Aristotle is crafty'. Furthermore, in this case the word 'and', which connects the two sentences, is serving as a truth-functional connective. This compound sentence is true if both of its component sentences are true and is false otherwise. We shall use '&' (ampersand) as the sentential connective of *SL* that captures the force of this truth-functional use of 'and' in English. Instead of symbolizing 'Socrates is wise and Aristotle is crafty' as 'A', we can now symbolize it as

W & C

where 'W' abbreviates 'Socrates is wise' and 'C' abbreviates 'Aristotle is crafty'. Remember that the letters abbreviate entire sentences, not merely specific words like the words 'wise' and 'crafty'. The compound sentence 'W & C' is an example of a molecular sentence of *SL*.

A sentence of the form

P & Q

where **P** and **Q** are sentences of *SL*, is a *conjunction*.[1] **P** and **Q** are the *conjuncts* of the conjunction. Informally we shall use the terms "conjunction" and "conjunct" in talking of English sentences that can be symbolized as conjunctions of *SL*. The relation between the truth or falsity of a conjunction and the truth or falsity of its conjuncts can be simply put: A conjunction is true if and only if both of its conjuncts are true. This is summarized by the following table:

P	Q	P & Q
T	T	T
T	F	F
F	T	F
F	F	F

Such a table is called a *characteristic truth-table* because it defines the use of '&' in *SL*. The table is read horizontally, row by row. The first row contains three **T**'s. The first two indicate that we are considering the case in which **P** has the truth-value **T** and **Q** has the truth-value **T**. The last item in the first row is a **T**, indicating that the conjunction has the truth-value **T** under these conditions. The second row indicates that, when **P** has the truth-value **T** and **Q** has the truth-value **F**, the conjunction has the truth-value **F**. The third row shows that, when **P** has the truth-value **F** and **Q** has the truth-value **T**, the conjunction has the truth-value **F**. The last row indicates that when both **P** and **Q** have the truth-value **F**, the conjunction has the truth-value **F** as well.

Sometimes an English sentence that is not itself a compound sentence can be paraphrased as a compound sentence. The sentence

Fred and Nancy passed their driving examinations

can be paraphrased as

Both Fred passed his driving examination and Nancy passed her driving examination.

We underscore the connectives in paraphrases to emphasize that we are using those connectives truth-functionally. We use 'both . . . and . . .',

[1] Our use of boldface letters to talk generally about the sentences of *SL* is explained in Section 2.4.

rather than just 'and', to mark off the conjuncts unambiguously. Where the example being paraphrased is complex, we shall sometimes also use parentheses—'(' and ')'—and brackets—'[' and ']'—to indicate grouping. The foregoing paraphrase is an adequate paraphrase of the original sentence inasmuch as both the original sentence and the paraphrase are true if and only if 'Fred passed his driving examination' and 'Nancy passed her driving examination' are both true. The paraphrase is a conjunction and can be symbolized as

F & N

where 'F' abbreviates 'Fred passed his driving examination' and 'N' abbreviates 'Nancy passed her driving examination'.

Symbolizing English sentences in *SL* should be thought of as a two-step process. First, we construct in English a truth-functional paraphrase of the original English sentence; next, we symbolize that paraphrase in *SL*. The paraphrase stage serves to remind us that the compounds symbolized as molecular sentences of *SL* are always truth-functional compounds.

The preceding example illustrates that the grammatical structure of an English sentence is not a completely reliable indication of its logical structure. Key words like 'and' serve as clues but are not infallible guides to symbolization. The sentence

Two jiggers of gin and a few drops of dry vermouth make a great martini

cannot be fairly paraphrased as

Both two jiggers of gin make a great martini and a few drops of dry vermouth make a great martini.

Together these ingredients may make a great martini, but separately they make no martini at all. Such a paraphrase completely distorts the sense of the original sentence. Thus the original sentence must be regarded as a simple sentence and symbolized in *SL* as an atomic sentence, say

M

Many sentences generated by such other connectives of English as 'but', 'however', 'although', 'nevertheless', 'nonetheless', and 'moreover' can be closely paraphrased using 'and' in its truth-functional sense. Consider some examples:

Susan loves country music, but she hates opera

can be paraphrased as

Both Susan loves country music and Susan hates opera.

The paraphrase can be symbolized as 'L & H', where 'L' abbreviates 'Susan loves country music' and 'H' abbreviates 'Susan hates opera'.

The members came today; however, the meeting is tomorrow

can be paraphrased as

Both the members came today and the meeting is tomorrow

which can be symbolized as 'C & M', where 'C' abbreviates 'The members came today' and 'M' abbreviates 'The meeting is tomorrow'.

Although George purchased a thousand raffle tickets, he lost

can be paraphrased as

Both George purchased a thousand raffle tickets and George lost

which can be symbolized as 'P & L', where 'P' abbreviates 'George purchased a thousand raffle tickets' and 'L' abbreviates 'George lost'.

In each of these cases, the paraphrase perhaps misses part of the sense of the original English sentence. In the last example, for instance, there is the suggestion that it is surprising that George could have purchased a thousand raffle tickets and still have lost the raffle. Truth-functional paraphrases often fail to capture all the nuances present in the sentences of which they are paraphrases. This loss is usually not important for the purposes of logical analysis.

In symbolizing sentences of a natural language—in our case English—grammatical structure and key words provide important clues, but they are not infallible guides to correct symbolizations. Ultimately we have to ask ourselves, as speakers of English, whether the sentence can be reasonably paraphrased as a truth-functional compound. If so, we can symbolize it as a molecular sentence of *SL*. If not, we have to symbolize it as an atomic sentence of *SL*.

DISJUNCTION

Another sentential connective of English is 'or', used in such sentences as

Henry James was a psychologist or William James was a psychologist.

This English sentence contains two simple sentences as components: 'Henry James was a psychologist' and 'William James was a psychologist'. The truth-value of the compound wholly depends upon the truth-values of the component sentences. As long as at least one of the component sentences is true, the compound is true; but if both the components are false, then the compound is false. When used in this way, 'or' serves as a truth-functional connective of English. In *SL* '∨' (wedge) is the symbol that expresses this truth-functional relation. Thus the sentence about Henry and William James can be symbolized as

$$H \vee W$$

where 'H' abbreviates 'Henry James was a psychologist' and 'W' abbreviates 'William James was a psychologist'. 'H ∨ W' is true if 'H' is true or 'W' is true, and it is false only when both 'H' and 'W' are false.

A sentence of the form

$$\mathbf{P} \vee \mathbf{Q}$$

where **P** and **Q** are sentences of *SL*, is a *disjunction*. **P** and **Q** are the *disjuncts* of the sentence. Informally we shall use the terms "disjunction" and "disjunct" in talking of English sentences that can be symbolized as disjunctions of *SL*. A disjunction is true if and only if at least one of its disjuncts is true. This is summarized by the following characteristic truth-table:

P	**Q**	**P ∨ Q**
T	**T**	**T**
T	**F**	**T**
F	**T**	**T**
F	**F**	**F**

The only case in which a disjunction has the truth-value **F** is when both disjuncts have the truth-value **F**.

Some sentences of English that do not contain the word 'or' can be paraphrased as a disjunction. For instance,

> At least one of the two hikers, Jerry and Amy, will get to the top of the mountain

can adequately be paraphrased as

> Either Jerry will get to the top of the mountain or Amy will get to the top of the mountain.

This paraphrase can be symbolized as 'J ∨ A', where 'J' abbreviates 'Jerry will get to the top of the mountain' and 'A' abbreviates 'Amy will get to the top of the mountain'. Remember, the letters abbreviate the entire sentences, not just the words 'Jerry' and 'Amy'. In paraphrasing English sentences as disjunctions of *SL*, we use the 'either . . . or . . .' construction to mark off the two disjuncts unambiguously.

In English sentences that can be paraphrased as disjunctions, 'or' does not always occur between full sentences. For example,

Nietzsche is either a philosopher or a mathematician

can be paraphrased as

Either Nietzsche is a philosopher or Nietzsche is a mathematician.

This truth-functional paraphrase can be symbolized as '$P \vee M$', where 'P' abbreviates 'Nietzsche is a philosopher' and 'M' abbreviates 'Nietzsche is a mathematician'.

We use the wedge to symbolize disjunctions in the *inclusive* sense. Suppose the following appears on a menu:

With your meal you get apple pie or chocolate cake.

We might try to paraphrase this as

Either with your meal you get apple pie or with your meal you get chocolate cake.

Since we use 'or' only in the inclusive sense in paraphrases, this paraphrase is true if either or both of the disjuncts are true. In ordinary English, on the other hand, 'or' is sometimes used in a more restrictive sense. In the present example, if someone orders both pie and cake, the waiter is likely to point out that either cake or pie, but *not* both, comes with the dinner. This is the exclusive sense of 'or'—either one or the other but not both. Although this sense of 'or' cannot be captured by '$\vee$' alone, there is, as we shall soon see, a combination of connectives of *SL* that will allow us to express the exclusive sense of 'or'.

NEGATION

'It is not the case that' is a sentential connective of English. Consider the following compound generated by this connective:

It is not the case that Franklin Pierce was president.

This sentence is true if its component sentence, 'Franklin Pierce was president', is false, and it is false if that component sentence is true. 'It is not the case that' is a truth-functional connective because the truth-value of the generated sentence is wholly determined by the truth-value of the component sentence. In *SL* '$\sim$ ' (tilde) is the sentential connective that captures this truth-functional relationship. Thus the sentence in question can be symbolized as

~ F

where 'F' abbreviates 'Franklin Pierce was president'. The tilde is a *unary connective,* because it "connects" only one sentence. On the other hand, '&' and '∨' are *binary connectives* since each connects two sentences. When '~ ' is placed in front of a sentence, the truth-value of the generated sentence is the opposite of the truth-value of the original sentence. So the characteristic truth-table for negation is this:

P	**~ P**
T	**F**
F	**T**

Notice that, because '~ ' is a unary connective, we need a truth-table of only two rows to represent all the possible "combinations" of truth-values that a single sentence to which '~ ' is attached might have.

Putting a '~ ' in front of a sentence forms the negation of that sentence. Hence '~ A' is the negation of 'A' (though 'A' is *not* the negation of '~ A'), '~ ~ A' is the negation of '~ A' (though '~ A' is not the negation of '~ ~ A'), and so forth. Informally we shall use the term "negation" in talking about sentences of English that can be symbolized as negations in *SL.* Thus

It is not the case that Franklin Pierce was president

is the negation of

Franklin Pierce was president.

Whether an English sentence should be symbolized as a negation depends on the context. As before, grammar and key words give us clues. Consider some examples:

Not all sailors are good swimmers

is readily paraphrased as

It is not the case that all sailors are good swimmers.

This paraphrase can be symbolized as '~ G', where 'G' abbreviates 'All sailors are good swimmers'. But the following example is not as straightforward:

No doctors are rich.

One might be tempted to paraphrase this sentence as 'It is not the case that all doctors are rich', but to do so is to treat 'No doctors are rich' as the negation of 'All doctors are rich'. This is a mistake because a sentence and its negation are so related that, if one is true, the other is false, and vice versa. In fact, since some doctors are rich and some doctors are not rich, both 'All doctors are rich' and 'No doctors are rich' are false. Hence the latter cannot be the negation of the former. Rather, 'No doctors are rich' is the negation of 'Some doctors are rich'. 'No doctor are rich' is true if and only if 'Some doctors are rich' is false, so the former sentence can be paraphrased as

It is not the case that some doctors are rich.

This can be symbolized as '~ D', where 'D' abbreviates 'Some doctors are rich'.

Some further examples will be helpful:

Chlorine is not a metal

can plausibly be understood as

It is not the case that chlorine is a metal.

This paraphrase can be symbolized as '~ C', where 'C' abbreviates 'Chlorine is a metal'. Notice that 'Chlorine is a metal' and 'Chlorine is not a metal' are such that if either is true the other is false, which must be the case if the latter is to be the negation of the former. But now consider an apparently similar case:

Some humans are not male.

This sentence should not be paraphrased as 'It is not the case that some humans are male'. The latter sentence is true if and only if *no* humans are male, which is not the claim made by the original sentence. The proper paraphrase is

It is not the case that all humans are male

which can be symbolized as '~ H', where 'H' abbreviates 'All humans are male'. Often sentences containing words with such prefixes as 'un-', 'in-', and 'non-' are best paraphrased as negations. But we must be careful here.

Kant was unmarried

can be understood as

It is not the case that Kant was married

and then symbolized as '~ K', where 'K' abbreviates 'Kant was married'. 'Kant was unmarried' is the negation of 'Kant was married'. But

Some people are unmarried

should not be paraphrased as 'It is not the case that some people are married'. 'Some people are married' and 'Some people are unmarried' are both true. A proper paraphrase in this case is

It is not the case that all people are married

which can be symbolized as '~ M', where 'M' abbreviates 'All people are married'.

COMBINATIONS OF SENTENTIAL CONNECTIVES

So far we have discussed three types of truth-functional compounds—conjunctions, disjunctions, and negations—and the corresponding sentential connectives of *SL*— '&', '∨', and '~ '. These connectives can be used in combination to symbolize complex passages. Suppose we wish to symbolize the following:

> Either the steam engine or the computer was the greatest modern invention, but the zipper, although not the greatest modern invention, has made life much easier.

The main connective in this sentence is 'but', and the sentence can be paraphrased as a conjunction. The left conjunct can be paraphrased as a disjunction, and the right can be paraphrased as a conjunction making the claim that the zipper was not the greatest modern invention and the claim that the zipper has made life much easier. Finally the claim that the zipper was not the greatest modern invention can be paraphrased as a negation. The resulting truth-functional paraphrase is

> Both (either the steam engine was the greatest modern invention or the computer was the greatest modern invention) and (both it is not the case that the zipper was the greatest modern invention and the zipper has made life much easier).

For clarity we have inserted some parentheses in the paraphrase to emphasize the grouping of the components. The order of placement of 'both' and 'either' is important. In this case 'both' occurring before 'either' at the beginning shows that the overall sentence is a conjunction, not a disjunction. The paraphrase can be symbolized as

(S ∨ C) & (~ Z & E)

where 'S' abbreviates 'The steam engine was the greatest modern invention', 'C' abbreviates 'The computer was the greatest modern invention', 'Z' abbreviates 'The zipper was the greatest modern invention', and 'E' abbreviates 'The zipper has made life much easier'.

The connectives '&', '∨', and '~ ' can be used in combination to symbolize English sentential connectives such as 'neither . . . nor . . .'. The sentence

Neither Sherlock Holmes nor Watson is fond of criminals

can be paraphrased as

Both it is not the case that Sherlock Holmes is fond of criminals and it is not the case that Watson is fond of criminals.

This can be symbolized as

~ H & ~ W

where 'H' abbreviates 'Sherlock Holmes is fond of criminals' and 'W' abbreviates 'Watson is fond of criminals'.

Another equally good paraphrase of the original sentence is

It is not the case that either Sherlock Holmes is fond of criminals or Watson is fond of criminals.

This paraphrase can be symbolized using the above abbreviations as

~ (H ∨ W)

Note that the original sentence, the paraphrases, and the symbolic sentences are all true if Sherlock Holmes is not fond of criminals and Watson is not fond of criminals, and they are all false otherwise.

A similar, but nonequivalent, connective is 'not both . . . and . . .'. Consider this claim:

A Republican and a Democrat will not both become president.

Truth-functionally paraphrased this becomes

It is not the case that both a Republican will become president and a Democrat will become president

which is symbolized as

~ (R & D)

This sentence does not maintain that neither a Republican nor a Democrat will become president but only that not both of them will become president. '~ (R ∨ D)' is not an acceptable symbolization, but '~ (R & D)' is. Another possible and acceptable paraphrase of this particular 'not both . . . and . . .' claim is

> Either it is not the case that a Republican will become president or it is not the case that a Democrat will become president

which when symbolized becomes

> ~ R ∨ ~ D

Here is a table summarizing the truth conditions for 'neither . . . nor . . .'. Notice that a 'neither . . . nor . . .' expression is true only when both of its components, **P** and **Q**, are false.

Truth Conditions for
'Neither . . . nor . . .'

P	**Q**	**~ P & ~ Q**	**~ (P ∨ Q)**
T	**T**	**F**	**F**
T	**F**	**F**	**F**
F	**T**	**F**	**F**
F	**F**	**T**	**T**

Compare this table with the next table, which shows the truth conditions for 'not both . . . and . . .':

Truth Conditions for
'Not both . . . and . . .'

P	**Q**	**~ (P & Q)**	**~ P ∨ ~ Q**
T	**T**	**F**	**F**
T	**F**	**T**	**T**
F	**T**	**T**	**T**
F	**F**	**T**	**T**

A 'not both . . . and . . .' expression is false only when both of its components, **P** and **Q**, are true.

A combination of the sentential connectives of *SL* can also be used to capture the exclusive sense of 'or' discussed earlier. Recall that the sentence

> With your meal you get apple pie or chocolate cake

is true in the exclusive sense of 'or' if with your meal you get apple pie or chocolate cake but not both apple pie and chocolate cake. We now know how to paraphrase the 'not both . . . and . . .' portion of the sentence. The paraphrase of the whole sentence is

> Both (either with your meal you get apple pie or with your meal you get chocolate cake) and it is not the case that (both with your meal you get apple pie and with your meal you get chocolate cake).

This can be symbolized as

$$(A \vee C) \ \& \sim (A \ \& \ C)$$

where 'A' abbreviates 'With your meal you get apple pie' and 'C' abbreviates 'With your meal you get chocolate cake'. Here is a table showing the truth conditions for exclusive 'or':

Truth Conditions for Exclusive 'Or'

P	**Q**	**(P ∨ Q) & ~ (P & Q)**
T	**T**	**F**
T	**F**	**T**
F	**T**	**T**
F	**F**	**F**

MATERIAL CONDITIONAL

One of the most common sentential connectives of English is 'if . . . then . . .'. A simple example is

> If Jones got the job then he applied for it.

This can be paraphrased as

> Either it is not the case that Jones got the job or Jones applied for the job

which can be symbolized as

$$\sim G \vee A$$

where 'G' abbreviates 'Jones got the job' and 'A' abbreviates 'Jones applied for the job'. It will be convenient to have a symbol in *SL* that expresses the truth-functional sense of 'if . . . then . . .'; we introduce '⊃' (horseshoe) for this purpose. The sentence 'If Jones got the job then Jones applied for the job' can then be symbolized as

$$G \supset A$$

A sentence of the form **P** ⊃ **Q**, where **P** and **Q** are sentences of *SL*, is a *material conditional.* **P**, the sentence on the left of the '⊃', is the *antecedent,* and **Q**, the sentence on the right of the '⊃', is the *consequent* of the conditional. It is important to remember that, whenever we write a sentence of the form **P** ⊃ **Q**, we could express it as ~ **P** ∨ **Q**. A sentence of the form ~ **P** ∨ **Q** is a disjunction, and a disjunction is false in only one case—when both disjuncts are false. Thus a sentence of the form ~ **P** ∨ **Q** is false when ~ **P** is false and **Q** is false, that is, when **P** is true and **Q** is false. This is also the only case in which a sentence of the form **P** ⊃ **Q** is false, that is, when the antecedent is true and the consequent is false. The characteristic truth-table is shown here:

P	Q	P ⊃ Q
T	T	T
T	F	F
F	T	T
F	F	T

Informally we can regard the 'if' clause of an English conditional as the antecedent of that conditional and the 'then' clause as the consequent. Here is an example of an English conditional converted to a truth-functional paraphrase that is symbolized by the material conditional:

If Michelle is in Paris then she is in France.

Expressed in a truth-functional paraphrase this becomes

<u>If</u> Michelle is in Paris <u>then</u> Michelle is in France.

The truth-functional paraphrase can be symbolized as a material conditional

$$P \supset F$$

Notice that the truth-functional paraphrase is false if Michelle is in Paris but is not in France—that is, if the antecedent is true and the consequent is false. But the truth-functional paraphrase is true under all other conditions. Thus, if Michelle is in Paris and in France, the paraphrase is true. If Michelle is not in Paris but is somewhere else in France, the paraphrase is true. If Michelle is not in Paris and not in France, the paraphrase is true.

However, the material conditional is not adequate as a complete treatment of conditional sentences in English. Material conditionals are truth-functional, but conditionals in English frequently convey information that exceeds a truth-functional analysis. For instance, 'if . . . then . . .' constructions sometimes have a causal force that is lost in a truth-functional paraphrase. Consider:

1. If this rod is made of metal then it will expand when heated.
2. If this rod is made of metal then it will contract when heated.

Each of these sentences can be used to make a causal claim, to assert a causal relation between the substance of which the rod in question is composed and the reaction of the rod to heat. But sentence 1 is in accord with the laws of nature, and sentence 2 is not. So, as used to make causal claims, sentence 1 is true and sentence 2 is false, even if it is false that the rod is made of metal.

Now suppose we paraphrase these two sentences as material conditionals:

1a. <u>If</u> this rod is made of metal <u>then</u> this rod will expand when heated.

2a. <u>If</u> this rod is made of metal <u>then</u> this rod will contract when heated.

These paraphrases can be symbolized as

1b. $M \supset E$

2b. $M \supset C$

where 'M' abbreviates 'The rod is made of metal', 'E' abbreviates 'This rod will expand when heated', and 'C' abbreviates 'This rod will contract when heated'. Remember that a material conditional is true if the antecedent is false. If the rod in the example is not made of metal, then both sentences 1a and 2a, and consequently their symbolizations 1b and 2b, are true. Sentence 1 says more than either 1a or 1b, and sentence 2 says more than either 2a or 2b. The fact that sentence 2 is false, whereas 2a and 2b are both true, shows this. It follows that when they are used to assert a causal relation, sentences 1 and 2, like many other English conditionals, are not truth-functional compounds. When it is and when it is not appropriate to paraphrase such sentences as material conditionals will be discussed further in Section 2.3.

Here are further examples of English sentences that can be paraphrased by using 'if . . . then . . .', but here and elsewhere we must keep in mind that sometimes information contained in the English conditionals will be lost in truth-functional paraphrasing.

Larry will become wealthy provided that he inherits the family fortune

can be paraphrased as

<u>If</u> Larry inherits the family fortune <u>then</u> Larry will become wealthy

which can be symbolized as

$F \supset W$

where 'F' abbreviates 'Larry inherits the family fortune' and 'W' abbreviates 'Larry will become wealthy'.

The Democratic candidate will win the election if he wins in the big cities

can be paraphrased as

If the Democratic candidate wins in the big cities then the Democratic candidate will win the election

which can be symbolized as '$C \supset E$', where 'C' abbreviates 'The Democratic candidate wins in the big cities' and 'E' abbreviates 'The Democratic candidate will win the election'.

Betty is in London only if Betty is in England

can be paraphrased as

If Betty is in London then Betty is in England

which can be symbolized as '$L \supset E$', where 'L' abbreviates 'Betty is in London' and 'E' abbreviates 'Betty is in England'. In this case be sure to notice the order in which the sentences are paraphrased. A common mistake in paraphrasing the sentential connective 'only if' is to ignore the word 'only' and reverse the order of the sentences. It is *incorrect* to paraphrase the original as 'If Betty is in England then Betty is in London'.

A connective that can be paraphrased either as a disjunction or as a conditional is 'unless'. Consider the sentence

This plant will die unless it is watered.

The only circumstance under which this sentence is false is the situation in which this plant does not die and is not watered. If either of the sentences that 'unless' connects is true, then the whole sentence is true. The simplest paraphrase is to treat the sentence as the disjunction

Either this plant will die or it is watered

which can be symbolized as

$$D \vee W$$

We can also understand the sentence 'This plant will die unless it is watered' as expressing a conditional:

If it is not the case that it is watered, then this plant will die which can be symbolized as

$\sim W \supset D$

Equally well, we can understand the sentence as expressing the equivalent conditional:

If it is not the case that this plant will die, then it is watered

which when symbolized is

$\sim D \supset W$

The two conditional paraphrases look different from each other and from the disjunction, but they make identical truth-functional claims. The disjunction claims that at least one of its component sentences is true. Each of the conditionals claims that, if one of two component sentences is not true, the other one is true. Here is a table that shows the truth-functional equivalence of the symbolizations for 'unless':

Truth Conditions for 'Unless'

P	**Q**	**P ∨ Q**	**~ P ⊃ Q**	**~ Q ⊃ P**
T	**T**	**T**	**T**	**T**
T	**F**	**T**	**T**	**T**
F	**T**	**T**	**T**	**T**
F	**F**	**F**	**F**	**F**

MATERIAL BICONDITIONAL

In English the connective 'if and only if' is used to express more than either the connective 'if' or the connective 'only if'. For example

John will get an A in the course if and only if he does well on the final examination

can be paraphrased as

Both (if John will get an A in the course then John does well on the final examination) and (if John does well on the final examination then John will get an A in the course).

We can symbolize the paraphrase as

$(C \supset E) \ \& \ (E \supset C)$

where 'C' abbreviates 'John will get an A in the course' and 'E' abbreviates 'John does well on the final examination'. The original sentence can also be paraphrased as

> Either (both John will get an A in the course and John does well on the final examination) or (both it is not the case that John will get an A in the course and it is not the case that John does well on the final examination).

Using the same abbreviations, this paraphrase is symbolized as

$$(C \& E) \vee (\sim C \& \sim E)$$

Both of these paraphrases and their corresponding symbolizations are truth-functional compounds. Each is true just in case either both atomic sentences are true or both atomic sentences are false. We introduce the connective '≡' (triple bar) to capture the truth-functional use of the connective 'if and only if'. The original English sentence can be symbolized as

$$C \equiv E$$

A sentence of the form

$$\mathbf{P} \equiv \mathbf{Q}$$

where **P** and **Q** are sentences of *SL*, is a *material biconditional.* Informally we shall use the term "material biconditional" when describing English sentences that can be symbolized as material biconditionals in *SL*. Here is the characteristic truth-table for '≡':

P	**Q**	**P ≡ Q**
T	T	T
T	F	F
F	T	F
F	F	T

The connective 'just in case' is sometimes used in English as an equivalent to 'if and only if'.

> Andy will win the lottery just in case Andy has the winning ticket

can be properly paraphrased as

> Andy will win the lottery if and only if Andy has the winning ticket

and symbolized as

$$W \equiv T$$

However, care must be taken when paraphrasing 'just in case' because this connective sometimes is used in ways *not* equivalent to 'if and only if'. Consider

Marty takes her umbrella to work just in case it rains.

This does not mean 'Marty takes her umbrella to work if and only if it rains'. Rather, the sentence means

Marty takes her umbrella to work because it may rain.

SUMMARY OF SOME COMMON CONNECTIVES

Note that we use lowercase boldface '**p**' and '**q**' to designate sentences of English and uppercase boldface '**P**' and '**Q**' to designate sentences of *SL*.

English Connectives	*Paraphrases*	*Symbolizations*
not **p**	it is not the case that **p**	~ **P**
p and **q** **p** but **q** **p** however **q** **p** although **q** **p** nevertheless **q** **p** nonetheless **q** **p** moreover **q**	both **p** and **q**	**P** & **Q**
p or **q**	either **p** or **q**	**P** ∨ **Q**
p or **q** [*exclusive*]	both either **p** or **q** and it is not the case that both **p** and **q**	(**P** ∨ **Q**) & ~ (**P** & **Q**)
if **p** then **q** **p** only if **q** **q** if **p** **q** provided that **p** **q** given **p**	if **p** then **q**	**P** ⊃ **Q**
p if and only if **q** **p** if but only if **q** **p** just in case **q**	**p** if and only if **q**	**P** ≡ **Q**
neither **p** nor **q**	both it is not the case that **p** and it is not the case that **q** it is not the case that either **p** or **q**	~ **P** & ~ **Q** ~ (**P** ∨ **Q**)
not both **p** and **q**	it is not the case that both **p** and **q** either it is not the case that **p** or it is not the case that **q**	~ (**P** & **Q**) ~ **P** ∨ ~ **Q**
p unless **q**	either **p** or **q** if it is not the case that **p** then **q** if it is not the case that **q** then **p**	**P** ∨ **Q** ~ **P** ⊃ **Q** ~ **Q** ⊃ **P**

The connective 'because' is not truth-functional. ('Because' can join two true sentences resulting in a true sentence and 'because' can join two true sentences resulting in a false sentence.) Hence 'Marty takes her umbrella to work just in case it rains' should be symbolized by a single sentence letter such as 'M'.

In our discussion of the material conditional and the material biconditional, we have been careful to distinguish among connectives such as 'if', 'only if', and 'if and only if'. These distinctions are very important in logic, philosophy, and mathematics. However, in everyday discourse people speak casually. For example, people may use 'if' or 'only if' when they mean 'if and only if'. Our general policy in this book is to take disjunctions and conditionals in their weaker rather than their stronger senses. That is, normally 'or' will be read in the inclusive sense, and 'if . . . then . . .' (and other conditional connectives) will be taken in the material conditional sense (not the biconditional sense). When stronger readings are intended, we will indicate that by explicitly using expressions such as 'either . . . or . . . but not both' and 'if and only if'.

2.1**E** EXERCISES

1. For each of the following sentences, construct a truth-functional paraphrase and symbolize the paraphrase in *SL*. Use these abbreviations:

A: Albert jogs regularly.
B: Bob jogs regularly.
C: Carol jogs regularly.

a. Bob and Carol jog regularly.
*b. Bob does not jog regularly, but Carol does.
c. Either Bob jogs regularly or Carol jogs regularly.
*d. Albert jogs regularly and so does Carol.
e. Neither Bob nor Carol jogs regularly.
*f. Bob does jog regularly; however, Albert doesn't.
g. Bob doesn't jog regularly unless Carol jogs regularly.
*h. Albert and Bob and also Carol do not jog regularly.
i. Either Bob jogs regularly or Albert jogs regularly, but they don't both jog regularly.
*j. Although Carol doesn't jog regularly, either Bob or Albert does.
k. It is not the case that Carol or Bob jogs regularly; moreover Albert doesn't jog regularly either.
*l. It is not the case that Albert, Bob, or Carol jogs regularly.
m. Either Albert jogs regularly or he doesn't.
*n. Neither Albert nor Carol nor Bob jogs regularly.

2. Using the abbreviations given in Exercise 1, construct idiomatic English sentences from the following sentences of *SL*:

a. A & B
*b. $A \vee \sim A$

c. A ∨ C
*d. ~ (A ∨ C)
e. ~ A & ~ C
*f. ~ ~ B
g. B & (A ∨ C)
*h. (A ∨ C) & ~ (A & C)
i. (A & C) & B
*j. ~ A ∨ (~ B ∨ ~ C)
k. (B ∨ C) ∨ ~ (B ∨ C)

3. Assuming that 'Albert jogs regularly' is true, 'Bob jogs regularly' is false, and 'Carol jogs regularly' is true, which of the symbolic sentences in Exercise 2 are true and which are false? Use your knowledge of the characteristic truth-tables in answering.

4. Paraphrase each of the following using the phrase 'it is not the case that'. Symbolize the results, indicating what your abbreviations are.

a. Some joggers are not marathon runners.
*b. Bob is not a marathon runner.
c. Each and every marathon runner is not lazy.
*d. Some joggers are unhealthy.
e. Nobody is perfect.

5. For each of the following sentences, construct a truth-functional paraphrase and symbolize the paraphrase in *SL*. Use these abbreviations:

A: Albert jogs regularly.
B: Bob jogs regularly.
C: Carol jogs regularly.
L: Bob is lazy.
M: Carol is a marathon runner.
H: Albert is healthy.

a. If Bob jogs regularly he is not lazy.
*b. If Bob is not lazy he jogs regularly.
c. Bob jogs regularly if and only if he is not lazy.
*d. Carol is a marathon runner only if she jogs regularly.
e. Carol is a marathon runner if and only if she jogs regularly.
*f. If Carol jogs regularly, then if Bob is not lazy he jogs regularly.
g. If both Carol and Bob jog regularly, then Albert does too.
*h. If either Carol or Bob jogs regularly, then Albert does too.
i. If either Carol or Bob does not jog regularly, then Albert doesn't either.
*j. If neither Carol nor Bob jogs regularly, then Albert doesn't either.
k. If Albert is healthy and Bob is not lazy, then both jog regularly.
*l. If Albert is healthy, he jogs regularly if and only if Bob does.
m. Assuming Carol is not a marathon runner, she jogs regularly if and only if Albert and Bob both jog regularly.
*n. Although Albert is healthy he does not jog regularly, but Carol does jog regularly if Bob does.
o. If Carol is a marathon runner and Bob is not lazy and Albert is healthy, then they all jog regularly.

*p. If Albert jogs regularly, then Carol does provided Bob does.
q. If Albert jogs regularly if Carol does, then Albert is healthy and Carol is a marathon runner.
*r. If Albert is healthy if he jogs regularly, then if Bob is lazy he doesn't jog regularly.
s. If Albert jogs regularly if either Carol or Bob does, then Albert is healthy and Bob isn't lazy.
*t. If Albert is not healthy, then Bob and Albert do not both jog regularly.

6. Using the abbreviations given in Exercise 5, construct idiomatic English sentences from the following sentences of *SL*.
a. L ∨ ~ L
*b. M ⊃ C
c. A ≡ H
*d. C & ~ B
e. ~ B & ~ C
*f. [A ∨ (B ∨ C)] ⊃ [A & (B & C)]
g. (~ A ∨ ~ C) ⊃ B
*h. ~ (A ∨ C) ⊃ B
i. C ⊃ (A & ~ B)
*j. B ≡ (~ L & A)
k. C & ~ C
*l. A & (C ≡ B)
m. (L ⊃ L) & B
*n. ~ ~ H & ~ A
o. ~ A ⊃ (~ B ⊃ ~ C)
*p. (C ⊃ A) & (A ⊃ B)
q. ~ A & (B ≡ ~ L)
*r. (H ⊃ A) ⊃ (~ L ⊃ B)

7. Give a truth-functional paraphrase for each of the following, and symbolize the paraphrase in *SL*.
a. Neither men nor women are from Mars or Venus.
*b. This dog won't hunt; moreover he is not even a good pet.
c. Not both Butch Cassidy and the Sundance Kid escaped.
*d. The tea will not taste robust unless it steeps for a while.
e. That lady was both cut in half and torn asunder unless it was a magic trick.
*f. Neither wind nor rain nor dark of night will stop the mail.
g. The prisoner will receive either a life sentence or the death penalty.
*h. Unless snowstorms arrive, skiing and snowboarding will be impossible.

8. What are the truth-conditions for the exclusive 'or'? How might the exclusive 'or' be expressed as a biconditional?

2.2 COMPLEX SYMBOLIZATIONS

Going through the paraphrase stage is useful when learning how to symbolize sentences. The paraphrases serve as reminders of exactly what is being symbolized in *SL*. Each sentence of a paraphrase will be either a simple sentence, a truth-functionally compound sentence, or a non-truth-functionally compound sentence. The simple sentences and non-truth-functionally compound sentences are to be symbolized as atomic sentences of *SL*. The truth-functionally compound sentences are to be symbolized as molecular sentences of *SL*. In constructing a paraphrase, we must be alert to the grammar, wording, and context of the original passage. Sometimes there will be a loss of information in moving from the original passage to the paraphrase, but often the loss of information will not matter.

GUIDELINES FOR PARAPHRASING

In paraphrasing sentences, following several guidelines will be useful:

1. Any sentence of the original passage that is going to be treated as a simple sentence, that will eventually be abbreviated as an atomic sentence in *SL*, can be copied as its own paraphrase.
2. Any sentence of the original passage that is going to be paraphrased as a truth-functionally compound sentence can be paraphrased using one or more of the connectives 'both . . . and . . .', 'either . . . or . . .', 'it is not the case that', 'if . . . then . . .', and 'if and only if'. We underscore these connectives in the paraphrases to emphasize their truth-functional usage.
3. Ambiguities should be eliminated in the paraphrase. For instance, sometimes it may be clearer to insert parentheses in the paraphrase to establish how sentences are to be grouped. If the connective 'it is not the case that' is applied to an entire material biconditional, rather than just to the first component, parentheses will show this, as in 'It is not the case that (the Republican candidate will win if and only if he is supported by big business)'.
4. If the passage is an argument, put the paraphrased argument in standard form. That is, list the paraphrased premises first, draw a line, and then list the paraphrased conclusion.
5. Where an English passage contains two or more different wordings of the same claim, use just one wording in constructing a paraphrase of that passage.

The intent of the last of these guidelines can be made clear through the use of examples. Suppose someone offers the following rather trivial argument:

> If Sue and Bill got married yesterday, they are honeymooning today. They did get married yesterday. So they are honeymooning today.

The sentence 'They did get married yesterday' is not the antecedent of 'If Sue and Bill got married yesterday, they are honeymooning today'. Yet, in the context of this passage, 'they' refers to Sue and Bill. So the second premise of our paraphrase should be 'Sue and Bill got married yesterday', *not* 'They did get married yesterday'. The full paraphrase will be

> If Sue and Bill got married yesterday, then Sue and Bill are honeymooning today.
>
> Sue and Bill got married yesterday.
>
> ---
>
> Sue and Bill are honeymooning today.

Note that we have replaced 'they' with 'Sue and Bill' throughout. Here is another example in which rewording is necessary in constructing a paraphrase:

> Either Jim will not pass the test or Jim spent last night studying logic. Jim's night was not spent poring over his logic text. Hence Jim will fail the test.

In constructing a paraphrase of this argument, it is important to word the premises and conclusion so that we can use a minimum number of sentential letters to symbolize the paraphrase. Suppose someone gives the following paraphrase:

> Either it is not the case that Jim will pass the test or Jim spent last night studying logic.
>
> It is not the case that Jim's night was spent poring over his logic text.
>
> ---
>
> Jim will fail the test.

To symbolize this argument, we need four sentence letters: 'J', 'S', 'O', and 'F'.

> $\sim J \vee S$
>
> $\sim O$
>
> ---
>
> F

Here 'J' abbreviates 'Jim will pass the test', 'S' abbreviates 'Jim spent last night studying logic', 'O' abbreviates 'Jim's night was spent poring over his logic text', and 'F' abbreviates 'Jim will fail the test'. Symbolized in this way our argument is invalid. But the original English argument is valid. The following is a far better paraphrase:

> Either it is not the case that Jim will pass the test or Jim spent last night studying logic.
>
> It is not the case that Jim spent last night studying logic.
>
> ---
>
> It is not the case that Jim will pass the test.

'Jim will not pass the test' and 'Jim will fail the test' express the same claim in this context. So do 'He spent last night studying logic' and 'Jim's night was spent poring over his logic text'. Our second paraphrase reflects this and allows us to give the following symbolization:

$$\sim J \vee S$$
$$\sim S$$
$$\overline{}$$
$$\sim J$$

This symbolic argument is valid, as our formal techniques will show.

We shall now present and symbolize more complex sentences and groups of sentences. In our first series of examples, we shall consider sentences about an international yacht race in which there are just three major competitors: the Americans, the British, and the Canadians. In symbolizing these sentences we shall make use of the following abbreviations:

M: The Americans win the race.
R: The British win the race.
N: The Canadians win the race.
A: The Americans have good luck.
B: The British have good luck.
C: The Canadians have good luck.
E: Everyone is surprised.
T: A major tradition is broken.

Our first two examples illustrate the important difference between sentences compounded by 'if . . . then . . .' and those compounded by 'only if':

1. The British will win if neither of the other two major competitors wins.
2. The British will win only if neither of the other two major competitors wins.

The first of these sentences tells us, in effect, that the British do not have to worry about the minor competitors. According to sentence 1, for the British to win all that is needed is that the Americans and Canadians not win. The second sentence makes a more modest claim—it expresses only the truism that for the British to win the other major competitors must not win. Here are our truth-functional paraphrases of these sentences:

1a. If both it is not the case that the Americans win the race and it is not the case that the Canadians win the race, then the British win the race.

2a. If the British win the race, then both it is not the case that the Americans win the race and it is not the case that the Canadians win the race.

The rule to remember here is that a sentence compounded by 'if' rather than by 'only if' should be paraphrased as a conditional whose *antecedent* is the sentence following 'if' in the original compound. A sentence compounded by 'only if' should be paraphrased as a conditional whose *consequent* is the sentence following 'only if' in the original compound. The symbolizations of these paraphrases will be

1b. $(\sim M \ \& \sim N) \supset R$

2b. $R \supset (\sim M \ \& \sim N)$

In sentences 1 and 2 some of the verbs are in the present tense and some are in the future tense. But in these particular examples, the difference in tense does not reflect a difference in the temporal order of the events under discussion. ('The British will win if neither of the other two major competitors wins' does *not* mean that if neither of the other two major competitors wins *now,* then the British will win *later.*) Accordingly in our paraphrases we have made all the verbs present tense. We could, alternatively, have made them all future tense. In giving paraphrases it is often useful to make as many of the verbs as possible the same tense; but this should be done *only* when doing so does not distort the truth-functional connections between the sentences in the passage.

Often there is more than one correct paraphrase of a sentence. For example, in paraphrasing both sentence 1 and sentence 2, we could have used 'or' instead of 'and'. For sentence 1 we would then have

<u>If</u> <u>it is not the case that</u> <u>either</u> the Americans win the race <u>or</u> the Canadians win the race <u>then</u> the British win the race.

Here the symbolization is

$\sim (M \vee N) \supset R$

Recall that 'neither . . . nor . . .' after paraphrasing will be symbolized by a sentence of the form

$\sim \mathbf{P} \ \& \sim \mathbf{Q}$ or $\sim (\mathbf{P} \vee \mathbf{Q})$

and 'not both . . . and . . .' by a sentence of the form

$\sim (\mathbf{P} \ \& \ \mathbf{Q})$ or $\sim \mathbf{P} \vee \sim \mathbf{Q}$

Further examples will help illustrate.

3. The Canadians will win if both the other major competitors do not have good luck.

4. The Canadians will win if either of the other major competitors does not have good luck.
5. The Canadians will win if not both of the other major competitors have good luck.

These are best paraphrased as

3a. If (both it is not the case that the Americans have good luck and it is not the case that the British have good luck) then the Canadians win the race.

4a. If (either it is not the case that the Americans have good luck or it is not the case that the British have good luck) then the Canadians win the race.

5a. If it is not the case that (both the Americans have good luck and the British have good luck) then the Canadians win the race.

In *SL* these become

3b. $(\sim A \ \& \sim B) \supset N$

4b. $(\sim A \vee \sim B) \supset N$

5b. $\sim (A \ \& \ B) \supset N$

Sentences 4a and 5a are equivalent, as are 4b and 5b. To say that either one or the other of the major competitors does not have good luck is to say only that they will *not both* have good luck. Where 'not' goes in relation to 'both' is important, as we shall see if we compare sentences 3 and 5. The phrase 'both . . . not . . .' means that each of the two things in question does not have the property in question. But the phrase 'not both' means only that at least one of those two things does not have the property in question.

Here are two more examples:

6. The Americans will win unless the British have good luck, in which case the British will win.
7. A major tradition will be broken if but only if no major competitor wins.

In sentence 6 the phrase 'in which case' is to be understood as 'in case the British have good luck'. The proper paraphrase is thus

6a. Both if it is not the case that the British have good luck then the Americans win the race and if the British have good luck then the British win the race.

This is symbolized as

6b. $(\sim B \supset M) \ \& \ (B \supset R)$

In paraphrasing sentence 7 we need only remember that there are exactly three major competitors: the Americans, the British, and the Canadians.

7a. A major tradition will be broken if and only if it is not the case that [either (either the Americans win the race or the British win the race) or the Canadians win the race].

In symbols this becomes

7b. $T \equiv \sim [(M \vee R) \vee N]$

Sometimes sentences containing such quantity terms as 'at least', 'at most', and 'all' can be paraphrased as truth-functional compounds. This will be the case when the number of things or events or cases we are talking about is finite. All the following can be given truth-functional paraphrases:

8. At least one of the major competitors will have good luck.
9. Exactly one of the major competitors will have good luck.
10. At least two of the major competitors will have good luck.
11. Exactly two of the major competitors will have good luck.

Since there are three major competitors, to say that at least one of them will have good luck is equivalent to saying that either the first, the second, or the third will have good luck. So

8a. Either the Americans have good luck or (either the British have good luck or the Canadians have good luck).

And in symbols we have

8b. $A \vee (B \vee C)$

The grouping here is arbitrary. We could just as well have written '$(A \vee B) \vee C$'. But grouping is necessary, since '$A \vee B \vee C$' is not a sentence of *SL*. (The connectives of *SL* are all, except for '~', *binary* connectives; that is, each connects *two* sentences. When the parentheses are removed from sentence 8b, it is unclear which sentences the first '∨' connects. So the expression is not well formed; that is, it is not a sentence of *SL*.)

Since '∨' is used to capture the inclusive sense of disjunction, we have to work some to say that one and only one of the three major competitors will have good luck. One way of doing it is this:

9a. Either [both the Americans have good luck and it is not the case that (either the British have good luck or the Canadians have good luck)] or (either [both the British have good luck and it is not the case that (either the Americans have good luck or the Canadians have good luck)] or [both the Canadians have good luck and it is not the case that (either the Americans have good luck or the British have good luck)]).

The symbolic version of sentence 9 is a good deal more perspicuous than is the paraphrase:

9b. $[A \,\&\, \sim (B \vee C)] \vee ([B \,\&\, \sim (A \vee C)] \vee [C \,\&\, \sim (A \vee B)])$

As sentence 9a illustrates, truth-functional paraphrases of complex English passages can themselves become very complex. Constructing truth-functional paraphrases is of most value when one is first learning to symbolize English sentences in *SL*. After some facility with the techniques of symbolization has been gained, the paraphrase stage can be skipped, except when there is something especially difficult or interesting about the passage being symbolized. Hence hereafter we shall sometimes omit the paraphrase stage. Sentence 10 is fairly readily symbolized as

10b. $(A \,\&\, B) \vee [(A \,\&\, C) \vee (B \,\&\, C)]$

Sentence 11 is a repeat of sentence 10 with the additional proviso that not all the teams have good luck. One appropriate symbolization is

11b. $[(A \,\&\, B) \vee [(A \,\&\, C) \vee (B \,\&\, C)]] \,\&\, \sim [A \,\&\, (B \,\&\, C)]$

We can symbolize an argument using the following abbreviations:

R: The Australians raise their spinnaker.
I: The wind increases.
A: The Australians win the race.
C: The Australians capsize.
L: The Australians look foolish.
J: The Australians strike their jib.
M: The Australians reef their main.

If the Australians raise their spinnaker then if the wind doesn't increase they will win the race, but if they raise their spinnaker and the wind does increase they will lose the race and look foolish. The wind will increase and the Australians will reef their main and strike their jib, and will not raise their spinnaker. So if they don't capsize the Australians will win the race.

In symbolizing this argument we shall identify losing the race with not winning the race. In the context this is surely permissible. Here is our symbolization of the argument:

$$[R \supset (\sim I \supset A)] \;\&\; [(R \;\&\; I) \supset (\sim A \;\&\; L)]$$
$$[I \;\&\; (M \;\&\; J)] \;\&\; \sim R$$
$$\overline{\sim C \supset A}$$

Our formal techniques will reveal that this argument is truth-functionally invalid.

2.2E EXERCISES

1. Paraphrase the following sentences about the performance of the French, German, and Danish teams in the next Olympics, and symbolize the paraphrases as sentences in *SL* using these abbreviations:

F: The French team will win at least one gold medal.
G: The German team will win at least one gold medal.
D: The Danish team will win at least one gold medal.
P: The French team is plagued with injuries.
S: The star German runner is disqualified.
R: It rains during most of the competition.

a. At least one of the French, German, or Danish teams will win a gold medal.
*b. At most one of them will win a gold medal.
c. Exactly one of them will win a gold medal.
*d. They will not all win gold medals.
e. At least two of them will win gold medals.
*f. At most two of them will win gold medals.
g. Exactly two of them will win gold medals.
*h. They will all win gold medals.

2. Using the abbreviations given in Exercise 1, construct idiomatic English sentences from the following sentences of *SL*.

a. $\sim F \;\&\; (\sim G \;\&\; \sim D)$
*b. $\sim (F \;\&\; (G \;\&\; D))$
c. $\sim (F \vee (G \vee D))$
*d. $\sim (F \vee G) \vee (\sim (G \vee D) \vee \sim (F \vee D))$
e. $(F \vee G) \vee ((G \vee D) \vee (F \vee D))$
*f. $(F \;\&\; G) \vee ((G \;\&\; D) \vee (F \;\&\; D))$
g. $F \;\&\; ((G \vee D) \;\&\; \sim (G \;\&\; D))$
*h. $(F \;\&\; G) \vee (F \;\&\; D)$

3. Paraphrase the following and, using the abbreviations given in Exercise 1, symbolize the resulting paraphrases as sentences in *SL*.

a. If any of them wins a gold medal so will the other two.

*b. The French will win a gold medal only if they are not plagued with injuries, in which case they won't win.

c. If the star German runner is disqualified, the Germans will win a gold medal only if neither of the other two teams does.

*d. Provided it doesn't rain during most of the competition and their star runner isn't disqualified, the Germans will win a gold medal if either of the other teams does.

e. The Danes will win a gold medal if and only if the French are plagued with injuries and the star German runner is disqualified.

*f. The Germans will win a gold medal only if it doesn't rain during most of the competition and their star runner is not disqualified.

g. If the French are plagued with injuries, they will win a gold medal only if neither of the other teams does and it rains during most of the competition.

*h. The Danes will win a gold medal unless it rains during most of the competition, in which case they won't but the other two teams will win gold medals.

4. Using the abbreviations given in Exercise 1, construct idiomatic English sentences from the following sentences of *SL*.

a. $(S \supset \sim G) \ \& \ S$

*b. $\sim (F \vee G) \supset D$

c. $\sim G \equiv (D \ \& \ F)$

*d. $(P \ \& \ S) \supset D$

e. $[(G \supset F) \ \& \ (F \supset D)] \supset (G \supset D)$

*f. $R \supset [(\sim F \ \& \sim G) \ \& \sim D]$

g. $[F \vee (G \vee D)] \vee [P \vee (S \vee R)]$

*h. $D \vee [(F \ \& \sim P) \vee (G \ \& \sim S)]$

5. Paraphrase and then symbolize the following passages, being careful to indicate the abbreviations you are using.

a. *Robert's Rules of Order* was written by an engineer or a clergyman if it was not written by a politician. The author of *Robert's Rules of Order* was motivated to write the book by an unruly church meeting but was not a clergyman. The book's author was not a politician and could not persuade a publisher that the book would make money, forcing him to publish the book himself. *Robert's Rules of Order* was written by an engineer.

*b. Either George doesn't have a high cholesterol level or cholesterol is trapped in the walls of his arteries. If cholesterol is trapped in his arteries, then plaque will build up and block his arteries, and with such a buildup and blockage, he is a candidate for a heart attack. Hence George is a candidate for a heart attack.

c. Either the maid or the butler committed the murder unless the cook did it. The cook did it only if a knife was the murder weapon; moreover, if a knife was used, neither the butler nor the maid did it. The murder weapon was a knife. Therefore the cook did it.

*d. If neither Henry nor Fred will play the lawyer, then Morris will not be upset; and moreover, if Morris will not be upset the drama will be successful. Thus the drama will get good reviews. After all, both Henry and Fred will not play the part of the lawyer, and the drama will get good reviews if and only if the drama will be a success.

e. The candidate will win at least two of three states—California, New York, and Texas—for if the candidate is perceived as conservative, she will not win New York but will win the other two. She is perceived as conservative if her advertising campaign is effective; and she has an effective advertising campaign.

*f. Assuming Betty is the judge, Peter won't get a suspended sentence. The trial will be long unless the district attorney is brief, but the district attorney is not brief. Fred is the defense lawyer. However, if Fred is the defense lawyer, Peter will be found guilty; and if Peter will be found guilty, he will be given a sentence. Consequently after a long trial Peter will be given a sentence, which won't be suspended by the judge.

2.3 NON-TRUTH-FUNCTIONAL CONNECTIVES

As stated in Section 2.1,

> A sentential connective is used *truth-functionally* if and only if it is used to generate a compound sentence from one or more sentences in such a way that the truth-value of the generated compound is wholly determined by the truth-values of those one or more sentences from which the compound is generated, no matter what those truth-values may be.

The sentential connectives of *SL* have only truth-functional uses. Many sentential connectives of English have truth-functional uses, but many do not. And many of those that do are not always used truth-functionally.

Determining whether a particular connective is or is not being used in a truth-functional sense is a complex matter. But a good rule of thumb is this: If the connective is being used truth-functionally, we should be able to construct a truth-table that adequately characterizes that use. (This is just what we did for standard uses of the English connectives introduced in Section 2.1.) If a truth-table that adequately characterizes the use of a connective in a particular sentence cannot be constructed, then that connective is not being used truth-functionally in the sentence in question.

To see how this rule of thumb operates, consider the use of 'if . . . then . . .' in the following sentence:

> If Germany's U-boats had been able to shut off the flow of supplies to Great Britain, then Germany would have won the war.

If 'if . . . then . . .' is being used truth-functionally in this conditional, it is probably being used in the sense captured by the horseshoe of *SL*, in the sense characterized by this table:

P	Q	P ⊃ Q
T	T	T
T	F	F
F	T	T
F	F	T

The truth-functional paraphrase of the sentence would be

> If Germany's U-boats were able to shut off the flow of supplies to Great Britain then Germany won the war.

In fact, Germany's U-boats were not able to shut off the flow of supplies to Great Britain; that is, the antecedent of this material conditional is false. The material conditional is therefore true. But historians do not all think the original conditional is true. Some think it true, and some false, depending upon their appraisal of the historical evidence.

One might still argue that in the example 'if . . . then . . .' is being used in some truth-functional sense. If so, we should be able to construct a paraphrase and a truth-table that express that sense. But a little reflection will show that no rearrangement of the **T**s and **F**s in the final column will produce such a table. This is because such conditionals are claims about what would happen in certain situations, regardless of whether those specified situations actually obtain. That is, knowledge of whether the situation described by the antecedent and consequent obtain is not sufficient to determine the truth-value of such conditionals. Some of these conditionals are true when the situations described do not hold ('If Germany had won World War II, Britain would have lost' is one), and some are false ('If Germany had invaded Spain, Germany would have won World War II').

Conditionals such as we have just been discussing are called *subjunctive conditionals* (because they are in the subjunctive, rather than the indicative, mood), and 'if . . . then . . .' as used in subjunctive conditionals is not truth-functional. In this case and others in which connectives are not being used truth-functionally, the safest course is to abbreviate the compounds generated by the connectives as atomic sentences of *SL*.

But being safe has it costs. Many arguments do make use of subjunctive conditionals, and we do want to evaluate the validity of these arguments whenever it is possible to do so. Consider the case of a doctor testifying at an inquest. He claims that the deceased did not die of strychnine poisoning and, when asked by the coroner to support his claim, argues as follows:

> Had the deceased died of strychnine poisoning, there would have been traces of that poison in the body. The autopsy would have found those traces had they been there. The autopsy did not reveal any traces of strychnine. Hence the deceased did not die of strychnine poisoning.

Here the following truth-functional paraphrase seems appropriate:

> If the deceased died of strychnine poisoning, then there were traces of strychnine in the body.
>
> If there were traces of strychnine in the body, then the autopsy found traces of strychnine in the body.
>
> It is not the case that the autopsy found traces of strychnine in the body.
>
> ---
>
> It is not the case that the deceased died of strychnine poisoning.

Symbolizing this argument yields

$$S \supset T$$
$$T \supset R$$
$$\sim R$$
$$\overline{}$$
$$\sim S$$

This symbolic argument is valid, and so is the English paraphrase of our original argument. In constructing that paraphrase, we weakened the premises but not the conclusion. A sentence **p** is *weaker* than a sentence **q** if and only if the truth of **q** guarantees the truth of **p**, but not vice versa. If **p** is weaker than **q**, **q** is *stronger* than **p**. Sentences **p** and **q** are *equivalent* if and only if **p** guarantees the truth of **q** and **q** guarantees the truth of **p**. Consequently, if the premises of the original argument are true, then so are those of the paraphrase. And, since the paraphrase is valid, its conclusion is true if its premises are. The conclusion of the paraphrase is merely a rewording of the conclusion of the original argument. Hence, if the premises of the original argument are true, the conclusion of that argument is also true. That is, the original argument is also valid.

Here is another argument using subjunctive conditionals:

> If Hitler had kept his treaty with Stalin, he would have defeated England. Hitler did not keep his treaty with Stalin. Therefore, if Hitler had kept his treaty with Stalin, he would have freed all the Jews and disbanded the SS.

Suppose we construct the following truth-functional paraphrase:

> If Hitler kept his treaty with Stalin then Hitler defeated England.
> It is not the case that Hitler kept his treaty with Stalin.
>
> ---
>
> If Hitler kept his treaty with Stalin, then both Hitler freed all the Jews and Hitler disbanded the SS.

This paraphrase can be readily symbolized as

$$
\begin{array}{l}
K \supset E \\
\sim K \\
\hline
K \supset (F \,\&\, D)
\end{array}
$$

Here the conclusion is equivalent to '$\sim K \vee (F \,\&\, D)$' and hence accurately symbolizes only 'Either Hitler did not keep his treaty with Stalin or Hitler did free all the Jews and Hitler disbanded the SS'. This claim does validly follow from the second premise of the argument. So our paraphrase is valid (as, of course, is the symbolic version of it). But the original English argument is clearly invalid. What has happened is that in paraphrasing that argument we made the conclusion, which is a subjunctive conditional, a material conditional. And if we weaken a conclusion in constructing a truth-functional paraphrase, there can be no guarantee that the symbolic argument we obtain by symbolizing that paraphrase will be valid *only if* the original English argument is valid. It may well be impossible for certain premises to be true and a weak conclusion false, where it is *not* impossible for those same premises to be true and a stronger conclusion false.

Although it may appear from the examples so far that truth-functional paraphrases will always be equivalent to or weaker than the original passages, this is not always the case. Sometimes the truth-functional paraphrase will be stronger. Consider this argument:

> It is not the case that if astronauts were to travel to Venus, they would find the surface of the planet hospitable. Hence astronauts travel to Venus.

Here the premise is the negation of a subjunctive conditional. Because the surface conditions of Venus are most unpleasant, astronauts would not find the planet hospitable if they traveled there. Therefore the premise is true. The conclusion of the argument is false because astronauts do not travel to Venus. The argument is invalid. But now consider a truth-functional paraphrase of the argument:

> <u>It is not the case that</u> <u>if</u> astronauts travel to Venus, <u>then</u> astronauts find the surface of the planet hospitable.
>
> ---
>
> Astronauts travel to Venus.

This paraphrased argument is valid. Suppose the conclusion is false. The conclusion, 'Astronauts travel to Venus', is also the antecedent of the embedded conditional in the premise. If the antecedent of a truth-functional conditional is false, then the conditional is true. And, if the conditional is true, its negation is false. Therefore, whenever the conclusion is false, the premise will be false as well. Hence the paraphrased argument and its symbolization

$$\frac{\sim (V \supset H)}{V}$$

are valid!

Why is the original argument invalid but its truth-functional paraphrase and symbolization valid? The answer is that, because subjunctive conditionals are usually stronger than material conditionals, negated subjunctive conditionals are generally weaker than their truth-functional counterparts. Because the truth-functional premise is stronger, it can support a conclusion the original premise cannot. In such cases the validity of a truth-functionally paraphrased argument and its symbolization will not establish the validity of the original argument containing the negated subjective conditional.

In view of these examples a further guideline for paraphrasing and symbolizing non-truth-functional compounds is in order:

6. The safest policy in dealing with non-truth-functional compounds is to paraphrase them as single sentences. In constructing a paraphrase for an argument, if non-truth-functional compounds are paraphrased as truth-functional compounds, be sure that the paraphrased premises are equivalent to or weaker than the original premises and that the paraphrased conclusion is equivalent to or stronger than the original conclusion.[2]

There are many connectives of English that have no truth-functional senses. One such connective is 'before'. When placed between two English sentences, 'before' does generate a further sentence (through sometimes an awkward one). From the sentences 'Nixon was elected president' and 'Bush's son was elected president' we can in this way obtain

Nixon was elected president before Bush's son was elected president.

This compound is true. But writing 'before' between two true sentences does not always produce a true sentence. A case in point is

Nixon was elected president before Kennedy was elected president.

This compound is false though the sentences from which it is generated are both true. Reflection should show that there is no truth-functional use of

[2]For this policy, which differs from the one we proposed in earlier editions, we are indebted to David Sherry. In his article "Note on the Scope of Truth-Functional Logic," (*Journal of Philosophical Logic*, 28 [1999], 327–328), Sherry explains why our earlier policy was inadequate.

'before' because there is no use of 'before' in which the truth-value of

> **p** before **q**

is determined, given only that **p** and **q** are both true. Similar considerations will show that 'after', 'when', and 'because' lack truth-functional senses in English.

There are also unary connectives of English that operate only non-truth-functionally. 'It is well known that' is one such connective. There is no use of this connective in which knowing only the truth-value of **p** always allows one to calculate the truth-value of

> It is well known that **p**.

For example, both 'Cleveland is a city in Ohio' and 'Arcadia is a town in Ohio' are true. And, though 'It is well known that Cleveland is a city in Ohio' is true, 'It is well known that Arcadia is a town in Ohio' is false. Such considerations show that this unary connective has no truth-functional use. Similar reasoning will show that such other unary connectives as 'necessarily', 'probably', 'possibly', 'it is alleged that', and 'many people fear that' have no truth-functional senses.

Such expressions as 'Tom believes that', 'Tom knows that', and 'Tom hopes that' can be attached to sentences to generate further sentences. But sentences generated in this way are not truth-functionally compound sentences. For example, 'Paris is in France' is true, but knowing this does not allow us to calculate the truth-value of

> Tom believes that Paris is in France.

For all we know, Tom may believe that Paris is in Belgium, not France. Tom, like most of us, has some true beliefs and some false beliefs.

We have yet to consider the rather special case of a non-truth-functional connective generating a compound sentence from sentences that are themselves truth-functionally compound. For example,

> Either Mary is late or the clock is wrong

is clearly a truth-functionally compound sentence. But

> Tom believes that either Mary is late or the clock is wrong

is not. Nor should it be paraphrased as a truth-functional compound—for example,

> Either Tom believes that Mary is late or Tom believes that the clock is wrong.

Tom may well believe the disjunction about Mary and the clock without believing either disjunct, just as one might believe that one will either pass or fail a given course, without either believing that one will pass or believing that one will fail. (We can often reasonably predict that one or the other of two events will happen, without being able to predict *which* one will happen.)

Similarly

> Probably the coin will come up heads or tails

cannot fairly be paraphrased as

> Either the coin will probably come up heads or the coin will probably come up tails.

In fact, if the coin is a fair coin the odds are very high that it will come up either heads or tails (that it will not stand on edge). But the odds that it will come up heads are slightly less than one in two, as are the odds that it will come up tails (it just might stand on edge). So the truth-functional paraphrase is false, even though the claim it allegedly paraphrases is true.

But now consider

> Probably Alice and Tom will both pass the course.

It certainly seems appropriate to paraphrase this sentence as

> Both probably Alice will pass the course and probably Tom will pass the course.

If a conjunction is probable, then each conjunct is probable. But a disjunction can be probable without either disjunct alone being probable. The same reasoning holds for such sentence-compounding expressions as 'necessarily' and 'certainly'. Roughly speaking, when either 'necessary' or 'probably' is attached to a sentence that can be paraphrased as a conjunction, the result can itself be paraphrased as a conjunction; but this is not the case when one of these terms is attached to a sentence that is a disjunction or to other kinds of truth-functional compounds.

2.3E EXERCISES

1. Decide which of the following sentences are truth-functional compounds, and explain why the remaining sentences are not. Symbolize all the sentences in *SL*.

a. It's possible that every family on this continent owns a television set.

*b. Rocky knows who will arrive on the train or George knows.

c. Necessarily, the coin will come up heads or tails.

*d. Tamara won't be visiting tonight because she is working late.

e. Although Tamara won't stop by, she has promised to phone early in the evening.

*f. If the defendant had originally pleaded guilty, the trial would have lasted twice as long.

g. John believes that our manuscript has been either lost or stolen.

*h. John believes that our manuscript has been stolen, and Howard believes that it has been lost.

i. The defendant relented only after much testimony was discredited.

2. Symbolize the following arguments in *SL*, being sure to state the abbreviations you are using.

a. The murder was committed by the maid only if she believed her life was in danger. Had the butler done it, it would have been done silently and the body would not have been mutilated. As a matter of fact it was done silently; however, the maid's life was not in danger. The butler did it if and only if the maid failed to do it. Hence the maid did it.

*b. If this piece of metal is gold, then it has atomic number 79. Nordvik believes this piece of metal is gold. Therefore Nordvik believes this piece of metal has atomic number 79.

c. If Charles Babbage had had the theory of the modern computer and had had modern electronic parts, then the modern computer would have been developed before the beginning of the twentieth century. In fact, although he lived in the early nineteenth century, Babbage had the theory of the modern computer. But he did not have access to modern electronic parts, and he was forced to construct his computers out of mechanical gears and levers. Therefore, if Charles Babbage had had modern electronic parts available to him, the modern computer would have been developed before the beginning of the twentieth century.

2.4 THE SYNTAX OF *SL*

Symbolic languages have a precision that everyday languages lack and that facilitates examination of the logical properties of sentences and arguments. We have already seen a large sample of sentences of *SL*. In this section a precise specification of the expressions of *SL* will be given. To ensure that our discussion of *SL* is as clear as possible, it will be helpful to draw some distinctions that are usually neither formulated nor observed in everyday language.

OBJECT LANGUAGE AND METALANGUAGE, USE AND MENTION

We have been talking about the language *SL* in this chapter. When we talk about a language, we call that language the *object language*. In this text *SL* is an object language, and English is the metalanguage used to discuss it. A *metalanguage* is a language used to discuss or describe some object language. The distinction between object language and metalanguage is a relative one. If we talk about the German language in English, German is the object language and English the metalanguage; if we talk about the English language in German, then English is the object language and German the metalanguage.

Ordinarily we employ words and expressions to talk about something other than those words themselves. But occasionally we do want to talk about expressions themselves, and we must use words to do so. For instance, in the sentence

Minnesota was the thirty-second state admitted to the Union

the word 'Minnesota' is being used to designate a political subdivision of the United States. On the other hand, in the sentence

'Minnesota' is an Indian word

the word 'Minnesota' itself is under discussion. When a word or expression is being talked about, we say that that word or expression is being *mentioned* rather than *used*. One way to mention an expression is to use a name of that expression, and the standard way to form the name of an expression is to enclose that expression in single quotation marks. Throughout this text we use this method of forming the names of expressions. Thus in

'Saratoga' contains four syllables

the word 'Saratoga' is mentioned, not used. Omitting the single quotation marks produces a false sentence:

Saratoga contains four syllables.

Saratoga is a city, not a word; it contains buildings and people, not syllables.

In discussing the object language *SL*, we often need to refer to, that is, to mention, specific expressions. We do so by using names of those expressions. One way to form the name of an expression is to enclose that expression in single quotation marks. The sentence

'~ B' is a negation

is about the expression of *SL* enclosed within single quotation marks. We also mention expressions by displaying them. The expression

(A ∨ B)

is a sentence of *SL* and is mentioned here by being displayed.

Note that the names of expressions in the language we are talking about do not themselves have to be part of that language. In fact, the *names* of expressions of *SL* are not part of the language *SL*. So an expression like

'(A ∨ B)'

is not an expression of *SL* although the expression named

(A ∨ B)

is an expression *SL*. This is because single quotation marks are not part of the vocabulary of the language *SL*. We use names of expressions of *SL* in order to talk about those expressions; hence in this text these names are part of the metalanguage that we are using.

METAVARIABLES

Besides naming specific expressions of *SL*, we sometimes want to talk about these expressions more generally. For this purpose we use *metalinguistic variables,* or *metavariables* for short. A metavariable is an expression in the metalanguage that is used to talk generally about expressions of the object language. In this text we use the boldface letters '**P**', '**Q**', '**R**', and '**S**' as metavariables that range over the expressions of our symbolic languages. (We used these metavariables in Section 2.1 in giving the characteristic truth-tables for the truth-functional connectives of *SL*.)

When we say

> If '~ (H ∨ I)' is an expression of *SL* consisting of a tilde followed by a sentence of *SL*, then '~ (H ∨ I)' is a negation

we are making a claim about a specific sentence of *SL*. But by using metavariables we can talk generally about expressions of *SL*. Thus we may write

> If **P** is an expression of *SL* consisting of a tilde followed by a sentence of *SL*, then **P** is a negation.

Here '**P**' is a metavariable that ranges over (is used to talk about) expressions of the object language. The displayed sentence means: Every expression of *SL* that consists of a tilde followed by a sentence is a *negation*. The displayed sentence is not about the metavariable '**P**', for '**P**' is not an expression of *SL*. Rather, the sentence is about all the *values* of **P**, that is, all those expressions that *are* expressions of *SL*. (When we want to talk about a metavariable, that is, to mention a metavariable, we place that metavariable in single quotation marks.)

THE LANGUAGE SL

We are now in a position to provide a rigorous definition of the sentences of the language *SL*. This is done in two steps: The vocabulary of *SL* is specified, and then the grammar is specified. The specification of the vocabulary involves stating what the basic expressions of *SL* are. These are like the words and punctuation marks of English, in the sense that the items in the vocabulary of basic expressions of *SL* are the building blocks from which all sentences of *SL* are generated. The difference is that in *SL* we do not have words and punctuation marks; rather, we have sentence letters, truth-functional connectives, and punctuation marks. The sentence letters are capitalized Roman letters (nonboldface) with or without positive-integer subscripts:

$$A, B, C, \ldots, A_1, B_1, C_1, \ldots, A_2, B_2, C_2, \ldots$$

Note that a capitalized Roman letter with a numerical subscript counts as *one* sentence letter, so 'A_1' is a *single* sentence letter. The connectives of *SL* are the five truth-functional connectives:

$$\sim \ \& \ \vee \ \supset \ \equiv$$

The connective '~' is a *unary* connective; the others are *binary* connectives. The punctuation marks consist of the left and right parentheses:

( )

Other expressions of *SL* are formed by writing one basic expression after another. But, just as the expression 'Some and vanity men will left' is not a sentence of the English language even though it is formed entirely of English words, so there are expressions that consist entirely of basic expressions of *SL* but are not themselves sentences of *SL*. We specify the grammar of *SL* by specifying what expressions of *SL* count as sentences of *SL*. The sentences of *SL* are defined as follows:

1. Every sentence letter is a sentence.
2. If **P** is a sentence, then ~ **P** is a sentence.[3]
3. If **P** and **Q** are sentences, then (**P** & **Q**) is a sentence.
4. If **P** and **Q** are sentences, then (**P** ∨ **Q**) is a sentence.

---

[3]The expression '~ **P**' is a hybrid insofar as the connective '~ ' belongs to the object language *SL*, whereas the metavariable '**P**' does not. We use the expression

~ **P**

as an expression of our metalanguage to stand for any sentence of *SL* that consists of a tilde followed by a sentence of *SL*. Similarly

(**P** ∨ **Q**)

is a metalinguistic expression that we use to stand for any sentence of *SL* that consists of the following sequence of expressions: a left parenthesis, a sentence of *SL*, a wedge, a sentence of *SL*, a right parenthesis.

In such contexts we do not place single quotes around these metalinguistic expressions because we want to talk about sentences of *SL* rather than about the metalinguistic expressions. That is,

'~ **P**' is a sentence of *SL*

says *falsely* that the metavariable '**P**' preceded by a tilde is a sentence of *SL*. When we do place single quotes around an expression containing a metavariable, it is because we want to talk about that expression, not about a sentence of *SL*.

We adopt the following conventions: Whenever we use expressions consisting of both metavariables and expressions of *SL*, we let the expressions of *SL* occurring therein function as their own names, while the metavariables continue to function as metavariables (*not* as their own names). Thus each symbol that occurs in such an expression is being used to designate some expression(s) of *SL*. Moreover the order of the symbols in such an expression indicates the order of the symbols in the object language sentences that the expression stands for. (We shall observe the same conventions in the second half of this book when we discuss the language *PL*.)

5. If **P** and **Q** are sentences, then (**P** ⊃ **Q**) is a sentence.
6. If **P** and **Q** are sentences, then (**P** ≡ **Q**) is a sentence.
7. Nothing is a sentence unless it can be formed by repeated application of clauses 1–6.

The sentences specified by the first clause—the sentence letters of *SL*—are the *atomic sentences* of *SL*. Clauses 1–6 specify how sentences are built up from shorter sentences. The final clause specifies that only expressions that can be formed in accordance with clauses 1–6 are sentences. This is an example of a *recursive* definition, in which complex cases are defined in terms of simpler ones.

The definition provides the basis for an *effective* method of determining whether an expression is a sentence. This means that we can determine in a finite number of mechanical steps whether an expression is a sentence. We may show that an expression is a sentence by beginning with the sentence letters that occur in the expression and continually using the clauses of the definition until we have generated the sentence in question. To illustrate this, we shall use this definition to show that '(~ B & (~ B ∨ A))' is a sentence. By clause 1, 'A' and 'B' are sentences. By clause 2, '~ B' is a sentence. By clause 4, '(~ B ∨ A)' is a sentence. Finally, by clause 3, '(~ B & (~ B ∨ A))' is a sentence.

The following expressions are not sentences of *SL*:

(B ∨ C ∨ D)
~ & A
(BC ⊃ D)
(B ⊂ (C ∨ D))
(p ≡ q)
(((A & B) & (C ∨ D))

The reasons in each case are as follows:

'(B ∨ C ∨ D)' needs another pair of parentheses because it contains two binary connectives.

'& A' is not a sentence since '&' is a *binary* connective; so '~ & A' cannot be a sentence.

'(BC ⊃ D)' contains two consecutive sentence letters, but no rule allows us to form a sentence in which sentence letters appear consecutively.

'(B ⊂ (C ∨ D))' is not a sentence because '⊂' is not an expression of *SL*.

'(p ≡ q)' contains symbols that are not expressions of *SL*—the two lowercase letters.

'(((A & B) & (C ∨ D))' contains more left parentheses than right, and the clauses that introduce parentheses introduce them in pairs.

We adopt the convention that the *outermost* parentheses of a sentence may be dropped whenever that sentence occurs by itself (when it is not part of another sentence). We followed this convention in earlier sections of this chapter. So we may write 'A ⊃ (B & C)' instead of '(A ⊃ (B & C))', but we may *not* write '~ B ∨ C' instead of '~ (B ∨ C)'. The second sentence is a negation; the first is not. Our convention also covers the *outermost* parentheses of metalinguistic expressions ranging over sentences of *SL*; for example, we write '**P** ∨ **Q**' instead of '(**P** ∨ **Q**)'. Finally we adopt the convention, for both sentences of *SL* and metalinguistic expressions, that brackets may be used in place of parentheses. Thus '(A ∨ B) & C' may be written as '[A ∨ B] & C'.

In this section we have been discussing *SL* syntactically. The *syntactical* study of a language is the study of the expressions of the language and the relations among them, without regard to possible *interpretations* of these expressions. Thus, for example, we have defined sentences of *SL* only in terms of expressions of *SL*; nowhere in the definition are the possible interpretations of the expressions mentioned. Of course, we have certain interpretations of these expressions in mind. We intend the connective '&' to symbolize the English connective 'and' in its truth-functional sense, the sentence letters to abbreviate sentences of English, and so on. But we could have presented this syntactic discussion of *SL* without regard to the possible interpretations of the expressions. When we specify and investigate interpretations of the expressions of a language, we are looking at the *semantics* of the language. For instance, the specification of the characteristic truth-tables for the truth-functional connectives is part of the specification of a *semantics* for *SL*.

Before closing this section, we shall introduce four more syntactic concepts: the *main connective* of a sentence and the *immediate sentential components*, *sentential components*, and *atomic components* of a sentence. These are defined in terms of the specification of sentences as follows:

1. If **P** is an atomic sentence, **P** contains no connectives and hence does not have a main connective. **P** has no immediate sentential components.
2. If **P** is of the form ~ **Q**, where **Q** is a sentence, then the main connective of **P** is the tilde that occurs before **Q**, and **Q** is the immediate sentential component of **P**.
3. If **P** is of the form **Q** & **R**, **Q** ∨ **R**, **Q** ⊃ **R**, or **Q** ≡ **R**, where **Q** and **R** are sentences, then the main connective of **P** is the connective that occurs between **Q** and **R**, and **Q** and **R** are the immediate sentential components of **P**.

The *sentential components* of a sentence include the sentence itself, its immediate sentential components, and the sentential components of its immediate sentential components. The *atomic components* of a sentence are all the sentential components that are atomic sentences.

2.4E EXERCISES

1. Which of the following are true and which are false?

a. Copper is copper.
*b. 'Copper' is the name of copper.
c. The chemical symbol 'Cu' names 'copper'.
*d. 'Copper' is copper.
e. Copper is the name of copper.
*f. Some coins are made of copper.
g. 'Copper' is a metal.

2. In each of the following sentences, 'Deutschland' is either used or mentioned. Indicate where that word is being used or mentioned and explain how this is being done.

a. The only German word mentioned in the instructions to these exercises contains eleven letters.
*b. Some people think Deutschland and Germany are two different countries, but actually 'Deutschland' is the German name of Germany.
c. The German name of Germany is mentioned several times in these examples but only is used once.
*d. 'Deutschland' is 'Deutschland'.
e. The word 'Deutschland' is not being used in this sentence.
*f. Deutschland is the German name of Germany.

3. Which of the following are sentences of *SL* and which are not? For those that are not explain why they are not.

a. B & Z
*b. & H
c. ~ O
*d. M ~ N
e. J ⊃ (K ⊃ (A ∨ N))
*f. **P** ∨ **Q**
g. (I ∨ [T & E])
*h. (U & C & ~ L)
i. (F ≡ K) ⊃ [M ∨ K]
*j. [(G ∨ E) ⊃ (~ H & (K ∨ B)]

4. For each of the following sentences, specify the main connective and the immediate sentential components. Then list all the sentential components, indicating which ones are atomic.

a. ~ A & H
*b. ~ (A & H)
c. ~ (S & G) ∨ B
*d. K ⊃ (~ K ⊃ K)
e. (C ≡ K) ∨ (~ H ∨ (M & N))
*f. M ⊃ [~ N ⊃ ((B & C) ≡ ~ [(L ⊃ J) ∨ X])]

5. Which of the following sentences are of the form ~ **P** ⊃ **Q**? In each case justify your answer.

a. A ⊃ B
*b. ~ A ⊃ B
c. ~ A ⊃ ~ B
*d. ~ ~ A ⊃ B
e. ~ (A ⊃ B)
*f. ~ ~ A ⊃ ~ B
g. ~ (~ A ⊃ B)
*h. ~ ~ (A ⊃ B) ⊃ (C ⊃ D)
i. ~ (A ∨ ~ B) ⊃ ~ (C & ~ D)
*j. ~ (A ≡ B) & (~ C ⊃ D)

6. Which of the following characters can occur immediately to the left of '~ ' in a sentence of *SL*? When one can so occur, give a sentence of *SL* in which it does; when it cannot so occur, explain why. Which of these characters could occur immediately to the right of 'A' in a sentence of *SL*. When one can so occur, give a sentence of *SL* in which it does; when it cannot so occur, explain why.

a. H
*b. &
c. (
*d.)
e. [
*f. ~

GLOSSARY

TRUTH-FUNCTIONAL USE OF A CONNECTIVE: A sentential connective is used truth-functionally if and only if it is used to generate a compound sentence from one or more sentences in such a way that the truth-value of the generated compound is wholly determined by the truth-values of those one or more sentences from which the compound is generated, no matter what those truth-values may be.

Chapter 3

SENTENTIAL LOGIC: SEMANTICS

3.1 TRUTH-VALUE ASSIGNMENTS AND TRUTH-TABLES FOR SENTENCES

In Chapter 1 we introduced logical concepts such as logical truth and deductive validity and used them to evaluate sentences and arguments stated in English. In this chapter we shall develop formal tests for truth-functional versions of the concepts introduced in Section 1.4—specifically truth-functional truth, falsity, and indeterminacy; truth-functional consistency; truth-functional entailment; and truth-functional validity. All these concepts fall within the realm of *semantics:* They concern the truth-values and truth-conditions of sentences. Before defining these truth-functional concepts for sentences and arguments of *SL*, our first task is to specify how truth-values and truth-conditions for sentences of *SL* are determined.

Every sentence of *SL* can be built up from its atomic components in accordance with the definition of sentences. Similarly the truth-value of a sentence of *SL* is determined completely by the truth-values of its atomic components in accordance with the characteristic truth-tables for the connectives. We repeat the characteristic truth-tables here:

P	**~ P**
T	**F**
F	**T**

P	**Q**	**P & Q**
T	**T**	**T**
T	**F**	**F**
F	**T**	**F**
F	**F**	**F**

P	**Q**	**P ∨ Q**
T	**T**	**T**
T	**F**	**T**
F	**T**	**T**
F	**F**	**F**

P	Q	$P \supset Q$
T	T	T
T	F	F
F	T	T
F	F	T

P	Q	$P \equiv Q$
T	T	T
T	F	F
F	T	F
F	F	T

These tables tell us how to determine the truth-value of a truth-functionally compound sentence given the truth-values of its immediate sentential components. And, if the immediate sentences of a truth-functionally compound sentence are themselves truth-functionally compound, we can use the information in the characteristic truth-tables to determine how the truth-value of each immediate component depends on the truth-values of *its* immediate components, and so on until we arrive at atomic components.

The truth-values of atomic sentences are fixed by truth-value assignments:

> A truth-value assignment is an assignment of truth-values (**T**s or **F**s) to the atomic sentences of *SL*.

Truth-value assignment is the basic semantic concept of *SL*. Intuitively each truth-value assignment gives us a description of a way the world *might* be, for in each we consider a combination of truth-values that atomic sentences might have. We assume that the atomic sentences of *SL* are truth-functionally independent—that is, that the truth-value assigned to one does not affect the truth-value assigned to any other. For generality we stipulate that a truth-value assignment must assign a truth-value to every atomic sentence of *SL*. Thus a truth-value assignment gives a *complete* description of a way the world might be. It tells us of each atomic sentence of *SL* whether or not that sentence is true. The truth-values of truth-functionally compound sentences of *SL* are determined uniquely and completely by the truth-values of their atomic components. Because every atomic sentence of *SL* is assigned a truth-value by a truth-value assignment, it follows that every truth-functionally compound sentence also has a truth-value on each truth-value assignment.

A truth-table for a sentence of *SL* is used to record its truth-value on each truth-value assignment. Because each truth-value assignment assigns truth-values to an infinite number of atomic sentences (*SL* has infinitely many atomic sentences), we cannot list an entire truth-value assignment in a truth-table. Instead, we list all the possible combinations of truth-values that the sentence's atomic components may have on a truth-value assignment. As an example here is the beginning of a truth-table for '$\sim B \supset C$':

B	C	$\sim B \supset C$
T	T	
T	F	
F	T	
F	F	

The atomic components of the sentence are ‘B’ and ‘C’, and there are four combinations of truth-values that these components might have, as indicated in the four rows of the table. (Rows in truth-tables go from left to right; columns go from top to bottom.) Each row represents an infinite number of truth-value assignments, namely, all the truth-value assignments that assign to ‘B’ and ‘C’ the values indicated in that row. Since the truth-value of ‘~ B ⊃ C’ on a truth-value assignment depends upon only the truth-values that its atomic components have on that assignment (and not, say, on the truth-value of ‘D’), the four combinations that we have displayed will allow us to determine the truth-value of ‘~ B ⊃ C’ on any truth-value assignment. That is, no matter which of the infinitely many truth-value assignments we might select, that truth-value assignment will assign one of the four pairs of truth-values displayed in the table to ‘B’ and ‘C’.

The first step in constructing a truth-table for a sentence **P** of *SL* is to determine the number of different combinations of truth-values that its atomic components might have. There is a simple way to do this. Consider first the case in which **P** has one atomic component. There are two different combinations of truth-values that the single atomic component may have: **T** and **F**. Now suppose that **P** is a sentence with two atomic components. In this case there are four combinations of truth-values that the atomic components of **P** might have, as we have seen in the case of ‘~ B ⊃ C’ above.

If **P** has three atomic components, there are eight combinations of truth-values that its atomic components might have. To see this, suppose we were to add a third sentence letter to the truth-table for ‘~ B ⊃ C’:

A	B	C	(~ B ⊃ C) & (A ≡ B)
	T	**T**	
	T	**F**	
	F	**T**	
	F	**F**	

What truth-tables do we enter in the first row under ‘A’? The combination of truth-values that would be displayed by entering **T** there is different from the combination that would be displayed by entering **F**. And we see that the same holds for each row. So we need to list each of the four combinations of truth-values that ‘B’ and ‘C’ may have *twice* in order to represent all combinations of truth-values for the three atomic components.

A	B	C	(~ B ⊃ C) & (A ≡ B)
T	**T**	**T**	
T	**T**	**F**	
T	**F**	**T**	
T	**F**	**F**	
F	**T**	**T**	
F	**T**	**F**	
F	**F**	**T**	
F	**F**	**F**	

Extending this reasoning, we find that every time we add a new atomic sentence to the list the number of rows in the truth-table doubles. If **P** has **n** atomic components, there are $2^{\mathbf{n}}$ different combinations of truth-values for its atomic components.[1] (If the same sentence letter occurs more than once in **P**, we do not count each occurrence as a different atomic component of **P**. To determine the number of atomic components, we count the number of *different* sentence letters that occur in **P**.)

In constructing a truth-table, we adopt a systematic method of listing the combinations of truth-values that the atomic components of a sentence **P** might have. We first list the atomic components of **P** to the left of the vertical line at the top of the truth-table, in alphabetical order.[2]

Under the first sentence letter listed, write a column of $2^{\mathbf{n}}$ entries, the first half of which are **T**s and the second half of which are **F**s. In the second column the number of **T**s and **F**s being alternated is half the number alternated in the first column. In the column under the third sentence letter listed, the number of **T**s and **F**s being alternated will again be half the number in the second column. We repeat this process until a column has been entered under each sentence letter to the left of the vertical line. The column under the last sentence letter in this list will then consist of single **T**s alternating with single **F**s. Thus, for a truth-table with **n** sentence letters, the first column consists of $2^{\mathbf{n}-1}$ **T**s alternating with $2^{\mathbf{n}-1}$ **F**s, the second of $2^{\mathbf{n}-2}$ **T**s alternating with $2^{\mathbf{n}-2}$ **F**s, and in general the *i*th column consists of $2^{\mathbf{n}-i}$ **T**s alternating with $2^{\mathbf{n}-i}$ **F**s. (Note that $2^0 = 1$.)

Now we can complete the rest of the truth-table for '(~ B ⊃ C) & (A ≡ B)'. We first repeat under 'A', 'B', and 'C', wherever these occur, the columns we have already entered to the left of the vertical line:

A	B	C	(~ B	⊃	C)	&	(A	≡	B)
T	**T**	**T**	**T**		**T**		**T**		**T**
T	**T**	**F**	**T**		**F**		**T**		**T**
T	**F**	**T**	**F**		**T**		**T**		**F**
T	**F**	**F**	**F**		**F**		**T**		**F**
F	**T**	**T**	**T**		**T**		**F**		**T**
F	**T**	**F**	**T**		**F**		**F**		**T**
F	**F**	**T**	**F**		**T**		**F**		**F**
F	**F**	**F**	**F**		**F**		**F**		**F**

Next we may enter the column for the component '~ B' under its main connective, the tilde. In each row in which 'B' has the truth-value **T**, '~ B' has the

[1] $2^{\mathbf{n}}$ is 2 if $\mathbf{n} = 1$, 2×2 if $\mathbf{n} = 2$, $2 \times 2 \times 2$ if $\mathbf{n} = 3$, and so on.

[2] This is an extended sense of 'alphabetical order' since some sentence letters have subscripts. In this order all the nonsubscripted letters appear first, then all letters subscripted with '1', then all letters subscripted with '2', and so on.

truth-value **F**, and in each row in which 'B' has the truth-value **F**, '~ B' has the truth-value **T**:

A	B	C	(~	B	⊃	C)	&	(A	≡	B)
T	**T**	**T**	**F**	**T**		**T**		**T**		**T**
T	**T**	**F**	**F**	**T**		**F**		**T**		**T**
T	**F**	**T**	**T**	**F**		**T**		**T**		**F**
T	**F**	**F**	**T**	**F**		**F**		**T**		**F**
F	**T**	**T**	**F**	**T**		**T**		**F**		**T**
F	**T**	**F**	**F**	**T**		**F**		**F**		**T**
F	**F**	**T**	**T**	**F**		**T**		**F**		**F**
F	**F**	**F**	**T**	**F**		**F**		**F**		**F**

The column for '~ B ⊃ C' is entered under the horseshoe:

A	B	C	(~	B	⊃	C)	&	(A	≡	B)
T	**T**	**T**	**F**	**T**	**T**	**T**		**T**		**T**
T	**T**	**F**	**F**	**T**	**T**	**F**		**T**		**T**
T	**F**	**T**	**T**	**F**	**T**	**T**		**T**		**F**
T	**F**	**F**	**T**	**F**	**F**	**F**		**T**		**F**
F	**T**	**T**	**F**	**T**	**T**	**T**		**F**		**T**
F	**T**	**F**	**F**	**T**	**T**	**F**		**F**		**T**
F	**F**	**T**	**T**	**F**	**T**	**T**		**F**		**F**
F	**F**	**F**	**T**	**F**	**F**	**F**		**F**		**F**

The truth-values of the immediate components of 'A ≡ B' for each row have been recorded, so we can now complete the column for 'A ≡ B' in accordance with the characteristic truth-table for '≡':

A	B	C	(~	B	⊃	C)	&	(A	≡	B)
T	**T**	**T**	**F**	**T**	**T**	**T**		**T**	**T**	**T**
T	**T**	**F**	**F**	**T**	**T**	**F**		**T**	**T**	**T**
T	**F**	**T**	**T**	**F**	**T**	**T**		**T**	**F**	**F**
T	**F**	**F**	**T**	**F**	**F**	**F**		**T**	**F**	**F**
F	**T**	**T**	**F**	**T**	**T**	**T**		**F**	**F**	**T**
F	**T**	**F**	**F**	**T**	**T**	**F**		**F**	**F**	**T**
F	**F**	**T**	**T**	**F**	**T**	**T**		**F**	**T**	**F**
F	**F**	**F**	**T**	**F**	**F**	**F**		**F**	**T**	**F**

Remember that a material biconditional has the truth-value **T** on all truth-value assignments on which its immediate components have the same truth-value, and the truth-value **F** on all other truth-value assignments. Finally we enter the column for '(~ B ⊃ C) & (A ≡ B)' under its main connective, the ampersand:

								↓			
A	B	C	(~	B	⊃	C)	&	(A	≡	B)
T	T	T	F	T	T	T	T	T	T	T
T	T	F	F	T	T	F	T	T	T	T
T	F	T	T	F	T	T	F	T	F	F
T	F	F	T	F	F	F	F	T	F	F
F	T	T	F	T	T	T	F	F	F	T
F	T	F	F	T	T	F	F	F	F	T
F	F	T	T	F	T	T	T	F	T	F
F	F	F	T	F	F	F	F	F	T	F

We use arrows to indicate the main connective of the sentence for which a truth-table has been constructed. Each row of the truth-table displays, underneath the arrow, the truth-value that the sentence has on every truth-value assignment that assigns to the atomic components of that sentence the truth-values displayed to the left of the vertical line.

Here is the truth-table for the sentence '[A ≡ (B ≡ A)] ∨ ~ C':

								↓		
A	B	C	[A	≡	(B	≡	A)]	∨	~	C
T	T	T	T	T	T	T	T	T	F	T
T	T	F	T	T	T	T	T	T	T	F
T	F	T	T	F	F	F	T	F	F	T
T	F	F	T	F	F	F	T	T	T	F
F	T	T	F	T	T	F	F	T	F	T
F	T	F	F	T	T	F	F	T	T	F
F	F	T	F	F	F	T	F	F	F	T
F	F	F	F	F	F	T	F	T	T	F

The column for '~ C' is constructed in accordance with the characteristic truth-table for the tilde. '~ C' has the truth-value **T** on all and only those truth-value assignments on which 'C' has the truth-value **F**, and '~ C' has the truth-value **F** on every assignment on which 'C' has the truth-value **T**. The column for '~ C' appears directly underneath the tilde. The immediate components of '(B ≡ A)' are 'B' and 'A'. The characteristic truth-value for '≡' tells us that a material biconditional has the truth-value **T** on all and only those truth-value assignments on which both of its immediate sentential components have the same truth-value (both have the truth-value **T** or both have the truth-value **F**). Thus '(B ≡ A)' has the truth-value **T** for the combinations of truth-values displayed in the first two and last two rows of the truth-table and the truth-value **F** for the other combinations.

Similarly '[A ≡ (B ≡ A)]' has the truth-value **T** on exactly those truth-value assignments on which 'A' and '(B ≡ A)' have the same truth-value. The column for '[A ≡ (B ≡ A)]' appears directly underneath its main connective, which is the first occurrence of the triple bar. '[A ≡ (B ≡ A)] ∨ ~ C' has the truth-value **T** on exactly those truth-value assignments on which at least one disjunct has the truth-value **T**. The disjuncts are '[A ≡ (B ≡ A)]' and '~ C'. So [A ≡ (B ≡ A)] ∨ ~ C' has the truth-value **T** on every truth-value assignment on which either '[A ≡ (B ≡ A)]' or '~ C' has the truth-value **T**. Where both disjuncts have the truth-value **F**, so does '[A ≡ (B ≡ A)] ∨ ~ C'. The truth-value of the entire sentence for each combination of truth-values assigned to its atomic components is written in the column directly underneath the wedge, the sentence's main connective.

Here is the truth-table for the sentence '~ [(U ∨ (W ⊃ ~ U)) ≡ W]':

U	W	↓ ~	[(U	∨	(W	⊃	~	U))	≡	W]
T	**T**	**F**	**T**	**T**	**T**	**F**	**F**	**T**	**T**	**T**
T	**F**	**T**	**T**	**T**	**F**	**T**	**F**	**T**	**F**	**F**
F	**T**	**F**	**F**	**T**	**T**	**T**	**T**	**F**	**T**	**T**
F	**F**	**T**	**F**	**T**	**F**	**T**	**T**	**F**	**F**	**F**

The column under the first occurrence of the tilde represents the truth-value of the entire sentence '~ [(U ∨ (W ⊃ ~ U)) ≡ W]' for each combination of truth-values that its atomic components might have. The truth-table tells us that '~ [(U ∨ (W ⊃ ~ U)) ≡ W]' has the truth-value **T** on those truth-value assignments on which either 'U' is assigned the truth-value **T** and 'W' is assigned the truth-value **F** or both 'U' and 'W' are assigned the truth-value **F**; the sentence is false on every other truth-value assignment.

Sometimes we are not interested in determining the truth-values of a sentence **P** for every truth-value assignment but are interested only in the truth-value of **P** on a particular truth-value assignment. In that case we may construct a shortened truth-table for **P** that records only the truth-values that its atomic components are assigned by that truth-value assignment. For example, suppose we want to know the truth-value of '(A & B) ⊃ B' on a truth-value assignment that assigns **F** to 'A' and **T** to 'B' and all the other atomic sentences of *SL*. We head the shortened truth-table as before, with the atomic components of the sentence to the left of the vertical line and '(A & B) ⊃ B' itself to the right. We list only one combination of truth-values for 'A' and 'B', namely, the truth-values they have on the assignment we are interested in:

A	B	(A	&	B)	↓ ⊃	B
F	**T**	**F**	**F**	**T**	**T**	**T**

The truth-values of '(A & B)' and '(A & B) ⊃ B' are determined in accordance with the characteristic truth-tables, as before. Thus '(A & B)' has the truth-value **F** on this truth-value assignment, for 'A' has the truth-value **F**. Since the antecedent of '(A & B) ⊃ B' has the truth-value **F** and the consequent the truth-value **T**, '(A & B) ⊃ B' has the truth-value **T**.

We emphasize that, when we want to determine the truth-value of a sentence on a particular truth-value assignment, we do not display the full truth-value assignment in question. Truth-value assignments assign truth-values to *every* atomic sentence of *SL*. Rather, we display only the combinations of truth-values that the atomic components of the sentence in question have on the assignment. There is no loss here because the truth-value of a sentence on a truth-value assignment depends *only* upon the truth-values of its atomic components on that assignment. Conversely each row of a truth-table for a sentence gives information about infinitely many truth-value assignments. It tells us the truth-value of the sentence on every truth-value assignment that assigns to the atomic components of the sentence the combination of truth-values displayed in that row (there are infinitely many such assignments).

To review: The truth-value of a sentence **P** on a truth-value assignment is determined by starting with the truth-values of the atomic components of **P** on the truth-value assignment and then using the characteristic truth-tables for the connectives of *SL* to compute the truth-values of larger and larger sentential components of **P** on the truth-value assignment. Ultimately we determine the truth-value of the largest sentential component of **P**, namely, **P** itself. This procedure is used in the construction of a truth-table for **P**, where each row displays a different combination of truth-values for the atomic components of **P**. The truth-value of **P** for each such combination is recorded directly underneath the main connective of **P** in the row representing that combination. (If **P** is atomic, the truth-value is recorded under **P**.)

We also define the notions of being true on a truth-value assignment and false on a truth-value assignment:

> A sentence is *true on a truth-value assignment* if and only if it has the truth-value **T** on the truth-value assignment.
>
> A sentence is *false on a truth-value assignment* if and only if it has the truth-value **F** on the truth-value assignment.

3.1**E** EXERCISES

1. How many rows will be in the truth-table for each of the following sentences?

a. A ≡ (~ A ≡ A)

*b. [~ D & (B ∨ G)] ⊃ [~ (H & A) ∨ ~ D]

c. (B & C) ⊃ [B ∨ (C & ~ C)]

2. Construct truth-tables for the following sentences.

a. ~ ~ (E & ~ E)
*b. (A & B) ≡ ~ B
c. A ≡ [J ≡ (A ≡ J)]
*d. [A ⊃ (B ⊃ C)] & [(A ⊃ B) ⊃ C]
e. [~ A ∨ (H ⊃ J)] ⊃ (A ∨ J)
*f. (~ ~ A & ~ B) ⊃ (~ A ≡ B)
g. ~ (A ∨ B) ⊃ (~ A ∨ ~ B)
*h. ~ D & [~ H ∨ (D & E)]
i. ~ (E & [H ⊃ (B & E)])
*j. ~ (D ≡ (~ A & B)) ∨ (~ D ∨ ~ B)
k. ~ [D & (E ∨ F)] ≡ [~ D & (E & F)]
*l. (J & [(E ∨ F) & (~ E & ~ F)]) ⊃ ~ J
m. (A ∨ (~ A & (H ⊃ J))) ⊃ (J ⊃ H)

3. Construct shortened truth-tables to determine the truth-value of each of the following sentences on the truth-value assignment that assigns **T** to 'B' and 'C', and **F** to 'A' and to every other atomic sentence of *SL.*

a. ~ [~ A ∨ (~ C ∨ ~ B)]
*b. ~ [A ∨ (~ C & ~ B)]
c. (A ⊃ B) ∨ (B ⊃ C)
*d. (A ⊃ B) ⊃ (B ⊃ C)
e. (A ≡ B) ∨ (B ≡ C)
*f. ~ A ⊃ (B ≡ C)
g. ~ [B ⊃ (A ∨ C)] & ~ ~ B
*h. ~ [~ A ≡ ~ (B ≡ ~ [A ≡ (B & C)])]
i. ~ [~ (A ≡ ~ B) ≡ ~ A] ≡ (B ∨ C)
*j. ~ (B ⊃ ~ A) & [C ≡ (A & B)]

4. Construct a truth-table for each of the sentences in Exercise 1 in Section 2.2E.

5. Construct a truth-table for each of the sentences in Exercise 3 in Section 2.2E.

3.2 TRUTH-FUNCTIONAL TRUTH, FALSITY, AND INDETERMINACY

In Chapter 1 we introduced the concepts of logical truth, logical falsity, and logical indeterminacy. A logically true sentence of English, it will be remembered, is one that cannot possibly be false. A sentence that is logically true (or logically false) may be so on purely truth-functional grounds. For example, we may symbolize 'Either Cynthia will get a job or Cynthia will not get a job' as 'C ∨ ~ C', and the truth-table for this sentence shows that it is true on every truth-value assignment:

C	C	∨ ↓	~	C
T	**T**	**T**	**F**	**T**
F	**F**	**T**	**T**	**F**

Thus the sentence cannot possibly be false. A sentence that is logically true on truth-functional grounds is a truth-functionally true sentence.

> A sentence **P** of *SL* is *truth-functionally true* if and only if **P** is true on every truth-value assignment.[3]

Since every sentence of *SL* has exactly one of the two truth-values on any truth-value assignment, it follows that a sentence **P** is truth-functionally true if and only if there is no truth-value assignment on which **P** is false.

Once the truth-table for a sentence has been constructed, it is a simple matter to determine whether the sentence is truth-functionally true. Simply examine the column of truth-values under its main connective. The sentence is truth-functionally true if and only if that column consists solely of **T**s. Since the rows of the truth-table represent *all* combinations of truth-values that may be assigned to the atomic components of the sentence by any truth-value assignment, the absence of **F**s under the sentence's main connective shows that there is no truth-value assignment on which the sentence is false.

Here is the truth-table for another truth-functionally true sentence:

X	Z	Z	↓ ⊃	(X	∨	Z)
T	**T**	**T**	**T**	**T**	**T**	**T**
T	**F**	**F**	**T**	**T**	**T**	**F**
F	**T**	**T**	**T**	**F**	**T**	**T**
F	**F**	**F**	**T**	**F**	**F**	**F**

The column under the main connective of '$Z \supset (X \vee Z)$' contains only **T**s. Note that the immediate sentential components of a truth-functionally true sentence need not themselves be truth-functionally true.

Truth-functional falsity is also defined in terms of truth-value assignments.

> A sentence **P** of *SL* is *truth-functionally false* if and only if **P** is false on every truth-value assignment.

It follows that if **P** is truth-functionally false then there is no truth-value assignment on which **P** is true. We can show that a sentence of *SL* is truth-functionally false by constructing a truth-table for the sentence; if the column of truth-values under the sentence's main connective contains only **F**s, then the sentence is

[3]Truth-functionally true sentences are sometimes called *tautologies* or *truth-functionally valid* sentences. Truth-functionally false sentences (introduced shortly) are sometimes called *contradictions,* or *self-contradictory* sentences. Truth-functionally indeterminate sentences (also to be introduced) are sometimes called *contingent* sentences.

truth-functionally false. Here are truth-tables for two truth-functionally false sentences:

A	A	↓ &	~	A
T	T	F	F	T
F	F	F	T	F

H	K	[(H	∨	K)	⊃	~	(H	∨	K)]	↓ &	H
T	T	T	T	T	F	F	T	T	T	F	T
T	F	T	T	F	F	F	T	T	F	F	T
F	T	F	T	T	F	F	F	T	T	F	F
F	F	F	F	F	T	T	F	F	F	F	F

Note that the immediate sentential components of a truth-functionally false sentence need not themselves be truth-functionally false. When we negate a truth-functionally true sentence, we end up with a truth-functionally false sentence:

A	↓ ~	(A	∨	~	A)
T	F	T	T	F	T
F	F	F	T	T	F

If we add another tilde to obtain '~ ~ (A ∨ ~ A)', we will have a truth-functionally true sentence again.

Although the two sentences 'A ⊃ (B ⊃ A)' and '(A ⊃ B) ⊃ A' look very much alike, one is truth-functionally true and the other is not:

A	B	A	↓ ⊃	(B	⊃	A)
T	T	T	T	T	T	T
T	F	T	T	F	T	T
F	T	F	T	T	F	F
F	F	F	T	F	T	F

A	B	(A	⊃	B)	↓ ⊃	A
T	T	T	T	T	T	T
T	F	T	F	F	T	T
F	T	F	T	T	F	F
F	F	F	T	F	F	F

'A ⊃ (B ⊃ A)' is true on every truth-value assignment, whereas '(A ⊃ B) ⊃ A' is not. The latter sentence is truth-functionally indeterminate.

> A sentence **P** of *SL* is *truth-functionally indeterminate* if and only if **P** is neither truth-functionally true nor truth-functionally false.

A truth-functionally indeterminate sentence is true on at least one truth-value assignment and false on at least one truth-value assignment. We can use a truth-table to show that a truth-functionally compound sentence is truth-functionally indeterminate by showing that the column under its main connective contains at least one **T** and at least one **F**. Every atomic sentence of *SL* is truth-functionally indeterminate. For example, the truth-table for 'H' is

H	↓ H
T	**T**
F	**F**

'H' is true on every truth-value assignment on which it is assigned the truth-value **T**, and false on every other truth-value assignment. Truth-tables for several truth-functionally indeterminate sentences appeared in Section 3.1. Every sentence of *SL* is either truth-functionally true, truth-functionally false, or truth-functionally indeterminate.

Sometimes we can show that a sentence is not truth-functionally true or is not truth-functionally false by displaying only one row of the sentence's truth-table—that is, by constructing a shortened truth-table. Consider the sentence '(A & ~ A) ∨ ~ A'. If this sentence is truth-functionally true, then there is no truth-value assignment on which it is false. So, if we can show that the sentence is false for some combination of truth-values its atomic components might have, then we can conclude that it is not truth-functionally true. The following shortened truth-table represents such a combination:

A	(A	&	~ A)	↓ ∨	~ A
T	**T**	**F**	**F T**	**F**	**F T**

This shortened truth-table shows that the sentence '(A & ~ A) ∨ ~ A' is false on every truth-value assignment that assigns the truth-value **T** to 'A'. Note that the shortened table shows only that '(A & ~ A) ∨ ~ A' is not truth-functionally true. The table does not show whether the sentence is true on those truth-value assignments on which 'A' is assigned the truth-value **F**. If it is, then the sentence is truth-functionally indeterminate; if not, the sentence is truth-functionally false.

Similarly we may construct a shortened truth-table in order to show that 'J & (~ K ∨ ~ J)' is not truth-functionally false:

			↓			
J	K	J	&	(~ K	∨	~ J)
T	**F**	**T**	**T**	**T F**	**T**	**F T**

This truth-table shows that the sentence is true on every truth-value assignment that assigns **T** to 'J' and **F** to 'K'. We thus know that the sentence is either truth-functionally indeterminate or truth-functionally true.

There is a systematic way to develop a shortened truth-table that shows that a sentence is true on at least one truth-value assignment or false on at least one truth-value assignment. Let's first consider the previous example, in which we wanted to show that 'J & (~ K ∨ ~ J)' is true on at least one truth-value assignment. We start by placing a **T** under the main connective:

			↓			
J	K	J	&	(~ K	∨	~ J)
			T			

Because the main connective is an ampersand, we know that each conjunct must be true as well:

			↓			
J	K	J	&	(~ K	∨	~ J)
		T	**T**		**T**	

Whenever we place a **T** or **F** under a sentence letter, we repeat it under all occurrences of that sentence letter:

			↓			
J	K	J	&	(~ K	∨	~ J)
T		**T**	**T**		**T**	**T**

Once we have placed a **T** under 'J', we know that we must fill in an **F** under the last tilde, since a negation is false if the negated sentence is true:

			↓			
J	K	J	&	(~ K	∨	~ J)
T		**T**	**T**		**T**	**F T**

Now we have a true disjunction with one false disjunct, so we know that the other disjunct must be true (otherwise the disjunction could not be true):

			↓					
J	K	J	&	(~	K	∨	~	J)
T		**T**	**T**	**T**		**T**	**F**	**T**

And if '~K' is true, then 'K' must be false:

			↓					
J	K	J	&	(~	K	∨	~	J)
T	**F**	**T**	**T**	**T**	**F**	**T**	**F**	**T**

Note that we also placed an **F** under the occurrence of 'K' to the left of the vertical bar. This completes our shortened truth-table.

Now consider the earlier example, in which we wanted to show that '(A & ~ A) ∨ ~ A' is false on at least one truth-value assignment. We begin by placing an **F** under the sentence's main connective:

					↓		
A	(A	&	~	A)	∨	~	A
					F		

If a disjunction is false, both of its disjuncts must be false:

					↓		
A	(A	&	~	A)	∨	~	A
		F			**F**	**F**	

We have just recorded an **F** for '~ A', and since '~ A' occurs elsewhere in the sentence, we repeat the **F** there:

					↓		
A	(A	&	~	A)	∨	~	A
		F	**F**		**F**	**F**	

Note that we have now assigned the value **F** to one of the conjuncts of '(A & ~ A)', thus ensuring that the conjunction is false, so it won't matter if we end up assigning the value **T** to the other conjunct. Next we note that if '~ A' is false then 'A' must be true:

							↓		
A		(A	&	~	A)		∨	~	A
T		**T**	**F**	**F**	**T**		**F**	**F**	**T**

And this completes the shortened truth-value.

In these two examples every addition to the table is dictated by some previous truth-value that had been entered: If a conjunction is true, both conjuncts must be true; if a disjunction is false, both disjuncts must be false; a negation is true if and only if the negated sentence is false; and a component of a sentence must have the same truth-value for each its occurrences. But sometimes we have examples where choices need to be made. For example, suppose we want to show that the sentence '(A ⊃ B) ≡ (B ⊃ A)' is not truth-functionally true. We can begin constructing a shortened truth-table with an **F** under the sentence's main connective as follows:

					↓			
A	B	(A	⊃	B)	≡	(B	⊃	A)
					F			

At this point we have to make a choice, because there are two ways that a biconditional can be false. Either the first immediate component is true and the second false, or the first immediate component is false and the second true. There is no simple rule of thumb to follow in this case. So we'll try one of the possibilities and see where it leads:

					↓			
A	B	(A	⊃	B)	≡	(B	⊃	A)
			T		**F**		**F**	

Since '(B ⊃ A)' is false, we know that 'B' must be true and 'A' false. We'll add these values in two steps. First, we have

					↓			
A	B	(A	⊃	B)	≡	(B	⊃	A)
F	**T**		**T**		**F**	**T**	**F**	**F**

We also need to add the values under the other occurrences of 'A' and 'B'—but in doing so we must make sure that these values are consistent with the assignment of **T** to the conditional '(A ⊃ B)':

					↓			
A	B	(A	⊃	B)	≡	(B	⊃	A)
F	**T**	**F**	**T**	**T**	**F**	**T**	**F**	**F**

Fortunately they are: A conditional with a false antecedent and a true consequent is itself true. So we have successfully completed the shortened table.

It turns out that we could have assigned **F** to the first immediate component of the biconditional and **T** to the second and produced another shortened truth-table representing a different set of truth-value assignments on which the biconditional is false. But sometimes, when we have a choice, one possible way of assigning truth-values won't work while another one will. Suppose, for example, that we want to show that the sentence '(A ⊃ B) ⊃ (B ⊃ ~ A)' is not truth-functionally false—that is, that there is at least one truth-value assignment on which it is true. We start with

					↓				
A	B	(A	⊃	B)	⊃	(B	⊃	~	A)
					T				

There are three ways in which a conditional can be true: Both the antecedent and consequent are true, or the antecedent is false and the consequent is true, or the antecedent is false and the consequent is false. We might try the first case first:

					↓				
A	B	(A	⊃	B)	⊃	(B	⊃	~	A)
			T		**T**		**T**		

We now have two true conditionals whose immediate components do not have truth-values. We'll work with the first one, and again, let's make its antecedent true and its consequent true:

					↓				
A	B	(A	⊃	B)	⊃	(B	⊃	~	A)
		T	**T**	**T**	**T**		**T**		

Filling in **T** under each 'A' and 'B'—because 'A' and 'B' have each been assigned the truth-value **T**—we get

					↓				
A	B	(A	⊃	B)	⊃	(B	⊃	~	A)
T	**T**	**T**	**T**	**T**	**T**	**T**	**T**		**T**

Now we must put **F** under the tilde:

A	B	(A	⊃	B)	↓ ⊃	(B	⊃	~ A)
T	**T**	**T**	**T**	**T**	**T**	**T**	**T**	**F T**

FAILURE!

The problem is that the conditional '(B ⊃ ~ A)' cannot be true if 'B' is true and '~ A' is false—there is no such truth-value assignment.

But we must not conclude that the sentence *cannot* be true. All we conclude is that we haven't come up with a way of assigning truth-values that will make it true. We can go back to

A	B	(A	⊃	B)	↓ ⊃	(B	⊃	~ A)
			T		**T**		**T**	

and try another way to make the conditional '(A ⊃ B)' true—say, by making 'A' false and 'B' true. This yields

A	B	(A	⊃	B)	↓ ⊃	(B	⊃	~ A)
F	**T**	**F**	**T**	**T**	**T**	**T**	**T**	**F**

and we can fill in a **T** under the tilde:

A	B	(A	⊃	B)	↓ ⊃	(B	⊃	~ A)
F	**T**	**F**	**T**	**T**	**T**	**T**	**T**	**T F**

Note that this time the conditional '(B ⊃ ~ A)' will be true since both of its immediate components are, so we have correctly produced a shortened truth-table. But even if this hadn't worked, there are still other possibilities, including trying to make the entire sentence true by a different assignment of truth-values to its immediate components.[4]

Of course, we may fail even when we try all the possibilities—which means that, although we thought a sentence might be true (or false) on some truth-value assignment, we were incorrect. The sentence is, in fact, truth-functionally false (or true), so there is no such assignment. Here's a simple

[4]Sometimes we have to try every possibility before coming up with a correct shortened truth-table (or concluding that there is no such table). The problem in constructing a shortened truth-table to show that a sentence can be true or that it can be false is one of a class of problems known to theoreticians as "NP-complete problems." These are problems for which the only known solutions guaranteed to produce a correct result are solutions that require us, in the worst case, to try every possibility.

example: We'll try to produce a shortened truth-table with an assignment of truth-values that makes the sentence 'A ⊃ A' false:

A	A	⊃	A
		↓	
		F	

If the conditional is false, the antecedent must be true and the consequent false:

A	A	⊃	A
		↓	
	T	**F**	**F**

FAILURE!

We failed because 'A' cannot have two different truth-values on the same truth-value assignment. Here we have, in fact, tried all the possibilities for making the conditional false (the antecedent must be true and the conclusion must be false)—unsuccessfully. That's as it should be, since the sentence is truth-functionally true.

3.2E EXERCISES

1. Determine whether each of the following sentences is truth-functionally true, truth-functionally false, or truth-functionally indeterminate by constructing truth-tables.

a. ~ A ⊃ A
*b. J ⊃ (K ⊃ J)
c. (A ≡ ~ A) ⊃ ~ (A ≡ ~ A)
*d. (E ≡ H) ⊃ (~ E ⊃ ~ H)
e. (~ B & ~ D) ∨ ~ (B ∨ D)
*f. ([(C ⊃ D) & (D ⊃ E)] & C) & ~ E
g. [(A ∨ B) & (A ∨ C)] ⊃ ~ (B & C)
*h. ~ [[(A ∨ B) & (B ∨ B)] & (~ A & ~ B)]
i. (J ∨ ~ K) ≡ ~ ~ (K ⊃ J)
*j. ~ B ⊃ [(B ∨ D) ⊃ D]
k. [(A ∨ ~ D) & ~ (A & D)] ⊃ ~ D
*l. (M ≡ ~ N) & (M ≡ N)

2. For each of the following sentences, either show that the sentence is truth-functionally true by constructing a full truth-table or show that the sentence is not truth-functionally true by constructing an appropriate shortened truth-table.

a. (F ∨ H) ∨ (~ F ≡ H)
*b. (F ∨ H) ∨ ~ (~ F ⊃ H)
c. ~ A ⊃ [(B & A) ⊃ C]
*d. A ≡ (B ≡ A)
e. [(C ∨ ~ C) ⊃ C] ⊃ C
*f. [C ⊃ (C ∨ ~ D)] ⊃ (C ∨ D)

3. For each of the following sentences, either show that the sentence is truth-functionally false by constructing a full truth-table or show that the sentence is not truth-functionally false by constructing an appropriate shortened truth-table.

a. $(B \equiv D)$ & $(B \equiv \sim D)$

*b. $(B \supset H)$ & $(B \supset \sim H)$

c. $A \equiv (B \equiv A)$

*d. $[(F$ & $G) \supset (C$ & $\sim C)]$ & F

e. $[(C \vee D) \equiv C] \supset \sim C$

*f. $[\sim (A$ & $F) \supset (B \vee A)]$ & $\sim [\sim B \supset \sim (F \vee A)]$

4. Which of the following are true? Explain.

a. A conjunction with one truth-functionally true conjunct must itself be truth-functionally true.

*b. A disjunction with one truth-functionally true disjunct must itself be truth-functionally true.

c. A material conditional with a truth-functionally true consequent must itself be truth-functionally true.

*d. A conjunction with one truth-functionally false conjunct must itself be truth-functionally false.

e. A disjunction with one truth-functionally false disjunct must itself be truth-functionally false.

*f. A material conditional with a truth-functionally false consequent must itself be truth-functionally false.

g. A sentence is truth-functionally true if and only if its negation is truth-functionally false.

*h. A sentence is truth-functionally indeterminate if and only if its negation is truth-functionally indeterminate.

i. A material conditional with a truth-functionally true antecedent must itself be truth-functionally true.

*j. A material conditional with a truth-functionally false antecedent must itself be truth-functionally false.

5. Answer the following questions; explain your answers.

a. Suppose that **P** is a truth-functionally true sentence and **Q** is a truth-functionally false sentence. On the basis of this information, can you determine whether **P** ≡ **Q** is truth-functionally true, false, or indeterminate? If so, which is it?

*b. Suppose that **P** and **Q** are truth-functionally indeterminate sentences. Does it follow that **P** & **Q** is truth-functionally indeterminate?

c. Suppose that **P** and **Q** are truth-functionally indeterminate. Does it follow that **P** ∨ **Q** is truth-functionally indeterminate?

*d. Suppose that **P** is a truth-functionally true sentence and that **Q** is truth-functionally indeterminate. On the basis of this information, can you determine whether **P** ⊃ **Q** is truth-functionally true, false, or indeterminate? If so, which is it?

3.3 TRUTH-FUNCTIONAL EQUIVALENCE

We now introduce the concept of truth-functional equivalence.

> Sentences **P** and **Q** of *SL* are *truth-functionally equivalent* if and only if there is no truth-value assignment on which **P** and **Q** have different truth-values.

Hence, to show that **P** and **Q** are truth-functionally equivalent, we construct a single truth-table for both **P** and **Q** and show that in each row the two sentences have the same truth-value. The columns under the *main* connectives must be identical.

The sentences 'A & A' and 'A ∨ A' are truth-functionally equivalent, as shown by the following truth-table:

		↓			↓	
A	A	&	A	A	∨	A
T	**T**	**T**	**T**	**T**	**T**	**T**
F	**F**	**F**	**F**	**F**	**F**	**F**

On any truth-value assignment that assigns **T** to 'A', both 'A & A' and 'A ∨ A' are true. On any truth-value assignment that assigns **F** to 'A', both 'A & A' and 'A ∨ A' are false. The sentences '(W & Y) ⊃ H' and 'W ⊃ (Y ⊃ H)' are also truth-functionally equivalent:

						↓			↓			
H	W	Y	(W	&	Y)	⊃	H	W	⊃	(Y	⊃	H)
T	**T**	**T**	**T**	**T**	**T**	**T**	**T**	**T**	**T**	**T**	**T**	**T**
T	**T**	**F**	**T**	**F**	**F**	**T**	**T**	**T**	**T**	**F**	**T**	**T**
T	**F**	**T**	**F**	**F**	**T**	**T**	**T**	**F**	**T**	**T**	**T**	**T**
T	**F**	**F**	**F**	**F**	**F**	**T**	**T**	**F**	**T**	**F**	**T**	**T**
F	**T**	**T**	**T**	**T**	**T**	**F**	**F**	**T**	**F**	**T**	**F**	**F**
F	**T**	**F**	**T**	**F**	**F**	**T**	**F**	**T**	**T**	**F**	**T**	**F**
F	**F**	**T**	**F**	**F**	**T**	**T**	**F**	**F**	**T**	**T**	**F**	**F**
F	**F**	**F**	**F**	**F**	**F**	**T**	**F**	**F**	**T**	**F**	**T**	**F**

The columns under the main connectives of '(W & Y) ⊃ H' and 'W ⊃ (Y ⊃ H)' are identical, which shows that the two sentences have the same truth-value on every truth-value assignment.

It is important to remember that two sentences are truth-functionally equivalent only if they have the same truth-value on every truth-value assignment. That is, their truth-table columns (in the same truth-table) must be identical. Consider the following truth-table:

				↓					↓	
E	H	J	E	∨	H	(H	∨	J)	∨	E
T	**T**	**T**	**T**	**T**	**T**	**T**	**T**	**T**	**T**	**T**
T	**T**	**F**	**T**	**T**	**T**	**T**	**T**	**F**	**T**	**T**
T	**F**	**T**	**T**	**T**	**F**	**F**	**T**	**T**	**T**	**T**
T	**F**	**F**	**T**	**T**	**F**	**F**	**F**	**F**	**T**	**T**
F	**T**	**T**	**F**	**T**	**T**	**T**	**T**	**T**	**T**	**F**
F	**T**	**F**	**F**	**T**	**T**	**T**	**T**	**F**	**T**	**F**
F	**F**	**T**	**F**	**F**	**F**	**F**	**T**	**T**	**T**	**F**
F	**F**	**F**	**F**	**F**	**F**	**F**	**F**	**F**	**F**	**F**

The table shows that the sentences 'E ∨ H' and '(H ∨ J) ∨ E' are not truth-functionally equivalent, for they have different truth-values on any truth-value assignment that assigns **F** to 'E' and 'H' and **T** to 'J'. The fact that 'E ∨ H' and '(H ∨ J) ∨ E' have the same truth-value for all *other* truth-value assignments is irrelevant to the question of whether the two sentences are truth-functionally equivalent. When we want to show that two sentences are not truth-functionally equivalent, we will circle at least one row of the truth-table in which the sentences do not have the same truth-value.

All truth-functionally true sentences are truth-functionally equivalent. This is because every truth-functionally true sentence has the truth-value **T** on every truth-value assignment. In a table for two truth-functionally true sentences, the columns under the main connectives of those sentences are always identical. For example, '~ (C & ~ C)' and 'A ⊃ (B ⊃ A)' are truth-functionally equivalent:

A	B	C	↓ ~	(C	&	~ C)	↓ A ⊃	(B	⊃	A)
T	T	T	T	T	F	F T	T T	T	T	T
T	T	F	T	F	F	T F	T T	T	T	T
T	F	T	T	T	F	F T	T T	F	T	T
T	F	F	T	F	F	T F	T T	F	T	T
F	T	T	T	T	F	F T	F T	T	F	F
F	T	F	T	F	F	T F	F T	T	F	F
F	F	T	T	T	F	F T	F T	F	T	F
F	F	F	T	F	F	T F	F T	F	T	F

Likewise all truth-functionally false sentences are truth-functionally equivalent.

But not all truth-functionally indeterminate sentences are truth-functionally equivalent—for example,

B	D	B	↓ &	D	~ B	↓ &	D
T	T	T	T	T	F T	F	T
T	F	T	F	F	F T	F	F
F	T	F	F	T	T F	T	T
F	F	F	F	F	T F	F	F

On any truth-value assignment on which 'B' and 'D' are both true, or 'B' is false and 'D' is true, the sentences 'B & D' and '~ B & D' have different truth-values. Hence they are not truth-functionally equivalent.

If **P** and **Q** are not truth-functionally equivalent, we can construct a shortened truth-table to show this. The shortened truth-table will display a combination of truth-values for which one sentence is true and the other false. For example, the following shortened truth-table shows that 'A' and 'A ∨ B' are not truth-functionally equivalent:

A	B	↓ A	A	↓ ∨	B
F	**T**	**F**	**F**	**T**	**T**

The shortened truth-table shows that, on any truth-value assignment that assigns **F** to 'A' and **T** to 'B', 'A' is false and 'A ∨ B' is true. Hence the sentences are not truth-functionally equivalent. Note that, if we construct a shortened truth-table that displays a row in which both sentences have the same truth-value, this is not sufficient to show that they are truth-functionally equivalent. This is because they are truth-functionally equivalent if and only if they have the same truth-value on *every* truth-value assignment. To show this, we must consider every combination of truth-values that their atomic components might have.

We may construct our shortened truth-tables for two (or more) sentences in a systematic way, just as we did for single sentences in Section 3.2. For example, we could begin constructing the previous table by assigning the sentence 'A' the truth-value **F** and 'B' the truth-value **T**:

A	B	↓ A	A	↓ ∨	B
		F		**T**	

(We might first have tried to make 'A' true and 'A ∨ B' false, but this would not lead to a correct truth-table since we would have a false disjunction with a true disjunct.) Filling in **F** under all the other occurrences of 'A' yields

A	B	↓ A	A	↓ ∨	B
F		**F**	**F**	**T**	

Now we can make 'B' true, which will secure the truth of the disjunction:

A	B	↓ A	A	↓ ∨	B
F	**T**	**F**	**F**	**T**	**T**

3.3**E** EXERCISES

1. Decide, by constructing truth-tables, in which of the following pairs the sentences are truth-functionally equivalent.

a.	~ (A & B)	~ (A ∨ B)
*b.	A ⊃ (B ⊃ A)	(C & ~ C) ∨ (A ⊃ A)
c.	K ≡ H	~ K ≡ ~ H
*d.	C & (B ∨ A)	(C & B) ∨ A

e.	$(G \supset F) \supset (F \supset G)$	$(G \equiv F) \vee (\sim F \vee G)$
*f.	$\sim C \supset \sim B$	$B \supset C$
g.	$\sim (H \,\&\, J) \equiv (J \equiv \sim K)$	$(H \,\&\, J) \supset \sim K$
*h.	$\sim (D \vee B) \supset (C \supset B)$	$C \supset (D \,\&\, B)$
i.	$[A \vee \sim (D \,\&\, C)] \supset \sim D$	$[D \vee \sim (A \,\&\, C)] \supset \sim A$
*j.	$A \supset [B \supset (A \supset B)]$	$B \supset [A \supset (B \supset A)]$
k.	$F \vee \sim (G \vee \sim H)$	$(H \equiv \sim F) \vee G$

2. For each of the following pairs of sentences, either show that the sentences are truth-functionally equivalent by constructing a full truth-table or show that they are not truth-functionally equivalent by constructing an appropriate shortened truth-table.

a.	$G \vee H$	$\sim G \supset H$
*b.	$\sim (B \,\&\, \sim A)$	$A \vee B$
c.	$(D \equiv A) \,\&\, D$	$D \,\&\, A$
*d.	$F \,\&\, (J \vee H)$	$(F \,\&\, J) \vee H$
e.	$A \equiv (\sim A \equiv A)$	$\sim (A \supset \sim A)$
*f.	$\sim (\sim B \vee (\sim C \vee \sim D))$	$(D \vee C) \,\&\, \sim B$

3. Symbolize each of the following pairs of sentences and determine whether the sentences are truth-functionally equivalent by constructing truth-tables.

a. Unless the sky clouds over, the night will be clear and the moon will shine brightly.
The moon will shine brightly if and only if the night is clear and the sky doesn't cloud over.

*b. Although the new play at the Roxy is a flop, critics won't ignore it unless it is canceled.
The new play at the Roxy is a flop, and if it is canceled critics will ignore it.

c. If the *Daily Herald* reports on our antics, then the antics are effective.
If our antics aren't effective, then the *Daily Herald* won't report on them.

*d. The year 1972 wasn't a good vintage year, 1973 was, and neither 1974 nor 1975 was.
Neither 1974 nor 1972 was a good vintage year, and not both 1973 and 1975 were.

e. If Mary met Tom and she liked him, then Mary didn't ask George to the movies.
If Mary met Tom and she didn't like him, then Mary asked George to the movies.

*f. Either the blue team or the red team will win the tournament, and they won't both win.
The red team will win the tournament if and only if the blue team won't win the tournament.

4. Answer the following questions; explain your answers.

a. Suppose that two sentences **P** and **Q** are truth-functionally equivalent. Are $\sim$ **P** and $\sim$ **Q** truth-functionally equivalent as well?

*b. Suppose that two sentences **P** and **Q** are truth-functionally equivalent. Show that it follows that **P** and **P** & **Q** are truth-functionally equivalent as well.

c. Suppose that two sentences **P** and **Q** are truth-functionally equivalent. Show that it follows that $\sim$ **P** $\vee$ **Q** is truth-functionally true.

To define truth-functional consistency, we need the notion of a *set* of sentences, informally introduced in Chapter 1. A set of sentences of *SL* is a group, or collection, of sentences of *SL*. We have special notation for representing finite sets of sentences (sets consisting of a finite number of sentences): We write the names of the sentences, separated by commas, and enclose the whole list in braces. Thus {'A', 'B ⊃ H', 'C ∨ A'} is the set of sentences consisting of 'A', 'B ⊃ H', and 'C ∨ A'. We say that these three sentences are *members* of the set. For convenience we will drop the single quotes from names of sentences when they are written between the braces; our convention is that this is merely a way of abbreviating the set notation. So we may write

{A, B ⊃ H, C ∨ A}

instead of

{'A', 'B ⊃ H', 'C ∨ A'}

All sets of sentences that have at least one member are nonempty sets of sentences. '∅' is the name of the empty set; the empty set of sentences of *SL* is the set that contains no members at all. In what follows we shall use the variable 'Γ' (gamma), with or without a subscript, to range over sets of sentences of *SL*.

Truth-functional consistency may now be introduced.

> A set of sentences of *SL* is *truth-functionally consistent* if and only if there is at least one truth-value assignment on which all the members of the set are true. A set of sentences of *SL* is *truth-functionally inconsistent* if and only if it is not truth-functionally consistent.

The set {A, B ⊃ H, B} is truth-functionally consistent, as is shown by the following truth-table:

A	B	H	↓ A	B	↓ ⊃	H	↓ B
T	T	T	T	T	T	T	T
T	T	F	T	T	F	F	T
T	F	T	T	F	T	T	F
T	F	F	T	F	T	F	F
F	T	T	F	T	T	T	T
F	T	F	F	T	F	F	T
F	F	T	F	F	T	T	F
F	F	F	F	F	T	F	F

The truth-table shows that, on any truth-value assignment on which 'A', 'B', and 'H' are all true, all three set members are true. So the set is truth-functionally consistent. We have circled the row of the truth-table that shows this. (Sometimes when we construct a truth-table to test a set of sentences for truth-functional consistency, we will find that there is more than one row in which all the members of the set are true. In such cases we shall circle only one of these rows of the truth-table.)

The set of sentences {L, L ⊃ J, ~ J} is truth-functionally inconsistent:

		↓		↓		↓
J	L	L	L	⊃	J	~ J
T	**T**	**T**	**T**	**T**	**T**	**F T**
T	**F**	**F**	**F**	**T**	**T**	**F T**
F	**T**	**T**	**T**	**F**	**F**	**T F**
F	**F**	**F**	**F**	**T**	**F**	**T F**

In each row at least one of the three sentences has the truth-value **F** in the column under its main connective. Hence there is no single truth-value assignment on which all three set members are true. The following set of sentences is also truth-functionally inconsistent: {C ∨ ~ C, ~ C & D, ~ D}.

			↓			↓		↓
C	D	C	∨	~ C	~ C	&	D	~ D
T	**T**	**T**	**T**	**F T**	**F T**	**F**	**T**	**F T**
T	**F**	**T**	**T**	**F T**	**F T**	**F**	**F**	**T F**
F	**T**	**F**	**T**	**T F**	**T F**	**T**	**T**	**F T**
F	**F**	**F**	**T**	**T F**	**T F**	**F**	**F**	**T F**

In this case it does not matter that one of the sentences, 'C ∨ ~ C', is true on every truth-value assignment. All that matters for establishing truth-functional inconsistency is that there is no single truth-value assignment on which all three members are true.

We can show that a set of sentences is truth-functionally consistent by constructing a shortened truth-table that lists one row in which all the set members are true. For instance, the following shortened truth-table shows that the set {(E ≡ H) ≡ E, H & ~ E} is truth-functionally consistent:

					↓			↓	
E	H	(E	≡	H)	≡	E	H	&	~ E
F	**T**	**F**	**F**	**T**	**T**	**F**	**T**	**T**	**T F**

The table shows that, on any truth-value assignment on which 'E' is false and 'H' is true, the set members will all be true. Note that if we construct a shortened table that lists a row in which not all the members of the set are true, this is not sufficient to show that the set is truth-functionally inconsistent. This is because a set of sentences is truth-functionally inconsistent if and only if there is *no* truth-value assignment on which every member of the set is true. To show this, we would have to consider every combination of truth-values that the atomic components of the set members might have.

3.4E EXERCISES

1. Using truth-tables, determine which of the following sets are truth-functionally consistent.

a. {A ⊃ B, B ⊃ C, A ⊃ C}
*b. {B ≡ (J & K), ~ J, ~ B ⊃ B}
c. {~ [J ∨ (H ⊃ L)], L ≡ (~ J ∨ ~ H), H ≡ (J ∨ L)}
*d. {(A & B) & C, C ∨ (B ∨ A), A ≡ (B ⊃ C)}
e. {(J ⊃ J) ⊃ H, ~ J, ~ H}
*f. {U ∨ (W & H), W ≡ (U ∨ H), H ∨ ~ H}
g. {A, B, C}
*h. {~ (A & B), ~ (B & C), ~ (A & C), A ∨ (B & C)}
i. {(A & B) ∨ (C ⊃ B), ~ A, ~ B}
*j. {A ⊃ (B ⊃ (C ⊃ A)), B ⊃ ~ A}

2. For each of the following sets of sentences, either show that the set is truth-functionally consistent by constructing an appropriate shortened truth-table or show that the set is truth-functionally inconsistent by constructing a full truth-table.

a. {B ⊃ (D ⊃ E), ~ D & B}
*b. {H ≡ (~ H ⊃ H)}
c. {F ⊃ (J ∨ K), F ≡ ~ J}
*d. {~ (~ C ∨ ~ B) & A, A ≡ ~ C}
e. {(A ⊃ B) ≡ (~ B ∨ B), A}
*f. {H ⊃ J, J ⊃ K, K ⊃ ~ H}

3. Symbolize each of the following passages and determine whether the set consisting of those sentences is truth-functionally consistent by constructing a truth-table.

a. If space is infinitely divisible, then Zeno's paradoxes are compelling. Zeno's paradoxes are neither convincing nor compelling. Space is infinitely divisible.
*b. Newtonian mechanics can't be right if Einsteinian mechanics is. But Einsteinian mechanics is right if and only if space is non-Euclidean. Space is non-Euclidean, or Newtonian mechanics is correct.
c. Eugene O'Neil was an alcoholic. His plays show it. But *The Iceman Cometh* must have been written by a teetotaler. O'Neill was an alcoholic unless he was a fake.
*d. Neither sugar nor saccharin is desirable if and only if both are lethal. Sugar is lethal if and only if saccharin is desirable. Sugar is undesirable if and only if saccharin isn't lethal.
e. If the Red Sox win next Sunday, then if Joan bet $5 against them she'll buy Ed a hamburger. The Red Sox won't win, and Joan won't buy Ed a hamburger.
*f. Either Johnson or Hartshorne pleaded guilty, or neither did. If Johnson pleaded guilty, then the newspaper story is incorrect. The newspaper story is correct, and Hartshorne pleaded guilty.

4.a. Prove that {**P**} is truth-functionally inconsistent if and only if ~ **P** is truth-functionally true.

*b. If {**P**} is truth-functionally consistent, must {~ **P**} be truth-functionally consistent as well? Show that you are right.

c. If **P** and **Q** are truth-functionally indeterminate, does it follow that {**P**, **Q**} is truth-functionally consistent? Explain your answer.

*d. Prove that if **P** ≡ **Q** is truth-functionally true then {**P**, ~ **Q**} is truth-functionally inconsistent.

3.5 TRUTH-FUNCTIONAL ENTAILMENT AND TRUTH-FUNCTIONAL VALIDITY

Truth-functional entailment is a relation that may hold between a sentence of *SL* and a set of sentences of *SL*.

> A set Γ of sentences of *SL* *truth-functionally entails* a sentence **P** if and only if there is no truth-value assignment on which every member of Γ is true and **P** is false.

In other words Γ truth-functionally entails **P** just in case **P** is true on every truth-value assignment on which every member of Γ is true. We have a special symbol for truth-functional entailment: the double turnstile '⊨'. The expression

Γ ⊨ **P**

is read

Γ truth-functionally entails **P**.

To indicate that Γ does not truth-functionally entail **P**, we write

Γ ⊭ **P**

Thus

{A, B & C} ⊨ 'B'

and

{A, B ∨ C} ⊭ 'B'

mean, respectively,

{A, B & C} truth-functionally entails 'B'

and

{A, B ∨ C} does not truth-functionally entail 'B'.

Henceforth we adopt the convention that, when using the turnstile notation, we drop the single quotation marks around the sentence following the turnstile. We also have a special abbreviation to indicate that a sentence is truth-functionally entailed by the empty set of sentences:

$\models$ **P**

The expression '$\models$ **P**' is an abbreviation for '∅ $\models$ **P**'. All and only truth-functionally true sentences are truth-functionally entailed by the empty set of sentences; the proof of this is left as an exercise in Section 3.6.

If Γ is a finite set, we can determine whether Γ truth-functionally entails **P** by constructing a truth-table for the members of Γ and for **P**. If there is a row in the truth-table in which all the members of Γ have the truth-value **T** and **P** has the truth-value **F**, then Γ does not truth-functionally entail **P**. If there is no such row, then Γ truth-functionally entails **P**. We can see that {A, B & C} $\models$ B by checking the following truth-table:

			↓		↓		↓
A	B	C	A	B	&	C	B
T	T	T	T	T	T	T	T
T	T	F	T	T	F	F	T
T	F	T	T	F	F	T	F
T	F	F	T	F	F	F	F
F	T	T	F	T	T	T	T
F	T	F	F	T	F	F	T
F	F	T	F	F	F	T	F
F	F	F	F	F	F	F	F

There is only one row in which both members of {A, B & C} are true, namely, the row in which 'A', 'B', and 'C' all have the truth-value **T**. But since 'B' is true in this row, it follows that there is no combination of truth-values for the atomic components of all these sentences that will make both 'A' and 'B & C' true and 'B' false. Hence there is no truth-value assignment on which 'A' and 'B & C' are true and 'B' is false: {A, B & C} $\models$ B.

In the same way we can show that {W ∨ J, (W ⊃ Z) ∨ (J ⊃ Z), ~ Z} $\models$ ~ (W & J):

				↓					↓				↓		↓			
J	W	Z	W	∨	J	(W	⊃	Z)	∨	(J	⊃	Z)	~	Z	~	(W	&	J)
T	T	T	T	T	T	T	T	T	T	T	T	T	F	T	F	T	T	T
T	T	F	T	T	T	T	F	F	F	T	F	F	T	F	F	T	T	T
T	F	T	F	T	T	F	T	T	T	T	T	T	F	T	T	F	F	T
T	F	F	F	T	T	F	T	F	T	T	F	F	T	F	T	F	F	T
F	T	T	T	T	F	T	T	T	T	F	T	T	F	T	T	T	F	F
F	T	F	T	T	F	T	F	F	T	F	T	F	T	F	T	T	F	F
F	F	T	F	F	F	F	T	T	T	F	T	T	F	T	T	F	F	F
F	F	F	F	F	F	F	T	F	T	F	T	F	T	F	T	F	F	F

The fourth and sixth rows are the only ones in which all the set members are true; '~ (W & J)' is true in these rows as well. The following truth-table shows that {K ∨ J, ~ (K ∨ J)} ⊨ K:

		↓			↓				↓
J	K	K	∨	J	~	(K	∨	J)	K
T	T	T	T	T	F	T	T	T	T
T	F	F	T	T	F	F	T	T	F
F	T	T	T	F	F	T	T	F	T
F	F	F	F	F	T	F	F	F	F

There is no row in which 'K ∨ J' and '~ (K ∨ J)' are both true, and hence no truth-value assignment on which the set members are both true. Consequently there is no truth-value assignment on which the members of the set are both true and 'K' is false; so the set truth-functionally entails 'K'.

On the other hand, {A, B ∨ C} does *not* truth-functionally entail 'B'. The following truth-table shows this:

			↓		↓		↓
A	B	C	A	B	∨	C	B
T	T	T	T	T	T	T	T
T	T	F	T	T	T	F	T
T	F	T	T	F	T	T	F
T	F	F	T	F	F	F	F
F	T	T	F	T	T	T	T
F	T	F	F	T	T	F	T
F	F	T	F	F	T	T	F
F	F	F	F	F	F	F	F

The circled row shows that 'A' and 'B ∨ C' are both true and 'B' is false on any truth-value assignment that assigns **T** to 'A' and 'C' and **F** to 'B'.

An *argument of SL* is a group of two or more sentences of *SL*, one of which is designated as the conclusion and the others as the premises.

An argument of *SL* is *truth-functionally valid* if and only if there is no truth-value assignment on which all the premises are true and the conclusion is false. An argument of *SL* is *truth-functionally invalid* if and only if it is not truth-functionally valid.

Thus an argument of *SL* is truth-functionally valid just in case on every truth-value assignment on which the premises are true the conclusion is true as well. This means that an argument is truth-functionally valid if and only if the set consisting of the premises of the argument truth-functionally entails the conclusion.

The argument

F ≡ G
F ∨ G
―――――
F & G

is truth-functionally valid, as the following truth-table shows:

F	G	F	↓ ≡	G	F	↓ ∨	G	F	↓ &	G
T	T	T	T	T	T	T	T	T	T	T
T	F	T	F	F	T	T	F	T	F	F
F	T	F	F	T	F	T	T	F	F	T
F	F	F	T	F	F	F	F	F	F	F

The first row lists the only combination of truth-values for the atomic components of these sentences for which the premises, 'F ≡ G' and 'F ∨ G', are both true; the conclusion, 'F & G', is true in this row as well. Similarly the argument

(A & G) ∨ (B ⊃ G)
~ G ∨ B
―――――――――――
~ B ∨ G

is truth-functionally valid:

A	B	G	(A	&	G)	↓ ∨	(B	⊃	G)	~	G	↓ ∨	B	~	B	↓ ∨	G
T	T	T	T	T	T	T	T	T	T	F	T	T	T	F	T	T	T
T	T	F	T	F	F	F	T	F	F	T	F	T	T	F	T	F	F
T	F	T	T	T	T	T	F	T	T	F	T	F	F	T	F	T	T
T	F	F	T	F	F	T	F	T	F	T	F	T	F	T	F	T	F
F	T	T	F	F	T	T	T	T	T	F	T	T	T	F	T	T	T
F	T	F	F	F	F	F	T	F	F	T	F	T	T	F	T	F	F
F	F	T	F	F	T	T	F	T	T	F	T	F	F	T	F	T	T
F	F	F	F	F	F	T	F	T	F	T	F	T	F	T	F	T	F

The conclusion, '~ B ∨ G', is true on every truth-value assignment on which the premises are true.

The following argument is truth-functionally invalid:

D ≡ (~ W ∨ G)
G ≡ ~ D
――――――――
~ D

This is shown by the following truth-table:

				↓						↓				↓
D	G	W	D	≡	(~	W	∨	G)	G	≡	~	D	~	D
T	**T**	**T**	**T**	**T**	**F**	**T**	**T**	**T**	**T**	**F**	**F**	**T**	**F**	**T**
T	**T**	**F**	**T**	**T**	**T**	**F**	**T**	**T**	**T**	**F**	**F**	**T**	**F**	**T**
T	**F**	**T**	**T**	**F**	**F**	**T**	**F**	**F**	**F**	**T**	**F**	**T**	**F**	**T**
T	**F**	**F**	**T**	**T**	**T**	**F**	**T**	**F**	**F**	**T**	**F**	**T**	**F**	**T**
F	**T**	**T**	**F**	**F**	**F**	**T**	**T**	**T**	**T**	**T**	**T**	**F**	**T**	**F**
F	**T**	**F**	**F**	**F**	**T**	**F**	**T**	**T**	**T**	**T**	**T**	**F**	**T**	**F**
F	**F**	**T**	**F**	**T**	**F**	**T**	**F**	**F**	**F**	**F**	**T**	**F**	**T**	**F**
F	**F**	**F**	**F**	**F**	**T**	**F**	**T**	**F**	**F**	**F**	**T**	**F**	**T**	**F**

The premises, 'D ≡ (~ W ∨ G)' and 'G ≡ ~ D', are both true on every truth-value assignment that assigns **T** to 'D' and **F** to 'G' and 'W', and the conclusion, '~ D', is false on these truth-value assignments.

Where an argument is truth-functionally invalid, we can show this by constructing a shortened truth-table that displays a row in which the premises are true and the conclusion false. The argument

~ (B ∨ D)
~ H
―――――
B

is truth-functionally invalid, as the following shortened truth-table shows:

			↓					↓		↓
B	D	H	~	(B	∨	D)		~	H	B
F	**F**	**F**	**T**	**F**	**F**	**F**		**T**	**F**	**F**

For any argument of *SL* that has a finite number of premises, we may form a sentence called the *corresponding material conditional*, and that sentence is truth-functionally true if and only if the argument is truth-functionally valid. First, we may form an *iterated conjunction* (. . . ($\mathbf{P}_1$ & $\mathbf{P}_2$) & . . . & $\mathbf{P}_n$) from the sentences $\mathbf{P}_1$, . . . , $\mathbf{P}_n$. The iterated conjunction for the sentences '~ (A ⊃ B)', 'D', and 'J ∨ H' is '((~ (A ⊃ B) & D) & (J ∨ H))'. The corresponding material conditional for an argument is then formed by constructing a material conditional with the iterated conjunction of the premises as antecedent and the conclusion of the argument as consequent. The corresponding material conditional for the argument

~ (A ⊃ B)
D
J ∨ H
―――――
~ H ∨ ~ A

is '[[~ (A ⊃ B) & D] & (J ∨ H)] ⊃ (~ H ∨ ~ A)', and the corresponding material conditional for the argument

A
A ⊃ B

B

is '[A & (A ⊃ B)] ⊃ B'.[5]

An argument with a finite number of premises is truth-functionally valid if and only if its corresponding material conditional is truth-functionally true (see Exercise 5). We can show that the argument

A
A ⊃ B

B

is truth-functionally valid by showing that the corresponding material conditional '[A & (A ⊃ B)] ⊃ B' is truth-functionally true:

A	B	[A	&	(A	⊃	B)]	↓ ⊃	B
T	T	T	T	T	T	T	T	T
T	F	T	F	T	F	F	T	F
F	T	F	F	F	T	T	T	T
F	F	F	F	F	T	F	T	F

There is no truth-value assignment on which 'A & (A ⊃ B)' is true and 'B' is false, which means that there is no truth-value assignment on which 'A' and 'A ⊃ B' are both true and 'B' is false. And we can show that the argument

~ A ≡ ~ B
B ∨ A

~ A

[5]Strictly speaking, an argument with more than one premise will have more than one corresponding material conditional. This is because the premises of an argument can be conjoined in more than one order. But all the corresponding material conditionals for any one argument are truth-functionally equivalent, and so we speak loosely of *the* corresponding material conditional for a given argument.

is truth-functionally invalid by showing that the corresponding material conditional is not truth-functionally true:

A	B	[(~ A	≡	~ B)	&	(B	∨	A)]	⊃ ↓	~ A
T	T	F T	T	F T	T	T	T	T	F	F T
T	F	F T	F	T F	F	F	T	T	T	F T
F	T	T F	F	F T	F	T	T	F	T	T F
F	F	T F	T	T F	F	F	F	F	T	T F

The first row represents truth-value assignments on which the antecedent is true and the consequent false. On these truth-value assignments the premises of the argument, '~ A ≡ ~ B' and 'B ∨ A', are both true and the conclusion, '~ A', is false. Hence the argument is truth-functionally invalid.

3.5E EXERCISES

1. Use truth-tables to determine whether the following arguments are truth-functionally valid.

a. A ⊃ (H & J)
J ≡ H
~ J
―――――
~ A

*b. B ∨ (A & ~ C)
(C ⊃ A) ≡ B
~ B ∨ A
―――――
~ (A ∨ C)

c. (D ≡ ~ G) & G
(G ∨ [(A ⊃ D) & A]) ⊃ ~ D
―――――
G ⊃ ~ D

*d. ~ (Y ≡ A)
~ Y
~ A
―――――
W & ~ W

e. (C ⊃ D) ⊃ (D ⊃ E)
D
―――――
C ⊃ E

*f. $B \vee B$

$[\sim B \supset (\sim D \vee \sim C)] \;\&\; [(\sim D \vee C) \vee (\sim B \vee C)]$

C

g. $(G \equiv H) \vee (\sim G \equiv H)$

$(\sim G \equiv \sim H) \vee \sim (G \equiv H)$

*h. $[(J \;\&\; T) \;\&\; Y] \vee (\sim J \supset \sim Y)$

$J \supset T$

$T \supset Y$

$Y \equiv T$

i. $\sim\sim F \supset \sim\sim G$

$\sim G \supset \sim F$

$G \supset F$

*j. $[A \;\&\; (B \vee C)] \equiv (A \vee B)$

$B \supset \sim B$

$C \vee A$

2. For each of the following arguments, either show that the argument is truth-functionally invalid by constructing an appropriate shortened truth-table or show that the argument is truth-functionally valid by constructing a full truth-table.

a. $(J \vee M) \supset \sim (J \;\&\; M)$

$M \equiv (M \supset J)$

$M \supset J$

*b. $B \;\&\; F$

$\sim (B \;\&\; G)$

G

c. $A \supset \sim A$

$(B \supset A) \supset B$

$A \equiv \sim B$

*d. $J \vee [M \supset (T \equiv J)]$

$(M \supset J) \;\&\; (T \supset M)$

$T \;\&\; \sim M$

e. $A \;\&\; \sim [(B \;\&\; C) \equiv (C \supset A)]$

$B \supset \sim B$

$\sim C \supset C$

3. Construct the corresponding material conditional for each of the following arguments. For each of the arguments, either show that the argument is truth-functionally invalid by constructing an appropriate shortened truth-table for the corresponding material conditional or show that the argument is truth-functionally valid by constructing a full truth-table for the corresponding material conditional.

a. B & C

B ∨ C

*b. K ≡ L

L ⊃ J

~ J

~ K ∨ L

c. (J ⊃ T) ⊃ J

(T ⊃ J) ⊃ T

~ J ∨ ~ T

*d. (A ∨ C) & ~ H

~ C

e. B & C

B ∨ D

D

*f. ~ [A ∨ ~ (B ∨ ~ C)]

B ⊃ (A ⊃ C)

~ A ≡ ~ B

4. Symbolize each of the following arguments and use truth-tables to test for truth-functional validity.

a. 'Stern' means the same as 'star' if 'Nacht' means the same as 'day'. But 'Nacht' doesn't mean the same as 'day'; therefore 'Stern' means something different from 'star'.

*b. Many people believe that war is inevitable. But war is inevitable if and only if our planet's natural resources are nonrenewable. So many people believe that our natural resources are nonrenewable.

c. Thirty days hath September, April, and November. But February has forty days, since April has thirty days if and only if May doesn't, and May has thirty days if November does.

*d. The town hall is now a grocery store, and, unless I'm mistaken, the little red schoolhouse is a movie theater. No, I'm not mistaken. The old schoolhouse is a boutique, and the old theater is an elementary school if the little red schoolhouse is a movie theater. So the little red schoolhouse is a movie theater.

e. Computers can think if and only if they can have emotions. If computers can have emotions, then they can have desires as well. But computers can't think if they have desires. Therefore computers can't think.

*f. If the butler murdered Devon, then the maid is lying, and if the gardener murdered Devon, then the weapon was a slingshot. The maid is lying if and only if the weapon wasn't a slingshot, and if the weapon wasn't a slingshot, then the butler murdered Devon. Therefore the butler murdered Devon.

5.a. Show that $(\ldots(\mathbf{P}_1 \,\&\, \mathbf{P}_2) \,\&\, \ldots \,\&\, \mathbf{P}_n) \supset \mathbf{Q}$ is truth-functionally true if and only if

$\mathbf{P}_1$

$\vdots$

$\mathbf{P}_n$

$\mathbf{Q}$

is truth-functionally valid.

*b. Show that $\{\mathbf{P}\} \models \mathbf{Q}$ and $\{\mathbf{Q}\} \models \mathbf{P}$ if and only if **P** and **Q** are truth-functionally equivalent.

c. Suppose that $\{\mathbf{P}\} \models \mathbf{Q} \vee \mathbf{R}$. Does it follow that either $\{\mathbf{P}\} \models \mathbf{Q}$ or $\{\mathbf{P}\} \models \mathbf{R}$? Show that you are right.

*d. Show that if $\{\mathbf{P}\} \models \mathbf{Q}$ and $\{\mathbf{Q}\} \models \mathbf{R}$, then $\{\mathbf{P}\} \models \mathbf{R}$.

3.6 TRUTH-FUNCTIONAL PROPERTIES AND TRUTH-FUNCTIONAL CONSISTENCY

In this section we show that the truth-functional concepts of truth-functional truth, truth-functional falsehood, truth-functional indeterminacy, truth-functional entailment, and truth-functional validity can all be explicated in terms of truth-functional consistency. This is important because in Chapter 4 we shall introduce an alternative test for truth-functional consistency, and the possibility of explicating the other concepts in terms of truth-functional consistency means that we shall be able to use the test to determine other truth-functional properties of sentences and sets of sentences as well.

> A sentence **P** is truth-functionally false if and only if {**P**} is truth-functionally inconsistent.

(We call {**P**} the *unit set* of **P**.) To prove that this is so, we first assume that **P** is truth-functionally false. Then, by definition, there is no truth-value assignment on which **P** is true. Consequently, as **P** is the only member of the unit set {**P**}, there is no truth-value assignment on which every member of that set is true. So {**P**} is truth-functionally inconsistent. Now assume that {**P**} is truth-functionally inconsistent. Then, by definition, there is no truth-value assignment on which every member of {**P**} is true. Since **P** is the only member of its unit set, there is no truth-value assignment on which **P** is true. Hence **P** is truth-functionally false.

The corresponding relation for truth-functionally true sentences is more complicated:

> A sentence **P** is truth-functionally true if and only if {~ **P**} is truth-functionally inconsistent.

We first assume that **P** is truth-functionally true. Then, by definition, **P** is true on every truth-value assignment. We know that a sentence is true on a truth-value assignment if and only if the negation of the sentence is false on that truth-value assignment. So it follows from our assumption that ~ **P** is false on every truth-value assignment; that is, there is no truth-value assignment on which ~ **P** is true. But then there is no truth-value assignment on which every member of {~ **P**} is true, which means that {~ **P**} is truth-functionally inconsistent. The proof of the converse, that if {~ **P**} is truth-functionally inconsistent then **P** is truth-functionally true, is left as an exercise.

Since a sentence **P** is truth-functionally true if and only if {~ **P**} is truth-functionally inconsistent and **P** is truth-functionally false if and only if {**P**} is truth-functionally inconsistent, it follows that

> A sentence **P** is truth-functionally indeterminate if and only if both {~ **P**} and {**P**} are truth-functionally consistent.

Now we turn to truth-functional equivalence. Where **P** and **Q** are sentences of *SL*, **P** ≡ **Q** is their *corresponding material biconditional.* **P** and **Q** are truth-functionally equivalent if and only if their corresponding material biconditional **P** ≡ **Q** is truth-functionally true. If we assume that **P** and **Q** are truth-functionally equivalent, then, by definition, **P** and **Q** have the same truth-value on every truth-value assignment. But we know that a material biconditional has the truth-value **T** on every truth-value assignment on which its immediate sentential components have the same truth-value. So, on our assumption, **P** ≡ **Q** is true on every truth-value assignment and hence is truth-functionally true. The converse of this, that if **P** ≡ **Q** is truth-functionally true then **P** and **Q** are truth-functionally equivalent, is left as an exercise. It follows from these results that

> Sentences **P** and **Q** are truth-functionally equivalent if and only if {~ (**P** ≡ **Q**)} is truth-functionally inconsistent.

Consider: **P** ≡ **Q** is truth-functionally true if and only if {~ (**P** ≡ **Q**)} is truth-functionally inconsistent, by our previous result concerning truth-functional truths. Moreover we have just shown that **P** and **Q** are truth-functionally equivalent if and only if **P** ≡ **Q** is truth-functionally true.

To make these results more concrete, we shall consider an example. The set {~ [(A ∨ B) ≡ (~ A ⊃ B)]} is truth-functionally inconsistent, as shown by the following truth-table:

A	B	↓ ~	[(A	∨	B)	≡	(~	A	⊃	B)]
T	T	F	T	T	T	T	F	T	T	T
T	F	F	T	T	F	T	F	T	T	F
F	T	F	F	T	T	T	T	F	T	T
F	F	F	F	F	F	T	T	F	F	F

The set is truth-functionally inconsistent because there is no truth-value assignment on which every member of the set (in this case there is just one member) is true. From this we know the following:

1. '~ [(A ∨ B) ≡ (~ A ⊃ B)]' is truth-functionally false. (**P** is truth-functionally false if and only if {**P**} is truth-functionally inconsistent. Here {~ [(A ∨ B) ≡ (~ A ⊃ B)]} is truth-functionally inconsistent. Hence there is no truth-value assignment on which the only member of that set, '~ [(A ∨ B) ≡ (~ A ⊃ B)]', is true. That one member is thus truth-functionally false.)
2. '(A ∨ B) ≡ (~ A ⊃ B)' is truth-functionally true. (**P** is truth-functionally true if and only if {~ **P**} is truth-functionally inconsistent. We have just reasoned that '~ [(A ∨ B) ≡ (~ A ⊃ B)]' is truth-functionally false. Hence the sentence of which it is the negation, '(A ∨ B) ≡ (~ A ⊃ B)', is true on every truth-value assignment—it is a truth-functionally true sentence.)
3. 'A ∨ B' and '~ A ⊃ B' are truth-functionally equivalent. (**P** and **Q** are truth-functionally equivalent if and only if {~ (**P** ≡ **Q**)} is truth-functionally inconsistent. Since '(A ∨ B) ≡ (~ A ⊃ B)' is truth-functionally true, 'A ∨ B' and '~ A ⊃ B' have the same truth-value on every truth-value assignment—they are truth-functionally equivalent.)

Of course, each of these claims can be directly verified by examining the truth-table, but our general proofs show that this is not necessary.

Next we relate the concepts of truth-functional entailment and truth-functional consistency. Where Γ is a set of sentences of *SL* and **P** is any sentence of *SL*, we may form a set that contains **P** and all the members of Γ. This set is represented as

Γ ∪ {**P**}

which is read as

the union of gamma and the unit set of **P**

Thus, if Γ is {A, A ⊃ B} and **P** is 'J', then $\Gamma \cup$ {**P**}—that is, {A, A ⊃ B} ∪ {J}—is {A, A ⊃ B, J}. Of course, if **P** is a member of Γ, then $\Gamma \cup$ {**P**} is identical with Γ. So {A, A ⊃ B} ∪ {A ⊃ B} is simply {A, A ⊃ B}. In the case where Γ is ∅ (the empty set), $\Gamma \cup$ {**P**} is simply {**P**}. This follows because ∅ contains no members.

We may now prove that, if $\Gamma \models$ **P**, for some sentence **P** and set of sentences Γ, then $\Gamma \cup$ {~ **P**} is truth-functionally inconsistent. Suppose that $\Gamma \models$ **P**. Then, by definition, there is no truth-value assignment on which every member of Γ is true and **P** is false. But we know that ~ **P** is true on a truth-value assignment if and only if **P** is false on that truth-value assignment. So it follows from our assumption that there is no truth-value on which every member of Γ is true and ~ **P** is true. But then there is no truth-value assignment on which every member of the set $\Gamma \cup$ {~ **P**} is true—so the set is truth-functionally inconsistent. It follows from this proof that since {J ∨ C} ⊨ ~ (~ J & ~ C) the set {J ∨ C, ~ ~ (~ J & ~ C)} is truth-functionally inconsistent. The converse, that if $\Gamma \cup$ {~ **P**} is truth-functionally inconsistent then $\Gamma \models$ **P**, holds as well. The proof is left as an exception.

It follows from this result, as well as the fact that an argument is truth-functionally valid if and only if the set consisting of the argument's premises truth-functionally entails the conclusion, that

> An argument of *SL* is truth-functionally valid if and only if the set containing as its only members the premises of the argument and the negation of the conclusion is truth-functionally inconsistent.

So the argument

(A ⊃ D) & H
F ∨ H
———————
D

is truth-functionally valid if and only if {(A ⊃ D) & H, F ∨ H, ~ D} is truth-functionally inconsistent.

3.6E EXERCISES

1. Prove each of the following:

a. If {~ **P**} is truth-functionally inconsistent, where **P** is a sentence of *SL*, then **P** is truth-functionally true.

*b. If **P** ≡ **Q** is truth-functionally true, where **P** and **Q** are sentences of *SL*, then **P** and **Q** are truth-functionally equivalent.

c. If $\Gamma \cup$ {~ **P**} is truth-functionally inconsistent, where Γ is a set of sentences of *SL* and **P** is a sentence of *SL*, then $\Gamma \models$ **P**.

2. Prove each of the following:

a. A sentence **P** is truth-functionally true if and only if $\varnothing \vDash$ **P**.

*b. $\Gamma \vDash$ **P** $\supset$ **Q**, where Γ is a set of sentences of *SL* and **P** and **Q** are sentences of *SL*, if and only if $\Gamma \cup$ {**P**} $\vDash$ **Q**.

c. If Γ is truth-functionally inconsistent, where Γ is a set of sentences of *SL*, then Γ truth-functionally entails every sentence of *SL*.

*d. For any set Γ of sentences of *SL* and any truth-functionally false sentence **P** of *SL*, $\Gamma \cup$ {**P**} is truth-functionally inconsistent.

3. Prove each of the following:

a. If a set Γ of sentences of *SL* is truth-functionally consistent and **P** is a truth-functionally true sentence of *SL*, then $\Gamma \cup$ {**P**} is truth-functionally consistent.

*b. If $\Gamma \vDash$ **P** and $\Gamma \vDash$ ~ **P**, for some sentence **P** and set Γ of sentences of *SL*, then Γ is truth-functionally inconsistent.

4. Prove each of the following:

a. If {**P**} $\vDash$ **Q** and {~ **P**} $\vDash$ **R**, where **P**, **Q**, and **R** are sentences of *SL*, then **Q** $\vee$ **R** is truth-functionally true.

*b. If **P** and **Q** are truth-functionally equivalent, where **P** and **Q** are sentences of *SL*, then for any sentence **R** of *SL*, {**P**} $\vDash$ **R** if and only if {**Q**} $\vDash$ **R**.

c. If $\Gamma \vDash$ **P** and $\Gamma' \vDash$ **Q**, where Γ and Γ' are sets of sentences of *SL* and **P** and **Q** are sentences of *SL*, then $\Gamma \cup \Gamma' \vDash$ **P** & **Q**, where $\Gamma \cup \Gamma'$ is the set that contains all the sentences in Γ and all the sentences in Γ'.

GLOSSARY

TRUTH-FUNCTIONAL TRUTH: A sentence **P** of *SL* is *truth-functionally true* if and only if **P** is true on every truth-value assignment.

TRUTH-FUNCTIONAL FALSITY: A sentence **P** of *SL* is *truth-functionally false* if and only if **P** is false on every truth-value assignment.

TRUTH-FUNCTIONAL INDETERMINACY: A sentence **P** of *SL* is *truth-functionally indeterminate* if and only if **P** is neither truth-functionally true nor truth-functionally false.

TRUTH-FUNCTIONAL EQUIVALENCE: Sentences **P** and **Q** of *SL* are *truth-functionally equivalent* if and only if there is no truth-value assignment on which **P** and **Q** have different truth-values.

TRUTH-FUNCTIONAL CONSISTENCY: A set of sentences of *SL* is *truth-functionally consistent* if and only if there is at least one truth-value assignment on which all the members of the set are true. A set of sentences of *SL* is *truth-functionally inconsistent* if and only if the set is not truth-functionally consistent.

TRUTH-FUNCTIONAL ENTAILMENT: A set Γ of sentences of *SL* *truth-functionally entails* a sentence **P** of *SL* if and only if there is no truth-value assignment on which every member of Γ is true and **P** is false.

TRUTH-FUNCTIONAL VALIDITY: An argument of *SL* is *truth-functionally valid* if and only if there is no truth-value assignment on which all the premises are true and the conclusion is false. An argument of *SL* is *truth-functionally invalid* if and only if it is not truth-functionally valid.

'hapter

4

SENTENTIAL LOGIC: TRUTH-TREES

4.1 THE TRUTH-TREE METHOD

In Chapter 3 we used the notion of a truth-value assignment to give formal accounts of the important semantic concepts of truth-functional logic. At the end of Chapter 3, we saw that, once truth-functional consistency has been explicated by means of the notion of a truth-value assignment, the remaining semantic concepts of sentential logic can be explicated in terms of truth-functional consistency. In this chapter we make use of this fact to provide an additional method, the truth-tree method, of determining whether truth-functional properties hold of sentences and finite[1] sets of sentences of *SL*. Truth-trees provide a systematic method of searching for truth-value assignments that are of special interest—for example, a truth-value assignment on which a given sentence of *SL* is false, or a truth-value assignment on which the premises of a given argument of *SL* are true and the conclusion false. The truth-tree method also reveals when no such truth-value assignments exist.

[1] This restriction is necessary because truth-trees, as we shall develop them, can only be constructed for finite sets of sentence. Hence in this chapter we restrict ourselves to arguments with a finite number of premises, to cases of alleged entailment involving finite sets, and to consistency as applied to finite sets. However, some implications can be drawn concerning infinite sets, as we shall explain.

The truth-table method is mechanical. And the truth-tree method we develop in this chapter can easily be made so. The advantage of truth-tables is that they graphically display how the truth-values of truth-functionally compound sentences are generated from the truth-values of their components. The disadvantage of truth-tables is that they become unwieldy when the number of distinct atomic components of the sentence or sentences being tested is much greater than 3. Truth-trees, it must be admitted, can also become unwieldy. However, the size and complexity of truth-trees are not as direct a function of the number of distinct atomic components of the sentences being tested as are the size and complexity of truth-tables. Sets of sentences with a large number of distinct atomic components frequently have reasonably concise truth-trees. What is of theoretical importance here, as with truth-tables, is that the truth-tree system can be used, for any finite set of sentences of *SL*, to yield, in a finite number of steps, an answer to the question 'Is this set truth-functionally consistent?' We establish this claim in Chapter 11.

The rules we will use in constructing truth-trees are derived directly from the characteristic truth-tables for the five truth-functional connectives. For this reason, and because truth-value assignments on which all the members of the set being tested are true can readily be recovered from truth-trees for consistent sets, we take truth-trees to constitute a second semantic method of determining whether the truth-functional properties defined in Chapter 3 hold of sentences and finite sets of sentences of *SL*.

4.2 TRUTH-TREE RULES FOR SENTENCES CONTAINING '~', '∨', AND '&'

Recall that a set of sentences is truth-functionally consistent if and only if there is at least one truth-value assignment on which all the members of that set are true. Sometimes we can tell at a glance that a set is truth-functionally consistent or that it is truth-functionally inconsistent. For example, {A & ~ B, C} is fairly obviously a consistent set, and {A & ~ B, ~ A} is fairly obviously an inconsistent set. But most of us cannot tell immediately whether {(~ B & C) & (A ∨ B), A & C} is consistent or inconsistent. Truth-trees provide us with a systematic method for determining, for any finite set of sentences of *SL*, whether that set is truth-functionally consistent.

We begin with some easy examples. First, we show that {A & ~ B, C} is indeed truth-functionally consistent. In constructing a truth-tree, the first step is to display the members of the set being tested, one above another, in a column:

A & ~ B
C

What we want to know is whether there is a truth-value assignment on which all the sentences in the column are true. The first sentence in the column is a conjunction, and we know that a conjunction is true on a truth-value assignment if and only if both its conjuncts are true on that assignment. So we can break down or decompose 'A & ~ B' into its conjuncts, adding these conjuncts, one below the other, to our column:

A & ~ B✓
C
A
~ B

We put a check mark after 'A & ~ B' to indicate that we are finished with it. We have, in effect, replaced it in our list of sentences with two simpler sentences. This replacement is appropriate inasmuch as 'A & ~ B' is true if and only if both 'A' and '~ B' are true. All the sentences on the tree either have been decomposed (and checked off) or are atomic sentences or negations of atomic sentences. We shall call a sentence that is either an atomic sentence or the negation of an atomic sentence a *literal*. Once we have a tree on which the only undecomposed sentences are literals, it is easy to determine whether there is a truth-value assignment on which all the members of the set we are testing are true—that is, whether the set is truth-functionally consistent. We try to generate the desired assignment by reading up the column of sentences, starting at the bottom. We pay attention only to the literals. If a literal is an atomic sentence, we assign the truth-value **T** to that atomic sentence. If the literal is the *negation* of an atomic sentence, we assign the truth-value **F** to the atomic sentence (not to the literal). Applying this procedure to the tree, we generate the following fragment of an assignment:

A	B	C
T	**F**	**T**

Clearly every member of the set we are testing, {A & ~ B, C}, is true on every truth-value assignment that assigns these truth-values to 'A', 'B', and 'C'. Hence the set we are testing is truth-functionally consistent.

Next we shall use the truth-tree method to show that {A & ~ B, ~ A} is truth-functionally inconsistent. We begin, as before, by listing the members of the set in a column. Then we decompose the conjunction 'A & ~ B'.

A & ~ B✓
~ A
A
~ B

All the literals on this tree must be true for the members of our set to be true. '~ B' occurs on the tree. To make it true, we assign 'B' the truth-value **F**. 'A' and '~ A' both occur on the tree. To make the former true, we must assign 'A' the truth-value **T**. To make the latter true, we must assign 'A' the truth-value **F**. But clearly there is no truth-value assignment on which 'A' is assigned both the truth-value **T** and the truth-value **F**. Hence there is no truth-value assignment on which all the literals on our tree are true. We entered the literals 'A' and '~ B' because they must be true if the first sentence, 'A & ~ B', is to be true. Thus it follows that there is no truth-value assignment on which the members of the set we are testing—that is, 'A & ~ B' and '~ A'—are both true. So the set is truth-functionally inconsistent.

The truth-trees we have constructed so far both consist of single branches, that is, of single columns of sentences of *SL*. However, many trees are more complex. We can illustrate how multiple branches are formed by constructing a tree for {A & ~ B, C, ~ A ∨ ~ C}. We formed this set from the first set we tested by adding one more sentence, '~ A ∨ ~ C'. Thus we can use our tree for the first set as a model for the first part of our tree for this set:

```
A & ~ B✓
   C
~ A ∨ ~ C✓
   A
  ~ B
```

Our tree is not yet complete; it contains a truth-functionally compound sentence, '~ A ∨ ~ C', that is not a literal and that has not been decomposed. We must decompose this sentence in such a way as to show what sentences must be true for this disjunction to be true. For a disjunction to be true, only one of its disjuncts need be true (though both may be true). If we add both disjuncts to our list, one below the other, we shall wrongly be *requiring* that both those disjuncts be true. But we can represent the fact that there are *alternative* ways in which a disjunction can be made true by *branching* our tree:

```
 A & ~ B✓
    C
~ A ∨ ~ C✓
    A
   ~ B
   / \
~ A   ~ C
```

By displaying '~ A' and '~ C' on the same line, rather than one below the other, we show that making either of them true is sufficient to make the sentence we are decomposing true. We now have two branches, and we have to inspect each to see whether there is a way of making all the sentences we are testing true. If there is such a way, it will involve either making all the literals on the left branch true or making all the literals on the right branch true (or both, since our '∨' is inclusive). A *branch,* in our sense, consists of all the sentences that can be reached by starting with a sentence at the bottom of the tree and tracing a path upward through the tree, never moving down or horizontally, and ending with the first sentence listed in our original column of sentences. A sentence may thus occur just once on a tree but still be on several branches. In our present example the members of the set we are testing, along with the literals 'A' and '~ B', occur on both branches of our tree—the one ending in '~ A' and the one ending in '~ C'.

When we inspect the branches of our tree, we immediately see that neither branch will yield a truth-value assignment on which all the members of the set we are testing are true. The left-hand branch shows us that to obtain such an assignment we would have to assign 'A' the truth-value **F** and the truth-value **T** since both '~ A' and 'A' occur on that branch. Similarly the right-hand branch shows us that to obtain such an assignment we would have to assign 'C' the truth-value **F** and the truth-value **T** since both '~ C' and 'C' occur on that branch. Neither alternative is possible. So there is no truth-value assignment on which all the members of the set we are testing are true; hence that set is truth-functionally inconsistent.

In constructing truth-trees we decompose truth-functionally compound sentences that are not literals in such a way as to display the truth-conditions for those compounds. Truth-trees are, in effect, ways of searching for truth-value assignments on which the sentences in the set being tested are true. A branch that contains both an atomic sentence and the negation of that sentence represents a failure to find such an assignment, for no truth-value assignment assigns any atomic sentence both the truth-value **T** and the truth-value **F**. A branch that does contain both an atomic sentence and the negation of that sentence is a closed branch. A branch that is not closed is open. Eventually each branch will either close or become a completed open branch, that is, an open branch such that every sentence on it either is a literal or has been decomposed. Note that since a completed open branch is a kind of open branch it will not contain an atomic sentence and the negation of that sentence. Any truth-value assignment on which all the literals on a completed open branch are true is, by the nature of the tree rules, also an assignment on which the members of the set being tested are all true.[2] To generate such an assignment from an open branch, we assign **T** to every atomic sentence occurring on that branch, **F** to every atomic sentence whose negation occurs on that branch, and either **T** or **F** (it does not matter which) to every other atomic sentence. Accordingly:

> A finite set Γ of sentences of *SL* is *truth-functionally consistent* if and only if Γ has a truth-tree with at least one completed open branch.

[2]These results are proven in Chapter 11.

We will call a truth-tree each of whose branches is closed a *closed truth-tree.* Accordingly we can also say this:

> A finite set Γ of sentences of *SL* is *truth-functionally inconsistent* if and only if Γ has a closed truth-tree.[3]

A *completed tree* is a tree each of whose branches is either closed or is a completed open branch. An *open tree* is a tree that is not closed. (Note that an open tree need not be a completed tree, and that an open tree that is not completed may become a closed tree.)[4]

In summary we shall use the following vocabulary for truth-trees:

Branch:	All the sentences that can be reached by starting with a sentence at the bottom of a tree and tracing an upwards path through the tree, ending with the first sentence listed at the top of the tree
Closed branch:	A branch containing both an atomic sentence and the negation of that sentence
Closed truth-tree:	A tree each of whose branches is closed
Open branch:	A branch that is not closed
Completed open branch:	An open branch such that every sentence on it is either a literal or has been decomposed
Completed truth-tree:	A tree each of whose branches is either closed or is a completed open branch
Open truth-tree:	A tree that is not closed

For the sake of clarity, we adopt the convention of numbering the lines of our truth-trees in a column on the left. We also include a justification column on the right. The column of line numbers and the column of justifications are not, strictly speaking, parts of truth-trees. They are notational devices we use to make the structure and logic of trees more transparent. The lines containing the members of the set we are testing for truth-functional consistency will all be justified by entering the abbreviation 'SM' for 'set member'. Later lines will be justified by entering a line number and a rule abbreviation. The two rules we have presented so far are *Conjunction Decomposition* and *Disjunction*

[3]If a finite set Γ of sentences is truth-functionally inconsistent, then so is every set of which Γ is a subset—that is, every set that contains all the members of Γ and possibly additional members. (We prove this in Chapter 6.) Hence it follows that, if an infinite set has a subset that is truth-functionally inconsistent, so is that infinite set.

[4]The truth-tree for the empty set is the null tree, that is, the truth-tree that has no sentences on its single null branch, each one of which is, trivially, either a literal or has been decomposed. Hence, by the above account, the empty set is consistent, a desired result.

Decomposition, abbreviated '&D' and '∨D', respectively. When these conventions are followed, our last tree appears as follows:

```
1.              A & ~ B✓              SM
2.                  C                 SM
3.             ~ A ∨ ~ C✓             SM
4.                  A                 1 &D
5.                 ~ B                1 &D
                 /     \
6.       ~ A                 ~ C      3 ∨D
          ×                   ×
```

For the sake of clarity, no line of the justification column is allowed to contain more than one rule abbreviation or reference to more than one previous line. An '×' under a branch of a tree indicates that that branch is closed. As with line numbers and justifications, the check marks after decomposed sentences and closed branch indicators (the occurrences of '×' at the end of closed branches) are notational conveniences and are not literally parts of truth-trees.

We noted earlier that the set {(~ B & C) & (A ∨ B), A & C} is neither obviously consistent nor obviously inconsistent. We can now use the truth-tree method to test this set for truth-functional consistency. We begin our tree in the usual way:

```
1.     (~ B & C) & (A ∨ B)✓     SM
2.            A & C             SM
3.           ~ B & C            1 &D
4.            A ∨ B             1 &D
```

Here the results of using the rule Conjunction Decomposition are themselves truth-functionally compound sentences that will have to be decomposed. First we decompose 'A & C', and then we decompose '~ B & C' and 'A ∨ B'.

```
1.     (~ B & C) & (A ∨ B)✓     SM
2.            A & C✓            SM
3.           ~ B & C✓           1 &D
4.            A ∨ B✓            1 &D
5.              A               2 &D
6.              C               2 &D
7.             ~ B              3 &D
8.              C               3 &D
             /     \
9.     A                 B      4 ∨D
                         ×
```

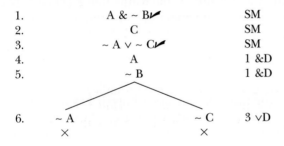

The only sentences on this tree that have not been decomposed are literals. There are no more sentences that can be decomposed. Yet we have a branch on the left that is not closed. This completed open branch displays the literals from which we can recover a truth-value assignment on which every member of our set is true. That assignment must make all those literals true, so it must assign 'A' and 'C' the truth-value **T** and 'B' the truth-value **F** (since '~ B' occurs on the open branch). The relevant fragment of the assignment is thus

A	B	C
T	**F**	**T**

That 'A' and 'C' each occur twice on our open branch has no special significance for the truth-value assignment we are looking for. They so occur because their truth is required by two different members of the set we are testing.

This tree is the first one we have encountered that has at least one completed open branch *and* at least one closed branch. A completed open tree often has one or more closed branches. The process of generating a truth-value assignment from a completed open branch is called *recovering a truth-value assignment.* Since truth-value assignments are, by definition, assignments of either **T** or **F** to each of the (infinitely many) sentence letters of *SL*, they are themselves infinite. Hence, when recovering truth-value assignments from truth-trees, we write down only the relevant (finite) fragment of the truth-value assignment. For a given sentence or set of sentences of *SL*, the relevant fragment of a truth-value assignment is that fragment that specifies the truth-values assigned to the atomic components of that sentence or set of sentences. When we talk of recovering a fragment of a truth-value assignment from a completed open branch, we mean the relevant fragment for the set of sentences being tested, that is, the fragment that specifies the assignments made to the atomic components of the set being tested.

In the previous example we decomposed the two conjunctions 'B & C' and 'A & C' before we decomposed the disjunction 'A ∨ B'. There is no rule stating that we must do this. Any order of decomposition would have led to a tree with a completed open branch. Altering the order of decomposition sometimes makes a tree more or less complex, but it never alters the final result. For a given set of sentences, if one order of decomposition generates an open tree, all orders of decomposition generate open trees. And if one order of decomposition generates a closed tree, all orders of decomposition generate closed trees. In the present case decomposing 'A ∨ B' earlier would produce the following tree:

1.	(~ B & C) & (A ∨ B)✓		SM
2.	A & C✓		SM
3.	~ B & C✓		1 &D
4.	A ∨ B✓		1 &D
5.	A	B	4 ∨D
6.	A	A	2 &D
7.	C	C	2 &D
8.	~ B	~ B	3 &D
9.	C		3 &D
	×		

In decomposing 'A ∨ B' before 'A & C and '~ B & C', we produced a branching early in our tree. Consequently we had to enter the results of decomposing the remaining sentences on both open branches, thus considerably complicating our tree. (It is important to remember that when a sentence is decomposed the results of that decomposition must be entered *on every open branch passing through the sentence being decomposed.*) But this more complex tree also has a completed open branch, so the end result is the same. The '×' was not placed under the right-hand branch until both '~ B' and 'C' had been entered on that branch. The closure here occurs because the branch contains the pair of literals 'B' and '~ B'. However, we do not stop halfway through the application of a decomposition rule to mark the closure. Rather, we finish decomposing '~ B & C' and then place an '×' below the branch.

So far we have presented the rules for decomposing conjunctions and disjunctions but not those for decomposing conditionals, biconditionals, and negations. To be able to construct truth-trees for all finite sets of sentences of *SL*, we need to know how to decompose these truth-functionally compound sentences as well. How a negation is to be decomposed depends upon the kind of sentence being negated, and we shall have separate rules for decomposing negated conjunctions, negated disjunctions, negated material conditionals, negated material biconditionals, and negated negations. Literals—that is, atomic sentences and negations of atomic sentences—are not decomposed.

We have already used the rules for decomposing conjunctions and disjunctions. Schematically these rules are

Conjunction Decomposition (&D)

P & **Q**✓
P
Q

Disjunction Decomposition (∨D)

P ∨ **Q**✓
P   **Q**

It is helpful to think of these rules in the following way: What is written below a sentence indicates what sentences must be true for that sentence to be true. That is, for **P** & **Q** to be true, both **P** and **Q** must be true, so both **P** and **Q** are written, one under the other, beneath **P** & **Q**. For **P** ∨ **Q** to be true, either **P** must be true or **Q** must be true, so these alternatives are displayed below **P** ∨ **Q**, but with both on the same line.

The rule for decomposing negated negations is also obvious. A sentence of the form ~ ~ **P** is true if and only if **P** is true. Hence we have the rule

Negated Negation Decomposition (~ ~ D)

~ ~ **P**✓
P

Consider next the rule for negated conjunctions. A sentence of the form ~ (**P** & **Q**) is truth-functionally equivalent to the corresponding sentence of the form ~ **P** ∨ ~ **Q**, and sentences of this latter form are disjunctions. The rule for decomposing disjunctions is a branching rule, that is, a rule that increases the number of branches on a tree. Hence

<u>*Negated Conjunction Decomposition* (~ &D)</u>

~ (**P** & **Q**)✓

~ **P**   ~ **Q**

Similarly we know that, for any sentences **P** and **Q**, ~ (**P** ∨ **Q**) and ~ **P** & ~ **Q** are truth-functionally equivalent sentences, and we already know how to decompose conjunctions. So we have

<u>*Negated Disjunction Decomposition* (~ ∨D)</u>

~ (**P** ∨ **Q**)✓
~ **P**
~ **Q**

We now have all the rules we need to decompose sentences that contain only the connectives '&', '∨', and '~'. It will be useful to pause here to construct a few truth-trees for sets consisting of sentences whose only connectives are those just mentioned. Consider first the set {A & ~ B, ~ (B ∨ ~ A), (B & A) ∨ (B & ~ A)}. This set is truth-functionally inconsistent, as the following truth-tree shows:

1.	A & ~ B✓		SM
2.	~ (B ∨ ~ A)✓		SM
3.	(B & A) ∨ (B & ~ A)✓		SM
4.	A		1 &D
5.	~ B		1 &D
6.	~ B		2 ~ ∨D
7.	~ ~ A✓		2 ~ ∨D
8.	A		7 ~ ~ D
9.	B & A✓	B & ~ A✓	3 ∨D
10.	B	B	9 &D
11.	A	~ A	9 &D
	×	×	

Both branches of this tree are closed, so the tree is closed, and no truth-value assignment can be recovered from it. Hence there is no truth-value assignment on which every member of the set being tested is true. Hence that set is truth-functionally inconsistent. Note that decomposing the sentences on lines 1 and 2 does not increase the number of branches, whereas decomposing the sentence on line 3 does. Since branching makes for complexity, we decomposed the sentences on lines 1 and 2 before we decomposed the sentence on line 3. This is a use of the first of several strategies we will develop for keeping trees simple.

> **Strategy 1:** Give priority to decomposing sentences whose decomposition does not require branching.

Note also that the justifications given for lines 10 and 11 actually apply to the decomposition of two sentences, 'B & A' and 'B & ~ A'. No confusion results here because both sentences occur on line 9, both are conjunctions, and both are therefore decomposed by the rule Conjunction Decomposition. For the sake of expository clarity, we shall avoid writing the products of multiple decompositions on the same line except where those products are, as here, obtained by applying the same decomposition rule multiple times to sentences occurring on the same earlier line.

Consider next a set whose members contain three distinct atomic sentences: {G ∨ (H ∨ I), ~ (G ∨ H), ~ (H ∨ I), ~ (I ∨ G)}. Here is a tree for this set:

1.		G ∨ (H ∨ I) ✓		SM
2.		~ (G ∨ H) ✓		SM
3.		~ (H ∨ I) ✓		SM
4.		~ (I ∨ G) ✓		SM
5.		~ G		2 ~ ∨D
6.		~ H		2 ~ ∨D
7.		~ H		3 ~ ∨D
8.		~ I		3 ~ ∨D
9.		~ I		4 ~ ∨D
10.		~ G		4 ~ ∨D
11.	G		H ∨ I ✓	1 ∨D
	×			
12.		H	I	11 ∨D
		×	×	

This tree has three branches, all of which are closed. Hence the set being tested is truth-functionally inconsistent.

Next we construct a truth-tree for the set {~ (~ S ∨ T) & ~ (T ∨ R), (T & ~ R) ∨ ~ (R & S), ~ ~ R ∨ (S & ~ T)}. Following our maxim of not using rules that produce branching until forced to do so, we obtain the following as the first part of our truth-tree for this set:

1.	~ (~ S ∨ T) & ~ (T ∨ R)✓	SM
2.	(T & ~ R) ∨ ~ (R & S)	SM
3.	~ ~ R ∨ (S & ~ T)	SM
4.	~ (~ S ∨ T)✓	1 &D
5.	~ (T ∨ R)✓	1 &D
6.	~ ~ S✓	4 ~ ∨D
7.	~ T	4 ~ ∨D
8.	~ T	5 ~ ∨D
9.	~ R	5 ~ ∨D
10.	S	6 ~ ~ D

Note that decomposing '~ (~ S ∨ T)' (using the rule Negated Disjunction Decomposition) yields '~ ~ S' and '~ T' on lines 6 and 7, respectively, *not* 'S' and '~ T'. The tree can be completed as follows:

11.	T & ~ R✓	~ (R & S)✓			2 ∨D
12.	T				11 &D
13.	~ R				11 &D
14.	×	~ ~ R✓	S & ~ T✓		3 ∨D
15.		R	|		14 ~ ~D
16.		×	S		14 &D
17.			~ T		14 &D
18.			~ R	~ S	
				×	11 ~ &D

Our tree has three closed branches and one completed open branch. The set we are testing is therefore truth-functionally consistent. Among the truth-value assignments that can be recovered from the open branch is the one that assigns **F** to 'R', **F** to 'T', **T** to 'S', and **T** to every other sentence letter. The relevant fragment of this truth-value assignment, for the set we are testing, is

R	S	T
F	**T**	**F**

Obviously, although an infinite number of truth-value assignments can be recovered from this one open branch, they will all be alike in their relevant fragments, that is, in what they assign to the sentence letters 'R', 'S', and 'T'.[5]

[5]Note that in this tree there are two lines (11 and 14) on which two sentences occur, both of which are ultimately decomposed. But in each case the results of the decomposition are entered on separate subsequent lines. This is because the two sentences on line 11, as well as the two sentences on line 14, are decomposed by separate rules. Hence, if we were to do the decompositions simultaneously, we could not, without engendering confusion, readily annotate what is happening in the justification column. In a pure tree, one that is not annotated with either line numbers or justifications, there would be no reason not to perform multiple decompositions, even ones using different rules, simultaneously.

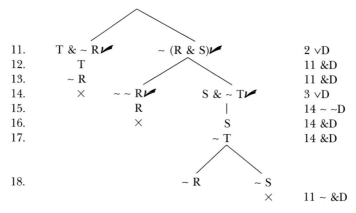

Completed truth-trees frequently contain more than one completed open branch. Consider the tree for {~ (H & G) & ~ (H & I), G ∨ I, ~ (H ∨ ~ I)):

1.	~ (H & G) & ~ (H & I)✔	SM
2.	G ∨ I✔	SM
3.	~ (H ∨ ~ I)✔	SM
4.	~ (H & G)✔	1 &D
5.	~ (H & I)✔	1 &D
6.	~ H	3 ~ ∨D
7.	~ ~ I✔	3 ~ ∨D
8.	I	7 ~ ~ D
9.	G I	2 ∨D
10.	~ H ~ G ~ H ~ G	4 ~ &D
11.	~ H ~ I ~ H ~ I ~ H ~ I	5 ~ &D

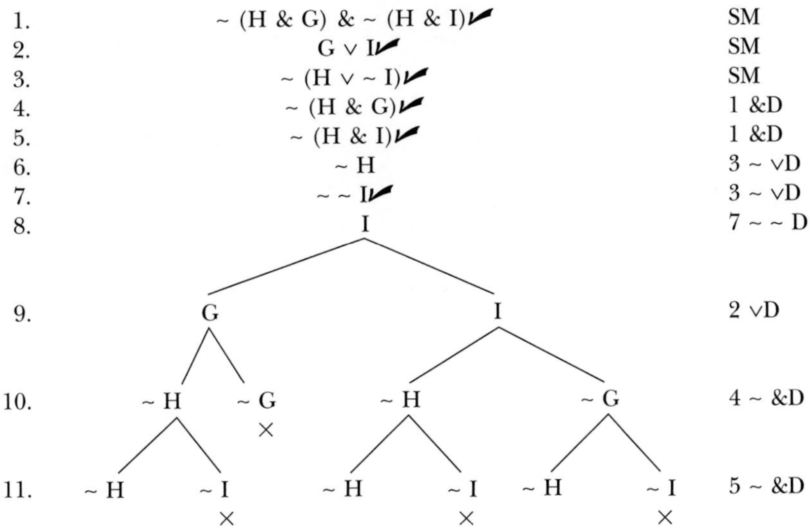

This tree has three open branches. From the leftmost open branch we can recover truth-value assignments of which the following is a fragment:

H	G	I
F	T	T

From the middle open branch we can recover truth-values for 'H' and for 'I', but that branch is mute concerning 'G':

H	G	I
F		T

The significance of this is that the members of the set being tested are all true on every truth-value assignment that assigns **F** to 'H' and **T** to 'I'. What is assigned to 'G', given these assignments to 'H' and 'I', does not matter. Hence we can recover *two* fragments of truth-value assignments from this branch, that is,

H	G	I
F	T	T
F	F	T

We complete this discussion by giving two additional sample trees. Both are closed, so in each case the set being tested is truth-functionally inconsistent.

1.	~ (~ B ∨ ~ C) ✓			SM
2.	B &(~ C ∨ ~ D) ✓			SM
3.	~ (C & ~ D) ✓			SM
4.	~ ~ B ✓			1 ~ ∨D
5.	~ ~ C ✓			1 ~ ∨D
6.	B			2 &D
7.	~ C ∨ ~ D ✓			2 &D
8.	B			4 ~ ~ D
9.	C			5 ~ ~ D
10.	~ C	~ ~ D ✓		3 ~ &D
11.	×	D		10 ~ ~ D
12.		~ C	~ D	
		×	×	7 ∨D

1.	~ [(A ∨ B) ∨ ~ C] ✓	SM
2.	C & ~ (A & B) ✓	SM
3.	(A ∨ C) & (A ∨ B) ✓	SM
4.	A	SM
5.	~ (A ∨ B) ✓	1 ~ ∨D
6.	~ ~ C	1 ~ ∨D
7.	C	2 &D
8.	~ (A & B)	2 &D
9.	A ∨ C	3 &D
10.	A ∨ B	3 &D
11.	~ A	5 ~ ∨D
12.	~ B	5 ~ ∨D
	×	

4.2E EXERCISES

1. Use the truth-tree method to test each of the following sets of sentences for truth-functional consistency. If a set is consistent, recover the relevant fragment of one truth-value assignment on which every member of the set is true.

a. {A & ~ (B ∨ A)}
*b. {A & ~ (B & A)}
c. {~ (A ∨ B) & (A ∨ ~ B)}
*d. {~ A & ~ (A & B), B}
e. {(A ∨ B) & (A ∨ ~ B)}
*f. {(J & ~ K) & I, ~ I ∨ K}
g. {(J ∨ ~ K) & I, ~ I ∨ K}
*h. {(H & ~ I) & (I ∨ ~ H)}
i. {(H ∨ ~ I) & I, ~ (H & I)}
*j. {(A & B) ∨ (A & C), ~ (A & B)}

k. {~ (A & B), ~ (~ C ∨ B), ~ (A & C)}
*l. {(A & B) ∨ (A & C), ~ (A ∨ B)}
m. {(A ∨ B) & (A ∨ C), ~ C & ~ A}
*n. {(A ∨ B) & (A ∨ C), C & ~ A, ~ B ∨ ~ A}
o. {(H & ~ I) ∨ (I ∨ ~ H), J ∨ I, ~ J}

2. Use the truth-tree method to test each of the following sets of sentences for truth-functional consistency. If a set is consistent, recover the relevant fragment of one truth-value assignment on which every member of the set is true.

a. {~ (H & I), H ∨ I}
*b. {~ [(F ∨ ~ F) & G]}
c. {~ (H & I) ∨ J, ~ (J ∨ ~ I)}
*d. {~ [(A ∨ B) ∨ C], ~ D ∨ C, D}
e. {A & (B & C), ~ [A & (B & C)]}
*f. {A & (B & ~ C), ~ [A & (B & C)]}
g. {~ C ∨ (A & B), C, ~ (A & B)}
*h. {~ (~ A ∨ B), A ∨ ~ B, ~ (~ B & ~ A)}
i. {(~ F & ~ G) & [(G ∨ ~ I) & (I ∨ ~ H)]}
*j. {~ (~ A ∨ ~ B), ~ [A & ~ (B & C)], A ∨ (B ∨ C)}
k. {(F ∨ ~ G) & [(G ∨ ~ I) & (I ∨ ~ H)])
*l. {~ [A & (~ B & ~ C)], ~ A ∨ ~ C, ~ (~ B ∨ ~ ~ C)}
m. {A ∨ (B ∨ C), ~ (A ∨ B), ~ (B & C), ~ (A & C)}
*n. {(H ∨ ~ I) & (I ∨ ~ G), ~ (H & G), H ∨ (~ I & ~ G)}

.3 RULES FOR SENTENCES CONTAINING '⊃' AND '≡'

We now need to develop decomposition rules for material conditionals, for material biconditionals, and for the negations of each. We know that, for any sentences **P** and **Q** of *SL*, **P** ⊃ **Q** is equivalent to ~ **P** ∨ **Q**. And we have already developed a rule for decomposing disjunctions:

Disjunction Decomposition (∨D)

Given this, and the fact that **P** ⊃ **Q** is equivalent to ~ **P** ∨ **Q**, the appropriate decomposition rule for **P** ⊃ **Q** is

Conditional Decomposition (⊃D)

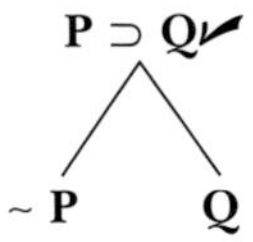

The negation of a material conditional, ~ (**P** ⊃ **Q**), is true if and only if that conditional is false, and a conditional is false if and only if its antecedent is true and its consequent is false. In other words, for any sentences **P** and **Q** in *SL*, ~ (**P** ⊃ **Q**) and **P** & ~ **Q** are truth-functionally equivalent sentences. Given the rule already developed for decomposing conjunctions, the appropriate rule for decomposing negated conditionals is clearly

Negated Conditional Decomposition (~ ⊃D)

~ (**P** ⊃ **Q**)✓
P
~ **Q**

The only rules we have left to present are those for material biconditionals and negated material biconditionals. A material biconditional is true if and only if either its immediate components are both true or its immediate components are both false. Alternatively, for any sentences **P** and **Q**, **P** ≡ **Q** is truth-functionally equivalent to (**P** & **Q**) ∨ (~ **P** & ~ **Q**). The rule for material biconditionals can thus be thought of as a combination of the rule for disjunctions and the rule for conjunctions. Decomposing a material biconditional splits every open branch running through that material biconditional into two branches, and on each new branch we enter two sentences:

Biconditional Decomposition (≡D)

P ≡ **Q**✓
/ \
P ~ **P**
Q ~ **Q**

The rule for decomposing negations of material biconditionals is also a branching rule. Since a material biconditional is true if and only if its immediate components have the same truth-value, the negation of a material biconditional will be true if and only if the immediate components of the material biconditional have different truth-values. In other words, for ~ (**P** ≡ **Q**) to be true, either **P** must be true and **Q** false, or **P** must be false and **Q** true. So, for any sentences **P** and **Q**, ~ (**P** ≡ **Q**) is truth-functionally equivalent to (**P** & ~ **Q**) ∨ (~ **P** & **Q**). Hence

Negated Biconditional Decomposition (~ ≡D)

~ (**P** ≡ **Q**)✓
/ \
P ~ **P**
~ **Q** **Q**

We present here our complete set of rules for decomposing sentences of *SL*:

Sentential Truth-Tree Rules

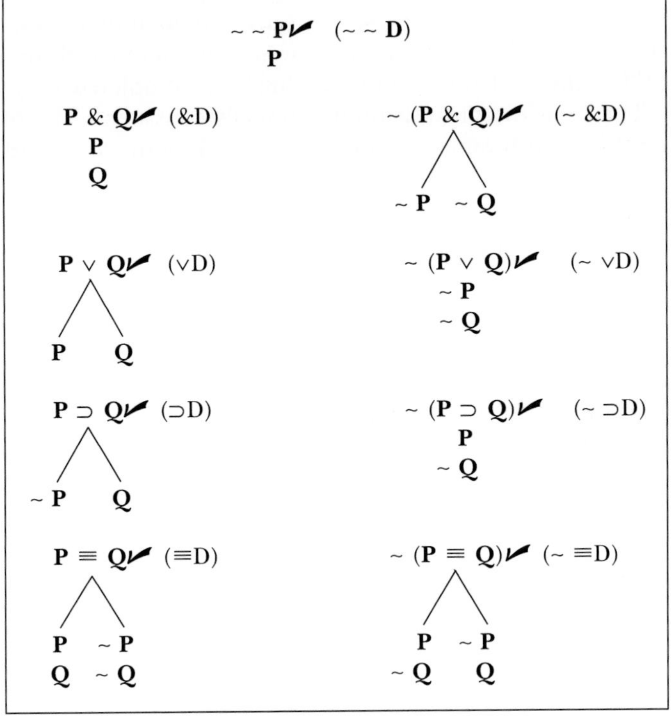

In learning how to construct trees, the best procedure is not simply to memorize the rules. Instead, try to grasp the rationale for the rules. One way to do this, as we have tried to show, is first to understand the bases for the simple rules for conjunctions, disjunctions, and negated negations and then to see how the other rules can be viewed as applications of these three simple rules.

We begin with a few straightforward examples. Here is a tree for the set {A ⊃ B, B ⊃ A, ~ A}:

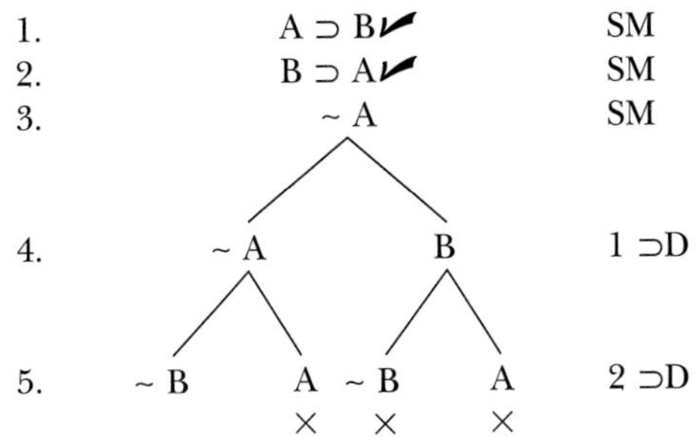

Earlier we noted that, when given a choice of decomposing a sentence that will produce branching or a sentence that will not, decomposing the latter generally produces a simpler tree. In this case we had no such choice, for the set consists of a literal and two conditionals, and the rule for decomposing conditionals is a branching rule, that is, a rule that produces branches. After decomposing the first member of the set, we have two open branches, one ending in '~ A', the other in 'B'. Decomposing the second member of the set yields four branches, but three of them close, leaving us a completed tree with one open branch. The set is therefore truth-functionally consistent. The one recoverable fragment of a truth-value assignment assigns **F** both to 'A' and to 'B'.

Here is another tree for the same set:

```
1.            A ⊃ B✔           SM
2.            B ⊃ A✔           SM
3.              ~ A            SM
               /   \
4.          ~ B     A          2 ⊃D
           /   \    ×
5.      ~ A     B              1 ⊃D
                ×
```

This tree is at least marginally simpler than the first; it has a total of three branches, whereas the first one had four branches. Although the sentences on lines 1 and 2 both produce multiple branches when decomposed, one of the branches produced by decomposing the sentence on line 2, the one ending in 'A', closes immediately. We can now formulate a second strategy for keeping trees simple.

> **Strategy 2:** Give priority to decomposing sentences whose decomposition results in the closing of one or more branches.

Here is a tree for {~ (A ⊃ B), B ⊃ A}:

```
1.        ~ (A ⊃ B)✔        SM
2.          B ⊃ A✔          SM
3.            A             1 ~ ⊃D
4.           ~ B            1 ~ ⊃D
            /   \
5.       ~ B     A          2 ⊃D
```

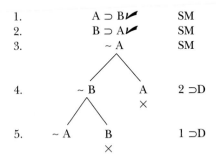

We decomposed the sentence on line 1 first because it does not branch. The tree has two completed open branches, so the set is truth-functionally consistent. Only one relevant fragment of a truth-value assignment is recoverable; it assigns **T** to 'A' and **F** to 'B'.

Next we construct a tree for {H ≡ G, G ≡ I, H, ~ I}:

1.		H ≡ G✓		SM
2.		G ≡ I✓		SM
3.		H		SM
4.		~ I		SM
5.	H		~ H	1 ≡D
6.	G		~ G	1 ≡D
			×	
7.	G ~ G			2 ≡D
8.	I ~ I			2 ≡D
	× ×			

The tree is closed, so the set is truth-functionally inconsistent. Here the order of decomposition makes no difference. Both the sentence on line 1 and the sentence on line 2 branch when decomposed; whichever is decomposed first produces one closed branch.

The set {~ (H ≡ I), I ≡ J, ~ H} yields an open tree:

1.		~ (H ≡ I)✓		SM
2.		I ≡ J✓		SM
3.		~ H		SM
4.	H		~ H	1 ~ ≡D
5.	~ I		I	1 ~ ≡D
	×			
6.			I ~ I	2 ≡D
7.			J ~ J	2 ≡D
			×	

Here the order of decomposition does matter. Decomposing the sentence on line 1 first produces two branches, one of which immediately closes. Decomposing the sentence on line 2 first would produce two branches, neither of which would close immediately. The one completed open branch yields a fragment of a truth-value assignment that assigns **F** to 'H' and **T** to 'I' and 'J'. The set is truth-functionally consistent. It is important to remember, as illustrated here, that both the rule for decomposing material biconditionals and the rule for decomposing negated material biconditionals branch, and both introduce tildes.

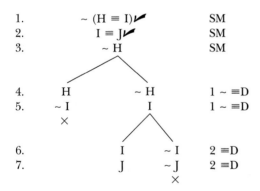

Finally consider the set {A ⊃ (B ≡ C), ~ (C ≡ A)}. Here is a tree:

1.		A ⊃ (B ≡ C)✓		SM
2.		~ (C ⊃ A)✓		SM
3.		C		2 ~ ⊃D
4.		~ A		2 ~ ⊃D
5.	~ A	B ≡ C✓		1 ⊃D
6.		B	~ B	5 ≡D
7.		C	~ C	5 ≡D
			×	

The tree has two completed open branches, so the set is truth-functionally consistent. Recoverable fragments are

A	B	C
F	**T**	**T**
F	**F**	**T**

What is of interest here is that the left-hand open branch becomes a completed open branch at line 5. At this point we know the set we are testing is truth-functionally consistent because we know the tree we are constructing has, and will continue to have, at least one completed branch, no matter what happens to the other open branch of the tree (the branch containing 'B ≡ C' on line 5). This suggests a third strategy:

Strategy 3: Stop when a tree yields an answer to the question being asked.

Of course, nothing less than a completed tree, with every branch closed, shows that a set is truth-functionally *inconsistent.* But if our only interest is in determining whether a set is consistent, and an incomplete tree for it has a completed open branch, there is no virtue in completing the tree. As soon as a branch becomes a completed open branch, we know the answer to the question we are asking: The set is consistent. We can recover a truth-value assignment demonstrating this from the completed open branch.[6] So in the present

[6] We will continue to give completed trees in our solutions to exercise problems. This is not because there is anything virtuous about completed trees. Rather, we do so because alternative orders of decomposition produce alternative trees, and the first completed open branch on one may not yield the same fragments of truth-value assignments yielded by the first completed open branch on another tree.

There is another way in which truth-trees could be shortened, namely, by defining a closed branch to be a branch that contains, for *any* sentence **P**, literal or not, both **P** and ~ **P**. Exactly the same sets would have closed trees, given this revised system, as do in the present system, and exactly the same sets would have trees with at least one completed open branch as do in the present system.

case we could just as well have stopped after line 5, that is, with the open but incomplete tree:

1.	A ⊃ (B ≡ C)✓		SM
2.	~ (C ⊃ A)✓		SM
3.	C		2 ~ ⊃D
4.	~ A		2 ~ ⊃D
5.	~ A	B ≡ C	1 ⊃D

4.3E EXERCISES

1. Use the truth-tree method to test each of the following sets of sentences for truth-functional consistency. If a set is consistent, recover one fragment of a truth-value assignment on which every member of the set is true.

a. {~ (A ⊃ B), ~ (B ⊃ A)}
*b. {~ [~ A ⊃ (B ⊃ C)], A ⊃ C}
c. {B ⊃ (D ⊃ E), D & B}
*d. {H ≡ G, ~ H, G}
e. {H ≡ G, ~ G}
*f. {(H ≡ G) ≡ ~ H}
g. {H ≡ G, ~ (H ⊃ G)}
*h. {H ≡ ~ G, H ⊃ G}
i. {H ≡ G, G ≡ I, ~ (H ⊃ I)}
*j. {A ⊃ ~ (A ≡ B), ~ (A ⊃ B)}
k. {L ≡ (J & K), ~ J, ~ L ⊃ L}
*l. {B ≡ D, B ≡ ~ D}
m. {~ [A ≡ (B ≡ A)]}
*n. {[B ⊃ (A ∨ C)] & ~ ~ B, A ≡ ~ B}
o. {H ⊃ J, J ⊃ K, K ⊃ ~ H}
*p. {A ⊃ (B ⊃ (C ⊃ A), ~ (B ⊃ ~ A)}

2. Use the truth-tree method to test each of the following sets of sentences for truth-functional consistency. If a set is consistent, recover one fragment of a truth-value assignment on which every member of the set is true.

a. {~ [(A ⊃ ~ B) ⊃ (B ⊃ A)], ~ (~ A ⊃ ~ B)}
*b. {~ [(A ⊃ ~ B) ⊃ (B ⊃ A)], ~ (~ A ⊃ ~ B)}
c. {(A & ~ C) ∨ (A & ~ B), A ⊃ B, C}
*d. {J ⊃ K, K ⊃ J, ~ (J ≡ K)}
e. {~ [A ⊃ (B ≡ C)], A ≡ ~ C, A ≡ B}
*f. {~ (A & ~ B) ⊃ ~ A, ~ (~ A & B) ⊃ ~ B, B & ~ A}
g. {~ (A ∨ B) ⊃ ~ A, ~ (A ∨ B) ⊃ ~ B, A}
*h. {~ (A ∨ B) ⊃ A, ~ (A ∨ B) ⊃ B, ~ B}
i. {A ≡ (B & ~ C), ~ A ∨ ~ B, ~ (~ B ≡ C)}
*j. {A ≡ (B & ~ C), ~ A ∨ ~ B, B ⊃ ~ C}
k. {A ≡ (~ B ≡ C), ~ A ⊃ (B ⊃ ~ C), ~ (A ⊃ ~ C)}

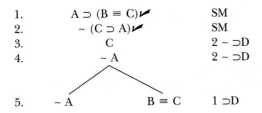

*l. {~ [A ⊃ (B ≡ C)], A ≡ ~ C, A ≡ B}
m. {J ⊃ (H ≡ ~ I), ~ (J ≡ H)}
*n. {(A & ~ B) ≡ (C & ~ E), ~ A ≡ E, B ≡ C}

4.4 MORE COMPLEX TRUTH-TREES

Consider the set {A ⊃ (B & ~ C), ~ (C ∨ A), C ≡ ~ A}. In constructing a truth-tree for this set, we start, as always, by listing the members of the set, one below the other:

1.	A ⊃ (B & ~ C)	SM
2.	~ (C ∨ A)	SM
3.	C ≡ ~ A	SM

No member of the set is a literal; hence all are candidates for decomposition. Which sentence should we decompose first? In one sense it does not matter: If any order of decomposition yields a completed open branch, all will; and, if any order of decomposition yields a closed tree, all will. However, as noted earlier, it is desirable to keep truth-trees as concise as possible, and one strategy for doing this is to decompose sentences that do not branch before decomposing those that do.

The sentence on line 1, a material conditional, will branch when decomposed. So will the sentence on line 3, a material biconditional. But the sentence on line 2, a negated disjunction, will not, so we decompose it first. There are now two undecomposed sentences on our tree that are not literals, 'A ⊃ (B & ~ C)' and 'C ≡ ~ A'. Both will yield new branches when decomposed. Decomposing the material conditional will yield two open branches, one ending in '~ A' and the other in 'B & ~ C'. Neither of these branches will close immediately. However, decomposing the material biconditional will yield an immediate closure:

```
1.        A ⊃ (B & ~ C)        SM
2.          ~ (C ∨ A)✓         SM
3.          C ≡ ~ A✓           SM
4.             ~ C             2 ~ ∨D
5.             ~ A             2 ~ ∨D
              /   \
6.          C       ~ C        3 ≡D
7.         ~ A     ~ ~ A       3 ≡D
            ×
```

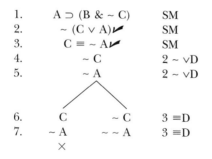

We are now left with just one open branch. There are two undecomposed non-literals on that branch, 'A ⊃ (B & ~ C)' and '~ ~ A'. We decompose '~ ~ A' first, since negated negations do not branch when decomposed. Moreover, when we decompose '~ ~ A', we add 'A' to the one open branch of our tree and thus close that branch and the tree:

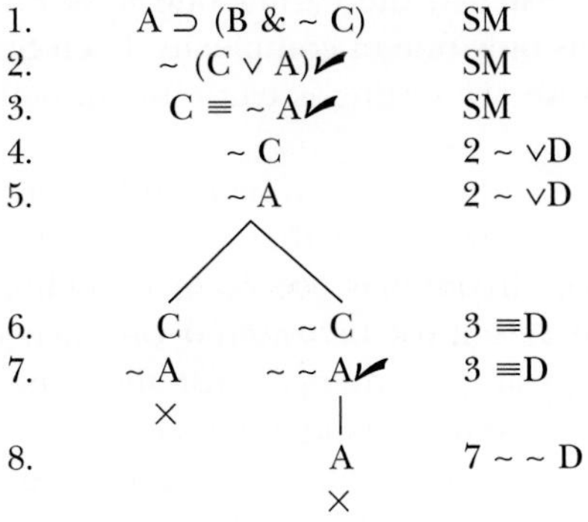

Several aspects of this tree are of interest. First, the tree is closed, and the set we are testing, {A ⊃ (B & ~ C), ~ (C ∨ A), C ≡ ~ A}, is therefore truth-functionally inconsistent. Every attempt to find a truth-value assignment on which every member of that set is true ended in failure. Second, we have shown that the set is inconsistent without decomposing every nonliteral on the tree. The sentence on line 1 was never decomposed, since decomposing the other nonliterals on the tree generated a closed tree. What this shows is that the set we are testing would be inconsistent even without its first member, 'A ⊃ (B & ~ C)'. Whenever a branch closes, we are through with that branch, even if it contains one or more undecomposed nonliterals.

This fairly concise tree was generated by following our strategies of giving priority to sentences whose decomposition does not require branching and to sentences whose decomposition generates one or more closed branches. Had we ignored these strategies and simply worked straight down the tree, always decomposing every nonliteral on a given level before moving to a lower level, the result would have been the following more complex tree:

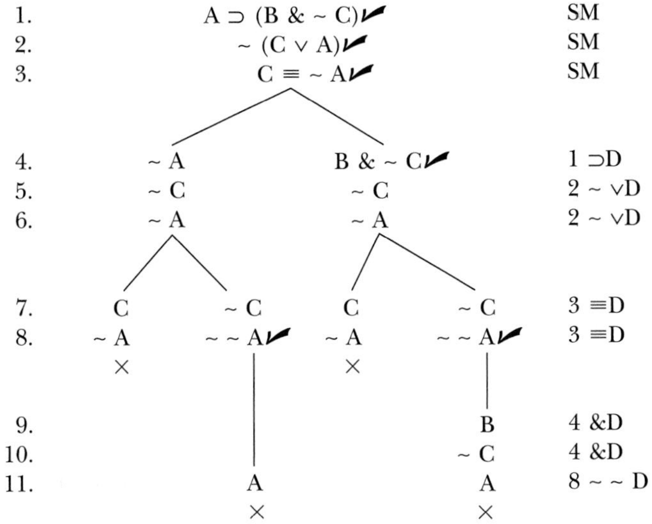

Here we have four branches, whereas in the earlier tree we had only two. Moreover this tree takes eleven lines to construct; the earlier one took only eight. But the difference between the trees is only one of complexity. Each tree shows equally well that the set of sentences we are testing is truth-functionally inconsistent, for each tree is closed.

The more complex of the preceding trees can be used to illustrate several important aspects of tree construction. Note that when we decompose '~ (C ∨ A)' at lines 5 and 6, the tree already has two open branches. Hence the results of decomposing this sentence must be entered on each of these open branches. The results of decomposing a sentence must always be entered on *every open branch that runs through the sentence being decomposed.*

Consider the tree after line 8 is completed: Two branches are closed, but two are open. We next decompose 'B & ~ C' on the right-hand branch only, at lines 9 and 10 (not on the left-hand branch because, although it is open, it does not go through 'B & ~ C'). We then decompose each occurrence of '~ ~ A' on line 8 by writing 'A' on line 11, at the end of each branch (since each branch does go through '~ ~ A'). Could we have put 'A' on the left-hand branch at line 9 at the same time that we put 'B' on the right-hand branch at line 9? We could not. The policy we follow is this: Trees are to be so constructed that every line of the tree is fully justified either by writing 'SM' in the justification column or by entering the number of one and only one earlier line and one and only one rule abbreviation in the justification column. All the entries made on line 7 come from line 3, and they are all obtained by one rule, Material Biconditional Decomposition. Had we tried to write 'A' on line 9 on the second branch from the left, we would have had two entries on that line coming from two different lines, by the use of two different rules and thus would have been forced to enter both '8 ~ ~ D' and '4 & D' in the justification column for line 9, in clear violation of this policy.

We have so far specified three strategies for keeping truth-trees concise. We repeat them here and add a fourth.

Strategies for Constructing Truth-Trees

1. Give priority to decomposing sentences whose decompositions do not require branching.
2. Give priority to decomposing sentences whose decompositions result in the closing of one or more branches.
3. Stop when a tree yields an answer to the question being asked.
4. Where strategies 1–3 are not applicable, decompose the more complex sentences first.

The rationale for the first three strategies should be clear by now. The fourth strategy is designed to save tedious work, for a complex sentence takes more work to decompose than does a less complex one. And, if a complex sentence is decomposed early in a tree, chances are there will be only a few open branches on which the results must be entered. But, if complex sentences are left until the end, it is likely that the results of decomposing them will have to be entered on many open branches. Roughly speaking, a sentence **P** is more complex than a sentence **Q** if decomposing **P** requires entering more sentences or longer sentences on a tree than does decomposing **Q**. In this sense longer sentences are generally more complex than shorter ones, and material biconditionals and negations of material biconditionals are more complex than other sentences of approximately the same length.

The strategies we have presented provide guidelines, not rules, for constructing truth-trees.[7] Disregarding one or more of them may produce a more complex tree than is necessary but will never yield a completed open branch where following them would yield a closed tree, or vice versa.

As a final example we shall do a truth-tree for {(C & ~ D) ≡ A, (A & C) ⊃ ~ (D ∨ A)}:

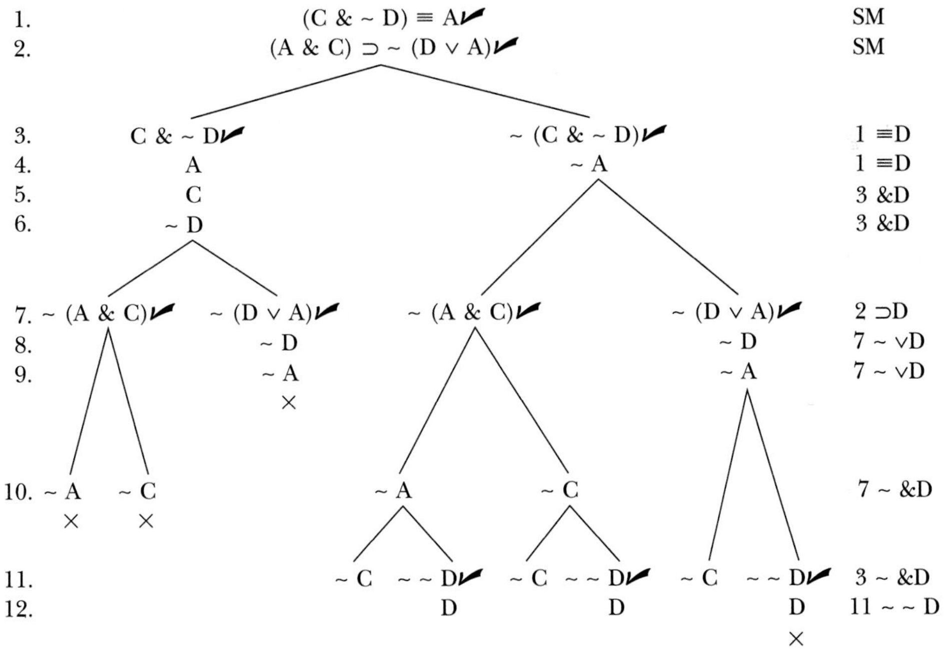

This tree has five completed open branches. The literals occurring on the left-most completed open branch are '~ C' and '~ A'. Hence this branch tells us that, to make all the sentences in the set we are testing true, it is sufficient to make '~ C' and '~ A' both true, and, to do this, we must assign the truth-value **F** to both 'A' and 'C'. But note that 'D' is an atomic component of both

[7]We said earlier that the truth-tree method could easily be made mechanical. We can do so by replacing our guidelines for decomposing sentences with some mandatory order of decomposition.

members of that set, and no assignment has yet been made to 'D'. This is because neither 'D' nor '~ D' occurs on the open branch just examined. The significance of the nonoccurrence of both 'D' and '~ D' is this: It does not matter which truth-value we assign to 'D'; the sentences we are testing will both be true as long as we assign the truth-value **F** to 'A' and to 'C', no matter what we assign to 'D'. Of course, we must assign some truth-value to 'D', but which one we assign is of no consequence. Thus we can recover *two* fragments of truth-value assignments from the left-hand open branch:

A	C	D
F	**F**	**T**
F	**F**	**F**

The next open branch we come to contains the literals 'D' and '~ A'. Neither 'C' nor '~ C' occurs on this second open branch. Hence we can expect to recover two fragments of truth-value assignments from it as well. They are

A	C	D
F	**T**	**T**
F	**F**	**T**

In fact, only the first of these is a new fragment; the second we also obtained from the first open branch, and the third open branch contains the same literals as the first. The fourth open branch contains the literals 'D', '~ C', and '~ A' and yields the fragment

A	C	D
F	**F**	**T**

which was also yielded by all the other open branches we have examined. The last open branch contains the literals '~ C', '~ A', and '~ D' and so yields just one fragment:

A	C	D
F	**F**	**F**

This is also not a new fragment; it was yielded by the first and third open branches as well. In sum, we have five completed open branches on our tree, and these branches yield three distinct fragments of truth-value assignments. The number of open branches on a completed truth-tree is, again, no guide to the number of distinct fragments of truth-value assignments that can be recovered from that tree. Of course, to show that a set of sentences is consistent, we need only show that there is at least one truth-value assignment on which all the members of the set are true. And, to show that there *is* such an assignment, it suffices to recover one fragment of a truth-value assignment.

Fragments of truth-value assignments can be recovered only from completed open branches. Closed branches represent unsuccessful attempts to find such fragments. Thus the branches of a truth-tree should not be thought of as corresponding to the rows of a truth-table. They do not. However, constructing a truth-tree for a set of sentences does tell us a lot about what the truth-table for the same set of sentences would be like. If the tree is closed, we know that there is no row in the corresponding truth-table in which every member of the set in question has a **T** under its main connective. If the tree has a completed open branch, we know that there is at least one row in that table in which every member of the set in question has a **T** under its main connective. And, if we count the number of distinct fragments of truth-value assignments we can recover, we know that there will be exactly that many rows in the corresponding truth-table in which every member of the set in question has a **T** under its main connective.

4.4E EXERCISES

1. Construct truth-trees to test each of the following sets of sentences for truth-functional consistency. If a set is consistent, recover one fragment of a truth-value assignment from your tree that shows this.

a. {H ∨ G, ~ G & ~ H}
*b. {K ∨ (M & ~ M), J & ~ C)
c. {~ ~ C, C & [U ∨ (~ C & B)]}
*d. {~ (M & ~ N), ~ (K ∨ M) & ~ ~ M, ~ ~ ~ K}
e. {~ [~ (E ∨ ~ C) & A], ~ (E ∨ ~ C) & A}
*f. {~ [~ (L ∨ ~ L) & (N ∨ ~ N)])
g. (~ A ∨ ~ ~ [~ (K & ~ A) ∨ R], ~ [D ∨ (A & ~ K)], A & (R ∨ K)}
*h. {~ [~ (J ⊃ M) ≡ (J & ~ M)]}
i. {B ⊃ J, H ≡ J, ~ H ∨ B}
*j. {H & (~ K ⊃ M), ~ K, ~ (H ⊃ M)}
k. {~ [(B & J) ≡ ~ (W ∨ Z)], ~ (J & W)}
*l. {~ ~ ~ [(K ∨ M) ⊃ ~ G], G ≡ (J & U), U ⊃ (~ G & K), K & ~ U}

2. Which of the following claims are true? Explain your reasoning.

a. If a completed truth-tree contains at least one open branch, then at least one truth-value assignment on which all the members of the set being tested are true can be recovered from that open branch.
*b. A completed open branch of a truth-tree yields at most one fragment of a truth-value assignment on which every member of the set being tested is true.
c. If a set of sentences has a truth-tree with a completed open branch, then that set is truth-functionally consistent.
*d. If a truth-tree is closed, there are no open branches on the tree.
e. If a truth-tree is closed, the set of sentences being tested is truth-functionally inconsistent.

*f. If a truth-tree is closed, every sentence on the tree either has been decomposed or is a literal.

g. If there are eight distinct atomic components of the members of a set Γ of sentences of *SL*, then a completed tree for Γ will have eight branches.

*h. A completed truth-tree with at least one open branch and at least one closed branch is an open tree.

i. If a tree has a closed branch, then there is a truth-value assignment for which all the members of the set being tested are false.

*j. If a set Γ of sentences of *SL* has an open tree, then every nonempty subset of Γ also has an open tree.

k. If no member of a set Γ of sentences of *SL* contains a tilde, then no tree for Γ will have a closed branch.

3. Use the truth-tree method to test symbolizations of the following passages for truth-functional consistency. If your symbolization is truth-functionally consistent, recover one fragment of a truth-value assignment from your tree that shows this.

a. Poison caused the victim's death if and only if there was a change in his blood chemistry or a residue of poison in the stomach. There was neither a change in blood chemistry nor a residue of poison in his stomach, but there were puncture marks on the body. Poison was injected by a needle only if there were puncture marks on the body. Either poison was the cause of the victim's death or there were no puncture marks on the body.

*b. Either the bullet was fired from an intermediate distance or it wasn't. If it wasn't, there are powder burns on the body (provided the bullet was fired at close range) or signs of a rifle bullet (provided the bullet was fired at a great distance). Although there are no powder burns on the body, there are signs of a rifle bullet. Unless the angle at which the bullet entered the body was elevated, the bullet wasn't fired from an intermediate distance, and the angle wasn't elevated.

c. The murder was committed by at least one of the staff—the butler, the maid, and the gardener—but not by all three. The butler did it only if the crime was committed indoors; and if it was not committed indoors, the gardener didn't do it. If poison was used, then the butler did it unless the maid did; but the maid didn't do it. Poison was used; moreover the crime was not committed indoors.

*d. Exactly two of Albert, Betty, and Christine will find employment when they graduate from law school. If Albert gets a job, Betty and Christine surely will too. Betty will not get a job unless Albert does. Christine is a first-rate lawyer and will certainly be hired by a good law firm.

4.5 USING TRUTH-TREES TO TEST FOR TRUTH-FUNCTIONAL TRUTH, FALSITY, AND INDETERMINACY

We know that each sentence of *SL* is either truth-functionally true, truth-functionally false, or truth-functionally indeterminate. Truth-trees can be used to determine into which of these categories a particular sentence of *SL* falls. Truth-trees test for the consistency of finite sets of sentences of *SL*. Suppose that we want to know whether a sentence **P** is truth-functionally false. Remember that, if **P** is not truth-functionally false, there is some truth-value assignment on which it is true; hence the unit set of **P**, {**P**}, will be truth-functionally consistent. However, if **P** is truth-functionally false, there is no truth-value assignment on which it is true; hence there is no assignment on which every member of {**P**} is true, and so {**P**} is truth-functionally inconsistent.

> A sentence **P** of *SL* is *truth-functionally false* if and only if the set {**P**} has a closed truth-tree.

Here is a tree for the set {[A ⊃ (B & C] & [~ (A ⊃ B) ∨ ~ (A ⊃ C)]}:

```
1.  [A ⊃ (B & C)] & [~ (A ⊃ B) ∨ ~ (A ⊃ C)]✓   SM
2.              A ⊃ (B & C)✓                    1 &D
3.         ~ (A ⊃ B) ∨ ~ (A ⊃ C)✓               1 &D
                  /            \
4.       ~ (A ⊃ B)✓          ~ (A ⊃ C)✓         3 ∨D
5.           A                    A             4 ~ ⊃D
6.          ~ B                  ~ C            4 ~ ⊃D
           /    \               /    \
7.    ~ A      B & C✓       ~ A      B & C✓     2 ⊃D
       ×          |          ×          |
8.                B                     B       7 &D
9.                C                     C       7 &D
                  ×                     ×
```

All the branches of this tree do close, so there is no truth-value assignment on which the one member of the set we are testing is true. Hence the set is truth-functionally inconsistent, and its single member is truth-functionally false. In constructing this tree we were able to save work at lines 5 and 6 by decomposing two sentences, '~ (A ⊃ B)' and '~ (A ⊃ C)', in one step. We could do so because these sentences occur on the same line, line 4, and are decomposed by the same rule, Negated Conditional Decomposition. This is acceptable because, in doing them both at once, we are not required to enter two line numbers or two rule abbreviations in our justification column. Of course, we also could have done them separately.

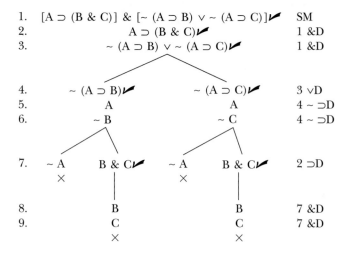

Next we use the tree method to determine whether 'A ⊃ [B ⊃ (A ⊃ B)]' is truth-functionally false:

1.	A ⊃ [B ⊃ (A ⊃ B)] ✓	SM
2.	~ A B ⊃ (A ⊃ B) ✓	1 ⊃D
3.	~ B A ⊃ B ✓	2 ⊃D
4.	~ A B	3 ⊃D

This tree obviously has a completed open branch (in fact it has four), so the unit set we are testing is truth-functionally consistent. Hence there is at least one truth-value assignment on which the one member of that set is true, and that sentence is thus not truth-functionally false. (Note that we could have stopped at line 2, where the first completed open branch ends.)

Although we know that 'A ⊃ [B ⊃ (A ⊃ B)]' is not truth-functionally false, we do not yet know whether that sentence is truth-functionally indeterminate or truth-functionally true. We can find out by constructing another tree. Suppose the sentence we are concerned with, 'A ⊃ [B ⊃ (A ⊃ B)]', is truth-functionally true. Then its negation, '~ (A ⊃ [B ⊃ (A ⊃ B)])', must be truth-functionally false. So we can determine whether the sentence is truth-functionally true by seeing if its negation is truth-functionally false, that is, by seeing if the unit set of its negation has a closed tree. Here is that tree:[8]

1.	~ (A ⊃ [B ⊃ (A ⊃ B)]) ✓	SM
2.	A	1 ~ ⊃D
3.	~ [B ⊃ (A ⊃ B)] ✓	1 ~ ⊃D
4.	B	3 ~ ⊃D
5.	~ (A ⊃ B) ✓	3 ~ ⊃D
6.	A	5 ~ ⊃D
7.	~ B	5 ~ ⊃D
	×	

The tree is closed. So there is no truth-value assignment on which the sentence '~ (A ⊃ [B ⊃ (A ⊃ B)])' is true. Since that sentence is a negation, there is no truth-value assignment on which the sentence of which it is a negation,

[8]Strictly speaking, there is more than one truth-tree for this set, as well as for most sets of sentences of *SL* (since there is usually more than one order of decomposition). However, since all the trees for any given set of sentences yield the same result, we sometimes speak informally of *the tree* for a set of sentences.

'A ⊃ [B ⊃ (A ⊃ B)]', is false. That sentence is therefore truth-functionally true.

> A sentence **P** of *SL* is *truth-functionally true* if and only if the set {~ **P**} has a closed tree.

A sentence is truth-functionally indeterminate if and only if it is neither truth-functionally true nor truth-functionally false. Therefore

> A sentence **P** of *SL* is *truth-functionally indeterminate* if and only if neither the set {**P**} nor the set {~ **P**} has a closed tree.

When we are interested in determining the truth-functional status of a sentence, the trees we construct will be trees for unit sets of sentences. However, we shall allow ourselves to talk informally of doing the tree for **P** or for ~ **P**. Such talk is to be understood as shorthand for talk about trees for unit sets.

When determining the truth-functional status of a sentence **P**, we shall sometimes end up constructing two trees, one for **P** and one for ~ **P**. Of course, if we suspect that **P** is truth-functionally true, we should first do the truth-tree for ~ **P**; if we suspect that **P** is truth-functionally false, we should first do the truth-tree for **P** itself.

Recall that our tree for 'A ⊃ [B ⊃ (A ⊃ B)]' has all open branches. One might think that it follows from this alone that 'A ⊃ [B ⊃ (A ⊃ B)]' is truth-functionally true, for surely, if that sentence were not truth-functionally true, the tree for it would have at least one closed branch. But this reasoning is mistaken. Many sentences that are not truth-functional truths have trees all of whose branches are completed open branches, and many truth-functional truths have trees with some closed branches. Consider the truth-tree for a simple disjunction 'A ∨ B':

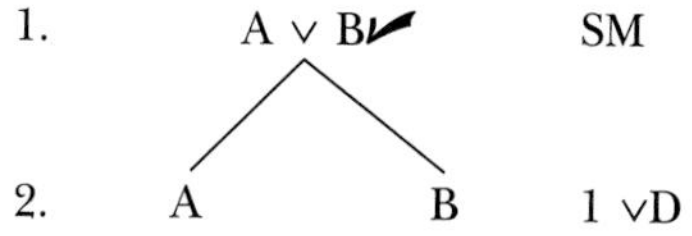

Both branches of this tree are completed open branches. Yet we know that 'A ∨ B' is not a truth-functional truth. Its truth-table will mirror the characteristic truth-table for disjunctions; that is, the first three rows under its main connective will contain **T**, and the fourth row will contain **F**.

We can see that not all truth-functional truths have truth-trees with all open branches by considering the sentence '(A ∨ ~ A) ⊃ (B ⊃ B)'. This sentence is a truth-functionally true inasmuch as its consequent is a truth-functional truth (its antecedent is as well), and there is thus no truth-value assignment on which this conditional is false. But the tree for this sentence does have one closed branch:

1.	(A ∨ ~ A) ⊃ (B ⊃ B)✓			SM
2.	~ (A ∨ ~ A)✓	B ⊃ B✓		1 ⊃D
3.	~ A			2 ~ ∨D
4.	~ ~ A✓			2 ~ ∨D
5.	A			4 ~ ~ D
6.	×	~ B	B	2 ⊃D

There is a way we can avoid constructing two truth-trees for one sentence. Suppose we do a tree for a sentence **P**, thinking it may be truth-functionally false, but the tree does not close. We now know that **P** is either truth-functionally true or truth-functionally indeterminate. If it is true on all truth-value assignments, it is truth-functionally true; if it is true on only some assignments, it is truth-functionally indeterminate. We can find out which is the case by counting the number of distinct fragments of truth-value assignments that are recoverable from our completed open tree—for these fragments correspond to the rows of the truth-table for the sentence being tested in which there is a **T** under that sentence's main connective. If **P** has **n** atomic components, we shall get back $2^{\mathbf{n}}$ distinct fragments of truth-value assignments from our tree if and only if **P** is truth-functionally true.

Recall our tree for 'A ∨ B', which has two open and no closed branches. The only literal occurring on the left-hand branch is 'A', so from that branch we can recover two fragments, one that assigns the truth-value **T** to 'B' and one that assigns the truth-value **F** to 'B':

A	B
T	**T**
T	**F**

We can also recover two fragments from the right-hand open branch. But only one of these is a new fragment:

A	B
F	**T**

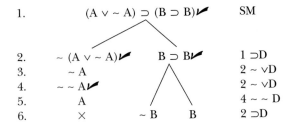

The one relevant fragment that we do not recover is the one that assigns the truth-value **F** to both 'A' and 'B', and this is just what we expected, for a disjunction is false when and only when both its disjuncts are false. By recovering fragments of truth-value assignments, we have shown that 'A ∨ B' is truth-functionally indeterminate, without having to construct two trees for that sentence.

We can use this same procedure with our last truth-tree to verify that '(A ∨ ~ A) ⊃ (B ⊃ B)' is indeed truth-functionally true. This sentence has two atomic components, so we can expect to recover four distinct fragments of truth-value assignments from the tree for this sentence. The tree has two completed open branches. The only literal on the left-hand branch is '~ B', so this branch yields two fragments:

A	B
T	**F**
F	**F**

The only literal occurring on the right-hand branch is 'B', so this branch yields two new fragments:

A	B
T	**T**
F	**T**

We have recovered all the expected fragments of truth-value assignments, thus showing that the sentence being tested is true on every truth-value assignment. We have verified that it is truth-functionally true, even though the tree for that sentence has one closed branch.

Suppose we suspect that a sentence **P** is truth-functionally true and accordingly construct a tree for the negation of that sentence, ~ **P**. Suppose also that our tree has at least one completed open branch, and thus that in this case our suspicions were wrong: **P** is not truth-functionally true. The standard procedure would now be to do a tree for **P** to see whether that sentence is truth-functionally false or truth-functionally indeterminate. Instead, we can see what distinct fragments of truth-value assignments can be recovered from the tree we have already done for ~ **P**. The fragments we recover are fragments of truth-value assignments on which ~ **P** is true. If we recover all relevant fragments, we know that ~ **P** is true on every truth-value assignment and is thus truth-functionally true. And if ~ **P** is truth-functionally true, **P** is truth-functionally false. If we do not recover all the distinct relevant fragments from our tree, we know that there is at least one truth-value assignment on which ~ **P** is false, and hence on which **P** is true. In this case **P** is truth-functionally indeterminate.

The method of recovering fragments of truth-value assignments always allows us to avoid constructing a second tree. However, to use the method, we must complete the tree we are working with (rather than stopping when we have one completed open branch). As a result, when the tree is complex and the number of relevant fragments is relatively large—eight, sixteen, thirty-two, or more—it is often easier to do a second tree than to recover and count distinct relevant fragments.

4.5E EXERCISES

1. For each of the following sentences, use the truth-tree method to determine its truth-functional status—that is, whether it is truth-functionally true, truth-functionally false, or truth-functionally indeterminate.

a. $M \& \sim M$
*b. $M \vee \sim M$
c. $\sim M \vee \sim M$
*d. $(C \supset R) \supset [\sim R \supset \sim (C \& J)]$
e. $(C \supset R) \& [(C \supset \sim R) \& \sim (\sim C \vee R)]$
*f. $(K \equiv W) \vee (A \& W)$
g. $(\sim A \equiv \sim Z) \& (A \& \sim Z)$
*h. $[L \vee (J \vee \sim K)] \& (K \& [(J \vee L) \supset \sim K])$
i. $(A \vee B) \& \sim (A \vee B)$
*j. $(A \vee B) \supset \sim (A \vee B)$
k. $(A \vee B) \equiv \sim (A \vee B)$
*l. $\sim (D \vee F) \equiv \sim (D \& F)$
m. $\sim (D \vee F) \equiv (\sim D \vee \sim F)$
*n. $\sim (D \vee F) \equiv (\sim D \& \sim F)$

2. For each of the following sentences, use the truth-tree method to determine whether the sentence is truth-functionally true. Where appropriate, give a fragment of a truth-value assignment that supports your answer.

a. $(B \supset L) \vee (L \supset B)$
*b. $(B \supset L) \& (L \supset B)$
c. $(A \equiv K) \supset (A \vee K)$
*d. $(A \equiv K) \supset (\sim A \vee K)$
e. $[(J \supset Z) \& \sim Z] \supset \sim J$
*f. $[(J \supset Z) \& \sim J] \supset \sim Z$
g. $(B \supset (M \supset H)) \equiv [(B \supset M) \supset (B \supset H)]$
*h. $M \supset [L \equiv (\sim M \equiv \sim L)]$
i. $(A \& \sim B) \supset \sim (A \vee B)$
*j. $(A \& \sim B) \supset \sim (A \& B)$
k. $[(A \& B) \supset C] \equiv [(A \supset \sim B) \vee C]$
*l. $(D \equiv \sim E) \equiv \sim (D \equiv E)$
m. $[A \supset (B \& C)] \supset [A \supset (B \supset C)]$
*n. $[A \supset (B \& C)] \equiv [A \supset (B \supset C)]$
o. $[(A \& B) \supset C] \equiv [A \supset (B \supset C)]$

3. For each of the following sentences, use the truth-tree method to determine its truth-functional status—that is, whether it is truth-functionally true, truth-functionally false, or truth-functionally indeterminate. In each case do a tree only for the given sentence. If the tree does not close, determine the truth-functional status of the sentence by recovering and counting relevant fragments of truth-value assignments.

a. $\sim (\sim A \supset A)$
*b. $J \supset (K \supset L)$
c. $(A \equiv \sim A) \supset \sim (A \equiv \sim A)$
*d. $(E \equiv H) \supset (\sim E \supset \sim H)$
e. $(\sim B \ \& \sim D) \vee \sim (B \vee D)$
*f. $([(C \supset D) \ \& \ (D \supset E)] \ \& \ C) \ \& \sim E$
g. $[(A \vee B) \ \& \ (A \vee C)] \supset \sim (B \ \& \ C)$
*h. $\sim ([(A \vee B) \ \& \ (B \vee C)] \ \& \ (\sim A \ \& \sim B))$
i. $(J \vee \sim K) \equiv \sim \sim (K \supset J)$
*j. $\sim B \supset [(B \vee D) \supset D]$

4. Decide which of the following claims are true and which are false. In each case explain and defend your reasoning. Use examples where appropriate.

a. If a completed tree for the unit set of **P**, {**P**}, has at least one open branch and at least one closed branch, then **P** is truth-functionally indeterminate.
*b. If **P** is truth-functionally true and has four atomic components, then the tree for {**P**} will have four open branches.
c. If a completed tree for {**P**} has all open branches, then **P** is truth-functionally true.
*d. If {**P**} has a closed tree and {**Q**} has a closed tree, then the unit set of every truth-functionally compound sentence whose immediate components are **P** and **Q** will also have a closed tree.
e. If {**P**} has an open tree and {**Q**} has an open tree, then the unit set of every truth-functionally compound sentence that has **P** and **Q** as its immediate components will have an open tree.
*f. If the completed truth-tree for {**P**} has exactly one open branch, then ~ **P** is truth-functionally indeterminate.
g. If **P** and **Q** are both truth-functionally true, then **P** & **Q**, **P** ∨ **Q**, **P** ⊃ **Q**, and **P** ≡ **Q** will each have a completed tree all of whose branches are open.
*h. If **P** and **Q** are both truth-functionally true, then **P** & **Q**, **P** ∨ **Q**, **P** ⊃ **Q**, and **P** ≡ **Q** will each have a tree with at least two completed open branches.
i. If **P** and **Q** are both truth-functionally false, then **P** & **Q**, **P** ∨ **Q**, **P** ⊃ **Q**, and **P** ≡ **Q** will each have a closed tree.
*j. If **P** and **Q** are both truth-functionally false, then **P** & **Q**, **P** ∨ **Q**, **P** ⊃ **Q**, and **P** ≡ **Q** will each have a completed tree with at least one closed branch.
k. If **P** truth-functionally true and **Q** is truth-functionally false then **P** & **Q**, **P** ∨ **Q**, **P** ⊃ **Q**, and **P** ≡ **Q** will each have a completed tree with at least one open branch and one closed branch.

4.6 TRUTH-FUNCTIONAL EQUIVALENCE

Sentences **P** and **Q** of *SL* are truth-functionally equivalent if and only if there is no truth-value assignment on which **P** and **Q** have different truth-values. It follows that sentences **P** and **Q** are truth-functionally equivalent if and only if their corresponding material biconditional, **P** ≡ **Q**, is truth-functionally true. And a material biconditional **P** ≡ **Q** is truth-functionally true just in case the tree for the negation of that biconditional is closed. That is, to determine whether a biconditional is truth-functionally true, we simply apply the test for truth-functional truth developed in the previous section. More formally,

---

Sentences **P** and **Q** of *SL* are *truth-functionally equivalent* if and only if the set {~ (**P** ≡ **Q**)} has a closed tree.

In discussing truth-tables, we showed that '(W & Y) ⊃ H' is truth-functionally equivalent to 'W ⊃ (Y ⊃ H)' by producing a truth-table revealing that these two sentences have the same truth-value on every truth-value assignment. We can now use the truth-tree method to show the same result. To show that these sentences are equivalent, we need show only that their corresponding material biconditional is truth-functionally true:

1.	~ ([[(W & Y)] ⊃ H] ≡ [W ⊃ (Y ⊃ H)])✔		SM
2.	(W & Y) ⊃ H✔	~ [(W & Y) ⊃ H]✔	1 ~ ≡D
3.	~ [W ⊃ (Y ⊃ H)]✔	W ⊃ (Y ⊃ H)✔	1 ~ ≡D
4.	W		3 ~ ⊃D
5.	~ (Y ⊃ H)✔		3 ~ ⊃D
6.	Y		5 ~ ⊃D
7.	~ H		5 ~ ⊃D
8.	~ (W & Y)✔ H		2 ⊃D
		×	
9.	~ W ~ Y		8 ~ &D
	× ×		
10.		W & Y✔	2 ~ ⊃D
11.		~ H	2 ~ ⊃D
12.		W	10 &D
13.		Y	10 &D
14.		~ W Y ⊃ H✔	3 ⊃D
15.		~ Y H	14 ⊃D
		× ×	

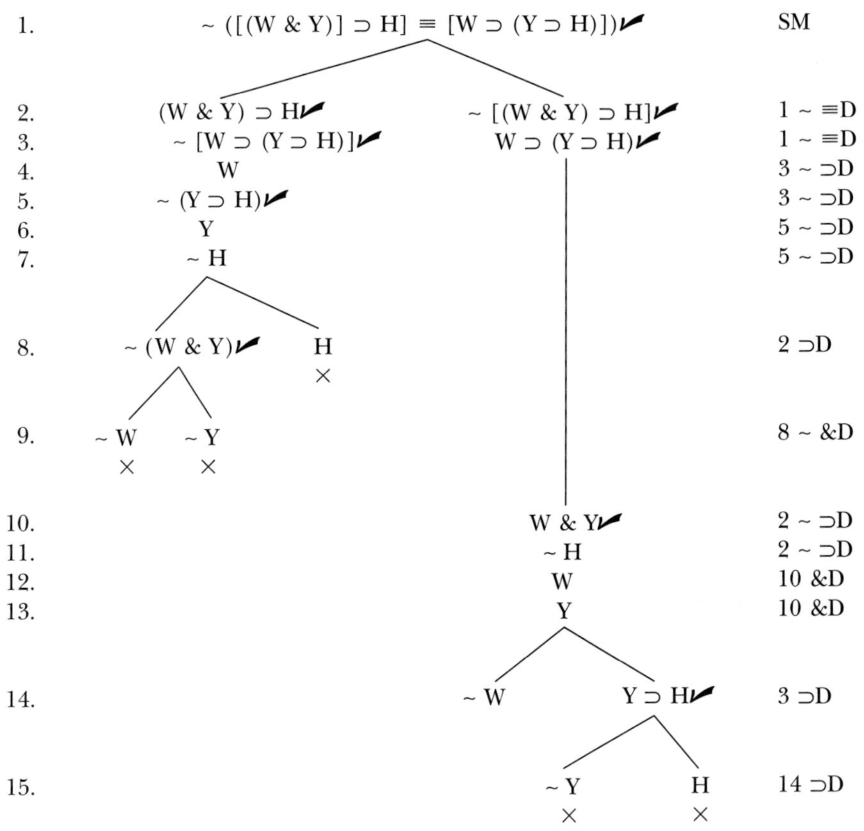

This tree is closed. The sentence at the top of the tree is therefore false on every truth-value assignment, and the biconditional of which it is the negation

is therefore true on every truth-value assignment. So the immediate components of that biconditional, '(W & Y) ⊃ H' and 'W ⊃ (Y ⊃ H)', are truth-functionally equivalent.

In the chapter on truth-tables (Chapter 3), we also showed that 'E ∨ H' and '(H ∨ J) ∨ E' are not truth-functionally equivalent. We can now show this by using the truth-tree method. These sentences are truth-functionally equivalent if and only if their corresponding material biconditional, '(E ∨ H) ≡ [(H ∨ J) ∨ E]', is truth-functionally true. And that biconditional is truth-functionally true if and only if the tree for its negation closes:

1.	~ ((E ∨ H) ≡ [(H ∨ J) ∨ E])✓				SM
2.	E ∨ H✓		~ (E ∨ H)✓		1 ~ ≡D
3.	~ [(H ∨ J) ∨ E]✓		(H ∨ J) ∨ E✓		1 ~ ≡D
4.	~ (H ∨ J)✓				3 ~ ∨D
5.	~ E				3 ~ ∨D
6.	~ H				4 ~ ∨D
7.	~ J				4 ~ ∨D
8.	E ×	H ×			2 ∨D
9.			~ E		2 ~ ∨D
10.			~ H		2 ~ ∨D
11.			H ∨ J✓	E ×	3 ∨D
12.			H (×) J		11 ∨D

Since this truth-tree has a completed open branch, there is at least one truth-value assignment on which the sentence at the top of the tree is true. That sentence is therefore not truth-functionally false, and the biconditional of which it is the negation is thus not truth-functionally true. It follows that the sentences that are the immediate components of that biconditional, 'E ∨ H' and '(H ∨ J) ∨ E', are not truth-functionally equivalent. They have different truth-values on every truth-value assignment of which

E	H	J
F	**F**	**T**

is a fragment.

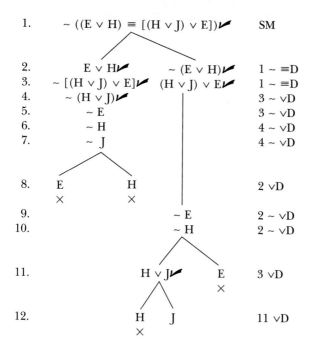

4.6E EXERCISES

1. Use the truth-tree method to determine whether the following pairs of sentences are truth-functionally equivalent. For those pairs that are not truth-functionally equivalent, give a fragment of a truth-value assignment that shows this.

a.	$\sim (Z \vee K)$	$\sim Z \,\&\, \sim K$
*b.	$\sim (Z \vee K)$	$\sim Z \vee \sim K$
c.	$(B \,\&\, C) \supset R$	$(B \supset R) \,\&\, (C \supset R)$
*d.	$(B \vee C) \supset R$	$(B \supset R) \,\&\, (C \supset R)$
e.	$A \,\&\, (B \vee C)$	$(A \,\&\, B) \vee (A \,\&\, C)$
*f.	$A \vee (B \,\&\, C)$	$(A \vee B) \,\&\, (A \vee C)$
g.	$D \supset (L \supset M)$	$(D \supset L) \supset M$
*h.	$J \supset (K \equiv L)$	$(J \supset K) \equiv (J \supset L)$
i.	$A \supset A$	$B \supset B$
*j.	$A \,\&\, \sim A$	$B \,\&\, \sim B$
k.	$A \,\&\, \sim B$	$\sim A \vee B$
*l.	$\sim (A \vee B)$	$\sim (A \,\&\, B)$
m.	$\sim (A \equiv B)$	$\sim A \equiv \sim B$
*n.	$A \supset (B \supset C)$	$(A \supset B) \supset C$
o.	$A \,\&\, (B \vee C)$	$(A \,\&\, B) \vee (A \,\&\, C)$
*p.	$A \supset (B \supset C)$	$A \supset (B \,\&\, C)$

2. Decide which of the following claims are true and which are false. In each case explain and defend your reasoning.

If **P** and **Q**, are truth-functionally equivalent, then

a. A completed truth-tree for {**P** $\equiv$ **Q**} will be open.
*b. A completed truth-tree for {**P** $\equiv \sim$ **Q**} will be open.
c. A completed truth-tree for the set {**P**, **Q**} will be open.
*d. A completed truth-tree for {$\sim$ **P** $\equiv \sim$ **Q**} will be open.

4.7 TRUTH-FUNCTIONAL ENTAILMENT AND TRUTH-FUNCTIONAL VALIDITY

We can use truth-trees to test for truth-functional entailment. Recall that, where **P** is a sentence and Γ is a set of sentences, Γ truth-functionally entails **P**—that is, $\Gamma \models$ **P** if and only if there is no truth-value assignment on which every member of Γ is true and **P** is false. Put another way, a set Γ of sentences truth-functionally entails a sentence **P** if and only if the set of sentences $\Gamma \cup$ {$\sim$ **P**} is truth-functionally inconsistent. Hence, to see if a finite set Γ truth-functionally entails **P**, we construct a tree for the members of $\Gamma \cup$ {$\sim$ **P**}. Here we have to be careful to negate the allegedly entailed sentence before doing a tree.

> A finite set Γ of sentences of *SL truth-functionally entails* a sentence **P** of *SL* if and only if the set $\Gamma \cup$ {$\sim$ **P**} has a closed truth-tree.

Does the set {B &, K, N ⊃ ~ K, K ∨ ~ K} truth-functionally entail 'B ⊃ N'?
We can find out by constructing a tree for {B &, K, N ⊃ ~ K, K ∨ ~ K, ~ B ⊃ N}:

1.	B & K✔	SM
2.	N ⊃ ~ K✔	SM
3.	K ∨ ~ K✔	SM
4.	~ (B ⊃ N)✔	SM
5.	B	1 &D
6.	K	1 &D
7.	B	4 ~ ⊃D
8.	~ N	4 ~ ⊃D

| 9. | K   ~ K | 3 ∨D |
| | ✗ | |

| 10. | ~ N   ~ K | 2 ⊃D |
| | ✗ | |

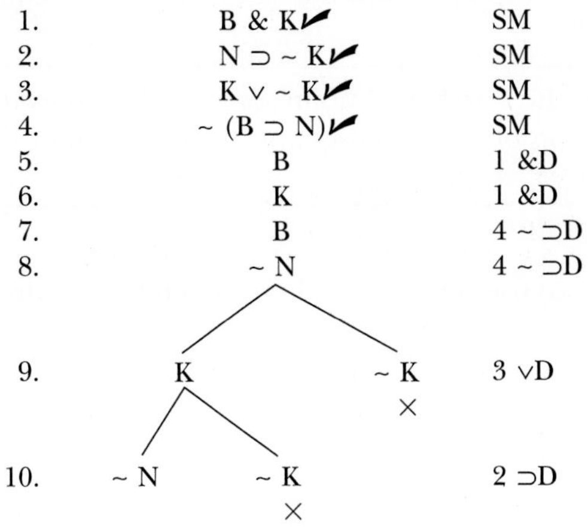

Since this truth-tree has a completed open branch, there is a truth-value assignment on which all the sentences we are testing are true. Hence there is an
assignment on which the members of the set {B & K, N ⊃ ~ K, K ∨ ~ K} are
all true and the allegedly entailed sentence, 'B ⊃ N', is false. So the entailment
does not in fact hold. The following fragment shows this:

B	K	N
T	T	F

On the other hand, {~ J ∨ S, S ⊃ E} does truth-functionally entail 'J ⊃ E', as
the following closed tree shows:

1.	~ J ∨ S✔	SM
2.	S ⊃ E✔	SM
3.	~ (J ⊃ E)✔	SM
4.	J	3 ~ ⊃D
5.	~ E	3 ~ ⊃D

| 6. | ~ J   S | 1 ∨D |
| | ✗ | |

| 7. | ~ S   E | 2 ⊃D |
| | ✗   ✗ | |

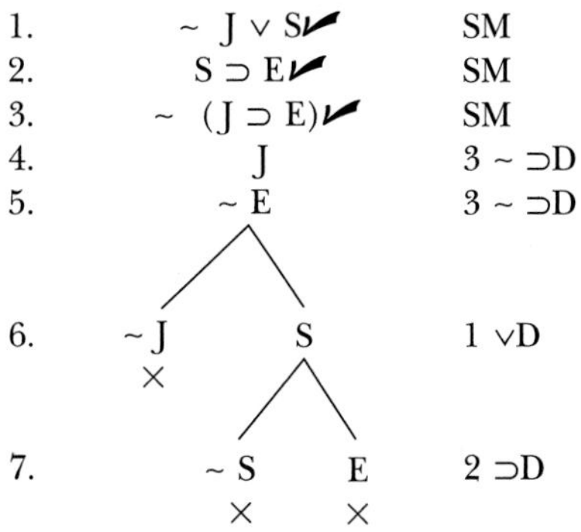

An argument is truth-functionally valid if and only if there is no truth-
value assignment on which the premises are true and the conclusion false. Alternatively an argument is truth-functionally valid if and only if there is no truth-
value assignment on which both the premises and the *negation* of the conclusion

are true. Hence an argument is truth-functionally valid if and only if the set consisting of the premises and the *negation* of the conclusion is truth-functionally inconsistent.

> An argument of *SL* with a finite number of premises is *truth-functionally valid* if and only if the set consisting of the premises and the negation of the conclusion has a closed truth-tree.

In our first example we use the tree method to determine whether the following argument is truth-functionally valid:

(~ B ∨ ~ H) ⊃ M

K & ~ M

B

Trees here are no different from the trees we have already constructed, but we must remember to do the tree for the premises and the *negation* of the conclusion, rather than for the premises and the conclusion:

1.	(~ B ∨ ~ H) ⊃ M✓		SM
2.	K & ~ M✓		SM
3.	~ B		SM
4.	K		2 &D
5.	~ M		2 &D
6.	~ (~ B ∨ ~ H)✓	M	1 ⊃D
		×	
7.	~ ~ B✓		6 ~ ∨D
8.	~ ~ H		6 ~ ∨D
9.	B		7 ~ ~ D
	×		

Our truth-tree is closed. So we know that the set consisting of the sentences we are testing is truth-functionally inconsistent, and hence that the argument from which the set was formed is truth-functionally valid. Our reasoning is this: The closed tree shows that there is no truth-value assignment on which the premises of our argument are all true and the negation of the conclusion is also true. Therefore there is no truth-value assignment on which those premises are true and the conclusion false, so the argument is truth-functionally valid.

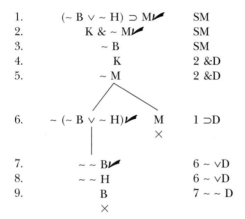

Here is another argument:

~ W & ~ L
(J ⊃ ~ W) ≡ ~ L
H

J & H

Our tree for this argument follows. Remember that it is the negation of the conclusion that we use along with the premises, not the conclusion itself:

1.	~ W & ~ L ✓				SM
2.	(J ⊃ ~ W) ≡ ~ L ✓				SM
3.	H				SM
4.	~ (J & H) ✓				SM
5.	~ W				1 &D
6.	~ L				1 &D
7.	J ⊃ ~ W ✓		~ (J ⊃ ~ W)		2 ≡D
8.	~ L		~ ~ L ✓		2 ≡D
9.			L ×		8 ~ ~ D
10.	~ J	~ W			7 ⊃D

11.	~ J ~ H
	         ×
		~ J ~ H
		         ×
					4 ~ &D

Because this tree has at least one completed open branch, we can recover a fragment of a truth-value assignment on which the premises and the negation of the conclusion are true, and hence on which the premises are true and the conclusion false. So the argument we are testing is truth-functionally invalid. The recoverable fragment is

H	J	L	W
T	**F**	**F**	**F**

An argument is truth-functionally valid if and only if the set consisting of the premises of that argument truth-functionally entails the conclusion of that argument. Thus the procedures for constructing truth-trees to test for truth-functionally validity and for truth-functional entailment are very similar. In the case of testing for truth-functional validity, the conclusion is negated; in the case of testing for truth-functional entailment, the allegedly entailed sentence is negated.

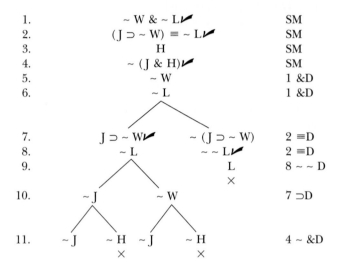

4.7E EXERCISES

1. Use the truth-tree method to determine which of the following claims are true and which are false. For those that are false, give the relevant fragment of a truth-value assignment that shows this.

a. $\{A \supset (B \,\&\, C),\ C \equiv B,\ \sim C\} \vDash\ \sim A$
*b. $\{K \supset H,\ H \supset L,\ L \supset M\} \vDash K \supset M$
c. $\{\sim (A \equiv B),\ \sim A,\ \sim B\} \vDash C \,\&\, \sim C$
*d. $\{\sim (\sim A \,\&\, \sim B)\} \vDash A \,\&\, B$
e. $\{\sim \sim F \supset \sim \sim G,\ \sim G \supset \sim F\} \vDash G \supset F$
*f. $\{A \,\&\, (B \supset C)\} \vDash (A \,\&\, C) \vee (A \,\&\, B)$
g. $\{[(C \vee D) \,\&\, H] \supset A,\ D\} \vDash H \supset A$
*h. $\{(G \equiv H) \vee (\sim G \equiv H)\} \vDash (\sim G \equiv \sim H) \vee \sim (G \equiv H)$
i. $\{(J \vee M) \supset \sim (J \,\&\, M),\ M \equiv (M \supset J)\} \vDash M \supset J$
*j. $\vDash [A \vee ((K \supset \sim H) \,\&\, \sim A)] \vee \sim A$
k. $\vDash\ \sim (A \equiv B) \supset (\sim A \equiv \sim B)$
*l. $\vDash\ \sim (C \equiv C) \equiv (C \vee \sim C)$
m. $\vDash [(A \supset B) \supset (C \supset D)] \supset [C \supset (B \supset D)]$

2. Use the truth-tree method to determine which of the following arguments are truth-functionally valid and which are truth-functionally invalid. For those that are truth-functionally invalid, give the relevant fragment of a truth-value assignment that shows this.

a. $M \supset (K \supset B)$
$\sim K \supset \sim M$
$L \,\&\, M$
———
B

*b. $(\sim J \vee K) \supset (L \,\&\, M)$
$\sim (\sim J \vee K)$
———
$\sim (L \,\&\, M)$

c. $A \,\&\, (B \vee C)$
$(\sim C \vee H) \,\&\, (H \supset \sim H)$
———
$A \,\&\, B$

*d. $(D \equiv \sim G) \,\&\, G$
$[G \vee ((A \supset D) \,\&\, A)] \supset \sim D$
———
$G \supset \sim D$

e. $(M \equiv K) \vee \sim (K \,\&\, D)$
$\sim M \supset \sim K$
$\sim D \supset \sim (K \,\&\, D)$
———
M

*f. $(J \supset T) \supset J$
$(T \supset J) \supset T$
———
$\sim J \vee \sim T$

g. $B \,\&\, (H \vee Z)$
$\sim Z \supset K$
$(B \equiv Z) \supset \sim Z$
$\sim K$
———
$M \,\&\, N$

*h. $A \vee \sim (B \,\&\, C)$
$\sim B$
$\sim (A \vee C)$
———
A

i. $A \& (B \supset C)$

$(A \& C) \vee (A \& \sim B)$

k. $A \supset \sim A$

$(B \supset A) \supset B$

$A \equiv \sim B$

*j. $(G \equiv H) \vee (\sim G \equiv H)$

$(\sim G \equiv \sim H) \vee \sim (G \equiv H)$

*l. $B \vee (A \& \sim C)$

$(C \vee A) \equiv B$

$\sim B \vee A$

$\sim (A \vee C)$

3. Symbolize each of the following arguments and then use the truth-tree method to determine whether the symbolized argument is truth-functionally valid. If an argument is not truth-functionally valid, recover one fragment of a truth-value assignment that shows this.

a. The social security system will succeed if and only if more money is collected through social security taxes. Unless the social security system succeeds, many senior citizens will be in trouble. Although members of Congress claim to be sympathetic to senior citizens, more money won't be collected through social security taxes. Hence the social security system will not succeed.

*b. Either the president and the senators will support the legislation, or the president and the representatives will support it. Moreover, the representatives will support the legislation, provided that a majority of the people support it. The people don't support it. Thus the senators will support the legislation.

c. If the president acts quickly the social security system will be saved, and if the social security system is saved, senior citizens will be delighted. If the president is pressured by members of the Senate, by members of the House of Representatives, or by senior citizens, he will act quickly. However, neither members of the Senate nor members of the House will pressure the President, but senior citizens will. Therefore senior citizens will be delighted.

*d. The president won't veto the bill if Congress passes it, and Congress will pass it if and only if both the Senate passes it and the House of Representatives passes it. But the House of Representatives will pass it only if a majority of Democrats will vote for it; and indeed, a majority of Democrats will vote for it. Therefore the president won't veto the bill.

e. At most, one of the two houses of Congress will pass the bill. If either the House of Representatives or the Senate passes it, the voters will be pleased; but if both houses of Congress pass the bill, the president will not be pleased. If the president is not pleased, not all the members of the White House will be happy. Hence some members of the White House will not be happy.

4. Show that constructing a tree for the premises and conclusion (not the negation of the conclusion) of an argument of *SL* yields no useful information concerning the validity of the argument by completing the following exercises.

a. Give two arguments of *SL*, one valid and the other invalid, such that the trees for the premises and conclusion of these arguments both have at least one completed open branch. Construct the trees and explain why they are not useful in determining whether the arguments in question are truth-functionally valid.

*b. Give two arguments of *SL*, one valid and the other invalid, such that the trees for the premises and conclusion of these arguments are both closed. Construct the trees and explain why they are not useful in determining whether the arguments in question are truth-functionally valid.

c. Explain why (a) and (b) together constitute a proof that there is no useful information concerning the validity of an argument to be obtained by doing a tree for the premises and conclusion of the argument.

5. Suppose we define a new connective, '|', thus:

P	**Q**	**P|Q**
T	**T**	**F**
T	**F**	**T**
F	**T**	**T**
F	**F**	**T**

To deal with this new connective, we have to add two new rules to our truth-tree system, one for decomposing sentences of the form **P|Q** and one for decomposing sentences of the form ~ **P|Q**.

a. Give the rules needed for sentences of these two forms.

b. Use the new rules to test the sentences 'A|B' and '(A|A) ∨ (B|B)' for truth-functional equivalence, using the truth-tree method. State your result.

SUMMARY

Key Semantic Properties

TRUTH-FUNCTIONAL CONSISTENCY: A finite set Γ of sentences of *SL* is *truth-functionally consistent* if and only if Γ has a truth-tree with at least one completed open branch.

TRUTH-FUNCTIONAL INCONSISTENCY: A set Γ of sentences of *SL* is *truth-functionally inconsistent* if and only if at least one finite subset of Γ has a closed truth-tree.

TRUTH-FUNCTIONAL FALSITY: A sentence **P** of *SL* is *truth-functionally false* if and only if the set {**P**} has a closed truth-tree.

TRUTH-FUNCTIONAL TRUTH: A sentence **P** of *SL* is *truth-functionally true* if and only if the set {~ **P**} has a closed truth-tree.

TRUTH-FUNCTIONAL INDETERMINACY: A sentence **P** of *SL* is *truth-functionally indeterminate* if and only if neither the set {**P**} nor the set {~ **P**} has a closed truth-tree.

TRUTH-FUNCTIONAL EQUIVALENCE: Sentences **P** and **Q** of *SL* are *truth-functionally equivalent* if and only if the set {~ (**P** ≡ **Q**)} has a closed truth-tree.

TRUTH-FUNCTIONAL ENTAILMENT: A finite set Γ of sentences of *SL* *truth-functionally entails* a sentence **P** of *SL* if and only if the set Γ ∪ {~ **P**} has a closed truth-tree.

TRUTH-FUNCTIONAL VALIDITY: An argument of *SL* with a finite number of premises is *truth-functionally valid* if and only if the set consisting of the premises and the negation of the conclusion has a closed truth-tree.

Key Truth-Tree Concepts

CLOSED BRANCH: A branch containing both an atomic sentence and the negation of that sentence.

CLOSED TRUTH-TREE: A tree each of whose branches is closed.

OPEN BRANCH: A truth-tree branch that is not closed.

COMPLETED TRUTH-TREE: A truth-tree each of whose branches either is closed or is a completed open branch.

OPEN TRUTH-TREE: A truth-tree that is not closed.

COMPLETED OPEN BRANCH: An open truth-tree branch on which every sentence either is a literal or has been decomposed.

Chapter 5

SENTENTIAL LOGIC: DERIVATIONS

5.1 THE DERIVATION SYSTEM *SD*

In Chapters 3 and 4 we developed techniques for, among other things, determining the truth-functional validity or invalidity of arguments of *SL* and the truth-functional status of sentences of *SL*. These techniques, based on truth-tables and truth-trees, are reliable, but they can hardly be said to parallel the informal kind of reasoning we do in everyday discourse when we are interested in discovering whether an argument is valid or whether a set of beliefs is inconsistent. In this chapter we develop techniques that parallel, at least to a considerable extent, the sort of informal reasoning we do in everyday discourse.

For example, when evaluating an argument we often try to show that its conclusion can be deduced or derived from its premises. Consider the argument

Whales breathe by lungs and whales are warm-blooded.

If whales breathe by lungs, then whales are not fish.

Whales are warm-blooded and whales are not fish.

A way of showing that the conclusion can be derived from the premises is to proceed through a series of inferences that lead from the premises to the conclusion. From the first premise we can infer that whales breathe by lungs. From this result and the second premise, we can infer that whales are not fish. Finally, since from the first premise we can infer that whales are warm-blooded and we have already inferred that whales are not fish, we conclude that whales are warm-blooded and are not fish. Here are the steps in the reasoning process:

1. Whales breathe by lungs and whales are warm-blooded.	Assumption
2. If whales breathe by lungs, then whales are not fish.	Assumption
3. Whales breathe by lungs.	From 1
4. Whales are not fish.	From 2 and 3
5. Whales are warm-blooded.	From 1
6. Whales are warm-blooded and whales are not fish.	From 4 and 5

We took the premises as assumptions and proceeded through a series of inferences that lead to the conclusion of the argument. The structure of the reasoning is clearly seen when the sentences are symbolized in *SL*:

1. L & W	Assumption
2. L ⊃ ~ F	Assumption
3. L	From 1
4. ~ F	From 2 and 3
5. W	From 1
6. W & ~ F	From 4 and 5

Semantics is concerned with the interpretation of a language, whereas *syntax* is concerned with the formal properties of a language. The reasoning in our example can be viewed as the application of a series of syntactic rules for deriving sentences. Rules are syntactic when they are applied on the basis of the forms, and not the truth-values or truth-conditions, of sentences. Syntactic rules for deriving sentences are called *derivation rules.* For example, a derivation rule might tell us that from a sentence of the form **P** & **Q** we can derive **P**. Another derivation rule might tell us that from **P** we can derive ~ **P**. Of course, for our purposes the former would be an acceptable rule, whereas the latter would not. The first rule would be acceptable because, whenever a sentence of the form **P** & **Q** is true, the left conjunct, **P**, is true. That is, the rule is truth-preserving. In contrast, the second rule is not truth-preserving. We shall employ only truth-preserving derivation rules, that is, derivation rules that never lead us from true sentences to false sentences.

It is important to realize that there is a connection between the derivation rules introduced in this chapter and the semantic results presented earlier. But it is equally important to realize that derivation rules can be applied without having any interpretation of the symbols in mind. In effect, a derivation rule tells us that, given a group of symbols with a certain structure, we can write down another group of symbols with a certain structure. This appeal to structure is what makes derivation rules syntactic.

Derivation rules are used to construct *derivations* that show, in a finite series of easily understood steps, how sentences are derived from other sentences. Systems that employ derivation rules like the ones we introduce in this chapter are called *natural deduction systems. SD* (for *s*entential *d*erivation) is the natural deduction system that is based on the sentential derivation rules introduced in this section.

REITERATION

The simplest derivation rule of *SD* is *Reiteration.*

<u>*Reiteration* (R)</u>

	P
▷	**P**

The pointer '▷' indicates which sentence we are allowed to derive according to the rule. This rule, Reiteration, permits us to derive a sentence of *SL* from itself. Here is a simple derivation that uses Reiteration:

1	(H ≡ K) & S	Assumption
2	G ∨ ~ H	Assumption
3	(H ≡ K) & S	1 R

In this derivation the sentences on lines 1 and 2 are taken as assumptions, and the sentence on line 3 is derived. For reasons to be explained later, the vertical line is called the *scope line* of the derivation. A horizontal line is drawn under the assumptions to mark them off from the derived sentences. That the sentence on line 3 is derived by Reiteration is indicated in the righthand column of the derivation by '1 R'—that is, by giving the line number of the sentence to which the rule was applied and the abbreviation of the rule name.

If Reiteration were the only derivation rule available, derivations would be rather uninteresting. To make *SL* an interesting system, we need rules that allow us to introduce and to eliminate each of the five sentential connectives of *SL.* So we shall employ five pairs of derivation rules—one pair for each of the sentential connectives. One member of each pair will allow us to introduce a connective, and one will allow us to eliminate it. For this reason such derivation rules are sometimes called *intelim rules.*[1]

[1]The standard form for expressing the rules and constructing derivations is largely due to Frederic Brenton Fitch, *Symbolic Logic: An Introduction* (New York: Ronald, 1952). The derivation rules are adaptations of rules derived by Gerhard Gentzen, "Untersuchungen über das logische Schliessen," *Mathematische Zeitschrift,* 39 (1934–1935), 176–210, 405–431; and Stanislaw Jaŝkowski, "On the Rules of Suppositions in Formal Logic," *Studia Logica,* 1 (1934), 5–32.

INTRODUCTION AND ELIMINATION RULES FOR '&'

The introduction rule for '&' is *Conjunction Introduction.*

Conjunction Introduction (&I)

	P
	Q
▷	**P & Q**

This rule allows us to derive **P & Q** from sentences **P** and **Q** of *SL* that occur on earlier lines. Where several sentences are appealed to in applications of this and the other derivation rules of *SD*, those sentences may occur in any order. Hence, if **P** occurs later than **Q**, we can still derive **P & Q** by Conjunction Introduction.

The elimination rule for '&' is *Conjunction Elimination.*

Conjunction Elimination (&E)

	P & Q	or		**P & Q**
▷	**P**		▷	**Q**

Conjunction Elimination allows us to derive **P** from **P & Q** and to derive **Q** from **P & Q**.

To illustrate the use of these derivation rules, we consider the following argument:

> The Parthenon is being damaged by pollution, and it will continue to be damaged as long as environmental standards are not imposed.
>
> The Parthenon is being damaged by tourists; each year millions of feet wear away the stone.
>
> Although the restoration efforts of the late nineteenth century were well intentioned, the iron bars installed are cracking the stone, and the Parthenon is being damaged by former restoration.
>
> ---
>
> The Parthenon is being damaged by pollution, tourists, and former restoration.

This argument can be symbolized in *SL* as

P & C

T & M

E & (I & R)

(P & T) & R

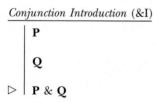

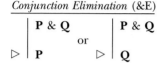

To show that the conclusion follows from the premises of the symbolized argument, we take the premises as assumptions and derive the conclusion from those assumptions. As a reminder of our goal, we list the sentence ultimately to be derived at the top of the derivation.

Derive: (P & T) & R

1	P & C	Assumption
2	T & M	Assumption
3	E & (I & R)	Assumption
4	P	1 &E
5	T	2 &E
6	P & T	4, 5 &I
7	I & R	3 &E
8	R	7 &E
9	(P & T) & R	6, 8 &I

5.1.1E EXERCISES

1. Complete the following derivations.

a. Derive: Q & R

1	R & Q	Assumption

*b. Derive: (~ ~ S & ~ ~ S) & ~ ~ S

1	~ ~ S	Assumption

c. Derive: K

1	S & [~ T & (K & ~ F)]	Assumption

*d. Derive: A & (B & C)

1	(C & B) & A	Assumption

e. Derive: [(J ⊃ T) & ~ R] & (~ U ∨ G)

1	N & ~ R	Assumption
2	K & (J ⊃ T)	Assumption
3	(~ U ∨ G) & ~ J	Assumption

INTRODUCTION AND ELIMINATION RULES FOR '⊃'

The elimination rule for '⊃' is *Conditional Elimination* (sometimes called 'Modus Ponens').

Conditional Elimination (⊃E)

	P ⊃ Q
	P
▷	**Q**

A sentence **Q** can be derived from sentences **P** and **P ⊃ Q** that occur on earlier lines of a derivation. To illustrate a use of this derivation rule, we recall this argument:

Whales breathe by lungs and whales are warm-blooded.
If whales breathe by lungs, then whales are not fish.
___
Whales are warm-blooded and whales are not fish.

A derivation for a symbolized version of the argument is

Derive: W & ~ F

1	L & W	Assumption
2	L ⊃ ~ F	Assumption
3	L	1 &E
4	~ F	2, 3 ⊃E
5	W	1 &E
6	W & ~ F	4, 5 &I

The introduction rule for '⊃' is *Conditional Introduction* (sometimes called 'Conditional Proof').

Conditional Introduction (⊃I)

		P
		Q
▷	**P ⊃ Q**	

In deriving **P ⊃ Q** a *subderivation* is constructed that has **P** as the assumption and **Q** as the sentence on the last line. Consider the argument

If Wendy is on the Eiffel Tower, then she is in Paris.
If she is in Paris, then she is in France.
___
If Wendy is on the Eiffel Tower, then she is in France.

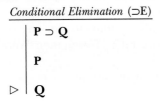

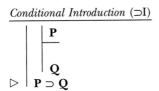

To show that the conclusion follows from the premises, we might reason as follows: Assume that Wendy is on the Eiffel Tower. On the basis of this assumption and the first premise, we can infer that Wendy is in Paris. If this is so, then, on the basis of the second premise, we can infer that Wendy is in France. Of course, we have shown that Wendy is in France not on the basis of the premises alone but rather on the basis of the premises and the additional assumption that Wendy is on the Eiffel Tower. But this amounts to showing that from the premises it follows that if Wendy is on the Eiffel Tower then Wendy is in France.

A derivation for a symbolized version of the argument is

Derive: E ⊃ F

```
1 | E ⊃ P          Assumption
2 | P ⊃ F          Assumption
  |------
3 |  | E           Assumption
  |  |---
4 |  | P           1, 3 ⊃E
5 |  | F           2, 4 ⊃E
6 | E ⊃ F          3–5 ⊃I
```

The subderivation occupies lines 3–5 of the derivation; this is indicated by the inner vertical line—the scope line of the subderivation. We have shown on the basis of the primary assumptions (lines 1 and 2) that if we assume 'E' (line 3) then 'F' (line 5) can be derived. Hence we can derive 'E ⊃ F' in the main derivation. A subderivation is terminated by ending the scope line of the subderivation and returning to the main scope line on the left. When a subderivation is terminated, the assumption of the subderivation is said to be *discharged,* and none of the lines constituting that subderivation is accessible; that is, none of those lines can be appealed to later in the derivation. However, the subderivation as a whole can be appealed to. This is done in the example, in the justification for the sentence on line 6, by using a dash to separate the first and last line numbers of the subderivation. In short, to derive a conditional sentence, construct a subderivation with the antecedent of the conditional as the assumption and with the consequent of the conditional as the sentence on the last line of the subderivation. Once the subderivation is terminated, the entire subderivation is cited in justifying the conditional entered below it.

All the assumptions that occur at the top and immediately to the right of the main scope line of the derivation are called *primary assumptions.* Each subderivation begins with an assumption, called an *auxiliary assumption,* and ends with a sentence that occurs immediately to the right of the scope line of the subderivation. The scope line of the subderivation indicates the scope of the auxiliary assumption that begins the subderivation. The following illustrates how subderivations can occur within subderivations:

Derive: G ⊃ (H ⊃ K)

1	(G & H) ⊃ K	Assumption
2	G	Assumption
3	H	Assumption
4	G & H	2, 3 &I
5	K	1, 4 ⊃E
6	H ⊃ K	3–5 ⊃I
7	G ⊃ (H ⊃ K)	2–6 ⊃I

Each of these subderivations begins with an auxiliary assumption and ends prior to the end of the derivation. Only the primary assumption on line 1 is not discharged.

5.1.2E EXERCISES

1. Complete the following derivations.

a. Derive: U

1	H ⊃ U	Assumption
2	S & H	Assumption

*b. Derive: E ∨ K

1	(Q & M) ⊃ (E ∨ K)	Assumption
2	M & (E ∨ C)	Assumption
3	Q & ~ N	Assumption

c. Derive: J ⊃ T

1	J ⊃ (S & T)	Assumption

*d. Derive: (Z & K) ⊃ (A & E)

1	(K & Z) ⊃ (E & A)	Assumption

e. Derive: (S & B) ⊃ ~ N

1	S ⊃ (L & ~ N)	Assumption

INTRODUCTION AND ELIMINATION RULES FOR '~'

The introduction rule for '~' is *Negation Introduction.*

<u>*Negation Introduction* (~ I)</u>

```
   |  | P
   |  |----
   |  |
   |  | Q
   |  |
   |  | ~ Q
▷  | ~ P
```

From a subderivation that has a sentence **P** as its assumption and sentences **Q** and ~ **Q** derived within it, ~ **P** can be derived. The sentences **Q** and ~ **Q** may be derived in either order, but one or the other must be the last sentence of the subderivation, and both must occur immediately to the right of the scope line of the subderivation. Consider the following argument:

> If the union votes for the contract and the management agrees to the terms of the contract, then the contract will be signed.
>
> The management agrees to the terms of the contract, but the contract will not be signed.
>
> ---
>
> The union does not vote for the contract.

Here is a derivation for a symbolized version of this argument:

Derive: ~ U

1	(U & M) ⊃ S	Assumption
2	M & ~ S	Assumption
3	U	Assumption
4	M	2 &E
5	U & M	3, 4 &I
6	S	1, 5 ⊃E
7	~ S	2 &E
8	~ U	3–7 ~ I

The elimination rule for '~' is *Negation Elimination.*

<u>*Negation Elimination* (~ E)</u>

```
   |  | ~ P
   |  |----
   |  |
   |  | Q
   |  |
   |  | ~ Q
▷  | P
```

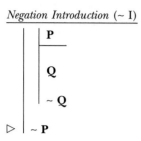

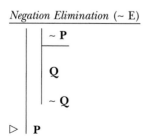

We can derive **P** if we can construct a subderivation that has ~ **P** as its assumption and sentences **Q** and ~ **Q** derived within the subderivation. The sentences **Q** and ~ **Q** may be derived in either order, but one or the other must be the last sentence of the subderivation, and both must occur immediately to the right of the scope line of the subderivation. This rule is useful in constructing a derivation for the following argument:

> If the soldier will not volunteer, then his superior officer will order him to volunteer.
>
> If his superior officer orders him to volunteer, then he will volunteer.
>
> ---
>
> The soldier will volunteer.

Derive: S

1	$\sim S \supset O$	Assumption
2	$O \supset S$	Assumption
3	$\quad \sim S$	Assumption
4	$\quad O$	1, 3 $\supset$E
5	$\quad S$	2, 4 $\supset$E
6	$\quad \sim S$	3 R
7	S	3–6 ~ E

Note that, when a subderivation is being constructed for use with Negation Introduction or Negation Elimination, the sentence and its negation that are derived in the subderivation may both be molecular, and one of these may be the same as the assumption. Again the sentence and its negation may be derived in any order. The following derivation illustrates these points:

Derive: $\sim \sim (J \equiv H)$

1	$\sim (J \equiv H) \supset \sim \sim (J \equiv H)$	Assumption
2	$\quad \sim (J \equiv H)$	Assumption
3	$\quad \sim \sim (J \equiv H)$	1, 2 $\supset$E
4	$\quad \sim (J \equiv H)$	2 R
5	$\sim \sim (J \equiv H)$	2–4 ~ I

Both Negation Introduction and Negation Elimination are akin to a strategy known as *reductio ad absurdum*. Intuitively, if we can derive both a sentence and its negation under an auxiliary assumption, the auxiliary assumption can be rejected on the grounds of leading to an absurdity. We require, for the sake of clarity, that when Negation Introduction or Negation Elimination is applied, both a sentence and its negation actually occur *under* and within the scope of the auxiliary assumption of the subderivation cited. Reiteration is often useful in obtaining the sentences needed for the application of these rules, as the following derivation illustrates:

Derive: K

1	~ ~ K	Assumption
2	~ K	Assumption
3	~ K	2 R
4	~ ~ K	1 R
5	K	2–4 ~ E

In this case '~ K' and '~ ~ K' have been reiterated so that they occur *under* the auxiliary assumption on line 2. Negation Elimination can then be applied at line 5.

5.1.3E EXERCISES

1. Complete the following derivations.

a. Derive: ~ G

1	(G ⊃ I) & ~ I	Assumption

*b. Derive: K

1	M & ~ M	Assumption

c. Derive: ~ ~ R

1	~ R ⊃ A	Assumption
2	~ R ⊃ ~ A	Assumption

*d. Derive: R & M

1	~ (R & M) ⊃ (L & ~ N)	Assumption
2	N	Assumption

e. Derive: P

1	(~ P ⊃ ~ L) & (~ L ⊃ L)	Assumption

INTRODUCTION AND ELIMINATION RULES FOR '∨'

The introduction rule for '∨' is *Disjunction Introduction.*

Disjunction Introduction (∨I)

```
  | P                 | P
  |         or        |
▷ | P ∨ Q           ▷ | Q ∨ P
```

This is an interesting rule in that **Q** and all its components may be completely new to the derivation. We are not really getting something for nothing, for if **P** is true, then **P** ∨ **Q** (as well as **Q** ∨ **P**) is true. So Disjunction Introduction is truth-preserving. The following derivation illustrates applications of this rule:

Business is booming although the cost of energy is up.

If either the cost of energy is up or food and clothing prices are increasing, then inflation will continue.

Manufacturing costs will level off, or inflation will continue.

Derive: M ∨ I

1	B & E	Assumption
2	[E ∨ (F & C)] ⊃ I	Assumption
3	E	1 &E
4	E ∨ (F & C)	3 ∨I
5	I	2, 4 ⊃E
6	M ∨ I	5 ∨I

The elimination rule for '∨' is *Disjunction Elimination.*

Disjunction Elimination (∨E)

```
  | P ∨ Q
  |
  |  | P
  |  |----
  |  |
  |  | R
  |  | Q
  |  |----
  |  |
  |  | R
  |
▷ | R
```

This rule tells us that we can derive a sentence **R** if we have a sentence of the form **P** ∨ **Q** and a subderivation that begins with the assumption **P** and ends with **R** and a subderivation that begins with the assumption **Q** and ends with **R**.

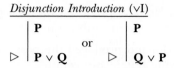

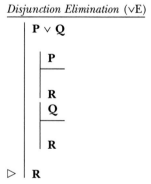

Disjunction Elimination is used in our derivation for the following argument:

> The greatest painter is either Rembrandt or van Gogh.
>
> If Rembrandt is the greatest, then Holland produced the best painter and the best painter lived during the seventeenth century.
>
> If van Gogh is the greatest, then Holland produced the best painter and the best painter lived during the nineteenth century.
>
> ---
>
> Holland produced the best painter, and the best painter lived during the seventeenth or nineteenth century.

Derive: H & (S ∨ N)

1	R ∨ V		Assumption
2	R ⊃ (H & S)		Assumption
3	V ⊃ (H & N)		Assumption
4		R	Assumption
5		H & S	2, 4 ⊃E
6		S	5 &E
7		S ∨ N	6 ∨I
8		H	5 &E
9		H & (S ∨ N)	8, 7 &I
10		V	Assumption
11		H & N	3, 10 ⊃E
12		N	11 &E
13		S ∨ N	12 ∨I
14		H	11 &E
15		H & (S ∨ N)	14, 13 &I
16	H & (S ∨ N)		1, 4–9, 10–15 ∨E

This derivation shows that if 'R' is assumed (line 4) then 'H & (S ∨ N)' follows and if 'V' is assumed (line 10) then 'H & (S ∨ N)' follows. Therefore we can be sure that 'H & (S ∨ N)' follows from the primary assumptions, for 'R ∨ V' (line 1) assures us that either 'R' or 'V' is the case. Disjunction Elimination allows us to enter 'H & (S ∨ N)' by appealing to line 1 and the two subderivations.

5.1.4E EXERCISES

1. Complete the following derivations.

a. Derive: B ∨ (K ∨ G)

1	K	Assumption

*b. Derive: Y

1	P ∨ C	Assumption
2	P ⊃ Y	Assumption
3	C ⊃ Y	Assumption

c. Derive: D

1	D ∨ D	Assumption

*d. Derive: ~ H

1	(K ∨ P) ⊃ ~ H	Assumption
2	P	Assumption

e. Derive: X

1	~ E ∨ X	Assumption
2	~ E ⊃ X	Assumption

INTRODUCTION AND ELIMINATION RULES FOR '≡'

The introduction rule for '≡' is *Biconditional Introduction.*

Biconditional Introduction (≡I)

```
|  | P
|  |---
|  |
|  | Q
|
|  | Q
|  |---
|  |
|  | P
▷ | P ≡ Q
```

To derive a biconditional **P** ≡ **Q**, construct two subderivations—one that has **P** as its assumption and ends with **Q** and one that has **Q** as its assumption and ends with **P**. Intuitively it may help to think of **P** ≡ **Q** as tantamount to (**P** ⊃ **Q**) & (**Q** ⊃ **P**). Each of these subderivations would allow us to derive one of these conjuncts. The derivation for the following argument uses Biconditional Introduction:

This solution is acidic only if it is neither basic nor neutral.
If this solution is not basic, then if it is not neutral it is acidic.
———
This solution is acidic if and only if it is neither basic nor neutral.

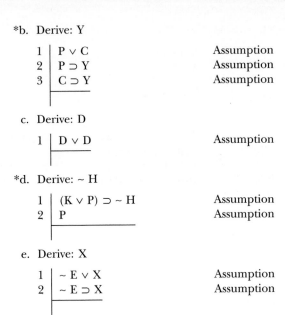

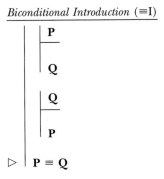

Derive: A ≡ (~ B & ~ N)

1	A ⊃ (~ B & ~ N)	Assumption
2	~ B ⊃ (~ N ⊃ A)	Assumption
3	A	Assumption
4	~ B & ~ N	1, 3 ⊃E
5	~ B & ~ N	Assumption
6	~ B	5 &E
7	~ N ⊃ A	2, 6 ⊃E
8	~ N	5 &E
9	A	7, 8 ⊃E
10	A ≡ (~ B & ~ N)	3–4, 5–9 ≡I

The elimination rule for '≡' is *Biconditional Elimination.*

Biconditional Elimination (≡E)

	P ≡ Q			**P ≡ Q**
	P	or		**Q**
▷	**Q**		▷	**P**

If a sentence **P** ≡ **Q** occurs on a line and **P** occurs on another line, then we can derive **Q**. Similarly, if a sentence **P** ≡ **Q** occurs on a line and **Q** occurs on another line, then we can derive **P**. Here are some applications of this rule:

Michelle will study for the final exam; moreover, if she studies for the final exam, she will pass it.

Michelle will pass the logic course if and only if she passes the final exam.

Michelle will pass the logic course if and only if she graduates.

Michelle will graduate.

Derive: G

1	S & (S ⊃ E)	Assumption
2	C ≡ E	Assumption
3	C ≡ G	Assumption
4	S	1 &E
5	S ⊃ E	1 &E
6	E	4, 5 ⊃E
7	C	2, 6 ≡E
8	G	3, 7 ≡E

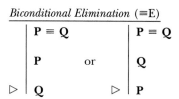

5.1.5E EXERCISES

1. Complete the following derivations.

a. Derive: Q

1	K ≡ (~ E & Q)	Assumption
2	K	Assumption

*b. Derive: ~ R ≡ E

1	(~ R ⊃ E) & (E ⊃ ~ R)	Assumption

c. Derive: S & ~ A

1	(S ≡ ~ I) & N	Assumption
2	(N ≡ ~ I) & ~ A	Assumption

*d. Derive: N

1	A ∨ L	Assumption
2	A ≡ N	Assumption
3	L ⊃ N	Assumption

e. Derive: (E ≡ O) & (O ≡ E)

1	(E ⊃ T) & (T ⊃ O)	Assumption
2	O ⊃ E	Assumption

5.2 APPLYING THE DERIVATION RULES OF *SD*

Several principles of application should be kept in mind when using the derivation rules. All the derivation rules of *SD* are rules of inference that appeal to *entire* sentences or to *entire* subderivations on earlier lines.

For example, in developing a derivation for the argument

(~ J & W) & Y
(N ∨ ~ B) & [~ J ⊃ (K ∨ G)]
———————————————
K ∨ G

it would be *incorrect* to use Conjunction Elimination as follows:

Derive: K ∨ G

1	(~ J & W) & Y	Assumption	
2	(N ∨ ~ B) & [~ J ⊃ (K ∨ G)]	Assumption	
3	~ J	1 &E	**MISTAKE!**

The mistake here is trying to derive '~ J' from '~ J & W' when the latter sentence occurs only as a component of another sentence. The sentence on line 1 is a conjunction; that is, it is a sentence of the form **P** & **Q** where **P** is '~ J & W' and **Q** is 'Y'. Conjunction Elimination only allows us to derive either of the conjuncts of a conjunction. So, though we cannot derive '~ J' from the sentence on line 1 by Conjunction Elimination, we can derive '~ J & W'. Because '~ J & W' is itself a conjunction, Conjunction Elimination can be applied to it to derive '~ J'.

Derive: K ∨ G

1	(~ J & W) & Y	Assumption
2	(N ∨ ~ B) & [~ J ⊃ (K ∨ G)]	Assumption
3	~ J & W	1 &E
4	~ J	3 &E

It is *incorrect* to continue this derivation as follows:

5	K ∨ G	2, 4 ⊃E	**MISTAKE!**

Again the mistake is in trying to apply a rule of inference to a component of a sentence, rather than to the entire sentence. Conditional Elimination licenses deriving **Q** from **P** and **P** ⊃ **Q**. Neither the sentence on line 2 nor the sentence on line 4 has '⊃' as the main connective. Hence Conditional Elimination cannot be applied to these sentences. However, the material conditional to which we want to apply the rule is a component of the sentence on line 2, and we can use Conditional Elimination if we first derive the conditional '~ J ⊃ (K ∨ G)' by Conjunction Elimination. Therefore the completed derivation is

Derive: K ∨ G

1	(~ J & W) & Y	Assumption
2	(N ∨ ~ B) & [~ J ⊃ (K ∨ G)]	Assumption
3	~ J & W	1 &E
4	~ J	3 &E
5	~ J ⊃ (K ∨ G)	2 &E
6	K ∨ G	4, 5 ⊃E

Similarly, it is *incorrect* to cite part of a subderivation.

Derive: ~ N

1	H ⊃ ~ N	Assumption	
2	(H ∨ G) & ~ M	Assumption	
3	~ N ≡ (G ∨ B)	Assumption	
4	H ∨ G	2 &E	
5	H	Assumption	
6	~ N	1, 5 ⊃E	
7	~ N ∨ H	6 ∨I	
8	G	Assumption	
9	G ∨ B	8 ∨I	
10	~ N	3, 9 ≡E	
11	~ N	4, 5–6, 8–10 ∨E	**MISTAKE!**

The entire subderivation must be cited; therefore the reference '5–6' on line 11 is a mistake. Line 7 can be eliminated. A proper derivation is

Derive: ~ N

1	H ⊃ ~ N	Assumption
2	(H ∨ G) & ~ M	Assumption
3	~ N ≡ (G ∨ B)	Assumption
4	H ∨ G	2 &E
5	H	Assumption
6	~ N	1, 5 ⊃E
7	G	Assumption
8	G ∨ B	7 ∨I
9	~ N	3, 8 ≡E
10	~ N	4, 5–6, 7–9 ∨E

If more than one line or subderivation is appealed to when applying a derivation rule, the relevant sentences or subderivations can occur in any order. For instance, on line 10 of the last derivation, appeal is made to an earlier line and to two subderivations. It would also be correct if the sentence on the line cited occurred between the subderivations or after them, or if the subderivations were reversed in order. Here is an example that illustrates this flexibility in order:

Derive: ~ N

```
1  | H ⊃ ~ N                 Assumption
2  | (H ∨ G) & ~ M           Assumption
3  | ~ N ≡ (G ∨ B)           Assumption
   |------------
4  |  | G                    Assumption
   |  |------
5  |  | G ∨ B                4 ∨I
6  |  | ~ N                  3, 5 ≡E
7  |  | H                    Assumption
   |  |------
8  |  | ~ N                  1, 7 ⊃E
9  | H ∨ G                   2 &E
10 | ~ N                     9, 7–8, 4–6 ∨E
```

It is essential that the lines and subderivations cited in justifying a sentence be accessible. In a derivation a sentence or subderivation is *accessible* at line **n**; that is, it can be appealed to when justifying a sentence on line **n**, if and only if that sentence or subderivation does not lie within the scope of an assumption that has been discharged prior to line **n**. In other words, every scope line to the left of a cited sentence or subderivation must be to the left of the sentence on line **n**. Some examples will make this clear. Consider the derivation

Derive: ~ U ⊃ ~ S

```
1 | ~ U ⊃ ~ W                Assumption
2 | ~ W ⊃ ~ S                Assumption
  |------------
3 |  | ~ U                   Assumption
  |  |------
4 |  | ~ W                   1, 3 ⊃E
5 |  | ~ S                   2, 4 ⊃E
6 | ~ U ⊃ ~ S                3–5 ⊃I
```

Line 4 cites lines 1 and 3, which are both accessible at line 4. The sentences on lines 1 and 3 do not lie within the scope of an assumption that has been discharged prior to line 4. (Neither the sentence on line 1 nor the sentence on line 3 has a scope line to its left that is not also to the left of the sentence on line 4.) Similarly line 5 cites lines 2 and 4, which are both accessible at line 5. Line 6 cites the subderivation from lines 3–5. This subderivation is accessible at line 6 because the subderivation does not lie within the scope of an assumption that has been discharged prior to line 6. (We consider the scope line of a subderivation to be part of that subderivation. Hence the scope line of a subderivation does not count as being to the left of that subderivation. In the present case every scope line to the left of the subderivation cited—there is only one—is also to the left of the sentence on line 6.)

Once an assumption has been discharged, none of the lines or subderivations *within* that subderivation is accessible for justifying sentences on later lines. In the example, once the assumption on line 3 is discharged, none of the lines within the scope of the assumption is accessible. The reason for this is that the sentences of the subderivation have been derived under the assumption of the subderivation, and this assumption has been discharged. There is no guarantee that sentences derived on the basis of an assumption can be derived without it. For instance, it is *incorrect* to continue the derivation as follows:

1	~ U ⊃ ~ W	Assumption	
2	~ W ⊃ ~ S	Assumption	
3	~ U	Assumption	
4	~ W	1, 3 ⊃E	
5	~ S	2, 4 ⊃E	
6	~ U ⊃ ~ S	3–5 ⊃I	
7	~ S	2, 4 ⊃E	**MISTAKE!**

The mistake at line 7 is citing line 4, which is not accessible at line 7. The sentence on line 4 does lie within the scope of an assumption (line 3) that has been discharged before line 7. (There is a scope line to the left of the sentence on line 4 that does not appear to the left of the sentence on line 7.)

Here is another example that illustrates mistakes in citing lines and subderivations that are not accessible:

1	(B ⊃ A) & C	Assumption	
2	(A ⊃ C) ⊃ B	Assumption	
3	A	Assumption	
4	A	Assumption	
5	C	1 & E	
6	A ⊃ C	4–5 ⊃I	
7	B	2, 6 ⊃E	
8	C	Assumption	
9	B	Assumption	
10	B ⊃ A	1 &E	
11	A	9, 10 ⊃E	
12	A ≡ B	3–7, 9–11 ≡I	
13	B	7 R	**MISTAKE!**
14	A	12, 13 ≡E	
15	A ≡ C	4–5, 8–14 ≡I	**MISTAKE!**

Line 13 contains a mistake because line 7, which is cited in justifying the entry of 'B' at line 13, is not accessible at line 13. The sentence on line 7 lies within the scope of an assumption (line 3) that has been discharged prior to line 13. The mistake on line 15 is citing the subderivation from lines 4–5. That subderivation lies within the scope of an assumption (line 3) that has been discharged prior to line 15. (There is a scope line to the left of that subderivation that ends before line 15—it ends at line 7.)

Citing a subderivation that occurs much earlier in the derivation is allowable as long as the subderivation is accessible. For instance, in the example the justification on line 12 is correct. Neither the subderivation from lines 3–7 nor the subderivation from lines 9–11 lies within the scope of an assumption that has been discharged prior to line 12. Scope lines show graphically which sentences are derived under which assumptions. Consequently scope lines give us a handy way of checking which lines and subderivations can be properly cited in justifications for derived sentences.

The Derivation Rules of SD

Reiteration (R)

```
  | P
  |
▷ | P
```

Conjunction Introduction (&I)

```
  | P
  |
  | Q
  |
▷ | P & Q
```

Conjunction Elimination (&E)

```
  | P & Q              | P & Q
  |          or        |
▷ | P                ▷ | Q
```

Disjunction Introduction (∨I)

```
  | P                  | P
  |          or        |
▷ | P ∨ Q            ▷ | Q ∨ P
```

Disjunction Elimination (∨E)

```
  | P ∨ Q
  |  | P
  |  |---
  |  | R
  |  | Q
  |  |---
  |  | R
▷ | R
```

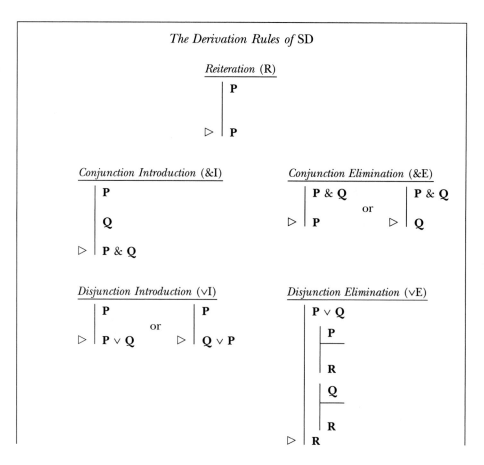

Negation Introduction (~ I)

	P (assumption)
	Q
	~ **Q**
▷	~ **P**

Negation Elimination (~ E)

	~ **P** (assumption)
	Q
	~ **Q**
▷	**P**

Conditional Introduction (⊃I)

	P (assumption)
	Q
▷	**P** ⊃ **Q**

Conditional Elimination (⊃E)

	P ⊃ **Q**
	P
▷	**Q**

Biconditional Introduction (≡I)

	P (assumption)
	Q
	Q (assumption)
	P
▷	**P** ≡ **Q**

Biconditional Elimination (≡E)

	P ≡ **Q**			**P** ≡ **Q**
	P	or		**Q**
▷	**Q**		▷	**P**

5.2E EXERCISES

1. Complete each of the following derivations by entering the appropriate justifications.

a. Derive: (A & C) ∨ (B & C)

1	(A ∨ B) & C
2	A ∨ B
3	C
4	A (assumption)
5	A & C
6	(A & C) ∨ (B & C)
7	B (assumption)
8	B & C
9	(A & C) ∨ (B & C)
10	(A & C) ∨ (B & C)

*b. Derive: A ⊃ (B ⊃ C)

1	(A & B) ⊃ C
2	A (assumption)
3	B (assumption)
4	A & B
5	C
6	B ⊃ C
7	A ⊃ (B ⊃ C)

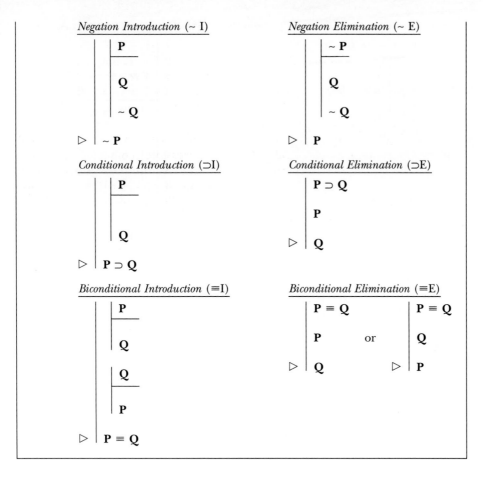

c. Derive: ~ B

```
 1 | B ⊃ (A & ~ B)
   |---------------
 2 | | B
   | |-------------
 3 | | A & ~ B
 4 | | ~ B
 5 | | B
 6 | ~ B
```

*d. Derive: A ⊃ B

```
 1 | (A & ~ B) ⊃ (~ B & C)
 2 | C ⊃ ~ A
   |-----------------------
 3 | | A
   | |---------------------
 4 | | | ~ B
   | | |-------------------
 5 | | | A & ~ B
 6 | | | ~ B & C
 7 | | | C
 8 | | | ~ A
 9 | | | A
10 | | B
11 | A ⊃ B
```

e. Derive: C ⊃ (~ A & B)

```
 1 | ~ D
 2 | C ⊃ (A ≡ B)
 3 | (D ∨ B) ⊃ ~ A
 4 | (A ≡ B) ⊃ (D & E)
 5 | ~ B ⊃ D
   |-------------------
 6 | | C
   | |-----------------
 7 | | A ≡ B
 8 | | D & E
 9 | | D
10 | | D ∨ B
11 | | ~ A
12 | | | ~ B
   | | |---------------
13 | | | D
14 | | | ~ D
15 | | B
16 | | ~ A & B
17 | C ⊃ (~ A & B)
```

*f. Derive: (A & ~ B) ∨ A

```
 1 | C ⊃ B
 2 | (~ C ⊃ A) ∨ E
 3 | F & ~ E
 4 | B ⊃ (A & ~ B)
   |---------------
 5 | | ~ C ⊃ A
   | |-------------
 6 | | | C
   | | |-----------
 7 | | | B
 8 | | | A & ~ B
 9 | | | ~ B
10 | | ~ C
11 | | A
12 | | E
   | |-------------
13 | | | ~ A
   | | |-----------
14 | | | E
15 | | | ~ E
16 | | A
17 | A
18 | (A & ~ B) ∨ A
```

g. Derive: A ≡ B

```
 1 | ~ A & ~ B
   |-----------
 2 | | A
   | |---------
 3 | | | ~ B
   | | |-------
 4 | | | ~ A
 5 | | | A
 6 | | B
 7 | | B
   | |---------
 8 | | | ~ A
   | | |-------
 9 | | | B
10 | | | ~ B
11 | | A
12 | A ≡ B
```

*h. Derive: $A \equiv (B \vee C)$

1	$(A \equiv B) \& (A \equiv C)$
2	$\quad A$
3	$\quad A \equiv B$
4	$\quad B$
5	$\quad B \vee C$
6	$\quad B \vee C$
7	$\qquad B$
8	$\qquad A \equiv B$
9	$\qquad A$
10	$\qquad C$
11	$\qquad A \equiv C$
12	$\qquad A$
13	$\quad A$
14	$A \equiv (B \vee C)$

2. For each of the following, find the *mistakes* in the application of the rules.

a. Derive: $\sim D$

1	$\sim\sim P \supset (W \& \sim D)$	Assumption
2	$\sim P$	Assumption
3	$W \& \sim D$	1, 2 $\supset$E
4	$\sim D$	3 &E

*b. Derive: B

1	$P \supset (S \equiv (A \& B))$	Assumption
2	$P \& S$	Assumption
3	S	2 &E
4	$A \& B$	1, 3 $\equiv$E
5	B	4 &E

c. Derive: H & A

1	$B \supset A$	Assumption
2	H	Assumption
3	$\quad B$	Assumption
4	$\quad A$	1, 3 $\supset$E
5	$\quad A \& A$	4, 4 &I
6	$B \supset (A \& A)$	3–5 $\supset$I
7	$H \& A$	2, 4 &I

*d. Derive: M

1	$(G \supset \sim\sim M) \;\&\; G$	Assumption
2	G	1 &E
3	$G \supset \sim\sim M$	1 &E
4	$\sim\sim M$	2, 3 $\supset$E
5	M	4 $\sim$ E

e. Derive: X

1	$(K \;\&\; H) \supset L$	Assumption
2	$X \equiv L$	Assumption
3	$\quad K \;\&\; H$	Assumption
4	$\quad L$	1, 3 $\supset$E
5	L	4 R
6	X	2, 5 $\equiv$E

*f. Derive: K

1	$S \vee J$	Assumption
2	$\quad K$	Assumption
3	$\quad\quad S$	Assumption
4	$\quad\quad K$	2 R
5	$\quad\quad J$	Assumption
6	$\quad\quad K$	2 R
7	K	1, 3–4, 5–6 $\vee$E

5.3 BASIC CONCEPTS OF *SD*

A *derivation in SD* is a series of sentences of *SL* in which each sentence either is taken as an assumption with an indication of its scope or is justified by one of the rules of *SD*. As the previous examples illustrate, our standard derivation format is to number each line on which a sentence occurs and to state the justification for that sentence on the right-hand side of the derivation. All primary assumptions are put at the beginning of a derivation, and one auxiliary assumption is put at the beginning of each subderivation. Horizontal lines are drawn below assumptions in a derivation as a way to mark off the assumptions more clearly. The main vertical derivation line serves as a scope line for all primary assumptions in a derivation, and the vertical subderivation lines serve as scope lines for auxiliary assumptions in a derivation. Scope lines show immediately which sentences and subderivations are in the scope of which assumptions. A sentence or subderivation is *in the scope of an assumption* if the scope line immediately to the left of the assumption is also to the left of the sentence or subderivation.

The concept of derivability is defined as follows:

> A sentence **P** of *SL* is *derivable in SD* from a set Γ of sentences of *SL* if and only if there is a derivation in *SD* in which all the primary assumptions are members of Γ and **P** occurs in the scope of only those assumptions.

The claim that **P** is derivable from Γ is often written using the single turnstile, '⊢':

$$\Gamma \vdash \mathbf{P}$$

We write that **P** is not derivable from Γ as

$$\Gamma \nvdash \mathbf{P}$$

Suppose we wish to show that 'D ∨ B' is derivable from {~ F ∨ D, F, J}, that is,

$$\{\sim F \vee D, F, J\} \vdash D \vee B$$

We begin by taking members of the set as the primary assumptions and then construct a derivation such that 'D ∨ B' occurs in the scope of only those assumptions. Here is such a derivation:

Derive: D ∨ B

```
 1  | ~ F ∨ D                Assumption
 2  | F                      Assumption
 3  | J                      Assumption
    |------
 4  |  | ~ F                 Assumption
    |  |-----
 5  |  |  | ~ D              Assumption
    |  |  |----
 6  |  |  | ~ F              4 R
 7  |  |  | F                2 R
 8  |  | D                   5–7 ~ E
 9  |  | D                   Assumption
    |  |-----
10  |  | D                   9 R
11  | D                      1, 4–8, 9–10 ∨E
12  | D ∨ B                  11 ∨I
```

Thus the sentence 'D ∨ B' is derivable from {~ F ∨ D, F, J}. Of course, there are many other derivations that demonstrate this claim equally well. Producing any one such derivation is sufficient to establish derivability.

Notice that, by the definition of derivability, every primary assumption must be a member of the set Γ, but not every member of the set Γ must be taken as a primary assumption. In the example the sentence 'J' was listed as a primary assumption but need not have been, for 'D ∨ B' can be derived from just the first two assumptions. Also, by the definition of derivability, the sentence to be derived must occur in the scope of only the primary assumptions. The following derivation would *not* demonstrate the previous derivability claim:

Derive: D ∨ B

1	∼ F ∨ D	Assumption
2	F	Assumption
3	J	Assumption
4	∼ F	Assumption
5	∼ D	Assumption
6	∼ F	4 R
7	F	2 R
8	D	5–7 ∼ E
9	D ∨ B	8 ∨I

Here 'D ∨ B' lies in the scope of '∼ F' (line 4), as well as in the scope of the primary assumptions, and therefore this derivation would not establish the derivability claim.

The definition for validity in *SD* is as follows:

> An argument of *SL* is *valid in SD* if and only if the conclusion of the argument is derivable in *SD* from the set consisting of the premises. An argument of *SL* is *invalid in SD* if and only if it is not valid in *SD*.

The argument

(∼ L ∨ K) ⊃ A
A ⊃ ∼ A
―――――――
L & ∼ K

is shown to be valid in *SD* by the following derivation:

Derive: L & ∼ K

1	(∼ L ∨ K) ⊃ A	Assumption
2	A ⊃ ∼ A	Assumption
3	∼ L	Assumption
4	∼ L ∨ K	3 ∨I
5	A	1, 4 ⊃E
6	∼ A	2, 5 ⊃E
7	L	3–6 ∼ E
8	K	Assumption
9	∼ L ∨ K	8 ∨I
10	A	1, 9 ⊃E
11	∼ A	2, 10 ⊃E
12	∼ K	8–11 ∼ I
13	L & ∼ K	7, 12 &I

A special case of deriving a sentence **P** from a set Γ of sentences arises when Γ is the empty set. The derivation shown below demonstrates that 'B ⊃ [C ⊃ (B & C)]' is derivable from the empty set.

Derive: B ⊃ [C ⊃ (B & C)]

1	B	Assumption
2	C	Assumption
3	B & C	1, 2 &I
4	C ⊃ (B & C)	2–3 ⊃I
5	B ⊃ [C ⊃ (B & C)]	1–4 ⊃I

There are no primary assumptions in this derivation, and every auxiliary assumption has been discharged. The sentence 'B ⊃ [C ⊃ (B & C)]' on the last line lies in the scope of only the primary assumptions (in this case none). Hence 'B ⊃ [C ⊃ (B & C)]' is derivable from the empty set.

A sentence **P** of *SL* is a *theorem in SD* if and only if **P** is derivable in *SD* from the empty set.

Thus the last derivation establishes that 'B ⊃ [C ⊃ (B & C)]' is a theorem in *SD*. Because a derivation of a theorem has no primary assumptions, a main derivation line can be omitted. However, our practice will be to draw a main derivation line in such derivations to show graphically that any assumptions that are made are auxiliary assumptions. The claim that a sentence **P** of *SL* is a theorem can be expressed as

⊢ **P**

Equivalence in *SD* is defined as follows:

Sentences **P** and **Q** of *SL* are *equivalent in SD* if and only if **Q** is derivable in *SD* from {**P**} and **P** is derivable in *SD* from {**Q**}.

The sentences '(G & S) ∨ N' and '(G ∨ N) & (S ∨ N)' are equivalent in *SD*. We can show this with two derivations. First, '(G & S) ∨ N' is taken as an assumption, and '(G ∨ N) & (S ∨ N)' is derived.

Derive: (G ∨ N) & (S ∨ N)

1	(G & S) ∨ N	Assumption
2	G & S	Assumption
3	G	2 &E
4	G ∨ N	3 ∨I
5	S	2 &E
6	S ∨ N	5 ∨I
7	(G ∨ N) & (S ∨ N)	4, 6 &I
8	N	Assumption
9	G ∨ N	8 ∨I
10	S ∨ N	8 ∨I
11	(G ∨ N) & (S ∨ N)	9, 10 &I
12	(G ∨ N) & (S ∨ N)	1, 2–7, 8–11 ∨E

Then the procedure is reversed, with '(G ∨ N) & (S ∨ N)' taken as an assumption and '(G & S) ∨ N' derived.

Derive: (G & S) ∨ N

1	(G ∨ N) & (S ∨ N)	Assumption
2	G ∨ N	1 &E
3	S ∨ N	1 &E
4	N	Assumption
5	(G & S) ∨ N	4 ∨I
6	G	Assumption
7	S	Assumption
8	G & S	6, 7 &I
9	(G & S) ∨ N	8 ∨I
10	(G & S) ∨ N	3, 7–9, 4–5 ∨E
11	(G & S) ∨ N	2, 6–10, 4–5 ∨E

Inconsistency in *SD* is defined as follows:

> A set Γ of sentences of *SL* is *inconsistent in SD* if and only if both a sentence **P** of *SL* and its negation ~ **P** are derivable in *SD* from Γ. A set Γ of sentences of *SL* is *consistent in SD* if and only if it is not inconsistent in *SD*.

So we can show that the set of sentences

{(M ∨ B) ⊃ B, A ⊃ M, A & ~ B}

is inconsistent in *SD* by constructing a derivation in which the members of the set are the primary assumptions and both a sentence and its negation are derived in the scope of only the primary assumptions. Here is such a derivation:

1	(M ∨ B) ⊃ B	Assumption
2	A ⊃ M	Assumption
3	A & ~ B	Assumption
4	~ B	3 &E
5	A	3 &E
6	M	2, 5 ⊃E
7	M ∨ B	6 ∨I
8	B	1, 7 ⊃E

In this derivation the sentence 'B' is derived in line 8 and its negation '~ B' is derived in line 4. Both these sentences are in the scope of only the primary assumptions; that is, both of these sentences occur immediately to the right of the main scope line. Hence the original set is inconsistent in *SD*.

If a set of sentences of *SL* is inconsistent in *SD*, any sentence of *SL* is derivable from the set. This is easy to see. Suppose that a set of sentences is inconsistent in *SL*. Then there must be a derivation in which all the primary assumptions are members of the set and a sentence **P** and its negation ~ **P** are derivable from them. Suppose that **P** occurs on line **i** of this derivation and ~ **P** occurs on line **j**. Continue the derivation from a later line **n**. Now, let **Q** be any sentence of *SL*. We can proceed to derive **Q** from the set as follows:

i	**P**	
j	~ **P**	
n	~ **Q**	Assumption
n + 1	**P**	**i** R
n + 2	~ **P**	**j** R
n + 3	**Q**	**n** − **n** + 2 ~ E

In other words, if both **P** and ~ **P** can be derived from a set of sentences, then any sentence of *SL* can be derived in merely four more steps! This is one reason a rational person would want to avoid beliefs which form a set that is inconsistent in *SD*. Actions cannot be guided well by a set of beliefs from which every possible belief follows.

The syntactic concepts of the system of *SD* parallel the semantic concepts introduced in Chapter 3, as we prove in Exercise 20 in Section 5.4E and in Chapter 6. That is,

1. A sentence **P** is derivable in *SD* from a set Γ of sentences of *SL* if and only if **P** is truth-functionally entailed by Γ.
2. An argument of *SL* is valid in *SD* if and only if the argument is truth-functionally valid.
3. A sentence **P** of *SL* is a theorem in *SD* if and only if P is truth-functionally true.

4. Sentences **P** and **Q** of *SL* are equivalent in *SD* if and only if **P** and **Q** are truth-functionally equivalent.
5. A set Γ of sentences of *SL* is inconsistent in *SD* if and only if Γ is truth-functionally inconsistent.

Although the syntactic system *SD* has been developed with an eye to semantics, it is important to remember that *SD* as a syntactic system is independent of semantics. For example, constructing a truth-table showing that 'A ∨ ~ A' is a truth-functional truth does not by itself show that 'A ∨ ~ A' is a theorem in *SD*.

5.4 STRATEGIES FOR CONSTRUCTING DERIVATIONS IN *SD*

An advantage of a natural deduction system such as *SD* is that we can show in a series of very natural steps that one sentence follows from other sentences. In this section we develop a technique for constructing derivations. If we cannot construct an appropriate derivation, it does not mean that no such derivation exists. It may be that an appropriate derivation can be constructed but that we have not been ingenious enough to find it.

The first step in constructing derivations is easy: Write the sentence to be derived, the *goal sentence,* well below any primary assumptions. How should we proceed? A very tempting, though unreliable, procedure is to apply the derivation rules rather randomly to the assumptions and other derived sentences in the hope that the goal sentence eventually will emerge. This approach may work, but it often leads to mindless application of the derivation rules and eventual frustration if the goal sentence is not derived. A better approach to constructing derivations is called *goal analysis.*

Goal analysis is a technique for generating a connected series of subgoals that guide the construction of derivations. Roughly speaking, goal analysis is a process that works backward from the goal sentence of a derivation to its assumptions. More precisely, goal analysis, when properly done, utilizes information about the goal sentence of a derivation, the accessible sentences on earlier lines of a derivation, and the rules of *SL* to select an appropriate series of subgoals to facilitate the complete construction of a derivation. Goal analysis is not a mechanical procedure for generating derivations but rather a system of useful guidelines. Goal analysis proceeds through a three-step cycle:

1. *Analyze the goal sentence.* Determine what kind of sentence it is. If it is not an atomic sentence, what is its main sentential connective? What kind of component sentences does it have?
2. *Analyze accessible sentences on earlier lines.* Determine what kinds of sentences they are. What are their main sentential connectives? Do they have sentential components similar to the components of the goal sentence? If the goal sentence can be derived immediately, derive it. Otherwise select a subgoal sentence.

3. *Enter a subgoal sentence.* A subgoal sentence is a sentence such that, if it were derived from accessible sentences on earlier lines in the derivation, then it would lead directly to a derivation of the goal sentence. Select either an introduction rule subgoal or an elimination rule subgoal (discussed next). Enter this subgoal into the derivation under construction, and regard that subgoal sentence as the new goal sentence. Now return to step 1 and repeat the process.

SUBGOALS FROM THE INTRODUCTION RULES

If the goal sentence has a main sentential connective, then consider entering a subgoal sentence that supports the application of the rule of *SD* that *introduces* that sentential connective.

If the goal sentence has the form **P** & **Q**, then consider entering the following subgoals:

Enter subgoal →	**P**	
Enter subgoal →	**Q**	
Goal sentence →	**P** & **Q**	—, — &I

Notice that these subgoals give us a new objective. We are no longer trying to derive **P** & **Q** but rather are aiming at deriving **P** and deriving **Q**. Once we have derived **P** and have derived **Q**, **P** & **Q** can be derived immediately by Conjunction Introduction. This is indicated by entering the abbreviated name, '&I', as part of the justification for **P** & **Q**. The underlined spaces in the justification will be filled in eventually with line numbers, when the rest of the derivation is completed.

If the goal sentence has the form **P** ∨ **Q**, then consider entering the following subgoal:

Enter subgoal →	**P**	
Goal sentence →	**P** ∨ **Q**	— ∨I

Similarly **Q** can be taken as the subgoal sentence for a later application of Disjunction Introduction.

If the goal sentence has the form **P** ⊃ **Q**, then consider entering the following subderivation and subgoal:

Enter assumption →	| **P**	Assumption
Enter subgoal →	| **Q**	
Goal sentence →	**P** ⊃ **Q**	—–— ⊃I

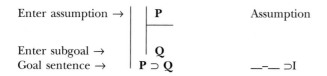

If the goal sentence has the form **P** ≡ **Q**, then consider entering the following subderivations and subgoals:

Enter assumption →	**P**	Assumption
Enter subgoal →	**Q**	
Enter assumption →	**Q**	Assumption
Enter subgoal →	**P**	
Goal sentence →	**P** ≡ **Q**	__–__, __–__ ≡I

If the goal sentence has the form ~ **P**, then consider entering the following subderivation:

Enter assumption →	**P**	Assumption
Subgoal? →	**Q**	
Subgoal? →	~ **Q**	
Goal sentence →	~ **P**	__–__ ~I

This introduction rule is less helpful than the others, for in this case we know only the form of the subgoals. We know we must derive some sentence **Q** and its negation. However, we are not given guidance about what the sentence **Q** is.

SUBGOALS FROM THE ELIMINATION RULES

If the goal sentence is a component of an accessible sentence on an earlier line or depends on removing a sentential connective in an accessible sentence on an earlier line, then consider entering a subgoal sentence that supports the application of the rule of *SD* that *eliminates* the relevant sentential connective.

If the goal sentence has the form **P**, and a sentential component of the form **P** & **Q** occurs in an earlier accessible sentence in the derivation, then consider entering the following subgoal:

Enter subgoal →	**P** & **Q**	
Goal sentence →	**P**	__ &E

A similar procedure applies if the goal sentence is the right conjunct of a conjunction.

If the goal sentence has the form **Q** and a sentential component of the form **P** ⊃ **Q** occurs in an earlier accessible sentence in the derivation, then consider entering the following subgoals:

Enter subgoal →	**P**	
Enter subgoal →	**P ⊃ Q**	
Goal sentence →	**Q**	—, — ⊃E

If the goal sentence has the form **Q** and a sentential component of the form **P ≡ Q** occurs in an earlier accessible sentence in the derivation, then consider entering the following subgoals:

Enter subgoal →	**P**	
Enter subgoal →	**P ≡ Q**	
Goal sentence →	**Q**	—, — ≡E

Because of the symmetry in the rule Biconditional Elimination, a similar approach is possible if **Q ≡ P** occurs as a sentential component rather than **P ≡ Q**.

If the goal sentence has the form **R**, and a sentential component of the form **P ∨ Q** occurs in an earlier accessible sentence in the derivation, then consider entering the following subderivations and subgoals:

Enter subgoal →	**P ∨ Q**	
Enter assumption →	**P**	Assumption
Enter subgoal →	**R**	
Enter assumption →	**Q**	Assumption
Enter subgoal →	**R**	
Goal sentence →	**R**	—, —–—, —–— ∨E

Finally, if the goal sentence has the form **P**, then consider entering the following subderivation:

Enter assumption →	**~ P**	Assumption
Subgoal? →	**Q**	
Subgoal? →	**~ Q**	
Goal sentence →	**P**	—–— ~E

Every goal sentence has the form **P**, and we can always take **~ P** as an assumption! In spite of the generality of Negation Elimination, this approach should be utilized only as a last resort when selecting subgoal sentences, for it hinders further goal analysis. We know we must derive some sentence **Q** and its negation, but we are not given guidance about which specific sentence **Q** to derive.

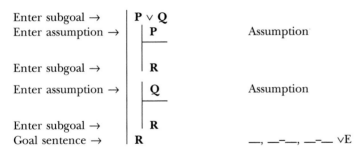

Whether an introduction rule subgoal or an elimination rule subgoal should be entered in a particular situation depends on what the analysis of the particular goal sentence and the accessible sentences on earlier lines reveals. A strength of the *SD* rules is that they suggest the conditions for their own application. That is, they suggest the kinds of subgoals to consider.

In addition, the use of goal analysis reduces the incidence of the common mistake of making random and ineffective auxiliary assumptions. Suppose we wish to construct a derivation for this problem:

Derive: (A & B) ⊃ C

1	A ⊃ C	Assumption
	(A & B) ⊃ C	

A beginner sometimes succumbs to the temptation to make many auxiliary assumptions hoping something will be helpful, as illustrated by this dubious start:

Derive: (A & B) ⊃ C

1	A ⊃ C	Assumption
2	A	Assumption?
3	B	Assumption?
4	C	Assumption?
	(A & B) ⊃ C	

The auxiliary assumptions on lines 2–4 are permissible, because any sentence of *SL* can be assumed, but these auxiliary assumptions are not aimed at deriving anything useful. Eventually we must abandon aimless auxiliary assumptions like these since they are not rooted in a plan that will lead to a goal or subgoal.

But now consider the problem in terms of goal analysis. We do need to make some auxiliary assumption for this problem, but what assumption should we make? Because our goal sentence, '(A & B) ⊃ C', is a conditional, we will derive it using the rule of Conditional Introduction. Realizing this, we know that we should assume the *antecedent* of the conditional and then derive its *consequent*.

Derive: (A & B) ⊃ C

1	A ⊃ C	Assumption
2	A & B	Assumption
	C	
	(A & B) ⊃ C	2–__ ⊃I

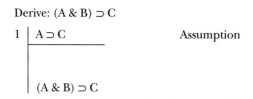

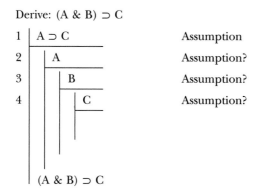

This illustrates an important principle in constructing derivations. Whenever we make an auxiliary assumption, it should be part of a subderivation, and we should know the purpose of the subderivation—that is, we should know the rule that will cite the subderivation. In this case we decided that Conditional Introduction is the rule that will cite the subderivation, and we listed it at the bottom in our derivation under construction. Setting up such a *subderivation framework* is an important technique in constructing derivations by goal analysis. When setting up a subderivation framework, we list the auxiliary assumption of the subderivation and justify it with the word 'Assumption', draw a subderivation scope line, and enter the last sentence in the subderivation at the bottom of the subderivation (if that sentence is known). We also list the sentence to be derived (our goal or subgoal) after the subderivation and enter the rule that will be used to justify the goal. In our current example the auxiliary assumption, 'A & B', is entered on line 2; then the scope line for the subderivation is drawn, and the last sentence of the subderivation, 'C', is listed. The sentence that we hope to derive by means of the subderivation, '(A & B) ⊃ C', is listed along with its justification, '2–__ ⊃I' (we do not yet know how long the subderivation will be—hence the blank). Drawing the subderivation structure and entering the information including the justification is important because it shows the purpose of the subderivation.

It is often not difficult to fill in the rest of the derivation once a subderivation framework has been set up. The framework guides us. The last sentence of the subderivation, in this case 'C', becomes a new subgoal. Here is the completed derivation for our problem:

Derive: (A & B) ⊃ C

1	A ⊃ C		Assumption
2		A & B	Assumption
3		A	2 &E
4		C	1, 3 ⊃E
5	(A & B) ⊃ C		2–4 ⊃I

Setting up subderivation frameworks forces us to pick auxiliary assumptions that will be useful in deriving specific sentences. It also assists in keeping the construction of the derivation on track. We should never be baffled by our auxiliary assumptions; we need only read the information off the subderivation framework. Of course, in the case of some rules, such as Disjunction Elimination and Biconditional Introduction, we need to set up *two* subderivation frameworks because the application of these rules requires citing two (usually different) subderivations.

Here are some more examples of how goal analysis works. Consider the argument

$\sim N$

$(\sim N \supset L) \mathbin{\&} (D \equiv \sim N)$

$(L \vee A) \mathbin{\&} D$

Our ultimate goal is to derive the conclusion of the argument. So we write 'Derive: (L ∨ A) & D' and then list the premises of the argument as assumptions. Since we know what the last line of the derivation must be, we enter it farther down the page, leaving as much room as we think necessary to complete the derivation.

Derive: $(L \vee A) \mathbin{\&} D$

1	$\sim N$	Assumption
2	$(\sim N \supset L) \mathbin{\&} (D \equiv \sim N)$	Assumption
	$(L \vee A) \mathbin{\&} D$	

Analysis of the goal sentence '(L ∨ A) & D' and the assumptions shows that the goal sentence is not a component of any of the assumptions and cannot be derived immediately. A subgoal should be selected. Because the main connective of this goal sentence is '&', the rule Conjunction Introduction indicates the proper subgoals. After each of the conjuncts is entered into the derivation as a subgoal, the abbreviated rule name '&I' is also entered along with two underlined spaces indicating that line numbers should be filled in later.

Derive: $(L \vee A) \mathbin{\&} D$

1	$\sim N$	Assumption
2	$(\sim N \supset L) \mathbin{\&} (D \equiv \sim N)$	Assumption
	$L \vee A$	
	D	
	$(L \vee A) \mathbin{\&} D$	—, — &I

The two conjuncts 'L ∨ A' and 'D' become our new goal sentences. We know that once we have derived them we can derive our original goal sentence '(L ∨ A) & D' in one step by Conjunction Introduction. 'D' occurs as one of the components of one of the assumptions. Specifically 'D' occurs in 'D ≡ ~ N'. Hence the sentential connective '≡' needs to be eliminated, which suggests the rule Biconditional Elimination. To apply the rule Biconditional Elimination, we need to set up two new subgoals. One of the subgoals is the sentence 'D ≡ ~ N', and the other is the sentence '~ N'. If we can derive both of these subgoals, then 'D' can be obtained immediately by Biconditional Elimination. Because '~ N' already occurs as an assumption, we need to enter only the subgoal 'D ≡ ~ N'.

Derive: (L ∨ A) & D

1	~ N	Assumption
2	(~ N ⊃ L) & (D ≡ ~ N)	Assumption
	D ≡ ~ N	
	L ∨ A	
	D	1, __ ≡E
	(L ∨ A) & D	__, __ &I

'D ≡ ~ N' is derived immediately from line 2 by Conjunction Elimination. But we are not finished with the derivation, for we still must derive 'L ∨ A'. This sentence cannot be derived immediately from the assumptions. However, its main connective, '∨', indicates that Disjunction Introduction is the rule to consider. We can take either 'L' or 'A' as the subgoal sentence; but because the assumptions do not contain any occurrence of 'A', it is reasonable to take 'L' as the subgoal sentence.

Derive: (L ∨ A) & D

1	~ N	Assumption
2	(~ N ⊃ L) & (D ≡ ~ N)	Assumption
	L	
	D ≡ ~ N	2 &E
	L ∨ A	__ ∨I
	D	1, __ ≡E
	(L ∨ A) & D	__, __ &I

'L' becomes our new goal sentence. 'L' occurs as a component of '~ N ⊃ L' in line 2. Hence '⊃' is the connective to eliminate, and Conditional Elimination is the rule to use. If we take '~ N' and '~ N ⊃ L' as subgoals, then we can derive

'L' by Conditional Elimination. '~ N' already occurs as an assumption on line 1, so we need to take only '~ N ⊃ L' as a new subgoal.

Derive: (L ∨ A) & D

1	~ N	Assumption
2	(~ N ⊃ L) & (D ≡ ~ N)	Assumption
	~ N ⊃ L	
	L	1, — ⊃E
	D ≡ ~ N	2 &E
	L ∨ A	— ∨I
	D	1, — ≡E
	(L ∨ A) & D	—, — &I

'~ N ⊃ L' becomes our new goal sentence. This sentence is a component of the assumption on line 2 and can be derived immediately using the rule Conjunction Elimination. We do this and follow the trail of our subgoals down the derivation, filling in the line numbers as we go.

Derive: (L ∨ A) & D

1	~ N	Assumption
2	(~ N ⊃ L) & (D ≡ ~ N)	Assumption
3	~ N ⊃ L	2 &E
4	L	1, 3 ⊃E
5	D ≡ ~ N	2 &E
6	L ∨ A	4 ∨I
7	D	1, 5 ≡E
8	(L ∨ A) & D	6, 7 &I

Suppose we wish to construct a derivation to show that the following argument is valid in *SD*:

~ L ≡ [X & (~ S ∨ B)]

(E & C) ⊃ ~ L

(E & R) & C

X & (~ S ∨ B)

We begin the derivation thus:

Derive: X & (~ S ∨ B)

1	~ L ≡ [X &(~ S ∨ B)]	Assumption
2	(E & C) ⊃ ~ L	Assumption
3	(E & R) & C	Assumption
	X &(~ S ∨ B)	

The goal sentence, 'X &(~ S ∨ B)', is a conjunction; this suggests using the rule Conjunction Introduction. However, a glance at the assumptions reveals that the goal sentence is a component of a biconditional on line 1. Thus a more promising strategy in this case is to use Biconditional Elimination to derive the conjunction. We can use Biconditional Elimination if '~ L' can be derived. Thus '~ L' is entered as a subgoal.

Derive: X & (~ S ∨ B)

1	~ L ≡ [X &(~ S ∨ B)]	Assumption
2	(E & C) ⊃ ~ L	Assumption
3	(E & R) & C	Assumption
	~ L	
	X &(~ S ∨ B)	1, __ ≡E

'~ L' is a component of the second assumption and can be obtained by using Conditional Elimination if 'E & C' can be derived. 'E & C' becomes our next subgoal.

Derive: X & (~ S ∨ B)

1	~ L ≡ [X &(~ S ∨ B)]	Assumption
2	(E & C) ⊃ ~ L	Assumption
3	(E & R) & C	Assumption
	E & C	
	~ L	2, __ ⊃E
	X & (~ S ∨ B)	1, __ ≡E

Our current goal sentence is the conjunction 'E & C'. This conjunction is a component of the second assumption, but we are using that assumption, along with 'E & C', to derive '~ L'. Since 'E & C' does not occur as a component of any other assumption, using Conjunction Introduction to derive this goal sentence is a good strategy. Hence 'E' and 'C' should be entered as subgoals.

Derive: X & (~ S ∨ B)

1	~ L ≡ [X &(~ S ∨ B)]	Assumption
2	(E & C) ⊃ ~ L	Assumption
3	(E & R) & C	Assumption
	E	
	C	
	E & C	__, __ &I
	~ L	2, __ ⊃E
	X & (~ S ∨ B)	1, __ ≡E

Deriving 'E' and deriving 'C' are the current goals, and they can be accomplished easily by using the rule Conjunction Elimination.

Derive: X & (~ S ∨ B)

1	~ L ≡ [X &(~ S ∨ B)]	Assumption
2	(E & C) ⊃ ~ L	Assumption
3	(E & R) & C	Assumption
4	E & R	3 &E
5	E	4 &E
6	C	3 &E
7	E & C	5, 6 &I
8	~ L	2, 7 ⊃E
9	X &(~ S ∨ B)	1, 8 ≡E

Goal analysis is helpful in constructing subderivations in that it guides the choice of assumptions. Suppose we wish to show the following:

⊢ (U & Y) ⊃ [L ⊃ (U & L)]

To prove that '(U & Y) ⊃ [L ⊃ (U & L)]' is a theorem, we must derive it from the empty set. We enter the sentence at the bottom, leaving plenty of room to fill in the derivation above it.

Derive: (U & Y) ⊃ [L ⊃ (U & L)]

	(U & Y) ⊃ [L ⊃ (U & L)]	

As our goal is a conditional sentence, using Conditional Introduction is a good strategy. We thus construct a subderivation that has as its assumption the antecedent of the conditional and as its last line the consequent of the conditional. If the consequent can be derived within the subderivation, then the subderivation can be terminated, and the conditional can be derived using Conditional Introduction.

Derive: (U & Y) ⊃ [L ⊃ (U & L)]

1	U & Y	Assumption
	L ⊃ (U & L)	
	(U & Y) ⊃ [L ⊃ (U & L)]	1–__ ⊃I

Hence our new goal is to derive 'L ⊃ (U & L)', which is itself a conditional. We should again consider using Conditional Introduction to derive it. We assume the antecedent of the conditional, and the derivation of its consequent becomes our new goal. If the consequent can be derived, then Conditional Introduction yields the desired conditional.

Derive: (U & Y) ⊃ [L ⊃ (U & L)]

1	U & Y	Assumption
2	L	Assumption
	U & L	
	L ⊃ (U & L)	2–__ ⊃I
	(U & Y) ⊃ [L ⊃ (U & L)]	1–__ ⊃I

Our current goal is to derive 'U & L', which is straightforward, given the assumptions. The complete derivation, with the line numbers properly filled in, is

Derive: (U & Y) ⊃ [L ⊃ (U & L)]

1	U & Y	Assumption
2	L	Assumption
3	U	1 &E
4	U & L	3, 2 &I
5	L ⊃ (U & L)	2–4 ⊃I
6	(U & Y) ⊃ [L ⊃ (U & L)]	1–5 ⊃I

All the assumptions have been discharged, and now we have a derivation of the theorem.

Remember that when we use Conditional Introduction the sentence we derive is a conditional whose antecedent is the sentence we assume. For example, if the goal sentence is of the form (**P** ⊃ **Q**) ⊃ **R**, we assume **P** ⊃ **Q**, not **P**, and try to derive **R**.

As another example, suppose we wish to show that

⊢ [(J ⊃ [(J ∨ B) ⊃ K]) & J] ⊃ K

Our ultimate goal is to derive this sentence. Since our goal sentence is a conditional, we can plan to use Conditional Introduction in deriving it. The proper assumption is the antecedent of this conditional, and the derivation of the consequent of the conditional becomes our new goal.

Derive: [(J ⊃ [(J ∨ B) ⊃ K]) & J] ⊃ K

1	(J ⊃ [(J ∨ B) ⊃ K]) & J	Assumption
	K	
	[(J ⊃ [(J ∨ B) ⊃ K]) & J] ⊃ K	1–__ ⊃I

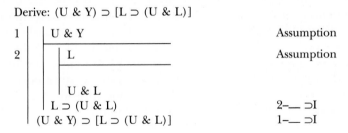

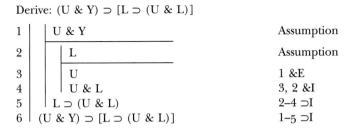

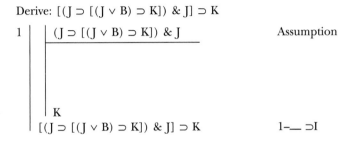

Notice that we do *not* take 'J' as the assumption, although 'J' is an antecedent of a conditional within the sentence. Nor do we take 'J ∨ B' as an assumption, although it, too, is an antecedent of a conditional within the sentence. The reason is that, if we assume 'J' or 'J ∨ B', the use of Conditional Introduction to discharge the assumption will generate a conditional whose antecedent is 'J' or 'J ∨ B'. But this would not accomplish our goal, for we want to derive a conditional whose antecedent is '(J ⊃ [J ∨ B) ⊃ K]) & J'. Our current goal sentence is 'K'. Because 'K' is atomic, the introduction rules will not provide reasonable subgoals. But 'K' does occur in the assumption in the component '(J ∨ B) ⊃ K'. Therefore we need to eliminate the '⊃', and Conditional Elimination indicates the subgoals 'J ∨ B' and '(J ∨ B) ⊃ K'.

Derive: [(J ⊃ [(J ∨ B) ⊃ K]) & J] ⊃ K

1	(J ⊃ [(J ∨ B) ⊃ K]) & J	Assumption
	(J ∨ B) ⊃ K	
	J ∨ B	
	K	—, — ⊃E
	[(J ⊃ [(J ∨ B) ⊃ K]) & J] ⊃ K	1–— ⊃I

'J ∨ B' is one of the new goal sentences. Disjunction Introduction suggests that either 'J' or 'B' be taken as a subgoal to introduce the '∨'. Because 'J' is easily derived from line 1 and 'B' is not, 'J' makes the better subgoal.

Derive: [(J ⊃ [(J ∨ B) ⊃ K]) & J] ⊃ K

1	(J ⊃ [(J ∨ B) ⊃ K]) & J	Assumption
	J	
	(J ∨ B) ⊃ K	
	J ∨ B	— ∨I
	K	—, — ⊃E
	[(J ⊃ [(J ∨ B) ⊃ K]) & J] ⊃ K	1–— ⊃I

The goal sentences are now 'J', which is derivable immediately from line 1 by Conjunction Elimination, and '(J ∨ B) ⊃ K'. This latter goal sentence is a component of 'J ⊃ [(J ∨ B) ⊃ K]' that occurs in the first assumption. Thus 'J', which we already have, and 'J ⊃ [(J ∨ B) ⊃ K]' become the new subgoals. When 'J ⊃ [(J ∨ B) ⊃ K]' is entered as a subgoal, the derivation can be completed immediately, as 'J ⊃ [(J ∨ B) ⊃ K]' can be obtained from line 1 by Conjunction Elimination.

Derive: [(J ⊃ [(J ∨ B) ⊃ K]) & J] ⊃ K

1	(J ⊃ [(J ∨ B) ⊃ K]) & J	Assumption
2	J ⊃ [(J ∨ B) ⊃ K]	1 &E
3	J	1 &E
4	(J ∨ B) ⊃ K	2, 3 ⊃E
5	J ∨ B	3 ∨I
6	K	4, 5 ⊃E
7	[(J ⊃ [(J ∨ B) ⊃ K]) & J] ⊃ K	1–6 ⊃I

In this next problem we note that the goal sentence, '~ (W & T)', is a negation and that this sentence does not appear as a component of the primary assumptions. So a good strategy is to try to derive the goal sentence by Negation Introduction.

Derive: ~ (W & T)

1	W ⊃ (H ⊃ ~ M)	Assumption
2	T ≡ ~ (H ⊃ ~ M)	Assumption
	~ (W & T)	

We proceed to set up a subderivation framework for application of Negation Introduction.

Derive: ~ (W & T)

1	W ⊃ (H ⊃ ~ M)	Assumption
2	T ≡ ~ (H ⊃ ~ M)	Assumption
3	W & T	Assumption
	~ (W & T)	3–___ ~ I

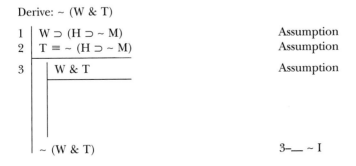

We enter part of the justification on the last line, but we do not have a subgoal sentence at the bottom of the subderivation. For the rule Negation Introduction, we need to derive a pair of sentences of the form **Q** and ~ **Q**. In this situation we should examine the accessible sentences for candidates for such a pair of sentences. '~ M' may tempt us briefly as a possibility, but there is no other sentence 'M' or "~ ~ M' available on any of the lines that would allow us to derive either 'M' and '~ M' as a pair or '~ M' and '~ ~ M' as a pair. We are seeking a sentence and its negation. In this case the pair 'H ⊃ ~ M' and '~ (H ⊃ ~ M)' presents itself as a good candidate, particularly since these are each the consequent of an accessible conditional and therefore are potentially derivable using Conditional Elimination. We enter these sentences as possible subgoals of the subderivation.

```
Derive: ~ (W & T)

1 | W ⊃ (H ⊃ ~ M)          Assumption
2 | T ≡ ~ (H ⊃ ~ M)        Assumption
  |-----------------
3 |  | W & T               Assumption
  |  |-----------
  |  |
  |  |
  |  | H ⊃ ~ M
  |  | ~ (H ⊃ ~ M)
  | ~(W & T)               3–__ ~ I
```

We can derive our subgoal '~ (H ⊃ ~ M)' from the sentence on line 2 if we can first derive 'T'. And we can derive 'H ⊃ ~ M' from the sentence on line 1 if we can first derive 'W'.

```
Derive: ~ (W & T)

1 | W ⊃ (H ⊃ ~ M)          Assumption
2 | T ≡ ~ (H ⊃ ~ M)        Assumption
  |-----------------
3 |  | W & T               Assumption
  |  |-----------
  |  | W
  |  | T
  |  | H ⊃ ~ M             1, __ ⊃E
  |  | ~ (H ⊃ ~ M)         2, __ ≡E
  | ~ (W & T)              3–__ ~ I
```

Our new subgoals, 'T' and 'W', are derived immediately from the sentence on line 3.

```
Derive: ~ (W & T)

1 | W ⊃ (H ⊃ ~ M)          Assumption
2 | T ≡ ~ (H ⊃ ~ M)        Assumption
  |-----------------
3 |  | W & T               Assumption
  |  |-----------
4 |  | W                   3 &E
5 |  | T                   3 &E
6 |  | H ⊃ ~ M             1, 4 ⊃E
7 |  | ~ (H ⊃ ~ M)         2, 5 ≡E
8 | ~ (W & T)              3–7 ~ I
```

Consider another example in which a negation rule plays a key role.

Derive: C

1	$\sim C \supset C$	Assumption
	C	

In the previous example the goal sentence was itself a negation for which goal analysis suggested using the rule Negation Introduction. In this case the goal sentence, 'C', is not a negation, but we can use a negation rule, Negation Elimination, to derive it. This is a good rule to consider when we are stumped as to how to derive a goal or subgoal. We begin by setting up the subderivation framework.

Derive: C

1	$\sim C \supset C$	Assumption
2	$\sim C$	Assumption
	C	2–__ $\sim$ E

We plan to use the rule Negation Elimination. What sentences will play the roles of **Q** and ~ **Q** in our subderivation? We are free to use the auxiliary assumption itself as one of these sentences. In fact, the auxiliary assumption often plays the role of **Q** or ~ **Q** in the subderivation. In this case the auxiliary assumption is a negation, and so we choose 'C' and '~ C' as the subgoal sentences in the subderivation. The derivation is then easy to complete.

Derive: C

1	$\sim C \supset C$	Assumption
2	$\sim C$	Assumption
3	C	1, 2 $\supset$E
4	$\sim C$	2 R
5	C	2–4 $\sim$ E

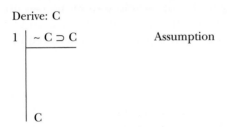

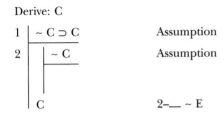

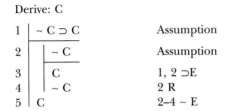

In general, if we do not know how to derive a goal or subgoal sentence, we can take the negation of the sentence as an auxiliary assumption and try to derive some sentence and its negation within the subderivation framework that is headed by this auxiliary assumption. Once we derive some sentence **Q** and its negation ~ **Q** within the subderivation, we can use Negation Elimination to derive the goal sentence. Any sentence and its negation will do, but sometimes finding such a pair of sentences requires some searching.

Here is another example. Suppose we wish to construct a derivation that shows

⊢ (~ A ∨ ~ B) ≡ ~ (A & B)

Since our goal sentence is a biconditional, using Biconditional Introduction is an appropriate strategy. This requires that two subderivations be constructed. One subderivation will have '~ A ∨ ~ B' as its assumption and '~ (A & B)' as its last sentence. The other will have '~ (A & B)' as its assumption and '~ A ∨ ~ B' as its last sentence.

Derive: (~ A ∨ ~ B) ≡ ~ (A & B)

1			~ A ∨ ~ B	Assumption
			~ (A & B)	
			~ (A & B)	Assumption
			~ A ∨ ~ B	
		(~ A ∨ ~ B) ≡ ~ (A & B)	1–___, ___–___ ≡I

Goal analysis can be applied to each subderivation. In the first subderivation a negation is our goal sentence. Thus it might seem that Negation Introduction is the obvious rule to use. However, it is a mistake to think that, whenever a goal sentence is a negation, Negation Introduction is the best rule to use. Since the assumption of the first subderivation is a disjunction, an alternative—and in this case slightly preferable—strategy is to use Disjunction Elimination to eliminate the '∨'. To follow this strategy, we set up two subderivations within the first subderivation.

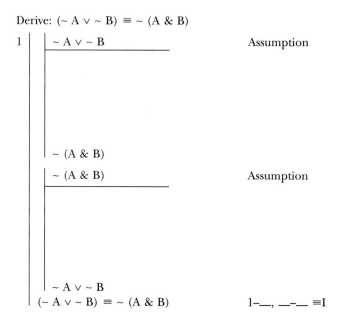

```
Derive: (~ A ∨ ~ B) ≡ ~ (A & B)

1  | | ~ A ∨ ~ B                  Assumption
   | |-------------
2  | | | ~ A                      Assumption
   | | |-----------
   | | |
   | | | ~ (A & B)
   | | | ~ B                      Assumption
   | | |-----------
   | | |
   | | | ~ (A & B)
   | | ~ (A & B)                  1, 2–__, __–__ ∨E
   | | ~ (A & B)                  Assumption
   | |-------------
   | |
   | | ~ A ∨ ~ B
   | (~ A ∨ ~ B) ≡ ~ (A & B)      1–__, __–__ ≡I
```

If each of the two subderivations within the first subderivation can be completed, then Disjunction Elimination can be used to complete the first subderivation. Our new goal is to derive '~ (A & B)' within each of these subderivations. Negation Introduction will allow us to derive a negation if we construct a subderivation with the unnegated sentence as the assumption and derive a sentence and its negation within the subderivation. Here is the derivation so far:

```
Derive: (~ A ∨ ~ B) ≡ ~ (A & B)

1  | | ~ A ∨ ~ B                  Assumption
   | |-------------
2  | | | ~ A                      Assumption
   | | |-----------
3  | | | | A & B                  Assumption
   | | | |---------
   | | | |
   | | | ~ (A & B)                3–__ ~ I
   | | | ~ B                      Assumption
   | | |-----------
   | | | | A & B                  Assumption
   | | | |---------
   | | | |
   | | | ~ (A & B)                __–__ ~ I
   | | ~ (A & B)                  1, 2–__, __–__ ∨E
   | | ~ (A & B)                  Assumption
   | |-------------
   | |
   | | ~ A ∨ ~ B
   | (~ A ∨ ~ B) ≡ ~ (A & B)      1–__, __–__ ≡I
```

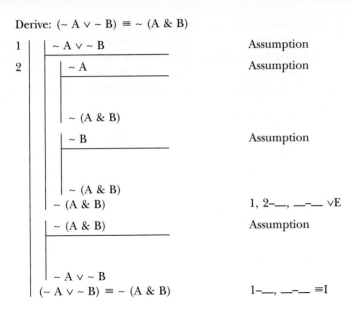

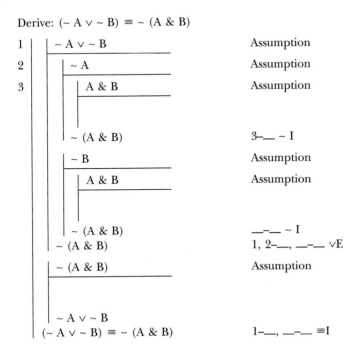

In using the negation rules, we must derive a sentence and its negation within a subderivation. It is generally wise to let a sentence that has been derived on an earlier line serve as one of these sentences, for such a sentence can easily be brought into the subderivation by Reiteration. If the sentence to be reiterated is a negation, so much the better. For example, to complete the first subderivation, we can obtain '~ A' by Reiteration from line 2 and then plan to derive 'A'. Here 'A' is easily derived by Conjunction Elimination on the assumption on line 3. Similarly, to complete the next subderivation, we can use Reiteration to obtain '~ B' and then derive 'B'.

```
Derive: (~ A ∨ ~ B) ≡ ~ (A & B)

 1  | | ~ A ∨ ~ B                Assumption
    | |----------
 2  | | | ~ A                    Assumption
    | | |------
 3  | | | | A & B                Assumption
    | | | |------
 4  | | | | A                    3 &E
 5  | | | | ~ A                  2 R
 6  | | | ~ (A & B)              3–5 ~ I
 7  | | | ~ B                    Assumption
    | | |------
 8  | | | | A & B                Assumption
    | | | |------
 9  | | | | B                    8 &E
10  | | | | ~ B                  7 R
11  | | | ~ (A & B)              8–10 ~ I
12  | | ~ (A & B)                1, 2–6, 7–11 ∨E
13  | | ~ (A & B)                Assumption
    | |----------
    | |
    | |
    | | ~ A ∨ ~ B
    | (~ A ∨ ~ B) ≡ ~ (A & B)    1–12, 13–__ ≡I
```

The second major subderivation is still unfinished. The goal sentence for it is a disjunction, '~ A ∨ ~ B'. A possible strategy is to use Disjunction Introduction. However, this requires that we derive one of the disjuncts of the goal sentence on a line by itself. In this case we can be sure that it is not possible since our derivation rules are truth-preserving and the assumption '~ (A & B)' can be true while '~ A' is false. Similarly '~ (A & B)' can be true while '~ B' is false. Therefore we reject using Disjunction Introduction as a strategy for obtaining the goal sentence. The only option left is to assume the negation of the goal sentence in a subderivation and to derive a sentence and its negation, so that the goal sentence can be derived by Negation Elimination. Here is the relevant portion of the derivation:

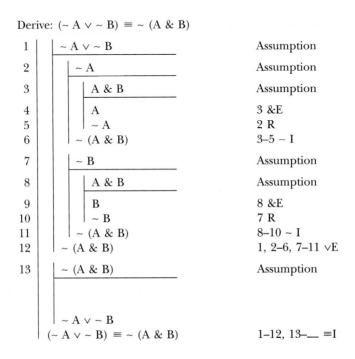

```
13  | | ~ (A & B)                      Assumption
    | |-----------
14  | | | ~ (~ A ∨ ~ B)                Assumption
    | | |-----------
    | | |
    | | |
    | | ~ A ∨ ~ B                      14–__ ~ E
    | (~ A ∨ ~ B) ≡ ~ (A & B)          1–12, 13–__ ≡I
```

Since we have a negation as an assumption, we can try to derive the corresponding unnegated sentence 'A & B'. Thus our current goal sentence is a conjunction that can be derived by the rule of Conjunction Introduction if we can first derive each of the conjuncts.

```
13  | | ~ (A & B)                      Assumption
    | |-----------
14  | | | ~ (~ A ∨ ~ B)                Assumption
    | | |-----------
    | | |
    | | | A
    | | |
    | | | B
    | | | A & B                        __, __ &I
    | | | ~ (A & B)                    13 R
    | | ~ A ∨ ~ B                      14–__ ~ E
    | (~ A ∨ ~ B) ≡ ~ (A & B)          1–12, 13–__ ≡I
```

Since our goal sentences are atomic, they cannot be derived by any of the introduction rules. The most promising elimination rule to use is Negation Elimination. Thus we proceed by assuming the negation of each of the atomic sentences and deriving a sentence and its negation within each subderivation. This will allow us to derive the goal sentences by Negation Elimination.

```
13  | | ~ (A & B)                      Assumption
    | |-----------
14  | | | ~ (~ A ∨ ~ B)                Assumption
    | | |-----------
15  | | | | ~ A                        Assumption
    | | | |-----------
    | | | |
    | | | A                            15–__ ~ E
    | | | | ~ B                        Assumption
    | | | |-----------
    | | | |
    | | | B                            __–__ ~ E
    | | | A & B                        __, __ &I
    | | | ~ (A & B)                    13 R
    | | ~ A ∨ ~ B                      14–__ ~ E
    | (~ A ∨ ~ B) ≡ ~ (A & B)          1–12, 13–__ ≡I
```

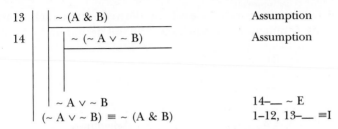

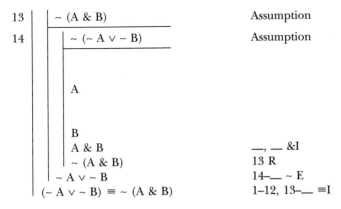

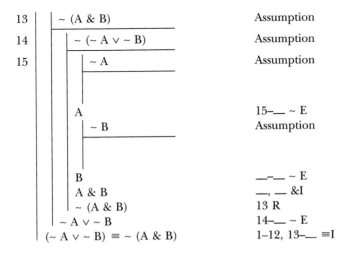

A sentence and its negation can now easily be derived within each of the subderivations by using Disjunction Introduction. The full derivation looks like this:

```
Derive: (~ A ∨ ~ B) ≡ ~ (A & B)

 1  | | ~ A ∨ ~ B                      Assumption
    | |----------
 2  | | | ~ A                          Assumption
    | | |------
 3  | | | | A & B                      Assumption
    | | | |------
 4  | | | | A                          3 &E
 5  | | | | ~ A                        2 R
 6  | | | ~ (A & B)                    3–5 ~ I
 7  | | | ~ B                          Assumption
    | | |------
 8  | | | | A & B                      Assumption
    | | | |------
 9  | | | | B                          8 &E
10  | | | | ~ B                        7 R
11  | | | ~ (A & B)                    8–10 ~ I
12  | | ~ (A & B)                      1, 2–6, 7–11 ∨E
13  | | ~ (A & B)                      Assumption
    | |----------
14  | | | ~ (~ A ∨ ~ B)                Assumption
    | | |--------------
15  | | | | ~ A                        Assumption
    | | | |------
16  | | | | ~ A ∨ ~ B                  15 ∨I
17  | | | | ~ (~ A ∨ ~ B)              14 R
18  | | | A                            15–17 ~ E
19  | | | | ~ B                        Assumption
    | | | |------
20  | | | | ~ A ∨ ~ B                  19 ∨I
21  | | | | ~ (~ A ∨ ~ B)              14 R
22  | | | B                            19–21 ~ E
23  | | | A & B                        18, 22 &I
24  | | | ~ (A & B)                    13 R
25  | | ~ A ∨ ~ B                      14–24 ~ E
26  | (~ A ∨ ~ B) ≡ ~ (A & B)          1–12, 13–25 ≡I
```

This derivation is complex, but it can be constructed systematically, as we have just done, by analyzing goal sentences along the way and asking what means we have for deriving them. Of course, constructing derivations is not a spectator sport; it requires active participation and lots of practice. But the time and energy spent are well worth it.

5.4E EXERCISES

1. First, using the techniques of goal analysis on each of the following, indicate the *goal* sentence at the current state of construction and specify a next plausible *subgoal* sentence or sentences. When appropriate, set up subderivation structures that will lead to the subgoal sentence(s). Remember to consider

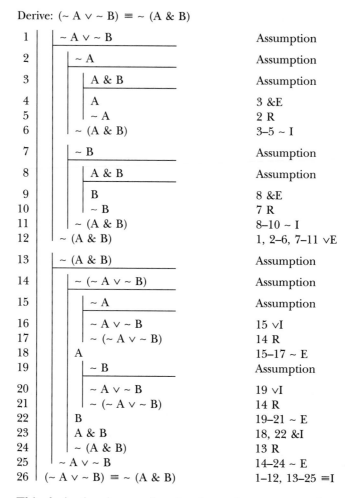

both the form of the goal sentence and the content of the accessible sentences in selecting proper subgoals. Second, continue to use the goal analysis method and complete each of the derivations.

a. Derive: L & ~ G

1	(L & T) & (~ G & S)	Assumption
	L & ~ G	

*b. Derive: A ∨ Q

1	R ⊃ A	Assumption
2	R	Assumption
	A ∨ Q	

c. Derive: S ⊃ ~ B

1	~ B ≡ S	Assumption
	S ⊃ ~ B	

*d. Derive: L ≡ K

1	(K ⊃ L) & (L ⊃ K)	Assumption
	L ≡ K	

e. Derive: ~ M

1	M ≡ P	Assumption
2	~ P	Assumption
	~ M	

*f. Derive: Z

1	B & (~ E ⊃ Z)	Assumption
2	~ E	Assumption
	Z	

g. Derive: S & I

1	~ G & ~ H	Assumption
2	G	Assumption
	S & I	

*h. Derive: W

1	~ T ⊃ W	Assumption
2	I ≡ W	Assumption
3	~ T ∨ I	Assumption
	W	

i. Derive: B

1	~ Q ⊃ (K ≡ (J & B))	Assumption
2	~ Q & K	Assumption
	J & B	
	B	— &E

*j. Derive: (Y & ~ H) & L

1	(C ∨ A) ⊃ (Y & ~ H)	Assumption
2	L & P	Assumption
3	A	Assumption
	Y & ~ H	
	L	2 &E
	(Y & ~ H) & L	—, — &I

k. Derive: N ⊃ (C ⊃ ~ D)

1	~ D & (N ∨ H)	Assumption
2	N	Assumption
	C ⊃ ~ D	
	N ⊃ (C ⊃ ~ D)	2–— ⊃I

*1. Derive: (~ F & H) ≡ K

1	K ⊃ (~ F & H)	Assumption
2	(~ F & H) ⊃ J	Assumption
3	J ⊃ K	Assumption
	| ~ F & H	Assumption
	|	
	| K	
	| K	Assumption
	| ~ F & H	1,__ ⊃I
	(~ F & H) ≡ K	__–__, __–__ ≡I

2. Show that the following derivability claims hold in *SD*.

a. {(Z ≡ R) & H, (K ⊃ J) & ~ ~ Y, D ∨ B} ⊢ H & (K ⊃ J)
*b. {K ⊃ R, B & K} ⊢ R ∨ T
c. {A ≡ (A ⊃ B)} ⊢ A ⊃ B
*d. {(A ∨ B) ⊃ (B ≡ D), B} ⊢ B & D
e. {B & F, ~ (B & G)} ⊢ ~ G
*f. {(~ B ∨ ~ H) ⊃ M, K & ~ M} ⊢ B

3. Show that each of the following arguments is valid in *SD*.

a. ~ (L & E)
~ (L & E) ≡ P
———
L ∨ P

*b. R & (C & ~ F)
(R ∨ S) ⊃ ~ W
———
~ W

c. R ⊃ S
S ⊃ T
———
R ⊃ T

*d. (A ⊃ F) & (F ⊃ D)
[(M ∨ H) ∨ C] ⊃ A
~ (M ∨ H) & C
———
D

e. A ⊃ (B & C)
~ C
———
~ (A & D)

*f. H
———
C ⊃ [A ⊃ (S ⊃ H)]

g. A ≡ B
B ≡ C
———
A ≡ C

*h. A ⊃ (B ⊃ C)
D ⊃ B
———
A ⊃ (D ⊃ C)

i. F ≡ G
F ∨ G
———
F & G

*j. ~ B ≡ Z
N ⊃ B
Z & N
———
~ H

4. Show that each of the following is a theorem in *SD*.

a. A ⊃ (A ∨ B)
*b. A ⊃ (B ⊃ A)
c. (A ≡ B) ⊃ (A ⊃ B)
*d. (A & ~ A) ⊃ (B & ~ B)
e. (A ⊃ B) ⊃ [(C ⊃ A) ⊃ (C ⊃ B)]
*f. A ∨ ~ A
g. [(A ⊃ B) & ~ B] ⊃ ~ A
*h. (A & A) ≡ A
i. A ⊃ [B ⊃ (A ⊃ B)]
*j. ~ A ⊃ [(B & A) ⊃ C]
k. (A ⊃ B) ⊃ [~ B ⊃ ~ (A & D)]

5. Show that the members of each of the following pairs of sentences are equivalent in *SD*.

a.	(A ∨ ~ ~ B) & C	(A ∨ ~ ~ B) & C
*b.	(A & B) & C	A & (B & C)
c.	A	~ ~ A
*d.	A & A	A ∨ A
e.	A ⊃ B	~ B ⊃ ~ A
*f.	A ≡ B	B ≡ A

6. Show that each of the following sets of sentences is inconsistent in *SD*.

a. {A ≡ ~ (A ≡ A), A}
*b. {P ⊃ ~ P, ~ P ⊃ P}
c. {M ⊃ (K ⊃ B), ~ K ⊃ ~ M, (L & M) & ~ B}
*d. {(E ∨ F) ⊃ (G & ~ I), (G ∨ F) ⊃ I, ~ F ⊃ E}
e. {~ (Y ≡ A), ~ Y, ~ A}
*f. {F ⊃ ~ G, ~ F ⊃ ~ H, (~ F ∨ G) & H}
g. {(~ C ⊃ ~ D) & (C ⊃ D), D ⊃ ~ C, ~ (B & ~ D), B ≡ (~ C ∨ D)}

7. Show that the following derivability claims hold in *SD*.

a. {F ⊃ A, (A & B) ≡ Z, B & F} ⊢ F & Z
*b. {C ⊃ (~ D ⊃ H), C & ~ D} ⊢ E ∨ H
c. {C ≡ A, A ⊃ G, ~ (G ∨ U)} ⊢ ~ C
*d. {A ⊃ ~ ~ B, I ⊃ ~ B} ⊢ ~ (A & I)
e. {B ∨ ~ Z, ~ Z ⊃ D, B ≡ D, D ≡ ~S} ⊢ ~ S

8. Show that each of the following arguments is valid in *SD*.

a. E ⊃ K

A ≡ G

A & E

(K & G) & (G & K)

*b. B ∨ Q

A ≡ B

Q ⊃ A

A

c. C ∨ ~ D

C ⊃ Y

D

Y

*d. [~ (M & F) ∨ N] ⊃ G

~ N ⊃ ~ G

G ≡ N

e. K ⊃ [K ⊃ (K ⊃ P)]

~ P ⊃ ~ K

9. Show that each of the following is a theorem in *SD*.

a. (A & ~ A) ⊃ ~ B
*b. (A ∨ B) ⊃ (B ∨ A)
c. A ⊃ [B ⊃ (A & B)]
*d. (A ≡ B) ⊃ (B ⊃ A)
e. A ⊃ [A ∨ (B & C)]

10. Show that the members of each of the following pairs of sentences are equivalent in *SD*.

a. A	(A ∨ A) ∨ A
*b. A ≡ A	A ⊃ (A ⊃ A)
c. (A ∨ B) ⊃ A	B ⊃ A
*d. (A ∨ B) & C	(A & C) ∨ (B & C)

11. Show that each of the following sets of sentences is inconsistent in *SD*.

a. {A ⊃ (B & ~ B), A}
*b. {~ G & Y, Y ⊃ G}
c. {Z ≡ W, Z, W ⊃ ~ Z}
*d. {P ⊃ (A & Y), Y ⊃ (~ A & P), P ∨ Y}
e. {~ ~ ~ D ⊃ D, ~ D}

12. Show the following derivability claims hold in *SD*.

a. {P ⊃ Q} ⊢ ~ Q ⊃ ~ P
*b. {K ∨ (K ∨ K)} ⊢ K
c. {H ⊃ M, ~ H ⊃ ~ M} ⊢ H ≡ M
*d. {A ∨ B, ~ B} ⊢ A
e. {~ (F ⊃ G), ~ (G ⊃ H)} ⊢ ~ I
*f. {A ≡ (~ B ∨ C), B ⊃ C} ⊢ A
g. {L ≡ ~ (Z ≡ ~ C), ~ (L ∨ Z)} ⊢ C
*h. {(P ∨ Q) ∨ R} ⊢ P ∨ (Q ∨ R)
i. {~ (Y ⊃ X), ~ (X ⊃ H)} ⊢ K
*j. {(R ∨ ~ H), (~ R ∨ ~ H)} ⊢ ~ H
k. {(L ⊃ X) ∨ B, (~ (L ⊃ X) & ~ B) ≡ (J ⊃ (E & ~ F))} ⊢ (J ⊃ (E & ~ F)) ⊃ Z
*l. {(S ⊃ L) ⊃ W, (S ⊃ L) ∨ ~ W} ⊢ ~ W ≡ ~ (S ⊃ L)
m. {P ≡ Q} ⊢ (R ≡ P) ≡ (R ≡ Q)
*n. {[E ∨ (L ∨ M)] & (E ≡ F), L ⊃ D, D ⊃ ~ L} ⊢ E ∨ M
o. {A ⊃ (Q & B), (~ Q ≡ B) & (C ⊃ A)} ⊢ (A ∨ B) ⊃ ~ C
*p. {~ (A ≡ B)} ⊢ ~ A ≡ B

13. Show that each of the following arguments is valid in *SD*.

a. $$\begin{array}{l} (H \& I) \vee (H \& S) \\ \hline H \end{array}$$

*b. $$\begin{array}{l} K \supset \sim \sim Q \\ \sim \sim K \\ \hline Q \end{array}$$

c. $$\begin{array}{l} B \equiv \sim B \\ \hline J \equiv \sim C \end{array}$$

*d. $$\begin{array}{l} A \equiv B \\ B \equiv \sim C \\ \hline \sim (A \equiv C) \end{array}$$

e. $$\begin{array}{l} M \supset I \\ \sim I \& L \\ M \vee B \\ \hline B \end{array}$$

*f. $$\begin{array}{l} Q \vee (J \equiv D) \\ \sim D \\ J \\ \hline Q \end{array}$$

g. $$\begin{array}{l} M \supset A \\ (M \equiv (A \& M)) \supset (C \& \sim (A \& D)) \\ \sim (A \& D) \equiv (C \& \sim D) \\ \hline \sim D \end{array}$$

*h. $$\begin{array}{l} A \vee \sim (\sim K \vee C) \\ \sim (\sim K \vee C) \supset \sim A \\ \hline \sim A \equiv \sim (\sim K \vee C) \end{array}$$

i. $$\begin{array}{l} (J \& Y) \supset \sim A \\ S \supset (A \& \sim A) \\ N \supset (A \& (J \& Y)) \\ \hline \sim S \equiv \sim N \end{array}$$

*j. $$\begin{array}{l} A \vee B \\ \sim B \vee C \\ \sim C \\ \hline A \end{array}$$

k. $$\begin{array}{l} (\sim H \vee J) \vee K \\ K \supset \sim I \\ \hline (H \& I) \supset J \end{array}$$

*l. $$\begin{array}{l} B \supset (E \supset F) \\ A \supset (C \supset D) \\ A \vee B \\ \sim D \& \sim F \\ \hline (P \& (G \equiv (A \& B))) \vee (\sim C \vee \sim E) \end{array}$$

m. $$\begin{array}{l} F \vee H \\ \sim H \equiv (L \vee G) \\ (G \& B) \vee [G \& (K \supset G)] \\ \hline F \end{array}$$

*n. $$\begin{array}{l} (A \vee B) \vee (C \& D) \\ (A \equiv E) \& (B \supset F) \\ K \equiv \sim (E \vee F) \\ C \supset B \\ \hline \sim K \end{array}$$

o. $$\begin{array}{l} (A \vee B) \& \sim C \\ \sim C \supset (D \& \sim A) \\ B \supset (A \vee E) \\ \hline E \vee F \end{array}$$

14. Show that each of the following is a theorem in *SD*.

a. $\sim [(A \& B) \& \sim (A \& B)]$

*b. $A \equiv \sim \sim A$

c. $(A \equiv \sim A) \supset \sim (A \equiv \sim A)$

*d. $[(A \supset B) \supset A] \supset A$

e. $(A \supset B) \vee (B \supset A)$

*f. $(A \equiv B) \equiv [(A \supset B) \& (B \supset A)]$

g. $[A \supset (B \supset C)] \equiv [(A \supset B) \supset (A \supset C)]$

*h. $[(A \vee B) \supset C] \equiv [(A \supset C) \& (B \supset C)]$

i. $[(A \equiv B) \supset C] \supset [\sim (A \& B) \vee C]$

15. Show that the members of each of the following pairs of sentences are equivalent in *SD*:

a.	$\sim A \vee B$	$A \supset B$
*b.	$A \& \sim A$	$B \& \sim B$
c.	$\sim (A \supset B)$	$A \& \sim B$
*d.	$A \equiv B$	$\sim A \equiv \sim B$
e.	$A \equiv B$	$(A \& B) \vee (\sim A \& \sim B)$
*f.	$\sim (A \equiv B)$	$(A \& \sim B) \vee (\sim A \& B)$

16. Show that each of the following sets of sentences is inconsistent in *SD*:

a. $\{(A \supset B) \& (A \supset \sim B), (C \supset A) \& (\sim C \supset A)\}$

*b. $\{B \equiv (A \& \sim A), \sim B \supset (A \& \sim A)\}$

c. $\{W \vee (Z \supset Y), \sim Y \& \sim (W \vee \sim Z)\}$

*d. $\{A \& (B \vee C), (\sim C \vee H) \& (H \supset \sim H), \sim B\}$

e. $\{[(A \equiv B) \equiv (D \& \sim D)] \equiv B, A\}$

17. Symbolize the following arguments in *SL*, and show that the symbolized arguments are valid in *SD*.

a. Spring has sprung, and the flowers are blooming. If the flowers are blooming, the bees are happy. If the bees are happy but aren't making honey, then spring hasn't sprung. So the bees are making honey.

*b. If Luscious Food Industries goes out of business, then food processing won't be improved. And if they go out of business, canned beans will be available if and only if Brockport Company stays in business. But Brockport Company is going out of business, and canned beans will be available. Hence Luscious Food Industries is staying in business unless food processing is improved.

c. If civil disobedience is moral, then not all resistance to the law is morally prohibited, although our legal code is correct if all resistance to the law is morally prohibited. But civil disobedience is moral if and only if either civil disobedience is moral or our legal code is correct. Our judges have acted well only if all resistance to the law is morally prohibited. So our judges haven't acted well.

*d. If oranges contain citric acid so do lemons, or if lemons don't contain citric acid neither do grapefruit. Thus, if oranges and grapefruit contain citric acid, so do lemons.

e. Neither rubber nor wood is a good conductor of electricity. But either rubber is a good conductor if and only if metal is, or if metal or glass is a good conductor then wood is a good conductor if and only if metal is. So metal isn't a good conductor of electricity.

*f. If the trains stop running then airline prices will increase, and buses will reduce their fares provided that trains don't stop running. If airline prices increase, then buses won't lose their customers. Hence buses will lose their customers only if they reduce their fares.

g. If the house is built and taxes increase, Jones will go bankrupt. If Smith becomes mayor, then the tax director will quit; and Smith will become mayor unless the tax director quits. But taxes won't increase if but only if the tax director doesn't quit and Smith becomes mayor. So if the house is built, Jones will go bankrupt.

*h. Jim is a Democrat only if Howard or Rhoda is. If Howard is a Democrat, so are Barbara and Allen. If Barbara is a Democrat, then Allen is a Democrat only if Freda is. But not both Freda and Jim are Democrats. Therefore Jim is a Democrat only if Rhoda is too.

i. If life is a carnival, then I'm a clown or a trapeze artist. But either life isn't a carnival or there are balloons, and either there aren't any balloons or I'm not a clown. So, if life is a carnival, then I'm a trapeze artist.

18. Symbolize the following passages in *SL* and show that the resulting sets of sentences are inconsistent in *SD*.

a. If motorcycling is dangerous sailboating is also dangerous, and if sailboating is dangerous parachuting is dangerous. Motorcycling is dangerous but parachuting is not.

*b. If the recipe doesn't call for flavoring or it doesn't call for eggs, it's not a recipe for tapioca. If the recipe calls for eggs, then it's a tapioca recipe and it doesn't call for flavoring. But this recipe calls for eggs.

c. Bach is popular only if Beethoven is ignored. If Bach is unpopular and Beethoven isn't ignored, then current musical tastes are hopeless. Current musical tastes aren't hopeless, and Beethoven isn't ignored.

*d. Historians are right just in case theologians are mistaken, if and only if Darwin's theory is correct. And if historians or philosophers are right, then Darwinian theory is correct and theologians are mistaken. Historians are right if and only if philosophers are wrong. But if Darwinian theory is correct, then historians are mistaken.

e. Either Martha was commissioned to write the ballet or, if the fund-raising sale was a failure, Tony was commissioned. Nancy will dance if and only if Tony wasn't commissioned. But the fund-raiser was a failure, Nancy will dance, and Martha wasn't commissioned.

19.a. Explain why we would not want to include the following derivation rule in *SD*.

```
  | P ∨ Q
  |
▷ | P
```

*b. Explain why Negation Introduction is a dispensable rule in *SD*.

c. Explain why Reiteration is a dispensable rule in *SD*.

*d. Why does the following *not* show that the set containing only 'A' and 'B ⊃ ~ A' is inconsistent in *SD*:

```
1 | A                 Assumption
2 | B ⊃ ~ A           Assumption
  |-------
3 |  | B              Assumption
  |  |----
4 |  | ~ A            2, 3 ⊃E
5 |  | A              1 R
```

e. Suppose that **P** is a theorem in *SD*. Explain why any argument of *SL* that has ~ **P** among its premises is valid in *SD*.

*f. Give a derivation showing that there is a sentence of *SL* such that the unit set of that sentence is inconsistent in *SD*.

20. In Chapter 6 we prove that, for any sentence **P** and set Γ of sentences of *SL*,

*Γ ⊢ **P** in *SD* if and only if Γ ⊨ **P**

Use this result to prove the following:

a. An argument of *SL* is valid in *SD* if and only if the argument is truth-functionally valid.

*b. A sentence **P** of *SL* is a theorem in *SD* if and only if **P** is truth-functionally true.

c. Sentences **P** and **Q** of *SL* are equivalent in *SD* if and only if **P** and **Q** are truth-functionally equivalent.

.5 THE DERIVATION SYSTEM *SD+*

Although there are important theoretical advantages to having a small set of derivation rules, there are definite practical advantages to having a larger set. With a larger set of rules, derivations are often easier to construct and much shorter. In this section we introduce a new natural deduction system, *SD+*, which contains all the derivation rules of *SD* plus some more. However, *SD+* is not a stronger system than *SD* in the sense that more arguments of *SL* can be shown to be valid or that more sentences of *SL* are theorems. A sentence is derivable in *SD+* from a set of sentences of *SL* if and only if it is derivable in *SD* from the set of sentences.

RULES OF INFERENCE

Suppose that prior to line **n** of a derivation two accessible lines, **i** and **j**, contain **P** ⊃ **Q** and ~ **Q**, respectively. We can derive ~ **P** as follows:

i	**P** ⊃ **Q**	
j	~ **Q**	
n	| **P**	Assumption
n + 1	| **Q**	i, n ⊃E
n + 2	| ~ **Q**	j, R
n + 3	~ **P**	n – n + 2 ~I

To avoid going through this routine every time such a situation arises, we introduce the rule *Modus Tollens.*

Modus Tollens (MT)

	P ⊃ **Q**
	~ **Q**
▷	~ **P**

Now suppose that prior to line **n** of a derivation two accessible lines, **i** and **j**, contain $\mathbf{P \supset Q}$ and $\mathbf{Q \supset R}$. A routine to derive $\mathbf{P \supset R}$ beginning at line **n** is as follows:

i	$\mathbf{P \supset Q}$		
j	$\mathbf{Q \supset R}$		
n		$\mathbf{P}$	Assumption
n + 1		$\mathbf{Q}$	**i, n** $\supset$E
n + 2		$\mathbf{R}$	**j, n** + 1 $\supset$E
n + 3	$\mathbf{P \supset R}$		**n** – **n** + 2 $\supset$I

To avoid this routine, we introduce the rule *Hypothetical Syllogism.*

Hypothetical Syllogism (HS)

	$\mathbf{P \supset Q}$
	$\mathbf{Q \supset R}$
▷	$\mathbf{P \supset R}$

Finally suppose that prior to the line **n** of a derivation two accessible lines, **i** and **j**, contain $\mathbf{P \vee Q}$ and $\sim \mathbf{P}$ and that we wish to derive **Q**. A routine for this is as follows:

i	$\mathbf{P \vee Q}$			
j	$\sim \mathbf{P}$			
n		$\mathbf{P}$		Assumption
n + 1			$\sim \mathbf{Q}$	Assumption
n + 2			$\sim \mathbf{P}$	**j** R
n + 3			$\mathbf{P}$	**n** R
n + 4		$\mathbf{Q}$		**n** + 1 – **n** + 3 $\sim$E
n + 5		$\mathbf{Q}$		Assumption
n + 6		$\mathbf{Q}$		**n** + 5 R
n + 7	$\mathbf{Q}$			**i, n** – **n** + 4, **n** + 5 – **n** + 6 $\vee$E

The rule of *Disjunctive Syllogism* allows us to avoid going through this routine for this and similar cases.

Disjunctive Syllogism (DS)

	$\mathbf{P \vee Q}$			$\mathbf{P \vee Q}$
	$\sim \mathbf{P}$	or		$\sim \mathbf{Q}$
▷	$\mathbf{Q}$		▷	$\mathbf{P}$

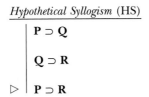

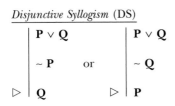

The three rules of inference just introduced can be thought of as derived rules. They are added for convenience only; whatever we can derive with them, we can derive without them, using only the rules of *SD*.

RULES OF REPLACEMENT

In addition to rules of inference, there are also derivation rules known as *rules of replacement*. Rules of replacement, as their name suggests, allow us to derive some sentences from other sentences by replacing sentential components. For example, from the sentence

G ∨ (H & K)

we can certainly infer

G ∨ (~ ~ H & K)

In this instance the sentential component 'H' has been replaced with '~ ~ H'. Similarly from

G ∨ (~ ~ H & K)

we can certainly infer

G ∨ (H & K)

Double Negation is the rule of replacement that licenses such moves within a derivation.

Double Negation (DN)
P ◁ ▷ ~ ~ **P**

That is, by using Double Negation, we can derive from a sentence **Q** that contains **P** as a sentential component another sentence that is like **Q**, except that one occurrence of the sentential component **P** has been replaced with ~ ~ **P**. And, by using Double Negation, we can derive from a sentence **Q** that contains ~ ~ **P** as a sentential component another sentence that is like **Q**, except that one occurrence of the sentential component ~ ~ **P** has been replaced with **P**.

Double Negation can be applied to any of the sentential components of a sentence. For instance, from

G ∨ (H & K)

Double Negation permits us to derive

G ∨ ~ ~ (H & K)

And from

$$G \vee \sim\sim (H \mathbin{\&} K)$$

Double Negation allows us to derive

$$G \vee (H \mathbin{\&} K)$$

Since every sentence is a sentential component of itself, Double Negation applies to the entire sentence as well. In a derivation Double Negation permits us to go from

$$G \vee (H \mathbin{\&} K)$$

to

$$\sim\sim [G \vee (H \mathbin{\&} K)]$$

and from

$$\sim\sim [G \vee (H \mathbin{\&} K)]$$

to

$$G \vee (H \mathbin{\&} K)$$

Here are the rules of replacement for *SD+*:

Commutation (Com)

$$\mathbf{P} \mathbin{\&} \mathbf{Q} \triangleleft\triangleright \mathbf{Q} \mathbin{\&} \mathbf{P}$$
$$\mathbf{P} \vee \mathbf{Q} \triangleleft\triangleright \mathbf{Q} \vee \mathbf{P}$$

Association (Assoc)

$$\mathbf{P} \mathbin{\&} (\mathbf{Q} \mathbin{\&} \mathbf{R}) \triangleleft\triangleright (\mathbf{P} \mathbin{\&} \mathbf{Q}) \mathbin{\&} \mathbf{R}$$
$$\mathbf{P} \vee (\mathbf{Q} \vee \mathbf{R}) \triangleleft\triangleright (\mathbf{P} \vee \mathbf{Q}) \vee \mathbf{R}$$

Implication (Impl)

$$\mathbf{P} \supset \mathbf{Q} \triangleleft\triangleright \sim \mathbf{P} \vee \mathbf{Q}$$

Double Negation (DN)

$$\mathbf{P} \triangleleft\triangleright \sim\sim \mathbf{P}$$

De Morgan (DeM)

$$\sim (\mathbf{P} \mathbin{\&} \mathbf{Q}) \triangleleft\triangleright \sim \mathbf{P} \vee \sim \mathbf{Q}$$
$$\sim (\mathbf{P} \vee \mathbf{Q}) \triangleleft\triangleright \sim \mathbf{P} \mathbin{\&} \sim \mathbf{Q}$$

Idempotence (Idem)

$$\mathbf{P} \triangleleft\triangleright \mathbf{P} \mathbin{\&} \mathbf{P}$$
$$\mathbf{P} \triangleleft\triangleright \mathbf{P} \vee \mathbf{P}$$

Transposition (Trans)

$$\mathbf{P} \supset \mathbf{Q} \triangleleft\triangleright \sim \mathbf{Q} \supset \sim \mathbf{P}$$

Exportation (Exp)

$$\mathbf{P} \supset (\mathbf{Q} \supset \mathbf{R}) \triangleleft\triangleright (\mathbf{P} \mathbin{\&} \mathbf{Q}) \supset \mathbf{R}$$

Distribution (Dist)

$$\mathbf{P} \mathbin{\&} (\mathbf{Q} \vee \mathbf{R}) \triangleleft\triangleright (\mathbf{P} \mathbin{\&} \mathbf{Q}) \vee (\mathbf{P} \mathbin{\&} \mathbf{R})$$
$$\mathbf{P} \vee (\mathbf{Q} \mathbin{\&} \mathbf{R}) \triangleleft\triangleright (\mathbf{P} \vee \mathbf{Q}) \mathbin{\&} (\mathbf{P} \vee \mathbf{R})$$

Equivalence (Equiv)

$\mathbf{P} \equiv \mathbf{Q} \lhd \rhd (\mathbf{P} \supset \mathbf{Q}) \ \& \ (\mathbf{Q} \supset \mathbf{P})$
$\mathbf{P} \equiv \mathbf{Q} \lhd \rhd (\mathbf{P} \ \& \ \mathbf{Q}) \vee (\sim \mathbf{P} \ \& \sim \mathbf{Q})$

Rules of replacement always allow the replacement of sentential components. In addition, all these rules of replacement are two-way rules; that is, a sentential component that has the form of the sentence on the left of '$\lhd \rhd$' can be replaced with a sentential component that has the form of the sentence on the right of '$\lhd \rhd$', and vice versa.

Consider the following derivation:

Derive: J ⊃ [M ∨ (G ∨ I)]

1	J ⊃ [K ∨ (L ∨ H)]	Assumption
2	[(K ∨ L) ∨ H] ⊃ [(M ∨ G) ∨ I]	Assumption
3	J ⊃ [(K ∨ L) ∨ H]	1 Assoc
4	J ⊃ [(M ∨ G) ∨ I]	2, 3 HS
5	J ⊃ [M ∨ (G ∨ I)]	4 Assoc

Here the replacement rule Association has been used twice—first to replace a sentential component of the form **P** ∨ (**Q** ∨ **R**) with a sentential component of the form (**P** ∨ **Q**) ∨ **R** and then to replace a sentential component of the form (**P** ∨ **Q**) ∨ **R** with a sentential component of the form **P** ∨ (**Q** ∨ **R**).

Since all the derivation rules of *SD* are derivation rules of *SD+*, the procedures for properly applying the rules of *SD* apply to *SD+* as well. The rules of inference of *SD+*, including Modus Tollens, Hypothetical Syllogism, and Disjunctive Syllogism, must be applied to entire sentences on a line. Rules of replacement, on the other hand, can be applied to sentential components. The following derivation illustrates the proper use of several of the rules of replacement:

Derive: ~ C ≡ E

1	(D ∨ B) ∨ (E ⊃ ~ C)	Assumption
2	~ B & [~ D & (~ E ⊃ C)]	Assumption
3	(~ B & ~ D) & (~ E ⊃ C)	2 Assoc
4	~ (B ∨ D) & (~ E ⊃ C)	3 DeM
5	~ (B ∨ D)	4 &E
6	~ (D ∨ B)	5 Com
7	E ⊃ ~ C	1, 6 DS
8	~ E ⊃ C	3 &E
9	~ C ⊃ ~ ~ E	8 Trans
10	~ C ⊃ E	9 DN
11	(~ C ⊃ E) & (E ⊃ ~ C)	10, 7 &I
12	~ C ≡ E	11 Equiv

Notice that each application of a derivation rule requires a separate line. Moreover care must be taken to apply each derivation rule only to sentences that have the proper form (or, in the case of rules of replacement, sentences that have components that have the proper form).

Here is an example in which these points are ignored:

Derive: ~ A ⊃ [B ⊃ (G ∨ D)]

1	(A ∨ ~ B) ∨ ~ C	Assumption	
2	(D ∨ G) ∨ C	Assumption	
3	~ (~ A & B) ∨ ~ C	1 DeM	**MISTAKE!**
4	(~ A & B) ⊃ ~ C	3 Impl	
5	C ∨ (G ∨ D)	2 Com	**MISTAKE!**
6	~ C ⊃ (G ∨ D)	5 Impl	**MISTAKE!**
7	(~ A & B) ⊃ (G ∨ D)	4, 6 HS	
8	~ A ⊃ [B ⊃ (G ∨ D)]	7 Exp	

De Morgan does not license entering the sentence on line 3. What De Morgan does allow is the replacement of a sentential component of the form ~ **P** ∨ ~ **Q** with a sentential component of the form ~ (**P** & **Q**), but the sentential component 'A ∨ ~ B' does not have the form ~ **P** ∨ ~ **Q**. However, by applying Double Negation to the first assumption, we can obtain '(~ ~ A ∨ ~ B) ∨ ~ C'. And this latter sentence does have a sentential component of the form ~ **P** ∨ ~ **Q**, namely, '~ ~ A ∨ ~ B'. Here **P** is '~ A', and **Q** is 'B'. Hence the derivation should begin this way:

Derive: ~ A ⊃ [B ⊃ (G ∨ D)]

1	(A ∨ ~ B) ∨ ~ C	Assumption
2	(D ∨ G) ∨ C	Assumption
3	(~ ~ A ∨ ~ B) ∨ ~ C	1 DN
4	~ (~ A & B) ∨ ~ C	3 DeM

The second mistake in our example, in line 5, is that Commutation is applied twice within the same line. Each application of a rule, even if it is the same rule, requires a separate line. Correctly done, the derivation proceeds:

5	(~ A & B) ⊃ ~ C	4 Impl
6	C ∨ (D ∨ G)	2 Com
7	C ∨ (G ∨ D)	6 Com

The third mistake, in line 6 of the example, also stems from our trying to apply a rule of replacement to a sentential component that does not have the form required by the rule. Implication permits the replacement of a sentential component of the form ~ **P** ∨ **Q** with a sentential component of the form **P** ⊃ **Q**, but 'C ∨ (G ∨ D)' does not have the form ~ **P** ∨ **Q**. However, applying Double Negation to 'C', a sentential component of 'C ∨ (G ∨ D)', generates '~ ~ C ∨ (G ∨ D)'. This latter sentence does have the form ~ **P** ∨ **Q**, where **P** is '~ C' and **Q** is 'G ∨ D'. Here is the entire derivation done correctly:

Derive: ~ A ⊃ [B ⊃ (G ∨ D)]

1	(A ∨ ~ B) ∨ ~ C	Assumption
2	(D ∨ G) ∨ C	Assumption
3	(~ ~ A ∨ ~ B) ∨ ~ C	1 DN
4	~ (~ A & B) ∨ ~ C	3 DeM
5	(~ A & B) ⊃ ~ C	4 Impl
6	C ∨ (D ∨ G)	2 Com
7	C ∨ (G ∨ D)	6 Com
8	~ ~ C ∨ (G ∨ D)	7 DN
9	~ C ⊃ (G ∨ D)	8 Impl
10	(~ A & B) ⊃ (G ∨ D)	5, 9 HS
11	~ A ⊃ [B ⊃ (G ∨ D)]	10 Exp

The definitions of the basic concepts of *SD+* are exactly like the definitions for the basic concepts of *SD*, except that '*SD*' is replaced with '*SD+*'. For example, the concept of derivability is defined as follows:

> A sentence **P** of *SL* is *derivable in SD+* from a set Γ of sentence of *SL* if and only if there is a derivation in *SD+* in which all the primary assumptions are members of Γ and **P** occurs in the scope of only those assumptions.

Consequently tests for the various syntactic properties are carried out in the same way. To show that an argument is valid in *SD+*, we construct a derivation in *SD+* showing that the conclusion of the argument is derivable in *SD+* from the set consisting of only the premises of the argument. To show that a sentence **P** of *SL* is a theorem in *SD+*, we show that **P** is derivable in *SD+* from the empty set. And so on for the other properties. Remember that, although technically *SD* and *SD+* are different syntactic systems, they are equally strong in the sense that whatever can be derived in one can be derived in the other. The practical advantage of *SD+* is that it enables us to construct shorter derivations.

The Derivation Rules of SD+

All the Derivation Rules of *SD* and Rules of Inference

Modus Tollens (MT)

	$\mathbf{P} \supset \mathbf{Q}$
	$\sim \mathbf{Q}$
▷	$\sim \mathbf{P}$

Hypothetical Syllogism (HS)

	$\mathbf{P} \supset \mathbf{Q}$
	$\mathbf{Q} \supset \mathbf{R}$
▷	$\mathbf{P} \supset \mathbf{R}$

Disjunctive Syllogism (DS)

	$\mathbf{P} \vee \mathbf{Q}$			$\mathbf{P} \vee \mathbf{Q}$
	$\sim \mathbf{P}$	or		$\sim \mathbf{Q}$
▷	$\mathbf{Q}$		▷	$\mathbf{P}$

Rules of Replacement

Commutation (Com)

$\mathbf{P} \,\&\, \mathbf{Q} \lhd\rhd \mathbf{Q} \,\&\, \mathbf{P}$
$\mathbf{P} \vee \mathbf{Q} \lhd\rhd \mathbf{Q} \vee \mathbf{P}$

Association (Assoc)

$\mathbf{P} \,\&\, (\mathbf{Q} \,\&\, \mathbf{R}) \lhd\rhd (\mathbf{P} \,\&\, \mathbf{Q}) \,\&\, \mathbf{R}$
$\mathbf{P} \vee (\mathbf{Q} \vee \mathbf{R}) \lhd\rhd (\mathbf{P} \vee \mathbf{Q}) \vee \mathbf{R}$

Implication (Impl)

$\mathbf{P} \supset \mathbf{Q} \lhd\rhd \sim \mathbf{P} \vee \mathbf{Q}$

Double Negation (DN)

$\mathbf{P} \lhd\rhd \sim \sim \mathbf{P}$

De Morgan (DeM)

$\sim (\mathbf{P} \,\&\, \mathbf{Q}) \lhd\rhd \sim \mathbf{P} \vee \sim \mathbf{Q}$
$\sim (\mathbf{P} \vee \mathbf{Q}) \lhd\rhd \sim \mathbf{P} \,\&\, \sim \mathbf{Q}$

Idempotence (Idem)

$\mathbf{P} \lhd\rhd \mathbf{P} \,\&\, \mathbf{P}$
$\mathbf{P} \lhd\rhd \mathbf{P} \vee \mathbf{P}$

Transposition (Trans)

$\mathbf{P} \supset \mathbf{Q} \lhd\rhd \sim \mathbf{Q} \supset \sim \mathbf{P}$

Exportation (Exp)

$\mathbf{P} \supset (\mathbf{Q} \supset \mathbf{R}) \lhd\rhd (\mathbf{P} \,\&\, \mathbf{Q}) \supset \mathbf{R}$

Distribution (Dist)

$\mathbf{P} \,\&\, (\mathbf{Q} \vee \mathbf{R}) \lhd\rhd (\mathbf{P} \,\&\, \mathbf{Q}) \vee (\mathbf{P} \,\&\, \mathbf{R})$
$\mathbf{P} \vee (\mathbf{Q} \,\&\, \mathbf{R}) \lhd\rhd (\mathbf{P} \vee \mathbf{Q}) \,\&\, (\mathbf{P} \vee \mathbf{R})$

Equivalence (Equiv)

$\mathbf{P} \equiv \mathbf{Q} \lhd\rhd (\mathbf{P} \supset \mathbf{Q}) \,\&\, (\mathbf{Q} \supset \mathbf{P})$
$\mathbf{P} \equiv \mathbf{Q} \lhd\rhd (\mathbf{P} \,\&\, \mathbf{Q}) \vee (\sim \mathbf{P} \,\&\, \sim \mathbf{Q})$

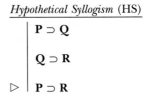

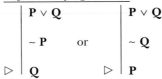

5.5E EXERCISES

1. Show that the following derivability claims hold in *SD+*.

a. {D ⊃ E, E ⊃ (Z & W), ~ Z ∨ ~ W} ⊢ ~ D
*b. {(H & G) ⊃ (L ∨ K), G & H} ⊢ K ∨ L
c. {(W ⊃ S) & ~ M, (~ W ⊃ H) ∨ M, (~ S ⊃ H) ⊃ K} ⊢ K
*d. {[(K & J) ∨ I] ∨ ~ Y, Y & [(I ∨ K) ⊃ F]} ⊢ F ∨ N
e. {(M ∨ B) ∨ (C ∨ G), ~ B & (~ G & ~ M)} ⊢ C
*f. {~ L ∨ (~ Z ∨ ~ U), (U & G) ∨ H, Z} ⊢ L ⊃ H

2. Show that each of the following is valid in *SD+*.

a. ~ Y ⊃ ~ Z
~ Z ⊃ ~ X
~ X ⊃ ~ Y
———
Y ≡ Z

*b. (~ A & ~ B) ∨ (~ A & ~ C)
(E & D) ⊃ A
———
~ E ∨ ~ D

c. (F & G) ∨ (H & ~ I)
I ⊃ ~ (F & D)
———
I ⊃ ~ D

*d. F ⊃ (~ G ∨ H)
F ⊃ G
~ (H ∨ I)
———
F ⊃ J

e. F ⊃ (G ⊃ H)
~ I ⊃ (F ∨ H)
F ⊃ G
———
I ∨ H

*f. G ⊃ (H & ~ K)
H ≡ (L & I)
~ I ∨ K
———
~ G

g. [(X & Z) & Y] ∨ (~ X ⊃ ~ Y)
X ⊃ Z
Z ⊃ Y
———
X ≡ Y

3. Show that each of the following is a theorem in *SD+*.

a. A ∨ ~ A
*b. ~ ~ ~ ~ ~ (A & ~ A)
c. A ∨ [(~ A ∨ B) & (~ A ∨ C)]
*d. [(A & B) ⊃ (B & A)] & [~ (A & B) ⊃ ~ (B & A)]
e. [A ⊃ (B & C)] ≡ [(~ B ∨ ~ C) ⊃ ~ A]
*f. [A ∨ (B ∨ C)] ≡ [C ∨ (B ∨ A)]
g. [A ⊃ (B ≡ C)] ≡ (A ⊃ [(~ B ∨ C) & (~ C ∨ B)])
*h. (A ∨ [B ⊃ (A ⊃ B)]) ≡ (A ∨ [(~ A ∨ ~ B) ∨ B])
i. [~ A ⊃ (~ B ⊃ C)] ⊃ [(A ∨ B) ∨ (~ ~ B ∨ C)]
*j. (~ A ≡ ~ A) ≡ [~ (~ A ⊃ A) ≡ (A ⊃ ~ A)]

4. Show that the members of each of the following pairs of sentences are equivalent in *SD+*.

a. A ∨ B
~ (~ A & ~ B)

*b. A & (B ∨ C)
(B & A) ∨ (C & A)

c. (A & B) ⊃ C
~ (A ⊃ C) ⊃ ~ B

*d. (A ∨ B) ∨ C
~ A ⊃ (~ B ⊃ C)

e. A ∨ (B ≡ C)
A ∨ (~ B ≡ ~ C)

*f. (A & B) ∨ [(C & D) ∨ A]
([(C ∨ A) & (C ∨ B)] & [(D ∨ A) & (D ∨ B)]) ∨ A

5. Show that the following sets of sentences are inconsistent in *SD+*.

a. {[(E & F) ∨ ~ ~ G] ⊃ M, ~ [[(G ∨ E) & (F ∨ G)] ⊃ (M & M)]}
*b. {~ [(~ C ∨ ~ ~ C) ∨ ~ ~ C]}
c. {M & L, [L & (M & ~ S)] ⊃ K, ~ K ∨ ~ S, ~ (K ≡ ~ S)}
*d. {B & (H ∨ Z), ~ Z ⊃ K, (B ≡ Z) ⊃ ~ Z, ~ K}
e. {~ [W & (Z ∨ Y)], (Z ⊃ Y) ⊃ Z, (Y ⊃ Z) ⊃ W}
*f. {[(F ⊃ G) ∨ (~ F ⊃ G)] ⊃ H, (A & H) ⊃ ~ A, A ∨ ~ H}

6. Symbolize the following arguments in *SL*, and show that they are valid in *SD+*.

a. If the phone rings Ed is calling, or if the beeper beeps Ed is calling. If not both Ed and Agnes are at home today, then it's not the case that if the phone rings, Ed is calling. Ed isn't home today, and he isn't calling. So the beeper won't beep.

*b. If Monday is a bad day, then I'll lose my job provided the boss doesn't call in sick. The boss won't call in sick. So I'll lose my job—since either Monday will be a bad day, or the boss won't call in sick only if I lose my job.

c. Army coats are warm only if they're either made of wool or not made of cotton or rayon. If army coats are not made of rayon, then they're made of cotton. Hence, if they're not made of wool, army coats aren't warm.

*d. If either the greenhouse is dry or the greenhouse is sunny if and only if it's not raining, the violets will wither. But if the violets wither the greenhouse is sunny, or if the violets wither the greenhouse isn't dry. It's raining, and the greenhouse isn't sunny. So the greenhouse is dry only if the violets won't wither.

e. It's not the case that John is rich and Hugo isn't. In fact, Hugo isn't rich, unless Moe is. And if Moe just emptied his bank account, then he isn't rich. Thus, if John is rich, then it's not the case that either Moe emptied his bank account or Moe isn't rich.

*f. Neither aspirin nor gin will ease my headache, unless it's psychosomatic. If it's psychosomatic and I'm really not ill, then I'll go out to a party and drink some martinis. So, if I'm not ill and don't drink any martinis, then aspirin won't ease my headache.

g. If I stay on this highway and don't slow down, I'll arrive in Montreal by 5:00. If I don't put my foot on the brake, I won't slow down. Either I won't slow down or I'll stop for a cup of coffee at the next exit. I'll stop for a cup of coffee at the next exit only if I'm falling asleep. So, if I don't arrive in Montreal by 5:00, then I'll stay on this highway only if I'm falling asleep and I put my foot on the brake.

*h. The weather is fine if and only if it's not snowing, and it's not snowing if and only if the sky is clear. So, either the weather is fine, the sky is clear, and it's not snowing; or it's snowing, the sky isn't clear, and the weather is lousy.

7. Symbolize the following passages in *SL*, and show that the resulting sets of sentences of *SL* are inconsistent in *SD+*.

a. Unless Stowe believes that all liberals are atheists, his claims about current politics are unintelligible. But if liberals are atheists only if they're not churchgoers, then Stowe's claims about current politics are nevertheless intelligible. Liberals are, in fact, churchgoers if and only if Stowe doesn't believe that they're all atheists, and if liberals aren't atheists, then Stowe doesn't believe that they are atheists. Liberals aren't atheists.

*b. Either Congress won't cut taxes or the elderly and the poor will riot, if but only if big business prospers. If the elderly don't riot, then Congress won't cut taxes. It won't happen that both the poor will riot and big business will prosper, and it won't happen that the poor don't riot and big business doesn't prosper. But if big business prospers, then Congress will cut taxes.

8. Answer the following.

a. Suppose we can derive **Q** from **P** by using only the rules of replacement. Why can we be sure that we can derive **P** from **Q**?

*b. Why must all arguments that are valid in *SD* be valid in *SD+* as well?

c. Suppose we develop a new natural deduction system *SD**. Let *SD** contain all the derivation rules of *SD* and in addition the derivation rule Absorption.

Absorption

| **P** ⊃ **Q**
▷ | **P** ⊃ (**P** & **Q**)

Using only the derivation rules of *SD*, develop a routine showing that any sentence derived by using Absorption could be derived in *SD* without using it.

GLOSSARY[2]

DERIVABILITY IN *SD*: A sentence **P** of *SL* is *derivable in SD* from a set Γ of sentences of *SL* if and only if there is a derivation in *SD* in which all the primary assumptions are members of Γ and **P** occurs in the scope of only those assumptions.

VALIDITY IN *SD*: An argument of *SL* is *valid in SD* if and only if the conclusion of the argument is derivable in *SD* from the set consisting of the premises. An argument of *SL* is *invalid in SD* if and only if it is not valid in *SD*.

THEOREM IN *SD*: A sentence **P** of *SL* is a *theorem in SD* if and only if **P** is derivable in *SD* from the empty set.

EQUIVALENCE IN *SD*: Sentences **P** and **Q** of *SL* are *equivalent in SD* if and only if **Q** is derivable in *SD* from {**P**} and **P** is derivable in *SD* from {**Q**}.

INCONSISTENCY IN *SD*: A set Γ of sentences of *SL* is *inconsistent in SD* if and only if both a sentence **P** of *SL* and its negation ~ **P** are derivable in *SD* from Γ. A set Γ of sentences of *SL* is *consistent in SD* if and only if it is not inconsistent in *SD*.

---

[2]Similar definitions hold for the derivation system *SD+*.

Chapter 6

SENTENTIAL LOGIC: METATHEORY

6.1 MATHEMATICAL INDUCTION

In the three previous chapters we concentrated on developing and using techniques of sentential logic, both semantic and syntactic. In this chapter we step back to prove some claims *about* the semantics and syntax of sentential logic. Such results constitute the *metatheory* of sentential logic.

For the language *SL* the semantic accounts of such logical properties of sentences and sets of sentences of *SL* as validity, consistency, and equivalence given in Chapter 3 are fundamental in the sense that they are the standards by which other accounts of these properties are judged. For instance, although the techniques of Chapter 5 are purely syntactical—all the derivation rules appeal to the structures or forms of sentences, not to their truth-conditions—those techniques are intended to yield results paralleling those yielded by the semantic techniques of Chapter 3. One of the important metatheoretic results that we shall prove in this chapter is that this parallel does hold. We shall prove this by proving that the natural deduction system *SL* allows us to construct all and only the derivations we want to be able to construct, given the semantics of Chapter 3. Specifically we shall prove that, given any set Γ of sentences and any sentence **P** of *SL*, **P** is derivable from Γ in *SD* if and only if **P** is truth-functionally entailed by Γ. The results mentioned at the end of Section 5.3 follow from this. For example, all and only the truth-functionally valid arguments of *SD* are valid in *SD*, and all and only the truth-functionally true sentences of *SL* are theorems in *SD*.

Before establishing the foregoing results, we introduce the method of proof known as *mathematical induction* and use that method to establish some other interesting results in the metatheory of sentential logic. We use mathematical induction in later sections to prove the claims made in the previous paragraph. Mathematical induction is an extremely powerful method in that it allows us to establish results holding for an infinite number of items.

We introduce mathematical induction with an example. It seems obvious that in each sentence of *SL* the number of left parentheses equals the number of right parentheses. How might we *prove* that this claim is true for every sentence of *SL*? We cannot show that it is true by considering the sentences of *SL* one at a time; there are infinitely many sentences of *SL*, and so we would never get through all of them. Rather, we shall reason more generally about the sentences of *SL*, using the recursive definition of those sentences that was presented in Chapter 2:

1. Every sentence letter is a sentence.
2. If **P** is a sentence, then ~ **P** is a sentence.
3. If **P** and **Q** are sentences, then (**P** & **Q**) is a sentence.
4. If **P** and **Q** are sentences, then (**P** ∨ **Q**) is a sentence.
5. If **P** and **Q** are sentences, then (**P** ⊃ **Q**) is a sentence.
6. If **P** and **Q** are sentences, then (**P** ≡ **Q**) is a sentence.
7. Nothing is a sentence unless it can be formed by repeated application of clauses 1–6.

It is trivial to show that every atomic sentence—that is, every sentence formed in accordance with clause 1—has an equal number of left and right parentheses (namely, zero), because atomic sentences contain no parentheses. All other sentences of *SL* are formed in accordance with clauses 2–6. We note that in each of these cases an equal number of outermost left and right parentheses are added to those already occurring in the sentence's immediate components to form the new sentence (zero of each in clause 2, one of each in clauses 3–6). Therefore, if we can be sure that the immediate components **P** and **Q** of sentences formed in accordance with clauses 2–6 themselves contain an equal number of parentheses, then we may conclude that the application of one of these clauses will result in a new sentence that also contains an equal number of left and right parentheses.

How can we be sure, though, that each of the immediate components of a molecular sentence *does* contain an equal number of left and right parentheses? Start with molecular sentences that contain one occurrence of a connective—sentences like '~ A', '(A ⊃ B)', and '(A & B)'. Every sentence that contains one occurrence of a connective has one of the forms ~ **P**, (**P** & **Q**), (**P** ∨ **Q**), (**P** ⊃ **Q**), or (**P** ≡ **Q**), in accordance with clauses 2–6. Moreover in each case the immediate components **P** and **Q** are atomic. We have already noted that every atomic sentence contains an equal number of left and right parentheses (namely, zero), and so, because clauses 2–6 each add an equal number of left and right parentheses to the ones already occurring in its immediate components, every molecular sentence with one occurrence of a connective must also have an equal number of left and right parentheses.

Now consider molecular sentences that contain two occurrences of connectives—sentences like '~ ~ A', '~ (A ∨ B)', '(A ∨ ~ B)', '((A ≡ B) ⊃ C)', and '(A ∨ (B & C))'. We may reason as we did in the previous paragraph. That is, every sentence that contains two occurrences of connectives has one of the forms ~ **P**, (**P** & **Q**), (**P** ∨ **Q**), (**P** ⊃ **Q**), or (**P** ≡ **Q**), in accordance with clauses 2–6. And in each case the immediate components **P** and **Q** each contain fewer than two occurrences of connectives. We have already found that, in all sentences containing fewer than two occurrences of connectives (atomic sentences or sentences containing one occurrence of a connective), the number of left parentheses equals the number of right parentheses. Therefore, because clauses 2–6 each add an equal number of left and right parentheses to those already occurring in its immediate components, we may conclude that every molecular sentence with two occurrences of connectives also has an equal number of left and right parentheses.

And in sentences containing *three* occurrences of connectives—sentences like '~ ~ ~ A', '~ (~ A ∨ B)', '((A ⊃ B) & (A ∨ C))', and '(~ (A ≡ B) ≡ C)' —the same pattern of reasoning emerges. In every sentence that contains three occurrences of connectives, the immediate components each contain fewer than three occurrences of connectives—either zero, one, or two occurrences. We have already shown that, in any sentence of *SL* that contains either zero, one, or two occurrences of connectives, the number of left parentheses equals the number of right parentheses. Therefore, because clauses 2–6 each add an equal number of left and right parentheses, we may conclude that the number of left parentheses in a sentence that contains three occurrences of connectives is equal to the number of right parentheses. Having established that the claim holds true for every sentence with three or fewer occurrences of connectives, we may show that it also holds for every sentence with four occurrences, then for every sentence with five, and so on—in each case using the same reasoning that we used for earlier cases. Generally, as soon as we have established that the claim holds for every sentence with **k** or fewer occurrences of connectives, the same pattern of reasoning shows that the claim also holds for every sentence that contains **k** + 1 occurrences of connectives.

We shall now present an argument by mathematical induction establishing that our claim is true of *every* sentence of *SL*:

> Every sentence of *SL* containing zero occurrences of connectives—that is, every atomic sentence of *SL*—is such that the number of left parentheses in that sentence equals the number of right parentheses.
>
> If every sentence of *SL* with **k** or fewer occurrences of connectives is such that the number of left parentheses in that sentence equals the number of right parentheses, then every sentence of *SL* with **k** + 1

occurrences of connectives is also such that the number of left parentheses in that sentence equals the number of right parentheses.

Therefore every sentence of *SL* is such that the number of left parentheses in that sentence equals the number of right parentheses.

(Here we use '**k**' as a variable ranging over the nonnegative integers, that is, the positive integers plus zero.) This argument is deductively valid—if the premises are true, then the conclusion is true as well. The first premise is our claim about parentheses for sentences with no connectives, and the second premise says that it follows that the claim also holds for sentences containing one occurrence of a connective. Having concluded that the claim holds for all sentences containing zero or one occurrences of connectives, we are assured by the second premise that the claim must also hold for sentences containing two occurrences of connectives. Having concluded that the claim holds for all sentences containing zero, one, or two occurrences of connectives, we are assured by the second premise that the claim also holds for sentences containing three occurrences of connectives, and so on for any number of occurrences of connectives that a sentence may contain. Because the argument is deductively valid, we can establish that its conclusion is true by showing that both premises are true.

We have already shown that the first premise is true. Sentences that contain zero occurrences of connectives are atomic sentences, and atomic sentences are simply sentence letters. The first premise is called the *basis clause* of the argument.

The second premise of the argument is called the *inductive step*. We shall prove that the inductive step is true by generalizing on the reasoning that we have already used. The antecedent of the inductive step is called the *inductive hypothesis*. We shall assume that the inductive hypothesis is true—that is, that every sentence of *SL* containing **k** or fewer occurrences of connectives contains an equal number of left and right parentheses—and we must show that on this assumption it follows that any sentence **P** that has **k** + 1 occurrences of connectives also contains an equal number of left and right parentheses. Since **k** is nonnegative, **k** + 1 is positive, and hence such a sentence **P** contains at least one occurrence of a connective. So **P** will be a molecular sentence, having one of the forms ~ **Q**, (**Q** & **R**), (**Q** ∨ **R**), (**Q** ⊃ **R**), or (**Q** ≡ **R**). We divide these forms into two cases.

Case 1: **P** has the form ~ **Q**. If ~ **Q** contains **k** + 1 occurrences of connectives, then **Q** contains **k** occurrences of connectives. By the inductive hypothesis (that every sentence containing **k** or fewer connectives has an equal number of left and right parentheses), the number of left parentheses in **Q** equals the number of right parentheses in **Q**. But ~ **Q** contains all the parentheses occurring in **Q** and no others. So ~ **Q** contains an equal number of left and right parentheses as well.

Case 2: **P** has one of the forms (**Q** & **R**), (**Q** ∨ **R**), (**Q** ⊃ **R**), or (**Q** ≡ **R**). In each instance, if **P** contains **k** + 1 occurrences of connectives, then each of its immediate components, **Q** and **R**, must contain **k** or fewer occurrences of connectives. By the inductive hypothesis, then, we have the following:

a. The number of left parentheses in **Q** equals the number of right parentheses in **Q**.
b. The number of left parentheses in **R** equals the number of right parentheses in **R**.

We also have this:

c. The number of left parentheses in **P** is the number of left parentheses in **Q** plus the number of left parentheses in **R** plus 1—the one for the outermost left parenthesis in **P**.
d. The number of right parentheses in **P** is the number of right parentheses in **Q** plus the number of right parentheses in **R** plus 1.

By simple arithmetic, using (a) and (b), it follows that (c) equals (d)—**P** therefore has an equal number of left and right parentheses as well.

This completes our proof that the second premise, the inductive step, is true. Having established that both premises are true, we may conclude that the conclusion is true as well. Every sentence of *SL* contains an equal number of left and right parentheses.

We may now generally characterize arguments by mathematical induction. In such an argument, we arrange the items about which we wish to prove some thesis in a series of groups. In our example, we arranged the sentences of *SL* into the series: all sentences containing zero occurrences of connectives, all sentences containing one occurrence of connectives, all sentences containing two occurrences of connectives, and so on. Every sentence of *SL* appears in some group in this series—any sentence with **k** occurrences of connectives is part of group **k** + 1 in the series. Having arranged the items in such a series, an argument by mathematical induction then takes the following form[1].

The thesis holds for every member of the first group in the series.

For each group in the series, if the thesis holds of every member of every prior group then the thesis holds for every member of that group as well.

The thesis holds for every member of every group of the series.

All arguments of this form are valid. Of course, only those with true premises are sound. Hence, to establish that the thesis holds for every member of every

[1] Strictly speaking, this is the form for arguments by *strong* mathematical induction. There is another type of mathematical induction, known as *weak* induction. We shall use only the strong variety of mathematical induction in this text. There is no loss here, for every claim that can be proved by weak mathematical induction can also be proved by strong mathematical induction.

group in the series, we must show first that the thesis does hold for every member of the first group and then that, no matter what group in the series we consider, the thesis holds for every member of that group if it holds for every member of every prior group. The first premise of such arguments is called the *basis clause,* and the second premise is called the *inductive step.* The antecedent of the second premise is called the *inductive hypothesis.*

We further illustrate mathematical induction with another example. Let **P** be a sentence that contains only '~ ', '∨', and '&' as connectives, and let **P′** be the sentence that results from doing this:

a. Replacing each occurrence of '∨' in **P** with '&'

b. Replacing each occurrence of '&' in **P** with '∨'

c. Adding a '~ ' in front of each atomic component of **P**

We shall call a sentence that contains only '~ ', '∨', and '&' as connectives a *TWA* sentence (short for '*t*ilde, *w*edge, and *a*mpersand'), and we shall call the sentence **P′** that results from **P** by (a), (b), and (c) the *dual* of **P**. Here are some examples of duals for TWA sentences:

P	*Dual of* **P**
A	~ A
((A ∨ F) & G)	((~ A & ~ F) ∨ ~ G)
(((B & C) & C) ∨ D)	(((~ B ∨ ~ C) ∨ ~ C) & ~ D)
~ ((A ∨ ~ B) ∨ (~ A & ~ B))	~ ((~ A & ~ ~ B) & (~ ~ A ∨ ~ ~ B))

We shall use mathematical induction to establish the following thesis:

Every TWA sentence **P** is such that **P** and its dual **P′** have opposite truth-values on each truth-value assignment (that is, if **P** is true then **P′** is false, and if **P** is false then **P′** is true).

As in the previous example, our series will classify sentences by the number of occurrences of connectives that they contain:

Basis clause: Every TWA sentence **P** of *SL* that contains zero occurrences of connectives is such that **P** and its dual **P′** have opposite truth-values on each truth-value assignment.

Inductive step: If every TWA sentence **P** of *SL* with **k** or fewer occurrences of connectives is such that **P** and its dual **P′** have opposite truth-values on each truth-value assignment, then every TWA sentence **P** of *SL* with **k** + 1 occurrences of connectives is such that **P** and its dual **P′** have opposite truth-values on each truth-value assignment.

Conclusion: Every TWA sentence **P** of *SL* is such that **P** and its dual **P′** have opposite truth-values on each truth-value assignment.

To show that the conclusion of this argument is true, we must show that the first premise, the basis clause, is true and also that the second premise, the inductive step, is true.

Proof of basis clause: A TWA sentence **P** that contains zero occurrences of connectives must be an atomic sentence, and its dual is ~ **P**—because there are no connectives to replace, we simply place a tilde in front of the atomic sentence. If **P** is true on a truth-value assignment, then according to the characteristic truth-table for the tilde, ~ **P** must be false. And if **P** is false on a truth-value assignment, then ~ **P** is true. We conclude that **P** and its dual have opposite truth-values on each truth-value assignment.

Proof of inductive step: We assume that the inductive hypothesis is true for all sentences that contain fewer than **k** + 1 connectives—that is, that every TWA sentence that contains fewer than **k** + 1 occurrences of connectives is such that it and its dual have opposite truth-values on each truth-value assignment. We must show that it follows from this assumption that the claim is also true of all TWA sentences that contain **k** + 1 occurrences of connectives. A TWA sentence **P** that contains **k** + 1 occurrences of connectives must be molecular, and because it is TWA, it has one of the three forms ~ **Q**, (**Q** ∨ **R**), or (**Q** & **R**). We will consider each form.

Case 1: **P** has the form ~ **Q**. If **P** contains **k** + 1 occurrences of connectives, then **Q** contains **k** occurrences of connectives, and **Q** is a TWA sentence (if it were not—if it contained a horseshoe or triple bar—then **P** would not be a TWA sentence either). Let **Q**′ be the dual of **Q**. Then the dual of **P** is ~ **Q**′, the sentence that results from ~ **Q** by making the changes (a), (b), and (c) of our definition of dual sentences within **Q** and leaving the initial tilde of ~ **Q** intact.

If **P**, that is, ~ **Q**, is true on a truth-value assignment, then **Q** is false. Because **Q** is a TWA sentence with fewer than **k** + 1 occurrences of connectives, it follows from the inductive hypothesis that **Q**′ is true. Therefore ~ **Q**′—the dual of **P**—is false. So, if **P** is true then its dual is false, and if **P** is false on a truth-value assignment then **Q** is true. It follows from the inductive hypothesis that **Q**′ is false, and therefore ~ **Q**′ is true. So, if **P** is false then its dual is true. We conclude that **P** and its dual have opposite truth-values on each truth-value assignment.

Case 2: **P** has the form (**Q** ∨ **R**). If **P** contains **k** + 1 occurrences of connectives, then **Q** and **R** each contain **k** or fewer occurrences of connectives. **Q** and **R** are also TWA sentences. Let **Q**′ be the dual of **Q** and **R**′ be the dual of **R**. Then the dual of **P** is (**Q**′ & **R**′)—the changes specified by (a), (b), and (c) must be made within **Q**, yielding its dual, and within **R**, yielding *its* dual, and the main connective '∨' of **P** must be replaced with '&'.

If **P** is true on a truth-value assignment, then by the characteristic truth-table for the wedge, either **Q** is true or **R** is true. Because **Q** and **R** each contain **k** or fewer occurrences of connectives, it follows from the inductive hypothesis that either **Q**′ is false or **R**′ is false. Either way, (**Q**′ & **R**′), the dual of **P**, must be false as well. But if **P** is false on a truth-value assignment, then both **Q** and **R** must be false. By the inductive hypothesis both **Q**′ and **R**′ are true. So (**Q**′ & **R**′) is true as well. We conclude that **P** and its dual have opposite truth-values on each truth-value assignment.

Case 3: **P** has the form (**Q** & **R**). If **P** contains **k** + 1 occurrences of connectives, then **Q** and **R** each contain **k** or fewer occurrences of connectives. And they are also TWA sentences. Let **Q**′ be the dual of **Q** and **R**′ be the dual of **R**. Then the dual of **P** is (**Q**′ ∨ **R**′); changes (a), (b), and (c) have to be made within each of **Q** and **R**, producing their duals, and the main connective '&' has to be replaced with '∨'.

If **P** is true on a truth-value assignment, then, by the characteristic truth-table for the ampersand, both **Q** and **R** are true. Because **Q** and **R** each contain **k** or fewer occurrences of connectives, it follows from the inductive hypothesis that **Q**′ and **R**′ are both false, and therefore that the dual of **P**, (**Q**′ ∨ **R**′), is false. If **P** is false on a truth-value assignment, then either **Q** is false or **R** is false. If **Q** is false, then it follows by the inductive hypothesis that **Q**′ is true. If **R** is false, then it follows by the inductive hypothesis that **R**′ is true. So at least one of **Q**′ and **R**′ is true, and (**Q**′ ∨ **R**′), the dual of **P**, must be true as well. We conclude that **P** and its dual have opposite truth-values on each truth-value assignment.

These three cases establish the inductive step of the argument by mathematical induction, and we may now conclude that its conclusion is true as well. Our argument shows that the thesis about duals is true of every TWA sentence of *SL*. The basis clause shows that the thesis is true of every TWA sentence with zero occurrences of connectives. It follows, from the inductive step, that the thesis is also true of every TWA sentence with one connective. Because the thesis holds for all TWA sentences with zero or one occurrences of connectives, it follows from the inductive step that the thesis is also true of every TWA sentence with two occurrences of connectives. And so on, for any number of occurrences of connectives that a TWA sentence may have. Together the basis clause and the inductive step take every TWA sentence into account.

6.1E EXERCISES

1. Prove the following theses by mathematical induction.

a. No sentence of *SL* that contains only binary connectives, if any, is truth-functionally false (that is, every truth-functionally false sentence of *SL* contains at least one '∼ ').

b. Every sentence of *SL* that contains no binary connectives is truth-functionally indeterminate.
c. If two truth-value assignments **A**′ and **A**″ assign the same truth-values to the atomic components of a sentence **P**, then **P** has the same truth-value on **A**′ and **A**″.
d. An iterated conjunction $(\ldots(\mathbf{P}_1 \,\&\, \mathbf{P}_2) \,\&\, \ldots \,\&\, \mathbf{P}_n)$ of sentences of *SL* is true on a truth-value assignment if and only if $\mathbf{P}_1, \mathbf{P}_2 \ldots, \mathbf{P}_n$ are all true on that assignment.
e. Where **P** is a sentence of *SL* and **Q** is a sentential component of **P**, let $[\mathbf{P}]\ (\mathbf{Q}_1//\mathbf{Q})$ be a sentence that is the result of replacing at least one occurrence of **Q** in **P** with the sentence $\mathbf{Q}_1$. If **Q** and $\mathbf{Q}_1$ are truth-functionally equivalent, then **P** and $[\mathbf{P}]\ (\mathbf{Q}_1//\mathbf{Q})$ are truth-functionally equivalent.

2. Consider this thesis:

No sentence of *SL* that contains only binary connectives is truth-functionally true.

Show that this thesis is false by producing a sentence that contains only binary connectives and that is truth-functionally true. Explain where an attempt to prove the thesis by mathematical induction (in the manner of the answer to Exercise 1.a) would fail.

6.2 TRUTH-FUNCTIONAL COMPLETENESS

In Chapter 2 we defined the truth-functional use of sentential connectives as follows:

> A sentential connective is used *truth-functionally* if and only if it is used to generate a compound sentence from one or more sentences in such a way that the truth-value of the generated compound is wholly determined by the truth-values of those one or more sentences from which the compound is generated, no matter what those truth-values may be.

The connectives of *SL* are used only truth-functionally since their intended interpretations are given wholly by their characteristic truth-tables. In Chapter 2 we constructed truth-functional paraphrases of many English sentences and showed how to symbolize these paraphrases in *SL*. Although *SL* contains only five sentential connectives, we found that a great variety of English compounds can nevertheless be adequately symbolized by using various combinations of these connectives. For instance, an English sentence of the form

Neither **p** nor **q**

can be appropriately symbolized either by a sentence of the form

$\sim (\mathbf{P} \vee \mathbf{Q})$

or by a sentence of the form

$$\sim \mathbf{P} \;\&\; \sim \mathbf{Q}$$

An interesting question now arises: Is *SL* capable of representing all the ways in which sentences can be built up from other sentences by truth-functional means? We want the answer to this question to be 'yes' because we want *SL* to be an adequate vehicle for all of truth-functional logic. If there is some way of truth-functionally compounding sentences that cannot be represented in *SL*, then there may be some truth-functionally valid arguments that do not have valid symbolizations in *SL* simply because they cannot be adequately symbolized in *SL*. Similarly there may be sets of sentences that are truth-functionally inconsistent but that cannot be shown to be inconsistent by the truth-table method, again because these sentences cannot be adequately symbolized in *SL*. And so on.

To settle this question, we might try to produce complicated examples of truth-functionally compound sentences of English and then show that each can be adequately symbolized in *SL*. But obviously we cannot in this way prove that every truth-functionally compound sentence can be adequately symbolized in *SL*. Rather, we must show that all the possible ways of truth-functionally compounding sentences—of building up sentences from sentences by truth-functional connectives—yield sentences that can be adequately symbolized in *SL*.

We must first formulate our question somewhat more precisely: Can every truth-function be expressed by a sentence of *SL*? A *truth-function* is a mapping, for some positive integer **n**, of each combination of truth-values that **n** sentences of *SL* may have to a truth-value. Functions are most familiar in mathematics. Addition and multiplication are, for example, both functions that map each pair of numbers to a unique number. Addition maps each pair of numbers to the sum of those numbers. Multiplication maps each pair of numbers to the product of those numbers. The members of the pairs of numbers that are mapped are the *arguments* of the function, and the number to which a pair is mapped is the *value* of the function for that pair of arguments. (Arguments in the sense of arguments of functions are not to be confused with arguments consisting of premises and conclusions.) Thus the addition function maps the pair of arguments 3 and 4 to the value 7, and the multiplication function maps that pair of arguments to the value 12.

Instead of mapping combinations of numbers to numbers, a truth-function maps each combination of truth-values that **n** atomic sentences of *SL* may have to a truth-value. The characteristic truth-table for '⊃' defines the material conditional truth-function:

P	Q	P ⊃ Q
T	T	T
T	F	F
F	T	T
F	F	T

This truth-function is a truth-function of *two* arguments. There are four distinct combinations of truth-values that two sentences may have, and the table defining the truth-function accordingly contains four rows. Each distinct combination of arguments is listed to the left of the vertical line, and the truth-value to which that combination of arguments is mapped is listed to the right of the vertical line.

The characteristic truth-table for '~ ' defines the negation truth-function:

P	**~ P**
T	**F**
F	**T**

The negation truth-function is a truth-function of *one* argument since it maps each combination of truth-values that one sentence of *SL* may have to a truth-value. There are only two such combinations; each consists of a single truth-value. The truth-value to which each combination is mapped is listed in the same row to the right of the vertical line.

A truth-function is said to be *expressed* in *SL* by any sentence whose truth-table contains (in the column under its main connective) exactly the column of **T**s and **F**s that occurs on the right-hand side of the characteristic truth-table for the truth-function in question. For example, each sentence of the form ~ **P**, where **P** is an atomic sentence of *SL*, expresses the negation truth-function—for every such sentence has a two-row truth-table in which the column under the main connective contains an **F** in the first row and a **T** in the second row. This truth-function is also expressed by other sentences of *SL*—for example, by all sentences of the form ~ **P** & ~ **P**, where **P** is an atomic sentence. Every such sentence has a two-row truth-table in which the column under the main connective is

F
T

The important question for us is not how many sentences of *SL* express the same truth-function but rather whether for each truth-function there is *at least one* sentence of *SL* that expresses that truth-function. There are an infinite number of truth-functions. This is most easily seen by considering that for every positive integer **n** there are truth-functions of **n** arguments (truth-functions that map each combination of truth-values that **n** sentences of *SL* may have to a truth-value), and there are infinitely many positive integers. In Chapter 2 we defined one truth-function of one argument and four truth-functions of two arguments via the five characteristic truth-tables for the connectives of *SL*. There are three other truth-functions of one argument:

P	
T	**T**
F	**F**

P	
T	**T**
F	**T**

P	
T	**F**
F	**F**

And there are twelve other truth-functions of two arguments (because there are sixteen different ways of arranging **T**s and **F**s in a column of a four-row truth-table). Generally, where **n** is any positive integer, there are $2^{(2^{\mathbf{n}})}$ truth-functions of **n** arguments. So there are 256 truth-functions of three arguments, 65,536 truth-functions of four arguments, and so on. What we want to show is that, given any truth-function of any finite number of arguments, there is at least one sentence of *SL* that expresses that truth-function. In fact, we shall prove something even stronger:

Metatheorem 6.2.1:[2] Every truth-function can be expressed by a sentence of *SL* that contains no sentential connectives other than '~ ', '∨', and '&'.

The connectives of a language in which every truth-function can be expressed form a *truth-functionally complete* set of connectives. In proving Metatheorem 6.2.1 we shall be proving that the set that contains the connectives '~ ', '&', and '∨', defined as they are defined in *SL*, is truth-functionally complete.

Characteristic truth-tables define truth-functions by giving an exhaustive list of the combinations of arguments that each truth-function takes and displaying the value to which each such combination is mapped. That is, it is the rows of **T**s and **F**s that serve to define truth-functions in characteristic truth-tables. It should now be clear that the following schema also specifies a truth-function:

T	**T**	**F**
T	**F**	**F**
F	**T**	**F**
F	**F**	**T**

To the left of the vertical line, the four distinct combinations of truth-values that two sentences of *SL* may have are displayed. The specified truth-function is thus a function of two arguments. The value of the function for each combination of arguments is displayed to the right of the vertical line. Since every truth-function maps only a finite number of combinations of arguments, every truth-function can be specified in a table like the previous one. We call such a table a *truth-function schema.* A truth-function schema is simply a truncated truth-table.

We shall now show that the set of connectives {'~ ', '&', '∨'} is truth-functionally complete by producing an *algorithm* for constructing, given any possible truth-function schema, a sentence of *SL* that contains no connectives other than '~ ', '&', and '∨' and that expresses the truth-function specified by the schema. An algorithm is an *effective* procedure for producing a desired result—that is, a mechanical procedure that, when correctly followed, yields the desired result in a finite number of steps. Given a truth-function schema, our algorithm will produce a sentence whose truth-table contains, under its

[2]We number our metatheoretic results in a way that makes clear where to find them in the text. The first two digits, '6.2', refer to the chapter and section. The third digit, '1', means that this is the first numbered metatheoretic result in this section.

main connective, exactly the same column of **T**s and **F**s as occurs to the right of the vertical line in the truth-function schema. Once we produce the algorithm, Metatheorem 6.2.1 will be proved; the construction of such an algorithm will show that every truth-function can be expressed by a sentence of *SL* containing no connectives other than '~ ', '&', and '∨'.

To begin, we need a stock of atomic sentences. If the truth-function is a function of **n** arguments, we use the alphabetically first **n** atomic sentences of *SL*. So for the truth-function schema

T	**T**	**F**
T	**F**	**F**
F	**T**	**F**
F	**F**	**T**

we start with the atomic sentences 'A' and 'B'. Next we form, for each row of the truth-table, a sentence that is true if and only if its atomic components have the truth-values indicated in that row. This sentence is called the *characteristic sentence* for the row in question. The characteristic sentence for row **i** is the iterated conjunction

$$(\ldots(\mathbf{P}_1 \;\&\; \mathbf{P}_2) \;\&\; \ldots \;\&\; \mathbf{P}_\mathbf{n})$$

where $\mathbf{P_j}$ is the **j**th atomic sentence if the **j**th value in row **i** (to the left of the vertical bar) is **T**, and $\mathbf{P_j}$ is the negation of the **j**th atomic sentence if the **j**th value in row **i** is **F**. Thus the characteristic sentences for the four rows in our sample truth-function schema are 'A & B', 'A & ~ B', '~ A & B', and '~ A & ~ B', respectively. The first sentence is true if and only if both 'A' and 'B' are true; the second sentence is true if and only if 'A' is true and 'B' is false; the third sentence is true if and only if 'A' is false and 'B' is true; and the fourth sentence is true if and only if both 'A' and 'B' are false. We leave it as an exercise to prove that the characteristic sentence for each row of a truth-function schema is true if and only if its atomic components have the truth-values presented in that row.

Finally we identify the rows in the truth-function schema that have a **T** to the right of the vertical bar. If there is only one such row, then the characteristic sentence for that row is a sentence that expresses the truth-function specified in the schema. In our example the fourth row is the only row that has a **T** to the right of the vertical bar, and the characteristic sentence for that row is '~ A & ~ B'. This sentence is true if and only if both 'A' and 'B' are false, and therefore this sentence expresses the truth-function specified by the truth-function schema:

A	B	~ A & ~ B
T	**T**	**F T F F T**
T	**F**	**F T F T F**
F	**T**	**T F F F T**
F	**F**	**T F T T F**

If the truth-function schema has more than one **T** to the right of the vertical bar, as does the following,

T	**T**	**F**
T	**F**	**T**
F	**T**	**F**
F	**F**	**T**

then we form an iterated disjunction of the characteristic sentences for the rows that have a **T** to the right of the vertical bar. In the present case the disjunction is '(A & ~ B) ∨ (~ A & ~ B)'—the disjunction of the characteristic sentences for the second and fourth rows. This sentence is true if and only if either 'A' is true and 'B' is false or both 'A' and 'B' are false, and it therefore expresses the truth-function specified in this schema:

A	B	(A	&	~ B)	∨	(~ A	&	~ B)
T	**T**	**T**	**F**	**F T**	**F**	**F T**	**F**	**F T**
T	**F**	**T**	**T**	**T F**	**T**	**F T**	**F**	**T F**
F	**T**	**F**	**F**	**F T**	**F**	**T F**	**F**	**F T**
F	**F**	**F**	**F**	**T F**	**T**	**T F**	**T**	**T F**

And if the schema is

T	**T**	**F**
T	**F**	**T**
F	**T**	**T**
F	**F**	**T**

then the disjunction of the characteristic sentences for the last three rows, '((A & ~ B) ∨ (~ A & B)) ∨ (~ A & ~ B)', expresses the truth-function in the schema.

In general, in the case where there is more than one **T** to the right of the vertical bar in a truth-function schema, the iterated disjunction that we form from the characteristic sentences for those rows will be true if and only if at least one of its disjuncts is true, and each disjunct is true only in the row for which it is a characteristic sentence. Therefore the iterated disjunction is true if and only if its atomic components have the truth-values specified by one of the rows that have a **T** to the right of the vertical bar, and so the disjunction expresses the truth-function specified by that schema.

If there are no **T**s in the column to the right of the vertical bar, then we conjoin the characteristic sentence for the first row of the truth-function schema with its negation. (Any other row's characteristic sentence would have done as well.) The result will be a sentence of the form **P** & ~ **P**, which is false on every truth-value assignment and hence expresses a truth-function that maps every combination of **n** truth-values into **F**. For example, if our schema is

T	**T**	**F**
T	**F**	**F**
F	**T**	**F**
F	**F**	**F**

then the sentence '(A & B) & ~ (A & B)' expresses the truth-function specified in the schema.

In sum, we have three cases. If a truth-function schema has exactly one row with a **T** to the right of the vertical bar, then the characteristic sentence for that row expresses the truth-function specified in the schema. If a truth-function schema has more than one row with a **T** to the right of the vertical bar, then an iterated disjunction of the characteristic sentences for all such rows will express the truth-function specified in the schema. If a truth-function schema has no **T**s to the right of the vertical bar, then the conjunction of the characteristic sentence for the first row and its negation will express the truth-function specified by the schema.

The algorithm tells us how to construct a sentence that expresses the truth-function indicated in a given truth-function schema, and we may use it for any truth-function schema. As a final example consider the schema

T	**T**	**T**	**F**
T	**T**	**F**	**F**
T	**F**	**T**	**T**
T	**F**	**F**	**T**
F	**T**	**T**	**F**
F	**T**	**F**	**F**
F	**F**	**T**	**T**
F	**F**	**F**	**F**

This falls under our second case; there is more than one **T** to the right of the vertical line. We shall use the first three sentence letters of *SL*, because the truth-function is a truth-function of three arguments. We form the characteristic sentences for rows 3, 4, and 7 and then disjoin those characteristic sentences to produce

(((A & ~ B) & C) ∨ ((A & ~ B) & ~ C)) ∨ ((~ A & ~ B) & C)

This sentence is true if and only if 'A', 'B', and 'C' have one of the combinations of truth-values represented in the third, fourth, and seventh rows of the schema.

Our algorithm shows how to construct, for any truth-function, a sentence of *SL* that expresses that truth-function. It therefore shows that for each truth-function there is *at least one* sentence of *SL* that expresses that truth-function. Moreover, because we have used only the three connectives '~ ', '&', and '∨', we have shown that the set of connectives {'~ ', '&', '∨'} is truth-functionally complete. This completes the proof of Metatheorem 6.2.1.

There is a consequence of the theorem that follows almost immediately: The smaller set {'~ ', '∨'} is also truth-functionally complete. Every conjunction **P** & **Q** is truth-functionally equivalent to ~ (~ **P** ∨ ~ **Q**), and so we may rewrite each sentence produced by the algorithm using only '~ ' and '∨'. For example, the sentence

(~ (~ A ∨ ~ ~ B) ∨ ~ (~ ~ A ∨ ~ ~ B))

expresses the same truth-function as

((A & ~ B) ∨ (~ A & ~ B))

Therefore every truth-function can be expressed by a sentence that contains only '~ ' and '∨' as connectives. It is also a consequence of Metatheorem 6.2.1 that the sets of connectives {'~ ', '&'} and {'~ ', '>'} are truth-functionally complete; we leave the proofs as an exercise.

On the other hand, the set of connectives {'∨', '&'} is *not* truth-functionally complete. To prove this, we must show that there is at least one truth-function that cannot be expressed by any sentence that contains at most the connectives '∨' and '&'. We call such a sentence a *W-A* sentence (short for '*w*edge and *a*mpersand'). A little reflection suggests that, no matter how many times we conjoin and disjoin, if we do not have the tilde available we can never produce a false sentence from atomic components that are all true. That is, every W-A sentence is true whenever its atomic components are all true. And if this is the case, then there are many truth-functions that cannot be expressed by any W-A sentence. Take the negation truth-function as an example. This truth-function maps the argument **T** into the value **F**. If our reflection is correct, there is no false W-A sentence with a single atomic component when that atomic component is true.

We shall therefore show that the set of connectives {'∨', '&'} is not truth-functionally complete by proving the following thesis:

> Every W-A sentence has the truth-value **T** on every truth-value assignment on which its atomic components all have the truth-value **T**.

This is a general claim about *all* W-A sentences, and so it cannot be proved by examining W-A sentences one by one (there are infinitely many). Instead, we shall prove the thesis by mathematical induction.

The shortest W-A sentences—that is, those with zero occurrences of connectives, are simply the atomic sentences of *SL*.

> *Basis clause:* Every atomic sentence of *SL* has the truth-value **T** on every truth-value assignment on which its atomic components all have the truth-value **T**.
>
> **Proof of basis clause:** The basis clause is obviously true, since an atomic sentence is itself its only component.

Inductive step: If every W-A sentence of *SL* with **k** or fewer occurrences of connectives is such that it has the truth-value **T** on every truth-value assignment on which its atomic components all have the truth-value **T**, then every W-A sentence with **k** + 1 occurrences of connectives has the truth-value **T** on every truth-value assignment on which its atomic components all have the truth-value **T**.

Proof of inductive step: We now assume that the inductive hypothesis is true for an arbitrary nonnegative integer **k**; that is, we assume that every W-A sentence with **k** or fewer occurrences of connectives is true whenever all its atomic components are true. We must show that it follows that the thesis also holds for any W-A sentence **P** with **k** + 1 occurrences of connectives. Since these sentences contain only '∨' and '&' as connectives, there are two cases.

Case 1: P has the form **Q** ∨ **R**. Then **Q** and **R** each contain fewer than **k** + 1 occurrences of connectives. They are also W-A sentences. So, by the inductive hypothesis, each disjunct is true on every truth-value assignment on which each of its atomic components is true. So, if all the atomic components of **Q** ∨ **R** are true, then both **Q** and **R** are true, and hence **Q** ∨ **R** is itself true.

Case 2: P has the form **Q** & **R**. Then each of **Q** and **R** is a W-A sentence with **k** or fewer occurrences of connectives. Hence the inductive hypothesis holds for both **Q** and **R**. Each conjunct is true on every truth-value assignment on which all its atomic components are true. So, if all the atomic components of **Q** & **R** are true, then both **Q** and **R** are true, and hence **Q** & **R** itself is true.

This proves the inductive step, and we can conclude that the thesis holds for every W-A sentence:

Conclusion: Every W-A sentence has the truth-value **T** on every truth-value assignment on which its atomic components all have the truth-value **T**.

It follows that no W-A sentence can express the negation truth-function as defined in the characteristic truth-table for the tilde since no W-A sentence can express a truth-function that maps the truth-value **T** to the truth-value **F**. (Whenever all the atomic components of a W-A sentence are true, the W-A sentence itself is true.)

6.2E EXERCISES

1. Show that a sentence constructed in accordance with our characteristic sentence algorithm is indeed a characteristic sentence for the row of the truth-function schema in question.
2. Using the algorithm in the proof of Metatheorem 6.2.1, construct a sentence containing at most '~ ', '&', and '∨' that expresses the truth-function defined in each of the following truth-function schemata.

a.

T	T	F
T	F	T
F	T	F
F	F	T

b.

T	F
F	F

*c.

T	T	F
T	F	T
F	T	T
F	F	F

d.

T	T	T	T
T	T	F	T
T	F	T	F
T	F	F	F
F	T	T	F
F	T	F	F
F	F	T	T
F	F	F	F

3. Give an algorithm analogous to that in Metatheorem 6.2.1 for constructing a characteristic sentence containing only '~ ' and '∨' for each row of a truth-function schema.

4. Using Metatheorem 6.2.1, prove that the sets {'~ ', '&'} and {'~ ', '⊃'} are truth-functionally complete.

5. Prove that the set consisting of the dagger '↓' is truth-functionally complete, where the dagger has the following characteristic truth-table:

P	Q	P ↓ Q
T	T	F
T	F	F
F	T	F
F	F	T

***6.** Prove that the set consisting of the stroke '|' is truth-functionally complete, where the stroke has the following characteristic truth-table:

P	Q	P | Q
T	T	F
T	F	T
F	T	T
F	F	T

7. Using the results of Exercises 1.a and 1.b in Section 6.1E, prove that the following sets of connectives are not truth-functionally complete: {'~ '}, {'&', '∨', '⊃', '≡'}.

8. Prove that the set {'~ ', '≡'} is not truth-functionally complete. *Hint:* Show that the truth-table for any sentence **P** that contains only these two connectives and just two atomic components will have, in the column under the main connective, an even number of **T**s and an even number of **F**s.

9. Prove that if a truth-functionally complete set of connectives consists of exactly one binary connective, then that connective has either the characteristic truth-table for '↓' or the characteristic truth-table for '|'. (That is, show that the connective must be either '↓' or '|', though possibly under a different name.) (*Hint:* In the proofs for Exercises 7 and 8 above, it became apparent that characteristic truth-tables for truth-functionally complete sets of connectives must have certain properties. Show that only two characteristic truth-tables with just four rows have these properties.)

6.3 THE SOUNDNESS OF *SD* AND *SD*+

We now turn to the results announced at the beginning of this chapter. In this section we shall prove that, if a sentence **P** is derivable in *SD* from a set of sentences Γ, then Γ truth-functionally entails **P**. A natural deduction system for which this result holds is said to be *sound* for sentential logic. In the next section we shall prove the converse—that if a set of sentences Γ truth-functionally entails a sentence **P**, then **P** is derivable in *SD* from Γ. A natural deduction system for which this second result holds is said to be *complete* for sentential logic. Soundness and completeness are important properties for natural deduction systems. A natural deduction system that is not sound will sometimes lead us from true sentences to false ones, and a natural deduction system that is not complete will not allow us to construct all the derivations that we want to construct. In either case the natural deduction system would not be adequate for the purposes of sentential logic.

Metatheorem 6.3.1 is the *Soundness Metatheorem* for *SD*. That is, for any set Γ of sentences of *SL* and any sentence **P** of *SL*, we have this:

Metatheorem 6.3.1: If Γ ⊢ **P** in *SD*, then Γ ⊨ **P**.[3]

Recall that Γ ⊨ **P** if and only if there is no truth-value assignment on which all the members of Γ are true and **P** is false. Metatheorem 6.3.1 therefore says that the derivation rules of *SD* are *truth-preserving;* that is, when correctly applied, they will never take us from true sentences to a false sentence. When we constructed *SD*, our intent was to pick out truth-preserving derivation rules, and we shall now prove that we were successful.

Our proof will use mathematical induction to establish that each sentence in a derivation is true if all the undischarged assumptions in whose scope the sentence lies are true. The basis clause will show that this claim is true

[3]In what follows we shall abbreviate 'Γ ⊢ **P** in *SD*' as 'Γ ⊢ **P**'.

of the first sentence in a derivation. And the inductive step will show that, if the claim is true for the first **k** sentences in a derivation, then the claim is also true for the (**k** + 1)th sentence—that is, each time we apply another derivation rule in the derivation, that application is truth-preserving. We will then be able to conclude that the last sentence in any derivation, no matter how long the derivation is, is true if all the undischarged assumptions in whose scope the sentence lies are true. And this conclusion is just what Metatheorem 6.3.1 says.

In the course of the proof, we shall use some set-theoretic terminology, which we here explain: Let Γ and Γ′ be sets. If every member of Γ is also a member of Γ′, then Γ is said to be a *subset* of Γ′. Note that every set is a subset of itself, and the empty set is trivially a subset of every set (because the empty set has no members, it has no members that are not members of every set). As an example, the set of sentences

{A, B, C}

has eight subsets: {A, B, C}, {A, B}, {B, C}, {A, C}, {A}, {B}, {C}, and ∅. If a set Γ is a subset of a set Γ′, then Γ′ is said to be a *superset* of Γ. Thus {A, B, C} is a superset of each of its eight subsets.

We will also make use of several semantic results, which we gather together here. First, if **P** is truth-functionally entailed by a set of sentences Γ, then **P** is truth-functionally entailed by every superset of Γ:

6.3.2: If Γ ⊨ **P**, then for every superset Γ′ of Γ, Γ′ ⊨ **P**.

Proof: Assume that Γ ⊨ **P** and let Γ′ be any superset of Γ. If every member of Γ′ is true, then every member of its subset Γ is true, and so, because Γ ⊨ **P**, **P** is also true. Therefore Γ′ ⊨ **P**.

Second, we have two results that were proved in the exercises for Chapter 3:

6.3.3: If Γ ∪ {**Q**} ⊨ **R**, then Γ ⊨ **Q** ⊃ **R** (see Exercise 2.b in Section 3.6E).

6.3.4: If Γ ⊨ **Q** and Γ ⊨ ~ **Q** for some sentence **Q**, then Γ is truth-functionally inconsistent (see Exercise 3.b in Section 3.6E).

Finally, if a set of sentences is truth-functionally inconsistent, then, for any sentence **Q** in the set, the set consisting of all the *other* sentences in the set truth-functionally entails ~ **Q**:

6.3.5: If Γ ∪ {**Q**} is truth-functionally inconsistent, then Γ ⊨ ~ **Q**.

Proof: Assume that Γ ∪ {**Q**} is truth-functionally inconsistent. Then there is no truth-value assignment on which every member of Γ ∪ {**Q**} is true. Therefore, if every member of Γ is true on some truth-value assignment, **Q** must be false on that assignment, and ~ **Q** will be true. So Γ ⊨ ~ **Q**.

We are now prepared to prove that each sentence in a derivation is truth-functionally entailed by the set of the undischarged assumptions in whose scope the sentence lies. We introduce the following notation: For any derivation, let $\mathbf{P_k}$ be the **k**th sentence in the derivation, and let $\Gamma_{\mathbf{k}}$ be the set of undischarged assumptions in whose scope $\mathbf{P_k}$ lies. Here is our argument by mathematical induction on the position **k** in a derivation:

Basis clause: $\Gamma_1 \vDash \mathbf{P}_1$.

Inductive step: If $\Gamma_{\mathbf{i}} \vDash \mathbf{P_i}$ for every positive integer $\mathbf{i} \leq \mathbf{k}$, then $\Gamma_{\mathbf{k}+1} \vDash \mathbf{P}_{\mathbf{k}+1}$.

Conclusion: For every positive integer **k**, $\Gamma_{\mathbf{k}} \vDash \mathbf{P_k}$.

Once we have established that the premises of this argument are true, and hence that the conclusion is true as well, we may then conclude that in every derivation the last sentence—which is $\mathbf{P_k}$ for some positive integer **k**—is truth-functionally entailed by the primary assumptions of the derivation; these are the undischarged assumptions in whose scope the last sentence lies.

Proof of basis clause: $\mathbf{P}_1$ is the first sentence in a derivation. Moreover, because every derivation in *SD* begins with one or more assumptions, $\mathbf{P}_1$ is an undischarged assumption that lies in its own scope. (We remind the reader that, by definition, every assumption of a derivation lies within its own scope.) That is, Γ_1, the set of undischarged assumptions in whose scope $\mathbf{P}_1$ lies, is $\{\mathbf{P}_1\}$. Because $\{\mathbf{P}_1\} \vDash \mathbf{P}_1$, we conclude that the basis clause is true.

Proof of inductive step: Let **k** be an arbitrary positive integer and assume the inductive hypothesis: for every positive integer $\mathbf{i} \leq \mathbf{k}$, $\Gamma_{\mathbf{i}} \vDash \mathbf{P_i}$. We must show that on this assumption it follows that $\Gamma_{\mathbf{k}+1} \vDash \mathbf{P}_{\mathbf{k}+1}$. We shall consider each way in which $\mathbf{P}_{\mathbf{k}+1}$ might be justified and show that our thesis holds whichever justification is used. We now turn to cases.

Case 1: $\mathbf{P}_{\mathbf{k}+1}$ is an Assumption. Then $\mathbf{P}_{\mathbf{k}+1}$ is a member of $\Gamma_{\mathbf{k}+1}$, the set of undischarged assumptions in whose scope $\mathbf{P}_{\mathbf{k}+1}$ lies. Therefore, if every member of $\Gamma_{\mathbf{k}+1}$ is true, $\mathbf{P}_{\mathbf{k}+1}$, being a member of the set, is true as well. So $\Gamma_{\mathbf{k}+1} \vDash \mathbf{P}_{\mathbf{k}+1}$.

Case 2: $\mathbf{P}_{\mathbf{k}+1}$ is justified by Reiteration. Then $\mathbf{P}_{\mathbf{k}+1}$ occurs earlier in the derivation as sentence $\mathbf{P_i}$ at some position **i**. Moreover every assumption that is undischarged at position **i** must remain undischarged at position **k** + 1—for if even one assumption in whose scope $\mathbf{P_i}$ lies were discharged before position **k** + 1, then $\mathbf{P_i}$ would not be accessible at position **k** + 1. Therefore $\Gamma_{\mathbf{i}}$ is a subset of $\Gamma_{\mathbf{k}+1}$; every member of $\Gamma_{\mathbf{i}}$ is still an undischarged assumption at position **k** + 1. By our inductive hypothesis $\Gamma_{\mathbf{i}} \vDash \mathbf{P_i}$. Because $\Gamma_{\mathbf{i}}$ is a subset of $\Gamma_{\mathbf{k}+1}$, it follows, by 6.3.2, that $\Gamma_{\mathbf{k}+1} \vDash \mathbf{P_i}$. And because $\mathbf{P}_{\mathbf{k}+1}$ is the same sentence as $\mathbf{P_i}$, $\Gamma_{\mathbf{k}+1} \vDash \mathbf{P}_{\mathbf{k}+1}$.

Case 3: $\mathbf{P_{k+1}}$ is justified by Conjunction Introduction. The conjuncts of $\mathbf{P_{k+1}}$ occur earlier in the derivation, say at positions **h** and **j**:

h	Q	
j	R	
k + 1	Q & R (= $\mathbf{P_{k+1}}$)	h, j &I

(There may be undischarged assumptions between positions **h** and **j** and between positions **j** and **k** + 1. Moreover it may be that **R** occurs earlier in the derivation than **Q** does—the order is immaterial.) By the inductive hypothesis, $\Gamma_{\mathbf{h}} \vDash \mathbf{Q}$ and $\Gamma_{\mathbf{j}} \vDash \mathbf{R}$. Moreover every member of $\Gamma_{\mathbf{h}}$ is a member of $\Gamma_{\mathbf{k+1}}$ and every member of $\Gamma_{\mathbf{j}}$ is a member of $\Gamma_{\mathbf{k+1}}$—for if this were not the case, then either **Q** or **R** would not be accessible at position **k** + 1. $\Gamma_{\mathbf{h}}$ and $\Gamma_{\mathbf{j}}$ are therefore subsets of $\Gamma_{\mathbf{k+1}}$ and so, by 6.3.2, $\Gamma_{\mathbf{k+1}} \vDash \mathbf{Q}$ and $\Gamma_{\mathbf{k+1}} \vDash \mathbf{R}$. But whenever both **Q** and **R** are true, $\mathbf{P_{k+1}}$, which is **Q** & **R**, is also true. So $\Gamma_{\mathbf{k+1}} \vDash \mathbf{P_{k+1}}$ as well.

Case 4: $\mathbf{P_{k+1}}$ is justified by Conjunction Elimination:

h	Q & $\mathbf{P_{k+1}}$		or	h	$\mathbf{P_{k+1}}$ & Q	
k + 1	$\mathbf{P_{k+1}}$	h &E		k + 1	$\mathbf{P_{k+1}}$	h &E

By the inductive hypothesis, $\Gamma_{\mathbf{h}}$ truth-functionally entails the conjunction at position **h**. And whenever the conjunction is true, both conjuncts must be true. So $\Gamma_{\mathbf{h}} \vDash \mathbf{P_{k+1}}$. $\Gamma_{\mathbf{h}}$ is a subset of $\Gamma_{\mathbf{k+1}}$—all assumptions that have not been discharged by position **h** must remain undischarged at position **k** + 1. It follows, by 6.3.2, that $\Gamma_{\mathbf{k+1}} \vDash \mathbf{P_{k+1}}$.

Case 5: $\mathbf{P_{k+1}}$ is justified by Disjunction Introduction:

h	Q		or	h	R	
k + 1	Q ∨ R (= $\mathbf{P_{k+1}}$)	h ∨I		k + 1	Q ∨ R (= $\mathbf{P_{k+1}}$)	h ∨I

By the inductive hypothesis, $\Gamma_{\mathbf{h}}$ truth-functionally entails the sentence at position **h**. That sentence is one of the disjuncts of **Q** ∨ **R**, so whenever it is true, so is **Q** ∨ **R**. Thus $\Gamma_{\mathbf{h}} \vDash \mathbf{P_{k+1}}$. $\Gamma_{\mathbf{h}}$ must be a subset of $\Gamma_{\mathbf{k+1}}$ if the sentence at position **h** is accessible at position **k** + 1, and so, by 6.3.2, $\Gamma_{\mathbf{k+1}} \vDash \mathbf{P_{k+1}}$.

Case 6: $\mathbf{P_{k+1}}$ is justified by Conditional Elimination:

h	Q	
j	Q ⊃ $\mathbf{P_{k+1}}$	
k + 1	$\mathbf{P_{k+1}}$	h, j ⊃E

By the inductive hypothesis, $\Gamma_{\mathbf{h}} \vDash \mathbf{Q}$ and $\Gamma_{\mathbf{j}} \vDash \mathbf{Q} \supset \mathbf{P}_{\mathbf{k}+1}$. Both $\Gamma_{\mathbf{h}}$ and $\Gamma_{\mathbf{j}}$ must be subsets of $\Gamma_{\mathbf{k}+1}$ if the sentences at positions **h** and **j** are accessible at position **k** + 1. By 6.3.2, then, $\Gamma_{\mathbf{k}+1} \vDash \mathbf{Q}$ and $\Gamma_{\mathbf{k}+1} \vDash \mathbf{Q} \supset \mathbf{P}_{\mathbf{k}+1}$. Because $\mathbf{P}_{\mathbf{k}+1}$ must be true whenever both **Q** and $\mathbf{Q} \supset \mathbf{P}_{\mathbf{k}+1}$ are true, $\Gamma_{\mathbf{k}+1} \vDash \mathbf{P}_{\mathbf{k}+1}$ as well.

Case 7: $\mathbf{P}_{\mathbf{k}+1}$ is justified by Biconditional Elimination:

h	**Q**			**h**	**Q**	
j	$\mathbf{Q} \equiv \mathbf{P}_{\mathbf{k}+1}$		or	**j**	$\mathbf{P}_{\mathbf{k}+1} \equiv \mathbf{Q}$	
k + 1	$\mathbf{P}_{\mathbf{k}+1}$	**h, j** ≡E		**k** + 1	$\mathbf{P}_{\mathbf{k}+1}$	**h, j** ≡E

By the inductive hypothesis, $\Gamma_{\mathbf{h}} \vDash \mathbf{Q}$ and $\Gamma_{\mathbf{j}}$ truth-functionally entails the biconditional at position **j**. $\Gamma_{\mathbf{h}}$ and $\Gamma_{\mathbf{j}}$ must be subsets of $\Gamma_{\mathbf{k}+1}$ if the sentences at positions **h** and **j** are accessible at position **k** + 1. By 6.3.2, then, $\Gamma_{\mathbf{k}+1}$ truth-functionally entails both **Q** and the biconditional at position **j**. Because the sentence $\mathbf{P}_{\mathbf{k}+1}$ must be true whenever both **Q** and the biconditional at position **j** are true, $\Gamma_{\mathbf{k}+1} \vDash \mathbf{P}_{\mathbf{k}+1}$ as well.

Case 8: $\mathbf{P}_{\mathbf{k}+1}$ is justified by Conditional Introduction:

h	**Q** (assumption)	
j	**R**	
k + 1	$\mathbf{Q} \supset \mathbf{R}\ (= \mathbf{P}_{\mathbf{k}+1})$	**h–j** ⊃I

By the inductive hypothesis, $\Gamma_{\mathbf{j}} \vDash \mathbf{R}$. Because the subderivation in which **R** is derived from **Q** is accessible at position **k** + 1, every assumption that is undischarged at position **j** is undischarged at position **k** + 1, except for the assumption **Q** that begins the subderivation. So the set of undischarged assumptions $\Gamma_{\mathbf{j}}$ is a subset of $\Gamma_{\mathbf{k}+1} \cup \{\mathbf{Q}\}$. Because $\Gamma_{\mathbf{j}} \vDash \mathbf{R}$, it follows, by 6.3.2, that $\Gamma_{\mathbf{k}+1} \cup \{\mathbf{Q}\} \vDash \mathbf{R}$. And from this it follows, by 6.3.3, that $\Gamma_{\mathbf{k}+1} \vDash \mathbf{Q} \supset \mathbf{R}$.

Case 9: $\mathbf{P}_{\mathbf{k}+1}$ is justified by Negation Introduction:

h	**Q** (assumption)	
j	**R**	
m	~ **R**	
k + 1	~ **Q** $(= \mathbf{P}_{\mathbf{k}+1})$	**h–m** ~ I

By the inductive hypothesis, $\Gamma_{\mathbf{j}} \vDash \mathbf{R}$ and $\Gamma_{\mathbf{m}} \vDash$ ~ **R**. Because the subderivation that derives **R** from **Q** is accessible at position **k** + 1, every assumption that is undischarged at position $\mathbf{j}$ is undischarged at position $\mathbf{k} + 1$ except for the assumption $\mathbf{Q}$ that begins the subderivation. That is, the set of undischarged assumptions $\Gamma_{\mathbf{j}}$ is a subset of $\Gamma_{\mathbf{k+1}} \cup \{\mathbf{Q}\}$. By similar reasoning $\Gamma_{\mathbf{m}}$ must be a subset of $\Gamma_{\mathbf{k+1}} \cup \{\mathbf{Q}\}$. Therefore, by 6.3.2, $\Gamma_{\mathbf{k+1}} \cup \{\mathbf{Q}\} \vDash \mathbf{R}$ and $\Gamma_{\mathbf{k+1}} \cup \{\mathbf{Q}\} \vDash \sim \mathbf{R}$. From this it follows, by 6.3.4, that $\Gamma_{\mathbf{k+1}} \cup \{\mathbf{Q}\}$ is truth-functionally inconsistent and then, by 6.3.5, that $\Gamma_{\mathbf{k+1}} \vDash \sim \mathbf{Q}$.

Case 10: $\mathbf{P_{k+1}}$ is justified by Negation Elimination. See Exercise 3.

Case 11: $\mathbf{P_{k+1}}$ is justified by Disjunction Elimination:

h	$\mathbf{Q} \vee \mathbf{R}$	
j	$\mathbf{Q}$	
m	$\mathbf{P_{k+1}}$	
n	$\mathbf{R}$	
p	$\mathbf{P_{k+1}}$	
k + 1	$\mathbf{P_{k+1}}$	h, j–m, n–p $\vee$E

By the inductive hypothesis, $\Gamma_{\mathbf{h}} \vDash \mathbf{Q} \vee \mathbf{R}$, $\Gamma_{\mathbf{m}} \vDash \mathbf{P_{k+1}}$, and $\Gamma_{\mathbf{p}} \vDash \mathbf{P_{k+1}}$. Because the two subderivations are accessible at position $\mathbf{k} + 1$, the undischarged assumptions $\Gamma_{\mathbf{m}}$ form a subset of $\Gamma_{\mathbf{k+1}} \cup \{\mathbf{Q}\}$ and the undischarged assumptions $\Gamma_{\mathbf{p}}$ form a subset of $\Gamma_{\mathbf{k+1}} \cup \{\mathbf{R}\}$. By 6.3.2, then, $\Gamma_{\mathbf{k+1}} \cup \{\mathbf{Q}\} \vDash \mathbf{P_{k+1}}$ and $\Gamma_{\mathbf{k+1}} \cup \{\mathbf{R}\} \vDash \mathbf{P_{k+1}}$. Moreover, because $\mathbf{Q} \vee \mathbf{R}$ at position $\mathbf{h}$ is accessible at position $\mathbf{k} + 1$, $\Gamma_{\mathbf{h}}$ is a subset of $\Gamma_{\mathbf{k+1}}$. So, because $\Gamma_{\mathbf{h}} \vDash \mathbf{Q} \vee \mathbf{R}$, it follows, by 6.3.2, that $\Gamma_{\mathbf{k+1}} \vDash \mathbf{Q} \vee \mathbf{R}$. Now consider any truth-value assignment on which every member of $\Gamma_{\mathbf{k+1}}$ is true. Because $\Gamma_{\mathbf{k+1}} \vDash \mathbf{Q} \vee \mathbf{R}$, $\mathbf{Q} \vee \mathbf{R}$ is also true on this assignment. So either $\mathbf{Q}$ or $\mathbf{R}$ is true. If $\mathbf{Q}$ is true, then every member of $\Gamma_{\mathbf{k+1}} \cup \{\mathbf{Q}\}$ is true and hence $\mathbf{P_{k+1}}$ is true as well because $\Gamma_{\mathbf{k+1}} \cup \{\mathbf{Q}\} \vDash \mathbf{P_{k+1}}$. Similarly, if $\mathbf{R}$ is true, then every member of $\Gamma_{\mathbf{k+1}} \cup \{\mathbf{R}\}$ is true, and hence $\mathbf{P_{k+1}}$ is true as well because $\Gamma_{\mathbf{k+1}} \cup \{\mathbf{R}\} \vDash \mathbf{P_{k+1}}$. Either way, it follows that $\mathbf{P_{k+1}}$ must be true on any truth-value assignment on which every member of $\Gamma_{\mathbf{k+1}}$ is true. So $\Gamma_{\mathbf{k+1}} \vDash \mathbf{P_{k+1}}$.

Case 12: $\mathbf{P_{k+1}}$ is justified by Biconditional Introduction:

h	$\mathbf{Q}$	
j	$\mathbf{R}$	
m	$\mathbf{R}$	
n	$\mathbf{Q}$	
k + 1	$\mathbf{Q} \equiv \mathbf{R}$ $(= \mathbf{P_{k+1}})$	h–j, m–n $\equiv$I

By the inductive hypothesis $\Gamma_j \vDash \mathbf{R}$ and $\Gamma_n \vDash \mathbf{Q}$. Because the two subderivations are accessible at position $\mathbf{k} + 1$, Γ_j is a subset of $\Gamma_{k+1} \cup \{\mathbf{Q}\}$ and Γ_n is a subset of $\Gamma_{k+1} \cup \{\mathbf{R}\}$. By 6.3.2, then, $\Gamma_{k+1} \cup \{\mathbf{Q}\} \vDash \mathbf{R}$ and $\Gamma_{k+1} \cup \{\mathbf{R}\} \vDash \mathbf{Q}$. Now consider any truth-value assignment on which every member of Γ_{k+1} is true. If **R** is also true on that assignment, then so is **Q** because $\Gamma_{k+1} \cup \{\mathbf{R}\} \vDash \mathbf{Q}$. If **R** is false on that assignment, then **Q** must also be false—if **Q** were true, then **R** would have to be true as well because $\Gamma_{k+1} \cup \{\mathbf{Q}\} \vDash \mathbf{R}$. Either way, **Q** and **R** have the same truth-value, and so $\mathbf{Q} \equiv \mathbf{R}$ is true on every truth-value assignment on which every member of Γ_{k+1} is true. So $\Gamma_{k+1} \vDash \mathbf{P}_{k+1}$.

This completes the proof of the inductive step; we have considered every way in which the sentence at position $\mathbf{k} + 1$ of a derivation might be justified and have shown that in each case $\Gamma_{k+1} \vDash \mathbf{P}_{k+1}$ if the same is true of all earlier positions in the derivation. We have therefore established that the conclusion of the argument by mathematical induction is also true: For any position in a derivation, the sentence at that position is truth-functionally entailed by the set of undischarged assumptions in whose scope it lies. In particular, this thesis is true of the last position in any derivation—the sentence that has been derived is truth-functionally entailed by the undischarged assumptions in whose scope it lies, and these are the primary assumptions of the derivation. So the soundness metatheorem for *SD* has been established: If $\Gamma \vdash \mathbf{P}$ in *SD*, then $\Gamma \vDash \mathbf{P}$. It follows from Metatheorem 6.3.1 that every sentence of *SL* that is a theorem in *SD* is truth-functionally true and that every argument that is valid in *SD* is truth-functionally valid (see Exercise 20 in Section 5.4E).

6.3E EXERCISES

1. List all the subsets of each of the following sets:

a. $\{A \supset B, C \supset D\}$
b. $\{C \vee \sim D, \sim D \vee C, C \vee C\}$
c. $\{(B \,\&\, A) \equiv K\}$
d. $\varnothing$

2. Of which of the following sets is $\{A \supset B, C \,\&\, D, D \supset A\}$ a superset?

a. $\{A \supset B\}$
b. $\{D \supset A, A \supset B\}$
c. $\{A \supset D, C \,\&\, D\}$
d. $\varnothing$
e. $\{C \,\&\, D, D \supset A, A \supset B\}$

***3.** Prove Case 10 of the inductive step in the proof of Metatheorem 6.3.1.

4.

a. Suppose that system *SD** is just like *SD* except that it also contains a new rule of inference:

Negated Biconditional Introduction ($\sim\equiv$I)

$$
\begin{array}{|l}
\mathbf{P} \\
\sim \mathbf{Q} \\
\sim (\mathbf{P} \equiv \mathbf{Q})
\end{array}
$$

Prove that system *SD** is a sound system for sentential logic; that is, prove that if $\Gamma \vdash \mathbf{P}$ in *SD** then $\Gamma \vDash \mathbf{P}$. (You may use Metatheorem 6.3.1.)

*b. Suppose that system *SD** is just like *SD* except that it also contains a new rule of inference:

Backward Conditional Introduction (B$\supset$I)

$$
\begin{array}{|l}
\begin{array}{|l}
\sim \mathbf{Q} \\
\hline
\sim \mathbf{P}
\end{array} \\
\mathbf{P} \supset \mathbf{Q}
\end{array}
$$

Prove that system *SD** is sound for sentential logic.

c. Suppose that system *SD** is just like *SD* except that it also contains a new rule of inference:

Crazy Disjunction Elimination (C$\vee$E)

$$
\begin{array}{|l}
\mathbf{P} \vee \mathbf{Q} \\
\mathbf{P} \\
\mathbf{Q}
\end{array}
$$

Prove that *SD** is not a sound system for sentential logic.

*d. Suppose that system *SD** is just like *SD* except that it also contains a new rule of inference:

Crazy Conditional Introduction (C$\supset$I)

$$
\begin{array}{|l}
\begin{array}{|l}
\sim \mathbf{P} \\
\hline
\mathbf{Q}
\end{array} \\
\mathbf{P} \supset \mathbf{Q}
\end{array}
$$

Prove that *SD** is not a sound system for sentential logic.

e. Suppose that the rules of a system *SD** form a subset of the rules of *SD*. Is *SD** a sound system for sentential logic? Explain.

5. Suppose that in our semantics for *SL* the characteristic truth-table for '&' is

P	Q	P & Q
T	T	T
T	F	T
F	T	F
F	F	F

while the characteristic truth-tables for the other sentential connectives remain the same. Would *SD* still be a sound system for sentential logic? Explain.

6. Using Metatheorem 6.3.1 and Exercise 1.e in Section 6.1E, prove that *SD+* is sound for sentential logic.

6.4 THE COMPLETENESS OF *SD* AND *SD+*

We proved in the last section that derivations in *SD* never lead from true premises to a false conclusion, and so every derivation in *SD* is semantically acceptable. This fact alone does not establish that *SD* is an adequate natural deduction system for sentential logic. In addition, it is to be hoped that if an argument is truth-functionally valid then we can derive its conclusion from its premises in *SD* and that every sentence that is truth-functionally true can be derived in *SD* from the empty set—in short, that everything that we want to derive in *SD* *can* be derived in *SD*. If there is even one argument that is truth-functionally valid but for which no derivation can be constructed in *SD*, then *SD* is not adequate to sentential logic. Our final metatheorem assures us that we can derive all that we want to derive in *SD*; it is called the Completeness Metatheorem:

Metatheorem 6.4.1: If $\Gamma \models \mathbf{P}$, then $\Gamma \vdash \mathbf{P}$ in *SD*.

That is, if a set Γ truth-functionally entails a sentence **P**, then **P** may be derived from Γ in *SD*. It follows from this metatheorem that every argument of *SL* that is truth-functionally valid is valid in *SD* and that every sentence of *SL* that is truth-functionally true is a theorem in *SD* (see Exercise 20 in Section 5.4E). A system for which Metatheorem 6.4.1 holds is said to be *complete* for sentential logic.

There are several well-known ways to establish a completeness metatheorem. Some of these are said to be *constructive*—they show, for any set Γ and sentence **P** such that $\Gamma \models \mathbf{P}$, how to construct a derivation of **P** from Γ. We shall present a *nonconstructive* proof of completeness.[4] The proof will establish that, for every truth-functional entailment, there is at least one corresponding derivation in *SD*. It will not, however, show how to construct such a derivation.

[4]The method that we use to prove completeness is due to Leon Henkin, "The Completeness of the First-Order Functional Calculus," *Journal of Symbolic Logic*, 14 (1949), 159–166.

Before diving into the details of the proof, we shall give an overview of the proof's structure. The proof of Metatheorem 6.4.1 relies on several results that we present here; we defer the lengthy proof of 6.4.3 to the following pages.

> **6.4.2:** For any set of sentences Γ and any sentence **P**, $\Gamma \models$ **P** if and only if $\Gamma \cup \{\sim$ **P**$\}$ is truth-functionally inconsistent. (This follows from result 6.3.5 and Exercise 1.c in Section 3.6E.)
>
> **6.4.3:** (The *Inconsistency Lemma*): If a set Γ of sentences of *SL* is truth-functionally inconsistent, then Γ is also inconsistent in *SD*.
>
> **6.4.4:** For any set of sentences Γ and any sentence **P**, $\Gamma \vdash$ **P** in *SD* if and only if $\Gamma \cup \{\sim$**P**$\}$ is inconsistent in *SD* (see Exercise 1).

Here is how the Completeness Theorem follows from these results. If the antecedent of Metatheorem 6.4.1, $\Gamma \models$ **P**, is true, it follows from 6.4.2 that $\Gamma \cup \{\sim$**P**$\}$ is truth-functionally inconsistent, from the Inconsistency Lemma (6.4.3) that $\Gamma \cup \{\sim$**P**$\}$ is inconsistent in *SD*, and from 6.4.4 that $\Gamma \vdash$ **P** in *SD*.

We shall prove 6.4.3, the Inconsistency Lemma, by proving the following equivalent claim:

> If a set Γ of sentences of *SL* is consistent in *SD*, then Γ is also truth-functionally consistent.

(The claim is equivalent because any sentence of the form $\sim$ **P** $\supset \sim$ **Q** is equivalent to the corresponding sentence of the form **Q** $\supset$ **P**.) Our strategy will be to show, for any set Γ that is consistent in *SD*, how to construct a truth-value assignment on which every member of Γ is true. We shall construct the truth-value assignment in two steps. First, we shall form a superset of Γ (a set that includes all the members of Γ and possibly other sentences) that is *maximally consistent in SD*. A maximally consistent set is, intuitively, a consistent set that contains as many sentences as it can without being inconsistent in *SD*:

> A set Γ of sentences of *SL* is *maximally consistent in SD* if and only if Γ is consistent in *SD* and, for every sentence **P** of *SL* that is not a member of Γ, $\Gamma \cup \{$**P**$\}$ is inconsistent in *SD*.

If a set is maximally consistent in *SD*, then if we add to the set any sentence that is not already a member, it will be possible to derive some sentence and its negation from the augmented set.

Having constructed a maximally consistent superset of Γ, we shall then construct a truth-value assignment on which every member of the maximally consistent superset is true. We use a superset of Γ that is maximally consistent in *SD*, rather than simply using the original set Γ, because there is a straightforward way to construct a truth-value assignment on which every member of a maximally consistent set is true. Of course, because every member of Γ will be in the maximally consistent superset, it follows that every member of Γ will be true on the truth-value assignment that we have constructed and therefore that Γ is truth-functionally consistent.

So, to begin with, we need to establish that we can form a maximally consistent superset of any set of sentences Γ that is consistent in *SD*; that is, we need to prove this:

> **6.4.5** (The *Maximal Consistency Lemma*): If Γ is a set of sentences of *SL* that is consistent in *SD*, then Γ is a subset of at least one set of sentences that is maximally consistent in *SD*.

This lemma is important, for we are then going to show how to construct the desired truth-value assignment for a maximally consistent set. If there were any sets of sentences that were consistent in *SD* but that were not subsets of any set that is *maximally* consistent in *SD*, our construction would fail to show that the Inconsistency Lemma (6.4.3) is true of these sets. At most, we would be able to conclude that some sets of sentences that are consistent in *SD*—those that can be expanded to maximally consistent supersets—are also truth-functionally consistent.

In proving the Maximal Consistency Lemma (6.4.5), we shall make use of the fact that the sentences of *SL* can be *enumerated,* that is, placed in a definite order in one-to-one correspondence with the positive integers so that there is a sentence for each positive integer. Here is one method of enumerating the sentences of *SL*. First, we associate with each symbol of *SL* the two-digit numeral occurring to its right:

Symbol	*Numeral*	*Symbol*	*Numeral*
~	10	A	30
∨	11	B	31
&	12	C	32
⊃	13	D	33
≡	14	E	34
(	15	F	35
)	16	G	36
0	20	H	37
1	21	I	38
⋮	⋮	⋮	⋮
9	29	Z	55

(The ellipses mean that the next two-digit numeral is assigned to the next digit or letter of the alphabet.) Next we associate with each sentence of *SL*, atomic or molecular, the number designated by the numeral that consists of the numerals associated with the symbols in the sentence, in the order in which those symbols occur. For example, the numbers associated with the sentences

$$(A \vee C_2) \qquad \sim\sim(A \supset (B \ \& \sim C))$$

are, respectively,

153011322216   101015301315311210321616

It is obvious that each sentence of *SL* will thus have a distinct number associated with it. Finally we enumerate all the sentences of *SL* by taking them in the order of their associated numbers: The first sentence in the enumeration is the sentence with the smallest associated number, the second sentence is the one with the next smallest associated number, and so on. In effect, we have imposed an alphabetical order on the sentences of *SL* so that we may freely talk of the first sentence of *SL* (which turns out to be 'A'—because only atomic sentences will have two-digit associated numbers, and the number for 'A' is the smallest of these), the second sentence of *SL* (which turns out to be 'B'), and so on.

We shall start with a set Γ of sentences that is consistent in *SD* (as provided for in the antecedent of the Maximal Consistency Lemma) and use our enumeration to construct a superset of Γ that is maximally consistent in *SD*. The construction considers in turn each sentence in the enumeration we have just described and adds it to the set if and only if the resulting set is consistent in *SD*. In the end the construction will have added as many sentences as can be added to the original set without producing a set that is inconsistent in *SD*. As the construction goes through the sentences of *SL*, deciding whether to add each sentence, it produces an infinite sequence Γ_1, Γ_2, Γ_3, . . . of sets of sentences of *SL*:

1. Γ_1 is Γ, the original set.
2. If $\mathbf{P_i}$ is the **i**th sentence in the enumeration, then $\Gamma_{\mathbf{i}+1}$ is $\Gamma_{\mathbf{i}} \cup \{\mathbf{P_i}\}$ if $\Gamma_{\mathbf{i}} \cup \{\mathbf{P_i}\}$ is consistent in *SD*; otherwise $\Gamma_{\mathbf{i}+1}$ is $\Gamma_{\mathbf{i}}$.

As an example, if $\Gamma_{\mathbf{i}}$ is {~ B, ~ C ∨ ~ B} and $\mathbf{P_i}$ is 'A', then $\Gamma_{\mathbf{i}} \cup \{\mathbf{P_i}\}$, which is {~ B, ~ C ∨ ~ B, A}, is consistent in *SD*. In this case $\Gamma_{\mathbf{i}+1}$ will be the expanded set $\Gamma_{\mathbf{i}} \cup \{\mathbf{P_i}\}$. If $\Gamma_{\mathbf{i}}$ is {A, ~ B, ~ C ∨ ~ B} and $\mathbf{P_i}$ is 'B', then $\Gamma_{\mathbf{i}} \cup \{\mathbf{P_i}\}$, which is {A, ~ B, ~ C ∨ ~ B, B}, is inconsistent in *SD* (this is readily verified). In this case $\mathbf{P_i}$ is not added to the set—$\Gamma_{\mathbf{i}+1}$ is merely the set {A, ~ B, ~ C ∨ ~ B}.

Because we have an infinite sequence of sets, we cannot take the last member of the series as the maximally consistent set desired—there is no last member. Instead, we form a set Γ* that is the union of all the sets in the series: Γ* is defined to contain every sentence that is a member of at least one set in the series and no other sentences. Γ* is a superset of Γ because it follows from the definition of Γ* that every sentence in Γ_1 (as well as Γ_2, Γ_3, . . .) is a member of Γ*, and Γ_1 is the original set Γ.

Having formed the set Γ*, it remains to be proved that Γ* is consistent in *SD* and that it is *maximally* consistent in *SD*. To prove the first claim, we note that every set in the sequence Γ_1, Γ_2, Γ_3, . . . is consistent in *SD*. This is easily established by mathematical induction:

Basis clause: The first member of the sequence, Γ_1, is consistent in *SD*.

Proof: Γ_1 is defined to be the original set Γ, which is consistent in *SD*.

Inductive step: If every set in the sequence prior to Γ_{k+1} is consistent in *SD*, then Γ_{k+1} is consistent in *SD*.

Proof: Γ_{k+1} was defined to be $\Gamma_k \cup \{\mathbf{P_k}\}$ if the latter set is consistent in *SD* and to be Γ_k otherwise. In the first case Γ_{k+1} is obviously consistent in *SD*. In the second case Γ_{k+1} is consistent because, by the inductive hypothesis, Γ_k is consistent in *SD*.

Conclusion: Every member of the series $\Gamma_1, \Gamma_2, \Gamma_3, \ldots$ is consistent in *SD*.

Now suppose, contrary to what we wish to prove, that Γ^* is *inconsistent* in *SD*.

6.4.6: If Γ is inconsistent in *SD*, then some finite subset of Γ is inconsistent in *SD* (see Exercise 2).

It follows that there is a finite subset Γ' of Γ^* that is inconsistent in *SD*. Γ' must be nonempty, for the empty set is consistent in *SD* (see Exercise 3). Moreover, because Γ' is finite, there is a sentence in Γ' that comes after all the other members of Γ' in our enumeration—call this sentence $\mathbf{P_j}$. (That is, any other member of Γ' is $\mathbf{P_h}$ for some $\mathbf{h} < \mathbf{j}$.) Then every member of Γ' is a member of Γ_{j+1}, by the way we constructed the series $\Gamma_1, \Gamma_2, \Gamma_3, \ldots$ (This is because we have constructed the sets in such a way that if a sentence that is the **i**th sentence in our enumeration is a member of *any* set in the sequence—and hence of Γ^*—it must be in the set Γ_{i+1} and every set thereafter. After the construction of Γ_{i+1}, the only sentences that are added are sentences at position $\mathbf{i} + 1$ in the enumeration or later.) But if Γ' is inconsistent in *SD*, and every member of Γ' is a member of Γ_{j+1}, then Γ_{j+1} is inconsistent in *SD* as well, by 6.4.7:

6.4.7: If Γ is inconsistent in *SD*, then every superset of Γ is inconsistent in *SD*.

Proof: Assume that Γ is inconsistent in *SD*. Then for some sentence **P** there is a derivation of **P** in which all the primary assumptions are members of Γ, and also a derivation of ~ **P** in which all the primary assumptions are members of Γ. The primary assumptions of both derivations are members of every superset of Γ, so **P** and ~ **P** are both derivable from every superset of Γ. Therefore every superset of Γ is inconsistent in *SD*.

But we have already proved by mathematical induction that every set in the infinite sequence is consistent in *SD*. So Γ_{j+1} *cannot* be inconsistent in *SD*, and our supposition that led to this conclusion is wrong—we may conclude that Γ^* is consistent in *SD*.

It remains to be proved not only that Γ^* is consistent in *SD* but that it is, in addition, *maximally* consistent. Suppose that Γ^* is not maximally consistent in *SD*. Then there is at least one sentence $\mathbf{P_k}$ of *SL* that is not a member of Γ^* and is such that $\Gamma^* \cup \{\mathbf{P_k}\}$ is consistent in *SD*. We showed, in 6.4.7, that every superset of a set that is inconsistent in *SD* is itself inconsistent, so every subset of a set that is *consistent* in *SD* must itself be consistent in *SD*. In particular, the subset $\Gamma_k \cup \{\mathbf{P_k}\}$ of $\Gamma^* \cup \{\mathbf{P_k}\}$ must be consistent in *SD*. But then, by step 2 of the construction of the sequence of sets, Γ_{k+1} is defined to be $\Gamma_k \cup \{\mathbf{P_k}\}$—$\mathbf{P_k}$ is a member of Γ_{k+1}. $\mathbf{P_k}$ is therefore a member of Γ^*, contradicting our supposition that it is not a member of Γ^*. Therefore Γ^* must be maximally consistent in *SD*—every sentence that can be consistently added to Γ^* is already a member of Γ^*. This and the result of the previous paragraph establish the Maximal Consistency Lemma (6.4.5); we have shown that, given any set of sentences that is consistent in *SD*, we can construct a superset that is maximally consistent in *SD*.

It remains to be shown that, for every set that is maximally consistent in *SD*, we can construct a truth-value assignment on which all the sentences in the set are true. From this we will have the following:

> **6.4.8** (the *Consistency Lemma*): Every set of sentence of *SL* that is maximally consistent in *SD* is truth-functionally consistent.

In establishing the Consistency Lemma, we shall appeal to the following important facts about sets that are maximally consistent in *SD*:

> **6.4.9:** If $\Gamma \vdash \mathbf{P}$ and Γ^* is a maximally consistent superset of Γ, then $\mathbf{P}$ is a member of Γ^*.

> **Proof:** Assume that $\Gamma \vdash \mathbf{P}$ and let Γ^* be a maximally consistent superset of Γ. By the definition of derivability in *SD*, $\Gamma^* \vdash \mathbf{P}$ as well. Now suppose, contrary to what we wish to prove, that $\mathbf{P}$ is *not* a member of Γ^*. Then, by the definition of maximal consistency, $\Gamma^* \cup \{\mathbf{P}\}$ is inconsistent in *SD*. Therefore by
>
> **6.4.10:** If $\Gamma \cup \{\mathbf{P}\}$ is inconsistent in *SD*, then $\Gamma \vdash {\sim}\,\mathbf{P}$ (see Exercise 1)
>
> it follows that $\Gamma^* \vdash {\sim}\,\mathbf{P}$. But then, because both $\mathbf{P}$ and ${\sim}\,\mathbf{P}$ are derivable in *SD* from Γ^*, it follows that Γ^* is inconsistent in *SD*. But this is impossible if Γ is maximally consistent in *SD*. We conclude that our supposition about $\mathbf{P}$, that it is not a member of Γ^*, is wrong—$\mathbf{P}$ *is* a member of Γ^*.

In what follows, we will use the standard notation

$$\mathbf{P} \in \Gamma$$

to mean

P is a member of Γ

and the standard notation

P $\notin \Gamma$

to mean

P is not a member of Γ.

The next result concerns the composition of the membership of any set that is maximally consistent in *SD*:

6.4.11: If Γ^* is maximally consistent in *SD* and **P** and **Q** are sentences of *SL*, then:

a. ~ **P** $\in \Gamma^*$ if and only if **P** $\notin \Gamma^*$.
b. **P** & **Q** $\in \Gamma^*$ if and only if both **P** $\in \Gamma^*$ and **Q** $\in \Gamma^*$.
c. **P** $\vee$ **Q** $\in \Gamma^*$ if and only if either **P** $\in \Gamma^*$ or **Q** $\in \Gamma^*$.
d. **P** $\supset$ **Q** $\in \Gamma^*$ if and only if either **P** $\notin \Gamma^*$ or **Q** $\in \Gamma^*$.
e. **P** $\equiv$ **Q** $\in \Gamma^*$ if and only if either **P** $\in \Gamma^*$ and **Q** $\in \Gamma^*$, or **P** $\notin \Gamma^*$ and **Q** $\notin \Gamma^*$.

Proof of (a): Assume that ~ **P** $\in \Gamma^*$. Then **P** $\notin \Gamma^*$ for, if it were a member, then Γ^* would have a finite subset that is inconsistent in *SD*, namely, {**P**, ~ **P**}, and according to 6.4.7 this is impossible if Γ^* is consistent in *SD*. Now assume that **P** $\notin \Gamma^*$. Then, by the definition of maximal consistency in *SD*, $\Gamma^* \cup$ {**P**} is inconsistent in *SD*. So, by reasoning similar to that used in proving 6.4.9, some finite subset Γ' of Γ^* is such that $\Gamma' \cup$ {**P**} is inconsistent in *SD*, and therefore such that $\Gamma' \cup$ {~ ~ **P**} is inconsistent in *SD* and hence that $\Gamma' \vdash$ ~ **P**, by 6.4.4. It follows, by 6.4.9, that ~ **P** $\in \Gamma^*$.

Proof of (b): Assume that **P** & **Q** $\in \Gamma^*$. Then {**P** & **Q**} is a subset of Γ^*. Because {**P** & **Q**} $\vdash$ **P** and {**P** & **Q**} $\vdash$ **Q** (both by Conjunction Elimination), it follows, by 6.4.9, that **P** $\in \Gamma^*$ and **Q** $\in \Gamma^*$. Now suppose that **P** $\in \Gamma^*$ and **Q** $\in \Gamma^*$. Then {**P**, **Q**} is a subset of Γ^* and, because {**P**, **Q**} $\vdash$ **P** & **Q** (by Conjunction Introduction), it follows, by 6.4.9, that **P** & **Q** $\in \Gamma^*$.

Proof of (c): See Exercise 5.

Proof of (d): Assume that **P** $\supset$ **Q** $\in \Gamma^*$. If **P** $\notin \Gamma^*$, then it follows trivially that either **P** $\notin \Gamma^*$ or **Q** $\in \Gamma^*$. If **P** $\in \Gamma^*$, then {**P**, **P** $\supset$ **Q**} is a subset of Γ^*. Because {**P**, **P** $\supset$ **Q**} $\vdash$ **Q** (by Conditional Elimination), it follows, by 6.4.9, that **Q** ∈ Γ*. So, if **P** ⊃ **Q** ∈ Γ*, then either **P** ∉ Γ* or **Q** ∈ Γ*. Now assume that either **P** ∉ Γ* or **Q** ∈ Γ*. In the former case, by (a), ~ **P** ∈ Γ*. So either {~ **P**} is a subset of Γ* or {**Q**} is a subset of Γ*. **P** ⊃ **Q** is derivable from either subset:

1	~ **P**	Assumption
2	**P**	Assumption
3	~ **Q**	Assumption
4	**P**	2 R
5	~ **P**	1 R
6	**Q**	3–5 ~ E
7	**P** ⊃ **Q**	2–6 ⊃I

1	**Q**	Assumption
2	**P**	Assumption
3	**Q**	1 R
4	**P** ⊃ **Q**	2–3 ⊃I

Either way, there is a finite subset of Γ* from which **P** ⊃ **Q** is derivable; so, by 6.4.9, it follows that **P** ⊃ **Q** ∈ Γ*.

Proof of (e): See Exercise 5.

Turning now to the Consistency Lemma (6.4.8), let Γ be a set of sentences that is maximally consistent in *SD*. We said earlier that it is easy to construct a truth-value assignment on which every member of a maximally consistent set is true, and it is; we need only consider the atomic sentences in the set. Let **A*** be the truth-value assignment that assigns the truth-value **T** to every atomic sentence of *SL* that is a member of Γ* and assigns the truth-value **F** to every other atomic sentence of *SL*. We shall prove by mathematical induction that each sentence of *SL* is true on the truth-value assignment **A*** if and only if it is a member of Γ*—from which it follows that every member of Γ* is true on **A***, thus establishing truth-functional consistency. The induction will be based on the number of occurrences of connectives in the sentences of *SL*:

Basis clause: Each atomic sentence of *SL* is true on **A*** if and only if it is a member of Γ*.

Inductive step: If every sentence of *SL* with **k** or fewer occurrences of connectives is such that it is true on **A*** if and only if it is a member of Γ*, then every sentence of *SL* with **k** + 1 occurrences of connectives is such that it is true on **A*** if and only if it is a member of Γ*.

Conclusion: Every sentence of *SL* is such that it is true on **A*** if and only if it is a member of Γ*.

The basis clause is obviously true; we defined **A*** to be an assignment that assigns **T** to all and only the atomic sentences of *SL* that are members of Γ*. To prove the inductive step, we will assume that the inductive hypothesis holds for an arbitrary integer **k**: That each sentence containing **k** or fewer occurrences of connectives is true on **A*** if and only if it is a member of Γ*.

We must now show that the same holds true of every sentence **P** containing **k** + 1 occurrences of connectives. We consider five cases, reflecting the five forms that a molecular sentence of *SL* might have.

Case 1: **P** has the form ~ **Q**. If ~ **Q** is true on **A***, then **Q** is false on **A***. Because **Q** contains fewer than **k** + 1 occurrences of connectives, it follows by the inductive hypothesis that **Q** $\notin$ Γ*. Therefore, by 6.4.11(a), ~ **Q** $\in$ Γ*. If ~ **Q** is false on **A***, then **Q** is true on **A***. It follows by the inductive hypothesis that **Q** $\in$ Γ*. Therefore, by 6.4.11(a), ~ **Q** $\notin$ Γ*.

Case 2: **P** has the form **Q** & **R**. If **Q** & **R** is true on **A***, then both **Q** and **R** are true on **A***. Because **Q** and **R** each contain fewer than **k** + 1 occurrences of connectives, it follows by the inductive hypothesis that **Q** $\in$ Γ* and **R** $\in$ Γ*. Therefore, by 6.4.11(b), **Q** & **R** $\in$ Γ*. If **Q** & **R** is false on **A***, then either **Q** is false on **A*** or **R** is false on **A***. Therefore, by the inductive hypothesis, either **Q** $\notin$ Γ* or **R** $\notin$ Γ* and so, by 6.4.11(b), **Q** & **R** $\notin$ Γ*.

Case 3: **P** has the form **Q** ∨ **R**. See Exercise 6.

Case 4: **P** has the form **Q** ⊃ **R**. If **Q** ⊃ **R** is true on **A***, then either **Q** is false on **A*** or **R** is true on **A***. Because **Q** and **R** each contain fewer than **k** + 1 occurrences of connectives, it follows from the inductive hypothesis that either **Q** $\notin$ Γ* or **R** $\in$ Γ*. By 6.4.11(d), then, **Q** ⊃ **R** $\in$ Γ*. If **Q** ⊃ **R** is false on **A***, then **Q** is true on **A*** and **R** is false on **A***. By the inductive hypothesis, then, **Q** $\in$ Γ* and **R** $\notin$ Γ*. And by 6.4.11(d), it follows that **Q** ⊃ **R** $\notin$ Γ*.

Case 5: See Exercise 6.

This completes the proof of the inductive step. Hence we may conclude that each sentence of *SL* is such that it is a member of Γ* if and only if it is true on **A***. So every member of a set Γ* that is maximally consistent in *SD* is true on **A***, and the set Γ* is therefore truth-functionally consistent. This establishes the Consistency Lemma (6.4.8).

We now know that the Inconsistency Lemma (6.4.3) is true. Because every set of sentences Γ that is consistent in *SD* is a subset of a set of sentences that is maximally consistent in *SD* (the Maximal Consistency Lemma (6.4.5)), and because every set of sentences that is maximally consistent in *SD* is truth-functionally consistent (the Consistency Lemma (6.4.8)), it follows that every set of sentences that is consistent in *SD* is a subset of a truth-functionally consistent set and is therefore itself truth-functionally consistent. So, if a set is truth-functionally *inconsistent,* it must be inconsistent in *SD*.

It now follows that Metatheorem 6.4.1:

If Γ ⊨ **P**, then Γ ⊢ **P**

is true. For if Γ ⊨ **P**, then, by 6.4.2, Γ ∪ {~ **P**} is truth-functionally inconsistent. Then, by the Inconsistency Lemma (6.4.3), Γ ∪ {~ **P**} is inconsistent in *SD*. And if $\Gamma \cup \{\sim \mathbf{P}\}$ is inconsistent in *SD*, then, by 6.4.4, $\Gamma \vdash \mathbf{P}$ in *SD*. So *SD* is complete for sentential logic—for every truth-functional entailment there is at least one corresponding derivation that can be constructed in *SD*. This, together with the proof of the Soundness Metatheorem in Section 6.3, shows that *SD* is an adequate system for sentential logic.

We conclude by noting that another important result, the Compactness Theorem for sentential logic, follows from the Inconsistency Lemma (6.4.3) and Metatheorem 6.3.1:

Metatheorem 6.4.12: A set Γ of sentences of *SL* is truth-functionally consistent if and only if every finite subset of Γ is truth-functionally consistent.

And, as a consequence, a set of sentences of *SL* is truth-functionally inconsistent if and only if at least one finite subset of Γ is inconsistent.

6.4E EXERCISES

1. Prove 6.4.4 and 6.4.10.

2. Prove 6.4.6.

***3.** Prove that the empty set is consistent in *SD*.

4. Using Metatheorem 6.4.1, prove that *SD+* is complete for sentential logic.

***5.** Prove that every set that is maximally consistent in *SD* has the following properties:
c. $\mathbf{P} \vee \mathbf{Q} \in \Gamma^*$ if and only if either $\mathbf{P} \in \Gamma^*$ or $\mathbf{Q} \in \Gamma^*$.
e. $\mathbf{P} \equiv \mathbf{Q} \in \Gamma^*$ if and only if either $\mathbf{P} \in \Gamma^*$ and $\mathbf{Q} \in \Gamma^*$, or $\mathbf{P} \notin \Gamma^*$ and $\mathbf{Q} \notin \Gamma^*$.

***6.** Establish Cases 3 and 5 of the inductive step in the proof of the Consistency Lemma 6.4.8.

7.a. Suppose that *SD** is like *SD* except that it lacks Reiteration. Show that *SD** is complete for sentential logic.
*b. Suppose that *SD** is like *SD* except that it lacks Negation Introduction. Show that *SD** is complete for sentential logic.

8. Suppose that *SD** is like *SD* except that it lacks Conjunction Elimination. Show where our completeness proof for *SD* will fail as a completeness proof for *SD**.

9. Using the Inconsistency Lemma 6.4.3 and Metatheorem 6.3.1, prove Metatheorem 6.4.12.

Chapter

7

PREDICATE LOGIC: SYMBOLIZATION AND SYNTAX

7.1 THE LIMITATIONS OF *SL*

In Chapter 2 we introduced the language *SL* and techniques for symbolizing sentences of English in *SL*. In subsequent chapters we presented various semantic and syntactic methods for testing sentences and sets of sentences of *SL* for the logical properties defined for that language, including both semantic and syntactic versions of deductive validity, logical consistency, and logical truth (the former defined in terms of truth-value assignments, the latter in terms of derivability). *SL* has a number of virtues. For example, any English language argument that has an acceptable symbolization in *SL* that is truth-functionally valid is itself deductively valid. So, too, a sentence of English that can be fairly symbolized as a truth-functionally true (or truth-functionally false) sentence of *SL* is itself logically true (or logically false); similarly for equivalence and entailment. And if a set of English sentences can be fairly symbolized as a set of sentences of *SL* that is truth-functionally *inconsistent,* then that set of English sentences is itself logically *inconsistent.*

A further advantage is that two of the test procedures we developed in conjunction with the language *SL*—that based on truth-tables and that based on truth-trees—can readily be made into mechanical procedures. (A procedure is "mechanical" in this sense if each step is dictated by some rule, given prior steps. Thus a procedure for which a computer program can be written is a mechanical procedure.) Some mechanical procedures have no stopping point; that is, once started, they run on indefinitely. For example, if someone is hired to scrape and paint a bridge, told to start at the west end of the bridge and, upon reaching the east bank, to go back and start over on the west bank, we have a procedure that will go on indefinitely. The continuous scraping and painting will stop when the painter quits or retires, the bridge is removed or abandoned, the supply of paint runs out, or whatever. But the parameters established by the instructions do not determine or even envision a stopping point. The mechanical procedures based on truth-tables and truth-trees for *SL* are not of this sort—they always come to a stop after a finite number of steps. Moreover, when they stop, they always provide either a "yes" or a "no" answer to the question being asked (for instance, 'Is this argument truth-functionally valid?' or 'Is this sentence truth-functionally true?'). The semantic properties of consistency, truth-functional truth, truth-functional falsity, truth-functional indeterminacy, truth-functional equivalence, truth-functional validity, and truth-functional entailment are termed *decidable* properties precisely because there are mechanical test procedures for these properties, procedures that always terminate after a finite number of steps and always yield either a "yes" or "no" answer to the question being asked ('Does this semantic property hold of this sentence, or argument, or pair of sentences, or set of sentences?').

One of the goals of formal logic is to develop tools that allow us to understand (and test for the holding of) various logical properties of sentences and sets of sentences *of natural languages.* Until well into the twentieth century many, if not most, logicians assumed that the way to meet this goal was to develop formal languages in which all natural language discourse, or at least all "important" discourse (for example, mathematics and physics), could be represented and then to develop test procedures for these formal languages. It was expected that the test procedures would be such that each of the logical properties defined for a formal system would be decidable in the above sense.

So *SL* has at least these two advantages: There are decidable test procedures associated with it, and at least some of the results of these tests can be carried over to English. (For example, again, if a fair symbolization of an English language argument is found to be truth-functionally valid, we may conclude that the English language argument is deductively valid.) But not all test results obtained for arguments, sentences, and sets of sentences of *SL* can be carried back to the English arguments, sentences, and sets of sentences from which they were derived. Specifically *it does not follow* from the fact that the most appropriate symbolization of an English language argument is truth-functionally invalid that the original English argument is invalid. If a sentence of *SL* is not truth-functionally true, *it does not follow* that the English sentence it symbolizes is not logically true. If a sentence of *SL* is not truth-functionally false, *it does not follow* that the English sentence it symbolizes is not logically false; so, too, for equivalence and entailment. And if a set of sentences of *SL* is truth-functionally consistent, *it does not follow* that the set of English sentences we are trying to evaluate is logically consistent.

The problem is not that we have no test for determining when a sentence of *SL* constitutes a "fair" or "most appropriate" symbolization of a sentence of English, although it is true that we do not have such a test. The problem is rather that the language *SL* is itself not sophisticated enough to allow adequate symbolization of a great deal of natural language discourse. Put another way, even the most appropriate symbolization of an English sentence by a sentence of *SL* frequently fails to capture much of the content of the English sentence. This is so because the syntactic structure of English, and of every natural language, is much more complex than the structure of purely truth-functional languages such as *SL*. No truth-functional language can mirror all or even all the important semantic relationships that hold among sentences and parts of sentences of natural languages. For example, while the sentence

Each citizen will either vote or pay a fine

might form part of a recommendation for rather dramatic reforms in our political system, the sentence

Each citizen either will vote or will not vote

is not similarly controversial. Rather, it smacks of being a logical truth. Each citizen—for example, Cynthia—obviously either will vote or will not vote. Indeed, the claim about Cynthia, or any other specified citizen, can be symbolized as a truth-functional truth of *SL*. Where 'C' abbreviates 'Cynthia will vote', 'C ∨ ~ C' says of Cynthia what the general claim says of each citizen. But there is, barring heroic measures, no symbolization of the general claim in *SL* that is truth-functionally true.[1]

Similarly the following argument should strike the reader as being deductively valid, although it has no symbolization in *SL* that is truth-functionally valid:

> None of David's friends supports Republicans. Sarah supports Breitlow, and Breitlow is a Republican. So Sarah is no friend of David's.

One attempt at a symbolization of this argument in *SL* is

N
S & B
———
~ F

Here 'S' abbreviates 'Sarah supports Breitlow', 'B' abbreviates 'Breitlow is a Republican', and 'F' abbreviates 'Sarah is a friend of David's'. 'None of David's friends supports Republicans' is treated as an atomic sentence and symbolized

[1] Since there are presumably only finitely many citizens, we could construct a very extended conjunction with as many conjuncts of the sort 'C ∨ ~ C' as there are citizens. But even such heroic measures fail when the items about which we wish to talk (for example, the positive integers) constitute an infinite, and not just an exceedingly large, set. See Section 7.4.

as 'N'. This argument of *SL* is truth-functionally invalid. We could have treated 'None of David's friends supports Republicans' as the negation of 'Some of David's friends support Republicans' and symbolized it as '~ D', but the result would still be truth-functionally invalid.

The problem is that we cannot show, via the syntax of *SL*, that there is a relation between supporting Breitlow, Breitlow's being a Republican, and supporting Republicans. This is because *SL*, in taking sentences to be the smallest linguistic units (other than sentential connectives), makes all *subsentential* relationships invisible.

In this chapter we shall develop a new language, *PL* (for predicate logic) that will allow us to express many subsentential relationships.[2] It will turn out that the preceding argument has a valid symbolization in *PL* and that 'Each citizen will either vote or not vote' has a symbolization in *PL* that is logically true. However, it will also turn out that *PL* and its associated test procedures do not constitute a *decidable* system. That is, there is no mechanical test procedure that always yields, in a finite number of steps, a "yes" or a "no" answer to such a question as 'Is this argument of *PL* valid?' In fact, we now know that there can be no formal system that is both decidable and powerful enough to allow the expression of even moderately complex natural language discourse, including the claims of mathematics and physics.[3] So, while in moving from *SL* to *PL* we gain expressive power and are able, for example, to demonstrate the validity of a wider range of English arguments, we lose decidability.

7.2 PREDICATES, INDIVIDUAL CONSTANTS, AND QUANTITY TERMS OF ENGLISH

A distinction between singular terms and predicates is central to understanding the subsentential structure of English discourse. A *singular term* is any word or phrase that designates or purports to designate (or denote or refer to) some one thing. Singular terms are of two sorts: proper names and definite descriptions. Examples of proper names include 'George Washington', 'Marie Curie', 'Sherlock Holmes', 'Rhoda', and 'Henry'. Generally speaking, proper names are attached to the things they name by simple convention. Definite descriptions—for example, 'the discoverer of radium', 'the person Henry is talking to', 'Mary's best friend', and 'James' only brother'—on the other hand, pick out or purport to pick out a thing by providing a unique description of that thing. A definite description is a description that, by its grammatical structure, purports to describe exactly one thing. Thus 'James' only brother' is a definite description whereas 'James' brother' is not—the latter could accurately describe many persons whereas the former can describe at most one.

[2]There are, as one might expect, arguments that are deductively valid but whose symbolizations in *PL* are not valid, sentences that are logically true but whose symbolizations in *PL* do not reflect this, and so on. To deal with natural language discourse that cannot be represented in *PL*, even more powerful formal systems are available—for example, tense logic and modal logic. A discussion of these systems is beyond the scope of this text.

[3]See Section 8.2 for further discussion of this point.

In English not every singular term designates. For example, in its normal use 'Sherlock Holmes' fails to designate because there is no such person as Sherlock Holmes. Similarly a definite description fails to designate if nothing satisfies—that is, if nothing is uniquely described by—that description. Both 'the largest prime number' and 'the present prime minister of the United States' are definite descriptions that for this reason fail to designate.

What thing, if any, a name or definite description designates clearly depends upon the context of use. In its most familiar use 'George Washington' designates the first president of the United States. But a historian may have named her dog after the first president, and if so there will be contexts in which she and her friends use the term 'George Washington' to designate a dog, not a figure from American history. In the same way 'the person Henry is talking to' may designate one person on one occasion, another on another occasion, and (Henry being a taciturn fellow) very often no one at all. Hereafter, when we use a sentence of English as an example or in an exercise set, we shall, unless otherwise noted, be assuming that a context is available for that sentence such that in that context all the singular terms in the sentence do designate. Moreover, when we are working with a group of sentences, the context that is assumed must be the same for all the sentences in the group. That is, we assume that a singular term that occurs several times in the piece of English discourse under discussion designates the same thing in each of its occurrences.

In English pronouns are often used in place of proper names and definite descriptions. When they are so used, their references are determined by the proper names or definite descriptions for which they substitute. For example, in the most straightforward reading of the conditional

If Sue has read Darwin, then she's no creationist

the reference of 'she' is established by the use of 'Sue' in the antecedent of that conditional. So it is clearly appropriate to paraphrase this sentence as

If Sue has read Darwin, then Sue's no creationist.

But not every pronoun can be replaced by a singular term. Replacing 'her or his' in

This test is so easy that if anyone fails the test, then it's her or his own fault

with a singular term, *any* singular term, creates a nonequivalent sentence, as in this example:

This test is so easy that if anyone fails the test then it's Cynthia's own fault.

The former claim places responsibility for failure on the test taker, the latter places it, no matter who the test taker is, on Cynthia (suggesting, perhaps, that

Cynthia is the instructor). (We shall return to uses of pronouns that cannot be replaced with singular terms shortly.)

Obviously a sentence can contain more than one singular term. For example,

New York is between Philadelphia and Boston

contains three singular terms: 'New York', 'Philadelphia', and 'Boston'.[4] *Predicates* of English are parts of English sentences that can be obtained by deleting one or more singular terms from an English sentence. Alternatively a predicate is a string of words with one or more holes or blanks in it such that when the holes are filled with singular terms, a sentence of English results. From the preceding example all the following predicates can be obtained:

__ is between Philadelphia and Boston.
New York is between __ and Boston.
New York is between Philadelphia and __.
__ is between __ and Boston.
__ is between Philadelphia and __.
New York is between __ and __.
__ is between __ and __.

A predicate with just one blank is a one-place predicate. A predicate with more than one blank is a many-place predicate. (A predicate with exactly two blanks is a two-place predicate, a predicate with exactly three blanks is a three-place predicate, and so on. Generally, where **n** is a positive integer, a predicate with **n** blanks is an **n**-place predicate.)

One way of generating a sentence from a predicate is to fill the blanks in the predicate with singular terms. Any singular term can be put in any blank, and the same singular term can be put in more than one blank. So, from the two-place predicate '__ works for __' and the singular terms 'Pat', 'Tom', '3M', 'IBM', and 'the smallest prime number', we can generate the following sentences:

Tom works for 3M.
Pat works for 3M.
Tom works for Pat.
Pat works for Tom.
Pat works for Pat.
3M works for Tom.
IBM works for 3M.
The smallest prime number works for IBM.

---

[4] We are here concerned only with isolating singular terms that do not occur as constituents of other singular terms. That is, we here take

The Roman general who defeated Pompey invaded both Gaul and Germany

to contain just three singular terms: 'The Roman general who defeated Pompey', 'Gaul', and 'Germany'. In Section 7.9 we shall introduce techniques that allow us to recognize and symbolize singular terms that are themselves constituents of singular terms—for example, 'Pompey' as it occurs in 'The Roman general who defeated Pompey'.

And so on. Note that all of these are sentences of English by the standard grammatical rules of English. When a sentence that consists of an **n**-place predicate with the blanks filled with **n** singular terms is true, we say that that predicate is true of the **n** things designated by those **n** singular terms. As it happens, '__ works for __' is true of the pair consisting of Tom and 3M but false of the pair consisting of 3M and Tom (pairs, and triples, and so on, have an order built in). That is, the Tom we have in mind does work for 3M, but 3M does not work for Tom.

It may be objected that not all the above sentences "make sense"—what would it mean for the smallest prime number—2—to work for anything or anyone? One approach here would be to declare such sentences as the last listed to be semantically deviant and therefore not candidates for truth, that is, neither true nor false. We, however, take the simpler approach of counting such sentences as meaningful but false. After all, on any normal understanding, the smallest prime number is not the sort of thing that works for anyone or anything, so the claim that it works for IBM is false. (The predicate '__ works for __' is not true of the pair consisting of the smallest prime number and IBM.) By this move we will gain an overall simplicity and generality when we come to develop the formal syntax and semantics for *PL*.

So far, in displaying predicates, we have been marking the blanks into which singular terms can be placed with underscores. It is time to adopt a more standard notation. Hereafter, in displaying predicates, we shall use the lowercase letters 'w', 'x', 'y', and 'z' (with numerical subscripts where necessary) to mark the blanks in those predicates. (These are, as we shall see, the variables of *PL*.) Using this convention, the three-place predicate of English discussed above can be displayed as

x is between y and z

(or as 'w is between x and y', or 'z is between x and y', and so on). We must use distinct variables to replace the different occurrences of singular terms, but which variables are used is immaterial.

Given a stock of predicates, singular terms, and the sentential connectives 'and', 'or', 'if . . . then . . .', 'if and only if', and 'not', we can generate a wide variety of sentences of English. For example, from the just enumerated sentential connectives, the singular terms 'Henry', 'Sue', 'Rita', and 'Michael' and the predicates 'x is easygoing', 'x likes y', and 'x is taller than y,' we can generate

Michael is easygoing.
Sue is easygoing.
Michael is taller than Sue and Sue is taller than Henry.
Sue likes Henry and Michael likes Rita.
If Rita likes Henry, then Rita is taller than Henry.
If Michael is easygoing, then Rita isn't easygoing.

But we cannot, with these limited resources, generate such simple but powerful claims as

Everyone is easygoing.
No one is easygoing.
Someone is easygoing.
Someone is not easygoing.
Michael likes everyone.
Michael does not like anyone.
Michael doesn't like everyone.
Someone likes Sue.
No one is taller than her or himself.

What is missing is an account of such "quantity" terms as 'every', 'all', 'each', 'some', and 'none'.

The first thing to note is that quantity terms are not singular terms. 'Everyone' is neither a proper name nor a definite description—there is no thing that is either named or described by the term 'everyone'. So, too, for 'everything', 'no one', 'nothing', 'anyone', 'anything', 'someone', and 'something'. These and other quantity terms serve to indicate *how many* of the persons or things under discussion are thus-and-so, not to name or refer to some single entity.

Consider the simple claim 'Someone is easygoing'. We can see this sentence as being composed of the one-place predicate 'x is easygoing' and the expression 'someone'. If this claim is true, then there is some person who is easygoing, that is, someone of whom the predicate 'x is easygoing' is true. But his or her name is not 'someone', nor is 'someone' a description of that person.

Similarly,

Everyone is easygoing

is true if and only if 'x is easygoing' is true of each and every person,

No one is easygoing

is true if and only if there is no person of whom the predicate 'x is easygoing' is true, and

Someone is not easygoing

is true if and only if there is at least one person of whom 'x is easygoing' is not true.[5]

---

[5]Instead of talking of a predicate's being true or false of a thing or an ordered collection of things, we shall hereafter frequently talk instead of a thing or ordered collection of things *satisfying* or *failing to satisfy* a predicate. Thus all and only red things *satisfy* the predicate 'x is red'. This notion of *satisfaction* will be used in the semantics for *PL*.

7.2E EXERCISES

1. Identify the singular terms in the following sentences, and then specify all the one or more place predicates that can be obtained from each sentence by deleting one or more singular terms.

a. The president is a Democrat.
*b. The speaker of the house is a Republican.
c. Sarah attends Smith College.
*d. Bob flunked out of U Mass.
e. Charles and Rita are brother and sister.
*f. Oregon is south of Washington and north of California.
g. 2 times 4 is 8.
*h. 3 times 4 equals 2 times 6.
i. 0 plus 0 equals 0.

2. List all the distinct sentences of English that can be generated using the following predicates and singular terms.

Singular terms:
Herman
Juan
Antonio

Predicates:
x is larger than y
x is to the right of y
x is larger than y but smaller than z

7.3 INTRODUCTION TO *PL*

It is time to introduce the basic elements of the formal language *PL*. We will need the sentential connectives of *SL* and analogs to the singular terms, predicates, and quantity terms of English. The sentential connectives are, to review, the five truth-functional connectives '&', '∨', '⊃', '≡', and '~'. As analogs to denoting singular terms of English—that is, singular terms that actually do, on the occasion of use in question, denote—*PL* contains *individual constants*. These are the lowercase Roman letters 'a' through 'v', with or without numerical subscripts. The predicates of *PL* are the uppercase Roman letters 'A' through 'Z', with or without numerical subscripts, followed by one or more primes. Predicates of *PL*, like predicates of English, come with holes or blanks, with the number of holes indicated by the number of primes. A predicate with one hole is called a 'one-place predicate', a predicate with two holes a 'two-place predicate', and so on. Hence

F′
G′
H′

are all one-place predicates and

F″
G″
H″

are all two-place predicates of *PL*. In specifying predicates, we shall, in practice, generally omit the primes and indicate that the predicate in question is an **n**-place predicate by writing **n** of the letters 'w', 'x', 'y', and 'z' (with subscripts if necessary) after the predicate letter. (For example, the predicate in 'Fx' is a one-place predicate and the predicate in 'Fxy' is a two-place predicate.) The letters 'w' through 'z', with and without subscripts, are called the *variables* of *PL* and have more than a hole-marking use.

In *SL* a single sentence letter can be used to symbolize or abbreviate different English sentences on different occasions. Analogously in *PL* we can use the two-place predicate 'Lxy' to symbolize, on different occasions, a variety of two-place predicates of English, including 'x likes y', 'x loves y', 'x loathes y', and 'x is less than y'. Of course, we could use 'Txy' to symbolize 'x likes y', but that would be harder to remember. Similarly on one occasion we might use the individual constant 'a' to designate Adriana, on another Alfred, and on another the number 1.

It will be useful to have a way of specifying how predicates and constants of *PL* are being used on a particular occasion, as well as what things are being talked about on that occasion. We call the set of things being talked about on a given occasion the *universe of discourse* for that occasion and use the abbreviation 'UD' in specifying a universe of discourse.[6] For this purpose we introduce the notion of a *symbolization key*. The following is an example of a symbolization key. We shall use it in symbolizing the English sentences discussed previously concerning Henry, Michael, Rita, and Sue.

UD: People in Michael's office
Lxy: x likes y
Ex: x is easygoing
Txy: x is taller than y
h: Henry
m: Michael
r: Rita
s: Sue

Note that, whereas in English proper names are capitalized and predicates written with lowercase letters, in *PL* lowercase letters are used to symbolize singular terms of English, including proper names, and uppercase letters are

[6]By stipulation, in *PL* universes of discourse must be nonempty; that is, discourse must always be about at least one thing. This is not a *very* restrictive stipulation because if the universe of discourse is the empty set, then there is nothing in that universe to say anything about.

used to symbolize predicates. In English sentences can be generated from predicates by filling the holes with singular terms. Similarly in *PL* sentences can be generated from predicates by filling the holes (replacing the variables that mark the holes) with individual constants. For example, 'Lsh' symbolizes, given the preceding symbolization key, 'Sue likes Henry'. 'Henry likes Sue' is symbolized as 'Lhs'. And 'Michael is easygoing' is symbolized as 'Em'. Still using the above symbolization key, the sentences

Sue is easygoing.
Michael is taller than Sue and Sue is taller than Henry.
Sue likes Henry and Michael likes Rita.
If Rita likes Henry, then Rita is taller than Henry.
If Michael is easygoing, then Rita is not easygoing.

can be symbolized as follows in *PL*:

Es
Tms & Tsh
Lsh & Lm
Lrh ⊃ Trh
Em ⊃ ~ Er

In *PL*, as in *SL*, when a binary connective is used to join sentences, the result must be enclosed within parentheses. So, for example, the official versions of 'Lsh & Lmr' and 'Em ⊃ ~ Er' are '(Lsh & Lmr)' and '(Em ⊃ ~ Er)'. But with *PL*, as with *SL*, we shall informally omit the outermost parentheses of a sentence whose main logical operator (what in *SL* is termed the 'main connective') is a binary connective. (Also, as in *SL*, we shall informally allow the use of square brackets in place of parentheses.)

We can use our present symbolization key to give English readings for the following sentences of *PL*:

Lhr & ~ Lrh
Lrh ⊃ Lrm
Trh & ~ Trs
Tsh ⊃ Lhs
(Lmh ∨ Lms) ⊃ (Lmh & Lms)

In English these become, respectively,

Henry likes Rita and Rita does not like Henry.
If Rita likes Henry, then Rita likes Michael.
Rita is taller than Henry and Rita is not taller than Sue.

If Sue is taller than Henry, then Henry likes Sue.
If Michael likes Henry or Michael likes Sue, then Michael likes Henry and Michael likes Sue.

We can, of course, improve on the English. For example, the last sentence can be more colloquially paraphrased as

If Michael likes either Henry or Sue he likes both of them.

We can symbolize some English sentences involving quantity terms using only the resources of *PL* so far available to us. If we are talking just about the people in Michael's office, that is, just about Michael, Sue, Rita, and Henry, then one way to symbolize 'Everyone is easygoing' in *PL* is

(Es & Eh) & (Er & Em)

Note that we are here taking the scope or range of application of 'Everyone' in 'Everyone is easygoing' to be all and only the people in Michael's office. We could use the same strategy to symbolize 'Michael likes someone' as

(Lms ∨ Lmh) ∨ (Lmr ∨ Lmm)

and 'Michael likes everyone' as

(Lms & Lmh) & (Lmr & Lmm)

Note that, since we are talking about *everyone* in Michael's office, and Michael is one of those persons, we have to include 'Lmm' in our symbolization; that is, we take 'Michael likes everyone' to mean, in part, that Michael likes himself.

7.3E EXERCISES

1. Use the following symbolization key to symbolize the English sentences given as answers to Exercise 2 in Section 7.2E.

UD: Herman, Juan, and Antonio
Sxyz: x is larger than y but smaller than z
Lxy: x is larger than y
Rxy: x is to the right of y
a: Antonio
h: Herman
m: Juan

2. Symbolize the following sentences in *PL* using the given symbolization key.

UD: Alfy, Barbara, Clarence, Dawn, Ellis, and the cities Houston, Indianapolis, Kalamazoo, Newark, Philadelphia, San Francisco, and Tulsa
Bxy: x was born in y
Lxy: x lives in y
Axy: x is larger than y
Txy: x is taller than y
a: Alfy
b: Barbara
c: Clarence
d: Dawn
e: Ellis
h: Houston
i: Indianapolis
k: Kalamazoo
n: Newark
p: Philadelphia
s: San Francisco
t: Tulsa

a. Alfy was born in Indianapolis.
*b. Clarence was born in Tulsa.
c. Barbara was born in Newark.
*d. Dawn was born in San Francisco.
e. Ellis was born in Houston.
*f. No one was born in Kalamazoo.
g. Philadelphia is larger than Houston, Houston is larger than Newark, and Newark is larger than Kalamazoo.
*h. Tulsa isn't larger than either Philadelphia or Houston.
i. Indianapolis is larger than Houston if and only if it is larger than Philadelphia.
*j. Barbara lives in Philadelphia only if Dawn does.
k. Everyone lives in Philadelphia, but no one was born there.
*l. Barbara is taller than Clarence and Clarence is taller than Alfy, but neither Barbara nor Clarence is taller than Ellis.
m. Dawn is the tallest person in the office.
*n. Alfy isn't taller than everyone else in the office.
o. Alfy isn't taller than anyone in the office, but he is larger than everyone else in the office.
*p. If Clarence is taller than Barbara, he's also larger than Alfy.

3. Symbolize the following sentences in *PL* using the given symbolization key.

UD: Andrea, Bentley, Charles, and Deirdre
Bx: x is beautiful
Ix: x is intelligent
Rx: x is rich
Axy: x is attracted to y
Dxy: x despises y
Lxy: x loves y
Sxy: x is shorter than y

a: Andrea
b: Bentley
c: Charles
d: Deirdre

a. Andrea is both intelligent and beautiful, but she is not rich.
*b. Charles is rich and beautiful but not intelligent.
c. Deirdre is beautiful, rich, and intelligent.
*d. Bentley is neither rich, nor beautiful, nor intelligent.
e. If Bentley is intelligent, so are both Deirdre and Andrea.
*f. Andrea is beautiful and intelligent, Bentley is intelligent but not beautiful, and neither is rich.
g. Andrea loves Bentley but despises Charles.
*h. Andrea loves both herself and Charles and despises both Bentley and Deirdre.
i. Charles neither loves nor despises Andrea but both loves and despises Deirdre.
*j. Neither Deirdre nor Bentley is attracted to Charles, but Charles is attracted to both of them.
k. Charles is attracted to Bentley if and only if Bentley both is shorter than Charles and is rich.
*l. Andrea is attracted to both Bentley and Deirdre but doesn't love either of them.
m. If Deirdre is shorter than Charles and Charles is shorter than Andrea, then Deirdre is shorter than Andrea.
*n. If Bentley is attracted to Deirdre and she is attracted to him, then they love each other.
o. If Charles loves Bentley and Bentley loves Andrea, then Charles both despises and is shorter than Andrea.
*p. If Charles is neither rich nor beautiful nor intelligent, then no one loves him.
q. Only Deirdre is rich.
*r. Only Deirdre is both rich and intelligent.

4. For each of the following passages, provide a symbolization key and then use it to symbolize the passage in *PL*.

a. Margaret and Todd both like skateboarding, but neither is good at it. Charles is good at skateboarding but doesn't like it. Sarah is both good at skateboarding and likes it. All of them wear headgear, but Charles and Sarah are the only ones who wear knee pads. Sarah is more reckless than the rest, and Charles is more skillful than the rest.
*b. Charles is a sailor but not a tennis player, while Linda is both. Linda is a yuppie, and while Charles wants to be one, he isn't. Everyone likes Charles, but everyone also likes someone else more. Stan is a yuppie, and although Linda likes Charles, she likes Stan more. Stan is a sailor, a tennis player, and a squash player, and he likes himself more than he likes either of the other two. (*Hint:* Take the universe of discourse to consist of just Charles, Linda, and Stan.)
c. Andrew and Christopher are both hikers, but neither is a mountain climber. Amanda is a hiker and a mountain climber and also a kayaker. One, but not both, of Andrew and Christopher is also a kayaker. None of them is a swimmer. Andrew, Christopher, and Amanda all like each other, and Amanda is nuts about Andrew, and vice versa.

*d. Joan, Mark, Alice, and Randy are all in law school. Joan and Randy are studying tax law; Mark and Alice medical malpractice law. Alice gets better grades than Randy, and Mark gets better grades than Joan. They will all finish in three years, and everyone but Mark will pass the bar exam. At least two of the three who pass the bar exam will get jobs as attorneys.

7.4 QUANTIFIERS INTRODUCED

In the preceding section we saw how quantity claims can sometimes be symbolized using conjunctions and/or disjunctions of sentences. For example, we symbolize 'Michael likes someone in his office' as '(Lms ∨ Lmh) ∨ (Lmr ∨ Lmm)'. But this is a bit awkward. This strategy will not, in practice, work if we want to symbolize claims such as 'Michael likes everyone' where the number of people encompassed by 'everyone' is even modestly large—for example, the several hundred people Michael has met in the last five years. Worse still, suppose Michael is a mathematician and likes the positive integers, all infinitely many of them. On the present strategy we would need an infinitely long sentence, and we require the sentences of both *SL* and *PL* to be finitely long.[7] We need, within *PL*, analogs to the quantity terms of English; that is, we need the quantifier symbols and variables of *PL*. There are two quantifier symbols: '∀' and '∃'. The variables of *PL* are the letters 'w' through 'z', with or without subscripts. A *quantifier* of *PL* consists of a quantifier symbol followed by a variable, both enclosed in parentheses. Thus '(∀x)' and '(∃y)' are both quantifiers.

Recalling that our universe of discourse consists of the people in Michael's office, we can now abandon the use of iterated conjunctions and disjunctions. For example, we can symbolize 'Michael likes everyone' as

(∀x)Lmx

Here we have a predicate with one hole filled by an individual constant and one filled by a variable. The predicate is prefaced with a quantifier built from the same variable that fills the second hole. Quantifiers formed from '∀' are called *universal quantifiers* and are used to claim that each of the things being talked about is of the sort specified by the expression following the quantifier. The things being talked about, the members of the current universe of discourse, are called the *values* of the variables—because they are the things the variables are used to talk about. Here the claim being made is that each thing being talked about, that is, each person in Michael's office (each value of the variable 'x'), is of the sort Lmx, that is, is such that Michael likes it.

To symbolize 'Michael likes someone', still talking exclusively about the people in Michael's office, we can use an *existential quantifier*, that is, a quantifier built from '∃'.

(∃x)Lmx

[7]The problem is even more serious than suggested here, for Michael might like all real numbers, and there are more real numbers than there are individual constants of *PL*.

says there is at least one x (at least one value of the variable 'x') such that Michael likes that x. Since we are talking exclusively of the people in Michael's office, this amounts to

There is at least one person Michael likes

or

Michael likes someone.

Note that we interpret 'some' to mean 'at least one'.[8]

Variables of *PL* serve some of the functions of English pronouns and of such place-holder terms as 'thing', 'body', and 'one'—as in, for example, 'something', 'somebody', and 'someone'. 'Something is out of place' means that at least one of the things, whatever they may be, we are currently discussing is out of place. 'Everything is out of place' means that each of the things we are currently discussing is out of place. It is more stilted, but still acceptable English, to paraphrase these claims as, respectively,

<u>At least one</u> of the things under discussion is such that it is out of place

and

<u>Each</u> of the things under discussion is such that it is out of place.[9]

These paraphrases have a syntax that closely mirrors that of *PL*. Using 'Ox' to express 'x is out of place', we can symbolize the foregoing sentences in *PL* as

$(\exists x)Ox$

and

$(\forall x)Ox$

Note that in each the variable 'x' occurs twice; the first occurrence corresponds to 'thing' in the stilted English version, the second to 'it'. We can paraphrase these sentences of *PL* in quasi-English as '<u>At least one</u> x is such that x is out of place' and '<u>Each</u> x is such that x is out of place', respectively.

---

[8]This is certainly appropriate for such English locutions as 'Someone is in the house' and John knows someone in the bursar's office'. But 'There are some cookies in the cookie jar' suggests to many that there are *at least two* cookies in that vessel. Nonetheless, we will always take the existential quantifier to mean 'at least one'. We will later introduce a way of saying 'at least two' when it is important to distinguish between 'at least one' and 'at least two'.

[9]In this chapter we frequently underline quantity expressions and truth-functional expressions in our paraphrases of sentences.

We now return to our example of Michael and his co-workers. This time we provide symbolizations that make use of quantifiers:

UD: People in Michael's office
Lxy: x likes y
Ex: x is easygoing
Txy: x is taller than y
h: Henry
m: Michael
r: Rita
s: Sue

The sentences to be symbolized are

Everyone is easygoing.
No one likes Michael.
Michael likes everyone.
Michael doesn't like anyone.
Michael doesn't like everyone.
Someone likes Sue.
No one is taller than herself or himself.

These can be symbolized in *PL* as, respectively,

$(\forall x)Ex$
$\sim (\exists x)Lxm$
$(\forall x)Lmx$
$\sim (\exists x)Lmx$
$\sim (\forall x)Lmx$
$(\exists x)Lxs$
$\sim (\exists x)Txx$

Points to Note

1. There is nothing sacrosanct about our choice of variables. In each of the preceding cases, every occurrence of 'x' can be replaced with any other variable. '$(\exists y)Lys$' says 'Someone likes Sue' just as well as '$(\exists x)Lxs$' does.
2. There is nothing sacrosanct about the variables used in specifying predicates in symbolization keys. Our symbolization key includes

   Ex: x is easygoing

   Any other variable would have done as well in specifying how the one-place predicate in question is to be interpreted. (For example, we could have used 'Ez: z is easygoing'.)
3. The variables used in specifying predicates in symbolization keys need not be used in constructing symbolizations based on those keys. Given the previous symbolization key, we are perfectly free to symbolize 'Everyone is easygoing' as '$(\forall y)Ey$'.

We are treating claims such as 'Everyone is easygoing' and 'Michael likes everyone' as ways of saying, in shorthand fashion, of each thing under discussion, in the first instance that it is easygoing and, in the second instance that Michael likes it. That is, we are *not* treating 'Everyone is easygoing' as being a sentence that has a subject term, 'Everyone', that denotes something (the collection of people being talked about) of which a property, easygoingness, is being predicated.

Note also that 'every' and 'all' function somewhat differently grammatically. Grammatically 'All people are mortal' has a plural subject term and thus requires a plural verb, 'are'. 'Everyone is mortal' has a singular term in subject position and thus requires a singular verb, 'is'.

Some uses of 'all' and 'every' can be confusing. Consider 'All the bricks are too heavy' uttered in response to the question 'Can you take all the bricks in one load?' Here 'All the bricks are too heavy' probably means, not that each brick, by itself, is too heavy to take in one load, but rather that the bricks taken collectively, all at once, are too heavy. Note that this ambiguity is absent from 'Every brick is too heavy'. Here there is no chance we mean anything other than that each brick, by itself, is too heavy. At any rate, in this text, we treat 'All such-and-such are thus-and-so', 'Every such-and-such is thus-and-so', and 'Each such-and-such is thus-and-so', as various ways of saying of each thing that is such-and-such that it is thus-and-so—that is, as claims about individual things, not as claims about collections of things (all the bricks taken together).

There is a very important difference between 'Michael doesn't like everyone' and 'Michael doesn't like anyone'. If Michael is like most of us, he likes some people and not others, and so it is true that he doesn't like everyone (he doesn't, for example, like Rita at all) but false that he doesn't like anyone (he likes Sue very much). The difference between 'doesn't like every' and 'doesn't like any' is very clearly marked by the syntax of *PL*: The first can be expressed by a '~' followed by a universal quantifier, and the second by a '~' followed by an existential quantifier.

So far the sentences of *PL* we have dealt with have contained only a single quantifier, one predicate, and in some cases a tilde. It is an easy next step to form truth-functional compounds of such sentences. Here are some examples:

1. Either everyone is easygoing or no one is.
2. If Rita is easygoing, everyone is.
3. Rita likes Sue if and only if everyone does.
4. Henry likes everyone but Sue doesn't.
5. Henry likes everyone and Sue doesn't like anyone.
6. Not everyone is easygoing, but everyone is ambitious.
7. If anyone is ambitious, Michael is.
8. Everyone is ambitious if and only if no one is easygoing.

We can symbolize these English sentences in *PL* using the symbolization key introduced previously, with the addition of

Ax: x is ambitious

The first sentence is a disjunction. We can symbolize the left disjunct, 'Everyone is easygoing' as '$(\forall y)Ey$' (remember, the fact that we specified the predicate for 'is easygoing' as 'Ex' in the symbolization key does *not* mean we can only use the variable 'x' when working with that predicate). We must be careful in symbolizing the second half of our disjunction—'no one is easygoing' is *not* the negation of 'Everyone is easygoing'. That is, the symbolization '$\sim (\forall y)Ey$' says, not that *no one is* easygoing', but rather that *not everyone is* easygoing. For the second disjunct of the sentence of *PL*, we are constructing, we can use either '$\sim (\exists w)Ew$' or '$(\forall w) \sim Ew$'. The first says it is not the case that there is even one person who is easygoing (hence no one is), and the second that each person is not easygoing (again, hence that no one is). So for a complete symbolization of our first example we might pick

$$(\forall y)Ey \vee \sim (\exists w)Ew$$

Note that in the left disjunct we used the variable 'y', and in the right disjunct the variable 'w'. This was an arbitrary selection; we could have used the same variable in both. But we cannot use two different variables within either disjunct. That is, '$(\forall y)Ex$' is not allowed since the purpose of the quantifier is to indicate how many things are of the sort specified by the predicate that follows it, and to do this the variable used in forming the quantifier must match the variable used with the predicate following it.

Sentence 2, 'If Rita is easygoing, everyone is', is a conditional whose antecedent is 'Rita is easygoing', or 'Er' in *PL*, and whose consequent is short for 'everyone is easygoing'. The latter can be symbolized as '$(\forall w)Ew$', and the whole sentence as

$$Er \supset (\forall w)Ew$$

The third sentence, 'Rita likes Sue if and only if everyone does', can be symbolized as a material biconditional

$$Lrs \equiv (\forall z)Lzs$$

Note that, while '$Lrs \equiv (\forall z)Lsz$' looks a lot like the above sentence of *PL*, it says something very different, namely, that Rita likes Sue if and only if Sue likes everyone.

Sentence 5, 'Henry likes everyone but Sue doesn't', becomes a conjunction of *PL*. '$(\forall y)Lhy$' is an appropriate left conjunct, and '$\sim (\forall x)Lsx$' an appropriate right conjunct, yielding the conjunction *PL*:

$$(\forall y)Lhy \;\&\; \sim (\forall x)Lsx$$

The second conjunct says of Sue that she doesn't like everyone, not that she doesn't like *anyone*, which is what the next example says of Sue. To symbolize the fifth example, we can replace the right conjunct of the preceding sentence of *PL* with either '(∀x) ~ Lsx' or '~ (∃x)Lsx'. The first of the foregoing can be paraphrased as 'each person is such that it is not the case that Sue likes that person', and the second as 'it is not the case that there is at least one person that Sue likes'. These amount to the same thing—that Sue doesn't like anyone. So we might pick for our symbolization of the fifth example

(∀y)Lhy & ~ (∃x)Lsx

'Not everyone is easygoing, but everyone is ambitious', our sixth example, can be symbolized as the conjunction of '~ (∀z)Ez' and '(∀y)Ay', or as

~ (∀z)Ez & (∀y)Ay

Sentence 7, 'If anyone is ambitious, Michael is', is a conditional. Here the 'anyone' of the antecedent means 'at least one', for the claim is that if anyone, anyone at all—that is, at least one person—is ambitious, Michael is. So an appropriate symbolization is

(∃w)Aw ⊃ Am

The last of our examples can be symbolized as a material biconditional linking 'Everyone is ambitious', or '(∀w)Aw', and 'no one is easygoing', or '~ (∃w)Ew'. So an appropriate symbolization in *PL* is

(∀w)Aw ≡ ~ (∃w)Ew

For 'no one is easygoing' we could also have used '(∀w) ~ Ew'; that is, each person is not easygoing.

Finally we do not really need both existential and universal quantifiers. Instead of saying 'Everything is thus-and-so' ('Everyone likes Michael', or '(∀x)Lxm'), we can say 'It is not the case that something is not thus-and-so' ('It is not the case that someone does not like Michael', or '~ (∃x) ~ Lxm'). And instead of saying 'Something is thus-and-so' ('Someone likes Michael', or '(∃x)Lxm'), we can say 'It is not the case that everything is not thus-and-so' ('It is not the case that everyone does not like Michael', or '~ (∀x) ~ Lxm'). However, having both quantifiers available does make symbolization somewhat easier and more natural.

7.4E EXERCISES

1. Symbolize the following sentences in *PL* using the given symbolization key.

UD: The jellybeans in the jar on the coffee table
Bx: x is black
Rx: x is red

a. All the jellybeans are black.
*b. Some of the jellybeans are black.
c. None of the jellybeans is black.
*d. Some of the jellybeans are not black.
e. Some of the jellybeans are black and some are red.
*f. If all the jellybeans are black then none is red.
g. If some are red some are black.
*h. If none is black all are red.
i. All are black if and only if none is red.
*j. Either all are black or all are red.

2. Symbolize the following sentences in *PL*. (*Note:* Not all of these sentences are true.)

UD: The integers 1–100
Ex: x is even
Ox: x is odd
Lxy: x is less than y
Px: x is prime
Gx: x is greater than 0
a: 1
b: 2
c: 4
d: 100

a. Some integers are odd and some are even.
*b. Some integers are both odd and even.
c. No integer is less than 1.
*d. No integer is greater than 100.
e. Every integer is greater than 0.
*f. 100 is greater than every odd integer.
g. There is a prime that is even.
*h. Some primes are not even.
i. All prime integers greater than 2 are odd.
*j. 1 is not prime and is not greater than any integer.
k. There is an integer that is greater than 2 and less than 4.

3. Symbolize the following sentences in *PL* using the given symbolization key.

UD: The students in a logic class
Px: x will pass
Sx: x will study
j: Jamie
r: Rhoda

a. If Jamie will pass everyone will pass.
*b. Either no one will pass or Jamie will pass.
c. If anyone passes both Jamie and Rhoda will.
*d. Not everyone will pass, but Rhoda will.
e. If Rhoda doesn't pass no one will.
*f. Some, but not all, of the students will pass.
g. Rhoda will pass if Jamie does, and if Rhoda passes everyone will pass.
*h. No one will pass if Jamie doesn't pass, and if she does everyone will.
i. Everyone will study but not everyone will pass.
*j. If everyone studies everyone will pass.
k. If everyone studies some will pass.

7.5 THE FORMAL SYNTAX OF *PL*

Before attempting more complex symbolizations, it will be useful to acquire a fuller understanding of the syntax of *PL*. To this end we now pause to present the formal syntax for the language of *PL* and to introduce some important syntactical concepts. While this material may at first seem difficult, it can be readily mastered, and doing so will make mastering the rest of this chapter much easier.

The vocabulary of *PL* consists of the following:

Sentence letters of PL: The capital Roman letters 'A' through 'Z', with or without positive-integer subscripts (These are just the sentence letters of *SL*.)	A, B, C, . . . , Z, A_1, B_1, C_1, . . . , Z_1, . . .
Predicates of PL: The capital Roman letters 'A' through 'Z', with or without positive-integer subscripts, followed by one or more primes (An **n**-place predicate is indicated by the presence of exactly **n** primes.)	A′, B′, C′ . . . , Z′, A_1', B_1', C_1', . . . , Z_1' . . .
Individual terms of PL:	
Individual constants of PL: The lowercase Roman letters 'a' through 'v', with or without positive-integer subscripts	a, b, c, . . . , v, a_1, b_1, c_1, . . . , v_1, . . .
Individual variables of PL: The lowercase Roman letters 'w' through 'z', with or without positive-integer subscripts.	w, x, y, z, w_1, x_1, y_1, z_1, ...
Truth-functional connectives:	$\sim$ & $\vee$ $\supset$ $\equiv$
Quantifier Symbols:	$\forall$ $\exists$
Punctuation marks:	( )

By informal convention we will continue to omit the primes from predicates of *PL* where no confusion results from doing so. By including the sentence letters of *SL* as sentence letters of *PL*, we make every sentence of *SL* a sentence of *PL*. Thus every English sentence that can be symbolized in *SL* can also be symbolized in *PL*. However, the content of English sentences is generally better captured by using predicates rather than sentence letters. Hence we shall rarely, if ever, have use for sentence letters in the rest of this text.[10]

We define an expression of *PL* to be a sequence of not necessarily distinct elements of the vocabulary of *PL*. The following are expressions of *PL*:

((((()(((a ⊃ bba)
(A ⊃ Bab))
(∀x)(∃x)Fxx

but

(({ABA)
(A ⊃ 3)
A # Bab
(∀ @)(Cab)

are not since '{', '3', '#', and '@' are not elements of the vocabulary of *PL*.

In what follows we will use the bold letters

P Q R

as metavariables ranging over expressions of *PL*. We will use a bold '**a**' as a metavariable ranging over individual constants of *PL* and a bold '**x**' as a metavariable ranging over individual variables of *PL*.

> *Quantifier of PL:* An expression of *PL* of the form (∀**x**) or (∃**x**). An expression of the first form is a universal quantifier, and one of the second form is an existential quantifier.

We will say that a quantifier *contains* a variable. Thus '(∀y)' and '(∃y)' both contain the variable 'y' (and are 'y-quantifiers'); '(∀z)' and '(∃z)' both contain the variable 'z' (and are 'z-quantifiers').

> *Atomic formulas of PL:* Every expression of *PL* that is either a sentence letter of *PL* or an **n**-place predicate of *PL* followed by **n** individual terms of *PL*.

---

[10]We could include among the predicates of *PL* zero-place predicates. Doing so would make the sentence letters of *SL* zero-place predicates and would obviate the need for the separate category 'Sentence letters of *PL*'.

We are now ready to give a recursive definition of 'formula of *PL*':

1. Every atomic formula of *PL* is a formula of *PL*.
2. If **P** is a formula of *PL*, so is ~ **P**.
3. If **P** and **Q** are formulas of *PL*, so are (**P** & **Q**), (**P** ∨ **Q**), (**P** ⊃ **Q**), and (**P** ≡ **Q**).
4. If **P** is a formula of *PL* that contains at least one occurrence of **x** and no **x**-quantifier, then (∀**x**)**P** and (∃**x**)**P** are both formulas of *PL*.
5. Nothing is a formula of *PL* unless it can be formed by repeated applications of clauses 1–4.

Last, we specify the logical operators of *PL*:

Logical operator of PL: An expression of *PL* that is either a quantifier or a truth-functional connective

Consider the following expressions of *PL*:

Rabz
~ (Rabz & Hxy)
(~ Rabz & Hxy)
(Hab ⊃ (∀z) (Fz ⊃ Gza))
(Haz ⊃ ~ (∀z) (Fz ⊃ Gza))
(∀z) (Haz ⊃ (∀z) (Fz ⊃ Gza))
(∀x) (Haz ⊃ (∀z) (Fz ⊃ Gza))
(∀y) (Hay ⊃ (Fy ⊃ Gya))

The first expression consists of a three-place predicate followed by three individual terms, the first two being individual constants and the third an individual variable. Hence it is an atomic formula of *PL* and, by clause 1 of the recursive definition of 'formula of *PL*', a formula of *PL*.

The second expression consists of a tilde, '~', followed by '(Rabz & Hxy)', and so it is a formula of *PL* by clause 2 if '(Rabz & Hxy)' is a formula of *PL*. And since 'Rabz' and 'Hxy' are both atomic formulas of *PL*, and hence formulas of *PL*, '(Rabz & Hxy)' is a formula of *PL* by clause 3 of the recursive definition. The third expression, '(~ Rabz & Hxy)', is a formula of *PL* by clause 3 if '~ Rabz' and 'Hxy' are both formulas of *PL*. They are: 'Hxy' is an atomic formula and hence a formula, and 'Rabz' is an atomic formula and hence a formula; and so '~ Rabz' is a formula by clause 2.

The fourth expression, '(Hab ⊃ (∀z) (Fz ⊃ Gza))', is a formula of *PL* by clause 3 if 'Hab' and '(∀z) (Fz ⊃ Gza)' are both formulas of *PL*. The first is an atomic formula, a two-place predicate followed by two individual terms (both constants), and hence a formula of *PL* by clause 1. The second is a formula of

PL by clause 4 if '(Fz ⊃ Gza)' is a formula containing at least one occurrence of 'z' and no z-quantifier. It clearly satisfies the last two conditions, and since 'Fz' and 'Gza' are both atomic formulas of *PL* and hence formulas of *PL*, '(Fz ⊃ Gza)' is a formula of *PL* by clause 3 of the recursive definition. So the whole expression is a formula of *PL*. For reasons parallel to those outlined above, the fifth expression, '(Haz ⊃ ~ (∀z)(Fz ⊃ Gza))', is also a formula of *PL*. The differences are that the antecedent of the conditional, 'Haz', is an atomic formula containing one constant and one variable instead of two constants, and the consequent is a negation, '~ (∀z)(Fz ⊃ Gza)'. Since '(∀z)(Fz ⊃ Gza)' is a formula, so is '~ (∀z)(Fz ⊃ Gza)' by clause 2 of the recursive definition.

The sixth expression, '(∀z)(Haz ⊃ (∀z)(Fz ⊃ Gza))', is not a formula of *PL*. It would be a formula, by clause 4, if '(Haz ⊃ (∀z)(Fz ⊃ Gza))' were a formula containing at least one occurrence of 'z' and no z-quantifier. The first two conditions are satisfied, but the third is not. '(Haz ⊃ (∀z)(Fz ⊃ Gza))' does contain a z-quantifier in '(∀z)(Fz ⊃ Gza)'. The seventh expression, '(∀x)(Haz ⊃ (∀z)(Fz ⊃ Gza))', is also not a formula. As we saw, '(Haz ⊃ (∀z)(Fz ⊃ Gza))' is a formula. But since it contains no occurrence of the variable 'x', prefixing it with an x-quantifier does not produce a formula of *PL*.

The last expression, '(∀y)(Hay ⊃ (Fy ⊃ Gya))', is a formula. While it looks rather similar to the two expressions just considered, it is built up in rather different ways. Note first that 'Fy' and 'Gya' are formulas of *PL*, so '(Fy ⊃ Gya)' is also a formula of *PL*. And since 'Hay' is an atomic formula, and therefore a formula, of *PL*, '(Hay ⊃ (Fy ⊃ Gya))' is also a formula of *PL*. Since this formula contains at least one occurrence of the variable 'y' and no y-quantifier, prefixing it with a y-quantifier, here '(∀y)', produces a formula of *PL*—that is, '(∀y)(Hay ⊃ (Fy ⊃ Gya))'.

Not all formulas of *PL* qualify as sentences of *PL*. But before we can explicitly state the relationship between formulas and sentences, we need to introduce the concepts of *subformula* and *main logical operator*. We do so by cases:

1. If **P** is an atomic formula of *PL*, then **P** contains no logical operator, and hence no main logical operator, and **P** is the only subformula of **P**.
2. If **P** is a formula of *PL* of the form ~ **Q**, then the tilde ('~') that precedes **Q** is the main logical operator of **P**, and **Q** is the immediate subformula of **P**.
3. If **P** is a formula of *PL* of the form (**Q** & **R**), (**Q** ∨ **R**), (**Q** ⊃ **R**), or (**Q** ≡ **R**), then the binary connective between **Q** and **R** is the main logical operator of **P**, and **Q** and **R** are the immediate subformulas of **P**.
4. If **P** is a formula of *PL* of the form (∀**x**)**Q** or of the form (∃**x**)**Q**, then the quantifier that occurs before **Q** is the main logical operator of **P**, and **Q** is the immediate subformula of **P**.
5. If **P** is a formula of *PL*, then every subformula (immediate or not) of a subformula of **P** is a subformula of **P**, and **P** is a subformula of itself.

We can classify formulas of *PL* (and later sentences) by their main logical operator. Atomic formulas have no main logical operator. Quantified formulas have a quantifier as their main logical operator. Truth-functional compounds have a truth-functional connective as their main logical operator. Consider again the eight expressions of *PL* displayed previously. The sixth and seventh are not formulas of *PL*, and hence the notions of main logical operator and subformula do not apply to them. For each of the rest we display its subformulas, identify the main logical operator (if any), and classify its subformula as either atomic, quantified, or a truth-functional compound.

Formula	*Subformula*	*Main Logical Operator*	*Type*
Rabz	Rabz	None	Atomic
~ (Rabz & Hxy)	~ (Rabz & Hxy)	~	Truth-functional
	(Rabz & Hxy)	&	Truth-functional
	Rabz	None	Atomic
	Hxy	None	Atomic
(~ Rabz & Hxy)	(~ Rabz & Hxy)	&	Truth-functional
	~ Rabz	~	Truth-functional
	Hxy	None	Atomic
	Rabz	None	Atomic
(Hab ⊃ (∀z)(Fz ⊃ Gza))	(Hab ⊃ (∀z)(Fz ⊃ Gza)	⊃	Truth-functional
	Hab	None	Atomic
	(∀z)(Fz ⊃ Gza)	(∀z)	Quantified
	(Fz ⊃ Gza)	⊃	Truth-functional
	Fz	None	Atomic
	Gza	None	Atomic
(Haz ⊃ ~ (∀z)(Fz ⊃ Gza))	(Haz ⊃ ~ (∀z)(Fz ⊃ Gza))	⊃	Truth-functional
	Haz	None	Atomic
	~ (∀z)(Fz ⊃ Gza)	~	Truth-functional
	(∀z)(Fz ⊃ Gza)	(∀z)	Quantified
	(Fz ⊃ Gza)	⊃	Truth-functional
	Fz	None	Atomic
	Gza	None	Atomic
(∀y)(Hay ⊃ (Fy ⊃ Gya))	(∀y)(Hay ⊃ (Fy ⊃ Gya))	(∀y)	Quantified
	(Hay ⊃ (Fy ⊃ (Gya))	⊃	Truth-functional
	Hay	None	Atomic
	(Fy ⊃ Gya)	⊃	Truth-functional
	Fy	None	Atomic
	Gya	None	Atomic

Earlier we talked informally of quantifiers serving to interpret variables. We can now make that notion explicit. The interpretive range of a quantifier is its scope.

> *Scope of a quantifier:* The scope of a quantifier in a formula **P** of *PL* is the subformula **Q** of **P** of which that quantifier is the main logical operator.

Recall, from the recursive definition of 'formula of *PL*', that the only way quantifiers get into formulas is by clause 4, which specifies the conditions under which a quantifier may be attached to a formula. So attaching a quantifier to a formula produces a new formula, of which the quantifier is the main logical operator. The scope of that quantifier is all of the new formula; that is, it is the quantifier itself and the formula to which it is being attached. For example, '(∀x)Fxy' is a quantified formula of which '(∀x)' is the main logical operator. The scope of that quantifier is all of '(∀x)Fxy'; that is, the scope includes the quantifier '(∀x)' and the formula immediately following the quantifier, namely, 'Fxy'.

Consider the formula '(Hx ⊃ (∀y)Fxy)'. This expression is a formula (by clause 3 of the recursive definition of 'formula of *PL*') inasmuch as 'Hx' is a formula (an atomic formula) and '(∀y)Fxy' is a formula by clause 4 ('Fxy' is a formula of *PL* in which x occurs and in which no x-quantifier occurs). The formula contains two distinct variables, 'x' and 'y', and a total of four occurrences of variables ('x' and 'y' each occur twice). The scope of '(∀y)' includes the occurrence of 'y' from which it is formed and the occurrences of 'x' and 'y' in 'Fxy', for the subformula of which '(∀y)' is the main logical operator is '(∀y)Fxy'. But the first occurrence of 'x', that in 'Hx', does not fall within the scope of '(∀y)', for it is not in the subformula '(∀y)Fxy'. In '((∀z)Gz ⊃ ~ Hz)' the scope of the quantifier '(∀z)' is '(∀z)Gz; hence the first two occurrences of 'z' in this formula fall within its scope, but the last occurrence, that in '~ Hz', does not. We can now introduce the notions of free and bound variables of *PL*.

> *Bound variable:* An occurrence of a variable **x** in a formula **P** of *PL* that is within the scope of an **x**-quantifier
>
> *Free variable:* An occurrence of a variable **x** in a formula **P** of *PL* that is not bound

At long last we are ready to formally introduce the notion of a sentence of *PL*:

> *Sentence of PL:* A formula **P** of *PL* is a sentence of *PL* if and only if no occurrence of a variable in **P** is free.

We shall speak of a formula of *PL* that is not a sentence of *PL* as an *open sentence* of *PL*.

We can now see that '(Hx ⊃ (∀y)Fxy)' is not a sentence of *PL* for two reasons: The first occurrence of 'x' does not fall within the scope of any quantifier and is therefore free, and the second occurrence of 'x', while falling within the scope of a quantifier, does not fall within the scope of an x-quantifier. And '((∀z)Gz ⊃ ~ Hz)' is not a sentence because the third occurrence of 'z' does not fall within the scope of a z-quantifier. The scope of '(∀z)' is limited to the subformula of which it is the main logical operator—that is, to '(∀z)Gz'.

Earlier we considered the following eight expressions of *PL*:

Rabz

~ (Rabz & Hxy)

(~ Rabz & Hxy)

(Hab ⊃ (∀z) (Fz ⊃ Gza))

(Haz ⊃ ~ (∀z) (Fz ⊃ Gza))

(∀z) (Haz ⊃ (∀z) (Fz ⊃ Gza))

(∀x) (Haz ⊃ (∀z) (Fz ⊃ Gza))

(∀y) (Hay ⊃ (Fy ⊃ Gya))

The first is not a sentence because it contains a free occurrence of 'z'. However, this formula can be made into a sentence by prefacing it with a z-quantifier; that is, both '(∀y)Rabz' and '(∃z)Rabz' are sentences of *PL*. Note that formulas that contain no variables—for example, 'Rabc', 'Hab', and '(Gd & Fab)'—are sentences of *PL*; they contain no occurrences of variables and hence no free occurrences of variables. It is individual variables, *not individual constants,* that need to be interpreted by quantifiers.

The second formula contains three free occurrences of variables—one each of 'z', 'x', and 'y'—and so is not a sentence of *PL*. We would have to add three quantifiers to this formula to make it a sentence: a z-quantifier, an x-quantifier, and a y-quantifier, in any order. So, too, for the third formula. The fourth formula is a sentence since the only variable it contains is 'z', and all occurrences of 'z' fall within the scope of '(∀z)'. (The scope of that quantifier is '(∀z) (Fz ⊃ Gza)'.)

The fifth formula is not a sentence of *PL* since it does contain a free variable, the first occurrence of 'z' (in 'Haz'). The sixth expression, '(∀z) (Haz ⊃ (∀z) (Fz ⊃ Gza))', is, as noted earlier, not a formula of *PL* because the initial z-quantifier is attached to an expression that is a formula that already contains a z-quantifier. Since it is not a formula of *PL*, it is not a sentence of *PL*. We can now see why the fourth clause of the recursive definition of 'formula of *PL*',

4. If **P** is a formula of *PL* that contains at least one occurrence of **x** and no **x**-quantifier, then (∀**x**)**P** and (∃**x**)**P** are both formulas of *PL*

is as complicated as it is. If we dropped the restriction 'and no **x**-quantifier' from clause 4, the expression '(∀z) (Haz ⊃ (∀z) (Fz ⊃ Gza))' would be a formula with two z-quantifiers with overlapping scopes. We would then need some further rule to determine which quantifier interprets the last two occurrences of 'z' for those occurrences of 'z' that fall within the scope of *both* quantifiers.

The seventh expression, '(∀x) (Haz ⊃ (∀z) (Fz ⊃ Gza))', is also not a formula, and hence not a sentence. It would be a formula if clause 4 of the recursive definition did not include the requirement that the formula to which a quantifier is added—here '(Haz ⊃ (∀z)(Fz ⊃ Gza))'—contain at least one occurrence of the variable from which the added quantifier—here '(∀x)'—is formed. Clause 4 is intentionally written so as to disallow the use of quantifiers that do no work, that is, quantifiers that bind no variables in the formula to which they are attached.

Since sentences of *PL* are formulas of *PL*, we can speak of sentences as being either quantified (sentences whose main logical operator is a quantifier), truth-functional (sentences whose main logical operator is a truth-functional connective), or atomic (sentences that have no main logical operator).

We have been omitting the primes that, by the formal requirements of *PL*, are parts of the predicates of *PL*, and we will continue to do so. We will also frequently omit the outermost parentheses of a formula of *PL*. On our usage outermost parentheses are a pair of left and right parentheses that are added, as a pair, when a binary connective is inserted between two formulas of *PL*. Thus we may write, 'Fa & ~ (∀x)Fx' instead of '(Fa & ~ (∀x)(Fx)'. Note that, while '~ (Fa & (∃x) ~ Fx)' is a truth-functionally compound formula (and sentence), it has no outermost parentheses. So, too, '(∀x)(Fx ⊃ Gx)' has as its first symbol a left parentheses and as its last a right parentheses, but these are not 'outermost parentheses', for the first and last symbols of this sentence were not added as a pair when formulas were joined by a binary connective.

The omission of outermost parentheses should cause no confusion. Note, however, that when outer parentheses are customarily dropped, it is not safe to assume that every sentence that begins with a quantifier is a quantified sentence. Consider

(∀x)(Fx ⊃ Ga)

and

(∀x)Fx ⊃ Ga

Both begin with quantifiers, but only the first is a quantified sentence. The scope of the x-quantifier in this sentence is the whole formula. The second sentence is a truth-functional compound; the scope of the x-quantifier is just '(∀x)Fx'. It turns out that the two sentences are not only syntactically distinct but also that they say very different things.

To make complicated formulas of *PL* easier to read, we also allow the use of square brackets, '[' and ']', in place of the parentheses required by clause 3 of the recursive definition of 'formula of *PL*', that is, by the use of truth-functional connectives. But we will not allow square brackets in place of parentheses in quantifiers. So, instead of

~(∀y)((∃z)Fzy ⊃ (∃x)Gxy)

we can write

$$\sim(\forall y)[(\exists z)Fzy \supset (\exists x)Gxy]$$

In later chapters we shall require one further syntactic concept, that of a substitution instance of a quantified sentence. We use the notation

$$\mathbf{P}(\mathbf{a}/\mathbf{x})$$

to specify the formula of *PL* that is like **P** except that it contains the individual constant **a** wherever **P** contains the individual variable **x**. Thus if **P** is

$$(Fza \vee \sim Gz)$$

P(c/z) is

$$(Fca \vee \sim Gc)$$

Substitution instance of **P**: If **P** is a sentence of *PL* of the form $(\forall \mathbf{x})\mathbf{Q}$ or $(\exists \mathbf{x})\mathbf{Q}$, and **a** is an individual constant, then $\mathbf{Q}(\mathbf{a}/\mathbf{x})$ is a substitution instance of **P**. The constant **a** is the *instantiating constant.*

For example, 'Fab', 'Fbb', and 'Fcb' are all substitution instances of '(∀z)Fzb'. In the first case 'a' has been substituted for 'z' in 'Fzb'; in the second case 'b' has been substituted for 'z'; and in the third case 'c' has been substituted for 'z'.

In forming a substitution instance of a quantified sentence, we drop the initial quantifier and replace all remaining occurrences of the variable that that quantifier contains with some one constant. Thus '(∃y)Hay' and '(∃y)Hgy' are both substitution instances of '(∀x)(∃y)Hxy', but 'Hab' is not. (In forming substitution instances *only* the initial quantifier is dropped, and every occurrence of the variable that becomes free when that quantifier is dropped is replaced by the *same* constant.) All the following are substitution instances of '(∃w)[Fw ⊃ (∀y)(~ Dwy ≡ Ry)]':

$$Fd \supset (\forall y)(\sim Ddy \equiv Ry)$$
$$Fa \supset (\forall y)(\sim Day \equiv Ry)$$
$$Fn \supset (\forall y)(\sim Dny \equiv Ry)$$

but

$$Fd \supset (\forall y)(\sim Dny \equiv Ry)$$

is not—for here we have used one constant to replace the first occurrence of 'w' and a different constant to replace the second occurrence of 'w'. Again, in generating substitution instances, each occurrence of the variable being replaced must be replaced by the same individual constant.

Only quantified sentences have substitution instances, and those instances are formed by dropping the initial quantifier. Thus '~ Fa' is *not* a substitution instance of '~ (∀x)Fx'. '~ (∀x)Fx' is a truth-functional compound, not a quantified sentence, and hence has no substitution instances. And '(∀x)Fxb' is not a substitution instance of '(∀x)(∀y)Fxy' because, while the latter is a quantified sentence, only the initial quantifier can be dropped in forming substitution instances, and here the initial quantifier is '(∀x)', not '(∀y)'.

7.5E EXERCISES

1. Which of the following are formulas of *PL*? (Here we allow the deletion of outer parentheses and the use of square brackets in place of parentheses.) For those that are not, explain why they are not. For those that are, state whether they are sentences or open sentences.

a. Ba & Zz
*b. (x)Px ∨ Py
c. (∃y) ~ Hyy & Ga
*d. (∀z)(Ex)(Fzx & Fxz)
e. (∀z)((∃x)Fzx & Fxz)
*f. (∀x)Faa
g. (∃z)(Fz & Bgz) ≡ (∃z)Gzb
*h. (∃x)[Fx & (∀x)(Px ⊃ Gx)]
i. (~ ∃x)(Fx ∨ Gx)
*j. ~ (∀x)(Gx ≡ (∃z)Fzx)
k. (∃x)(∃y)Lxx
*l. (∀x)[(∃y)Fyx ⊃ (∃y)Fxy]
m. (Bu & ~ Faa) ⊃ (∀w) ~ Fww
*n. (∃a)Fa
o. Fw ⊃ (∃w)Gww
*p. (∀z)(Hza ⊃ (∃z)Gaz)

2. For each of the following formulas, indicate whether it is a sentence of *PL*. If it is not a sentence, explain why it is not. Also list all its subformulas, identifying the main logical operator of each.

a. (∃x)(∀y)Byx
*b. (∃x) ~ (∀y)Byx
c. (∀x)(~ Fx & Gx) ≡ (Bg ⊃ Fx)
*d. (∀y)[(∀z) ~ Byz ∨ Byy]
e. ~ (∃x)Px & Rab
*f. Rax ⊃ ~ (∀y)Ryx
g. ~ [~ (∀x)Fx ≡ (∃w) ~ Gw] ⊃ Maa
*h. (∀x)(∀y)(∀z)Mxyz & (∀z)(∀x)(∀y)Myzx
i. ~ ~ ~ (∃x)(∀z)(Gxaz ∨ ~ Hazb)
*j. (∀z)[Fz ⊃ (∃w)(~ Fw & Gwaz)]
k. (∃x)[Fx ⊃ (∀w)(~ Gx ⊃ ~ Hwx)]
*l. ~ [(∀x)Fx ∨ (∀x) ~ Fx]

m. $(Hb \vee Fa) \equiv (\exists z)(\sim Fz \;\&\; Gza)$
*n. $(\exists w)(Fw \;\&\; \sim Fw) \equiv (He \;\&\; \sim He)$

3. Indicate, for each of the following sentences, whether it is an atomic sentence, a truth-functional compound, or a quantified sentence.

a. $(\forall x)(Fx \supset Ga)$
*b. $(\forall x) \sim (Fx \supset Ga)$
c. $\sim (\forall x)(Fx \supset Ga)$
*d. $(\exists w)Raw \vee (\exists w)Rwa$
e. $\sim (\exists x)Hx$
*f. Habc
g. $(\forall x)(Fx \equiv (\exists w)Gw)$
*h. $(\forall x)Fx \equiv (\exists w)Gw$
i. $(\exists w)(Pw \supset (\forall y)(Hy \equiv \sim Kyw))$
*j. $\sim (\exists w)(Jw \vee Nw) \vee (\exists w)(Mw \vee Lw)$
k. $\sim [(\exists w)(Jw \vee Nw) \vee (\exists w)(Mw \vee Lw)]$
*l. Da
m. $(\forall z)Gza \supset (\exists z)Fz$
*n. $\sim (\exists x)(Fx \;\&\; \sim Gxa)$
o. $(\exists z) \sim Hza$
*p. $(\forall w)(\sim Hw \supset (\exists y)Gwy)$
q. $(\forall x) \sim Fx \equiv (\forall z) \sim Hza$

4. For each of the following sentences, give the substitution instance in which 'a' is the instantiating term.

a. $(\forall w)(Mww \;\&\; Fw)$
*b. $(\exists y)(Mby \supset Mya)$
c. $(\exists z) \sim (Cz \equiv \sim Cz)$
*d. $(\forall x)[(Laa \;\&\; Lab) \supset Lax]$
e. $(\exists z)[Fz \;\&\; \sim Gb) \supset (Bzb \vee Bbz)]$
*f. $(\exists w)[Fw \;\&\; (\forall y)(Cyw \supset Cwa)]$
g. $(\forall y)[\sim (\exists z)Nyz \equiv (\forall w)(Mww \;\&\; Nyw)]$
*h. $(\forall y)[(Fy \;\&\; Hy) \supset [(\exists z)(Fz \;\&\; Gz) \supset Gy]]$
i. $(\exists x)(Fxb \equiv Gbx)$
*j. $(\forall x)(\forall y)[(\exists z)Hzx \supset (\exists z)Hzy]$
k. $(\forall x) \sim (\exists y)(Hxy \;\&\; Hyx)$
*l. $(\forall z)[Fz \supset (\exists w)(\sim Fw \;\&\; Gwaz)]$
m. $(\forall w)(\forall y)[(Hwy \;\&\; Hyw) \supset (\exists z)Gzw]$
*n. $(\exists z)(\exists w)(\exists y)[(Fzwy \equiv Fwzy) \equiv Fyzw]$

5. Which of the following examples are substitution instances of the sentence '$(\exists w)(\forall y)(Rwy \supset Byy)$'?

a. $(\forall y)Ray \supset Byy$
*b. $(\forall y)(Ray \supset Byy)$
c. $(\forall y)(Rwy \supset Byy)$
*d. $(\forall y)(Rcy \supset Byy)$
e. $(\forall y)(Ryy \supset Byy)$
*f. $(\exists y)(Ray \supset Byy)$
g. $(Ray \supset Byy)$
*h. $(\forall y)(Ray \supset Baa)$
i. $Rab \supset Bbb$

6. Which of the following examples are substitution instances of the sentence '$(\forall x)[(\forall y) \sim Rxy \equiv Pxa]$'?

a. $(\forall y) \sim Ray \equiv Paa$
*b. $(\forall y) \sim Raa \equiv Paa$
c. $(\forall y) \sim Ray \equiv Pba$
*d. $(\forall y) \sim Rpy \equiv Ppa$
e. $(\forall y)(\sim Ryy \equiv Paa)$
*f. $(\forall y) \sim Ray \equiv Pya$
g. $(\forall y) \sim Raw \equiv Paa$
*h. $(\forall y) \sim Rcy \equiv Pca$

7.6 A-, E-, I-, AND O-SENTENCES

In Section 7.4 we symbolized fairly simple sentences of English in *PL*. The quantified sentences of *PL* that we used each had as its immediate subformula either an atomic formula or the negation of an atomic formula. That is, we produced such sentences as '$(\forall x)Lmx$', '$(\exists x)Txx$', and '$(\forall y)Lhy \,\&\, \sim (\exists x)Lsx$', but *not* such sentences as '$(\forall z)(Fz \supset Gzz)$' or '$(\forall w)(\forall y)[Fxy \equiv (\exists z)Gzx]$'. In Section 7.5 we presented the syntax of *PL* and became familiar with the syntactic properties of complex sentences of *PL*, including sentences containing multiple quantifiers. Some of these contained quantifiers with *overlapping scope;* that is, some had a quantifier falling within the scope of another quantifier—for example, '$(\forall y)$' within the scope of '$(\forall x)$' in '$(\forall x)(Fx \supset (\forall y)Gxy)$'. In this and the following sections we shall learn to use the resources of *PL* to express a rich variety of English claims. In this section and the next we limit ourselves to sentences of *PL* *without* quantifiers with overlapping scope, though we will work with sentences having multiple quantifiers and many-place predicates.

Sentences of *PL* such as those we produced in Section 7.4 express English claims to the effect that it is, or is not, the case that everything, or something, is, or is not, of the sort such-and-such, where we capture the 'such-and-such' with a single predicate. We also produced truth-functional compounds of such sentences and of atomic sentences of *PL*. Such sentences allow us to express a substantial variety of English claims within *PL*. We can, for example, say that all bears are dangerous—by making our universe of discourse (UD) bears and using 'Dx' for 'x is dangerous', '$(\forall w)Dw$' will do the job. But with the resources so far used and a UD of *all* bears, we cannot say that grizzly bears are dangerous and black bears are not. The limitation is substantial, for our UD is frequently diverse and it is rare that we want to say that everything, or nothing, in such a UD is of the sort specified by an atomic formula. What is needed is a way of saying, not that *everything*, or *something*, or *nothing* is of the sort specified by a given atomic formula, but rather that *everything*, or *something*, or *nothing* of the sort specified by a given formula is (or is not) of the sort specified by a second formula. We want, for example, to be able to symbolize sentences such as the following in *PL*:

All dolphins are mammals.
All reptiles are cold-blooded.
Every cheese is a dairy product.
Every logic text bores Michael.

We also want to be able to symbolize such claims as these:

No fatty foods are conducive to good health.
No government is unbureaucratic.
No zebra is unicolored.
Some automobiles are Fords.
Some apples are Granny Smiths.
Some instructors are without a sense of humor.
Some horses are not racehorses.
Some lawyers are not rich.

The mechanism for symbolizing claims such as these is to let a quantifier's scope or interpretive range extend not just into an atomic formula or the negation of an atomic formula but also to more complex formulas. Consider the first of the examples, 'All dolphins are mammals'. Suppose our UD is all living things, 'Dy' symbolizes 'y is a dolphin', and 'My' symbolizes 'y is a mammal'. Here is an *unsuccessful* attempt at symbolizing 'All dolphins are mammals':

$$(\forall y)Dy \ \& \ (\forall y)My$$

This sentence, a conjunction, asserts both that all things are dolphins and that all things are mammals. This is patently false where the UD is *all* living things.

What we want is a way of saying, not that each thing is both a dolphin and a mammal, but rather that each thing that is a dolphin is also a mammal. The universal quantifier is, however, used to make a claim about each thing in the UD. So the trick is to figure out what claim we can make about each thing that will amount to our attributing being a mammal to each dolphin but not to everything. The puzzle is solved when we recall that the material conditional, a sentence of the form $\mathbf{P} \supset \mathbf{Q}$, asserts neither **P** nor **Q** but rather asserts **Q** on the condition that **P**. What we can say of each thing, dolphins and nondolphins alike, is that if the thing in question is a dolphin then it is a mammal. This claim is as true of rattlesnakes, bumblebees, and bacteria as it is of dolphins. So an appropriate sentence of *PL* is

$$(\forall z)(Dz \supset Mz)$$

Here we are saying, again, neither that each living thing is a dolphin nor that each living thing is a mammal, but rather that each living thing is such that *if* it is a dolphin *then* it is a mammal. So this claim applied to rattlesnakes comes to naught, but when applied to dolphins, it commits us to dolphins being mammals.

It is also important to note that '$(\forall y)(Dy \,\&\, My)$' is not an appropriate symbolization of 'All dolphins are mammals'. Given our UD and specification of predicates, this sentence of *PL* says that each living thing is of the sort specified by the conjunction 'Dy & My'—that is, that each living things is both a dolphin and a mammal. And this is equivalent to '$(\forall y)Dy \,\&\, (\forall y)My$', which is, as we pointed out, an incorrect symbolization of our English sentence.

With this model in hand, it is easy to symbolize the next three of our examples. Again taking our UD to be all living things and using 'Rx' for 'x is a reptile' and 'Cx' for 'x is cold-blooded', we can symbolize 'All reptiles are cold-blooded' as

$$(\forall w)(Rw \supset Cw)$$

The foregoing is as true of dolphins as it is of rattlesnakes, for what it says of a given dolphin is that *if* that thing is a reptile (which it is not) *then* it is cold-blooded. Changing our UD to foods and using 'Cy' for 'y is a cheese' and 'Dz' for 'z is a dairy product', we can symbolize 'Every cheese is a dairy product' as

$$(\forall x)(Cx \supset Dx)$$

And if we take our UD to be books and people, 'Lz' to represent 'z is a logic text', 'Bzw' to represent 'z bores w', and 'm' to stand for Michael, we can symbolize 'Every logic text bores Michael' as

$$(\forall y)(Ly \supset Bym)$$

In sentences of *PL* such as those we have just presented, it is essential that the quantifier's scope extend over the entire sentence. For example, removing the parentheses around '$(Ly \supset Bym)$' produces '$(\forall y)Ly \supset Bym$', which is a formula but not a sentence of *PL*. In the present examples it is also important that we use one and the same variable in the quantifier and in the atomic formulas it interprets. Doing otherwise also produces a nonsentence—for example, '$(\forall y)(Lx \supset Bym)$'. In the foregoing discussion we purposely used different variables in the specification of predicates of *PL* and in the symbolizations we gave using those predicates. We did so to illustrate that the variables used in specifying predicates, whether informally as above or in symbolization keys, are only place-holders, marking holes in predicates. In actual symbolizations using those predicates, other variables and/or individual constants may be used.

The claim, 'No fatty foods are conducive to good health', asserts that anything that is a fatty food is not conducive to good health. Taking foods as our UD and using 'Fz' for 'z is fatty' and 'Cw' as 'w is conducive to good health', we can symbolize this claim in *PL* as

$$(\forall x)(Fx \supset \sim Cx)$$

Alternatively, but equivalently, we can see 'No fatty foods are conducive to good health' as denying that there is a fatty food that is conducive to good health.

This suggests the symbolization

$\sim (\exists x)(Fx \,\&\, Cx)$

These two sentences of *PL*, as one would expect, turn out to be equivalent. The latter claim of *PL* is very different from '$\sim (\exists x)Fx \,\&\, \sim (\exists x)Cx$', which asserts both that nothing is fatty and that nothing is conducive to good health.

Next we can symbolize 'No government is unbureaucratic' by taking our UD to be organizations, 'Gx' to represent 'x is a government', and 'Bx' 'x is bureaucratic'. Since to say no government is unbureaucratic is just to say that every government is bureaucratic, an appropriate symbolization in *PL* is

$(\forall y)(Gy \supset By)$

An equally appropriate symbolization is

$\sim (\exists y)(Gy \,\&\, \sim By)$

Returning to a UD of living things and taking 'Zy' to represent 'y is a zebra' and 'Uw' to represent 'w is unicolored', we can symbolize the claim 'No zebra is unicolored' either as

$(\forall z)(Zz \supset \sim Uz)$

or as

$\sim (\exists w)(Zw \,\&\, Uw)$

The first says of each thing in the UD that <u>if</u> it is a zebra <u>then</u> it is <u>not</u> unicolored; the second says that <u>it is not the case that there is something</u> in the UD that is a zebra <u>and</u> unicolored. These are equivalent.

Now take our UD to be vehicles (including automobiles, bicycles, boats, airplanes, and so on). The claim 'Some automobiles are Fords' can be construed, not as making a conditional claim about each thing in the UD, but rather as saying that in the UD <u>there is at least one thing</u> that <u>both</u> is a car <u>and</u> is a Ford (remember, we take 'some' to mean 'at least one'). Where 'Ax' stands for 'x is an automobile' and 'Fx' for 'x is a Ford', an appropriate symbolization is

$(\exists y)(Ay \,\&\, Fy)$

Similarly, if we take our UD to be all fruits and vegetables, 'Ay' to represent 'y is an apple', and 'Gy' to represent 'y is a Granny Smith', we can symbolize the claim 'Some apples are Granny Smiths' as

$(\exists z)(Az \,\&\, Gz)$

Taking our UD to be people, 'Ix' to represent 'x is an instructor', and 'Hx' to represent 'x has a sense of humor', 'Some instructors are without a sense of humor' can be symbolized as

$$(\exists y)(Iy \ \& \sim Hy)$$

And the claim 'Some horses are not racehorses' can be symbolized as

$$(\exists w)(Hw \ \& \sim Rw)$$

if we take our UD to be living things, 'Hx' to represent 'x is a horse', and 'Rx' to represent 'x is a racehorse'. Finally 'Some lawyers are not rich' can be symbolized as

$$(\exists y)(Ly \ \& \sim Ry)$$

with a UD of living things and 'Lw' and 'Rw' representing, respectively, 'w is a lawyer' and 'w is rich'.

We noted in Chapter 1 that Aristotelian logic holds that syllogistic arguments are composed of sentences of the following sorts:

All As are Bs.
No As are Bs.
Some As are Bs.
Some As are not Bs.

where 'A' and 'B' are used as variables for general terms. Sentences of these types are traditionally classified as A-, E-, I-, and O-sentences, respectively. Using '**P**' and '**Q**' as variables for formulas containing the variable **x**, we can employ the following schema to present this traditional classification as it applies to sentences of *PL*:

A: $(\forall \mathbf{x})(\mathbf{P} \supset \mathbf{Q})$
E: $(\forall \mathbf{x})(\mathbf{P} \supset \sim \mathbf{Q})$
I: $(\exists \mathbf{x})(\mathbf{P} \ \& \ \mathbf{Q})$
O: $(\exists \mathbf{x})(\mathbf{P} \ \& \sim \mathbf{Q})$

The sentences of *PL* we have so far considered in this section can, in fact, each be seen as being of one of these four sorts, as can a very large number of other sentences. For example, we have symbolized 'All dolphins are mammals' as '$(\forall z)(Dz \supset Mz)$', an A-sentence; 'No fatty foods are conducive to good health' as '$(\forall x)(Fxr \supset \sim Cx)$', an E-sentence; 'Some automobiles are Fords' as '$(\exists y)(Ay \ \& \ Fy)$', an I-sentence; and 'Some horses are not racehorses' as '$(\exists w)(Hw \ \& \sim Rw)$', an O-sentence.

Aristotle believed that there are important logical relations among A-, E-, I-, and O-sentences. These are usually presented using a "square of opposition":

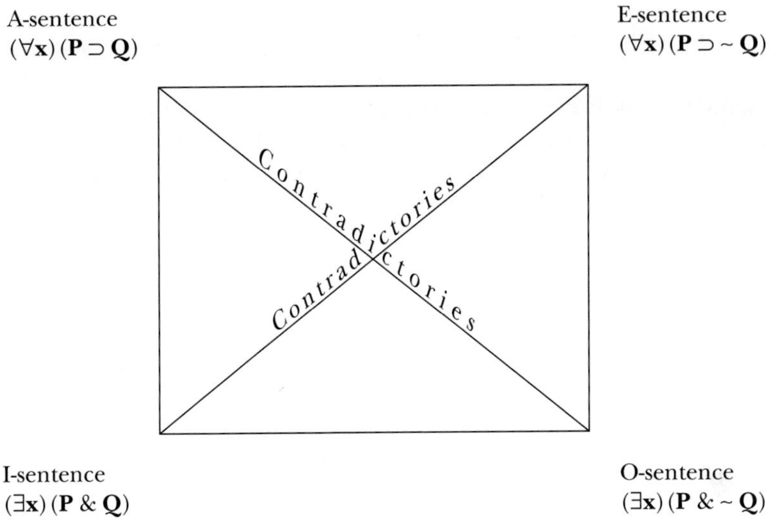

The following relationships hold: If an A-sentence is true, then the corresponding O-sentence is false, and vice versa; and if an E-sentence is true, the corresponding I-sentence is false, and vice versa. This is sometimes expressed by saying that the sentences connected by diagonal lines are *contradictories*—if either is true the other is false. It follows that each sentence on the square of opposition is equivalent to the negation of the sentence at the other end of the diagonal. Thus A-sentences are equivalent to the negation of O-sentences, and vice versa; and E-sentences are equivalent to the negation of I-sentences, and vice versa. This gives us four pairs of equivalences:

$(\forall \mathbf{x})(\mathbf{P} \supset \mathbf{Q})$	and	$\sim (\exists \mathbf{x})(\mathbf{P} \ \& \sim \mathbf{Q})$
$(\forall \mathbf{x})(\mathbf{P} \supset \sim \mathbf{Q})$	and	$\sim (\exists \mathbf{x})(\mathbf{P} \ \& \ \mathbf{Q})$
$(\exists \mathbf{x})(\mathbf{P} \ \& \ \mathbf{Q})$	and	$\sim (\forall \mathbf{x})(\mathbf{P} \supset \sim \mathbf{Q})$
$(\exists \mathbf{x})(\mathbf{P} \ \& \sim \mathbf{Q})$	and	$\sim (\forall \mathbf{x})(\mathbf{P} \supset \mathbf{Q})$

An example will help here. We will use the following symbolization key:

UD: The jawbreakers (hard, round candies) in a large glass jar
Yz: z is yellow
Sz: z is sweet

The following are examples of A-, E-, I-, and O-sentences of English and their symbolizations in *PL*:

All yellow jawbreakers are sweet.	$(\forall w)(Yw \supset Sw)$
No yellow jawbreakers are sweet.	$(\forall w)(Yw \supset \sim Sw)$
Some yellow jawbreakers are sweet.	$(\exists w)(Yw \,\&\, Sw)$
Some yellow jawbreakers are not sweet.	$(\exists w)(Yw \,\&\, \sim Sw)$

The A-sentence 'All yellow jawbreakers are sweet' is the contradictory of the O-sentence 'Some yellow jawbreakers are not sweet'. If it is true that all yellow jawbreakers are sweet, then it is clearly false that some yellow jawbreakers are not sweet, and vice versa. So '$(\forall w)(Yw \supset Sw)$' is equivalent to the negation of the corresponding O-sentence, that is, equivalent to '$\sim (\exists w)(Yw \,\&\, \sim Sw)$'. And the O-sentence '$(\exists w)(Yw \,\&\, \sim Sw)$' is equivalent to the negation of the corresponding A-sentence, that is, to '$\sim (\forall w)(Yw \supset Sw)$'. So, too, if the E-sentence 'No yellow jawbreakers are sweet' is true, then its contradictory, the I-sentence 'Some yellow jawbreakers are sweet', is false, and vice versa. So the E-sentence '$(\forall w)(Yw \supset \sim Sw)$' is equivalent to '$\sim (\exists)(Yw \,\&\, Sw)$'. And the I-sentence '$(\exists w)(Yw \,\&\, Sw)$' is equivalent to the negation of the corresponding E-sentence, that is, to '$\sim (\forall w)\ (Yw \supset \sim Sw)$'. These relationships explain why, in symbolizing the examples at the beginning of this section, we often came up with two alternative, equivalent symbolizations.

In some systems of logic, if an A-sentence is true then so is the corresponding I-sentence, and if an E-sentence is true then so is the corresponding O-sentence. These relationships do not hold in *PL*. This may *seem* counterintuitive, for it is very tempting to believe that if 'All rabbits are mammals' is true, then so must be 'Some rabbits are mammals', and that if 'No rabbits are cold-blooded' is true, then so must be 'Some rabbits are not cold-blooded'. The reason these relationships do not hold for A- and I- and for E- and O-sentences is that in *PL* we allow predicates that are not satisfied by any member of the universe of discourse.

Given that we treat universal claims as saying of each thing that if it is of this sort it is also of that sort, this is obviously a sensible policy. For example, when working with a culture of unknown bacteria, we might reasonably say, after having placed the culture in a hermetically sealed container for an appropriate length of time,

All the aerobic (air-dependent) bacteria in the culture are dead.

Our claim will be true even if there are no such bacteria in the culture, for we will paraphrase it as saying of each bacterium, of whatever sort, that *if* it is aerobic *then* it is dead. Since there may be no aerobic bacteria in the culture, dead or alive, we clearly do not want the corresponding I-sentence

Some aerobic bacteria in the culture are dead

to follow, for it says that there are bacteria in the culture that are both aerobic and dead. Again, in the system we are developing, A-sentences do not entail I-sentences and E-sentences do not entail O-sentences.

Aristotle also believed that A- and E-sentences are contraries and that I- and O-sentences are subcontraries. That is, an A- and the corresponding E-sentence cannot both be true, and an I- and the corresponding O-sentence cannot both be false. Neither of these relationships holds in *PL*, again because we allow predicates that are not satisfied by any member of the universe of discourse. Hence, if there are no things in the universe of discourse that are of the sort specified by the one-place predicate 'F', then both the A-sentence '$(\forall x)(Fx \supset Gx)$' and the corresponding E-sentence '$(\forall x)(Fx \supset \sim Gx)$' will be true, and both the I-sentence '$(\exists x)(Fx \ \& \ Gx)$' and the corresponding O-sentence '$(\exists x)(Fx \ \& \sim Gx)$' will be false.

Neither every sentence of English nor every sentence of *PL* can reasonably be construed as being of one of the four sorts of sentences we have been discussing. However, many can, and it is frequently helpful in symbolizing sentences of English to keep these four types of sentences in mind.

Not every sentence of English that can be symbolized as an A-sentence uses the quantity term 'all'. For example, in an introductory biology class an instructor might assert any one of the following sentences:

All mammals are warm-blooded.
Every mammal is warm-blooded.
Each mammal is warm-blooded.
Mammals are warm-blooded.
A mammal is warm-blooded.

In the envisioned context these sentences are interchangeable. They can all be symbolized as the A-sentence '$(\forall y)(My \supset Wy)$' given a UD of living things and using 'Mz' for 'z is a mammal' and 'Wz' for 'z is warm-blooded'. This is true of the fourth example, 'Mammals are warm-blooded', even though this sentence contains no quantity term. The context makes it clear that it is all, not just some, mammals that are under discussion. The fifth sentence, 'A mammal is warm-blooded', is about all mammals even though it uses the singular article 'a'. This is not uncommon. Consider 'A mind is a terrible thing to waste', 'An accident incurred while at work is covered by the employee insurance plan', or 'An unexcused absence on an examination day will result in a failure'. The claims just mentioned concern, respectively, *all* minds, *all* accidents incurred while at work, and *all* unexcused absences on examination days.

'Any' can also be used to make a claim about all things of the specified sort. The cynic's crack about the findings of modern medicine, "Anything that tastes good is bad," is equivalent to 'All things that taste good are bad'. Both can be symbolized as '$(\forall x)(Tx \supset Bx)$' given a UD of all foods and drinks and taking 'Tx' to represent 'x tastes good' and 'Bx' to represent 'x is bad'.

It is important to remember that claims of the sort we have been discussing, claims to the effect that all things of this sort (for example, mammals) are also of that sort (for example, warm-blooded), do not pick out or refer to a group of things and then predicate something of that group. It is not the group or set of mammals that is warm-blooded but each individual mammal. ('Supertankers are very large ships' means that each supertanker is a very large ship, not that the set of supertankers is very large, that is, not that there are a very large number of supertankers.) The claims we have been discussing are better analyzed as universal claims deriving from conditionals that apply to each thing in the given universe of discourse. They say of each thing under discussion that if it is of such-and-such a sort then it is also thus-and-so. Each living thing is such that if it is a mammal then it is warm-blooded. This is, again, true as much of a given reptile as it is of a given koala bear.[11]

E-sentences, which can be symbolized as sentences of *PL* of the form $(\forall \mathbf{x})(\mathbf{P} \supset \sim \mathbf{Q})$, are also universal claims. They say of each thing under discussion that if it is of the sort **P** then it is not of the sort **Q**. Again assuming the context of an introductory biology class, all of the following can be used to make the point that reptiles are not warm-blooded:

No reptile is warm-blooded.
Reptiles are not warm-blooded.
A reptile is not warm-blooded.

Taking our universe of discourse to be living things and using 'Rw' to represent 'w is a reptile' and 'Ww' to represent 'w is warm-blooded', we can symbolize all these claims as

$$(\forall y)(Ry \supset \sim Wy)$$

We claimed earlier that 'Mammals are warm-blooded' and 'All mammals are warm-blooded' make the same claim. So, too, one would expect 'Reptiles are not warm-blooded' and 'All reptiles are not warm-blooded' to make the same claim. And, literally speaking, they do. 'All reptiles are not warm-blooded' says, literally, that each thing that is a reptile is not a thing that is warm-blooded, and thus can be symbolized as above.

But there is a complication here. Imagine a conversation about future careers. Someone says, "I want to become a lawyer because lawyers are all rich"; someone more thoughtful replies, "While the stereotype of lawyers may be that they are rich, the fact is that all lawyers are not rich". The claims we want to contrast are 'All lawyers are rich' and 'All lawyers are not rich'. The first clearly

[11]But consider 'Insects are more numerous than mammals'. This is not a disguised conditional claim about each living thing—its force is not 'Each living thing is such that if it is an insect it is more numerous than' . . . The correct analysis here is rather something like 'The set consisting of all insects is larger than the set consisting of all mammals'—that is, a claim about a relation between two things, the set of insects and the set of mammals.

means that each lawyer is rich and can be symbolized, given a UD of people and using 'Ly' as 'y is a lawyer' and 'Ry' as 'y is rich', as

$(\forall z)(Lz \supset Rz)$

The second claim, 'All lawyers are not rich', literally means that each lawyer is not rich, a claim that can be symbolized as an E-sentence:

$(\forall z)(Lz \supset \sim Rz)$

But in the envisioned conversation 'All lawyers are not rich' is clearly intended, not as the claim that there are no rich lawyers, but rather merely as a denial of 'All lawyers are rich', that is, as equivalent to 'It is not the case that all lawyers are rich'. Thus it can reasonably be symbolized as

$\sim (\forall z)(Lz \supset Rz)$

And this sentence of *PL*, the denial of an A-sentence, is equivalent to the O-sentence '$(\exists z)(Lz \,\&\, \sim Rz)$', which says 'There is something that is a lawyer and is not rich'.

In practice we must rely on the context to determine whether what is literally an E-sentence—our example was 'All lawyers are not rich', and another is 'Every politician is not a scoundrel'—is being used as an E-sentence or as the negation of an A-sentence. In this text, whenever we do use a sentence of the sort 'All **P**s are not **Q**s' or 'Each **P** is not **Q**', and no context is provided, we mean the sentence to be interpreted literally as saying each and every **P** thing is not a **Q** thing.

I- and O-sentences of *PL* are existential claims. They do not make a claim about each thing in the universe of discourse; rather, they say that included within that universe is at least one thing of a specified sort, either the sort **P** & **Q** (an I-sentence) or the sort (**P** & ~ **Q**) (an O-sentence). Both

Some mammals are carnivorous

and

There are carnivorous mammals

can be symbolized as the O-sentence '$(\exists y)(My \,\&\, Cy)$', where our UD is living things, 'Mx' represents 'x is a mammal', and 'Cx' represents 'x is carnivorous'. Similarly 'Some mammals are not carnivorous' and 'There are mammals that are not carnivorous' can both be symbolized as

$(\exists z)(Mz \,\&\, \sim Cz)$

Note that 'Some mammals are carnivorous' does not identify a particular mammal and say of it that it is carnivorous. It says that there are carnivorous mammals but not which ones they are. Note also that the following are not symbolizations of 'Some mammals are carnivorous':

$(\exists x)Mx \ \& \ (\exists x)Cx$
$(\exists x)(Mx \supset Cx)$

The first is a truth-functional compound. It says that there is something that is a mammal and there is something (not necessarily the same thing) that is carnivorous. The second says that there is some living thing such that if it is a mammal then it is carnivorous. While this is true, it is a much weaker claim than is intended. It would, for example, be true even if the UD were limited to reptiles. For each reptile (and hence at least one) is such that *if* it is a mammal (which it is not) *then* it is warm-blooded. Remember that *material conditionals with false antecedents are true.*

Note that neither '$(\forall x)(Mx \supset Wx)$' nor '$(\exists x)(Mx \ \& \ Cx)$' contains outermost parentheses. The formulas to which the quantifiers attach, '$(Mx \supset Wx)$' and '$(Mx \ \& \ Cx)$', respectively, do contain outer parentheses, but these are not "outer" once the quantifiers are attached. '$(\forall x)Mx \supset Wx$' is therefore not an informal version of '$(\forall x)(Mx \supset Wx)$', and '$(\exists x)Mx \ \& \ Cx$' is not an informal version of '$(\exists x)(Mx \ \& \ Cx)$'. Rather, both are formulas that are not sentences of *PL*. The main logical operator of the first is '$\supset$', not '$(\forall x)$', and so the occurrence of 'x' in 'Wx' is not bound; and the main logical operator of the second is '&', not '$(\exists x)$', and so the occurrence of 'x' in 'Cx' is not bound.

We next symbolize a further group of sentences about the people in Michael's office:

1. Everyone whom Michael likes is easygoing.
2. Everyone who is taller than Rita is taller than Henry.
3. No one who likes Michael likes Henry.
4. Some of those whom Michael likes like Rita.
5. Some of those whom Michael likes don't like Rita.

We will use the symbolization key given in Section 7.3:

UD: People in Michael's office
Lxy: x likes y
Ex: x is easygoing
Txy: x is taller than y
h: Henry
m: Michael
r: Rita
s: Sue

The first of these claims is a straightforward A-sentence and can be symbolized as

$(\forall x)(Lmx \supset Ex)$

The only interesting difference between this and the A-sentences we symbolized earlier (for example, 'All mammals are warm-blooded') is that here the antecedent of the immediate subformula, 'Lmx', of '(Lmx ⊃ Ex)' is an atomic formula formed from a two-place rather than a one-place predicate. The second sentence is also an A-sentence, and here both the antecedent and the consequent of the immediate subformula are formed from two-place predicates:

(∀z) (Tzr ⊃ Tzh)

The third English sentence—'No one who likes Michael likes Henry'—can be parsed as 'Each thing is such that if it likes Michael then it is not the case that it likes Henry', an E-sentence, and symbolized as

(∀x) (Lxm ⊃ ~ Lxh)

This English sentence can also be symbolized as the negation of an I-sentence:

~ (∃x) (Lxm & Lxh)

which can be read as 'It is not the case that there is something that likes Michael and likes Henry'. The fourth and fifth sentences can be treated as I- and O-sentences, respectively. Appropriate symbolizations are

(∃w) (Lmw & Lwr)
(∃w) (Lmw & ~ Lwr)

Next we work through a series of symbolizations concerning the marbles being used in a marble game. We will symbolize these sentences:

1. All the marbles are blue.
2. None of the marbles is blue.
3. Some of the marbles are blue.
4. Some of the marbles are not blue.
5. Some but not all of the marbles are blue.
6. All the marbles are blue or all the marbles are green.
7. Some of the marbles are blue and some are green, but none is red.
8. If any marble is blue they all are.
9. If any marble is blue it's a cat's-eye.
10. All the shooters are red.

To illustrate how the choice of a UD affects the symbolizations required, we give two symbolizations for each of the above sentences, the first using the symbolization key:

UD: The marbles being used by Ashley, Clarence, Rhoda, and Terry
Bx: x is blue
Gx: x is green
Rx: x is red
Sx: x is a shooter
Cx: x is a cat's-eye

The second symbolization key we will use is like the above but with a UD of the marbles being used and the players, and the additional predicate 'Mx' for 'x is a marble'. Thus we have

UD: Marbles	UD: Marbles and marble players
1′. $(\forall y)By$	1″. $(\forall y)(My \supset By)$
2′. $\sim (\exists y)By$	2″. $\sim (\exists y)(My \& By)$
3′. $(\exists y)By$	3″. $(\exists y)(My \& By)$
4′. $(\exists y) \sim By$	4″. $(\exists y)(My \& \sim By)$
5′. $(\exists y)By \& \sim (\forall y)By$	5″. $(\exists y)(My \& By) \& \sim (\forall y)(My \supset By)$
6′. $(\forall z)Bz \vee (\forall y)Gy$	6″. $(\forall y)(My \supset By) \vee (\forall y)(My \supset Gy)$
7′. $[(\exists x)Bx \& (\exists x)Gx] \& \sim (\exists x)Rx$	7″. $[(\exists x)(Mx \& Bx) \& (\exists x)(Mx \& Gx)] \& \sim (\exists x)(Mx \& Rx)$
8′. $(\exists w)Bw \supset (\forall x)Bx$	8″. $(\exists w)(Mw \& Bw) \supset (\forall x)(Mx \supset Bx)$
9′. $(\forall x)(Bx \supset Cx)$	9″. $(\forall x)[(Mx \& Bx) \supset Cx]$
10′. $(\forall y)(Sy \supset Ry)$	10″. $(\forall y)[(My \& Sy) \supset Ry]$

If the universe of discourse is just marbles, then 1′, '$(\forall y)By$', is an appropriate symbolization of 'All the marbles are blue'. But 1′ will not suffice if the UD is marbles and marble players, for we want to say that the marbles are blue but not that the players are. So 1″ is called for, '$(\forall y)(My \supset By)$'. Generally, where the universe of discourse is severely restricted and we do want to attribute some property to, or deny a property of, every or at least one member of that universe, A-, E-, I-, and O-sentences can be specified as follows, where **P** may be an atomic formula:

A: $(\forall \mathbf{x})\mathbf{P}$
E: $(\forall \mathbf{x}) \sim \mathbf{P}$
I: $(\exists \mathbf{x})\mathbf{P}$
O: $(\exists \mathbf{x}) \sim \mathbf{P}$

Our 1′ and 1″ are thus both A-sentences, and 6′ and 6″ are both disjunctions of A-sentences; 2′ and 2″ are both O-sentences; 3′ and 3″ are both I-sentences, and 7′ and 7″ are both conjunctions of the conjunction of two I-sentences and an E-sentence; 4′ and 4″ are both O-sentences; 5′ and 5″ are both conjunctions of an I-sentence and the negation of an A-sentence; 6′ and 6″ are both disjunctions of A-sentences; and 8′ and 8″ are both material conditionals whose antecedents are I-sentences and whose consequents are A-sentences. The 'any' of sentence 9 has the force of 'every', for 'If any marble is blue it's a cat's-eye' says the same thing as 'Every blue marble is a cat's-eye'. Hence 9′ is an A-sentence, as is 10′. In addition, 9″ and 10″ are A-sentences of the form $(\forall \mathbf{x})(\mathbf{P} \supset \mathbf{Q})$, where **P** is itself a conjunction. (We shall discuss this sort of complexity further in Section 7.7.)

While 2′ and 2″ are negations of I-sentences, we could also have used E-sentences, '$(\forall y) \sim By$' and '$(\forall y)(My \supset \sim By)$', respectively. For 3′ and 3″ we could have used the negation of E-sentences instead of I-sentences, and so on. The notion of there being a single correct, or even "most intuitive", symbolization for each English sentence is even more inappropriate here than it was in *SL*.

7.6E EXERCISES

1. Identify each of the following sentences as either an A-, E-, I-, or O-sentence and symbolize each in *PL* using the given symbolization key.

UD: A pile of coins consisting of quarters, dimes, nickels, and pennies
Qz: z is a quarter
Dz: z is a dime
Nz: z is a nickel
Cz: z contains copper
Pz: z is a penny
Sz: z contains silver
Kz: z contains nickel
Zz: z contains zinc
Bz: z is a buffalo head coin
Iz: z is an Indian head coin
Mz: z was minted before 1965

a. All the pennies contain copper.
*b. Some of the dimes contain silver.
c. Some of the dimes do not contain silver.
*d. None of the quarters contains silver.
e. Some of the nickels are buffalo heads.
*f. All the nickels contain nickel.
g. No penny contains silver.
*h. Some of the nickels are not buffalo heads.
i. Every penny was minted before 1965.
*j. Some quarters were not minted before 1965.

k. Every coin containing silver contains copper.
*l. No penny contains silver.
m. No coin that contains nickel contains silver.
*n. Every coin minted during or after 1965 contains zinc.
o. None of the quarters contains zinc.
*p. Some of the pennies are not Indian heads.

2. Symbolize the following sentences in *PL* using the given symbolization key.

UD: The jellybeans in a larger glass jar
By: y is black
Ry: y is red
Gy: y is green
Ly: y is licorice-flavored
Cy: y is cherry-flavored
Sy: y is sweet
Oy: y is sour

a. All the black jellybeans are licorice-flavored.
*b. All the red jellybeans are sweet.
c. None of the red jellybeans is licorice-flavored.
*d. Some red jellybeans are cherry-flavored.
e. Some jellybeans are black and some are red.
*f. Some jellybeans are sour and some are not.
g. Some jellybeans are black and some are red, but none is both.
*h. The red jellybeans are sweet, and the green jellybeans are sour.
i. Some jellybeans are black, some are sweet, and some are licorice-flavored.
*j. No jellybeans are red and licorice-flavored.
k. All the cherry-flavored jellybeans are red, but not all the red jellybeans are cherry-flavored.
*l. Every jellybean is red, and some are cherry-flavored and some are not cherry-flavored.
m. Every jellybean is red or every jellybean is black or every jellybean is green.
*n. Not all the jellybeans are licorice-flavored, but all those that are, are black.
o. Some red jellybeans are sweet and some are not.
*p. Some jellybeans are sweet and some are sour, but none is sweet and sour.
q. Some of the jellybeans are sour, but none of the licorice ones is.

3. With respect to the square of opposition, answer the following:
a. Can an I-sentence of *PL* and the corresponding O-sentence both be true? Can two such sentences both be false? Explain.
*b. Can an A-sentence of *PL* and the corresponding E-sentence both be false? Can two such sentences both be true? Explain.

7.7 SYMBOLIZATION TECHNIQUES

So far most of the A- and E-sentences we have considered have had as immediate subformulas atomic formulas, negations of atomic formulas, or material conditionals (whose immediate subformulas have themselves been either atomic formulas or the negations of atomic formulas). Similarly most of the I- and O-sentences we have considered have had as immediate subformulas atomic formulas, the negations of atomic formulas, or conjunctions (whose immediate subformulas have been either atomic formulas or the negations of atomic formulas). But we need not restrict ourselves to these simple combinations. The **P** and **Q** of sentences of the forms

$(\forall \mathbf{x})(\mathbf{P} \supset \mathbf{Q})$
$(\forall \mathbf{x})(\mathbf{P} \supset \sim \mathbf{Q})$
$(\exists \mathbf{x})(\mathbf{P} \; \& \; \mathbf{Q})$
$(\exists \mathbf{x})(\mathbf{P} \; \& \sim \mathbf{Q})$

can themselves be any formulas of *PL*, including negations, conjunctions, disjunctions, material conditionals, and material biconditionals. Consider

Everyone that Michael likes likes either Henry or Sue.

Here, and in other, more complicated examples to come, it may help to first paraphrase the English sentence into a more explicit quasi-English sentence:

Each thing is such that if Michael likes it, then either it likes Henry or it likes Sue.

This sort of paraphrase uses 'it' where the symbolization in *PL* uses a variable. The paraphrase makes it clear that this sentence can be symbolized as a universally quantified sentence, the immediate subformula of which will be a material conditional, with the consequent of that conditional being a disjunction. Using a universe of discourse of people in Michael's office and the rest of the familiar symbolization key already specified, an appropriate symbolization is

$(\forall y)[Lmy \supset (Lyh \vee Lys)]$

This is an A-sentence, where **P** is 'Lmy' and **Q** is the disjunction '(Lyh ∨ Lys)'.

Here are some further sentences about Michael and his co-workers:

Michael likes everyone that both Sue and Rita like.
Michael likes everyone that either Sue or Rita likes.
Rita doesn't like Michael but she likes everyone that Michael likes.

The first can be paraphrased as

Each thing is such that if both Sue likes it and Rita likes it, then Michael likes it.

The paraphrase makes it clear that the *PL* symbolization of this sentence will be a universally quantified sentence whose immediate subformula is a material conditional, the antecedent of which will be a conjunction:

(∀z) [(Lsz & Lrz) ⊃ Lmz]

This is also an A-sentence, where **P** is '(Lsz & Lrz)' and **Q** is 'Lmz'.

The second sentence can be paraphrased as

Each thing is such that if either Sue likes it or Rita likes it, then Michael likes it.

An appropriate symbolization is

(∀w) [(Lsw ∨ Lrw) ⊃ Lmw]

This is an A-sentence, where **P** is '(Lyh ∨ Lys)', a disjunction, and **Q** is 'Lmw'.

The last of the sentences we are considering can be paraphrased as

Both it is not the case that Rita likes Michael and each thing is such that if Michael likes it then Rita likes it.

An appropriate symbolization here is

~ Lrm & (∀x) (Lmx ⊃ Lrx)

This sentence of *PL* is a conjunction of the negation of an atomic sentence and an A-sentence. We note that, if the foregoing sentence is true, if follows that Michael does not like himself, for if he did, Rita, who likes everyone Michael likes, would also like Michael, but she doesn't like Michael, so Michael must not like himself.

Lest we neglect bears, who figured briefly in the beginning of Section 7.6, we now consider

Grizzly bears are dangerous but black bears are not.

The grammatical structure of English sentences is often a good guide to what the structure of symbolizations in *PL* should be, and this is so in the present case. The foregoing sentence can be paraphrased as 'Both grizzly bears are dangerous and it is not the case that black bears are dangerous' and symbolized, as one would expect, as the conjunction of an A- and an E-sentence. When we take our UD to be living things, 'Gw' to represent 'w is a grizzly bear', 'Bw' to represent 'w is a black bear', and 'Dw' to represent 'w is dangerous', an appropriate symbolization is

(∀y) (Gy ⊃ Dy) & (∀z) (Bz ⊃ ~ Dz)

But consider next

Grizzly bears and polar bears are dangerous, but black bears are not.

The 'black bears are not' clearly becomes, as above, '$(\forall z)(Bz \supset \sim Dz)$'. But what of 'Grizzly bears and polar bears are dangerous'? If we add 'Pw' for 'w is a polar bear' to our symbolization key, we might, as a first attempt, try

$$(\forall x)[(Gx \,\&\, Px) \supset Dx]$$

But we can see that this first attempt misses the mark as soon as we read it back into quasi-English, for it says 'Each thing is such that if it both is a grizzly bear and is a polar bear, then it is dangerous'. But there are no things that are both grizzly bears and polar bears, and our intent was not to make a vacuous claim.

In a second attempt we might realize that the original sentence is a shortened form of the fuller claim

Grizzly bears are dangerous and polar bears are dangerous, but black bears are not

and then realize that an adequate symbolization is

$$[(\forall w)(Gw \supset Dw) \,\&\, (\forall w)(Pw \supset Dw)] \,\&\, (\forall w)(Bw \supset \sim Dw)$$

We have here the conjunction of a conjunction of A-sentences and an E-sentence. But there is also a shorter symbolization:

$$(\forall w)[(Gw \vee Fw) \supset Dw] \,\&\, (\forall w)(Bw \supset \sim Dw)$$

This sentence of *PL* is the conjunction of an A-sentence and an E-sentence. To say that grizzly bears *and* polar bears are dangerous is to say that everything in the group consisting of all grizzly bears *and* all polar bears is dangerous. And to be a member of that group, a creature need only be one or the other, a grizzly or a polar bear, not both.

Consider now 'Every self-respecting polar bear is a good swimmer'. Still taking our universe of discourse to be bears and adding as predicates 'Rxy' for 'x respects y' and 'Sx' for 'x is a good swimmer', we can symbolize this sentence as

$$(\forall z)[(Pz \,\&\, Rzz) \supset Sz]$$

We here illustrate that a thing can bear a relation to itself. (To be self-respecting is just to respect oneself.)

Here are two examples concerning the positive integers:

Every integer is either odd or even

and

Every integer is odd or every integer is even.

In the second sentence there are two quantity terms. Each falls within a disjunct of the overall sentence, which is clearly a disjunction. But in the first sentence the disjunction-indicating terms 'either' and 'or' both fall within the scope of the quantity term 'every'. This suggests, correctly, that the first sentence can be symbolized as a quantified sentence, and the second as a truth-functional compound of quantified sentences. If we restrict our universe of discourse to integers, appropriate paraphrases are

Each integer y is such that either y is odd or y is even

and

Either each integer y is such that y is odd or each integer y is such that y is even.

Using obvious predicates, we can now produce *PL* symbolizations:

$(\forall y)(Oy \vee Ey)$

$(\forall y)Oy \vee (\forall y)Ey$

There is a world of difference here. The first sentence of *PL* is clearly true: Each integer is either odd or even—one is odd, two is even, three is odd, four is even, and so on. The second sentence is just as clearly false: It is not the case that all integers are odd, and it is not the case that all integers are even. The great importance of the placement of quantifiers in relation to truth-functional connectives is here illustrated. (The first of the two sentences of *PL* is an A-sentence—it says each thing is of the sort specified by '$(Oy \vee Ey)$'; the second is a disjunction of A-sentences.)

Care must be taken when symbolizing English sentences using the quantity term 'any'. Consider these examples:

1. Anyone who likes Sue likes Rita.
2. Everyone who likes Sue likes Rita.
3. If anyone likes Sue, Michael does.
4. If everyone likes Sue, Michael does.
5. If anyone likes Sue, he or she likes Rita.

Assuming we restrict our UD to people, it is probably apparent that the first two of these sentences can each appropriately be symbolized as the A-sentence '$(\forall x)(Lxs \supset Lxr)$'. So in the first sentence the 'any' of 'anyone' has the force of 'every'. But in the third sentence 'anyone' does not have the force of 'everyone', for the third and fourth sentences clearly make different claims. (Sentence 3 may be very informative—we might suspect that someone likes Sue but have no idea that Michael does. But sentence 4 is not at all informative. Of course, Michael likes Sue if everyone does, for Michael is one of *everyone.*) Appropriate symbolizations for sentences 3 and 4 are, respectively,

$$(\exists x)Lxs \supset Lms$$

and

$$(\forall x)Lxs \supset Lms$$

Both of these sentences of *PL* are truth-functional compounds (material conditionals). It might be tempting to conclude that 'any' means 'every' except when it is used in the antecedent of an explicit conditional, in which case it means 'at least one'. But this rule is too simplistic, as sentence 5 makes clear. In 'If anyone likes Sue, he or she likes Rita', 'any' appears in the antecedent of an explicit English conditional. But here the force of 'any' cannot be captured by an existential quantifier, nor can the English sentence be symbolized as a conditional sentence of *PL*. Attempting to do so is likely to generate

$$(\exists x)Lxs \supset Lxr$$

which is a formula but not a sentence of *PL* (the third occurrence of 'x' is free). Changing the scope of the existential quantifier will not help either, for while

$$(\exists x)(Lxs \supset Lxr)$$

is a sentence of *PL* (albeit not a conditional), it says that there is someone such that if that person likes Sue then that person likes Rita. It is sufficient for the truth of this claim that there be someone who does not like Sue, for if a person does not like Sue, then '$(Lxs \supset Lxr)$' is true of that person—remember the weakness of the material conditional. To say what we want to say, we need a universally quantified sentence, that is, we need the symbolization we used for sentences 1 and 2:

$$(\forall x)(Lxs \supset Lxr)$$

This sentence of *PL* will be true if and only if each person who likes Sue also likes Rita. That we end up with this symbolization should not be surprising, for the force of sentence 5 ('If anyone likes Sue, he or she likes Rita') is, upon reflection, clearly the same as that of sentence 1 ('Anyone who likes Sue likes Rita').

A better rule can be formulated by appealing to the notion of *pronominal cross-reference.* In 'Sarah will deliver the lumber if she gets her truck fixed', the reference of 'she' is established by the earlier use of the noun 'Sarah'—there is pronominal cross-reference from the pronoun 'she' (as well as from 'her') back to the noun 'Sarah'. Pronominal cross-reference can be both to quantity terms and to nouns. In sentence 5, 'If anyone likes Sue, he or she likes Rita', the reference of 'he or she' is fixed by 'anyone who likes Sue'.

In sentence 3, 'If anyone likes Sue, Michael does', there is no pronominal cross-reference from the consequent of the English conditional back to the 'any' term in the antecedent. 'Michael does' in the consequent can be expanded to 'Michael likes Sue', a complete sentence that does not need further interpretation. But in 'If anyone likes Sue, he or she likes Rita', the consequent, 'he or she likes Rita', cannot be understood in isolation. This allows us to state the following rule:

> Where a quantity term is used in the antecedent of an English conditional and there is, in the consequent of that conditional, pronominal cross-reference to that quantity term, a universal quantifier is called for.

We can, with a little stretching, use this rule in dealing with such sentences as

> Anyone who fails the final examination flunks the course.

This sentence is not, on grammatical grounds, a conditional, and there is no obvious pronominal cross-reference. But since the person who flunks the course is the one who fails the final examination, we can paraphrase this sentence as a conditional in which there is pronominal cross-reference:

> <u>If</u> a person fails the final examination, <u>then</u> he or she flunks the course.

This is a sentence to which our new rule applies. Taking our universe of discourse to be students in the class and using 'Fx' for 'x fails the final examination' and 'Cx' for 'x flunks the course', we can, following this rule, offer

$$(\forall x)(Fx \supset Cx)$$

as an appropriate symbolization.

'Any' also functions differently from 'all', 'every', and 'each' when combined with a negation. For example, as noted in Section 7.4,

> Michael doesn't like everyone

and

> Michael doesn't like anyone

are very different claims. In general, 'not any' can be symbolized as the negation of an existential quantification ('not at least one'), whereas 'not every', 'not all', and 'not each' call for the negation of a universal quantification. In the present case, taking the people in Michael's office as our UD, 'm' as designating Michael, and 'Lxy' as 'x likes y', we can use '~ (∀x)Lmx' as a symbolization of the first sentence and '~ (∃x)Lmx' as a symbolization of the second.

Quantity constructions built from 'some' usually call for an existential quantifier. But some uses of 'some' constructions call for universal quantifiers, and the rule just developed helps in identifying them. Consider these two sentences:

If someone likes Sue, then he or she likes Rita.
If someone likes Sue, then someone likes Rita.

The first of these is a conditional with a quantity construction in the antecedent to which the 'he or she' in the consequent bears pronominal cross-reference. So a universal quantifier is called for, even though 'someone' usually signals an existential quantifier. A correct symbolization is '(∀x)(Lxs ⊃ Lxr)'. That this symbolization is correct becomes apparent when we reflect that the force of 'someone' in the first sentence is clearly that of 'anyone'. There is, in the second sentence, no pronominal cross-reference from the consequent back to the antecedent. The claim is not that if someone likes Sue then that very person likes Rita, but rather that if someone likes Sue then *someone*, quite possibly someone different, likes Rita. Here two existential quantifiers are called for:

(∃x)Lxs ⊃ (∃x)Lxr

Consider now some examples concerning runners:

UD: Runners
Bxy: x can beat y
Ay: y is on the American team
Sy: y is on the South African team
My: y is a marathon runner
Py: y is a sprinter
Dy: y has determination
Ey: y has endurance
Oy: y is over 50
Uy: y is under 20
j: Jim
k: Kerry
n: Noah
s: Seth
h: Shelly

Consider

Marathon runners have both endurance and determination.
Marathon runners are both over 50 and under 20.

The first example clearly attributes to marathon runners, and presumably to all marathon runners, two properties: endurance and determination. So an appropriate symbolization is

$$(\forall w)[Mw \supset (Ew \ \& \ Dw)]$$

Our symbolization is an A-sentence; it says that all things of this sort (marathon runners) are also of that sort (having endurance and determination). The second example should not be similarly taken to attribute two properties—being over 50 and being under 20—to all or even some marathon runners. Rather, this example has the force of 'Among marathon runners there are runners over 50 and runners under 20' and can be paraphrased as

There are marathon runners that are over 50 and there are marathon runners that are under 20.

One appropriate symbolization is thus a conjunction of two existentially quantified sentences (each of which is an I-sentence):

$$(\exists x)(Mx \ \& \ Ox) \ \& \ (\exists x)(Mx \ \& \ Ux)$$

For our next two examples we consider

There are no American sprinters over 50, but there are American marathon runners over 50.

There are sprinters under 20 on both the American team and the South African team.

Our symbolization of the first of these examples is a conjunction:

$$\sim (\exists y)[(Py \ \& \ Oy) \ \& \ Ay] \ \& \ (\exists y)[(My \ \& \ Oy) \ \& \ Ay]$$

Note that the first conjunct of this sentence of *PL* is the negation of an I-sentence, and the second is an I-sentence. I-sentences say there are members of the UD that are such-and-such, and sometimes it takes several predicates to capture the content of 'such-and-such'. The intent of the second example is clearly not that there are sprinters under 20 who are on both the American and the South African teams, but rather that on each team there are sprinters under 20. So an appropriate symbolization is

$$(\exists z)[(Pz \ \& \ Uz) \ \& \ Az] \ \& \ (\exists w)[(Pw \ \& \ Uw) \ \& \ Sw]$$

Consider next

Kerry and Shelly are both South African sprinters, and Shelly can beat every American sprinter Kerry can beat.

This example can be paraphrased, somewhat laboriously, as

Kerry is a sprinter and Kerry is on the South African team, and Shelly is a sprinter and Shelly is on the South African Team; and every runner is such that, if she or he is a sprinter and is on the American team and Kerry can beat her or him, then Shelly can beat her or him.

An appropriate symbolization is

$$[(Pk \ \& \ Sk) \ \& \ (Ph \ \& \ Sh)] \ \& \ (\forall z)([(Pz \ \& \ Az) \ \& \ Bkz] \supset Bsz)$$

Next we consider

If there is any marathon runner over 50 who can beat Seth, Jim can. Every South African sprinter can beat Jim, but they cannot all beat Seth. Noah is an American sprinter and marathon runner, and he can beat every sprinter, but not every marathon runner, on the South African team.

The first of these three sentences is fairly straightforward and can be symbolized either as

$$(\exists w)[(Mw \ \& \ Ow) \ \& \ Bws] \supset Bjs$$

or as

$$(\forall w)([(Mw \ \& \ Ow) \ \& \ Bws] \supset Bjs)$$

The second example *cannot* be symbolized as

$$(\forall x)[(Px \ \& \ Sx) \supset (Bxj \ \& \sim Bxs)]$$

for this sentence of *PL* says that all the South African sprinters are able to beat Jim and that they are all unable to beat Seth, whereas the original said merely that not all of them can beat Seth. The original contained two quantity expressions—'every' and 'all'—and we need a sentence of *PL* with two quantifiers:

$$(\forall x)[(Px \ \& \ Sx) \supset Bxj] \ \& \sim (\forall x)[(Px \ \& \ Sx) \supset Bxs]$$

This says that all the South African sprinters can beat Jim and that not all the South African sprinters can beat Seth (allowing that some may be able to do so), which is what was intended. The third example is a conjunction and can be paraphrased as

> Noah is on the American team and is a sprinter and a marathon runner, and Noah can beat every runner who is a sprinter and on the South African team, and Noah cannot beat every runner who is a marathon runner and on the South African team.

This can be symbolized as a conjunction, with the left conjunct being '[An & (Pn & Mn)]' and the right conjunct itself being a conjunction of an A-sentence and the negation of an A-sentence:

$$[An \ \& \ (Pn \ \& \ Mn)] \ \& \ ((\forall y)[(Py \ \& \ Sy) \supset Bny] \ \& \sim (\forall y)[(My \ \& \ Sy) \supset Bny])$$

For our next set of examples, we expand the symbolization key used at the end of Section 7.6 as follows. The UD includes marbles and people. Also, we encounter a three-place predicate for the first time.

UD:	Ashley, Clarence, Rhoda, Terry, and their marbles
a:	Ashley
c:	Clarence
r:	Rhoda
t:	Terry
Bx:	x is blue
Gx:	x is green
Rx:	x is red
Sx:	x is a shooter
Cx:	x is a cat's-eye
Tx:	x is a steely
Mx:	x is a marble
Bxy:	x belongs to y
Wxy:	x wins y
Gxyz:	x gives y to z

Here are our examples concerning an old-fashioned marble game:

1. All the cat's-eyes belong to Rhoda.
2. All the marbles but the shooters are cat's-eyes.
3. Some, but not all, of the cat's-eyes are green.
4. None of the steelies is red, green, or blue.
5. All of the shooters that are steelies belong to Terry.

6. Some green marbles and some blue marbles but no red ones belong to Clarence.
7. Ashley wins all Clarence's marbles.
8. Rhoda wins all Terry's cat's-eyes and shooters.
9. Terry doesn't have any marbles.
10. Rhoda gives all the red marbles she wins to Clarence.
11. Clarence gives all his green marbles to Ashley and all his blue marbles to Terry.

We now give one correct symbolization of each of these sentences. Then we shall discuss some of the noteworthy aspects of these examples.

1′. $(\forall y)(Cy \supset Byr)$

2′. $(\forall x)[(Mx \,\&\, \sim Sx) \supset Cx]$

3′. $(\exists x)(Cx \,\&\, Gx) \,\&\, \sim (\forall x)(Cx \supset Gx)$

4′. $(\forall w)[Tw \supset \sim (Rw \vee (Gw \vee Bw))]$

5′. $(\forall z)[(Sz \,\&\, Tz) \supset Bzt]$

6′. $[(\exists y)((My \,\&\, Gy) \,\&\, Byc) \,\&\, (\exists y)((My \,\&\, By) \,\&\, Byc)] \,\&\, \sim (\exists y)((My \,\&\, Ry) \,\&\, Byc)$

7′. $(\forall x)[(Mx \,\&\, Bxc) \supset Wax]$

8′. $(\forall x)([(Cx \vee Sx) \,\&\, Bxt] \supset Wrx)$

9′. $\sim (\exists z)(Mz \,\&\, Bzt)$

10′. $(\forall x)[((Mx \,\&\, Rx) \,\&\, Wrx) \supset Grxc]$

11′. $(\forall z)[(Mz \,\&\, Bzc) \supset ((Gz \supset Gcza) \,\&\, (Bz \supset Gczt))]$

Sentence 1 is unproblematic, and 1′ an obvious symbolization. Sentence 2 is not quite so straightforward. It does not claim that all the marbles are cat's-eyes—that can be symbolized as '$(\forall x)(Mx \supset Cx)$'—but that all the marbles but the *shooters* are cat's-eyes. Up to this point we have most commonly seen 'but' in contexts where it functions as a surrogate for 'and'. This is not the case here, where 'but' signals that the shooters are being exempted from the claim being made. Note that literally speaking no claim is being made about the shooters—either that they are or that they are not cat's-eyes. What is being said is merely that when the shooters are excluded the rest are cat's-eyes. (The context, for example, may be that someone asks whether all the marbles are cat's-eyes, and someone else replies as in example 2 and adds, when asked about the shooters, that she has examined all the marbles that are not shooters and found them all to be cat's-eyes but has not yet examined the shooters and hence has excluded them from consideration.) Analogously 'Everyone except Tom passed the test' does not *mean*—though it may *suggest*—that Tom did not pass. Tom's test may not yet be graded, or the speaker may not know how Tom fared or may simply not want to reveal whether Tom passed. In general 'All but such-and-such' and 'All except such-and-such' do not mean 'All and not such-and-such'. Rather, they mean 'All excluding such-and-such', to be followed or not by a separate comment about such-and-such.

Example 3 is also straightforward. An alternative and perhaps more intuitive, although longer, symbolization for example 4 is '$(\forall x)(Tx \supset \sim Rx)$ & $[(\forall x)(Tx \supset \sim Gx)$ & $(\forall x)(Tx \supset \sim Bx)]$'. But note that we really do not need three quantifiers. We can, as in 4′, single out the members of the UD we are concerned with (steelies) just once and then in one swoop deny that any such member is either red, or green, or yellow. Example 5 asserts, not that all the shooters belong to Terry, but that all those that are steelies do. So the group we need to single out consists of those things that are both shooters and steelies, and this is what we do in the antecedent of the conditional in 5.

We needed only one quantifier to symbolize example 4, but this is not so with example 6. Here even two quantifiers are not enough. For example, the force of

$$(\exists x)[(Mx \;\&\; Gx) \;\&\; (Bx \;\&\; Bxc)] \;\&\; \sim (\exists x)[(Mx \;\&\; Rx) \;\&\; Bxc]$$

is that Clarence possesses at least one marble that is both green and blue and that he possesses no red marbles, and this is not what example 6 claims.

Example 7 is easy enough once we realize that Clarence's marbles are just the marbles that belong to Clarence. What is of interest in example 8 is that it can be symbolized using only one quantifier, although Terry's cat's-eyes and her shooters may constitute mutually exclusive groups. For while we could use a conjunction, for example,

$$(\forall x)[(Cx \;\&\; Bxt) \supset Wrx] \;\&\; (\forall x)[(Sx \;\&\; Bxt) \supset Wrx]$$

doing so is being more verbose than we need to be. 'Cx & Bxt' applies to things that are cat's-eyes and belong to Terry. '$(Cx \vee Sx)$ & Bxt' picks out those things that are either cat's-eyes or shooters and that belong to Terry; that is, it *picks* out all the cat's-eyes and all the shooters that belong to Terry.

Examples 9 and 10 are straightforward. Example 11 is interesting in that it, like example 4, can be symbolized using just one quantifier. We could also have used two quantifiers:

$$(\forall x)[((Mx \;\&\; Gx) \;\&\; Bxc) \supset Gcxa] \;\&\; (\forall x)[((Mx \;\&\; Bx) \;\&\; Bxc) \supset Gcxt]$$

But if we first single out those things that are marbles and belong to Clarence, as we do in 11′, and then say that <u>if</u> such a thing is green, <u>then</u> Clarence gives it to Ashley, <u>and</u> that <u>if</u> it is blue, <u>then</u> Clarence gives it to Terry, we can get by with one quantifier.

Before ending this section we issue some cautionary notes about symbolizing sentences in *PL*. The first concerns the selection of predicates of *PL* for use in symbolizing English sentences. Frequently, but not always, English descriptions that consist of "stacked-up" adjectives, as in 'A second-hand, broken-down, uncomfortable, tan recliner is in the corner', can be captured by conjoining appropriate predicates of *PL*. Taking the furniture in the room to constitute the universe of discourse and using obvious predicates, we can symbolize the foregoing as

$$(\exists z)([(Sz \ \& \ Bz) \ \& \ (Uz \ \& \ Tz)] \ \& \ (Rz \ \& \ Cz))$$

This symbolization is appropriate because the recliner in question is secondhand, is broken-down, is uncomfortable, is tan, is a recliner, and is in the corner. In contrast, a bloody fool is presumably a very foolish person but not necessarily a person covered with blood. So, too, a counterfeit dollar is not something that both is counterfeit and is a dollar (because it is not a dollar). Similarly, while the animal in the corner may be a large mouse, it is not clear that there is something in the corner that is large, is an animal, and is a mouse—even large mice are not large as animals go. And a second-rate mathematician who is also a first-rate drama critic is not a second-rate person and a first-rate person. Rather, 'second-rate mathematician' and 'first-rate drama critic' should each normally be symbolized by a single predicate of *PL*, as should 'bloody fool', 'counterfeit dollar', and 'large mouse'.

This practice will cause problems in some contexts. For example, from 'Sue is a first-rate drama critic' we will not be able to infer 'Sue is a drama critic'. We can save such inferences by the admittedly ad hoc device of using one predicate for 'first-rate drama critic' and another for 'drama critic'. That is, using the symbolization key

UD: People
Fx: x is a first-rate drama critic
Dx: x is a drama critic
s: Sue

we can symbolize 'Sue is a first-rate drama critic' as

Fs & Ds

and 'Sue is a drama critic' as

Ds

And we can show that the second of these *PL* sentences follows from the first.

As this discussion illustrates, the appropriate selection of predicates commonly depends upon the context. For example, given just that the UD is animals and the sentence

Rabid bats are dangerous

and no context, we might decide to treat being a rabid bat as having a single property, use 'Rx' for 'x is a rabid bat', use 'Dx' for 'x is dangerous', and symbolize the example as

$$(\forall y)(Ry \supset Dy)$$

Alternatively we could treat being a rabid bat as having two properties: that of being a bat and that of being rabid (rabid bats are things that are both rabid and bats). Now, using 'Rx' for 'x is rabid' and 'Bx' for 'x is dangerous', we could symbolize the given sentence as

$$(\forall y)[(Ry \;\&\; By) \supset Dy]$$

Taken in isolation, neither symbolization is preferable to the other. But suppose that, instead of the foregoing single sentence, we are given a complete argument:

> Some bats are rabid. Rabid animals are dangerous. Therefore some bats are dangerous.

Here we want our symbolization to reveal as much as possible of what is common to the premises and the conclusion. To do this we clearly need to use separate predicates of *PL* for 'x is a bat' and 'x is rabid'. Where animals constitute the universe of discourse, an appropriate symbolization is

$$(\exists y)(Ry \;\&\; By)$$
$$(\forall z)(Rz \supset Dz)$$
$$\overline{(\exists y)(By \;\&\; Dy)}$$

We can show that this is a valid argument of *PL*. But had we chosen to use a single predicate, say, 'Rx', to symbolize being a rabid bat, we would have had to use a different predicate to symbolize being a rabid animal, say, 'Ax':

$$(\exists x)Rx$$
$$(\forall y)(Ay \supset Dy)$$
$$\overline{(\exists y)(By \;\&\; Dy)}$$

In this second symbolization we have made opaque the obvious fact that rabid bats are rabid animals and the obvious fact that rabid bats are bats. As a result, although the English language argument is valid, as is our first symbolization of it, the second symbolization is not valid.

There is a further complication in the selection of predicates. Suppose that the Spanish explorer Ponce de Leon did, as legend has it, spend a lot of time searching for the fountain of youth. How would we symbolize the following?

Ponce de Leon is searching for the fountain of youth.

We cannot use

Spf

where 'Sxy' is interpreted as 'x is searching for y', 'p' designates Ponce de Leon, and 'f' the fountain of youth, for while Ponce de Leon might believe there is a fountain of youth, there is, in fact, no such thing. We can interpret 'Yx' as 'x is searching for the fountain of youth' and symbolize the sentence as

Yp

Although things that do not exist cannot be found, it is unfortunately all too easy to search for them. For this reason

Ponce de Leon is searching for mermaids

also cannot be symbolized using the two-place 'Sxy' for 'x is searching for y'. We might indeed be tempted, using 'Mx' for 'x is a mermaid', to offer the following as possible symbolizations of 'Ponce de Leon is searching for mermaids':

(∃y) (My & Spy)
(∀y) (My ⊃ Spy)

But neither of these is adequate to the task. The problem is not with using 'Mx' for 'x is a mermaid' when there are no mermaids. As noted earlier, we do not presuppose that every predicate of *PL* we use is true of at least one member of the selected universe of discourse. Rather, one problem with the previous existentially quantified sentence is that it commits us, by its use of the existential quantifier, to there being at least one mermaid, whereas the sentence being symbolized does not. (One can search for what does not exist.) The universally quantified sentence of *PL* given earlier says not that there are mermaids—so here we escape a commitment to the existence of mermaids—but rather that anything that is a mermaid is such that Ponce de Leon is searching for it. This is too weak for, given the nonexistence of mermaids, it is true no matter what Ponce de Leon is doing, for it says only that if a thing is a mermaid (and nothing is) then Ponce de Leon is searching for it.

The way out of the present difficulty is to use a one-place predicate—for example, to interpret 'Mx' as 'x is searching for mermaids'—and to symbolize

Ponce de Leon is searching for mermaids

as

Mp

Difficulties arise in symbolizing sentences concerned with such activities as searching for, hunting, looking for, and . . . , even when what is being sought, hunted, desired, . . . , does exist. Suppose the sentence we want to symbolize is

Ponce de Leon is searching for a good harbor.

It might be thought that, if we interpret 'Sxy' as 'x is searching for y' and 'Gx' as 'x is a good harbor', a proper symbolization of this sentence would be

(∃x) (Gx & Spx)

This symbolization might be acceptable if Ponce de Leon is looking for a particular harbor, say, the harbor at Vera Cruz. But, if he is prowling the Florida coast and merely wants a haven from an impending storm, any good harbor, it is false to say that there is a good harbor such that he is looking for that harbor. Nor is '(∀x) (Gx ⊃ Spx)' a proper symbolization. Imagine that there are three good harbors in his vicinity. Ponce de Leon will be glad to reach any one of them, and he is not interested in reaching all of them. So neither '(∃x) (Gx & Spx)' nor '(∀x) (Gx ⊃ Spx)' is an acceptable symbolization—the first because it would be false to say of a good harbor our hero finds that he was searching for *that* harbor all along, and the second because he wants only one harbor and not all good harbors. So here, too, we should use a one-place predicate. If we interpret 'Hx' as 'x is searching for a good harbor', the proper symbolization is

Hp

On the other hand, if Ponce de Leon's ship got separated from an accompanying ship during the night, and Ponce de Leon is searching for *that* ship, a proper symbolization, using 'Sx' for 'x is a ship', would be

(∃x) (Sx & Spx)

Generally, unless what is being sought, hunted, searched for, hoped for, or desired is a particular thing, rather than a kind of thing, a one-place rather than a two-place predicate of *PL* should be used.[12]

---

[12]There are logics known as *intensional logics* in which problematic sentences of the sort just discussed can be further analyzed.

7.7E EXERCISES

1. Symbolize the following sentences in *PL* using the given symbolization key.

UD: Persons
Dx: x is at the door
Hx: x is honest
Ix: x is an influence peddler
Lx: x is likeable
Px: x is a politician
Rx: x is a registered lobbyist
h: Harrington

a. All politicians are honest.
*b. No politicians are honest.
c. Some politicians are honest.
*d. Some politicians are not honest.
e. An honest politician is not an influence peddler.
*f. An honest politician is at the door.
g. Politicians and influence peddlers are not all honest.
*h. Honest influence peddlers are nonexistent.
i. An influence peddler is honest only if he or she is a registered lobbyist.
*j. Some but not all registered lobbyists are honest.
k. If anyone is an influence peddler Harrington is.
*l. If anyone is an influence peddler, he or she is either a politician or a registered lobbyist.
m. If anyone is an influence peddler every registered lobbyist is.
*n. Harrington is no influence peddler but he is an honest politician.
o. No one is honest, a politician, and an influence peddler.
*p. Everyone is a politician but not everyone is honest.
q. If every politician is an influence peddler, then no politician is honest.
*r. Some politicians who are influence peddlers are honest, but none is likeable.
s. Registered lobbyists are likeable influence peddlers, but they are not honest.

2. Symbolize the following sentences in *PL* using the given symbolization key.

UD: Mammals
Cxy: x is chasing y
Lx: x is a lion
Ax: x is a formidable animal
Fx: is ferocious
Tx: x is a tiger
Bx: x is best avoided
b: Bruce Willis
d: Danny DeVito

a. A lion is a formidable animal.
*b. Lions are ferocious.
c. Lions are ferocious, but tigers are not.
*d. A lion is chasing Danny DeVito.
e. Danny DeVito is chasing a ferocious lion.

*f. Ferocious lions are best avoided.
g. Lions and tigers are ferocious.
*h. Lions and tigers are chasing Danny DeVito.
i. Some, but not all, tigers are ferocious.
*j. Ferocious lions and tigers are best avoided.
k. Any lion Bruce Willis is chasing is a formidable animal but is not ferocious.
*l. Danny DeVito and ferocious lions and tigers are all best avoided.
m. If any lion is ferocious, all tigers are.
*n. A lion is ferocious if and only if Danny DeVito is chasing it.
o. Bruce Willis is not ferocious, but he is best avoided.
*p. If Danny DeVito is ferocious, all lions are tigers.

3. Symbolize the following sentences in *PL* using the given symbolization key.

UD: Persons
Ex: x is a real estate agent
Lx: x is a lawyer
Px: x is a professor
Nx: x lives next door
Ix: x is rich
Sx: x can sell to yuppies
Yx: x is a yuppie
Rxy: x respects y
f: Fred

a. All real estate agents are yuppies.
*b. No real estate agents are yuppies.
c. Some but not all real estate agents are yuppies.
*d. Some real estate agents are yuppies and some are not.
e. If any real estate agent is a yuppie, all lawyers are.
*f. Any real estate agent who isn't a yuppie isn't rich.
g. If any real estate agent can sell to yuppies, he or she is a yuppie.
*h. If any real estate agent can sell to yuppies, Fred can.
i. Anyone who is a lawyer and a real estate agent is a yuppie and rich.
*j. Yuppies who aren't rich don't exist.
k. Real estate agents and lawyers are rich if they are yuppies.
*l. If Fred is a yuppie he's not a professor, and if he's a professor he's not rich.
m. No professor who isn't rich is a yuppie.
*n. No professor who is self-respecting is a yuppie.
o. Every self-respecting real estate agent is a yuppie.
*p. Real estate agents and lawyers who are rich are self-respecting.
q. Real estate agents and lawyers who are either rich or yuppies are self-respecting.
*r. A yuppie who is either a real estate agent or a lawyer is self-respecting.
s. A yuppie who is both a lawyer and a real estate agent is self-respecting.
*t. A yuppie who is both a lawyer and a real estate agent lives next door.

4. Symbolize the following sentences in *PL* using the given symbolization key.

UD: Persons
Ax: x is an administrator
Px: x is a professor

Ux: x is underpaid
Ox: x is overworked
Sx: x is a secretary

a. Professors are underpaid and overworked.
*b. Overworked professors are underpaid.
c. Administrators are neither overworked nor underpaid.
*d. Administrators are neither overworked nor underpaid, but professors are both.
e. A person is overworked if and only if he or she is underpaid.
*f. If any administrator is underpaid, all professors are; and if any professor is underpaid, all secretaries are.
g. Some professors are underpaid, but those who are administrators are not.
*h. Administrators are overworked but not underpaid; secretaries are underpaid but not overworked; and professors are both overworked and underpaid.
i. Some professors are overworked and underpaid, and all secretaries are.
*j. Some underpaid professors are also secretaries, and some overworked administrators are also professors, but no administrator is a secretary.
k. Some secretaries and some professors are underpaid, but no administrator is.

5. Use the following symbolization key to translate these sentences into fluent English. (*Note:* All of the following claims are true.)

UD: Positive integers
Lxy: x is larger than y
Dxy: x is evenly divisible by y
Ex: x is even
Ox: x is odd
Px: x is prime
a: 1
b: 2
c: 3
d: 4

a. Pb & Pc
*b. ~ (Pa ∨ Pd)
c. (∃x)Ex & (∃x)Ox
*d. ~ (∃y)(Ey & Oy)
e. (∀y)(Ey ∨ Oy)
*f. ~ (∃y)Lay
g. (∃x) ~ Lxa
*h. (∀z)(Pz ⊃ Lza)
i. (∀x)(Ex ⊃ Dxb)
*j. ~ (∃y)(Oy & Dyb)
k. (∀y)Dya
*l. ~ (∀x)Dxb
m. (∀y)(Dyb ≡ Ey)
*n. (∀x)(Dxb ⊃ ~ Dxc)
o. (∃y)Lay ⊃ (∀y)Lay
*p. (∃x)(Px & Dxb)
q. ~ (∃y)(Py & Dyd)
*r. (∀x)(Px ⊃ Lxa)

7.8 MULTIPLE QUANTIFIERS WITH OVERLAPPING SCOPE

In symbolizing sentences of English as sentences of *PL*, we have frequently encountered sentences of *PL* that contain more than one quantifier. But these have all been truth-functional compounds. In none of these sentences has one quantifier fallen within the scope of another quantifier. It is time to consider sentences of English whose *PL* symbolizations contain multiple quantifiers with *overlapping scope.*

Consider again the people in Michael's office. We symbolized 'Michael likes everyone' as '$(\forall x)Lmx$', but we did not attempt a symbolization of

Everyone likes everyone.

To symbolize 'Everyone likes everyone', we need to say of each person what '$(\forall x)Lmx$' says of Michael. To accomplish this we replace the constant 'm' with a second variable and add a second universal quantifier:

$$(\forall y)(\forall x)Lyx$$

In quasi-English this says 'Each person y is such that for each person x, y likes x' or 'Each person y is such that y likes everyone' or 'Everyone likes everyone'.

Similarly, just as '$(\exists x)Lmx$' symbolizes 'Michael likes someone',

$$(\exists y)(\exists x)Lyx$$

symbolizes 'Someone likes someone'. In each of these sentences of *PL*, the scope of the second quantifier falls within that of the first quantifier. It is also possible to mix universal and existential quantifiers. Consider

$$(\forall x)(\exists y)Lxy$$

and

$$(\exists y)(\forall x)Lxy$$

The first of the example sentences can be paraphrased as 'Each person x is such that x likes at least one person y' or 'Everyone likes someone'. For this claim to be true, it is sufficient that each person like at least one person. Perhaps Michael likes Rita, Rita likes Henry, Henry likes Sue, and Sue likes Michael. The second of the sentences looks very much like the first—only the order of the quantifiers is different. The second sentence says, however, not that everyone likes someone, but that someone is liked by everyone. If we limit our universe of discourse to the people in Michael's office or to any other reasonably small group, there may be such a lucky person. But if the UD is all people, there is no such person, for there is no person who is even known to everyone, let alone liked by everyone. The moral here is that we need to pay attention to the order of quantifiers in mixed quantification.

Generally, when we have two universal quantifiers, the order in which they occur does not matter. Similarly, when we have two existential quantifiers, the order in which they occur does not matter. More generally, when we have a series of quantifiers, all existential or all universal, the order in which they occur does not matter. But this is, again, not in general true where we have mixed quantification—that is, at least one universal and at least one existential quantifier.

There are four combinations in which pairs of quantifiers can occur. We display them here along with useful quasi-English paraphrases:

$(\exists x)(\exists y)$	There is an x and there is a y such that . . . [or] There is a pair x and y such that . . .
$(\forall x)(\forall y)$	For each x and for each y . . . [or] For each pair x and y . . .
$(\forall x)(\exists y)$	For each x there is a y such that . . .
$(\exists x)(\forall y)$	There is an x such that for each y . . .

So far we have been assuming that our universe of discourse is limited to persons, either just the persons in Michael's office or all persons. Suppose we now allow our UD to be more heterogeneous, including, say, all living things. To be able to say that, for example, everyone (as opposed to everything) likes someone (as opposed to something) we need a predicate that singles out persons. We will use 'Px', here interpreted as 'x is a person'. Appropriate symbolizations of

1. Everyone likes everyone
2. Someone likes someone
3. Everyone likes someone
4. Someone likes everyone
5. Everyone is liked by someone
6. Someone is liked by everyone

are, respectively,

1′. $(\forall x)(\forall y)[(Px \,\&\, Py) \supset Lxy]$
2′. $(\exists x)(\exists y)[(Px \,\&\, Py) \,\&\, Lxy]$
3′. $(\forall x)[Px \supset (\exists y)(Py \,\&\, Lxy)]$
4′. $(\exists x)[Px \,\&\, (\forall y)(Py \supset Lxy)]$
5′. $(\forall x)[Px \supset (\exists y)(Py \,\&\, Lyx)]$
6′. $(\exists x)[Px \,\&\, (\forall y)(Py \supset Lyx)]$

Note that in 1′ and 2′ both quantifiers occur at the beginning of the sentence, whereas in 3′–6′ the second quantifier occurs later in the sentence. We can move the y-quantifier closer to the first predicate containing 'y' in symbolizing sentences 1 and 2. That is, '(∀x)[Px ⊃ (∀y)(Py ⊃ Lxy)]' is also an appropriate symbolization of 1, as is '(∃x)[Px & (∃y)(Py & Lxy)]' of 2. Where quantifiers are placed, and when a quantifier can and cannot be moved, is a complicated issue, and we return to it below.

In symbolizing sentences of English that call for sentences of *PL* with multiple quantifiers with overlapping scope, it is especially important to learn to "read" the sentences of *PL* into quasi-English in order to check one's symbolization. In doing so, it is crucial that the role of each logical operator be identified—that is, that one identify the formula of which each logical operator is the main logical operator. In 1′ above, '(∀x)' is the main logical operator and '(∀y)' is the main logical operator of that sentence's immediate subformula, '(∀y)[(Px & Py) ⊃ Lxy]'. So we read '(∀x)' first and '(∀y)' second. The reading begins either 'Every x is such that every y is such that' or, perhaps more insightfully, 'Every pair x and y is such that'. The horseshoe is the main logical operator of '(Px & Py) ⊃ Lxy', so we read it next, then the antecedent of the conditional, and finally the consequent. The full quasi-English reading is

> Every pair x and y is such that if x is a person and y is a person then x likes y.

The main logical operator of 4′ is an existential quantifier, '(∃x)', and the immediate subformula of 4′ is a conjunction whose right conjunct is a universally quantified formula. So we read the existential quantifier first, and then the conjunction. The quasi-English reading is

> There is at least one thing x such that both x is a person and each thing y is such that if y is a person then x likes y.

In 5′ the main logical operator is again a universal quantifier, '(∀x)'. Here the main logical operator of the immediate subformula, 'Px ⊃ (∃y)(Py & Lyx)', is the horseshoe, so we read the universal quantifier first, and then the conditional, the consequent of which is itself an existentially quantified formula. The quasi-English reading is

> Each thing x is such that if x is a person then there is a y such that both y is a person and y likes x.

We next symbolize a series of claims concerning the positive integers, which we met briefly in Exercise Set 7.7. We pick positive integers as our UD because the relations among positive integers are very clear and easily stated and because a familiarity with positive integers and claims regarding them will be useful in Chapter 8. The positive integers are the numbers 1, 2, 3, 4, . . . (note that 0 is not a positive integer).

For our symbolization key we use

UD: Positive integers
Ex: x is even
Dx: x is odd
Px: x is prime
Lxy: x is larger than y
Exy: x times y is even
Oxy: x times y is odd
Pxy: x times y is prime
a: 1
b: 2

The claim 'Every positive integer is either odd or even and no positive integer is both' can be symbolized without using quantifiers with overlapping scope:

$$(\forall y)(Dy \vee Ey) \ \& \sim (\exists y)(Dy \ \& \ Ey)$$

But the claim 'There is no largest positive integer' does require use of quantifiers with overlapping scope. It says that each positive integer is such that there is a larger positive integer. A start at an appropriate symbolization is

(∀x)(there is an integer larger than x)

and a full symbolization is

$$(\forall x)(\exists y)Lyx$$

The sentence '~ (∃y)Lay' says that it is not the case that there is a positive integer such that 1 is larger than it. From here it is a short step to '(∃x) ~ (∃y)Lxy', which says that there is a positive integer x such that there is no positive integer y that x is larger than—that is, that there is a positive integer that is not larger than any positive integer or that there is a lower bound to the positive integers. This is true.

The sentence '2 is prime and there is no smaller prime' is equivalent to '2 is prime and 2 is not larger than any prime', which can be symbolized as

$$Pb \ \& \sim (\exists y)(Py \ \& \ Lby)$$

'An odd number times an odd number is odd' is clearly a claim about all positive integers—no matter what positive integers we select, if both are odd their product is odd. An appropriate paraphrase is

Each x and each y are such that if x is odd and y is odd then x times y is odd or, alternatively,

> Each pair of integers, x and y, is such that if x is odd and y is odd, then x times y is odd.

An appropriate *PL* symbolization is

$$(\forall w)(\forall x)[(Dw \;\&\; Dx) \supset Owx]$$

Similarly 'An even number times an even number is even' becomes '$(\forall x)(\forall y)[(Ex \;\&\; Ey) \supset Exy]$'. And 'An even number times an odd number is even' becomes '$(\forall z)(\forall y)[(Ez \;\&\; Dy) \supset Ezy]$'.

'No product of prime numbers is prime' means that there is no pair of positive integers, each of which is prime, whose product is also prime. An appropriate paraphrase is

> There is no w and z such that w is prime, z is prime, and w times z is prime.

In *PL* we have

$$\sim (\exists w)(\exists z)[(Pw \;\&\; Pz) \;\&\; Pwz]$$

Now consider

$$(\forall x)(\forall y)[Exy \supset (Ex \vee Ey)]$$

This sentence of *PL* says that for any pair of positive integers, if the first times the second is even, then at least one of the integers is even. This is true, for if neither integer were even, their product would be odd. Similarly

$$(\forall x)(\forall y)[Oxy \supset (Dx \;\&\; Dy)]$$

says that for any pair of positive integers, if the first times the second is odd, then both of those integers are odd. The sentence

$$\sim (\exists z)Ozb$$

says, truly, that there is no positive integer such that it times 2 is odd. And

$$(\forall x)(\forall y)(\forall z)[(Lxy \;\&\; Lyz) \supset Lxz]$$

says that for any triplet of positive integers, if the first is larger than the second and the second is larger than the third, then the first is larger than the third. This claim is true (see Section 7.9). The sentence

$$(\forall x)(Dx \equiv (\exists y)Oyx) \;\&\; (\forall x)(Ex \equiv \sim (\exists y)Oyx)$$

says that a positive integer is odd if and only if there is some positive integer such that it times the first integer is odd and that a positive integer is even if and only if there is no positive integer such that it times that integer is odd.

In Section 7.1 we presented a valid English language argument that cannot be shown to be valid by the techniques associated with *SL*:

> None of David's friends supports Republicans. Sarah supports Breitlow, and Breitlow is a Republican. So Sarah is no friend of David's.

We can now symbolize this argument in *PL*. An appropriate symbolization key is

UD: People
Fxy: x is a friend of y
Sxy: x supports y
Rx: x is a Republican
d: David
b: Breitlow
s: Sarah

The second premise, a conjunction, is readily symbolized as 'Ssb & Rb'. The conclusion is also easy to symbolize once we see that it simply amounts to the claim that Sarah is not a friend of David's: '~ Fsd'. It is only the first premise that seems to pose difficulties. That premise is of the general form

> No thing of such-and-such a sort is a thing of such-and-such a sort.

That is, it is an E-sentence. In Section 7.6 we saw that such sentences can be symbolized either as universally quantified sentences or as negations of existentially quantified sentences. If we opt for the former, an appropriate first step toward a symbolization is

> Each x is such that if x is a friend of David's then x does not support Republicans.

This quasi-English locution readily becomes

> (∀x)(Fxd ⊃ it is not the case that x supports Republicans)

What remains is to find a symbolization for 'It is not the case that x supports Republicans'. A quasi-English first step is

> It is not the case that there is a y such that y is a Republican and x supports y.

This can be symbolized as '$\sim (\exists y)(Ry \& Sxy)$'. The full symbolization of the first premise is thus

$$(\forall x)(Fxd \supset \sim (\exists y)(Ry \& Sxy))$$

The resulting argument of *PL* is

$$(\forall x)[Fxd \supset \sim (\exists y)(Ry \& Sxy)]$$
$$Ssb \& Rb$$

$$\sim Fsd$$

This argument is, as we shall see in later chapters, valid.

Note that, while we chose to treat the embedded clause 'It is not the case that x supports Republicans' as the negation of an I-claim, we could equally well have treated it as an E-claim, symbolizing it as '$(\forall y)(Ry \supset \sim Sxy)$'. Doing so would yield the following alternative symbolization of the first premise:

$$(\forall x)[Fxd \supset (\forall y)(Ry \supset \sim Sxy)]$$

Both of these symbolizations of the first premise, and many others we have not given, are equally acceptable. In constructing symbolizations it is often useful to start, as we did here, by determining whether the sentence to be symbolized fits one of the four patterns provided by the A-, E-, I-, O-sentence classification. If it does, the next step is to pick the overall structure to be used (for example, universal quantification of a conditional formula). Finally we fill in the missing pieces—successively replacing bits of English with formulas of *PL*.

Here is a somewhat more interesting argument:

> Anyone who is proud of anyone is proud of Samantha. Rhoda isn't proud of anyone who's proud of himself or herself, but she is proud of everyone who has mastered calculus. Therefore if Art has mastered calculus Samantha isn't proud of herself.

We will use the following symbolization key:

UD:	People in Samantha's class
Pxy:	x is proud of y
Mx:	x has mastered calculus
a:	Art
r:	Rhoda
s:	Samantha

The first occurrence of 'anyone' in the first premise clearly goes over to a universal quantifier in *PL*, as becomes apparent when we try to paraphrase the sentence

$$(\text{y is proud of anyone} \supset \text{y is proud of Samantha})$$

Here there is clear pronominal cross-reference—the y that is proud of Samantha is the y that is proud of anyone. So as a next step we have

$$(\forall y)(\text{y is proud of anyone} \supset Pys)$$

an A-sentence. What remains is to determine whether the second 'anyone' should go over to a universal or an existential quantifier in *PL*. Note that there is no pronominal cross-reference from the consequent of 'y is proud of anyone ⊃ Pys' back to 'anyone'. So we can use an existential quantifier. That a universal quantifier is not called for is also apparent when we consider that

$$(\forall y)(\text{y is proud of everyone} \supset Pys)$$

is clearly an inappropriate paraphrase of the first premise, while

$$(\forall y)(\text{y is proud of someone} \supset Pys)$$

is an appropriate paraphrase. To be proud of someone is for there to be someone of whom one is proud. So the missing formula is '$(\exists x)Pyx$'. The complete symbolization of the first premise is thus

$$(\forall y)[(\exists x)Pyx \supset Pys]$$

The second premise is a conjunction and should be symbolized as a conjunction of *PL*. The left conjunct will be a symbolization of 'Rhoda isn't proud of anyone who is proud of himself or herself', which can be treated as an E-sentence (as 'No person who is proud of himself or herself is a person of whom Rhoda is proud'). So an appropriate left conjunct for our *PL* symbolization is '$(\forall z)(Pzz \supset \sim Prz)$'. The right conjunct of the second premise can be treated as an A-sentence (as 'Everyone who has mastered calculus is a person of whom Rhoda is proud') and symbolized as '$(\forall z)(Mz \supset Prz)$'. The second premise of our symbolized argument is thus

$$(\forall z)(Pzz \supset \sim Prz) \ \& \ (\forall z)(Mz \supset Prz)$$

The conclusion of our English language argument is a conditional and can be symbolized as '$Ma \supset \sim Pss$'. The complete argument of *PL* is

$$(\forall y)[(\exists x)Pyx \supset Pys]$$
$$(\forall z)(Pzz \supset \sim Prz) \ \& \ (\forall z)(Mz \supset Prz)$$

$$Ma \supset \sim Pss$$

This is also a valid argument of *PL*.

We just symbolized 'Anyone who is proud of anyone is proud of Samantha' as '$(\forall y)[(\exists x)Pyx \supset Pys]$'. An alternative symbolization is

$$(\forall y)(\forall x)(Pyx \supset Pys)$$

A quasi-English reading of this second symbolization is

> Each y and each x is such that if y is proud of x then y is proud of Samantha.

The obvious difference between these two sentences of *PL* is that in the second the x-quantifier is a universal quantifier whose scope extends to the end of the sentence. A simpler example may be helpful here. Consider these sentences:

> If any student passes, Donna will pass.
> Each student is such that if that student passes Donna will pass.

If we restrict our UD to students in the class in question, interpret 'Tx' as 'x will pass', and let 'd' designate Donna, these sentences can be symbolized as

$$(\exists x)Px \supset Pd$$

and

$$(\forall x)(Px \supset Pd)$$

respectively. The first of these sentences of *PL* can be read

> If there is at least one student x such that x passes, then Donna passes.

Now suppose that some student, say, Art, does pass. Then, according to the first of the above sentences of *PL*, Donna also passes. The second sentence of *PL* can be read

> Each student x is such that if x passes then Donna passes.

Now, if each student is of this sort, then Art is of this sort. Therefore, if '$(\forall x)(Px \supset Pd)$' holds and Art passes, Donna passes. So '$(\exists x)Px \supset Pd$' and '$(\forall x)(Px \supset Pd)$' both commit us to Donna's passing if at least one student passes. These sentences are also false under just the same circumstances. The first will be false only if some student passes and Donna does not. Suppose, for example, that Bud passes but that Donna does not. Then '$(\exists x)Px \supset Pd$' is false and so is '$(\forall x)(Px \supset Pd)$', for the latter says that each student, including Bud, is such that if he or she passes Donna passes. And this is false if Bud passes but Donna does not.

The general rule is this: When an existential quantifier has only the antecedent of a material conditional within its scope and its scope is broadened to include the consequent of that conditional, the existential quantifier must be replaced with a universal quantifier. That is, where **P** is a formula in which x does not occur and **Ax** is a formula containing **x**,

$(\exists \mathbf{x})\mathbf{Ax} \supset \mathbf{P}$

and

$(\forall \mathbf{x})(\mathbf{Ax} \supset \mathbf{P})$

are equivalent sentence forms.

An analogous though less common case occurs when a universal quantifier has only the antecedent of a material conditional within its scope and its scope is broadened to include the entire conditional. When this happens, the universal quantifier must be replaced with an existential quantifier. That is, where **x** does not occur in **P** the following sentence forms are equivalent:

$(\forall \mathbf{x})\mathbf{Ax} \supset \mathbf{P}$

and

$(\exists \mathbf{x})(\mathbf{Ax} \supset \mathbf{P})$

The cases to watch out for, then, are cases where the consequent of a material conditional does not lie within the scope of a quantifier and is then brought within that scope, or vice versa. In these cases the quantifier in question must be replaced with a universal quantifier if it was an existential and with an existential quantifier if it was a universal.

Fortunately there are many cases in which quantifiers do not have to be changed when scopes are broadened or narrowed. If the scope of a quantifier extends over only one disjunct of a disjunction or over only one conjunct of a conjunction and that scope is broadened to include the entire disjunction or conjunction, the quantifier does not change. Similarly, when a quantifier has scope over only the consequent of a material conditional and its scope is broadened by relocating the quantifier so as to have scope over the entire conditional, the quantifier does not change. So where **x** does not occur in **P** the following are all pairs of equivalent sentence forms:

$(\exists \mathbf{x})\mathbf{Ax} \supset \mathbf{P}$	$(\forall \mathbf{x})(\mathbf{Ax} \supset \mathbf{P})$
$(\forall \mathbf{x})\mathbf{Ax} \supset \mathbf{P}$	$(\exists \mathbf{x})(\mathbf{Ax} \supset \mathbf{P})$
$\mathbf{P} \supset (\exists \mathbf{x})\mathbf{Ax}$	$(\exists \mathbf{x})(\mathbf{P} \supset \mathbf{Ax})$
$\mathbf{P} \supset (\forall \mathbf{x})\mathbf{Ax}$	$(\forall \mathbf{x})(\mathbf{P} \supset \mathbf{Ax})$
$(\exists \mathbf{x})\mathbf{Ax} \vee \mathbf{P}$	$(\exists \mathbf{x})(\mathbf{Ax} \vee \mathbf{P})$
$(\forall \mathbf{x})\mathbf{Ax} \vee \mathbf{P}$	$(\forall \mathbf{x})(\mathbf{Ax} \vee \mathbf{P})$
$\mathbf{P} \vee (\exists \mathbf{x})\mathbf{Ax}$	$(\exists \mathbf{x})(\mathbf{P} \vee \mathbf{Ax})$
$\mathbf{P} \vee (\forall \mathbf{x})\mathbf{Ax}$	$(\forall \mathbf{x})(\mathbf{P} \vee \mathbf{Ax})$
$(\exists \mathbf{x})\mathbf{Ax} \,\&\, \mathbf{P}$	$(\exists \mathbf{x})(\mathbf{Ax} \,\&\, \mathbf{P})$
$(\forall \mathbf{x})\mathbf{Ax} \,\&\, \mathbf{P}$	$(\forall \mathbf{x})(\mathbf{Ax} \,\&\, \mathbf{P})$
$\mathbf{P} \,\&\, (\exists \mathbf{x})\mathbf{Ax}$	$(\exists \mathbf{x})(\mathbf{P} \,\&\, \mathbf{Ax})$
$\mathbf{P} \,\&\, (\forall \mathbf{x})\mathbf{Ax}$	$(\forall \mathbf{x})(\mathbf{P} \,\&\, \mathbf{Ax})$

Material biconditionals are a special case. $(\forall \mathbf{x})\mathbf{Ax} \equiv \mathbf{P}$ is equivalent neither to $(\forall \mathbf{x})(\mathbf{Ax} \equiv \mathbf{P})$ nor to $(\exists \mathbf{x})(\mathbf{Ax} \equiv \mathbf{P})$. That is, the scope of a quantifier that does not extend over both sides of a material biconditional *cannot* be broadened to cover both sides, nor can the scope of a quantifier that does cover both sides of a material biconditional be narrowed to cover only one side.

We conclude this section by symbolizing a series of increasingly complex sentences in *PL*. The first three are as follows:

1. Everyone who understands either Bertrand Russell's *Principia Mathematica* or Lewis Carroll's *Alice in Wonderland* understands this text.
2. No one understands everything.
3. No one understands anything.

For these and subsequent sentences we will use the following symbolization key:

UD: Everything
Exy: x envies y
Uxy: x understands y
Px: x is a person
a: Lewis Carroll's *Alice in Wonderland*
p: Bertrand Russell's *Principia Mathematica*
t: this text

In symbolizing these sentences we shall again use the procedure of moving gradually from English to symbols.

Sentence 1 is an A-sentence, so it will be symbolized as a universally quantified sentence. We can start with

Each x is such that, if x is a person and x understands either Bertrand Russell's *Principia Mathematica* or x understands Lewis Carroll's *Alice in Wonderland*, then x understands this text

and move to

(∀x) (if Px and x understands either Bertrand Russell's *Principia Mathematica* or Lewis Carroll's *Alice in Wonderland*, then x understands this text)

We can now see that we can complete our symbolization without using any more quantifiers:

$(\forall x)([Px \,\&\, (Uxp \vee Uxa)] \supset Uxt)$

Sentence 2 is an E-sentence. So we symbolize it as a universal quantification that says of each thing that if it is a person then it doesn't understand everything. That is,

> Each y is such that if y is a person then y does not understand everything.

Next we move to

> $(\forall y)(Py \supset$ it is not the case that y understands everything)

The remaining bit of English obviously goes over to '$\sim (\forall z)Uyz$', and so the entire sentence of *PL* is

$$(\forall y)(Py \supset \sim (\forall z)Uyz)$$

Sentence 2, 'No one understands everything', and sentence 3, 'No one understands anything', are very different claims. The former is certainly true and the latter certainly false. Sentence 3 can, however, also be paraphrased and symbolized as an E-sentence:

> Each x is such that if x is a person, then it is not the case that x understands anything.

This gives way to

> $(\forall x)(Px \supset$ it is not the case that there is something x understands)

for to not understand anything is for there not to be something one understands. So a full symbolization is

$$(\forall x)(Px \supset \sim (\exists y)Uxy)$$

An alternative symbolization is '$(\forall x)(Px \supset (\forall y) \sim Uxy)$', for to not understand anything is for each thing to be such that one does not understand it.

Now consider this sentence:

4. If someone understands Bertrand Russell's *Principia Mathematica,* then that person understands Lewis Carroll's *Alice in Wonderland.*

We here have one of the rare uses of 'someone' that goes over to a universal quantifier. This becomes apparent when we realize that there is pronominal cross-reference from the consequent of this English conditional (from the phrase 'that person') back to the quantity term in the antecedent ('someone'). Seeing this, it becomes clear that an appropriate paraphrase and symbolization are

> Each x is such that if x is a person and x understands Bertrand Russell's *Principia Mathematica,* then x understands Lewis Carroll's *Alice in Wonderland*

and

$$(\forall x)[(Px \; \& \; Uxp) \supset Uxa]$$

Sentence 5 is somewhat more complex:

5. Only people who understand either Bertrand Russell's *Principia Mathematica* or Lewis Carroll's *Alice in Wonderland* understand this text.

We have here a quantificational analog of an 'only if' claim of sentential logic. That is, we are told, not that all those persons who understand either of the works in question understand this text, but rather that those who do understand this text also understand one of the other cited works. An appropriate paraphrase is thus

> Each y is such that if y is a person and y understand this text then y understands either Bertrand Russell's *Principia Mathematica* or Lewis Carroll's *Alice in Wonderland.*

And a correct symbolization is

$$(\forall y)([(Py \; \& \; Uyt) \supset (Uyp \vee Uya)]$$

In subsequent chapters we shall establish that this is equivalent to

$$(\forall y)[Py \; \& \sim (Uyp \vee Uya)] \supset \sim Uyt)$$

but not to

$$(\forall y)([Py \; \& \; (Uyp \vee Uya)] \supset Uyt)$$

Symbolizing our sixth example requires the use of three quantifiers:

6. Anyone who understands anything is envied by someone.

The first occurrence of 'anyone' yields a universal quantifier because 'is envied by someone' refers back to it; that is, the person who is envied by someone is the person who understands anything. So a paraphrase is

> Each x is such that if x is a person and x understands anything then x is envied by someone.

In this context to understand anything is to understand at least one thing, so a fuller paraphrase is

> Each x is such that if x is a person and there is at least one y such that x understands y then there is some z such that z is a person and z envies x.

An appropriate symbolization is

$(\forall x)[(Px \ \& \ (\exists y)Uxy) \supset (\exists z)(Pz \ \& \ Ezx)]$

Consider, finally,

7. Anyone who understands everything is envied by everyone.

We will use three universal quantifiers in symbolizing this sentence. An appropriate paraphrase is

> Each x is such that if x is a person and every y is such that x understands y then every z is such that if z is a person, then z envies x.

This yields the following sentence of *PL*:

$(\forall x)[(Px \ \& \ (\forall y)Uxy) \supset (\forall z)(Pz \supset Ezx)]$

7.8E EXERCISES

1. Symbolize the following sentences in *PL* using the given symbolization key.

UD: People
Sx: x is a sailor
Lx: x is lucky
Cx: x is careless
Yx: x dies young
Sxy: x is a son of y
Dxy: x is a daughter of y
Wx: x is Wilcox
d: Daniel Wilcox
j: Jacob Wilcox
r: Rebecca Wilcox

a. Some sailors are both careless and lucky.
*b. Some careless sailors aren't lucky.
c. Not all lucky sailors are careless.
*d. All careless sailors, except the lucky ones, die young.

e. Not all sons of sailors are sailors.
*f. Not all daughters of sailors are sailors.
g. Not all sons and daughters of sailors are sailors.
*h. Sailors who aren't lucky and are careless have neither daughters nor sons.
i. Sailors who have either sons or daughters are lucky.
*j. Sailors who have both daughters and sons are lucky.
k. Rebecca Wilcox is either a sailor or the daughter of a sailor.
*l. Every Wilcox is either a sailor or the offspring of a sailor.
m. Either Rebecca Wilcox and all her children are sailors or Jacob Wilcox and all his children are sailors.

2. Symbolize the following sentences in *PL* using the given symbolization key.

UD: The employees of this college
Exy: x earns more than y
Dxy: x distrusts y
Fx: x is a faculty member
Ax: x is an administrator
Cx: x is a coach
Ux: x is a union member
Rx: x should be fired
Mx: x is an MD
Px: x is paranoid
Ox: x is a union officer
p: the president
j: Jones

a. Every administrator earns more than some faculty member, and every faculty member earns more than some administrator.
*b. If any administrator earns more than every faculty member, Jones does.
c. No faculty member earns more than the president.
*d. Any administrator who earns more than every faculty member should be fired.
e. No faculty member earns more than the president, but some coaches do.
*f. Not all faculty members are union members, but all union members are faculty members.
g. No administrator is a union member, but some are faculty members.
*h. Every faculty member who is an administrator earns more than some faculty members who are not administrators.
i. At least one administrator who is not a faculty member earns more than every faculty member who is an administrator.
*j. Every faculty member who is an MD earns more than every faculty member who is not an MD.
k. Some faculty members distrust every administrator, and some administrators distrust every faculty member.
*l. There is an administrator who is a faculty member and distrusts all administrators who are not faculty members.
m. Anyone who distrusts everyone is either paranoid or an administrator or a union officer.
*n. Everyone distrusts someone, but only administrators who are not faculty members distrust everyone.

3. Symbolize the following sentences in *PL* using the given symbolization key.

UD: Everything
Axyz: x understands y as well as does z
Bxy: x bores y
Gxy: x gives a low grade to y
Lxy: x listens to y
Sxy: x is a student of y
Nxy: x understands y
Dx: x deserves to be fired
Px: x is a professor
Ux: x is unpopular
Wx: x is wasting x's time
t: this text

a. All professors bores some of their students.
*b. All professors who bore all their students deserve to be fired.
c. Any professor who is bored by everything bores all his or her students.
*d. Professors bore all and only those of their students they are bored by.
e. If all professors bore all their students, then all professors are wasting their time.
*f. If a professor bores a student, then both are wasting their time.
g. Professors don't understand the students they bore, and students don't listen to the professors they are bored by.
*h. No professor understands everything.
i. Some professors bore all professors.
*j. An unpopular professor either bores or gives a low grade to each of his or her students.
k. Unpopular professors either bore all of their students or give all of their students low grades.
*l. If a professor doesn't listen to a student, then that student is wasting his or her time.
m. If a student and his or her professor bore each other, then both are wasting their time.
*n. Some professors don't understand this text.
o. Some professors don't understand this text as well as some of their students do.
*p. No professor who understands this text bores any of his or her students.
q. Any student who doesn't listen to his or her professor doesn't understand that professor and bores that professor.

4. Construct fluent English readings for the following sentences of *PL* using the given symbolization key.

UD: Everything (including times)
Lxyz: x loves y at z
Px: x is a person
Tx: x is a time
h: Hildegard
m: Manfred
s: Siegfried

a. $(\exists x)(Tx \,\&\, Lhmx)$
*b. $(\forall y)[(Ty \,\&\, Lmhy) \supset Lhmy]$
c. $(\exists w)(Tw \,\&\, Lmha) \,\&\, (\forall z)(Tz \supset Lmsz)$
*d. $(\forall x)(Tx \supset Lshx)$
e. $(\exists x)(Tx \,\&\, Lmmx) \supset (\forall x)[(Tx \,\&\, Lhmx) \supset Lmmx]$
*f. $(\forall x)[Px \supset (\exists y)(Ty \,\&\, \sim (\exists z)(Pz \,\&\, Lzxy))]$
g. $(\exists x)[Px \,\&\, \sim (\exists y)(\exists z)(Ty \,\&\, (Pz \,\&\, Lzxy))]$
*h. $(\forall x)[Tx \supset (\exists y)(Py \,\&\, \sim (\exists z)(Pz \,\&\, Lzyx))]$
i. $(\exists x)[Tx \,\&\, (\exists y)(Py \,\&\, (\forall z)(Pz \supset Lyzx))]$
*j. $(\forall x)[Tx \supset (\exists y)(\exists z)((Py \,\&\, Pz) \,\&\, Lyzx)]$
k. $(\forall x)[Tx \supset (\exists y)(Py \,\&\, (\forall z)(Pz \supset Lyzx))]$
*l. $(\forall x)[Px \supset (\exists y)(\exists z)((Py \,\&\, Tz) \,\&\, Lxyz)]$
m. $\sim (\exists x)(\exists y)[(Px \,\&\, Py) \,\&\, (\forall z)(Tz \supset Lxyz)]$
*n. $(\exists x)[Px \,\&\, (\forall y)(\forall z)((Ty \,\&\, Pz) \supset Lxzy)]$
o. $(\forall x)[Px \supset (\exists y)(Ty \,\&\, Lxxy)]$

5. Use the following symbolization key to translate sentences a–r into fluent English. (*Note:* All of the following claims are true.)

UD: Positive integers
Dxy: the sum of x and y is odd
Exy: x times y is even
Lxy: x is larger than y
Oxy: x times y is odd
Sxy: x plus y is even
Ex: x is even
Ox: x is odd
Px: x is prime
Pxy: x times y is prime
a: 1
b: 2
c: 3

a. $(\forall x)[Ex \supset (\forall y)Exy]$
*b. $(\forall x)(\forall y)[(Ox \,\&\, Oy) \supset Oxy]$
c. $(\forall x)(\forall y)[Sxy \supset [(Ex \,\&\, Ey) \vee (Ox \,\&\, Oy)]]$
*d. $(\forall x)[(Px \,\&\, (\exists y)(Py \,\&\, Lxy)) \supset Ox]$
e. $\sim (\exists y)[Py \,\&\, (\forall x)(Px \supset Lyx)]$
*f. $(\forall y)(\forall z)([(Py \,\&\, Pz) \,\&\, (Lyb \,\&\, Lzb)] \supset Oyz)$
g. $\sim (\exists x)(\exists y)[(Px \,\&\, Py) \,\&\, Pxy]$
*h. $(\exists x)(Px \,\&\, Ex)$
i. $(\exists x)[Px \,\&\, (\forall y)Eyx]$
*j. $\sim (\forall x)(\exists y)Lxy \,\&\, (\forall x)(\exists y)Lyx$
k. $(\forall x)(\forall y)[Oxy \equiv (Ox \,\&\, Oy)]$
*l. $(\forall x)(\forall y)[Exy \equiv (Ex \vee Ey)]$
m. $(\forall x)(\forall y)[(Ox \,\&\, Oy) \supset (Oxy \,\&\, Sxy)]$
*n. $(\forall x)(\forall y)(Lxy \supset \sim Lyx)$
o. $(\forall x)(\forall y)[(Ox \,\&\, Ey) \supset (Dxy \,\&\, Exy)]$
*p. $(\forall x)(\forall y)[[(Px \,\&\, Py) \,\&\, Lcx] \supset Exy]$
q. $(\exists y)[(Lya \,\&\, Lcy) \,\&\, (Py \,\&\, Ey)]$
*r. $(\exists x)[(Px \,\&\, Ex) \,\&\, (\forall y)((Py \,\&\, Lyx) \supset Oy)]$

7.9 IDENTITY, DEFINITE DESCRIPTIONS, PROPERTIES OF RELATIONS, AND FUNCTIONS

Our standard reading of 'some' is 'at least one'. Some may object that this is not an accurate reading, that 'some' sometimes means something like 'at least two'. It is alleged, for example, that to say

There are still some apples in the basket

when there is only one apple in the basket is at best misleading and at worst false. In any event we clearly do want a means of symbolizing such claims as

There are at least two apples in the basket.

We can do this by interpreting one of the two-place predicates of *PL* as expressing the identity relation. For example, we could interpret 'Ixy' as 'x is identical with y'. Given the symbolization key

UD:	Everything
Nxy:	x is in y
Ixy:	x is identical with y
Ax:	x is an apple
b:	the basket

both

(∃x) (Ax & Nxb)

and

(∃x) [(Ax & Nxb) & (∃y) (Ay & Nyb)]

say 'There is at least one apple in the basket'. The latter merely says it twice, so to speak. But

(∃x) (∃y) ([(Ax & Ay) & (Nxb & Nyb)] & ~ Ixy)

does say 'There are at least two apples in the basket'. This sentence of *PL* says, in quasi-English, 'There is an x and there is a y such that both x and y are apples, both x and y are in the basket, and x and y are not identical'. This last clause is not redundant because using different variables does not commit us to there being more than one thing of the specified sort.

An alternative to interpreting one of the two-place predicates of *PL* as expressing identity is to introduce a special two-place predicate and specify that it *always* be interpreted as expressing the identity relation. This is the course we shall follow. In adding this predicate to *PL*, we generate a new language, *PLE*. As an extension of *PL*, it includes all the vocabulary of *PL* and an additional two-place predicate. *PLE* also includes, as we detail later in this section, functors (used to express functions). The formulas and sentences of *PL* are also formulas and sentences of *PLE*.

The new two-place predicate that is distinctive of *PLE* is the identity predicate,

=″

When using this predicate we shall, as we have been doing with other predicates, omit the two primes as the number of individual terms used (two) will show that this is a two-place predicate. This predicate is always interpreted as the identity predicate. For example, '= ab' says that a is identical to b. However, it is customary to write, informally, 'a = b', rather than '= ab'—that is to place one individual term before the predicate and one after it—and we shall follow this custom.

So, instead of '= ab', ' = xy', and ' = aa', we write 'a = b', 'x = y', and 'a = a'. And in place of, for example, '~ = ab', we write '~ a = b'. Since the interpretation of '=' is fixed, we never have to include an interpretation of this predicate in a symbolization key.

We can now symbolize 'There are at least two apples in the basket' in *PLE*, using the preceding symbolization key (but dispensing with the now superfluous 'Ixy'), as

(∃x) (∃y) ([(Ax & Ay) & (Nxb & Nyb)] & ~ x = y)

In *PLE* we can also say that there are just so many apples in the basket and no more—for example, that there is exactly one apple in the basket. An appropriate paraphrase is

> <u>There is</u> a y such that y is an apple <u>and</u> y is in the basket, <u>and</u> <u>each thing</u> z is such that <u>if</u> z is an apple <u>and</u> is in the basket <u>then</u> z is identical with y.

A full symbolization is

(∃y) [(Ay & Nyb) & (∀z) [(Az & Nzb) ⊃ z = y]]

What we are saying is that there is at least one apple in the basket and that anything that is an apple and is in the basket is *that very apple*.

Consider next

Henry hasn't read *Alice in Wonderland* but everyone else in the class has.

If we limit our universe of discourse to the students in the class in question, let 'h' designate Henry, and interpret 'Ax' as 'x has read *Alice in Wonderland*', we can symbolize this claim as

$$\sim Ah \ \& \ (\forall y)[\sim y = h \supset Ay]$$

And, using 'b' to designate Bob, we can symbolize 'Only Henry and Bob have not read *Alice in Wonderland*', as

$$\sim (Ah \vee Ab) \ \& \ (\forall x)[\sim (x = h \vee x = b) \supset Ax]$$

This says that neither Henry nor Bob has read *Alice in Wonderland* and that everyone else—that is, each person in the class who is neither identical to Henry nor identical to Bob—has read it.

We can also use the identity predicate to symbolize the following sentences of *PLE*:

1. There are apples and pears in the basket.
2. The only pear in the basket is rotten.
3. There are at least two apples in the basket.
4. There are two (and only two) apples in the basket.
5. There are no more than two pears in the basket.
6. There are at least three apples in the basket.

UD:	Everything
Ax:	x is an apple
Nxy:	x is in y
Px:	x is a pear
Rx:	x is rotten
b:	the basket

If we paraphrase sentence 1 as 'There is at least one apple and at least one pear in the basket', we can symbolize it without using the identity predicate:

$$(\exists x)(\exists y)[(Ax \ \& \ Py) \ \& \ (Nxb \ \& \ Nyb)]$$

However, if we take sentence 1 to assert that there are at least two apples and at least two pears in the basket, we do need the identity predicate:

$$(\exists x)(\exists y)[((Ax \ \& \ Ay) \ \& \ (Nxb \ \& \ Nyb)) \ \& \sim x = y] \ \&$$
$$(\exists x)(\exists y)[((Px \ \& \ Py) \ \& \ (Nxb \ \& \ Nyb)) \ \& \sim x = y]$$

Sentence 2 says that there is one and only one pear in the basket and that that one pear is rotten:

$$(\exists x)[((Px \& Nxb) \& Rx) \& (\forall y)[(Py \& Nyb) \supset y = x]]$$

Sentence 3 says only that there are *at least* two apples in the basket, not that there are *exactly* two. Hence

$$(\exists x)(\exists y)[((Ax \& Ay) \& (Nxb \& Nyb)) \& \sim x = y]$$

To symbolize sentence 4 we start with the symbolization for sentence 3 and add a clause saying there are no additional apples in the basket:

$$(\exists x)(\exists y)([((Ax \& Ay) \& (Nxb \& Nyb)) \& \sim x = y] \& \\ (\forall z)[(Az \& Nzb) \supset (z = x \vee z = y)])$$

The added clause says, in effect, 'and anything that is an apple and is in the basket is either x or y'. Sentence 5 does not say that there are two pears in the basket; rather, it says that there are *at most* two pears in the basket. We can express this in *PLE* by saying that of any pears, x, y, and z that are in the basket these are really at most two; that is, either x is identical to y, or x is identical to z, or y is identical to z. In other words

$$(\forall x)(\forall y)(\forall z)[([(Px \& Py) \& Pz] \& [(Nxb \& Nyb) \& Nzb]) \supset \\ ((x = y \vee x = z) \vee y = z)]$$

A shorter version is

$$(\forall x)(\forall y)(\forall z)[([(Px \& Py) \& Pz] \& [(Nxb \& Nyb) \& Nzb]) \supset \\ (z = x \vee z = y)]$$

This says, in effect, that any alleged third pear, z, is not a third pear but is the very same pear as either x or y. Finally sentence 6 can be symbolized by building on the symbolization for sentence 3:

$$(\exists x)(\exists y)(\exists z)(([(Ax \& Ay) \& Az] \& [(Nxb \& Nyb) \& Nzb]) \& \\ [(\sim x = y \& \sim y = z) \& \sim x = z)$$

We now return to our discussion of positive integers. This time we will use this symbolization key for the sentences that follow.

UD: Positive integers
Bxyz: x is between y and z
Lxy: x is larger than y
Sxy: x is a successor of y
Ex: x is even

Px: x is prime
a: 1
b: 2
c: 10
d: 14

1. There is no largest positive integer.
2. There is a unique smallest positive integer.
3. 2 is the only even prime.
4. There are exactly two primes between 10 and 14.
5. Every positive integer has exactly one successor.
6. 2 is the only prime whose successor is prime.

As we saw in our earlier discussion, we can symbolize sentence 1 without using the identity predicate, for to say that there is no largest positive integer it suffices to say that for every integer there is a larger integer (no matter what integer one might pick, there is an integer larger than it):

$$(\forall x)(\exists y)Lyx$$

It is also tempting to symbolize sentence 2 without using the identity predicate, for to say that there is a smallest positive integer seems to be to say that there is an integer that is not larger than any integer:

$$(\exists x) \sim (\exists y)Lxy$$

But while the foregoing does say that there is a smallest positive integer, it does not say that there is a unique such integer. So a better symbolization is

$$(\exists x)(\forall y)(\sim y = x \supset Lyx)$$

This sentence of *PL* says that there is an integer such that every integer not identical to it is larger than it. This does imply uniqueness.

Sentence 3, '2 is the only even prime', says that 2 is prime and is even and that all other primes are not even:

2 is prime <u>and</u> 2 is even, <u>and</u> <u>each</u> z is such that <u>if</u> z is prime <u>and</u> z is <u>not</u> identical with 2 <u>then</u> z is <u>not</u> even.

In *PLE*

$$(Pb \mathbin{\&} Eb) \mathbin{\&} (\forall z)[(Pz \mathbin{\&} \sim z = b) \supset \sim Ez]$$

This is equivalent to

$$(Pb \mathbin{\&} Eb) \mathbin{\&} (\forall z)[(Pz \mathbin{\&} Ez) \supset z = b]$$

Notice that we could equally well have paraphrased and symbolized sentence 3 as

> 2 is prime and 2 is even, and it is not the case that there is a z such that z is prime and z is even, and z is not identical with 2

and symbolized this claim as

$$(Pb \& Eb) \& \sim (\exists z)[(Pz \& Ez) \& \sim z = b]$$

Notice, too, that all three symbolic versions of sentence 3 are truth-functional compounds, not quantified sentences.

To symbolize sentence 4, 'There are exactly two primes between 10 and 14', we must say that there are at least two such primes and that there are no additional ones. So our paraphrase starts

> There is an x and there is a y such that x is prime and y is prime, x is between 10 and 14 and y is between 10 and 14, and x is not identical with y, . . .

This much can be symbolized as

$$(\exists x)(\exists y)((Px \& Py) \& [(Bxcd \& Bycd) \& \sim x = y])$$

What we now need to add is that any prime that is between 10 and 14 is one of these two primes:

> Each z is such that if z is prime and z is between 10 and 14 then z is either x or y.

That is,

$$(\forall z)[(Pz \& Bzcd) \supset (z = x \vee z = y)]$$

In joining the two fragments of our symbolization, we must be sure to extend the scope of our two existential quantifiers over the entire sentence, for we want to bind the occurrences of 'x' and 'y' in the last half of the sentence:

$$(\exists x)(\exists y)[((Px \& Py) \& [(Bxcd \& Bycd) \& \sim x = y]) \& \\ (\forall z)[(Pz \& Bzcd) \supset (z = x \vee z = y)]]$$

It is perhaps worth noting here that we could have symbolized sentence 4 without using the three-place predicate 'Bxyz'. To see this, note that to say a positive integer x is between 10 and 14 is just to say that x is larger than 10 and that 14 is larger than x. An appropriate symbolization is

$$(\exists x)(\exists y)[((Px \& Py) \& [((Lxc \& Ldx) \& (Lyc \& Ldy)) \& \sim x = y]) \& \\ (\forall z)([Pz \& (Lzc \& Ldz)] \supset (z = x \vee z = y))]$$

A successor of an integer is the sum of that integer and 1. Sentence 5, 'Every positive integer has exactly one successor', can be symbolized as

$$(\forall x)(\exists y)[Syx \;\&\; (\forall z)(Szx \supset z = y)]$$

This says that each positive integer x has a successor y and that any integer that is a successor of x is identical to y—that is, that each positive integer has exactly one successor.

Sentence 6, '2 is the only prime whose (only) successor is prime', can be paraphrased as a conjunction:

> 2 is prime and its only successor is prime, and any successor of any prime other than 2 is not prime.

The first conjunct can be symbolized as

$$Pb \;\&\; (\exists x)[(Sxb \;\&\; (\forall y)(Syb \supset y = x)) \;\&\; Px]$$

The second conjunct can be symbolized as

$$(\forall x)(\forall y)[(Sxy \;\&\; (Py \;\&\; \sim y = b)) \supset \sim Px]$$

Putting these together we obtain

$$(Pb \;\&\; (\exists x)[(Sxb \;\&\; (\forall y)(Syb \supset y = x)) \;\&\; Px]) \;\&\; (\forall x)(\forall y)[(Sxy \;\&\; (Py \;\&\; \sim y = b)) \supset \sim Px]$$

DEFINITE DESCRIPTIONS

In Section 7.1 we noted that there are two kinds of singular terms in English: proper names and definite descriptions. We subsequently noted that individual constants of *PL* can be used to symbolize both kinds of singular terms of English. But following this practice means that the internal structure of definite descriptions is not represented in *PL*. Consider, by way of illustration, this argument:

> The Roman general who defeated Pompey invaded both Gaul and Germany. Therefore Pompey was defeated by someone who invaded both Gaul and Germany.

This is fairly obviously a valid argument. But its symbolization in *PL* is not valid:

UD:	Persons and countries
Ixy:	x invaded y
Dxy:	x defeated y
r:	The Roman general who defeated Pompey
p:	Pompey
g:	Gaul
e:	Germany

Treating 'The Roman general who defeated Pompey' as an unanalyzable unit, to be symbolized by 'r', and paraphrasing the conclusion as 'There is an x such that x defeated Pompey and invaded Gaul and invaded Germany' yields this argument:

$$\begin{array}{l} \text{Irg} \;\&\; \text{Ire} \\ \hline (\exists \text{x})\,[\text{Dxp} \;\&\; (\text{Ixg} \;\&\; \text{Ixe})] \end{array}$$

The techniques we develop for testing arguments of *PL* will show that this argument of *PL* is invalid. This should not be surprising, for the premise tells us only that the thing designated by 'r' invaded both Gaul and Germany; it does not tell us that that thing is a thing that defeated Pompey, as the conclusion claims.

By using the identity predicate we can capture the structure of definite descriptions within *PLE*. Suppose we paraphrase the first premise of the preceding argument as

> There is exactly one thing that is a Roman general and defeated Pompey, and that thing invaded both Gaul and Germany.

Definite descriptions are, after all, descriptions that purport to specify conditions that are satisfied by exactly one thing. Using the symbolization key, plus 'Rx' for 'x is a Roman general', we can symbolize the first premise as

$$(\exists \text{x})\,[[(\text{Rx} \;\&\; \text{Dxp}) \;\&\; (\forall \text{y})\,[(\text{Ry} \;\&\; \text{Dyp}) \supset \text{y} = \text{x}]] \;\&\; (\text{Ixg} \;\&\; \text{Ixe})]$$

We shall later show that in *PLE* the conclusion '$(\exists x)[Dxp \,\&\, (Ixg \,\&\, Ixe)]$' does follow from this premise.

By transforming definite descriptions into unique existence claims, that is, claims that there is exactly one object of such-and-such a sort, we gain the further benefit of being able to symbolize English language definite descriptions that may, in fact, not designate anything. For example, taking the UD to be persons and using 'Dxy' for 'x is a daughter of y', 'Bx' for 'x is a biochemist', and 'j' to designate John, we might symbolize 'John's only daughter is a biochemist' as

$$(\exists \text{x})\,[(\text{Dxj} \;\&\; (\forall \text{y})\,(\text{Dyj} \supset \text{y} = \text{x})) \;\&\; \text{Bx}]$$

If it turns out that John has no, or more than one, daughter, or that his only daughter is not a biochemist, the above sentence of *PLE* will be false, not meaningless or truth-valueless. This is an acceptable result.

PROPERTIES OF RELATIONS

Identity is a relation with three rather special properties. First, identity is a *transitive* relation. That is, if an object x is identical with an object y, and y is identical with an object z, then x is identical with z. The following sentence of *PLE* says, in effect, that identity is transitive:

$$(\forall x)(\forall y)(\forall z)[(x = y \ \& \ y = z) \supset x = z]$$

Many relations other than identity are also transitive relations. The predicates

x is larger than y
x is taller than y
x is an ancestor of y
x is heavier than y
x occurs before y

all express transitive relations. But, 'x is a friend of y' does not represent a transitive relation. That is, 'Any friend of a friend of mine is a friend of mine' is a substantive claim, and one that is generally false. Where **x**, **y**, and **z** are all variables of *PL* or *PLE* and **A** is a two-place predicate of *PL* or *PLE*, the following says that **A** expresses a transitive relation:

$$(\forall \mathbf{x})(\forall \mathbf{y})(\forall \mathbf{z})[(\mathbf{Axy} \ \& \ \mathbf{Ayz}) \supset \mathbf{Axz}]$$

Identity is also a *symmetric* relation; that is, if an object x is identical with an object y, then y is identical with x. The following says that identity is a symmetric relation:

$$(\forall x)(\forall y)(Axy \supset Ayx)$$

The following predicates also express symmetric relations:

x is a sibling of y
x is a classmate of y
x is a relative of y
x has the same father as does y

Note that neither 'x is a sister of y' nor 'x loves y' expresses a symmetric relation. Jane Fonda is a sister of Peter Fonda, but Peter Fonda is not a sister of Jane Fonda. And, alas, it may be that Manfred loves Hildegard even though Hildegard does not love Manfred.

A relation is *reflexive* if and only if each object stands in that relation to itself. In *PL* and *PLE* the following says that **A** expresses a reflexive relation:

$$(\forall \mathbf{x})\mathbf{Axx}$$

Identity is a reflexive relation. In an unrestricted UD it is rather hard to find other reflexive relations. For example, a little thought should show that none of the following expresses a reflexive relation in an unrestricted universe of discourse:

x is the same age as y
x is the same height as y
x is in the same place as y

Since the number 48 is not of any age, it is not the same age as itself nor the same height as itself. Numbers have neither age nor height, though inscriptions of numerals usually have both. So, too, neither the number 93 nor the set of human beings is in any place. Numbers and sets do not have spatial positions; hence neither is in the same place as itself. However, the relations just discussed are reflexive relations in suitably restricted universes of discourse. For example, if the universe of discourse consists exclusively of people, then

x is the same age as y

expresses a reflexive relation (it is also transitive and symmetric). Every person is the same age as him- or herself. In this restricted universe 'x is the same height as y' and 'x is in the same place as y' also represent reflexive relations. Each person is the same height as him- or herself and is in the same place as him- or herself. And, if the universe of discourse is restricted to the positive integers, then

x is evenly divisible by y

expresses a reflexive relation, for every positive integer is evenly divisible by itself. This relation is not symmetric (not every positive integer evenly divides all the positive integers it is evenly divisible by). However, 'x is evenly divisible by y' does express a transitive relation.

FUNCTIONS

A *function* is an operation that takes one or more element of a set as arguments and returns a single value. *Addition, subtraction, multiplication, square,* and *successor* are all common functions of arithmetic. Each returns, for each number or pair of numbers, a single value. *Addition* takes a pair of numbers as arguments and returns their sum; *multiplication* takes a pair of numbers and returns the product of those numbers; *subtraction* returns, for each pair of numbers, the first number minus the second. The *square* function returns, for each number, the result of multiplying that number by itself; the *successor* function returns, for any positive integer **n**, the integer **n** + 1.

Not all functions are arithmetic functions. We have already encountered truth-functions—functions that map values from the set consisting of the truth-values (the set {**T**, **F**}) to truth-values. *Negation* is a function of one argument that returns **F** when given **T** as an argument and returns **T** when given **F** as an argument. *Conjunction, disjunction,* the *material conditional,* and the *material biconditional* are all functions that take two arguments (two truth-values) and return a single truth-value. Characteristic truth-tables display the value of each of these functions for each pair of truth-values.

Functions are also found outside of formal logic and mathematics. Consider a set of monogamously married individuals.[13] Here *spouse* is a function that takes a single member of the set as an argument and returns that person's spouse as its value. For the set of all twins, the function *twin* returns, for each member of the set, that member's twin. In *PLE* we shall use lowercase italicized Roman letters *a–z,* with or without a positive-integer subscript, followed by one or more prime marks to symbolize functions. We call these symbols *functors.* Where **n** is the number of prime marks after the functor, the function assigned to the functor takes **n** arguments. For example, in talking about the set of positive integers, we might assign the successor function to the functor *f*.[14] We specify this assignment in a symbolization key much the way we have been assigning interpretations to predicates. The following symbolization key assigns the successor function to f':

UD:	Positive integers
$f'(x)$:	the successor of x
Ex:	x is even
Ox:	x is odd
a:	2
b:	3

The variable x in parentheses indicates that we are assigning to f' a function that takes a single argument. The expression to the right of the colon assigns the successor function to f'. Given the above symbolization key,

$$\text{Ob}$$

says 3 is odd. The sentence

$$\text{O}f'(\text{a})$$

says the successor of 2, which is 3, is odd. Both claims are, of course, true. And

$$f'(\text{a}) = \text{b}$$

says the successor of 2 is 3, which it is. Similarly,

$$(\exists \text{x})\text{O}f'(\text{x}) \ \& \ (\exists \text{x})\text{E}f'(\text{x})$$

[13]The example is from Geoffrey Hunter, *Metalogic: An Introduction to the Metatheory of Standard First Order Logic* (Berkeley: University of California Press, 1973).

[14]It is customary to use, where only a few functors are needed, the letters '*f*', '*g*', '*h*', . . . We will follow this custom.

says there is a positive integer whose successor is odd and there is a positive integer whose successor is even. We can also use the symbolization key to symbolize 'The successor of an even number is odd'. A first step is the quasi-English

$(\forall x)(Ex \supset \text{the successor of x is odd})$

The successor of x is $f'(x)$, so the full symbolization is

$(\forall x)(Ex \supset Of'(x))$

We can add the following to our symbolization key

$h''(x,y)$: the sum of x and y

and symbolize 'The sum of an even number and an odd number is odd' as

$(\forall x)(\forall y)[(Ex \,\&\, Oy) \supset Oh''(x,y)]$

Since the number of distinct individual terms occurring within the parentheses after a functor indicates how many arguments the function assigned to that functor takes, we can informally omit the primes that officially follow functors, just as we do for predicate letters. Hereafter we will do so.

Returning to our example of the set of twins, we can use the following symbolization key

UD: Set of twins
$f(x)$: the twin of x
c: Cathy
h: Henry
j: Jose
s: Simone

to symbolize

Simone is Henry's twin

as

$s = f(h)$

and

Jose is Cathy's twin

as

$j = f(c)$

Using 'Bx' for 'x is bald', we can symbolize 'A twin is bald if and only if her or his twin is bald' as

$$(\forall x)[Bx \equiv Bf(x)]$$

and 'Some bald twins have twins that are not bald' as

$$(\exists x)Bx \,\&\, \sim Bf(x)$$

The symbolization

$$(\forall x)(\forall y)[(\exists z)(z = f(x) \,\&\, z = f(y)) \supset x = y]$$

says, in quasi-English, 'Any members of the UD x and y who are such that there is a z who is both a twin of x and a twin of y are in fact the same member of the UD', or 'No one is a twin of two different twins'.

We require that the functions we symbolize with functors have the following characteristics:

1. An **n**-place function must yield one and only one value for each **n**-tuple of arguments.[15]
2. The value of a function for an **n**-tuple of members of a UD must be a member of that UD.

If the UD is the set of integers, the square root operation does not meet condition 1 because it can yield more than one value for its arguments (there are two square roots of 4—2 and −2). (It also fails to meet condition 2 because not all square roots of integers are integers.) If the UD is the set of positive integers, the subtraction function does not meet condition 2, because when y is greater than x, x minus y yields a value that is not a positive integer (3 minus 9 is −6, and −6 is not a positive integer). Subtraction *does* meet condition 2 when the UD is the set of all integers—positive, zero, and negative. If the UD is the set of positive integers, division also fails to meet condition 2 (3 divided by 9 yields $\frac{1}{3}$, which is not a positive integer). Division *does* meet condition 2 when the UD is the set of positive rational numbers (positive integers plus numbers expressible as the ratio between positive integers). Finally division does not meet condition 1 when the UD is the set of *all* integers because it is undefined when the divisor is zero.

As we have just seen, functors can be used to generate a new kind of individual term (in addition to the individual constants and variables of *PL*). We call these new terms *complex terms*. Complex terms are of the form

$$f(\mathbf{t}_1, \mathbf{t}_2, \ldots \mathbf{t}_n)$$

[15] An **n**-tuple is an ordered set containing **n** members.

where f is an **n**-place functor and $\mathbf{t}_1, \mathbf{t}_2, \ldots \mathbf{t}_n$ are individual terms. Further examples of complex terms include

f(a,b)
h(a,b,c)
g(a)
f(b,b)
f(x,y)
f(a,y)
f(y,a)
g(x)
f(g(a),b)
f(a,g(x))

Complex terms are complex in that they are always formed from a functor and at least one individual term. Some complex terms contain variables, and some do not. We call individual terms that do not contain variables *closed terms,* and those that do *open terms.* This makes *both* individual constants and complex terms that contain no variables closed terms. Complex terms that do contain at least one variable, as well as variables themselves, are open terms. Individual terms that are not complex terms (the individual constants and individual variables) are *simple individual terms.* In the above list, the first four complex terms are closed, the next four open, the ninth closed, and the last open. Note the last two examples. In each, one of the individual terms from which the example is built is itself a complex term. This is wholly in order, as complex terms are individual terms and can occur anywhere a constant can occur. The kinds of individual terms included in *PLE* is summarized in the following table:

INDIVIDUAL TERMS OF *PLE*

	Open	*Closed*
Simple	Individual variables	Individual constants
Complex	Individual term formed from a functor and *at least one* individual variable—for example, f(x), f(a,x), g(f(a),y), g(h(x,y),a)	Individual term formed from a functor and containing *no* individual variable—for example, f(a), g(a,b), f(g(a,f(a,c)))

All of the following are formulas of *PLE*:

F af(x)
Ff(x)a
Ff(a)b
(∀x)Faf(x)
(∀x)(∃y)Fxf(y)

In each of these example 'F' is a two-place predicate. The first and second are formulas of *PLE* but are not sentences (because the x in 'f(x)' is not bound). The third, fourth, and fifth examples are all both formulas and sentences of *PLE*. The third says that f(a) bears the relation F to b. The fourth says that each thing x in the UD is such that a bears the relation F to f(x), that is, to the value of the function f as applied to x. The fifth says that each thing x in the UD is such that there is a thing y such that x bears the relation F to f(y). Every example contains a complex individual term, and all but the third an open complex individual term.

Consider this symbolization key:

UD:	Positive integers
Ox:	x is odd
Ex:	x is even
Px:	x is prime
Gxy:	x is greater than y
h(x,y):	the sum of x and y
f(x):	the successor of x
a:	1
b:	2

The sentence

$$(\forall x)[Ex \supset Of(x)]$$

says, truly, that each positive integer is such that if it is even then its successor is odd. And

$$(\forall x)[Ex \supset Ef(f(x))]$$

says, truly, that each positive integer is such that if it is even then the successor of its successor is also even. The sentence

$$(\forall x)(\forall y)[(Ex \& Ey) \supset Eh(x,y)]$$

can be read in quasi-English as 'For each x and each y, <u>if</u> both x and y are even, <u>then</u> the sum of x and y is even'. This is, of course, true.

Here are further sentences of *PLE* that can be read in English using the above symbolization key. The sentence

$$(\forall x)(\forall y)[Gh(x,y)x \& Gh(x,y)y]$$

says that for any positive integers x and y the sum of x and y is greater than x, and the sum of x and y is greater than y. This is true. The sentence

$$(\exists x)Gxh(a,b)$$

says that there is a positive integer, x, that is greater than the sum of 1 and 2—that is, there is a positive integer that is greater than 3. This is also true. The sentence

$$(\forall x)(\forall y)[(Ex \ \& \ Oy) \supset Oh(x,y)]$$

says that, for any pair of positive integers x and y, if the first is even and the second is odd, then their sum is odd. This is true as well. Finally the sentence

$$(\forall x)(\forall y)[Ph(x,y) \supset \sim (Px \ \& \ Py)]$$

says that, for any pair of positive integers, if their sum is prime then it is not the case that they are both prime, or, in other words, that there are no prime numbers x and y such that their sum is also prime. This sentence is false; 2 and 3 are both prime, and so is their sum, 5.

THE SYNTAX OF PLE

The language of *PLE* is an expansion of *PL* and as such includes all the vocabulary of *PL*. Every formula of *PL* is a formula of *PLE*, and every sentence of *PL* is a sentence of *PLE*. The vocabulary of *PLE* also includes

=": The two-place identity predicate (fixed interpretation)

Functors of PLE: Lowercase italicized Roman letters *a, b, c*, . . . , with or without a numeric subscript, followed by **n** primes.

Individual terms of PLE:

Individual constants are individual terms of *PLE*

Individual variables are individual terms of *PLE*

Expressions of the form $f(\mathbf{t}_1, \mathbf{t}_2, \ldots \mathbf{t}_\mathbf{n})$, where f is an **n**-place functor and $\mathbf{t}_1, \mathbf{t}_2, \ldots, \mathbf{t}_\mathbf{n})$ are individual terms of *PLE*, are individual terms of *PLE*

We can classify the individual terms of *PLE* as follows:

Simple terms of PLE: The individual constants and individual variables of *PLE*

Complex terms of PLE: Individual terms of the form $f(\mathbf{t}_1, \mathbf{t}_2, \ldots, \mathbf{t}_\mathbf{n})$, where f is an **n**-place functor

Closed individual term: An individual term in which no variable occurs

Open individual term: An individual term in which at least one variable occurs

Individual variables and functors that contain at least one individual variable are thus open terms. Individual constants and functors that contain no variables are thus closed terms.

In *PLE* a substitution instance is defined as follows:

Substitution instance of **P**: If **P** is a sentence of *PLE* of the form $(\forall \mathbf{x})\mathbf{Q}$ or $(\exists \mathbf{x})\mathbf{Q}$ and **t** is a closed individual term, then $\mathbf{Q}(\mathbf{t}/\mathbf{x})$ is a substitution instance of **P**. The individual term **t** is the *instantiating individual term.*

Note that every substitution instance of a sentence of *PL* is also a substitution instance of that same sentence in *PLE.*

7.9E EXERCISES

1. Symbolize the following sentences in *PLE* using the symbolization key given in Exercise 1 in Section 7.8E.

a. Every Wilcox except Daniel is a sailor.
*b. Every Wilcox except Daniel is the offspring of a sailor.
c. Every Wilcox except Daniel is either a sailor or the offspring of sailor.
*d. Daniel is the only son of Jacob.
e. Daniel is the only child of Jacob.
*f. All the Wilcoxes except Daniel are sailors.
g. Rebecca's only son is Jacob's only son.
*h. Rebecca Wilcox has only one son who is a sailor.
i. Rebecca Wilcox has at least two daughters who are sailors.
*j. There are two and only two sailors in the Wilcox family.
k. Jacob Wilcox has one son and two daughters, and they are all sailors.

2. Give fluent English readings for the following sentences of *PLE* using the given symbolization key.

UD:	Positive integers
Lxy:	x is less than y
Gxy:	x is greater than y
Ex:	x is even
Ox:	x is odd
Px:	x is prime
f(x,y):	the product of x and y
t:	2
f:	5
n:	9

a. $(\forall x)(\exists y)Lxy$
*b. $(\exists x)(\forall y)(\sim x = y \supset Lxy)$
c. $(\exists x)(\forall y) \sim Lyx$
*d. $\sim (\exists x)(Ex \;\&\; Lxt)$

e. $(Pt \,\&\, Et) \,\&\, (\forall x)[(Px \,\&\, Ex) \supset x = t]$
*f. $\sim (\exists x)(\exists y)[(Px \,\&\, Py) \,\&\, Pf(x,y)]$
g. $(\forall y)(\forall z)[(Oy \,\&\, Oz) \supset Of(y,z)]$
*h. $(\forall y)(\forall z)[(Ey \,\&\, Ez) \supset Ef(z,y)]$
i. $(\forall y)(\forall z)[(Ey \vee Ez) \supset Ef(y,z)]$
*j. $(\forall x)[Ex \supset (\exists y)(Oy \,\&\, Gxy)] \,\&\, \sim (\forall x)[Ox \supset (\exists y)(Ey \,\&\, Gxy)]$
k. $(\exists x)[[Px \,\&\, (Gxf \,\&\, Lxn)] \,\&\, (\forall y)([Py \,\&\, (Gyf \,\&\, Lyn)] \supset y = x)]$

3. For a–p, decide whether the specified relation is reflexive, whether it is symmetric, and whether it is transitive (in suitably restricted universes of discourse). In each case give the sentences of *PL* that assert the appropriate properties of the relation in question. If the relation is reflexive, symmetric, or reflexive in a restricted universe of discourse, specify such a universe of discourse.

a. Nxy: x is a neighbor of y
*b. Mxy: x is married to y
c. Axy: x admires y
*d. Nxy: x is north of y
e. Rxy: x is a relative of y
*f. Sxy: x is the same size as y
g. Txy: x is at least as tall as y
*h. Cxy: x coauthors a book with y
i. Exy: x enrolls in the same course as y
*j. Fxy: x fights y
k. Wxy: x weighs the same as y
*l. Cxy: x contracts with y
m. Axy: x is an ancestor of y
*n. Cxy: x is a cousin of y
o. Lxy: x and y have the same taste in food
*p. Rxy: x respects y

4. Symbolize the following sentences in *PLE* using the given symbolization key.

UD: People in Doreen's hometown
Dxy: x is a daughter of y
Sxy: x is a son of y
Bxy: x is a brother of y
Oxy: x is older than y
Mxy: x is married to y
Txy: x is taller than y
Px: x is a physician
Bx: x is a baseball player
Mx: x is a marine biologist
d: Doreen
c: Cory
j: Jeremy
h: Hal

a. Jeremy is Cory's son.
*b. Jeremy is Cory's only son.
c. Jeremy is Cory's oldest son.
*d. Doreen's only daughter is a physician.

e. Doreen's eldest daughter is a physician.
*f. Doreen is a physician and so is her eldest daughter.
g. Cory is Doreen's eldest daughter.
*h. Cory is married to Hal's only son.
i. Cory is married to Hal's tallest son.
*j. Doreen's eldest daughter is married to Hal's only son.
k. The only baseball player in town is the only marine biologist in town.
*l. The only baseball player in town is married to one of Jeremy's daughters.
m. Cory's husband is Jeremy's only brother.

5. Symbolize the following sentences in *PLE* using the given symbolization key.

UD:	Positive integers
Ox:	x is odd
Ex:	x is even
Px:	x is prime
a:	1
b:	2
f(x):	the successor of x
q(x):	x squared
t(x,y):	the product of x and y
s(x,y):	the sum of x and y

a. One is not the successor of any integer.
*b. One is not prime but its successor is.
c. There is a prime that is even.
*d. There is one and only one even prime.
e. Every integer has a successor.
*f. The square of a prime is not prime.
g. The successor of an odd integer is even.
*h. The successor of an even integer is odd.
i. If the product of a pair of positive integers is odd, then the product of the successors of those integers is even.
*j. If the product of a pair of positive integers is even, then one of those integers is even.
k. If the sum of a pair of positive integers is odd, then one member of the pair is odd and the other member is even.
*l. If the sum of a pair of positive integers is even, then either both members of the pair are even or both members are odd.
m. The product of a pair of prime integers is not prime.
*n. There are no primes such that their product is prime.
o. The square of an even number is even and the square of an odd number is odd.
*p. The successor of the square of an even number is odd.
q. The successor of the square of an odd number is even.
*r. 2 is the only even prime.
s. The sum of 2 and a prime other than 2 is odd.
*t. There is exactly one integer that is prime and is the successor of a prime.
u. There is a pair of primes such that their product is the successor of their sum.

Chapter **8**

PREDICATE LOGIC: SEMANTICS

8.1 INFORMAL SEMANTICS FOR *PL*

The basic semantic concept for the language of sentential logic, *SL*, is that of a truth-value assignment. The semantics for *PL* is more complex than truth-functional semantics. One source of the added complexity is this: Whereas the atomic sentences of *SL* are not analyzable in terms of more basic linguistic units of *SL*, the same does not hold for all atomic sentences of *PL*. Some atomic sentences of *PL*, such as 'Fa', are themselves complex expressions composed of predicates and individual constants. Consequently we do not directly assign truth-values to all the atomic sentences of *PL*; only the sentence letters are directly assigned truth-values. The truth-values of complex atomic sentences like 'Fa' depend on the interpretations of the predicates and individual constants that constitute such sentences. The basic semantic concept of *PL*, in terms of which other semantic concepts are defined, is that of an *interpretation*. Just as truth-value assignments for *SL* assign truth-values to every sentence of *SL*, an interpretation interprets *every* individual constant, predicate, and sentence letter of *PL*. Usually, however, we shall be interested only in that part of an interpretation that affects the truth-value of a particular sentence or set of sentences that we are looking at.

We can view the symbolization keys for sentences presented in Chapter 7 as embodying interpretations for those sentences. That is, the truth-conditions of sentences of *PL* are dependent upon the choice of universe of discourse and upon how each of the predicates and individual constants in the sentences is interpreted. In this section we shall discuss in an informal manner how interpretations determine the truth-conditions of sentences, appealing to the readings of sentences of *PL* that were used in Chapter 7.

Let us start with an example of an atomic sentence of *PL*: 'Fa'. Whether this sentence is true depends on how we interpret the predicate 'F' and the individual constant 'a'. If we interpret them as follows:

Fx: x is human
a: Socrates

then 'Fa' is true, for Socrates was human. But if we interpret them as

Fx: x is a potato
a: Socrates

then 'Fa' is false, for Socrates was not a potato. Similarly the truth-value of the sentence 'Bdc' depends upon the interpretation of the expressions that constitute the sentence. If we interpret them as

Bxy: x is bigger than y
c: the Statue of Liberty
d: the Empire State Building

then 'Bdc', which may be read as 'The Empire State Building is bigger than the Statue of Liberty', is true. But with the following interpretations:

Bxy: x is bigger than y
c: the moon
d: the Empire State Building

'Bdc' is false. The Empire State Building is not bigger than the moon.

Predicates are interpreted relative to a *universe of discourse.* Recall that a universe of discourse (UD) is simply a nonempty set. We may choose the set of natural numbers, the set of all people, the set of words in this chapter, the set of all the objects in the world, the set containing only Mark Twain, or any other nonempty set as the UD when we specify an interpretation. The UD that we choose includes all and only those things that we want to interpret sentences of *PL* as being about. Once we specify the UD, our interpretations of predicates are interpretations relative to that UD. For example, if an interpretation includes

UD: Set of living creatures
Fx: x is human

then 'F' picks out all the living creatures in the UD that are human. We call the set of those things that the predicate picks out the *extension* of the predicate for the interpretation. If an interpretation includes

UD: Set of living creatures in San Francisco
Fx: x is human

then the predicate 'F' picks out all those living creatures in San Francisco that are human. The set of such creatures is the extension of the predicate 'F'. And if an interpretation includes

UD: Set of living creatures
Fx: x is an automobile

then the predicate 'F' picks out nothing—no member of the UD is an automobile. In this case the extension of the predicate 'F' is the empty set.

Now let us consider two-place predicates. Suppose that an interpretation includes the following:

UD: Set of positive integers
Gxy: x is greater than y

In this case we cannot simply say that the predicate 'G' picks out members of the UD. We are interpreting 'G' as a *relational* predicate, so here the extension of the predicate is a set of *pairs* of objects rather than simply a set of objects. One of the pairs of positive integers that is in the extension of the predicate is the pair consisting of the number 5 and the number 2, in that order, since 5 is greater than 2. We must think of these pairs as ordered because, although the predicate picks out the pair whose first member is 5 and whose second member is 2, it does not pick out the pair whose first member is 2 and whose second member is 5—2 is not greater than 5. The extension of 'G' includes all and only those pairs of objects in the UD (pairs of positive integers) of which the first member is greater than the second.

On some interpretations the extension of a two-place predicate includes pairs in which the first and second members are the same. For example, on an interpretation that includes

UD: Set of positive integers
Lxy: x is less than or equal to y

the extension of 'L' includes the pair consisting of 1 and 1, the pair consisting of 2 and 2, the pair consisting of 3 and 3, and so on—because each positive integer is less than or equal to itself. (The extension includes other pairs as well—any pair of positive integers in which the first member is less than or equal to the second.)

Three-place predicates, four-place predicates, and all other many-place predicates are interpreted similarly. A three-place predicate has as its extension a set of ordered triples of objects in the UD; a four-place predicate has as its extension a set of ordered quadruples of members of the UD; and so on.

An individual constant is interpreted by assigning to the constant some member of the selected UD. So, if we choose as our UD the set of living creatures, then we may assign to 'a', as its interpretation, some specific living creature. Here are two examples of interpretations for the sentence 'Fa':

1. UD: Set of positive integers
   Fx: x is a prime number
   a: 4
2. UD: Set of animals in the Bronx Zoo
   Fx: x is a giraffe
   a: the oldest giraffe in the Bronx Zoo

Once we have given interpretations of the expressions in the sentence 'Fa', we may determine the truth-value of 'Fa' on that interpretation. The sentence 'Fa' is true on an interpretation just in case the object that the constant 'a' designates is a member of the set that is the extension of the predicate 'F' for that interpretation. The sentence 'Fa' is false on interpretation 1 and true on interpretation 2. (Actually neither 1 nor 2 is a full interpretation; a full interpretation interprets every constant, predicate, and sentence letter of *PL*. For example, 1 represents infinitely many interpretations. It represents all interpretations that have the specified UD, that interpret 'F' and 'a' as indicated, and that interpret all other predicates, constants, and sentence letters as they please. However, we shall continue to talk informally of our partial interpretations simply as interpretations.)

Here is an interpretation for 'Gab':

3. UD: Set of positive integers
   Gxy: x is greater than y
   a: 2
   b: 16

The sentence 'Gab' is false on interpretation 3, for on this interpretation 'Gab' says that 2 is greater than 16, which is not the case. But 'Gba', which may be read as 'The number 16 is greater than the number 2', is true on this interpretation because the pair of numbers whose first member is 16 and whose second member is 2 *is* in the extension of the predicate 'G'.

An interpretation may assign the same member of the UD to more than one constant. The following is a legitimate interpretation for 'Jln':

4. UD: Set of planets in the solar system
   Jxy: x is closer to the sun than is y
   l: Jupiter
   n: Jupiter

Here both 'l' and 'n' have been interpreted as designating Jupiter. The sentence is false on this interpretation since Jupiter is not closer to the sun than itself. Usually, when we *symbolize* English sentences in *PL*, we use different constants to designate different individuals. But, if we want to use different constants to designate the same individual, we may do so. This is similar to the case in which an object is referred to by more than one expression in the English language. For instance, 'the first U.S. president' and 'George Washington' designate the same person. But note that, whereas in English one name may stand for more than one object (in which case it is *ambiguous*), we do not allow this in *PL*. Two names may designate the same object, but *no one name may designate more than one object.*

The truth-conditions for compound sentences of *PL* that do not contain quantifiers are determined in accordance with the truth-functional reading of the connectives, so we use the information in the characteristic truth-tables for the truth-functional connectives to determine the truth-values of such sentences. Consider the sentence '(Bs ∨ ~ Fh) & Gsh'. Here is an interpretation for the sentence:

5. UD: Set of all things
   Bx: x is an author
   Fx: x is an animal
   Gxy: x owns y
   h: The Liberty Bell
   s: Stephen King

The sentence 'Bs' is true on this interpretation since Stephen King is an author. The sentence 'Fh' is false on this interpretation since the Liberty Bell is not an animal, so '~ Fh' is true. Since 'Bs' and '~ Fh' are both true, the sentence 'Bs ∨ ~ Fh' is true. Stephen King does not own the Liberty Bell, so 'Gsh' is false on this interpretation. Consequently '(Bs ∨ ~ Fh) & Gsh' has one false conjunct and is false on interpretation 5. Another interpretation may make the same sentence true:

6. UD: Set of people
   Bx: x is male
   Fx: x is a negative integer
   Gxy: x is the mother of y
   h: Jay Doe
   s: Jane Doe (who is the mother of Jay Doe)

On this interpretation 'Fh' is false. As we have interpreted the predicate 'F', its extension is the empty set. The predicate picks out nothing in the UD since no person is a negative integer, so '~ Fh' is true. 'Bs' is false since Jane Doe is not male, but 'Bs ∨ ~ Fh' is true—a disjunction with one true disjunct is itself true. Since Jane Doe is Jay Doe's mother, 'Gsh' is true. Thus the sentence '(Bs ∨ ~ Fh) & Gsh' has two true conjuncts and is true on interpretation 6.

We have yet to consider interpretations for the *quantified* sentences of *PL*. Quantified sentences are not atomic, and they are not truth-functions of smaller sentences of *PL* either. The quantified sentence

(∀x) (Fx ⊃ Gx)

is not truth-functionally compound; indeed, it contains no proper subformula that is itself a sentence. To give an interpretation for this sentence, we must specify a UD and interpret the predicate letters 'F' and 'G'. *We do not interpret individual variables.* As noted in Chapter 7, individual variables function in *PL* much as pronouns do in English. They are not names, so interpretations do not assign to them members of the UD.

We may read '(∀x) (Fx ⊃ Gx)' as 'Each x is such that if x is F then x is G' or 'Everything that is F is G'. When we specify a UD for interpreting the sentence, we thereby specify what 'everything' is, namely, everything in the UD. Here is an interpretation for '(∀x) (Fx ⊃ Gx)':

7. UD: Set of people
   Fx: x is a politician
   Gx: x is honest

With this interpretation we may read the sentence as 'Every person who is a politician is honest'. Unfortunately some politicians are not honest; the sentence is therefore false on interpretation 7. The part of the sentence that follows the universal quantifier, the open sentence 'Fx ⊃ Gx', specifies a condition that may or may not hold for the individual members of the UD; the function of the universal quantifier is to state that this condition holds for *each* member of the UD. Consequently the sentence is true if and only if every member of the UD meets that condition.

Consider the following interpretation for the sentence

(∀x) (Ax ≡ ~ Bx)

8. UD: Set of positive integers
   Ax: x is evenly divisible by 2
   Bx: x is an odd number

The universal quantifier states that the condition specified by 'Ax ≡ ~ Bx' holds for every member of the UD. The sentence, which we may read as 'Each positive integer is evenly divisible by 2 if and only if it is not an odd number', is true on this interpretation. But the interpretation

9. UD: Set of positive integers
   Ax: x is evenly divisible by 4
   Bx: x is an odd number

makes the same sentence false. A universally quantified sentence is false if there is at least one member of the UD for which the condition specified after the quantifier does not hold. The number 6 is one member for which the condition specified by 'Ax ≡ ~ Bx' does not hold. The number 6 is not evenly divisible by 4 and is not an odd number—so 6 does not meet the condition that it *is* evenly divisible by 4 if and only if it is *not* an odd number.

In determining the truth-conditions for universally quantified sentences, then, we should keep two points in mind. First, individual variables are *not* interpreted. The function of these variables is to range over the members of the UD; consequently it is the specification of the UD for an interpretation that is relevant in determining the contribution that individual variables and quantifiers make to the truth-conditions of sentences of *PL*. Second, the role of the universal quantifier in a sentence of *PL* is to indicate that *every* member of the UD satisfies a certain condition. The condition is specified by that part of the sentence that lies within the scope of the quantifier.

Existential quantifiers function in sentences of *PL* to indicate that at least one member of the UD satisfies a certain condition. Here is an interpretation for the existentially quantified sentence

(∃y) (Cy & By)

10. UD: Set of all things
    Cx: x is a car
    Bx: x is brown

The sentence is true on this interpretation. It may be read as 'At least one object (in the universe) is a brown car'. Because it is existentially quantified, the sentence is true just in case at least one object in the universe is a car and is brown, that is, just in case at least one object in the universe satisfies the condition specified by 'Cy & By'. Since there is at least one such object, '(∃y) (Cy & By)' is true on this interpretation. However, the same sentence is false on the following interpretation:

11. UD: Set of all things
    Cx: x is a car
    Bx: x has a brain

Marvelous as technology is, it has not yet produced cars with brains. Hence no object satisfies the condition specified by 'Cy & By', and so '(∃y) (Cy & By)' is false on the present interpretation.

The different sentence

(∃y)Cy & (∃y)By

is true on interpretation 11. This is because both '(∃y)Cy' and '(∃y)By' are true—there is an object that is a car and there is an object that has a brain. It is not one and the same object that has both these properties, however. That is why the sentence '(∃y)(Cy & By)' is false on this interpretation. Although 'y' occurs in both 'Cy' and 'By' of '(∃y)Cy & (∃y)By', these two occurrences of the variable are not in the scope of a single occurrence of the quantifier '(∃y)'. So the predicates 'is a car' and 'has a brain' do not have to hold for the same object for the sentence '(∃y)Cy & (∃y)By' to be true. In '(∃y)(Cy & By)', however, all occurrences of 'y' *are* within the scope of one occurrence of '(∃y)'; so, for '(∃y)(Cy & By)' to be true on interpretation 11, a single member of the UD must both be a car and have a brain.

Now we shall consider an interpretation for a sentence containing a two-place predicate and two quantifiers:

(∃x)(∀y)Fxy

12. UD: Set of people
    Fxy: x is acquainted with y

Since the whole sentence is existentially quantified, it is true on interpretation 12 if at least one person satisfies the condition specified by the rest of the sentence, that is, if at least one person is acquainted with every member of the UD. Obviously there is no such person, so '(∃x)(∀y)Fxy' is false on interpretation 12. Using the same interpretation, let us look at the sentence that is formed by reversing the order of the quantifiers:

(∀y)(∃x)Fxy

Prefixed with the universal quantifier, the sentence says that *each* member of the UD satisfies a certain condition. For this sentence to be true, each person y must be such that at least one person is acquainted with y. This is true (since every person is at least self-acquainted), so '(∀y)(∃x)Fxy' is true on interpretation 12. Note that the difference that accounts for the diverging truth-values of '(∃x)(∀y)Fxy' and '(∀y)(∃x)Fxy' is that in the first case it is one and the same person who must be acquainted with everyone. Another sentence that we may interpret using interpretation 12 is

(∃x)(∃y)Fxy

This sentence is true on interpretation 12 since there is at least one person who is acquainted with at least one person.

The following is an interpretation for the sentence

(∀x)(Fx ⊃ (∃y) ~ Gyy)

13. UD: Set of houses in the world
    Fx: x is made of brick
    Gxy: x is larger than y

Given this interpretation, the sentence may be read as 'For any brick house, there is at least one house that is not larger than itself'. This sentence is universally quantified and hence is true just in case every house x in the world satisfies the condition that if x is made of brick then at least one house is not larger than itself. Any house that is not made of brick trivially satisfies the condition since it does not fulfill the condition of being made of brick. That is, a house x that is not made of brick is such that if x is made of brick (which it is not) then some house is not larger than itself. Brick houses also satisfy the condition specified in the sentence. For since it is true that at least one house is not larger than itself, it is true of any brick house x that if x is made of brick (which it is) then some house is not larger than itself (which is true).

The sentence

$$(\forall y)(\forall x)(Fyx \supset Fxy)$$

is false on the following interpretation:

14. UD: Set of integers
Fxy: x is smaller than y

No integer y satisfies the condition specified by '$(\forall x)(Fyx \supset Fxy)$', which is that every integer that y is smaller than is, in turn, smaller than y. For any integer y there are (infinitely many) integers x that y is smaller than, but not even one of these integers is, in turn, smaller than y. But the sentence

$$(\forall y)(\forall x)(Fyy \supset Fxy)$$

is true on interpretation 14. Every integer y trivially satisfies the condition specified by '$(\forall x)(Fyy \supset Fxy)$', which is that every integer x is such that if y is smaller than itself (it is not) then x is also smaller than y.

Now we shall consider sentences that contain individual constants and sentence letters, as well as quantifiers. Consider

$$(\exists x)(Fx \ \& \ (\forall y)Gxy) \supset \sim Gsl$$

and this interpretation:

15. UD: Set of people
Fx: x is female
Gxy: x is the sister of y
l: Michael Jackson
s: Janet Jackson

On this interpretation the sentence may be read as 'If some person is a female and is everybody's sister (including her own) then Janet Jackson is not Michael Jackson's sister'. The consequent of this sentence, '~ Gsl', is false because Janet *is* Michael's sister. But the antecedent is also false; there is no female person who is everybody's sister. So the sentence '$(\exists x)(Fx \;\&\; (\forall y)Gxy) \supset \sim Gsl$' is true on this interpretation.

Here are two interpretations for the sentence

$\sim Dm \vee (\forall x)(\exists y)(Bx \supset Cyx)$

16. UD: Set of people
    Dx: x is a golf pro
    Bx: x is bald
    Cxy: x has seen y on television
    m: Tiger Woods

17. UD: Set of people
    Dx: x is a politician
    Bx: x is a banana
    Cxy: x votes for y
    m: Madonna

The sentence is false on interpretation 16 since both disjuncts are false on that interpretation. The disjunct '$\sim Dm$' is false since 'Dm' is true—Tiger Woods is a golf pro. '$(\forall x)(\exists y)(Bx \supset Cyx)$', which may be read as 'Every bald person has been seen on television by someone', is false. At least one bald person has not been seen on television by anyone. Interpretation 17 makes the sentence true because both disjuncts are true. Since 'Dm' is false—Madonna is not a politician—'$\sim Dm$' is true. And since no person is a banana, it follows trivially that each person x satisfies the condition that <u>if</u> x is a banana (which x is not) <u>then</u> someone votes for x. On interpretation 17 the sentence '$\sim Dm \vee (\forall x)(\exists y)(Bx \supset Cyx)$' may be read as 'Either Madonna is a politician or everybody who is a banana receives a vote from someone'.

As a final example here is an interpretation for the four sentences

$(\exists x)(Nx \supset (\exists y)Lyx)$
$(\forall x)(Nx \supset (\exists y)Lyx)$
$(\exists x)Nx \supset (\exists y)Lya$
$(\forall x)Nx \supset (\exists y)Lya$

18. UD: Set of positive integers
    Nx: x is odd
    Lxy: x is smaller than y
    a: 1

The first sentence, '$(\exists x)(Nx \supset (\exists y)Lyx)$', is true on this interpretation. It is existentially quantified, and there *is* at least one positive integer x such that <u>if</u> it is odd <u>then</u> some positive integer is smaller than x. Every even positive integer trivially satisfies this condition (because every even positive integer fails to satisfy the antecedent), and every odd positive integer except 1 satisfies it. Because the number 1 does not satisfy the condition specified by 'Nx ⊃ (∃y)Lyx', the second sentence is false. The positive integer 1 is odd, but there is no positive integer that is smaller than 1. So it is not true of every positive integer x that if x is odd then there is a positive integer that is smaller than x.

The third sentence, '(∃x)Nx ⊃ (∃y)Lya', is false on interpretation 18 because its antecedent, '(∃x)Nx', is true, whereas the consequent, '(∃y)Lya', is false. There is at least one odd positive integer, but there is no positive integer that is smaller than the integer 1. In contrast, '(∀x)Nx ⊃ (∃y)Lya' is true because its antecedent is false—some positive integers are not odd.

In summary, the truth-conditions for sentences of *PL* are determined by *interpretations*. Officially an interpretation consists of the specification of a UD and the interpretation of each sentence letter, predicate, and individual constant in the language *PL*. (This parallels the definition of truth-value assignments for *SL*, where a truth-value assignment assigns a truth-value to *every* atomic sentence of *SL*.) But for most purposes we can ignore most of the interpreting that each interpretation does. In *SL* we were able to determine the truth-value of a sentence on a truth-value assignment by considering only the relevant part of that assignment, that is, the truth-values assigned to the atomic components of the sentence in question. Similarly, in order to determine the truth-value of a sentence of *PL* on an interpretation, we need only consider the UD and the interpretation of those sentence letters, predicates, and constants that occur in the sentence in question. In what follows, we shall continue the practice of displaying only the relevant parts of interpretations and of informally referring to such partial interpretations simply as *interpretations*.

8.1E EXERCISES

1. Determine the truth-value of the following sentences on this interpretation:

UD: Set of integers
Ax: x is a positive number
Cx: x is a negative number
Bxy: x is a square root of y
a: 0
b: 39
c: −4

a. Cc & (Ac ∨ Bca)
*b. Ab ⊃ Ab
c. ~ Bcb ⊃ (Bba ∨ ~ Ac)
*d. Cb ≡ (~ Ab ≡ Ac)
e. (Cb & Cc) & ~ Baa
*f. ~ (~ Ab ∨ Cb) ⊃ Baa
g. Baa ≡ [Bca ⊃ (Cb ∨ ~ Ab)]
*h. ~ (Ab ∨ Bcc) & (Cc ⊃ ~ Ac)

2. Determine the truth-value of the following sentences on this interpretation:

UD: Set of countries, cities, and people
Bxyz: x is between y and z
Dxy: x lives in y
Fx: x is a large city
a: West Germany
b: the United States
c: Italy
d: the U.S. president
e: Tokyo
f: Rome

a. Fa ⊃ Dda
*b. Ff ⊃ Ddb
c. (~ Babc ∨ ~ Bbac) ∨ ~ Bcab
*d. (Fa ≡ Fe) ⊃ Dde
e. (~ Fe ∨ Ddf) & (Fe ∨ Fb)
*f. Baaa ⊃ Bfff
g. (Dda ∨ Ddc) ∨ (Dde ∨ Ddf)
*h. (Fa ≡ Dda) & ~ (Ddb ⊃ Bccc)

3. For each of the following sentences, construct an interpretation on which the sentence is true.
a. Nad ⊃ ~ Nda
*b. Da ≡ ~ (Fb ∨ Gc)
c. (Lm & ~ Lm) ∨ Chm
*d. ~ (Wab ⊃ (Wbb & Eb))
e. (Ma ∨ Na) ∨ (Mb ∨ Nb)
*f. ~ Fc & [(Fa ⊃ Na) & (Fb ⊃ Nb)]

4. For each of the following sentences, construct an interpretation on which the sentence is false.
a. (Crs ∨ Csr) ∨ (Css ∨ Crr)
*b. (Ka ≡ ~ Ma) ≡ Gh
c. (Li ∨ Lj) ∨ Lm
*d. Iap ⊃ (Ipa ⊃ Iaa)
e. (~ Ja ≡ Jb) & (~ Jc ≡ ~ Jd)
*f. (Ha ∨ ~ Ha) ⊃ (Fbb ⊃ Fba)

5. For each pair construct an interpretation on which one sentence is true and the other false.
a. Fab ⊃ Fba, Fba ⊃ Fab
*b. (Caa & Cab) ∨ Da, ~ Da ≡ ~ (Caa & Cab)
c. ~ Ma ∨ Cpqr, Capq ∨ ~ Mr
*d. Kac ∨ Kad, Kac & Kad
e. ~ Ljk ≡ (Mjk ∨ Mkj), (Mjk & Mkj) & Ljk
*f. Fab ⊃ (Fbc ⊃ Fac), Fac ⊃ (Fcb ⊃ Fab)

6.a. Explain why there is no interpretation on which 'Ba ∨ ~ Ba' is false.
*b. Can the sentence 'Eab & ~ Eba' be true on an interpretation for which the UD contains exactly one member? Explain.

7. Determine the truth-value of the following sentences on this interpretation:

UD: Set of people
Bx: x is a child
Cx: x is over 40 years old
Dxy: x and y are sisters
Fxy: x and y are brothers

a. $(\forall w)(Cw \supset (\exists x)Dxx)$
*b. $(\exists x)(\exists y)(Fxy \ \& \ Cx)$
c. $(\exists x)(\forall y)(By \vee Fxy)$
*d. $(\forall x)(\forall y)(Dxy \equiv Fxy)$
e. $(\exists x)Cx \supset ((\exists x)(\exists y)Fxy \supset (\exists y)By)$
*f. $\sim (\forall w)(Cw \vee Bw)$
g. $(\forall x)Bx \supset (\forall x)Cx$
*h. $(\forall x)[(\exists y)(Dxy \vee Fxy) \supset Bx]$
i. $(\exists x)[Cx \vee (\exists y)(Dxy \ \& \ Cy)]$
*j. $(\forall w)((Cw \vee Bw) \supset (\exists y)Fwy)$

8. Determine the truth-value of each of the following sentences on this interpretation:

UD: Set of U.S. presidents
Ax: x was the first U.S. president
Bx: x is a female
Ux: x is a U.S. citizen
Dxy: x held office after y's first term of office
g: George Washington

a. $(\forall w)Dwg$
*b. $(\forall x)(\forall y)((Bx \ \& \ Ay) \supset Dyx)$
c. $(\exists x)(Ax \ \& \ (\exists y)Dyx)$
*d. $((\exists x)Ax \ \& \sim (\exists z)Bz) \ \& \ (Ag \supset (\forall y)Uy)$
e. $(\forall y)(Uy \supset (\exists x)(Dyx \vee Dxy))$
*f. $(\forall w)(Bw \equiv \sim Uw)$
g. $(\forall x)(Dxg \supset (\exists y)(\sim Uy \ \& \ Dxy))$
*h. $(\exists x)(Ax \ \& \ Bx) \equiv (\forall y)(Ay \supset Uy)$
i. $\sim (Bg \vee (\exists x)(\forall y)Dxy)$
*j. $(\forall y)((By \ \& \ Ay) \supset Dgy)$

9. Determine the truth-value of each of the following sentences on this interpretation:

UD: Set of positive integers
Bx: x is an even number
Gxy: x is greater than y
Exy: x equals y
Mxyz: x minus y equals z
a: 1
b: 2
c: 3

a. $Bb \ \& \ (\forall w)(Gwb \supset \sim Ewb)$
*b. $(\forall x)(\forall z)(\sim Exz \equiv Gxz)$
c. $(\forall x)(\forall z)(Gxz \supset \sim Exz)$
*d. $(\forall x)(\exists w)(Gwx \ \& \ (\exists z)Mzxw)$
e. $\sim (\forall w)(\forall y)Gwy \supset Mcba$
*f. $(\forall y)(Eya \vee Gya)$
g. $(\forall z)(Bz \supset \sim (\exists y)(By \ \& \ Mzay))$
*h. $(\forall y)[(Bb \ \& \ (\exists x)Exb) \supset Mcby]$
i. $(\forall x)(Exx \equiv \sim (\exists y)(\exists z)Myzx)$
*j. $(\exists x)((Bx \ \& \ Gxc) \ \& \sim (\exists z)Mxcz)$

8.2 QUANTIFICATIONAL TRUTH, FALSEHOOD, AND INDETERMINACY

Using the concept of an interpretation, we may now specify the quantificational counterparts of various truth-functional concepts. Here are the relevant properties that individual sentences of *PL* may have:

A sentence **P** of *PL* is *quantificationally true* if and only if **P** is true on every interpretation.

A sentence **P** of *PL* is *quantificationally false* if and only if **P** is false on every interpretation.

A sentence **P** of *PL* is *quantificationally indeterminate* if and only if **P** is neither quantificationally true nor quantificationally false.

These are the quantificational analogs of truth-functional truth, falsehood, and indeterminacy. The definitions here, however, are stated in terms of interpretations rather than truth-value assignments.

A sentence **P** is quantificationally true if and only if it is true on every interpretation. The sentence '$(\exists x)(Gx \vee \sim Gx)$' is quantificationally true. We cannot hope to show this by going through each of the interpretations of the sentence since there are infinitely many. (To see this, it suffices to note that there are infinitely many possible universes of discourse for the sentence. We can, for instance, choose as our UD a set containing exactly one positive integer. Because there are an infinite number of positive integers, there are an infinite number of such universes of discourse.)

However, we may reason about the sentence as follows: Because the sentence is existentially quantified, it is true on an interpretation just in case at least one member of the UD satisfies the condition specified by '$Gx \vee \sim Gx$'—that is, just in case at least one member of the UD either is G or is not G. Without knowing what the interpretation of 'G' is, we know that every member of a UD satisfies this condition, for every member is either in or not in the extension of 'G'. And since by definition every interpretation has a nonempty set as its UD, we know that the UD for any interpretation has at least one member and hence at least one member that satisfies the condition specified by the open sentence '$Gx \vee \sim Gx$'. Therefore '$(\exists x)(Gx \vee \sim Gx)$' is true on every interpretation.

In general, to show that a sentence of *PL* is quantificationally true, we must use reasoning showing that, no matter what the UD is and no matter how the sentence letters, predicates, and individual constants are interpreted, the sentence always turns out to be true. Here is another example. The sentence

$$(\exists x)(\exists y)(Gxy \supset (\forall z)(\forall w)Gzw)$$

is quantificationally true. That is, given any UD and any interpretation of 'G', there are always members x and y of the UD that satisfy the condition specified by '$(Gxy \supset (\forall z)(\forall w)Gzw)$'. The sentence claims that there is a pair of members of the UD such that if they stand in the relation G then all members of the UD stand in the relation G. We will consider two possibilities for the interpretation of the predicate: Either every pair of members of the UD is in its extension or not every pair is in its extension.

If every pair *is* in the extension of 'G', then every pair x and y (hence at least one pair) satisfies the condition specified by '$(Gxy \supset (\forall z)(\forall w)Gzw)$' because the consequent is true in this case. Now consider the other possibility—that some (at least one) pair is not in the extension of 'G'. In this case that pair satisfies the condition specified by '$(Gxy \supset (\forall z)(\forall w)Gzw)$' because that pair *fails* to satisfy the antecedent 'Gxy'. Because either the interpretation of 'G' includes every pair of members of the UD in its extension or it does not (there are no other possibilities), we have just shown that whatever the interpretation of 'G' may be there will always be at least one pair of members of the UD that satisfies '$(Gxy \supset (\forall z)(\forall w)Gzw)$'. This being so, the sentence '$(\exists x)(\exists y)(Gxy \supset (\forall z)(\forall w)Gzw)$' is true on every interpretation. The sentence is therefore quantificationally true.

The sentence

$$(\forall y)By \ \& \ (\exists z) \sim Bz$$

is quantificationally false. If an interpretation makes the first conjunct true, then every member of the UD will be in the extension of 'B'. But if this is so, then no member of the UD satisfies the condition specified by '$\sim Bz$', and so the existentially quantified second conjunct is false. So on any interpretation on which the first conjunct is true, the entire sentence is false. The sentence is also false on any interpretation on which the first conjunct is false, just because that conjunct is false. Since any interpretation either makes the first conjunct true or makes the first conjunct false, it follows that on every interpretation the sentence '$(\forall y)By \ \& \ (\exists z) \sim Bz$' is false.

The sentence

$$(\forall x)(\exists y)(Fx \supset Gy) \equiv ((\exists x)Fx \ \& \ (\forall y) \sim Gy)$$

is also quantificationally false. Because the sentence is a biconditional, it is false on any interpretation on which its immediate components have different truth-values, and we can show that this is the case for every interpretation. Consider first an interpretation on which the immediate component, '$(\forall x)(\exists y)(Fx \supset Gy)$', is true. For this to be true, every member x of the UD must satisfy the condition specified by '$(\exists y)(Fx \supset Gy)$'. That is, every member x must be such that if it is in the extension of 'F' then there is some member y of the UD that is in the extension of 'G'. It follows that the second immediate component of the biconditional, '$((\exists x)Fx \,\&\, (\forall y) \sim Gy)$', cannot be true. If it *were* true, then some member of the UD would be in the extension of 'F' (to satisfy the first conjunct), and no member of the UD would be in the extension of 'G'. But the truth of '$(\forall x)(\exists y)(Fx \supset Gy)$', as we have seen, requires that if any object is in the extension of 'F' then at least one object must be in the extension of 'G'. It follows that if '$(\forall x)(\exists y)(Fx \supset Gy)$' is true on an interpretation then '$((\exists x)Fx \,\&\, (\forall y) \sim Gy)$' is false on that interpretation.

Now let us consider an interpretation on which '$(\forall x)(\exists y)(Fx \supset Gy)$' is false. In this case some member x of the UD must fail to satisfy the condition specified by '$(\exists y)(Fx \supset Gy)$'—x must be in the extension of 'F' (to satisfy the antecedent of the conditional), and the extension of 'G' must be empty (so the consequent is not satisfied). But in this case '$((\exists x)Fx \,\&\, (\forall y) \sim Gy)$' must be true because both conjuncts are true. '$(\exists x)Fx$' is true because some member of the UD is in the extension of 'F', and '$(\forall y) \sim Gy$' is true because the extension of 'G' is empty. So any interpretation that makes '$(\forall x)(\exists y)(Fx \supset Gy)$' false makes '$((\exists x)Fx \,\&\, (\forall y) \sim Gy)$' true. Combined with the results of the previous paragraph, this establishes that on any interpretation the immediate components of '$(\forall x)(\exists y)(Fx \supset Gy) \equiv ((\exists x)Fx \,\&\, (\forall y) \sim Gy)$' have different truth-values. So the biconditional must be false on every interpretation and therefore is quantificationally false.

Unfortunately it is not always so easy to show that a sentence is quantificationally true or that it is quantificationally false. However, because a quantificationally true sentence must be true on every interpretation, we can show that a sentence is *not* quantificationally true by showing that it is false on at least one interpretation. Take as an example the sentence

$$(Ga \,\&\, (\exists z)Bz) \supset (\forall x)Bx$$

This sentence is not quantificationally true. To show this, we shall construct an interpretation on which the sentence is false. The sentence is a material conditional, and so our interpretation must make its antecedent true and its consequent false. For the antecedent to be true, 'Ga' must be true and at least one member of the UD must be in the extension of 'B'. For the consequent to be false, at least one member of the UD must fail to be in the extension of 'B'. Using the set of positive integers as our UD, we shall interpret 'G' and 'a' so that 'Ga' comes out true, and we shall interpret 'B' so that at least one member of the UD, but not all, falls into the extension of 'B'. The following interpretation will do the trick:

19. UD: Set of positive integers
    Gx: x is odd
    Bx: x is prime
    a: 1

The antecedent '(Ga & (∃z)Bz)' is true because the number 1 is odd and at least one positive integer is prime, but '(∀x)Bx' is false because not all positive integers are prime.

As a second example '(∀x)[(Fx ∨ Gx) ∨ (∃y)Hxy]' is not quantificationally true. We shall show this by constructing an interpretation on which the sentence is false. Because the sentence is universally quantified, the UD must have at least one member that fails to satisfy the condition specified by '(Fx ∨ Gx) ∨ (∃y)Hxy'. We choose the set of positive integers as our UD and choose 2 as the member of the UD that does not satisfy the condition. (There is no particular reason for using 2, but choosing a number helps us develop the rest of the interpretation.) We interpret 'F' and 'G' so that the number 2 has neither property (otherwise it would satisfy either 'Fx' or 'Gx'). We must also interpret 'H' so that the number 2 does not stand in the relation H to any positive integer:

20. UD: Set of positive integers
    Fx: x is odd
    Gx: x is greater than 4
    Hxy: x is equal to y squared

Because 2 is neither odd nor greater than 4, and it is not the square of any positive integer, it fails to satisfy the condition specified by '(Fx ∨ Gx) ∨ (∃y)Hxy'. Therefore the universally quantified sentence is false on interpretation 20. Having shown that there is at least one interpretation on which the sentence is false, we may conclude that it is not quantificationally true.

We may show that a sentence is not quantificationally *false* by constructing an interpretation on which it is true. The sentence

~ (~ Ga & (∃y)Gy)

is not quantificationally false. To construct an interpretation on which it is true, we must make '~ Ga & (∃y)Gy' false. To do so, we must make one or both conjuncts false. We choose the first and interpret 'G' and 'a' so that '~ Ga' is false:

21. UD: Set of positive integers
    Gx: x is even
    a: 2

Because the number 2 is even, 'Ga' is true. Hence '~ Ga' is false and so is '~ Ga & (∃y)Gy'. (The fact that the second conjunct turns out to be true on our interpretation is irrelevant—the conjunction as a whole is still false.) Therefore the negation of the conjunction is true on interpretation 21, and we may conclude that the sentence is not quantificationally false.

Note that we cannot show that a sentence *is* quantificationally true or that it *is* quantificationally false by constructing a single interpretation. To show that a sentence is quantificationally true, we must demonstrate that it is true on every interpretation, and to show that a sentence is quantificationally false, we must show that it is false on every interpretation.

A quantificationally indeterminate sentence is one that is neither quantificationally true nor quantificationally false. We may show that a sentence is quantificationally indeterminate by constructing two interpretations: one on which it is true (to show that the sentence is not quantificationally false) and one on which it is false (to show that the sentence is not quantificationally true). The sentence

~ (~ Ga & (∃y)Gy)

is quantificationally indeterminate. We have already constructed an interpretation (interpretation 21) on which it is true; all that is left is to construct an interpretation on which it is false. For the sentence to be false, '~ Ga & (∃y)Gy' must be true. To make '~ Ga' true, our UD must contain at least one member that is not in the extension of 'G', and 'a' will designate this member. But the UD must also contain another member that is in the extension of 'G', to make '(∃y)Gy' true:

22. UD: Set of positive integers
Gx: x is odd
a: 2

The number 2 is not odd, but at least one positive integer is, and so '~ Ga & (∃y)Gy' is true and '~ (~ Ga & (∃y)Gy)' is false on interpretation 22. The sentence is therefore not quantificationally true. Having shown that the sentence is neither quantificationally true nor quantificationally false, we may conclude that it is quantificationally indeterminate.

Sometimes it takes ingenuity to find either an interpretation on which a sentence is true or an interpretation on which a sentence is false. Examine the sentence itself for guidelines, as we have just done. If it is a truth-functional compound, then use your knowledge of the truth-conditions for that type of compound. If the sentence is universally quantified, then the sentence will be true if and only if the condition specified after the quantifier is satisfied by all members of the UD you choose. If the sentence is existentially quantified, then it will be true if and only if the condition specified after the quantifier is satisfied by at least one member of the UD. As you examine the components of the sentence, you may reason in the same way—are they truth-functional compounds or quantified? Sometimes the desired interpretation cannot be obtained. For example, a quantificationally true sentence is not false on any interpretation; therefore any attempt to construct an interpretation that makes the sentence false fails.

Two theoretical points are of interest here. The first is that, if a sentence of predicate logic without identity is true on at least one interpretation, then it is true on some interpretation that has the set of positive integers as its UD. This result is known as the *Löwenheim Theorem* (it will be proved in the exercises in Chapter 11). It follows from this result that, if a sentence of *PL* is true on some interpretation with a finite UD, then it is true on some interpretation that has the set of positive integers as its UD. And if a sentence of *PL* is true on some interpretation for which the UD is *larger* than the set of positive integers (for example, the set of real numbers), then it is true on at least one interpretation that has the set of positive integers as its UD.

Note that this result means that the set of positive integers is always a good choice for your UD as you construct interpretations. In fact, there are sentences of *PL* that are not quantificationally true but that are nevertheless true on every interpretation with a finite UD, and there are sentences of *PL* that are not quantificationally false but are false on every interpretation with a finite UD. For instance, the following sentence is not quantificationally false:

$$(\forall x)(\forall y)(\forall z)[(Bxy \ \& \ Byz) \supset Bxz] \ \& \ [(\forall x)(\exists y)Bxy \ \& \ (\forall z) \sim Bzz]$$

But it is false on every interpretation with a finite UD. To show that it is not quantificationally false, then, you must choose a UD that has infinitely many members—and the set of positive integers is a good choice.

In fact, in this section all our interpretations have used the set of positive integers as the UD. Although this was not necessary—we could have constructed interpretations using the set of all people, the set of all countries in the world, the set consisting of the three authors of this book, or whatever—we now see why it is a good choice. We shall therefore continue to use this particular UD for our examples in the remainder of this chapter. In addition, we shall make repeated use of very simple interpretations of predicates for this UD—for example, the properties of being even and of being prime, the relation of being greater than, and so on. Again this is not necessary—other properties and relations could be used—but it is convenient to reuse the same interpretations for predicates.

The second point is that there is no decision procedure for deciding, for each sentence of *PL*, whether that sentence is quantificationally true, quantificationally false, or quantificationally indeterminate. (We shall not prove the result here.) This is a very important way in which the semantics for *PL* differs from the semantics for *SL*. For *SL* the construction of truth-tables gives a decision procedure for whether a sentence is truth-functionally true, false, or indeterminate. That is, in a finite number of mechanical steps, we can always correctly answer the questions 'Is this sentence truth-functionally true?', 'Is this sentence truth-functionally false?', and 'Is this sentence truth-functionally indeterminate?' The previous result mentioned in this paragraph, due to Church, is that there is no analogous method for predicate logic—we have no such general method now, and no such general method will ever be found. This result does not mean that we cannot ever show that some sentences of *PL* are quantificationally true, false, or indeterminate; rather, it shows that there is no decision procedure (mechanical, certain, and requiring only a finite number of steps) for determining the quantificational status of *every* sentence of *PL*. However, it is interesting to note that there *is* such a procedure for determining the quantificational status of sentences of *PL* that contain no many-place predicates, that is, in which the predicates are all one-place predicates. This follows from a result by the logicians Bernays and Schönfinkel.[1]

8.2.E EXERCISES

1. Show that each of the following sentences is not quantificationally true by constructing an interpretation on which it is false.

a. (∀x)(Fx ⊃ Gx) ⊃ (∀x)Gx
*b. (∃x)(Fx ∨ Gx) ⊃ ((∃x)Fx ⊃ (∃x) ~ Gx)
c. (∀x)(∃y)Bxy ⊃ (∃y)(∀x)Bxy
*d. (∀x)(Fxb ∨ Gx) ⊃ [(∀x)Fxb ∨ (∀x)Gx]
e. [(∀x)Fx ⊃ (∀w)Gw] ⊃ (∀z)(Fz ⊃ Gz)
*f. (∀x)(Ax ⊃ (∀y)By) ⊃ (∀y)(By ⊃ (∀x)Ax)
g. ~ (∃x)Gx ⊃ (∀y)(Fyy ⊃ Gy)
*h. (∀x)(Bx ≡ Hx) ⊃ (∃x)(Bx & Hx)

2. Show that each of the following sentences is not quantificationally false by constructing an interpretation on which it is true.

a. ~ (∀w)(∀y)Bwy ≡ (∀z)Bzz
*b. (∃x)Fx & (∃x) ~ Fx
c. ((∃x)Fx & (∃x)Gx) & ~ (∃x)(Fx & Gx)
*d. (∃x)((∃y)Fy ⊃ ~ Fx)
e. (∀x)(Fx ⊃ Gx) & (∀x)(Gx ⊃ ~ Fx)
*f. (∃x)(∀y)(Dyx ⊃ ~ Dxy)
g. (∀x)(Bx ≡ Hx) ⊃ (∃x)(Bx & Hx)
*h. (∃x)(∀y)Dxy ∨ ~ (∀y)(∃x)Dxy
i. (∀x)(∀y)(∀z) [(Bxy & Byz) ⊃ Bxz] & [(∀x)(∃y)Bxy & (∀z) ~ Bzz]

3. Show that each of the following sentences is quantificationally indeterminate by constructing an interpretation on which it is true and an interpretation on which it is false.

a. (∃x)(Fx & Gx) ⊃ (∃x) ~ (Fx ∨ Gx)
*b. (∃x)Fx ⊃ (∀w)(Cw ⊃ Fw)
c. (∀x)Bnx ⊃ (∀x) ~ Bnx
*d. (∃x)(Fx ⊃ Gx) ⊃ (∃x)(Fx & Gx)
e. (∀x)(∀w)[(Nwx ∨ Nxw) ⊃ Nww]
*f. (Ma & Mb) & (∃x) ~ Mx
g. (∀x)(Cx ∨ Dx) ≡ (∃y)(Cy & Dy)
*h. [~ (∃x)Hx ∨ ~ (∃x)Gx] ∨ (∀x)(Hx & Gx)

---

[1] "Zum Entscheidungsproblem der mathematischen Logik," *Mathematische Annalen*, 99 (1928), 342–372. The result mentioned in the previous paragraph is from Alonzo Church, "A Note on the Entscheidungsproblem," *Journal of Symbolic Logic*, 1 (1936), 40–41, 101–102.

4. Each of the following sentences is quantificationally true. Explain why.

a. $(\exists x)(\forall y)Bxy \supset (\forall y)(\exists x)Bxy$
*b. $[(\forall x)Fx \vee (\forall x)Gx] \supset (\forall x)(Fx \vee Gx)$
c. $Fa \vee [(\forall x)Fx \supset Ga]$
*d. $(\forall x)(\exists y)Mxy \supset (\exists x)(\exists y)Mxy$
e. $(\exists x)Hx \vee (\forall x)(Hx \supset Jx)$

5. Each of the following sentences is quantificationally false. Explain why.

a. $(\exists w)(Bw \equiv \sim Bw)$
*b. $(\forall w)(Fw \supset Gw)$ & $[(\forall w)(Fw \supset \sim Gw)$ & $(\exists w)Fw]$
c. $[(\forall x)Fx \supset (\exists y)Gy]$ & $[\sim (\exists x)Gx$ & $\sim (\exists x) \sim Fx]$
*d. $(\exists x)(Fx$ & $\sim Gx)$ & $(\forall x)(Fx \supset Gx)$
e. $((\forall w)(Aw \supset Bw)$ & $(\forall w)(Bw \supset (Cw))$ & $(\exists y)(Ay$ & $\sim Cy)$

6. For each of the following sentences, decide whether it is quantificationally true, quantificationally false, or quantificationally indeterminate. If the sentence is quantificationally true or quantificationally false, explain why. If it is quantificationally indeterminate, construct interpretations that establish this.

a. $((\exists x)Gx$ & $(\exists y)Hy)$ & $(\exists z) \sim (Gz$ & $Hz)$
*b. $((\exists x)Gx$ & $(\exists y)Hy)$ & $\sim (\exists z)(Gz$ & $Hz)$
c. $(\forall x)(Fx \supset Gx) \supset (\forall x)(\sim Gx \supset \sim Fx)$
*d. $(\forall x)Fx \supset \sim (\exists x) \sim (Fx \vee Gx)$
e. $(\forall x)(Dx \supset (\exists z)Hxz) \supset (\exists z)(\forall x)(Dx \supset Hxz)$
*f. $(\exists z)(\forall x)(Dx \supset Hxz) \supset (\forall x)(Dx \supset (\exists z)Hxz)$

8.3 QUANTIFICATIONAL EQUIVALENCE AND CONSISTENCY

The next concept to be introduced is that of quantificational equivalence.

> Sentences **P** and **Q** of *PL* are *quantificationally equivalent* if and only if there is no interpretation on which **P** and **Q** have different truth-values.

The sentences

$$(\exists x)Fx \supset Ga$$

and

$$(\forall x)(Fx \supset Ga)$$

are quantificationally equivalent. We may reason as follows: First suppose that '$(\exists x)Fx \supset Ga$' is true on some interpretation. Then '$(\exists x)Fx$' is either true or false on this interpretation. If it is true, then so is 'Ga' (by our assumption that '$(\exists x)Fx \supset Ga$' is true). But then, since 'Ga' is true, every object x in the UD is such that if x is F then a is G. So '$(\forall x)(Fx \supset Ga)$' is true. If '$(\exists x)Fx$' is false, however, then every object x in the UD is such that if x is F (which, on our assumption, it is not) then a is G. Again '(∀x)(Fx ⊃ Ga)' is true. Hence, if '(∃x)Fx ⊃ Ga' is true on an interpretation, '(∀x)(Fx ⊃ Ga)' is also true on that interpretation.

Now suppose that '(∃x)Fx ⊃ Ga' is false on some interpretation. Since the sentence is a conditional, it follows that '(∃x)Fx' is true and 'Ga' is false. But if '(∃x)Fx' is true, then some object x in the UD is in the extension of 'F'. This object then does not satisfy the condition that if it is F (which it is) then a is G (which is false on our present assumption). So '(∀x)(Fx ⊃ Ga)' is false if '(∃x)Fx ⊃ Ga' is. Taken together with our previous result, this demonstrates that the two sentences are quantificationally equivalent.

The sentences

~ (∃x)(∀y)(Gxy ∨ Gyx)

and

(∀x)(∃y)(~ Gxy & ~ Gyx)

are also quantificationally equivalent. As in the previous example, we will show that if the first sentence is true on an interpretation then so is the second sentence, and that if the first sentence is false on an interpretation then so is the second sentence. First consider an interpretation on which '~ (∃x)(∀y)(Gxy ∨ Gyx)' is true. '(∃x)(∀y)(Gxy ∨ Gyx)' must be false on this interpretation, so no member x of the UD satisfies the condition specified by '(∀y)(Gxy ∨ Gyx)'. That is, no member x of the UD is such that for every object y either the pair x and y or the pair y and x is in the extension of 'G'. Put another way, for each member x of the UD, there is at least one object y such that both '~ Gxy' and '~ Gyx' hold. And that is exactly what the second sentence says, so it is true as well.

Now consider an interpretation on which the first sentence is false; '(∃x)(∀y)(Gxy ∨ Gyx)' is true on such an interpretation. So there is at least one member x of the UD such that for every object y, either 'Gxy' or 'Gyx' holds. Such a member x therefore does *not* satisfy the condition specified by '(∃y)(~ Gxy & ~ Gyx)' (there is *no* y such that neither 'Gxy' nor 'Gyx' holds). And so the universally quantified sentence '(∀x)(∃y)(~ Gxy & ~ Gyx)' is also false. From this and the result of the preceding paragraph, we conclude that the two sentences are quantificationally equivalent.

If we want to establish that two sentences are *not* quantificationally equivalent, we can construct an interpretation to show this. The interpretation must make one of the two sentences true and the other sentence false. For example, the sentences

(∀x)(Fx ⊃ Ga)

and

(∀x)Fx ⊃ Ga

are not quantificationally equivalent. We shall construct an interpretation on which the first sentence is false and the second sentence is true. To make the first sentence false, 'Ga' has to be false, and there must be at least one object in the extension of 'F'—for then this object will fail to satisfy '(Fx ⊃ Ga)'. But we can still make '(∀x)Fx ⊃ Ga' true on our interpretation if the extension of 'F' does not include the entire UD—because then the antecedent '(∀x)Fx' will be false. Here is our interpretation:

23. UD: Set of positive integers
Fx: x is prime
Gx: x is even
a: 1

The number 3 (as one example) does not satisfy the condition that if it is prime (which it is) then the number 1 is even (which is false). So '(∀x)(Fx ⊃ Ga)' is false on the interpretation. But '(∀x)Fx ⊃ Ga' is true because its antecedent, '(∀x)Fx', is false—not every positive integer is prime. Once again we see that the scope of quantifiers is very important in determining the truth-conditions of sentences of *PL*.

The sentences

(∀x)(∃y)(Hy ⊃ Lx)

and

(∀x)[(∃y)Hy ⊃ Lx]

are also not quantificationally equivalent. We shall show this by constructing an interpretation on which the first sentence is true and the second sentence is false. To make '(∀x)[(∃y)Hy ⊃ Lx]' false, some member of the UD must fail to satisfy '(∃y)Hy ⊃ Lx'. Therefore the UD must contain at least one object in the extension of 'H' (so that '(∃y)Hy' is satisfied) and at least one object x that is not in the extension of 'L' (so that this object does not satisfy 'Lx'). To make '(∀x)(∃y)(Hy ⊃ Lx)' true, every member of the UD must satisfy '(∃y)(Hy ⊃ Lx)' —for every member x of the UD, there must be an object y such that if y is H then x is L. We have already decided that at least one object x will not be in the extension of 'L'. So, if x (along with all other members of the UD) is to satisfy '(∃y)(Hy ⊃ Lx)', then at least one member of y of the UD must not be in the extension of 'H'—for then y will be such that if it is H (it is not) then x is L.

To sum up, we need at least one object that is in the extension of 'L' and at least one object that is not in the extension of 'H'. Here is our interpretation:

24. UD: Set of positive integers
Hx: x is odd
Lx: x is prime

The sentence '$(\forall x)[(\exists y)Hy \supset Lx]$' is false—every positive integer x that is not prime fails to satisfy the condition that i̲f̲ some positive integer is odd (which at least one positive integer is) t̲h̲e̲n̲ x is prime. The sentence '$(\forall x)(\exists y)(Hy \supset Lx)$' is true because at least one positive integer is not odd. For any positive integer x there is at least one positive integer y that is not odd, and hence at least one positive integer y such that i̲f̲ y is odd (which y is not) t̲h̲e̲n̲ x is prime.

While we may construct single interpretations to show that two sentences are not quantificationally equivalent, we may not use the same method to show that sentences *are* quantificationally equivalent. In the latter case we must reason about every interpretation as we did in the examples at the beginning of this section.

Quantificational consistency is our next concept.

A set of sentences of *PL* is *quantificationally consistent* if and only if there is at least one interpretation on which all the members of the set are true. A set of sentences of *PL* is *quantificationally inconsistent* if and only if the set is not quantificationally consistent.

The set of sentences

$\{(\forall x)Gax, \sim Gba \vee (\exists x) \sim Gax\}$

is quantificationally consistent. The following interpretation shows this:

25. UD: Set of positive integers
    Gxy: x is less than or equal to y
      a: 1
      b: 2

On this interpretation '$(\forall x)Gax$' is true since 1 is less than or equal to every positive integer. '$\sim Gba$' is true since 2 is neither less than nor equal to 1; so '$\sim Gba \vee (\exists x) \sim Gax$' is true. Since both members of the set are true on this interpretation, the set is quantificationally consistent.

The set

$\{(\forall w)(Fw \supset Gw), (\forall w)(Fw \supset \sim Gw)\}$

is also quantificationally consistent. This may seem surprising since the first sentence says that everything that is F is G and the second sentence says that everything that is F is not G. But the set is consistent because, if no object in the UD of an interpretation is in the extension of 'F', then every object w in the UD will be such that i̲f̲ w is F (which w is not) t̲h̲e̲n̲ w is both G and not G. The following interpretation illustrates this.

26. UD: Set of positive integers
Fx: x is negative
Gx: x is even

No positive integer is negative, so each positive integer w is such that if w is negative (which w is not) then w is even, and each positive integer w is such that if w is negative (which w is not) then w is not even. Both '$(\forall w)(Fw \supset Gw)$' and '$(\forall w)(Fw \supset \sim Gw)$' are true on this interpretation.

Note that, while a single interpretation may be produced to show that a set of sentences is quantificationally consistent, a single interpretation *cannot* be used to show that a set of sentences is quantificationally *in*consistent. To show that a set is quantificationally inconsistent, we must show that on every interpretation at least one sentence in the set is false. In some cases simple reasoning shows that a set of sentences is quantificationally inconsistent. The set

$$\{(\exists y)(Fy \ \& \sim Ny),\ (\forall y)(Fy \supset Ny)\}$$

is quantificationally inconsistent. For if '$(\exists y)(Fy \ \& \sim Ny)$' is true on some interpretation then some member y of the UD is F and is not N. But then that member is *not* such that if it is F (which it is) then it is N (which it is not). Hence the universally quantified sentence '$(\forall y)(Fy \supset Ny)$' is false on such an interpretation. So there is no interpretation on which both set members are true; the set is quantificationally inconsistent.

8.3E EXERCISES

1. Show that the sentences in each of the following pairs are not quantificationally equivalent by constructing an interpretation on which one of the sentences is true and the other is false.

a. $(\exists x)Fx \supset Ga$, $(\exists x)(Fx \supset Ga)$
*b. $(\exists x)Fx \ \& \ (\exists x)Gx$, $(\exists x)(Fx \ \& \ Gx)$
c. $(\forall x)Fx \vee (\forall x)Gx$, $(\forall x)(Fx \vee Gx)$
*d. $(\exists x)(Fx \vee Ga)$, $(\exists x)(Fx \vee Gb)$
e. $(\forall x)(Fx \equiv Gx)$, $(\exists x)Fx \equiv (\exists x)Gx$
*f. $(\forall x)(Fx \supset Gx)$, $(\forall y)((\forall x)Fx \supset Gy)$
g. $(\exists x)(Bx \ \& \ (\forall y)Dyx)$, $(\forall x)(Bx \supset (\forall y)Dyx)$
*h. $(\exists y)(My \equiv Ny)$, $(\exists y)My \equiv (\exists y)Ny$
i. $(\forall x)(\exists y)(Fx \supset Kyx)$, $(\exists x)(\exists y)(Fx \supset Kyx)$

2. In each of the following pairs the sentences are quantificationally equivalent. Explain why.

a. $(\forall x)Fx \supset Ga$, $(\exists x)(Fx \supset Ga)$
*b. $(\forall x)(Fx \supset Gx)$, $\sim (\exists x)(Fx \ \& \sim Gx)$
c. $(\exists x)(Fx \vee Gx)$, $\sim (\forall y)(\sim Fy \ \& \sim Gy)$
*d. $(\forall x)(\forall y)(Mxy \ \& \ Myx)$, $\sim (\exists x)(\exists y)(\sim Mxy \vee \sim Myx)$
e. $(\forall x)(\forall y)Gxy$, $(\forall y)(\forall x)Gxy$
*f. $(\forall x)(\forall y)(Fxy \supset Hyx)$, $\sim (\exists x)(\exists y)(Fxy \ \& \sim Hyx)$

3. Decide, for each of the following pairs of sentences, whether the sentences are quantificationally equivalent. If they are quantificationally equivalent, explain why. If they are not quantificationally equivalent, construct an interpretation that shows this.

a. (∃x)(Fx ∨ Gx), (∀x) ~ (Fx & Gx)
*b. (∃x)(Fx & Gx), ~ (∀x) ~ (Fx ∨ Gx)
c. (∀w)(∀y)(Gyw ∨ Gwy), (∀w)(∀y)(Gww ∨ Gwy)
*d. (∀y)((∃z)Hzy ⊃ Hyy), (∀y)((∃z)(Hzz ⊃ Hzy)

4. Show that each of the following sets of sentences is quantificationally consistent by constructing an interpretation on which every member of the set is true.

a. {(∃x)Bx, (∃x)Cx, ~ (∀x)(Bx ∨ Cx)}
*b. {(∃x)Fx ∨ (∃x)Gx, (∃x) ~ Fx, (∃x) ~ Gx}
c. {(∀x)(Fx ⊃ Gx), (∀x)(Nx ⊃ Mx), (∀x)(Gx ⊃ ~ Mx)}
*d. {(∀x)(Dax ≡ Bax), ~ Dab, ~ Bba}
e. {(∀w)(Nw ⊃ (∃z)(Mz & Cwz), (∀z)(∀w)(Mz ⊃ ~ Cwz)}
*f. {(∃w)Fw, (∀w)(Fw ⊃ (∃x)Bxw), (∀x) ~ Bxx}
g. {~ (∀y)(Ny ⊃ My), ~ (∀y) ~ (Ny ⊃ My)}
*h. {(∀x)(Bx ≡ (∀y)Cxy), (∃x) ~ Bx, (∃x)(∃y)Cxy}
i. {(∃y)Fay, (∃y) ~ Gay, (∀y)(Fay ∨ Gay)}

5. Each of the following sets of sentences is quantificationally inconsistent. Explain why.

a. {(∃x)(Bx & Cx), (∀x) ~ (Bx ∨ Cx)}
*b. {(∃x)(∃y)(Bxy ∨ Byx), ~ (∃x)(∃y)Bxy}
c. {(∀x)(∀y)(Byx ∨ Bxy), (∃y) ~ Byy}
*d. {Ba, (∃y)Day, (∀x)(Bx ⊃ (∀y) ~ Dxy)}
e. {(∃x)(∀y)Gxy, (∀x)(∀y) ~ Gxy}
*f. {(∀x)Fx ∨ (∀x) ~ Fx, (∃x)Fx ≡ (∃x) ~ Fx}

6. Decide, for each of the following sets of sentences, whether the set is quantificationally consistent. If the set is quantificationally consistent, construct an interpretation that shows this. If it is quantificationally inconsistent, explain why.

a. {(∃x)Fx ⊃ (∀x)Fx, (∃x) ~ Fx, (∃x) Fx}
*b. {(∃x)(∃y)Gxy, (∀y) ~ Gyy}
c. {(∀x) ~ (∀y)Gxy, (∀x)Gxx}
*d. {(∃x)Px, (∀y)(Py ⊃ Hya), ~ (∀x) ~ Hxa}

7. Explain why sentences **P** and **Q** of *PL* are quantificationally equivalent if and only if **P** ≡ **Q** is quantificationally true.

8.4 QUANTIFICATIONAL ENTAILMENT AND VALIDITY

Our last two semantic concepts for the language *PL* are the concepts of quantificational entailment and quantificational validity.

> A set Γ of sentences of *PL* *quantificationally entails* a sentence **P** of *PL* if and only if there is no interpretation on which every member of Γ is true and **P** is false.

An argument of *PL* is *quantificationally valid* if and only if there is no interpretation on which every premise is true and the conclusion is false. An argument of *PL* is *quantificationally invalid* if and only if the argument is not quantificationally valid.

The set

$\{(\forall x)(Bx \supset Ga), (\exists x)Bx\}$

quantificationally entails the sentence 'Ga'. As in *SL* we may use the double turnstile and write this as

$\{(\forall x)(Bx \supset Ga), (\exists x)Bx\} \vDash Ga$

Suppose that '$(\forall x)(Bx \supset Ga)$' and '$(\exists x)Bx$' are both true on some interpretation. Since '$(\forall x)(Bx \supset Ga)$' is true, we know that every object x in the UD is such that if x is B then a is G. Since '$(\exists x)Bx$' is true, we know that at least one object x in the UD of the interpretation is in the extension of 'B'. Since it is true that, if that object is B (which it is) then a is G, 'Ga' must therefore be true. So, on any interpretation on which '$(\forall x)(Bx \supset Ga)$' and '$(\exists x)Bx$' are both true, 'Ga' is also true. So the entailment does hold.

The set

$\{(\forall y)(\sim Jy \vee (\exists z)Kz), (\exists y)Jy\}$

quantificationally entails the sentence

$(\exists z)Kz$

We shall show that any interpretation that makes the two sentences in the set true also makes '$(\exists z)Kz$' true. If an interpretation makes the first sentence in the set true, then every member y of the UD satisfies the condition specified by '$(\sim Jy \vee (\exists z)Kz)$'. Every member is such that either it is not J or some member of the UD is K. If the second sentence is also true on the interpretation, then some member of the UD is J. Because this member must satisfy the disjunction '$\sim Jy \vee (\exists z)Kz$' and, being J, it does not satisfy the disjunct '$\sim Jy$', the second disjunct must be true. And the second disjunct is '$(\exists z)Kz$', so it is true whenever the two set members are true.

The argument

$(\exists x)(Fx \vee Gx)$
$(\forall x) \sim Fx$
―――――――
$(\exists x)Gx$

is quantificationally valid. Suppose that on some interpretation both premises are true. If the first premise is true, then some member x of the UD is either F or G. If the premise '$(\forall x) \sim Fx$' is true, then no member of the UD is F. Therefore, because the member that is either F or G is not F, it must be G. Thus '$(\exists x)Gx$' will also be true on such an interpretation.

We can show that a set of sentences does *not* quantificationally entail a sentence by constructing an interpretation. For example, the set

$$\{\sim(\forall x)(Gx \equiv Fx), \sim Fb\}$$

does not quantificationally entail the sentence

$$(\forall x) \sim Gx$$

We will construct an interpretation on which the members of the set are true and '$(\forall x) \sim Gx$' is false. For the sentence '$\sim (\forall x)(Gx \equiv Fx)$' to be true, the UD must contain at least one member that fails to satisfy '$Gx \equiv Fx$'—the member must be in the extension of one of the two predicates but not in the extension of the other. For '$\sim Fb$' to be true, 'b' must designate an object that is not in the extension of 'F'. And '$(\forall x) \sim Gx$', which claims that everything is not G, will be false if at least one object in the UD is in the extension of 'G'. Here is an interpretation that satisfies these conditions:

27. UD: Set of positive integers
Fx: x is greater than 5
Gx: x is prime
b: 3

Not all positive integers are prime if and only if they are greater than 5—take 2 as an example—and 3 is not greater than 5. Therefore the set members are both true on this interpretation. On the other hand, '$(\forall x) \sim Gx$' is false, because some positive integers are prime.

To show that an argument is quantificationally invalid, we can construct an interpretation on which its premises are true and its conclusion is false. The argument

$(\exists x)[(\exists y)Fy \supset Fx]$
$(\exists y) \sim Fy$

$\sim (\exists x)Fx$

is quantificationally invalid. We can make the first premise true by interpreting 'F' so that at least one member of the UD is in its extension—for then that object will satisfy the condition specified by '$(\exists y)Fy \supset Fx$' because it will satisfy its consequent. The second premise will be true if at least one member of the

UD is not in the extension of 'F'. So 'F' will have some, but not all, of the members of the UD in its extension. Because some members will be in the extension, the conclusion will turn out to be false. Here is an interpretation:

28. UD: Set of positive integers
Fx: x is prime

Some positive integer x is such that if there exists a prime positive integer then x is prime—for example, the integer 5 satisfies this condition—and some positive integer is not prime, but it is false that no positive integer is prime.

Note that we cannot prove that a quantificational entailment *does* hold or that an argument *is* quantificationally valid by constructing a single interpretation. Proving either of these involves proving something about the truth-value of sentences on every interpretation, not just a select few.

And, once again, there are limitations on deciding questions of quantificational equivalence, consistency, entailment, and validity. Owing to Church's result, mentioned at the end of Section 8.2, we know that there is no procedure for deciding these questions for every group of sentences of *PL*.[2] However, our method of producing interpretations to establish quantificational consistency, nonequivalence, nonentailment, and invalidity, although not a decision procedure, often produces the desired result. We have, for instance, just used this method to show that an argument is quantificationally invalid. Ingenuity in choosing an appropriate interpretation for sentences containing quantifiers is once again generally required.

8.4E EXERCISES

1. Establish each of the following by constructing an appropriate interpretation.

a. $\{(\forall x)(Fx \supset Gx), (\forall x)(Hx \supset Gx)\} \not\models (\exists x)(Hx \,\&\, Fx)$

*b. $\{(\forall y)(Fy \equiv Fa), Fa\} \not\models \sim Fb$

c. $\{(\forall x)Fx\} \not\models Fa$

*d. $\{(\forall x)(Bx \supset Cx), (\exists x)Bx\} \not\models (\forall x)Cx$

e. $\{(\exists x)(Bx \supset Cx), (\exists x)Cx\} \not\models (\exists x)Bx$

*f. $\{(\forall x)(Fx \supset Gx), (\forall x)(Hx \supset \sim Fx)\} \not\models (\forall x)(Hx \supset Gx)$

g. $\{(\forall x)(\exists y) \sim Lxy\} \not\models (\forall x) \sim Lxx$

*h. $\{(\exists x)(\forall y)(Hxy \vee Jxy), (\exists x)(\forall y) \sim Hxy\} \not\models (\exists x)(\forall y)Jxy$

2. Show that each of the following arguments is quantificationally invalid by constructing an appropriate interpretation.

[2] Moreover some arguments can be proved quantificationally invalid and some sets quantificationally consistent only by means of interpretations with universes of discourse containing an infinite number of members. However, there is a result for sets of sentences analogous to the Löwenheim Theorem (mentioned in Section 8.2), which says that if a set of sentences is quantificationally consistent—or an argument quantificationally invalid—then this can be shown by means of interpretations with the set of positive integers as the UD. It is not necessary in any case to check interpretations with larger universes of discourse. This result is known as the *Löwenheim-Skolem Theorem* and is assigned as an exercise in Chapter 11.

a. $(\forall x)(Fx \supset Gx) \supset (\exists x)Nx$

$(\forall x)(Nx \supset Gx)$

$(\forall x)(\sim Fx \vee Gx)$

*b. $(\sim (\exists y)Fy \supset (\exists y)Fy) \vee \sim Fa$

$(\exists z)Fz$

c. $(\exists x)(Fx \mathbin{\&} Gx)$

$(\exists x)(Fx \mathbin{\&} Hx)$

$(\exists x)(Gx \mathbin{\&} Hx)$

*d. $(\forall x)(Fx \supset Gx)$

Ga

Fa

e. $(\forall x)(Fx \supset Gx)$

$\sim (\exists x)Fx$

$\sim (\exists x)Gx$

*f. $(\forall x)(\forall y)(Mxy \supset Nxy)$

$(\forall x)(\forall y)(Mxy \supset (Nxy \mathbin{\&} Nyx))$

g. $(\exists x)Gx$

$(\forall x)(Gx \supset Dxx)$

$(\exists x)(\forall y)(Gx \mathbin{\&} Dxy)$

*h. $Fa \vee (\exists y)Gya$

$Fb \vee (\exists y) \sim Gyb$

$(\exists y)Gya$

i. $(\forall x)(Fx \supset Gx)$

$(\forall x)(Hx \supset Gx)$

$(\forall x)(Fx \vee Hx)$

3. Using the given symbolization keys, symbolize the following arguments in *PL*. Then show that the first symbolized argument in each pair is quantificationally valid while the second is not.

a. UD: Set consisting of all things
Bx: x is beautiful
Px: x is a person

Everything is beautiful. Therefore something is beautiful.

Everyone is beautiful. Therefore someone is beautiful.

*b. UD: Set of people
Rx: x roller skates
Dx: x can dance

Not everyone can dance. Therefore someone can't dance.

No one who roller skates can dance. Therefore some roller skater can't dance.

c. UD: Set of people
Lxy: x loves y

There is a person who loves everyone. Therefore everyone is loved by someone.

Everyone is loved by someone. Therefore there is a person who loves everyone.

*d. UD: Set of numbers
Ex: x is even
Dx: x is divisible by 2

Some numbers are even and some numbers are divisible by 2. Therefore some numbers are even if and only if some numbers are divisible by 2.

A number is even if and only if it is divisible by 2. Therefore some number is even.

e. UD: Set of people
Tx: x is a student
Sx: x is smart
Hx: x is happy

Some students are smart and some students are not happy. Therefore there is a student who is smart or not happy.

All students are smart, and no student is happy. Therefore there is a student who is smart or not happy.

*f. UD: Set of people
Sx: x is a senator
Rx: x is a Republican
Dx: x is a Democrat

Any senator who is not a Republican is a Democrat. There is a senator who is not a Republican. Therefore some senator is a Democrat.

There is a senator who is not a Republican. Therefore some senator is a Democrat.

g. UD: Set of people
Ax: x likes asparagus
Sx: x likes spinach
Cx: x is crazy

Anyone who likes asparagus is crazy, and anyone who is crazy likes spinach. Therefore anyone who likes asparagus also likes spinach.

Anyone who likes spinach is crazy, and anyone who is crazy likes asparagus. Therefore anyone who likes asparagus also likes spinach.

4. Decide, for each of the following arguments, whether it is quantificationally valid. If the argument is quantificationally valid, explain why. If the argument is not quantificationally valid, construct an interpretation that shows this.

a. $(\forall x)((Lx \,\&\, Dx) \supset Fx)$
$(\exists x)(Dx \,\&\, \sim Fx)$

$\sim(\exists x)Lx$

*b. $(\forall x)(Sx \supset (Gx \vee Bx))$
$(\exists x)(Sx \,\&\, \sim Bx)$

$(\exists x)Gx$

c. $(\exists x)(Hx \equiv (Rx \vee Sx))$

$(\exists x)((Hx \,\&\, Rx) \vee (Hx \,\&\, Sx))$

*d. $(\exists x)(\exists y)((Rx \,\&\, Sy) \,\&\, Pxy)$
$(\forall x)(Rx \supset Tx)$

$(\exists x)(\exists y)(Tx \,\&\, Pxy)$

.5 TRUTH-FUNCTIONAL EXPANSIONS

In the preceding sections we constructed interpretations for sentences of *PL* to establish various semantic results: A sentence is not quantificationally true, a set of sentences is quantificationally consistent, and so on. When we give an interpretation for a sentence or a set of sentences of *PL*, the UD we select may be very large or even infinite. However, when we ask whether certain sentences have various semantic properties, we can often find the answer by considering only interpretations with a relatively small UD. Truth-functional expansions enable us to reason about the truth-values of sentences for interpretations with small UDs.

We shall introduce truth-functional expansions with an example. Consider the sentence

$$(\forall x)(Wx \supset (\exists y)Cxy)$$

and the interpretation

29. UD: The set {1, 2}
Wx: x is even
Cxy: x is greater than y

The sentence is true on this interpretation; every even member of the UD (in this case the number 2) is greater than some member of the UD. If we designate each member of the UD with a constant, for example,

a: 1
b: 2

then we can use these constants to produce a sentence without quantifiers that says the same thing about our UD as the sentence above. We can eliminate the universal quantifier and use a conjunction instead to say that each member of the UD is such that if it is even then it is greater than some member of the UD:

$$(\mathrm{Wa} \supset (\exists y)\mathrm{Cay}) \ \& \ (\mathrm{Wb} \supset (\exists y)\mathrm{Cby})$$

We can now eliminate the existential quantifier in '(∃y)Cay' and use a disjunction instead to say that 1 is greater than some member of the UD:

$$(\mathrm{Wa} \supset (\mathrm{Caa} \vee \mathrm{Cab})) \ \& \ (\mathrm{Wb} \supset (\exists y)\mathrm{Cby})$$

Because 'a' and 'b' designate the two objects in the UD, '(Caa ∨ Cab)' makes the same claim about the UD as '(∃y)Cay' does—the claim that 1 is greater than at least one member of the UD. We can eliminate the remaining existential quantifier in a similar way:

$$(\mathrm{Wa} \supset (\mathrm{Caa} \vee \mathrm{Cab})) \ \& \ (\mathrm{Wb} \supset (\mathrm{Cba} \vee \mathrm{Cbb}))$$

The sentence that we have just produced says the same thing about our UD as the original sentence. It is called a *truth-functional expansion* of the original sentence for the set of constants {'a', 'b'}.

Although we introduced interpretation 29 for illustration, we may generalize what we have just said about the quantified sentence and its truth-functional expansion. On *any* interpretation in which each member of the UD is designated by one of the constants 'a' and 'b', the quantified sentence has the same truth-value as its truth-functional expansion using those constants.

The principles behind truth-functional expansions are simple. A universally quantified sentence says something about each member of the UD. If we have a finite UD and a set of constants such that each member of the UD is designated by at least one of these constants, then we can reexpress a universally quantified sentence as a conjunction of its substitution instances formed from the constants. As long as every member of the UD is designated by at least one of the constants, the conjunction ends up saying the same thing as the universally quantified sentence—that every member of the UD satisfies some condition. An existentially quantified sentence says that there is at least one member of the UD of which such-and-such is true and can be reexpressed as a disjunction of its substitution instances: The sentence says that such-and-such is true of *this* object or of *that* object or . . . As long as every member of the UD is designated by at least one of the constants, the disjunction of substitution instances makes the same claim about the UD as did the existentially quantified sentence.

In constructing a truth-functional expansion, we first choose a set of individual constants. If the sentence contains any constants, they must be among the constants chosen. To expand a universally quantified sentence $(\forall \mathbf{x})\mathbf{P}$, we remove the initial quantifier from the sentence and replace the resulting open sentence with the iterated conjunction

$$(\ldots (\mathbf{P}(\mathbf{a}_1/\mathbf{x}) \ \& \ \mathbf{P}(\mathbf{a}_2/\mathbf{x})) \ \& \ldots \& \ \mathbf{P}(\mathbf{a}_n/\mathbf{x}))$$

where $\mathbf{a}_1, \ldots, \mathbf{a}_n$ are the chosen constants and $\mathbf{P}(\mathbf{a}_i/\mathbf{x})$ is a substitution instance of $(\forall \mathbf{x})\mathbf{P}$. Each of the conjuncts is a substitution instance of $(\forall \mathbf{x})\mathbf{P}$, differing from one another only in that each is formed from a different constant, and there is one substitution instance for each of the individual constants.

We shall expand the sentence '(∀x)Nx' for the set of constants {'a', 'b'}. Removing the quantifier gives us the open sentence 'Nx', and we replace 'Nx' with the conjunction 'Na & Nb'. We can expand '(∀y)(My ⊃ Jyy)' for the same set of constants by first dropping the quantifier and then replacing 'My ⊃ Jyy' with an iterated conjunction. In the first conjunct 'a' replaces the free variable 'y', and in the second conjunct 'b' replaces that variable. The truth-functional expansion

(Ma ⊃ Jaa) & (Mb ⊃ Jbb)

has the same truth-value as the unexpanded sentence on every interpretation in which each member of the UD is named by at least one of the two constants. If we have an interpretation with a two-member UD, for example, in which 'a' designates one member and 'b' designates the other, then '(Ma ⊃ Jaa) & (Mb ⊃ Jbb)' makes the same claim about the UD as '(∀y)(My ⊃ Jyy)'—namely, that each of the two members is such that if it is M then it stands in the relation J to itself.

We have claimed that a truth-functional expansion has the same truth-value as the unexpanded sentence on any interpretation on which each member of the UD is named *by at least one* of the constants used in the expansion. We note two points about this claim, using the previous example to illustrate. The first is that the interpretations in question may assign the same object to several of the constants as long as each object in the UD is named by at least one of them. So, if we have an interpretation with a one-member UD, both 'a' and 'b' must refer to that one member. In this case every object in the UD is named by at least one of the two constants. Our expanded sentence says twice that the one member of the UD is such that if it is M then it stands in the relation J to itself, and this is equivalent to the universal claim that every member of the UD satisfies that condition.

The second point is that, if a UD for an interpretation has even one member that is not designated by one of the two constants, then the two sentences may fail to have the same truth-value. The following interpretation shows this:

30. UD: The set {1, 2}
Mx: x is positive
Jxy: x equals y squared
a: 1
b: 1

The expanded sentence '(Ma ⊃ Jaa) & (Mb ⊃ Jbb)', which says twice that if 1 is positive then it equals itself squared, is true on this interpretation. But the universally quantified sentence '(∀y)(My ⊃ Jyy)' is false on this interpretation because 2, which was not mentioned in the expansion, does not satisfy the condition specified after the quantifier. If, however, interpretation 30 had interpreted 'b' to designate 2 (leaving 'a' to designate 1), our requirement that each member of the UD be designated by at least one of the constants would have been met. In this case the two sentences would have had the same truth-value (false).

Now we shall expand the sentence

(∀x)(Gac ∨ Fx)

We have stipulated that the set of constants we use for an expansion must include all the individual constants that occur in the sentence being expanded. So any set of constants for which we expand the sentence must include 'a' and 'c'. We can expand the sentence for the set containing just those constants, in which case removing the initial quantifier and replacing 'x' with each constant in turn results in the expansion

(Gac ∨ Fa) & (Gac ∨ Fc)

If we expand the sentence for the larger set {'a', 'c', 'e'} we obtain

((Gac ∨ Fa) & (Gac ∨ Fc)) & (Gac ∨ Fe)

If the sentence we want to expand contains more than one universal quantifier, we can start with the leftmost one and remove each in turn. To expand

(∀y)(Ly & (∀z)Bzy)

for the set of constants {'a', 'b'}, we first eliminate the quantifier '(∀y)' and expand the resulting open sentence, '(Ly & (∀z)Bzy)', to obtain

[La & (∀z)Bza] & [Lb & (∀z)Bzb]

The expanded sentence now contains two occurrences of the quantifier '(∀z)'; this is because '(∀z)Bzy' was part of the open sentence obtained by removing the quantifier '$(\forall y)$' and hence became part of each conjunct. We now expand each of the universally quantified sentences that are components of '[La & $(\forall z)$Bza] & [Lb & $(\forall z)$Bzb]' by eliminating each occurrence of '$(\forall z)$' and expanding the resulting open sentences, to obtain first

[La & (Baa & Bba)] & [Lb & $(\forall z)$Bzb]

and then

[La & (Baa & Bba)] & [Lb & (Bab & Bbb)]

Here we replaced '$(\forall z)$Bza' with '(Baa & Bba)' and '$(\forall z)$Bzb' with '(Bab & Bbb)'. Note that when we expand a quantified sentence that is a component of another sentence—as with '$(\forall z)$Bza' and '$(\forall z)$Bzb'—we replace that component exactly where it occurred in the sentence being expanded.

We may expand existentially quantified sentences just as we expand universally quantified sentences, except in this case we construct an iterated *disjunction* rather than an iterated conjunction. A sentence of the form $(\exists \mathbf{x})\mathbf{P}$ expands to the disjunction

$$(\ldots(\mathbf{P}(\mathbf{a}_1/\mathbf{x}) \vee \mathbf{P}(\mathbf{a}_2/\mathbf{x})) \vee \ldots \vee \mathbf{P}(\mathbf{a}_\mathbf{n}/\mathbf{x}))$$

where $\mathbf{a}_1, \ldots, \mathbf{a}_\mathbf{n}$ are the constants in the chosen set and $\mathbf{P}(\mathbf{a}_\mathbf{i}/\mathbf{x})$ is a substitution instance of $(\forall \mathbf{x})\mathbf{P}$. We construct an iterated disjunction because an existential quantification indicates that at least one member of the UD satisfies the specified condition: *This* member satisfies the condition, or *that* member satisfies the condition, and so on.

We can expand the sentence

$(\exists x)(Fx \supset Gx)$

for the set of constants {'a', 'b', 'c'} as

$[(Fa \supset Ga) \vee (Fb \supset Gb)] \vee (Fc \supset Gc)$

On any interpretation on which all the members of the UD are named by at least one of 'a', 'b', and 'c', the expanded sentence has the same truth-value as the existentially quantified sentence. If the existentially quantified sentence is true, for example, then some member of the UD is such that if it is F then it is G. As long as at least one of 'a', 'b', or 'c' designates this object, the disjunct that contains that constant is true as well. If the existentially quantified sentence is false, then no object in the UD satisfies the condition, and hence none of the disjuncts is true.

As with universally quantified sentences, our claims require that *each* member of the UD be designated by at least one of the constants. For example,

'$(\exists x)(Fx \supset Gx)$' is true but its expansion, '$[(Fa \supset Ga) \vee (Fb \supset Gb)] \vee (Fc \supset Gc)$', is false on interpretation 31:

31. UD: The set {1, 2}
Fx: x is prime
Gx: x is odd
a: 2
b: 2
c: 2

The number 1 satisfies the condition that if it is prime then it is odd, so the existentially quantified sentence is true. However, the expansion mentions the number 2 only on interpretation 31; it is false because 2 does not satisfy the condition that if it is prime (it is) then it is odd. The existentially quantified sentence and its expansion will have the same truth-value on an interpretation *only if* every member of the UD is named by at least one of the constants used in the expansion.

We expand the sentence

$$(\exists x)(\exists w)Zwx$$

for the set of constants {'a', 'b'} as follows: First, we eliminate '$(\exists x)$' and replace '$(\exists w)Zwx$' with an iterated disjunction:

$$(\exists w)Zwa \vee (\exists w)Zwb$$

Then we eliminate '$(\exists w)$' in each of its occurrences, first to obtain

$$(Zaa \vee Zba) \vee (\exists w)Zwb$$

and then to obtain

$$(Zaa \vee Zba) \vee (Zab \vee Zbb)$$

To expand the sentence

$$(\exists w)[Gw \supset \sim (Fw \vee (\exists z)Bz)]$$

for the set of constants {'a', 'b'}, we first eliminate '$(\exists w)$' to obtain

$$[Ga \supset \sim (Fa \vee (\exists z)Bz)] \vee [Gb \supset \sim (Fb \vee (\exists z)Bz)]$$

and then eliminate both occurrences of '$(\exists z)$' to obtain

$$[Ga \supset \sim (Fa \vee (Ba \vee Bb))] \vee [Gb \supset \sim (Fb \vee (Ba \vee Bb))]$$

The sentence

$(\forall x)(Fx \vee (\exists z)[Fz \ \& \sim Izx])$

can also be expanded by systematic elimination of its quantifiers. We shall expand it for the set of constants {'b', 'f'}. First, the universal quantifier is eliminated to obtain the conjunction

$[Fb \vee (\exists z)[Fz \ \& \sim Izb]] \ \& \ (Ff \vee (\exists z)[Fz \ \& \sim Izf])$

Next we eliminate the first occurrence of '$(\exists z)$' to obtain

$(Fb \vee [(Fb \ \& \sim Ibb) \vee (Ff \ \& \sim Ifb)] \ \& \ (Ff \vee (\exists z)[Fz \ \& \sim Izf])$

Now we eliminate the second occurrence of '$(\exists z)$', again using a disjunction since we are eliminating an existential quantifier:

$(Fb \vee [(Fb \ \& \sim Ibb) \vee (Ff \ \& \sim Ifb)]) \ \&$
$(Ff \vee [(Fb \ \& \sim Ibf) \vee (Ff \ \& \sim Iff)])$

When we expand a sentence, we may choose a set containing only one constant for the expansion. In this case we simply remove the quantifier and replace the free variable in the resulting open sentence with that constant. '$(\forall x)Fx$' is expanded for the set of constants {'a'} as 'Fa', and '$(\exists x)Fx$' is also expanded as 'Fa'. With the same set of constants, '$(\exists y)Gyy$' is expanded as 'Gaa' and '$(\forall x)(Fx \vee (\exists y)Gyy)$' is expanded first to obtain '$(Fa \vee (\exists y)Gyy)$' and then to obtain '$(Fa \vee Gaa)$'.

As a final example we expand the sentence

$Dg \vee (\forall y)(\exists x)Cyx$

for the set of constants {'a', 'g'} (we must include 'g' in the set because it occurs in the sentence to be expanded). We first replace '$(\forall y)(\exists x)Cyx$' with its expansion to obtain

$Dg \vee [(\exists x)Cax \ \& \ (\exists x)Cgx]$

Then we replace '$(\exists x)Cax$' with its expansion to obtain

$Dg \vee [(Caa \vee Cag) \ \& \ (\exists x)Cgx]$

Finally we replace '$(\exists x)Cgx$' with its expansion to obtain

$Dg \vee [(Caa \vee Cag) \ \& \ (Cga \vee Cgg)]$

When we have expanded a sentence of *PL* to eliminate every quantifier, the truth-functional expansion that results is always an atomic sentence or a truth-functional compound of atomic sentences of *PL*. Because of this, we can construct truth-tables for truth-functional expansions. And the truth-tables, in turn, tell us something about the truth-conditions of the sentences that have been expanded. For example, the truth-functional expansion of the sentence '(∀x) (Fx & ~ Bx)' for the set of constants {'a', 'b'} is '(Fa & ~ Ba) & (Fb & ~ Bb)'. Here is a truth-table for the expansion:

Ba	Bb	Fa	Fb	(Fa	&	~ Ba)	↓ &	(Fb	&	~ Bb)
T	T	T	T	T	F	F T	F	T	F	F T
T	T	T	F	T	F	F T	F	F	F	F T
T	T	F	T	F	F	F T	F	T	F	F T
T	T	F	F	F	F	F T	F	F	F	F T
T	F	T	T	T	F	F T	F	T	T	T F
T	F	T	F	T	F	F T	F	F	F	T F
T	F	F	T	F	F	F T	F	T	T	T F
T	F	F	F	F	F	F T	F	F	F	T F
F	T	T	T	T	T	T F	F	T	F	F T
F	T	T	F	T	T	T F	F	F	F	F T
F	T	F	T	F	F	T F	F	T	F	F T
F	T	F	F	F	F	T F	F	F	F	F T
F	F	T	T	T	T	T F	T	T	T	T F
F	F	T	F	T	T	T F	F	F	F	T F
F	F	F	T	F	F	T F	F	T	T	T F
F	F	F	F	F	F	T F	F	F	F	T F

This truth-table tells us that the quantified sentence is true on some interpretations with one- or two-member UDs and false on some interpretations with one- or two-member UDs. We shall now explain why.

If each object in a UD is designated by either 'a' or 'b', then each of the combinations of truth-values to the left of the vertical line represents an interpretation of 'B' and 'F'. (This assumption means that we are restricting our attention to UDs with at most two members because the number of constants is not enough for naming more than two members.) For example, the first row represents interpretations with one- or two-member UDs in which all objects are in the extension of 'B' and also are in the extension of 'F'. If all objects are named by either 'a' or 'b', then the assignment of **T** to both 'Ba' and 'Bb' means that all objects are in the extension of 'B', and the assignment of **T** to both 'Fa' and 'Fb' means that all objects are in the extension of 'F'. The second row represents interpretations with two-member UDs in which both objects are in the extension of 'B' (because both 'Ba' and 'Bb' are true), one object is in the extension of 'F' (because 'Fa' is true), and one object is not in the extension of 'F' (because 'Fb' is false). Note that, because one object is in the extension of 'F' and one is not, the UD for any interpretation represented by this row cannot have just one member—the single object in a one-member UD cannot both be in the extension of 'F' and not be in the extension of 'F'.

In fact, the sixteen rows between them represent all the combinations of extensions that the two predicates may have for a one- or two-member UD. For example, we have the following possibilities for a one-member UD: The one object is in the extension of both 'B' and 'F' (row 1), the one object is in the extension of 'B' but not of 'F' (row 4), the one object is in the extension of 'F' but not of 'B' (row 13), or the one object is not in the extension of either predicate (row 16). For a two-member UD we have the following possibilities: Both members are in the extensions of both 'B' and 'F' (row 1), both members are in the extension of 'B' but only one is in the extension of 'F' (rows 2 and 3), both members are in the extension of 'B' but neither is in the extension of 'F' (row 4), and so on.

The truth-value assigned to the truth-functional expansion in each row is the truth-value that '(∀x)(Fx & ~ Bx)' receives for the interpretations of 'B' and 'F' represented by that row. The expansion has the truth-value **F** in the first row, from which we may conclude that, on every interpretation with a one- or two-member UD in which every member is in the extension of 'B' and also in the extension of 'F', '(∀x)(Fx & ~ Bx)' is false. The expansion also has the truth-value **F** in the second row, from which we may conclude that, on every interpretation with a two-member UD (recall that this row cannot represent interpretations with one-member UDs) in which both members are in the extension of 'B' but only one member is in the extension of 'F', the sentence '(∀x)(Fx & ~ Bx)' is false.

The thirteenth row is the only one on which the expansion is true. From this we may conclude that every interpretation with a one- or two-member UD in which every member is in the extension of 'B' and no member is in the extension of 'F' makes '(∀x)(Fx & ~ Bx)' true, and that every other interpretation with a one- or two-member UD makes the sentence false.

We can use the information in the thirteenth row to construct an interpretation on which the unexpanded quantified sentence is true. Because neither 'a' nor 'b' appears in the quantified sentence, we need only specify a UD (we will choose one with two members rather than one), an interpretation of 'B' that holds for neither member of the UD (because 'Ba' and 'Bb' are both false), and an interpretation of 'F' that holds for both members of the UD (because 'Fa' and 'Fb' are both true). Here is a candidate:

32. UD: The set {3, 5}
 Bx: x is an even integer
 Fx: x is a positive integer

Both objects in the UD satisfy the condition of being positive and not even, so '(∀x)(Fx & ~ Bx)' is true on this interpretation.

We can use the information in the first row to construct an interpretation on which the sentence is false. For convenience we will choose the same UD. We shall interpret 'B' and 'F' so that both the number 3 and the number 5 are in the extension of both predicates—because the four atomic sentences in the first row are all true:

33. UD: The set {3, 5}
    Bx: x is an odd integer
    Fx: x is a positive integer

Any row in the truth-table in which ‘Ba’ has the same truth-value as ‘Bb’ and ‘Fa’ has the same truth-value as ‘Fb’ can be used to construct an interpretation with a one-member UD. For example, using the first row, we can construct an interpretation on which our quantified sentence is false by making sure that the one object in the UD is in the extension of both ‘B’ and ‘F’:

34. UD: The set {3}
    Bx: x is an odd integer
    Fx: x is a positive integer

A truth-functional expansion of the sentence ‘(∃x)(∀y)Nyx’ for the set of constants {‘a’, ‘b’} is ‘(Naa & Nba) ∨ (Nab & Nbb)’. We may show that the sentence ‘(∃x)(∀y)Nyx’ is true on at least one interpretation with a two-member UD by producing a shortened truth-table in which the expansion is true:

							↓			
Naa	Nab	Nba	Nbb	(Naa	&	Nba)	∨	(Nab	&	Nbb)
T	T	F	T	T	F	F	T	T	T	T

(The table in this case gives us information only about two-member UDs, because if there were only one member in the UD then it would be named by both ‘a’ and ‘b’, and hence the four atomic sentences would have to have the same truth-value since each would in that case make the same claim—that the one object stands in the relation N to itself.) We do not have to give an actual interpretation on which the sentence is true; the shortened truth-table suffices to show that there is such an interpretation. It shows that the quantified sentence is true on any interpretation with a two-member UD in which both members stand in the relation N to themselves and one stands in the relation N to the other, but not vice versa. And the following shortened truth-table shows that the quantified sentence is false on at least one interpretation with a one- or two-member UD:

							↓			
Naa	Nab	Nba	Nbb	(Naa	&	Nba)	∨	(Nab	&	Nbb)
F	F	F	F	F	F	F	F	F	F	F

(Because the four atomic sentences have the same truth-value in this table, the row of assignments may represent an interpretation with a one-member UD.)

From these two shortened truth-tables we may conclude that '(∃x)(∀y)Nyx' is quantificationally indeterminate. The tables show that the sentence is true on at least one interpretation and false on at least one interpretation.

We may use truth-functional expansions and truth-tables to demonstrate that sentences of *PL* have, or fail to have, some other semantic properties as well. For example, to show that a sentence is not quantificationally true, we must show that the sentence is false on at least one interpretation. And we can show this by producing a shortened truth-table in which a truth-functional expansion of the sentence is false. We will have to choose a set of constants first—ideally a small set, to save us work. An expansion of the sentence '(Ga & (∃z)Bz) ⊃ (∀x)Bx' for the set of constants {'a', 'b'} is '(Ga & (Ba ∨ Bb) ⊃ (Ba & Bb)', and the expansion is false in the following shortened truth-table:

Ba	Bb	Ga	(Ga	&	(Ba	∨	Bb))	↓ ⊃	(Ba	&	Bb)
T	**F**	**T**	**T**	**T**	**T**	**T**	**F**	**F**	**T**	**F**	**F**

The table shows that there is at least one interpretation on which the sentence '(Ga & (∃z)Bz) ⊃ (∀x)Bx' is false. This sentence is therefore not quantificationally true.

Note that we cannot in general use truth-functional expansions to show that a sentence *is* quantificationally true. Even if we construct a full truth-table for a truth-functional expansion and find that the expansion is true in every row of the truth-table, all that we may generally conclude is that the sentence is true on every interpretation with a UD that is the same size as or smaller than the number of constants in the set that was used for the expansion. (An exception will be noted at the end of this section.)

The sentence '~ (~ Ga & (∃y)Gy)' is not quantificationally false. The truth-functional expansion of this sentence for the set of constants {'a'}('a' must be in this set because it occurs in the sentence) is '~ (~ Ga & Ga)', and this expansion is true in the following shortened truth-table:

Ga	↓ ~	(~	Ga	&	Ga)
T	**T**	**F**	**T**	**F**	**T**

This shows that the sentence '~ (~ Ga & (∃y)Gy)' is true on at least one interpretation and hence that the sentence is not quantificationally false. As with quantificational truth we cannot in general use truth-functional expansions to show that a sentence is quantificationally false, for that would involve showing that the sentence is false on every interpretation, not just those with a particular size UD.

The sentences

(∀x)(Fx ⊃ Ga)

and

$$(\forall x)Fx \supset Ga$$

are not quantificationally equivalent. To show this, we shall expand both sentences for the same set of constants (which must include 'a') and produce a shortened truth-table in which the expansions have different truth-values. Expanding the sentences for the set {'a', 'b'}, we obtain

$$(Fa \supset Ga) \mathbin{\&} (Fb \supset Ga)$$

and

$$(Fa \mathbin{\&} Fb) \supset Ga$$

The first sentence is false and the second is true in the following shortened truth-table:

Fa	Fb	Ga	(Fa	⊃	Ga)	↓ &	(Fb	⊃	Ga)	(Fa	&	Fb)	↓ ⊃	Ga
T	**F**	**F**	**T**	**F**	**F**	**F**	**F**	**T**	**F**	**T**	**F**	**F**	**T**	**F**

This shows that there is at least one interpretation on which '$(\forall x)(Fx \supset Ga)$' is false and '$(\forall x)Fx \supset Ga$' is true.

The set of sentences

$$\{(\forall x)Gax, \sim Gba \vee (\exists x) \sim Gax\}$$

is quantificationally consistent. The truth-functional expansions of these sentences for the set {'a', 'b'} are '$Gaa \mathbin{\&} Gab$' and '$\sim Gba \vee (\sim Gaa \vee \sim Gab)$'. Both expansions are true in the following shortened truth-table, and so we may conclude that there is at least one interpretation on which both members of the set are true:

Gaa	Gab	Gba	Gaa	↓ &	Gab	~	Gba	↓ ∨	(~	Gaa	∨	~	Gab)
T	**T**	**F**	**T**	**T**	**T**	**T**	**F**	**T**	**F**	**T**	**F**	**F**	**T**

The set of sentences

$$\{\sim (\forall x)(Ga \equiv Fx), \sim Fb\}$$

does not quantificationally entail the sentence

$$(\forall x) \sim Gx$$

We shall expand the sentences for the set of constants {'a', 'b'} to obtain

$\sim [(Ga \equiv Fa) \& (Gb \equiv Fb)]$

and

$\sim Fb$

for the set members ('~ Fb' expands to itself because it contains no quantifiers), and

$\sim Ga \& \sim Gb$

for the sentence '(∀x) ~ Gx'. Here is a shortened truth-table in which the expanded set members are true and the expansion of '(∀x) ~ Gx' is false:

Fa	Fb	Ga	Gb	↓ ~	[(Ga	≡	Fa)	&	(Gb	≡	Fb)]	↓ ~ Fb	~ Ga	↓ &	~ Gb
F	**F**	**F**	**T**	**T**	**F**	**T**	**F**	**F**	**T**	**F**	**F**	**TF**	**TF**	**F**	**FT**

We thus know that there is at least one interpretation on which the set members are both true and '(∀x) ~ Gx' is false, so '(∀x) ~ Gx' is not quantificationally entailed by the set.

Finally we may use truth-functional expansions to show that some arguments are not quantificationally valid. The expansions of the premises and conclusion of the argument

$(\exists x)[(\exists y)Fy \supset Fx]$
$(\exists y) \sim Fy$
$\overline{\sim (\exists x)Fx}$

for the set of constants {'a', 'b'} are

$[(Fa \vee Fb) \supset Fa] \vee [(Fa \vee Fb) \supset Fb]$
$\sim Fa \vee \sim Fb$
$\overline{\sim (Fa \vee Fb)}$

The premises of this expanded argument are true and the conclusion false in the following shortened truth-table:

Fa	Fb	[(Fa	∨	Fb)	⊃	Fa]	↓ ∨	[(Fa	∨	Fb)	⊃	Fb]	~ Fa	↓ ∨	~ Fb	↓ ~	(Fa	∨	Fb)
T	**F**	**T**	**T**	**F**	**T**	**T**	**T**	**T**	**T**	**F**	**F**	**F**	**FT**	**T**	**TF**	**F**	**T**	**T**	**F**

There is thus an interpretation on which the premises of the original argument are true and the conclusion is false.

Note once again that truth-functional expansions cannot generally be used to show that a set of sentences of *PL* is quantificationally inconsistent, that a set of sentences *does* quantificationally entail some sentence, or that an argument of *PL* is quantificationally valid. In each of these cases we must prove something about every interpretation, not just those represented in the truth-table for a particular set of expansions.

However, there is an exception to our claims about the limitations of using truth-functional expansions to test for semantic properties. We noted at the end of Section 8.2 that there is a decision procedure (based on a result by Bernays and Schönfinkel) for determining the quantificational status of sentences of *PL* that contain no many-place predicates, that is, in which the predicates are all one-place predicates. A decision procedure allows us to answer correctly in a finite number of mechanical steps the question 'Is this sentence quantificationally true?' and hence also questions like 'Is this sentence quantificationally false?' (it is if its negation is quantificationally true) and 'Is this finite set of sentences quantificationally consistent?' (it is if the conjunction of the sentences in the set is not quantificationally false). It allows us to answer these questions correctly for sentences that do not contain many-place predicates.

Bernays and Schönfinkel's result is that a sentence that contains no many-place predicates and that contains **k** distinct one-place predicates is quantificationally true if and only if the sentence is true on every interpretation with a UD containing exactly $2^{\mathbf{k}}$ members. This being the case, we can truth-functionally expand the sentence for a set of at least $2^{\mathbf{k}}$ constants, produce a truth-table for the expanded sentence, and determine whether it is quantificationally true by examining the truth-table. If the expanded sentence is true in every row of the truth-table, we may conclude that the sentence is true on every interpretation with a UD that is the same size as the set of constants or smaller. In particular, we may conclude that the sentence is true on every interpretation with a UD that contains exactly $2^{\mathbf{k}}$ members. And, by Bernays and Schönfinkel's result, we may finally conclude that the sentence is quantificationally true.

8.5E EXERCISES

1. Give a truth-functional expansion of each of the sentences in Exercise 7 in Section 8.1E for a set containing one constant.

2. Give a truth-functional expansion of each of the sentences in Exercise 8 in Section 8.1E for a set containing two constants.

3. Give a truth-functional expansion of each of the sentences in Exercise 9 in Section 8.1E for a set containing two constants.

4. Give a truth-functional expansion of each of the following sentences for the set {'a', 'b', 'c'}.

a. (∀w) (Gw ⊃ Nww)
*b. (Na ∨ (∃z)Bz)
c. (∃z) (Na ≡ Bz)
*d. (∀w)Bw ∨ ~ (∃w)Bw

5. Construct truth-functional expansions of the sentence

'((∃x)Fx & (∃y) ~ Fy) ⊃ (∀x) ~ Fx'

for the sets {'a'} and {'a', 'b'}. Construct a truth-table for each expansion. What information does the first truth-table give you about this sentence? What information does the second truth-table give you?

6. For each of the following sentences, construct a truth-functional expansion for the set of constants ('a', 'n'). Show that the expansion is true on at least one truth-value assignment. Then use the information in the truth-table to construct an interpretation on which the original sentence is true.

a. (∀x) (Nxx ∨ (∃y)Nxy)
*b. (∃x)Fx ≡ (∀x)Fx
c. (∀y)Syyn

7. Show that each of the sentences in Exercise 1 in Section 8.2E is not quantificationally true by producing a shortened truth-table in which a truth-functional expansion of the sentence is false.

8. Show that each of the sentences in Exercise 2 in Section 8.2E is not quantificationally false by producing a shortened truth-table in which a truth-functional expansion of the sentence is true.

9. Show that each of the sentences in Exercise 3 in Section 8.2E is quantificationally indeterminate by producing a shortened truth-table in which a truth-functional expansion of the sentence is true and a shortened truth-table in which a truth-functional expansion of the sentence is false.

***10.** In this section it was claimed that in general a sentence of *PL* that contains quantifiers cannot be shown to be quantificationally true by producing truth-tables for truth-functional expansions. Does the claim hold for sentences of *PL* that do not contain quantifiers, such as 'Fa ⊃ (Gb ⊃ Fa)'? Explain.

11. The truth-functional expansion of the sentence '(∃y)Gy & (∃y) ~ Gy' for the set {'a'} is 'Ga & ~ Ga'. The expanded sentence is quantificationally false. Explain this and then explain why this does *not* show that the original sentence '(∃y)Gy & (∃y) ~ Gy' is quantificationally false.

12. Show that the sentences in each pair in Exercise 1 in Section 8.3E are not quantificationally equivalent by producing a shortened truth-table in which a truth-functional expansion of one sentence of the pair is true and a truth-functional expansion of the other sentence (for the same set of constants) is false.

13. Show that each set of sentences in Exercise 4 in Section 8.3E is quantificationally consistent by producing a shortened truth-table in which a truth-functional expansion of each sentence in the set (for the same set of constants) is true.

*14. a. Is the set {Ba, Bb, Bc, Bd, Be, Bf, Bg, ~ (∀x)Bx} quantificationally consistent? Explain.
b. For the set in Exercise 14.a, what is the minimum size set of constants for which the sentences in the set must be expanded in order to show that the set is quantificationally consistent? Explain.
c. Can all the sentences in the set in Exercise 14.a be true on an interpretation with a UD smaller than the set of constants indicated in the answer to Exercise 14.b? Explain.

15. Show that each argument in Exercise 2 in Section 8.4E is quantificationally invalid by producing a shortened truth-table in which truth-functional expansions of the premises are true and a truth-functional expansion of the conclusion for the same set of constants is false.

8.6 SEMANTICS FOR PREDICATE LOGIC WITH IDENTITY AND FUNCTORS

In *PLE* interpretations for sentences containing the identity predicate but no functors are the same as interpretations for *PL*, because the *identity* predicate, '=', is *not* explicitly given an interpretation. This is because we always want its extension to be the set of ordered pairs of members of the UD in which the first member is identical to the second, no matter what the UD is. The extension of the identity predicate is determined once the UD has been determined. If the UD is the set of positive integers, for example, then the extension of the identity predicate will include the pair whose first and second members are 1, the pair whose first and second members are 2, and so on for each positive integer—and no other pairs.

Every atomic sentence of the form **a** = **a**, where **a** is an arbitrary individual constant, is true on every interpretation. This is because **a** designates exactly one member of the UD on a given interpretation, and the identity predicate must include the pair consisting of that object and itself in its extension. On the other hand, the truth-value of an atomic sentence of the form **a** = **b**, where **a** and **b** are different individual constants, depends on the interpretations of **a** and **b**. Interpretation 35 makes the sentence 'g = k' true, while interpretation 36 makes the sentence false:

35. UD: Set of positive integers
g: 1
k: 1

36. UD: Set of positive integers
g: 1
k: 2

The sentence '$(\forall x)(\forall y)(\sim x = y \supset Gxy)$' is true on interpretation 37 and false on interpretation 38:

37. UD: Set of positive integers
    Gxy: the sum of x and y is positive

38. UD: Set of positive integers
    Gxy: x is greater than y

On interpretation 37 the sentence may be read as 'The sum of any pair of nonidentical positive integers is a positive integer'—which is true. On interpretation 38 the sentence claims that for any pair of nonidentical positive integers the first is greater than the second. This is false—1 and 2 are nonidentical positive integers, for example, but 1 is not greater than 2.

We can show that various sentences and sets of sentences that contain the identity predicate have, or fail to have, semantic properties much as we did for *PL*. We shall give a few examples for the semantic properties of quantificational truth and quantificational validity. We can show that the sentence

$$(\forall x)(\forall y)(\sim x = y \vee (Fx \supset Fy))$$

is quantificationally true by reasoning generally about interpretations, showing that on every interpretation the sentence turns out to be true. The sentence is universally quantified and is true on an interpretation when, for every pair x and y of members of the UD, either they satisfy the condition specified by '$\sim x = y$' or they satisfy the condition specified by '$Fx \supset Fy$'. So let us consider two members x and y of an arbitrary UD. If x and y are not the same member, then the first disjunct '$\sim x = y$' is satisfied because the extension of the identity predicate includes only pairs in which the first and second members are the same. If, however, x and y *are* the same member of the UD (and hence do not satisfy the first disjunct), they satisfy the second disjunct. If x is in the extension of 'F', then so is y—because y is identical to x, and so x and y satisfy the condition '$Fx \supset Fy$'. Because x and y either are or are not the same member of the UD, we have shown that each pair of members of any UD satisfy the condition '$\sim x = y \vee (Fx \supset Fy)$' no matter what the interpretation of 'F' may be. Therefore the sentence '$(\forall x)(\forall y)(\sim x = y \vee (Fx \supset Fy))$' must be true on any interpretation; it is quantificationally true.

On the other hand, the sentence

$$(\forall x)(\forall y)(x = y \vee (Fx \supset Fy))$$

is not quantificationally true. To show this, we construct an interpretation on which the sentence is false. The sentence claims that every pair of members of the UD x and y satisfies '$x = y \vee (Fx \supset Fy)$'—that is, that either x and y are the same member or if x is F then so is y. If we choose a two-member UD, then a pair consisting of the two members will not satisfy the condition 'x = y'. If the first member is F but the other is not, then this pair also will not satisfy 'Fx ⊃ Fy'. Here is our interpretation:

39. UD: The set {1, 2}
    Fx: x is odd

The pair consisting of the numbers 1 and 2 does not satisfy 'x = y ∨ (Fx ⊃ Fy)'. The two numbers are not identical, and it is not true that <u>if</u> the number 1 is odd (which it is) <u>then</u> the number 2 is odd (it is not).

The argument

(∀x)(Fx ≡ Gx)

(∀x)(∀y)x = y

Ga

(∀x)Fx

is quantificationally valid. We shall show that any interpretation that makes the three premises true also makes '(∀x)Fx' true. If '(∀x)(Fx ≡ Gx)' is true, then every member of the UD that is F is also G, and every member of the UD that is G is also F. If '(∀x)(∀y)x = y' is also true, then there is exactly one object in the UD. The sentence says that, for any object x and any object y, x and y are identical—and this cannot be the case if there is more than one member of the UD. If 'Ga' is also true, then because there is exactly one object in the UD this object must be designated by 'a' and must therefore be in the extension of 'G'. It follows, from the truth of the first sentence, that this object is also in the extension of 'F'. Therefore it follows that '(∀x)Fx' is true—every object in our single-member UD is F.

On the other hand, the argument

(∀x)(∃y)x = y

---

a = b

is not quantificationally valid. The premise, it turns out, is quantificationally true—every member of any UD is identical to something (namely, itself). But the conclusion is false on any interpretation on which 'a' and 'b' designate different objects, such as the following:

40. UD: Set of positive integers
    a: 6
    b: 7

It is true that every positive integer is identical to some positive integer, but it is false that 6 is identical to 7.

Readers who have worked through the section on truth-functional expansions may wonder whether sentences containing the identity predicate may be expanded and truth-tables used to check for various semantic properties. The answer is yes, although we shall see that there is a complication. Sentences that contain the identity predicate are expanded in the same way as sentences without the identity predicate: Quantifiers are eliminated in favor of iterated conjunctions or disjunctions. The sentence '$(\forall x)(\exists y)x = y$' can be expanded for the set of constants {'a', 'b'} first to obtain

$$(\exists y)a = y \ \& \ (\exists y)b = y$$

and then to obtain

$$(a = a \lor a = b) \ \& \ (b = a \lor b = b)$$

But if we freely assign truth-values to the atomic components of this sentence, we end up with this truth-table:

a = a	a = b	b = a	b = b	(a = a	∨	a = b)	↓ &	(b = a	∨	b = b)
T	**T**	**T**	**T**	**T**	**T**	**T**	**T**	**T**	**T**	**T**
T	**T**	**T**	**F**	**T**	**T**	**T**	**T**	**T**	**T**	**F**
T	**T**	**F**	**T**	**T**	**T**	**T**	**T**	**F**	**T**	**T**
T	**T**	**F**	**F**	**T**	**T**	**T**	**F**	**F**	**F**	**F**
T	**F**	**T**	**T**	**T**	**T**	**F**	**T**	**T**	**T**	**T**
T	**F**	**T**	**F**	**T**	**T**	**F**	**T**	**T**	**T**	**F**
T	**F**	**F**	**T**	**T**	**T**	**F**	**T**	**F**	**T**	**T**
T	**F**	**F**	**F**	**T**	**T**	**F**	**F**	**F**	**F**	**F**
F	**T**	**T**	**T**	**F**	**T**	**T**	**T**	**T**	**T**	**T**
F	**T**	**T**	**F**	**F**	**T**	**T**	**T**	**T**	**T**	**F**
F	**T**	**F**	**T**	**F**	**T**	**T**	**T**	**F**	**T**	**T**
F	**T**	**F**	**F**	**F**	**T**	**T**	**F**	**F**	**F**	**F**
F	**F**	**T**	**T**	**F**	**F**	**F**	**F**	**T**	**T**	**T**
F	**F**	**T**	**F**	**F**	**F**	**F**	**F**	**T**	**T**	**F**
F	**F**	**F**	**T**	**F**	**F**	**F**	**F**	**F**	**T**	**T**
F	**F**	**F**	**F**	**F**	**F**	**F**	**F**	**F**	**F**	**F**

MISTAKE!

There is something wrong with this truth-table! The sentence '$(\forall x)(\exists y)x = y$' is quantificationally true, and yet we have assigned its expansion the truth-value **F** in seven rows. Let us look at the first row where this happened: row 4. In this row we have assigned **T** to '$a = b$' and **F** to '$b = a$', and that is the problem. If an interpretation makes '$a = b$' true then it must make '$b = a$' true as well; a and b are the same object. So row 4 does not correspond to any interpretation at all. By the same reasoning we find that none of rows 3–6 or 11–14 correspond to interpretations, for each of these rows assigns different truth-values to '$a = b$' and '$b = a$'. However, this still leaves us with problematic rows 8, 15, and 16—all of which make the expanded sentence false. The problem with each of these rows is that the truth-value **F** has been assigned to one or both of ‘a = a’ and ‘b = b’—thus claiming that some object is not the same as itself. Because every interpretation makes every sentence of the form $\mathbf{a} = \mathbf{a}$ true, rows 8, 15, and 16, as well as all other rows that make one or both of ‘a = a’ and ‘b = b’ false, do not correspond to interpretations. In fact, we have just ruled out all rows in the truth-table except rows 1 and 7. These are the only rows in which ‘a = a’ and ‘b = b’ are both true and in which ‘a = b’ and ‘b = a’ have the same truth-value—and, as we should have expected for a quantificationally true sentence, the expanded sentence is true in both rows.

The rows of a truth-table that do not correspond to any interpretation cannot be used to establish semantic properties of the sentence that has been expanded. We therefore require that each row in the truth-table we construct for an expansion of a sentence containing the identity predicate must meet two conditions:

1. Every sentence of the form $\mathbf{a} = \mathbf{a}$ has the truth-value **T**.
2. If a sentence of the form $\mathbf{a} = \mathbf{b}$ has the truth-value **T**, then for each atomic sentence **P** that contains **a**, every atomic sentence **P**(**b**//**a**) that results from replacing one or more occurrences of **a** in **P** with **b** must have the same truth-value as **P**.

If conditions 1 and 2 are met, then if a sentence containing $\mathbf{a} = \mathbf{b}$ has the truth-value **T** in a row, $\mathbf{b} = \mathbf{a}$ will also have the truth-value **T**. Condition 1 requires that $\mathbf{a} = \mathbf{a}$ have the truth-value **T**, and because $\mathbf{b} = \mathbf{a}$ can be obtained from $\mathbf{a} = \mathbf{a}$ by replacing the first occurrence of **a** with **b**, condition 2 requires that $\mathbf{b} = \mathbf{a}$ is true since $\mathbf{a} = \mathbf{b}$ and $\mathbf{a} = \mathbf{a}$ are. Condition 2 also rules out rows like the one in the following shortened truth-table for the expansion

$$[(a = a \supset (Fa \supset Fa)) \;\&\; (a = b \supset (Fa \supset Fb))] \;\&\; [(b = a \supset (Fb \supset Fa)) \;\&\; (b = b \supset (Fb \supset Fb))]$$

of the sentence

$$(\forall x)(\forall y)(x = y \supset (Fx \supset Fy))$$

for the set of constants {‘a’, ‘b’}:

a = a	a = b	b = a	b = b	Fa	Fb	[(a = a ⊃ (Fa ⊃ Fa)) & (a = b ⊃ (Fa ⊃ Fb))]
T	T	T	T	T	F	T T T T T F T F T F F

↓

& [(b = a ⊃ (Fb ⊃ Fa)) & (b = b ⊃ (Fb ⊃ Fb))]
F   T   T F T T   T   T   T F T F

Once again we have expanded a quantificationally true sentence and produced a row of a truth-table in which the truth-functional expansion is false. We have ensured that both sentences ‘a = a’ and ‘b = b’ are true and that ‘a = b’ and ‘b = a’ have the same truth-value. The problem is that we have assigned ‘Fa’ and ‘Fb’ different truth-values, although ‘a = b’ is true. Condition 2 rules out this combination: ‘Fb’ results from replacing ‘a’ in ‘Fa’ with ‘b,’ and so, because ‘a = b’ is true, ‘Fb’ must have the same truth-value as ‘Fa’. Our second condition reflects the fact that when the identity predicate occurs in a truth-functional expansion the atomic sentences that are components of the expansion may not be truth-functionally independent. Once a sentence of the form **a** = **b**, where **a** and **b** are different constants, has been made true, certain other atomic sentences must agree in truth-value.

The following truth-table shows the only combinations of truth-values for the atomic components of our sentence that correspond to interpretations with one- or two-member UDs:

a = a	a = b	b = a	b = b	Fa	Fb	[(a = a ⊃ (Fa ⊃ Fa)) & (a = b ⊃ (Fa ⊃ Fb))]										
T	T	T	T	T	T	T	T	T	T	T	T	T	T	T	T	T
T	T	T	T	F	F	T	T	F	T	F	T	T	T	F	T	F
T	F	F	T	T	T	T	T	T	T	T	T	F	T	T	T	T
T	F	F	T	T	F	T	F	T	T	T	T	F	T	T	F	F
T	F	F	T	F	T	T	T	F	T	F	T	F	T	F	T	T
T	F	F	T	F	F	T	T	F	T	F	T	F	T	F	T	F

↓

& [(b = a ⊃ (Fb ⊃ Fa)) & (b = b ⊃ (Fb ⊃ Fb))]											
T	T	T	T	T	T	T	T	T	T	T	T
T	T	T	F	T	F	T	T	T	F	T	F
T	F	T	T	T	T	T	T	T	T	T	T
T	F	T	F	T	T	T	T	T	F	T	F
T	F	T	T	F	F	T	T	T	T	T	T
T	F	T	F	T	F	T	T	T	F	T	F

All other rows are excluded by one or both of our conditions. And again we find that the expanded sentence is true in all six rows—we have shown that there are no interpretations with one- or two-member UDs on which the sentence is false.

Adhering to our two conditions, we now produce a shortened truth-table that shows that the sentence

(∀z)((Fz & (∃y)z = y) ⊃ (∀x)Fx)

is not quantificationally true. The sentence claims that, for each member of the UD, if it is F and is identical to something then everything is F. Certainly the sentence will be true if the UD contains exactly one object—but for larger

UDs it will be true only if either no member is F or all members are. We shall expand the sentence for the set of constants {'a', 'b'} and produce a shortened truth-table in which the expansion is false:

a = a	a = b	b = a	b = b	Fa	Fb	[(Fa	&	(a = a	∨	a = b))	⊃	(Fa	&	Fb)]
T	**F**	**F**	**T**	**T**	**F**	**T**	**T**	**T**	**T**	**F**	**F**	**T**	**F**	**F**

↓

&	[(Fb	&	(b = a	∨	b = b))	⊃	(Fa	&	Fb)]
F	**F**	**F**	**F**	**T**	**T**	**T**	**T**	**F**	**F**

Condition 1 has been met—both 'a = a' and 'b = b' are true. Condition 2 has also been met, trivially. The two identity statements that are true are 'a = a' and 'b = b', and the result of substituting 'a' for 'a' in any sentence is just that sentence itself and the same holds for 'b'. Here is an interpretation that has been constructed using the truth-values in the truth-table as a guide:

41. UD: The set {2, 3}
    Fx: x is even

We have chosen a UD with two members because the identity statements 'a = b' and 'b = a' are false in the shortened table, and so 'a' and 'b' must designate different objects. We have interpreted 'F' so that one member of the UD, but not the other, is in its extension.

We now turn to the semantics for functors in *PLE.* A one-place functor is interpreted as a function that maps each ordered set of one member of the UD to a single member of the UD, namely, the member that is the value of the function for that ordered set. A two-place functor is interpreted as a function that maps each ordered pair of members of the UD to a single member of the UD, a three-place functor is interpreted as a function that maps each ordered triple of members of the UD to a single member of the UD, and so on. Here is an interpretation for the sentence '(∀x)(Px ⊃ H*f*(x))':

42. UD: Set of positive integers
    Px: x is even
    Hx: x is odd
    f(x): the successor of x (the number that results from adding 1 to x)

On this interpretation the sentence may be read as 'The successor of any even positive integer is an odd positive integer', which is true. The sentence is false on the following interpretation:

43. UD: Set of positive integers
Px: x is even
Hx: x is odd
f(x): the square of x

On this interpretation the sentence may be read as 'The square of any even positive integer is an odd positive integer'.

Here is an interpretation for the sentence '$(\forall x)(\exists y)y = g(x) \supset (\forall x)(\exists y)Pf(x,y)$':

44. UD: Set of positive integers
Px: x is odd
g(x): the successor of x
f(x,y): the sum of x and y

On this interpretation the sentence may be read as 'If every positive integer has a successor, then for every positive integer x there is a positive integer y such that the sum of x and y is odd'. On this interpretation the sentence is true since both the antecedent and the consequent are true. The following interpretation makes the same sentence false:

45. UD: Set of positive integers
Px: x is prime
g(x): the successor of x
f(x,y): x raised to the power y

On this interpretation the sentence may be read as 'If every positive integer has a successor, then for every positive integer there is some positive power such that the integer raised to that power is prime'. While the antecedent remains true, the consequent in this case is false.

Here is an interpretation for the sentence '$(\forall x)(\forall y)f(x,y) = f(y,x)$':

46. UD: Set of positive integers:
f(x,y): the sum of x and y

On this interpretation the sentence may be read as 'The sum of any two positive integers x and y is equal to the sum of y and x', which is true. The same sentence is false on the following interpretation:

47. UD: Set of positive integers
f(x,y): x raised to the power y

It is not true that, for any two positive integers x and y, x raised to the power y equals y raised to the power x. For example, 2 cubed equals 8, but 3 squared equals 9.

The sentence '$(\forall x)Dh(x,f(x))$' is true on interpretation 48 and false on interpretation 49:

48. UD: Set of positive integers
Dx: x is even
$f(x)$: x cubed
$h(x,y)$: the sum of x and y

49. UD: Set of positive integers
Dx: x is even
$f(x)$: x doubled
$h(x,y)$: the sum of x and y

It is true that the sum of any positive integer and that same integer cubed is even, for the cube of an even integer is even and the cube of an odd integer is odd. But it is false that the sum of any positive integer and that same integer doubled is even, for the result of doubling an odd integer is even, and so the sum of an odd integer and its double is odd.

When we produce an interpretation for sentences containing functors, it is important that we really have interpreted the functors as functions. For example, it may be tempting to come up with an interpretation with the set of positive integers as UD on which '$f(x)$' means 'the integer greater than x'. But this is not a function, for there are (infinitely!) many integers greater than any positive integer. A one-place function cannot map a member of the UD to more than one value. Similarly we cannot interpret '$h(x,y)$' (with the same UD) as 'the integer that is a factor of both x and y', because two positive integers can have more than one factor in common.

It is also important, when we produce an interpretation for sentences containing functors, that the interpretation assigns a function that meets the following two conditions. First, a one-place function that is used to interpret a one-place functor must be defined for every member of the UD, and an **n**-place function that is used to interpret an **n**-place functor must be defined for every ordered set of members of the UD. For example, with the set of positive integers as the UD, we cannot interpret '$f(x)$' to mean 'the integer that is the square root of x', since not every positive integer has an integral square root. Similarly we cannot interpret '$h(x,y)$' to mean 'the integer that is the result of dividing x by y', since, for example, no integer is the result of dividing 5 by 3.

Second, even when the function is defined for every member or ordered set of members of the UD, we also require that the value of the function in each case be a member of the UD. So, if our UD is the set of positive integers, we also cannot interpret '$h(x,y)$' to mean 'the *number* that is the result of dividing x by y'. Thus, although the division function is defined for every pair of positive integers, the resulting value is not in every case a positive integer. For example, the result of dividing 5 by 3, namely, $\frac{5}{3}$, is not a positive integer. Nor can we interpret '$h(x,y)$' to mean 'x minus y' if our UD is the set of positive integers, because, for example, 2 minus 3 is not a positive integer.

Similarly, with the UD of positive integers, we cannot interpret 'f(x)' to mean 'the predecessor of x'. Not every positive integer has a positive integer as its predecessor, for the predecessor of the positive integer 1 is 0.

We may show semantic results for sentences containing functors either by producing interpretations that are sufficient to prove the result or by arguing generally that the sentences will have certain truth-values on every interpretation. For example, interpretations 45 and 46, respectively, established that the sentence '(∀x) (∀y)f(x,y) = f(y,x)' is quantificationally indeterminate. On the other hand, the sentence '(∀x) (∃y)y = f(x)' is quantificationally true. The sentence is universally quantified and is true on an interpretation if for each x there is at least one y such that the pair x and y satisfies 'y = f(x)'. This must be the case for any interpretation, since 'f' must be interpreted as a function that maps each member x of the UD to a member y of the UD.

The argument

(∀x) Pf(x)
―――――――
Pf(f(a))

is quantificationally valid. We must show that any interpretation that makes the premise true also makes the conclusion true. If '(∀x) Pf(x)' is true, then every member x of the UD is such that f(x) has the property P. Now, f(a) is a member of the UD by our requirements for functor interpretations, so it follows from the universally quantified sentence that f(f(a)) must also have the property P, making the conclusion true as well.

The similar argument

(∀x) Pf(f(x))
―――――――
Pf(a)

is quantificationally invalid. Here is an interpretation on which the premise is true and the conclusion false:

50. UD: Set of positive integers
Px: x is greater than or equal to 3
f(x): the successor of x
a: 1

For any positive integer x the successor of the successor of x is greater than or equal to 3, but the successor of 1 is 2, which is not greater than or equal to 3.

We may also expand sentences containing functors in order to use truth-tables to check for various properties, although again there will be a complication. We first note that the rules for expanding sentences containing complex terms are the same as the rules for expanding sentences without complex terms. For example, the sentence '(∀x) (Px ⊃ Hf(x))' is expanded for the set of constants {'a'} by eliminating the universal quantifier and substituting 'a' for 'x' to obtain

$$Pa \supset Hf(a)$$

and expanding the same sentence for the set of constants {'a', 'b'} results in the conjunction

$$(Pa \supset Hf(a)) \ \& \ (Pb \supset Hf(b))$$

The expansion of the sentence

$$(\forall x)(\exists y)y = g(x) \supset (\forall x)(\exists y)Pf(x,y)$$

for the set of constants {'a'} results in

$$a = g(a) \supset Pf(a,a)$$

To expand the same sentence for the set of constants {'a', 'b'}, we expand the antecedent first to obtain

$$(\exists y)y = g(a) \ \& \ (\exists y)y = g(b)$$

and then to obtain

$$(a = g(a) \vee b = g(a)) \ \& \ (a = g(b) \vee b = g(b))$$

we expand the consequent first to obtain

$$(\exists y)Pf(a,y)) \ \& \ (\exists y)Pf(b,y)$$

and then to obtain

$$(Pf(a,a) \vee Pf(a,b)) \ \& \ (Pf(b,a) \vee Pf(b,b))$$

resulting in the expansion

$$((a = g(a) \vee b = g(a)) \ \& \ (a = g(b) \vee b = g(b))) \supset$$
$$((Pf(a,a) \vee Pf(a,b)) \ \& \ (Pf(b,a) \vee Pf(b,b)))$$

for the entire sentence.

Suppose now that we want to develop a truth-table for the expansion '$Pa \supset Pf(a)$' of the sentence '$(\forall x)(Px \supset Pf(x))$' for the set of constants {'a'} and, that since 'Pa' and 'Pf(a)' are distinct sentences involving the distinct individual terms 'a' and 'f(a)', we decide that we can assign **T** to the antecedent and **F** to the consequent:

Pa	Pf(a)	Pa ⊃ Pf(a) ↓	
T	**F**	**T F F**	**MISTAKE!**

Something is wrong here—because the sentence '(∀x) (Px ⊃ Pf(x))' *cannot* be false on any interpretation with a one-member UD. If there is only one member of the UD, then the only candidate for the value of function f applied to that one member is that one member—since we require that the value of a function applied to any member of a UD must be a member of the UD.

Our method of using truth-functional expansions to determine possible truth-values assumes that every member of the UD is named by one of the constants used in the expansion. For this reason we cannot assume that terms containing functors might refer to individuals other than those referred to by the constants used in the expansion. To the contrary, we must assume that each term containing a functor refers to the same individual as at least one constant. Thus in the above example we must assume that 'a' refers to the same individual as 'f(a)', if the expansion is to tell us something about one-member UDs. We will make this explicit in our truth-table: The truth-value assignment must make the sentence 'a = f(a)' true.

Pa	Pf(a)	Pa ⊃ Pf(a) ↓	a = f(a) ↓
			T

And now our conditions 1 and 2 for truth-tables containing expansions of sentences with the identity predicate must apply. In particular, condition 2 requires that, since 'a = f(a)' is true, the sentences 'Pa' and 'Pf(a)' must have the same truth-value. So the only shortened truth-tables we can obtain are

a = f(a)	Pa	Pf(a)	Pa ⊃ Pf(a) ↓	a = f(a) ↓
T	**T**	**T**	**T T T**	**T**

and

a = f(a)	Pa	Pf(a)	Pa ⊃ Pf(a) ↓	a = f(a) ↓
T	**F**	**F**	**F T F**	**T**

The shortened truth-tables show that the sentence '(∀x)(Px ⊃ P*f*(x))' must be true on any interpretation with a one-member UD.

Generalizing, when we construct a truth-table for the truth-functional expansion of a sentence or set of sentences containing functors, the following condition must be met in addition to those for sentences containing the identity predicate:

> 3. For each **n**-place functor *f* occurring in one or more of the sentences being expanded and each sequence of **n** constants $\mathbf{a}_1, \ldots, \mathbf{a}_\mathbf{n}$ from the set of constants $\{\mathbf{b}_1, \ldots, \mathbf{b}_\mathbf{m}\}$ for which the sentence(s) is (are) being expanded, the sentence $(\ldots(f(\mathbf{a}_1, \ldots, \mathbf{a}_\mathbf{n}) = \mathbf{b}_1 \vee f(\mathbf{a}_1, \ldots, \mathbf{a}_\mathbf{n}) = \mathbf{b}_2) \vee \ldots \vee f(\mathbf{a}_1, \ldots, \mathbf{a}_\mathbf{n}) = \mathbf{b}_\mathbf{m})$ must be true.

That is, the value that the function produces when applied to $\mathbf{a}_1, \ldots, \mathbf{a}_\mathbf{n}$ must be named by one of the constants in the set of constants for which we are producing an expansion.

Let us now construct a truth-table for the truth-functional expansion of '(∀x)(Px ⊃ P*f*(x))' for the set of constants {'a', 'b'}. We begin by adding two sentences to the right of the vertical line in order to satisfy condition 3, and we add the atomic components of those sentences to the left of the vertical line:

f(a) = a	*f*(a) = b	*f*(b) = a	*f*(b) = b	Pa	Pb	P*f*(a)	P*f*(b)

	↓			↓			↓	
(Pa ⊃ P*f*(a))	&	(Pb ⊃ P*f*(b))	*f*(a) = a	∨	*f*(a) = b	*f*(b) = a	∨	*f*(b) = b
				T			T	

Let us now assign truth-values to the four identity sentences:

f(a) = a	*f*(a) = b	*f*(b) = a	*f*(b) = b	Pa	Pb	P*f*(a)	P*f*(b)
T	F	F	T				

	↓			↓			↓	
(Pa ⊃ P*f*(a))	&	(Pb ⊃ P*f*(b))	*f*(a) = a	∨	*f*(a) = b	*f*(b) = a	∨	*f*(b) = b
			T	T	F	F	T	T

By condition 2 for truth-tables for the expansions of sentences containing the identity predicate, 'Pa' and 'P*f*(a)' must have the same truth-value, because we have made '*f*(a) = a' true. And since we have made '*f*(b) = b' true, both 'Pb' and 'P*f*(b)' must have the same truth-value. Here, then, is one way of completing the assignment of values:

f(a) = a	*f*(a) = b	*f*(b) = a	*f*(b) = b	Pa	Pb	P*f*(a)	P*f*(b)
T	**F**	**F**	**T**	**T**	**F**	**T**	**F**

(Pa	⊃	P*f*(a))	↓ &	(Pb	⊃	P*f*(b))	*f*(a) = a	↓ ∨	*f*(a) = b	*f*(b) = a	↓ ∨	*f*(b) = b
T	**T**	**T**	**T**	**F**	**T**	**F**	**T**	**T**	**F**	**F**	**T**	**T**

And here is another (there are two additional ways, which we won't display):

f(a) = a	*f*(a) = b	*f*(b) = a	*f*(b) = b	Pa	Pb	P*f*(a)	P*f*(b)
T	**F**	**F**	**T**	**F**	**F**	**F**	**F**

(Pa	⊃	P*f*(a))	↓ &	(Pb	⊃	P*f*(b))	*f*(a) = a	↓ ∨	*f*(a) = b	*f*(b) = a	↓ ∨	*f*(b) = b
F	**T**	**F**	**T**	**F**	**T**	**F**	**T**	**T**	**F**	**F**	**T**	**T**

Note that the expansion '(Pa ⊃ P*f*(a)) & (Pb ⊃ P*f*(b))' had to come out true in both cases, since we have decided that a and *f*(a) are the same member of the UD and that b and *f*(b) are the same member of the UD.

Other ways of assigning truth-values to the identity sentences will make the expansion false—for example,

f(a) = a	*f*(a) = b	*f*(b) = a	*f*(b) = b	Pa	Pb	P*f*(a)	P*f*(b)
F	**T**	**T**	**F**	**T**	**F**	**F**	**T**

(Pa	⊃	P*f*(a))	↓ &	(Pb	⊃	P*f*(b))	*f*(a) = a	↓ ∨	*f*(a) = b	*f*(b) = a	↓ ∨	*f*(b) = b
T	**F**	**F**	**F**	**F**	**T**	**T**	**F**	**T**	**T**	**T**	**T**	**F**

We may also choose to make '*f*(a) = a', '*f*(a) = b', '*f*(b) = a', and '*f*(b) = b' all true. In this case we are required also to make the sentence 'a = b' true, because of the former two identities and condition 2; to make '*f*(a) = *f*(b)' true, because of the latter two identities; and to make '*f*(b) = a' true, by virtue of the truth of '*f*(b) = b' and 'a = b'. As a consequence, 'Pa', 'Pb', 'P*f*(a)', and 'P*f*(b)' must all have the same truth-table, so in this case there are only two distinct shortened truth-tables:

f(a) = a	*f*(a) = b	*f*(b) = a	*f*(b) = b	Pa	Pb	P*f*(a)	P*f*(b)
T	**T**	**T**	**T**	**T**	**T**	**T**	**T**

(Pa	⊃	P*f*(a))	↓ &	(Pb	⊃	P*f*(b))	*f*(a) = a	↓ ∨	*f*(a) = b	*f*(b) = a	↓ ∨	*f*(b) = b
T	**T**	**T**	**T**	**T**	**T**	**T**	**T**	**T**	**T**	**T**	**T**	**T**

and

$f(a) = a$	$f(a) = b$	$f(b) = a$	$f(b) = b$	Pa	Pb	$Pf(a)$	$Pf(b)$
T	**T**	**T**	**T**	**F**	**F**	**F**	**F**

(Pa	⊃	$Pf(a)$)	& ↓	(Pb	⊃	$Pf(b)$)	$f(a) = a$	∨ ↓	$f(a) = b$	$f(b) = a$	∨ ↓	$f(b) = b$
F	**T**	**F**	**T**	**F**	**T**	**F**	**T**	**T**	**T**	**T**	**T**	**T**

The expanded sentence is true in both cases because the truth of 'a = b' means that our UD contains only one member, given the requirement that every member of the UD be named by one of the constants.

As a second and final example, we expand the sentence '$(\forall x)(\forall y)(Dg(f(x), h(y)) \supset Dx)$' for the set of constants {'a', 'b'} to obtain

$$((Dg(f(a), h(a)) \supset Da) \;\&\; (Dg(f(a), h(b)) \supset Da)) \;\&$$
$$((Dg(f(b), h(a)) \supset Db) \;\&\; (Dg(f(b), h(b)) \supset Db))$$

Condition 3 requires us to make all of the following sentences true:

$f(a) = a \vee f(a) = b$
$f(b) = a \vee f(b) = b$
$h(a) = a \vee h(a) = b$
$h(b) = a \vee h(b) = b$
$g(a,a) = a \vee g(a,a) = b$
$g(a,b) = a \vee g(a,b) = b$
$g(b,a) = a \vee g(b,a) = b$
$g(b,b) = a \vee g(b,b) = b$

Let us suppose that we make all of these true by making the following identity sentences true:

1. $f(a) = a$
2. $f(b) = b$
3. $h(a) = b$
4. $h(b) = b$
5. $g(a,a) = a$
6. $g(b,a) = a$
7. $g(a,b) = b$
8. $g(b,b) = b$

and the rest of the atomic identity statements false. By conditions 1 and 2 we will then have the following true identities as well:

9.	*g*(*f*(a), *h*(a)) = *g*(a,b)	from *g*(a,b) = *g*(a,b) and 1 and 3
10.	*g*(*f*(a), *h*(b)) = *g*(a,b)	from *g*(a,b) = *g*(a,b) and 1 and 4
11.	*g*(*f*(b), *h*(a)) = *g*(b,b)	from *g*(b,b) = *g*(b,b) and 2 and 3
12.	*g*(*f*(b), *h*(b)) = *g*(b,b)	from *g*(b,b) = *g*(b,b) and 2 and 4
13.	*g*(*f*(a), *h*(a)) = *g*(*f*(a), *h*(b))	from 9 and 10
14.	*g*(*f*(b), *h*(a)) = *g*(*f*(b), *h*(b))	from 11 and 12

So 'D*g*(*f*(a), *h*(a))' and 'D*g*(*f*(a), *h*(b))' must have the same truth-value, and 'D*g*(*f*(b), *h*(a))' and 'D*g*(*f*(b), *h*(b))' must have the same truth-value. Here, then, is one shortened truth-table for the truth-functional expansion reflecting our choice of identities 1–8 and the consequences that follow by condition 2:

f(a) = a	*f*(a) = b	*f*(b) = a	*f*(b) = b	*h*(a) = a	*h*(a) = b	*h*(b) = a	*h*(b) = b
T	F	F	T	F	T	F	T

g(a,a) = a	*g*(a,a) = b	*g*(a,b) = a	*g*(a,b) = b	*g*(b,a) = a	*g*(b,a) = b	*g*(b,b) = a
T	F	F	T	T	F	F

g(b,b) = b	Da	Db	D*g*(*f*(a), *h*(a))	D*g*(*f*(a), *h*(b))	D*g*(*f*(b), *h*(a))	D*g*(*f*(b), *h*(b))
T	T	F	F	F	T	T

							↓				
((D*g*(*f*(a), *h*(a))	⊃	Da)	&	(D*g*(*f*(a), *h*(b))	⊃	Da))	&	((D*g*(*f*(b), *h*(a))	⊃	Db)	&
F	T	T	T	F	T	T	F	T	F	F	F

				↓				↓	
(D*g*(*f*(b), *h*(b))	⊃	Db))	*f*(a) = a	∨	*f*(a) = b		*f*(b) = a	∨	*f*(b) = b
T	F	F	T	T	F		F	T	T

	↓			↓			↓	
h(a) = a	∨	*h*(a) = b	*h*(b) = a	∨	*h*(b) = b	*g*(a,a) = a	∨	*g*(a,a) = b
F	T	T	F	T	T	T	T	F

	↓			↓			↓	
g(a,b) = a	∨	*g*(a,b) = b	*g*(b,a) = a	∨	*g*(b,a) = b	*g*(b,b) = a	∨	*g*(b,b) = b
F	T	T	T	T	F	F	T	T

This shortened truth-table, albeit not very short, shows that the sentence '$(\forall x)(\forall y)(Dg(f(x), h(y)) \supset Dx)$' is false on at least one interpretation with a one- or two-member UD. There are other shortened truth-tables showing that the sentence is true on at least one interpretation with a one- or two-member UD; and producing one of those will suffice to establish that the sentence is truth-functionally indeterminate.

8.6E EXERCISES

1. Determine the truth-values of the following sentences on this interpretation:

UD:	Set of positive integers
Ex:	x is even
Gxy:	x is greater than y
Ox:	x is odd
Pxyz:	x plus y equals z

a. $(\exists x)(\forall y)(x = y \supset Gxy)$
*b. $(\forall x)(\forall y) \sim x = y$
c. $(\forall x)(\exists y)(Oy \supset Gyx)$
*d. $(\forall x)(\forall y)(\forall z)[(Gxy \,\&\, Gyz) \supset \sim x = z]$
e. $(\exists w)[Ew \,\&\, (\forall y)(Oy \supset \sim w = y)]$
*f. $(\forall y)(\forall z)[(Oy \,\&\, y = z) \supset \sim Ez]$
g. $(\exists z)(\exists w)(z = w \,\&\, Gzw)$
*h. $(\forall x)(\forall y)(\exists z)[(Pxyz \,\&\, \sim x = z) \,\&\, \sim y = z]$
i. $(\forall x)(\forall y)(Pxyy \vee \sim x = y)$

2. Show that each of the following sentences is not quantificationally true by producing an interpretation on which it is false.
a. $(\exists x)(\forall y)x = y$
*b. $(\forall w)(w = b \supset Fw)$
c. $(\forall x)(\forall y)(\forall z)[(x = y \vee y = z) \vee x = z]$
*d. $(\exists w)[Gw \,\&\, (\forall z)(\sim Hzw \supset z = w)]$
e. $(\exists x)(\exists y)(\sim x = y \vee Gxy)$
*f. $(\forall x)(\forall y)(\exists z)(x = y \supset \sim x = z)$

3. Each of the following sentences is quantificationally true. Explain why.
a. $(\forall x)(\forall y)(\forall z)[(x = y \,\&\, y = z) \supset x = z]$
*b. $(\forall x)(\forall y)(\exists z)(x = z \vee y = z)$
c. $(\forall x)(\forall y)[x = y \supset (Gxy \equiv Gyx)]$

4. Show that the sentences in each of the following pairs are not quantificationally equivalent by constructing an interpretation on which one sentence is true and the other is false.
a. $(\forall x)(\exists y)\ x = y$, $(\forall x)(\forall y)x = y$
*b. $(\forall x)(\forall y)[x = y \supset (Fx \equiv Fy)]$, $(\forall x)(\forall y)[(Fx \equiv Fy) \supset x = y]$
c. $(a = b \vee a = c) \supset a = d$, $a = c \supset (a = b \vee a = d)$
*d. $(\exists x)(\forall y)(\sim x = y \supset Gy)$, $(\exists x)(\forall y)(Gy \supset \sim x = y)$

5. Show that each of the following sets of sentences is quantificationally consistent by constructing an interpretation on which each sentence in the set is true.

a. $\{a = b, a = c, \sim a = d\}$
*b. $\{(\forall x)(\forall y)x = y, (\exists x)Fx, (\forall y)Gy\}$
c. $\{(\exists x)(\exists z) \sim x = z, (\forall x)(\exists z)(\exists w)(x = z \vee x = w)\}$
*d. $\{(\forall x)(Gx \supset (\forall y)(\sim y = x \supset Gy)), (\forall x)(Hx \supset Gx), (\exists z)Hz\}$

6. Establish each of the following by producing an interpretation on which the set members are true and the sentence after the double turnstile is false.
a. $\{(\forall x)(\forall y)[(x = y \vee x = z) \vee y = z]\} \nvDash (\forall x)(\forall y)(x = y)$
*b. $\{(\exists w)(\exists z) \sim w = z, (\exists w)Hw\} \nvDash (\exists w) \sim Hw$
c. $\{(\exists w)(\forall y)Gwy, (\exists w)(\forall y)(\sim w = y \supset \sim Gwy)\} \nvDash (\exists z) \sim Gzz$
*d. $\{(\forall x)(\forall y)[(Fx \equiv Fy) \equiv x = y], (\exists z)Fz\} \nvDash (\exists x)(\exists y)[\sim x = y \,\&\, (Fx \,\&\, \sim Fy)]$

7. Using the given symbolization key, symbolize each of the following arguments in *PLE*. Then, for each symbolized argument, decide whether it is quantificationally valid and defend your answer.

UD: Set of all people
Fx: x is female
Mx: x is male
Lxy: x loves y
Pxy: x is a parent of y

a. Every male loves someone other than himself, and every male loves his children. Therefore no male is his own parent.
*b. Everyone loves her or his parents, and everyone has two parents. Therefore everyone loves at least two people.
c. A female who loves her children loves herself as well. Therefore every female loves at least two people.
*d. Everybody has exactly two parents. Therefore everybody has exactly four grandparents.
e. Nobody has three parents. Everybody has more than one parent. Therefore everybody has two parents.

8. Use truth-functional expansions to establish each of the following claims. Be sure that the truth-value assignments you produce meet the first two conditions discussed in this section.
a. The sentence '$(\exists x)(\exists y) \sim x = y$' is quantificationally indeterminate.
*b. The sentence '$(\forall w)(Fw \supset (\exists y) \sim y = w) \,\&\, (\exists w)Fw$' is quantificationally indeterminate.
c. The sentences '$(\forall y)(\forall z)[(Gyz \vee Gzy) \vee y = z]$' and '$(\forall y)(\exists z)Gyz$' are not quantificationally equivalent.
*d. The set of sentences $\{(\forall x)(\forall y)(\forall z)[(Gxy \vee Gyz) \vee x = z], (\forall y)(\exists z)Gyz\}$ is quantificationally consistent.
e. The set of sentences $\{(\forall y)y = y, (\exists z)(\exists w) \sim w = z\}$ does not quantificationally entail the sentence '$(\exists z)(\forall w) \sim z = w$'.
*f. The argument

$$(\forall y)(\forall z)(Gyz \supset y = z)$$

$$\overline{(\forall y)(\forall z)(y = z \supset Gyz)}$$

is quantificationally invalid.

9. Determine the truth-values of the following sentences on this interpretation:

UD:	Set of positive integers
Ex:	x is even
Gxy:	x is greater than y
$f(x)$:	the successor of x
$g(x)$:	x squared
$h(x,y)$:	the sum of x and y

a. $(\forall x)Gf(x)x$
*b. $(\forall x)Eg(x)$
c. $(\forall x)(\exists y)y = h(x,x)$
*d. $(\forall x)(\forall y)(y = h(x,x) \supset Ey)$
e. $(\exists x)(\exists y)((Ex \ \& \ {\sim}Ey) \ \& \ Eh(x,y))$
*f. $(\forall x)(\forall y)(\forall z)(Eh(h(x,y), z) \supset ((Ex \vee Ey) \vee Ez))$
g. $(\forall x)(\exists z)(Eh(g(x), z) \vee Eh(x,g(z)))$
*h. $(\forall x)(\forall y)Gh(f(x), f(y), h(x,y))$

10. Show that each of the following sentences is not quantificationally true by producing an interpretation on which it is false.
a. $(\forall x)(Pf(x) \supset Px)$
*b. $(\forall x)(\forall y)(x = g(y) \vee y = g(x))$
c. $(\exists x)(\forall y)x = g(y)$
*d. $(\forall x)(\forall y)(\forall z)((x = f(y) \ \& \ y = f(z)) \supset x = f(z))$
e. $(\forall x) \sim x = f(x)$
*f. $(\forall x)(\forall y)(Dh(x,y) \supset Dh(y,x))$

11. Each of the following sentences is quantificationally true. Explain why.
a. $(\forall x)(\exists y)y = f(f(x))$
*b. $(\forall x)(\forall y)(\forall z)((y = f(x) \ \& \ z = f((x)) \supset y = z)$
c. $((\forall x) \ Hxf(x) \ \& \ (\forall x)(\forall y)(\forall z)((Hxy \ \& \ Hyz) \supset Hxz)) \supset (\forall x)Hxf(f(x))$

12. Show that the sentences in each of the following pairs are not quantificationally equivalent by constructing an interpretation on which one sentence is true and the other false.
a. $Labf(b)$, $Laf(b)b$
*b. $(\forall x)B(h(x), x)$, $(\forall x)B(x,h(x))$
c. $(\forall x)(\exists y)y = f(h(x))$, $(\exists z)z = f(h(z))$
*d. $(\exists x)(\exists y)(\exists z)(x = f(y) \ \& \ y = f(z))$, $(\forall x)(\exists y)(\exists z)(x = f(y) \ \& \ y = f(z))$

13. Show that each of the following sets of sentences is quantificationally consistent by constructing an interpretation on which each sentence in the set is true.
a. $\{a = f(b), b = f(c), c = f(a)\}$
*b. $\{(\forall x)Lxf(x), (\exists y) \sim Lf(y)y\}$
c. $\{(\exists x)(\forall y)x = f(y), (\exists x)(\forall y) \sim x = f(y)\}$
*d. $\{(\forall x)(Gx \supset \sim Gh(x), (\exists x)(\sim Gx \ \& \sim Gh(x)\}$

14. For each of the following arguments, decide whether it is quantificationally valid. If it is quantificationally valid, explain why. If it is not quantificationally valid, construct an interpretation on which the premises are true and the conclusion false.

a. $(\forall x)(Fx \vee Fg(x))$

$\overline{(\forall x)(Fx \vee Fg(g(x)))}$

*b. $(\forall x)(Fx \vee Fg(x))$

$\overline{(\forall x)(Fg(x) \vee Fg(g(x)))}$

c. $(\forall x)(\exists y)(\exists z)Lf(x)yz$

$\overline{(\exists x)(\forall y)(\forall z)Lxf(y)f(z)}$

*d. $(\forall x)(Lxf(x) \ \& \sim Lf(x)x)$

$\overline{(\forall x)(\forall y)(y = f(x) \supset (Lxy \vee Lyx))}$

e. $(\forall x)(Bg(x) \supset (\forall y) \sim Hyg(x))$

$\overline{(a = g(b) \ \& \ Hca) \supset \sim Ba}$

15. Use truth-functional expansions to establish each of the following. Be sure that the truth-value assignments you produce meet all three conditions discussed in this section.

a. The sentence '$(\forall x)(Fx \vee Fg(x))$' is quantificationally indeterminate.

*b. The sentences '$(\exists x)(\exists y)Hg(x,y)x$' and '$(\exists x)(\exists y)Hg(y,x)x$' are not quantificationally equivalent.

c. The set of sentences $\{(\forall x) \sim x = f(x), (\exists x)x = f(f(x))\}$ is quantificationally consistent.

*d. The argument

$a = f(b) \ \& \ b = f(a)$

$\overline{(\exists x)(\exists y) \sim x = y}$

is quantificationally invalid.

8.7 FORMAL SEMANTICS OF *PL* AND *PLE*

The semantics for *PL* and *PLE* used so far in this chapter have been informal in the sense that strict definitions of truth on an interpretation and falsehood on an interpretation have not been specified. For example, we explained the truth-conditions for quantified sentences by saying that all or some of the members of the UD in question must satisfy the condition specified by that part of the sentence following the quantifier. But we have not as yet given a formalized account of how we determine what that condition is or how we determine whether it is satisfied as required. In this section we specify the formal semantics first for *PL* and then for *PLE*.

To do so, we first need to regiment the definition of an interpretation. Every interpretation must have a nonempty set as its UD. Interpreting an individual constant consists in the assignment of a member of the UD to that constant, and interpreting a sentence letter consists in the assignment of a truth-value to that sentence letter.

In the first section of this chapter, we pointed out that, when we give an English reading for an **n**-place predicate of *PL*, that reading determines the *extension* of the predicate. The extension of an **n**-place predicate is a set of **n**-*tuples* of members of the UD that are picked out by the predicate. An **n**-tuple is an ordered set containing **n** members—it is ordered in the sense that one member is designated as the first, one as the second, and so on. A 2-tuple is an ordered pair, a 3-tuple is an ordered triple, a 4-tuple is an ordered quadruple, and so on.

For instance, if we take the set of positive integers as our UD and interpret 'Gxy' as 'x is greater than y', then the *extension* of 'G' is the set of ordered pairs (2-tuples) of positive integers such that the first member of each pair is greater than the second. A sentence containing the predicate 'G'—say, the sentence 'Gab'—is then true if and only if the ordered pair of positive integers whose first member is designated by 'a' and whose second member is designated by 'b' is a member of the extension of 'G'. It is possible to give 'G' a different English reading that determines the same extension; for example, we might interpret 'Gxy' to mean 'x plus 1 is greater than y plus 1'. Since, for any numbers x and y, x plus 1 is greater than y plus 1 if and only if x is greater than y, it follows that the extension of 'G' for these two English readings of the predicate is the same. And, since the extension is the same in each case, the truth-conditions of 'Gab' on the latter interpretation of 'G' coincide with the truth-conditions of 'Gab' on the former interpretation. It is thus the *extension* of the predicate, not the particular English reading we use to specify the extension, that is important in determining the truth-conditions of any sentence in which the predicate occurs. So, in our formal account, we take the interpretation of a predicate of *PL* to be the set that is the extension of that predicate.[3]

An interpretation of an **n**-place predicate in a UD thus consists in the assignment of a set of **n**-tuples (ordered sets containing **n** members) of members of the UD to that predicate. For example, in the UD that consists of all people, years, and cities, we may wish to interpret the four-place predicate 'D' so that 'Dwxyz' reads 'w marries x in the year y in the city z'. We would then have the interpretation assign to 'D' the set of 4-tuples of members of the UD such that the first two members are people who marry each other, the third member is the year in which they marry, and the fourth member is the city in which they marry. Thus, if John Doe and Jane Doe marry in 1975 in Kansas City, then one of the 4-tuples that the interpretation assigns to 'D' is

⟨John Doe, Jane Doe, 1975, Kansas City⟩

[3] And when we assign an extension, which is simply a set, to a predicate, we need not have any natural English reading in mind. It is important to realize this, for when we say, for example, that a quantificationally true sentence is true on *every* interpretation, we include those interpretations that have no obvious English language renderings.

(the **n**-tuple whose first, second, third, and fourth members, respectively, are John Doe, Jane Doe, 1975, Kansas City).

Note that we designate an **n**-tuple by listing names of the members of the **n**-tuple, in the order in which the members occur in the **n**-tuple, between the angle brackets '⟨' and '⟩'. Thus we may designate the 3-tuple whose first member is the number 1, whose second member is Arthur Conan Doyle, and whose third member is Yankee Stadium as

⟨1, Arthur Conan Doyle, Yankee Stadium⟩

and the 5-tuple all of whose members are the fraction $\frac{1}{2}$ as

$\langle \frac{1}{2}, \frac{1}{2}, \frac{1}{2}, \frac{1}{2}, \frac{1}{2} \rangle$

A special case of the interpretation of predicates deserves attention here. The interpretation of a one-place predicate assigns to that predicate a set of 1-tuples of members of the UD. A 1-tuple is an ordered set containing exactly one member. It might seem more natural simply to assign to a one-place predicate a set of members of the UD—namely, those members we want the predicate to pick out. But, for the sake of generality in our definition of truth on an interpretation, it is convenient to assign to a one-place predicate a set of 1-tuples of members of the UD. We may designate the 1-tuple of John Doe by

⟨John Doe⟩

We may now formally define the concept of an interpretation:

> An *interpretation* for *PL* consists in the specification of a UD and the assignment of a truth-value to each sentence letter of *PL*, a member of the UD to each individual constant of *PL*, and a set of **n**-tuples of members of the UD to each **n**-place predicate of *PL*.

The next concept we need is that of a variable assignment. This concept plays an important role in the specification of truth-conditions for the sentences of *PL*, and the idea is this: We are going to explain the truth-conditions of sentences like '(∀x)(Fx ∨ Gx)' in terms of the semantics of their subformulas. But 'Fx ∨ Gx' is an open sentence, and for us open sentences are neither true nor false—because free variables are not names. We have noted several times that variables function as pronouns do. Here we exploit that feature of variables in order to determine the truth-conditions of quantified sentences. That is, we determine the truth-conditions of quantified sentences by exploring whether the things to which a variable in its role as pronoun can refer satisfy the condition specified by the formula in which the variable occurs. Our concept of variable assignments will be used to regiment the informal notion of satisfaction that we have used throughout this chapter.

A *variable assignment for an interpretation* **I** assigns to each individual variable of *PL* a member of the UD. Intuitively a variable assignment captures one way in which the variables of *PL*, in their role as pronouns, can refer to objects in the UD. If an interpretation has a one-member UD, there is exactly one variable assignment for that interpretation, the variable assignment that assigns the one member of the UD to each individual variable of *PL*. If an interpretation has more than one member in its UD, there will be infinitely many different variable assignments. For a two-member UD consisting of the integers 1 and 2, for example, there is a variable assignment that assigns the integer 1 to every individual variable, and a variable assignment that assigns the integer 2 to every individual variable, and there are infinitely many variable assignments that assign the integer 1 to only some of the individual variables and the integer 2 to the remaining variables (there are infinitely many ways of choosing which of the infinite number of variables of *PL* designate 1 and which designate 2). Note that it is not required that distinct variables be assigned different members of the UD; some variable assignments assign the same member to two or more variables—in fact, every variable assignment for an interpretation with a finite UD must do so. Nor is it required that every member of the UD be assigned to a variable; some variable assignments leave some members unnamed.

We will use the letter '**d**' to range over variable assignments (think of '**d**' as shorthand for 'designates'). If **d** is a variable assignment and **x** is an individual variable of *PL*, then **d**(**x**) designates the member of the UD that **d** assigns to **x**. So **d**(**x**) is 2 if and only if **d** assigns 2 to **x**. We need some additional notation that will be used in regimenting our informal notion of satisfaction. If **d** is a variable assignment for an interpretation, **u** is a member of the interpretation's UD, and **x** is an individual variable of *PL*, then **d**[**u**/**x**] is a variable assignment that assigns the same value to each variable as **d** does *except that* it assigns **u** to **x**. **d**[**u**/**x**] is called a *variant* of the assignment **d**. More generally, if **d** is a variable assignment for an interpretation, $\mathbf{u}_1$, $\mathbf{u}_2$, . . . , $\mathbf{u}_\mathbf{n}$ are (not necessarily distinct) members of the interpretation's UD, and $\mathbf{x}_1$, $\mathbf{x}_2$, . . . , $\mathbf{x}_\mathbf{n}$ are (not necessarily distinct) individual variables of *PL*, then $\mathbf{d}[\mathbf{u}_1/\mathbf{x}_1, \mathbf{u}_2/\mathbf{x}_2, \ldots, \mathbf{u}_\mathbf{n}/\mathbf{x}_\mathbf{n}]$ is shorthand for the variable assignment $\mathbf{d}[\mathbf{u}_1/\mathbf{x}_1]\ [\mathbf{u}_2/\mathbf{x}_2] \ldots [\mathbf{u}_\mathbf{n}/\mathbf{x}_\mathbf{n}]$—the variable assignment that starts out like **d** and results from successive stipulations that $\mathbf{u}_1$ will be assigned to $\mathbf{x}_1$, $\mathbf{u}_2$ to $\mathbf{x}_2$, . . . , and $\mathbf{u}_\mathbf{n}$ to $\mathbf{x}_\mathbf{n}$.

As an example let us assume that an interpretation has the set of positive integers as its UD and that the variable assignment **d** assigns 1 to every individual variable of *PL*. Then **d**[5/'x', 8/'z'] is the variable assignment that assigns 5 to 'x' and 8 to 'z' and assigns 1 to all other individual variables of *PL*. It assigns 1 to all other individual variables because, aside from the assignments it makes to 'x' and 'z', our definition requires that **d**[5/'x', 8/'z'] assign the same values to variables as **d** does. Note that **d**[1/'x', 1/'y'] is the same variable assignment as **d** because the values that we specified for the variables 'x' and 'y' are the same values that **d** assigns to them. Also note that if a variable occurs more than once between the square brackets, the value it receives on

$\mathbf{d}[\mathbf{u}_1/\mathbf{x}_1, \mathbf{u}_2/\mathbf{x}_2, \ldots, \mathbf{u}_n/\mathbf{x}_n]$ is the last value that appears for the variable in that list. For example, where **d** is as above, **d**[1/'x', 2/'y', 3/'x'] assigns 3, not 1, to 'x'. For notational convenience we shall drop the single quotes around names of individual variables when they appear between the square brackets; thus **d**[5/'x', 8/'z'] may be written as **d**[5/x, 8/z].

Relative to an interpretation and variable assignment, we define the *denotation of a term with respect to an interpretation **I** and variable assignment **d**,* symbolically $den_{I,d}(t)$:

1. If **t** is a variable, then $\text{den}_{\mathbf{I,d}}(\mathbf{t}) = \mathbf{d}(\mathbf{t})$.
2. If **t** is an individual constant, then $\text{den}_{\mathbf{I,d}}(\mathbf{t}) = \mathbf{I}(\mathbf{t})$.

The denotation of a term is the member of the UD that the variable assignment or interpretation says it designates.

Truth and falsehood of sentences on an interpretation are not defined directly; rather, they are defined in terms of *satisfaction* by variable assignments. We shall first recursively define the concept of satisfaction, then define truth and falsehood, and afterward illustrate through examples the role of the intermediate step. Here, as in Chapter 7, we use '**P**', '**Q**' and '**R**' as metavariables ranging over formulas of *PL*, '**A**' as a metavariable ranging over predicates of *PL*, '**t**' with or without subscripts as a metavariable ranging over individual terms (individual constants and individual variables of *PL*) and '**x**' as a metavariable ranging over individual variables of *PL*. We shall use **I**(**X**) to mean the value that the interpretation **I** assigns to the symbol **X**.

Let **I** be an interpretation, **d** a variable assignment for **I**, and **P** a formula of *PL*. Then

1. If **P** is a sentence letter, then **d** satisfies **P** on interpretation **I** if and only if **I**(**P**) = **T**.

Note that the values that **d** assigns to variables play no role in this case.

2. If **P** is an atomic formula of the form $\mathbf{At}_1 \ldots \mathbf{t}_n$ (where **A** is an **n**-place predicate), then **d** satisfies **P** on interpretation **I** if and only if $<\text{den}_{\mathbf{I,d}}(\mathbf{t}_1), \text{den}_{\mathbf{I,d}}(\mathbf{t}_2), \ldots, \text{den}_{\mathbf{I,d}}(\mathbf{t}_n)>$ is a member of **I**(**A**).

So **d** satisfies 'Gxa', for example, if ⟨**d**('x'), **I**('a')⟩—the 2-tuple whose first member is the object that **d** assigns to the variable 'x' and whose second member is the object that **I** assigns to the constant 'a'—is a member of the extension that **I** assigns to 'G'.

3. If **P** is of the form ~ **Q**, then **d** satisfies **P** on interpretation **I** if and only if **d** does not satisfy **Q** on interpretation **I**.

4. If **P** is of the form **Q** & **R**, then **d** satisfies **P** on interpretation **I** if and only if **d** satisfies **Q** on interpretation **I** and **d** satisfies **R** on interpretation **I**.
5. If **P** is of the form **Q** ∨ **R**, then **d** satisfies **P** on interpretation **I** if and only if either **d** satisfies **Q** on interpretation **I** or **d** satisfies **R** on interpretation **I**.
6. If **P** is of the form **Q** ⊃ **R**, then **d** satisfies **P** on interpretation **I** if and only if either **d** does not satisfy **Q** on interpretation **I** or **d** satisfies **R** on interpretation **I**.
7. If **P** is of the form **Q** ≡ **R**, then **d** satisfies **P** on interpretation **I** if and only if either **d** satisfies **Q** on interpretation **I** and **d** satisfies **R** on interpretation **I**, or **d** does not satisfy **Q** on interpretation **I** and **d** does not satisfy **R** on interpretation **I**.
8. If **P** is of the form (∀**x**)**Q**, then **d** satisfies **P** on interpretation **I** if and only if for every member **u** of the UD, **d**[**u**/**x**] satisfies **Q** on interpretation **I**.
9. If **P** is of the form (∃**x**)**Q**, then **d** satisfies **P** on interpretation **I** if and only if there is at least one member **u** of the UD such that **d**[**u**/**x**] satisfies **Q** on interpretation **I**.

Finally, the definitions of truth and falsehood are

> A sentence **P** of *PL* is *true on an interpretation* **I** if and only if every variable assignment **d** (for **I**) satisfies **P** on **I**. A sentence **P** of *PL* is *false on an interpretation* **I** if and only if no variable assignment **d** (for **I**) satisfies **P** on **I**.

In Chapter 11 we shall prove that for each sentence **P** and interpretation **I** either all variable assignments for **I** satisfy **P** or none do. (This is not generally true for *open* formulas.) This being the case, each sentence is true or false on any interpretation according to our definitions.

Our definitions have been long, so we shall look at some examples. Consider the sentence

(∀y)(By ⊃ ~ (∃z)Dyz)

and an interpretation that makes the following assignments:

51. UD: Set of positive integers
B: {<**u**>: **u** is prime}
D: {<$\mathbf{u}_1$, $\mathbf{u}_2$>: $\mathbf{u}_1$ is greater than $\mathbf{u}_2$}

Note that we no longer write variables after predicates when indicating their interpretations. This is because an interpretation makes an assignment to the predicate alone. Note also that we explicitly display the sets that are the interpretations of predicates. The notation used in displaying the interpretation of 'B' means: the set of 1-tuples of prime numbers. Because it would be cumbersome, we do not explicitly indicate that the prime numbers must be members of the UD—that is, the prime numbers in this set are all positive integers. The notation used in displaying the interpretation of 'D' means: the set of 2-tuples in which the first member is greater than the second. Again it is implicit that these 2-tuples contain only positive integers.

The interpretation must assign values to all other predicates, individual constants, and sentence letters of *PL* as well, but as we shall see, only the values assigned to 'B' and 'D' are used in determining the truth-value of the sentence. As we apply our definitions, it may be helpful to keep in mind the reading of the sentence on this interpretation: 'Every positive integer y is such that if it is prime then there is no positive integer than which it is greater'. The sentence is obviously false on this interpretation; what we shall now show is that we come to exactly this conclusion by using our definitions.

To show that the sentence is false, we must show that no variable assignment **d** (for **I**) satisfies the sentence. Let **d** be any variable assignment for **I**. According to clause 8 of the definition of satisfaction,

a. **d** satisfies '(∀y)(By ⊃ ~ (∃z)Dyz)' if and only if for every member **u** of the UD, **d**[**u**/y] satisfies '(By ⊃ ~ (∃z)Dyz)'.

So **d**[1/y] must satisfy the open sentence, **d**[2/y] must satisfy the open sentence, **d**[3/y] must satisfy the open sentence, and so on for every positive integer. Intuitively this means that no matter what we may take y to be, y must satisfy the condition specified by that open sentence. We must consider all possible values that might be assigned to 'y' rather than just the value that **d** itself assigns to 'y'—that is, all values that variants of **d** might assign to 'y'—because the variable 'y' is universally quantified.

But not every member **u** of the UD is such that **d**[**u**/y] satisfies '(By ⊃ ~ (∃z)Dyz)'—for example, 2 is not such that if it is prime then there is no positive integer than which it is greater. We shall show formally that **d**[2/y] does not satisfy '(By ⊃ ~ (∃z)Dyz)'. According to clause 6,

b. **d**[2/y] satisfies '(By ⊃ ~ (∃z)Dyz)' if and only if either **d**[2/y] does not satisfy 'By' or **d**[2/y] does satisfy '~ (∃z)Dyz'.

According to clause 2,

c. **d**[2/y] satisfies 'By' if and only if ⟨**d**[2/y](y)⟩ is a member of **I**(B).

The 1-tuple ⟨**d**[2/y](y)⟩ is ⟨2⟩—the set consisting of the integer that the variant assignment **d**[2/y] assigns to 'y', and **I**(B) is the set of 1-tuples of positive integers that are prime. Because ⟨2⟩ is a member of this set, **d**[2/y] does satisfy 'By'. We now turn to '~ (∃z)Dyz'. According to clause 3,

d. **d**[2/y] satisfies '~ (∃z)Dyz' if and only if it does not satisfy '(∃z)Dyz'.

And clause 9 tells us that

e. **d**[2/y] satisfies '(∃z)Dyz' if and only if there is at least one member **u** of the UD such that **d**[2/y, **u**/z], the variable assignment that is just like **d**[2/y] except that it assigns **u** to 'z', satisfies 'Dyz'

that is, if and only if there is a member **u** of the UD that is smaller than 2. There is such a member—the integer 1. Let us consider the variable assignment **d**[2/y, 1/z]. By clause 2,

f. **d**[2/y, 1/z] satisfies 'Dyz' if and only if the 2-tuple ⟨2, 1⟩ (this is the pair ⟨**d**[2/y, 1/z](y), **d**[2/y, 1/z](z)⟩) is a member of **I**(D).

I(D) is the set of 2-tuples of positive integers in which the first member is greater than the second—and ⟨2, 1⟩ is indeed a member of this set. Thus **d**[2/y, 1/z] satisfies 'Dyz'. Returning to step e, this shows that **d**[2/y] satisfies '(∃z)Dyz', and so, by step d, **d**[2/y] does not satisfy '~ (∃z)Dyz'. We now have a variable assignment, **d**[2/y], that satisfies 'By' but does not satisfy '~ (∃z)Dyz'. Therefore, by step b, **d**[2/y] does not satisfy '(By ⊃ ~ (∃z)Dyz)'. The number 2 is *not* such that if it is prime then it is not larger than any positive integer. We may conclude from step a that **d** does not satisfy '(∀y)(By ⊃ ~ (∃z)Dyz)', because we have found a variant of **d** that does not satisfy the open sentence following the universal quantifier.

We may also conclude that the sentence is *false* on interpretation 51 because we have just shown that every variable assignment for **I** fails to satisfy '(∀y)(By ⊃ ~ (∃z)Dyz)'. The value that the original assignment **d** assigned to 'y' did not come into play in our proof, for when we removed the universal quantifier in step a we considered all values that might be assigned to 'y' by variants of **d**. The universally quantified sentence is satisfied by a variable assignment **d** if and only if the open sentence following the quantifier is satisfied no matter what value is assigned to 'y'. Similarly, when we removed the existential quantifier in step e, we considered all values that might be assigned to 'z'—not just the value assigned by **d** or its variant **d**[2/y]. The values that **d** itself assigned to the variables 'y' and 'z' therefore played no role in showing that **d** did not satisfy the sentence. Moreover, because no other individual variables appear in the sentence, the values that **d** assigned to the other individual variables of *PL* also played no role. In sum, it does not matter which variable assignment we started with because, when we removed the quantifiers, we had to consider variants that explicitly assigned values to the variables thus freed.

We conclude that, no matter which variable assignment **d** we choose, **d** will fail to satisfy the sentence.

The sentence '(∀y)(By ⊃ ~ (∃z)Dyz)' is true, however, on interpretation 52:

52. UD: The set {2, 4}
    B: {<**u**>: **u** is prime}
    D: {<$\mathbf{u}_1$, $\mathbf{u}_2$>: $\mathbf{u}_1$ is greater than $\mathbf{u}_2$}

Consider any variable assignment **d** for this interpretation. By clause 8, **d** satisfies the sentence if and only if, for every member **u** of the UD, **d**[**u**/y] satisfies '(By ⊃ ~ (∃z)Dyz)'—that is, if and only if both **d**[2/y] and **d**[4/y] satisfy the open sentence, because 2 and 4 are the only members of the UD. We shall examine each variant. **d**[2/y] satisfies the consequent of the open sentence (in addition to its antecedent) because it fails to satisfy '(∃z)Dyz'. There is no member **u** of the set {2, 4} such that **d**[2/y, **u**/z] satisfies 'Dyz'. **d**[2/y, 2/z] does not satisfy 'Dyz' because ⟨**d**[2/y, 2/z](y), **d**[2/y, 2/z](z)⟩, which is ⟨2, 2⟩, is not in the extension of 'D'. **d**[2/y, 4/z] does not satisfy 'Dyz' because ⟨2, 4⟩ is not in the extension of 'D'. We have exhausted the possible values for 'z', so there is no member **u** of the UD such that **d**[2/y, **u**/z] satisfies 'Dyz'. Hence '(∃z) Dyz' is not satisfied by **d**[2/y], and its negation is satisfied. This established that **d**[2/y] satisfies '(By ⊃ ~ (∃z)Dyz)'. The variant **d**[4/y] also satisfies '(By ⊃ ~ (∃z)Dyz)' because it fails to satisfy the antecedent (it also fails to satisfy the consequent). The 1-tuple ⟨**d**[4/y](y)⟩ is just ⟨4⟩, and this 1-tuple is not a member of **I**(B), which is the set of 1-tuples of prime positive integers. So **d**[4/y] fails to satisfy 'By' and therefore does satisfy '(By ⊃ ~ (∃z)Dyz)'. Having shown that both **d**[2/y] and **d**[4/y] satisfy '(By ⊃ ~ (∃z)Dyz)', we have established that, for every member **u** of the UD, **d**[**u**/y] satisfies the conditional open sentence, and we may conclude that **d** satisfies '(∀y)(By ⊃ ~ (∃z)Dyz)'. Once again, because we used no specific values assigned to variables by our original variable assignment **d**, we have shown that every variable assignment for **I** satisfies the sentence. It is therefore true on interpretation 52.

As another example, we may use our definitions to prove that the sentence '(∀x)(Bx ≡ ~ Bx)' is quantificationally false. We will begin by assuming that there is an interpretation on which the sentence is true and then show that this is impossible. Suppose that **I** is an interpretation on which '(∀x)(Bx ≡ ~ Bx)' is true. By definition every variable assignment **d** for **I** must therefore satisfy '(∀x)(Bx ≡ ~ Bx)'. And because the sentence is universally quantified, for every member **u** of **I**'s UD, the variant **d**[**u**/x] for each variable assignment **d** must satisfy '(Bx ≡ ~ Bx)' (by clause 8). We shall show that not even one variant of one variable assignment can do so. Suppose that **u** is a member of the UD such that ⟨**u**⟩ is in the extension of 'B'. Then, no matter which variable assignment **d** we started with, **d**[**u**/x] satisfies 'Bx' according to clause 2, because ⟨**d**[**u**/x](x)⟩ is a member of **I**(B). But then, by clause 3, **d**[**u**/x] does not satisfy '~ Bx', and hence, by clause 7, it does not satisfy '(Bx ≡ ~ Bx)'. Suppose, on the other hand, that **u** is a member of the UD such that ⟨**u**⟩ is not in the extension of 'B'. In this case $\mathbf{d}[\mathbf{u}/x]$ does not satisfy 'Bx' because $\langle \mathbf{d}[\mathbf{u}/x](x) \rangle$ is not a member of $\mathbf{I}(B)$ and therefore does satisfy '~ Bx'. So, once again, '(Bx ≡ ~ Bx)' is not satisfied. Because each member of the UD either is or is not in the extension of 'B', we conclude that there is no member **u** such that $\mathbf{d}[\mathbf{u}/x]$ satisfies '(Bx ≡ ~ Bx)'. This being the case, no variable assignment for any interpretation **I** satisfies '(∀x)(Bx ≡ ~ Bx)'. The sentence is false on every interpretation and is therefore quantificationally false.

It should now be clear why the definition of truth was given in terms of the concept of satisfaction rather than directly in terms of interpretations. For the language of *SL* we were able to define the truth-conditions of a sentence directly in terms of the truth-conditions of its atomic components, for the atomic components were themselves sentences and so had truth-values on truth-value assignments. But consider the sentence of *PL* '(∀y)(By ⊃ ~ (∃z)Dyz)', which we used as an example in this section. There is no proper subformula of this sentence that is itself a sentence. The largest proper subformula is '(By ⊃ ~ (∃z)Dyz)', which is an *open sentence.* We do not consider open sentences to be true or false on interpretations because their free variables are not given values on interpretations. So we cannot define the truth-conditions of '(∀y)(By ⊃ ~ (∃z)Dyz)' in terms of the truth or falsehood of its subformula '(By ⊃ ~ (∃z)Dyz)'. But variable assignments, which do assign values to variables, can satisfy or fail to satisfy open formulas for interpretations, and so we have defined the truth-conditions of sentences in terms of the satisfaction conditions of their subformulas.[4]

To accommodate sentences of *PLE* containing the identity predicate, we need to add the following clause to our definition of satisfaction:

10. If **P** is an atomic formula of the form $\mathbf{t}_1 = \mathbf{t}_2$, then **d** satisfies **P** on interpretation **I** if and only if $\text{den}_{\mathbf{I},\mathbf{d}}(\mathbf{t}_1) = \text{den}_{\mathbf{I},\mathbf{d}}(\mathbf{t}_2)$.

This clause implicitly defines an extension for the identity predicate: The extension includes $\langle \mathbf{u}, \mathbf{u} \rangle$ for each member **u** of the UD, and that is all that it includes. We can use clause 10, along with others, to show that the sentence

(∃x)(Fx & (∀y)(Fy ⊃ y = x))

is false on interpretation 53:

53. UD: Set of positive integers
    F: {<**u**>: **u** is odd}

[4]Some authors allow all open sentences to be true or false on interpretations, so the concept of satisfaction is not needed in their truth-definitions. Other authors use a type of semantics for quantificational languages known as *substitution semantics;* in this type of semantics the concept of satisfaction is also unnecessary. For obvious reasons the semantics we have presented is known as *satisfaction semantics* (or sometimes as *referential* or *objectual semantics*). Satisfaction semantics was first presented by Alfred Tarski in "Der Wahrheitsbegriff in den formalisierten Sprachen," *Studia Philosophica,* 1 (1936), 261–405.

On this interpretation, the sentence may be read as 'Exactly one positive integer is odd'. To show that the sentence is false, we must show that no variable assignment for **I** satisfies it. Let **d** be a variable assignment. Then, by clause 9, **d** satisfies the sentence if and only if there is some member **u** of the UD such that **d**[**u**/x] satisfies '(Fx & (∀y)(Fy ⊃ y = x))'. Because at least one positive integer is odd, there is at least one member **u** such that **d**[**u**/x] does satisfy the first conjunct 'Fx'—for example, ⟨**d**[3/x](x)⟩, which is ⟨3⟩, is a member of **I**(F). However, no matter which odd integer **u** may be, **d**[**u**/x] cannot satisfy '(∀y)(Fy ⊃ y = x)'. If **d**[**u**/x] *did* satisfy this formula, then, according to clause 8, it would do so because, for every positive integer $\mathbf{u}_1$, **d**[**u**/x, $\mathbf{u}_1$/y] satisfies '(Fy ⊃ y = x)'. But for any odd positive integer **u**, there is at least one positive integer $\mathbf{u}_1$ such that **d**[**u**/x, $\mathbf{u}_1$/y] does *not* satisfy '(Fy ⊃ y = x)'—let $\mathbf{u}_1$ be any odd integer other than **u**. Here **d**[**u**/x, $\mathbf{u}_1$/y] satisfies 'Fy' because ⟨$\mathbf{u}_1$⟩ is in the extension of 'F', but according to clause 10 it does not satisfy 'y = x' because **d**[**u**/x, $\mathbf{u}_1$/y](x)—which is **u**—and **d**[**u**/x, $\mathbf{u}_1$/y](y)—which is $\mathbf{u}_1$—are different integers. It follows that no positive integer **u** is such that **d**[**u**/x] satisfies '(∀y)(Fy ⊃ y = x)', and so **d** does not satisfy the existentially quantified sentence '(∃x)(∀y)(Fy ⊃ y = x)'. The sentence is therefore false on interpretation 53.

Finally we shall complete our semantics for sentences of *PLE* that contain functors by amending our definition of an interpretation and of the denotation of a term with respect to an interpretation **I** and variable assignment **d**. We first define precisely the concept of an **n**-*place function on a UD:* An **n**-place function on a UD maps each **n**-tuple of members of the UD to a single member of the UD (not necessarily the same one in each case). So, if the UD consists of the integers 1 and 2, for example, there are four distinct 1-place functions: the function that maps each of 1 and 2 to itself, the function that maps both 1 and 2 to 1, the function that maps both 1 and 2 to 2, and the function that maps 1 to 2 and 2 to 1. We can represent each of these functions as a set of ordered pairs, where for each member **u** of the UD there is exactly one ordered pair with **u** as its first member, and the second member of that ordered pair is the value of the function for **u**. Here are the four sets of ordered pairs:

{<1, 1>, <2, 2>} (the function that maps each of 1 and 2 to itself)
{<1, 1>, <2, 1>} (the function that maps both 1 and 2 to 1)
{<1, 2>, <2, 2>} (the function that maps both 1 and 2 to 2)
{<1, 2>, <2, 1>} (the function that maps 1 to 2 and 2 to 1)

Similarly a 2-place function can be represented as a set of ordered triples, where for each pair of members $\mathbf{u}_1$ and $\mathbf{u}_2$ of the UD there is one ordered triple with $\mathbf{u}_1$ and $\mathbf{u}_2$ as the first two members, and the third member of that ordered triple is the value of the function for $\mathbf{u}_1$ and $\mathbf{u}_2$. So the multiplication function for the set of integers {0, 1} can be represented as the set {<0,0,0>, <0,1,0>, <1,0,0>, <1,1,1>}. (Note that multiplication is not a function on the set {1, 2} because we require that the value of the function for each pair of members of the UD itself be a member of the UD, but 2 × 2 is not a member of {1, 2}. On the other hand, multiplication *is* a function on the set of positive integers.)

We may now amend our definition of an interpretation:

> An interpretation for *PLE* consists in the specification of a UD and the assignment of a truth-value to each sentence letter of *PLE*, a member of the UD to each individual constant of *PLE*, an **n**-place function on the UD to each **n**-place functor of *PLE*, and a set of **n**-tuples of members of the UD to each **n**-place predicate of *PLE*.

We extend the definition of the *denotation of a term with respect to an interpretation* ***I*** *and variable assignment* **d** as follows, to accommodate terms containing functors:

1. If **t** is a variable, then $\text{den}_{\mathbf{I,d}}(\mathbf{t}) = \mathbf{d}(\mathbf{t})$.
2. If **t** is an individual constant, then $\text{den}_{\mathbf{I,d}}(\mathbf{t}) = \mathbf{I}(\mathbf{t})$.
3. If **t** is a term $f(\mathbf{t}_1, \ldots, \mathbf{t_n})$ where f is an **n**-place functor and $\mathbf{t}_1, \ldots, \mathbf{t_n}$ are terms, then if $<\text{den}_{\mathbf{I,d}}(\mathbf{t}_1), \ldots, \text{den}_{\mathbf{I,d}}(\mathbf{t_n}), \mathbf{u}>$ is a member of $\mathbf{I}(f)$, $\text{den}_{\mathbf{I,d}}(\mathbf{t}) = \mathbf{u}$.

Recall that for any members $\mathbf{u}_1, \ldots, \mathbf{u_n}$ of the UD, there will be a unique **n**-tuple $<\mathbf{u}_1, \ldots, \mathbf{u_n}, \mathbf{u}>$ that is a member of the function $\mathbf{I}(f)$, so clause 3 identifies exactly one member of the UD as $\text{den}_{\mathbf{I,d}}(\mathbf{t})$.

Using our new definitions, we can show that the sentence

$$(\forall x)(Gxa \supset Gf(x)a)$$

is true on interpretation 54:

54. UD: Set of positive integers
    Gxy: x is greater than y
    f(x): the successor of x
    a: 5

On this interpretation the sentence may be read as 'The successor of any positive integer that is greater than 5 is itself greater than 5'. To show that the sentence is true, we must show that it is satisfied by every variable assignment. Let **d** be a variable assignment. Then, by clause 8, **d** satisfies the sentence if and only if every member **u** of the UD is such that **d**[**u**/x] satisfies 'Gxa ⊃ Gf(x)a', and according to clause 6 this is the case if, whenever **d**[**u**/x] satisfies 'Gxa', **d**[**u**/x] also satisfies 'Gf(x)a'. So assume that **u** is such that **d**[**u**/x] satisfies 'Gxa'. It follows from clause 2 that $<\mathbf{d}[\mathbf{u}/x](x), \mathbf{I}(a)>$, which is $<\mathbf{u}, 5>$, is a member of **I**(G)—that is, **u** is greater than 5. But then $\text{den}_{\mathbf{I,d}}(f(x))$, which is the successor of **u**, is also greater than 5, so $<\text{den}_{\mathbf{I,d}}(f(x)), 5>$, which is

$<\text{den}_{\mathbf{I},\mathbf{d}}(f(x)), \mathbf{I}(a)>$, is also a member of **I**(G). It follows from clause 2, then, that **d**[**u**/x] also satisfies 'G*f*(x)a'. Therefore every variable assignment **d**[**u**/x] that satisfies the antecedent of 'Gxa ⊃ G*f*(x)a' also satisfies the consequent; so every variable assignment **d**[**u**/x] satisfies the conditional, and hence every variable assignment **d** satisfies the universally quantified '(∀x)(Gxa ⊃ G*f*(x)a)'. This establishes that the sentence is therefore true on interpretation 54.

8.7E EXERCISES

1. Using the definitions in this section, determine the truth-value of each of the following sentences on an interpretation that makes these assignments:

UD: Set of positive integers
K: {<**u**>: **u** is negative}
E: {<**u**>: **u** is even}
L: {<$\mathbf{u}_1$, $\mathbf{u}_2$>: $\mathbf{u}_1$ is less than $\mathbf{u}_2$}
o: 1

a. ~ (∀x)Ex ⊃ (∃y)Lyo
*b. ~ Loo & ~ (∀y) ~ Loy
c. (∃x)(Ko ∨ Ex)
*d. (∀x)(Lox ⊃ (∀y)Lxy)
e. (Ko ≡ (∀x)Ex) ⊃ (∃y)(∃z)Lyz
*f. (∀x)[Ex ⊃ (∃y)(Lyx ∨ Lyo)]

2. Using the definitions in this section, determine the truth-value of each of the following sentences on an interpretation that makes these assignments:

UD: Set of positive integers
E: {<**u**>: **u** is even}
G: {<$\mathbf{u}_1$, $\mathbf{u}_2$>: $\mathbf{u}_1$ is greater than $\mathbf{u}_2$}
T: {<**u**>: **u** is less than 2}
t: 3

a. (∃x)(Ex ⊃ (∀y)Ey)
*b. (∀x)(∀y)(Gxy ∨ Gyx)
c. (∀x)(Tx ⊃ (∃y)Gyx)
*d. (∀x)(Et ⊃ Ex)
e. (∀x)[(∀y)Gxy ∨ (∃y)Gxy]
*f. (∀y)[Ty ∨ (∀x)(Ex ⊃ Gxy)]

3. Using the definitions in this section, determine the truth-value of each of the following sentences on an interpretation that makes these assignments:

UD: Set of positive integers
M: {<$\mathbf{u}_1$, $\mathbf{u}_2$, $\mathbf{u}_3$>: $\mathbf{u}_1$ minus $\mathbf{u}_2$ equals $\mathbf{u}_3$}
P: {<$\mathbf{u}_1$, $\mathbf{u}_2$, $\mathbf{u}_3$>: $\mathbf{u}_1$ plus $\mathbf{u}_2$ equals $\mathbf{u}_3$}
o: 1

a. $Mooo = Pooo$
*b. $(\forall x)(\forall y)(Mxyo \equiv Pyox)$
c. $(\forall x)(\forall y)(\forall z)(Mxyz \equiv Pxyz)$
*d. $(\exists x)(\forall y)(\forall z)(Mxyz \vee Pzyx)$
e. $(\forall y)(\exists z)(Pyoz \supset Pooo)$

***4.** Using the definitions in this section, explain why the following two sentences are quantificationally equivalent:

$(\forall x)Fx$
$\sim (\exists x) \sim Fx$

5. Using the definitions in this section, explain why the following sentence is quantificationally true:

$(\forall x)((\forall y)Fy \supset Fx)$

***6.** Using the definitions in this section, explain why $\{(\forall x)Fx\}$ quantificationally entails every substitution instance of '$(\forall x)Fx$'.

7. Using the definitions in this section, explain why 'Fa' quantificationally entails '$(\exists x)Fx$'.

***8.** Using the definitions in this section, explain why '$(\exists x)Fx \& (\forall x) \sim Fx$' is quantificationally false.

9. Using the definitions in this section, determine the truth-value of each of the following sentences on an interpretation that makes these assignments:

UD: Set of positive integers
Ex: x is even
Gxy: x is greater than y

a. $(\forall x)(\forall y)[\sim x = y \supset (Ex \supset Gxy)]$
*b. $(\forall x)(\forall y)(x = y \vee \sim Ey)$
c. $(\forall x)[Ex \supset (\exists y)(\sim x = y \& \sim Gxy)]$

10.a. Using the definitions in this section, explain why every sentence of the form $(\forall \mathbf{x})\mathbf{x} = \mathbf{x}$ is quantificationally true.
*b. Using the definitions in this section, explain why '$(\forall x)(\forall y)(x = y \supset Fxy) \supset (\forall x)Fxx$' is quantificationally true.

11. Using the definitions in this section, determine the truth-value of each of the following sentences on an interpretation that makes the following assignments:

UD: Set of positive integers
Ox: x is odd
$h(x)$: x squared
$g(x,y)$: the sum of x and y

a. $(\forall x)(Oh(x) \supset Og(x,x))$
*b. $(\forall x)(\forall y)(Og(x,y) \supset (Ox \vee Oy))$
c. $(\exists x)(\exists y)(Ox \& x = h(y))$

12.a. Using the definitions in this section, explain why every sentence of the form $(\forall \mathbf{x})(\exists \mathbf{y})\mathbf{y} = f(\mathbf{x})$ is quantificationally true.

*b. Using the definitions in this section, explain why '$(\forall x)Pf(x) \supset (\forall x)Pf(f(x))$' is quantificationally true.

GLOSSARY

QUANTIFICATIONAL TRUTH: A sentence **P** of *PL/PLE* is *quantificationally true* if and only if **P** is true on every interpretation.

QUANTIFICATIONAL FALSITY: A sentence **P** of *PL/PLE* is *quantificationally false* if and only if **P** is false on every interpretation.

QUANTIFICATIONAL INDETERMINACY: A sentence **P** of *PL/PLE* is *quantificationally indeterminate* if and only if **P** is neither quantificationally true nor quantificationally false.

QUANTIFICATIONAL EQUIVALENCE: Sentences **P** and **Q** of *PL/PLE* are *quantificationally equivalent* if and only if there is no interpretation on which **P** and **Q** have different truth-values.

QUANTIFICATIONAL CONSISTENCY: A set of sentences of *PL/PLE* is *quantificationally consistent* if and only if there is at least one interpretation on which all the members of the set are true. A set of sentences of *PL/PLE* is *quantificationally inconsistent* if and only if the set is not quantificationally consistent.

QUANTIFICATIONAL ENTAILMENT: A set Γ of sentences of *PL/PLE quantificationally entails* a sentence **P** of *PL/PLE* if and only if there is no interpretation on which every member of Γ is true and **P** is false.

QUANTIFICATIONAL VALIDITY: An argument of *PL/PLE* is *quantificationally valid* if and only if there is no interpretation on which all the premises are true and the conclusion is false. An argument of *PL/PLE* is *quantificationally invalid* if and only if the argument is not quantificationally valid.

Chapter

9

PREDICATE LOGIC: TRUTH-TREES

9.1 EXPANDING THE RULES FOR TRUTH-TREES

Truth-trees, as developed in Chapter 4, provide the basis for an effective method of testing for truth-functional consistency and thus for all the properties of sentences and groups of sentences that can be explicated in terms of truth-functional consistency (for example, truth-functional validity, truth-functional truth, and truth-functional equivalence). In this chapter we shall extend the truth-tree method to make it applicable to sets of sentences of *PL*. The result will be a method of testing for quantificational consistency and thus for those properties of sentences and groups of sentences that can be explicated in terms of quantificational consistency.

Some sets of sentences of *PL* consist exclusively of sentences whose only logical operators are truth-functional connectives. We can test these sets for consistency by using the truth-tree rules of Chapter 4. For the set

$$\{Fab, Gac \& Rab, Fab \supset (\sim Gac \vee \sim Rab)\}$$

we can construct the following tree:

1.	Fab		SM
2.	Gac & Rab ✓		SM
3.	Fab ⊃ (~ Gac ∨ ~ Rab) ✓		SM
4.	Gac		2 &D
5.	Rab		2 &D
6.	~ Fab ×	~ Gac ∨ ~ Rab ✓	3 ⊃D
7.		~ Gac × ~ Rab ×	6 ∨D

The various branches represent abortive attempts to discover a way in which all the members of the set being tested might come to be true. Where the set being considered contains sentences whose only logical operators are truth-functional connectives, there is an interpretation on which all the members of the set being tested are true if and only if the tree for the set has at least one completed open branch. (It will turn out that from a completed open branch we can recover or construct an interpretation on which all the members of the set being tested are true.) The above tree contains only closed branches; that is, each branch of this tree contains an atomic sentence and the negation of that sentence. We know that there is no interpretation on which both a sentence and its negation are true. Hence there is no interpretation on which the sentences composing the set being tested are all true. So this set is, on truth-functional grounds, quantificationally inconsistent.

However, many sets that are quantificationally inconsistent are not inconsistent on truth-functional grounds. The rules we presently have for constructing truth-trees do not allow us to construct closed trees for such sets. For example, using the decomposition rules we presently have, we can obtain only the following tree for the set {(∀x) (Fxc ⊃ Gxb), Fac & ~ Gab}:

1.	(∀x) (Fxc ⊃ Gxb)	SM
2.	Fac & ~ Gab ✓	SM
3.	Fac	2 &D
4.	~ Gab	2 &D

We cannot decompose the quantified sentence '(∀x) (Fxc ⊃ Gxb)' using only the truth-tree rules given in Chapter 4. In fact, there are four varieties of nonatomic sentences of *PL* that cannot be decomposed by those rules. These are sentences of the forms

(∀**x**)**P**
(∃**x**)**P**
~ (∀**x**)**P**
~ (∃**x**)**P**

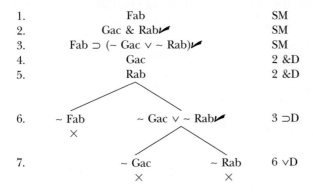

In this section we introduce one new tree rule for each of these kinds of sentences. We begin with the rules for negations of quantified sentences. Both are nonbranching rules.

Negated Existential Decomposition (~ ∃D)	*Negated Universal Decomposition* (~ ∀D)
~ (∃**x**)**P**✓	~ (∀**x**)**P**✓
(∀**x**) ~ **P**	(∃**x**) ~ **P**

In each case the sentence entered is equivalent to the sentence being decomposed. ('It is not the case that something is such-and-such' is equivalent to 'Each thing is such that it is not such-and-such', and 'It is not the case that each thing is such-and-such' is equivalent to 'Something is not such-and-such'.) Note that negations of quantified sentences are truth-functionally compound sentences. Hence Negated Existential Decomposition and Negated Universal Decomposition count as rules for decomposing truth-functionally compound sentences.

If a universally quantified sentence (∀**x**)**P** is true, then so is each substitution instance **P**(**a**/**x**) of that sentence. We want a rule that allows us to "decompose" a universally quantified sentence into the appropriate substitution instances of that sentence. Recall the tree we started for the set {(∀x)(Fxc ⊃ Gxb), Fac & ~ Gab}. The only sentence on that tree remaining to be decomposed is '(∀x)(Fxc ⊃ Gxb)'. Since that sentence is true on an interpretation only if all its substitution instances are true on that interpretation, we are justified in entering on line 5 *any* substitution instance of that sentence we may choose. So we add the following to our set of tree rules:

Universal Decomposition (∀D)
(∀**x**)**P**
P(**a**/**x**)

where **a** is an individual constant

At any point in the construction of a tree, any universally quantified sentence (∀**x**)**P** may be decomposed by entering any substitution instance **P**(**a**/**x**) of that sentence on *one or more* open branches passing through (∀**x**)**P**. Because a universally quantified sentence has an infinite number of substitution instances, we can never "finish" decomposing such a sentence. (Consequently universally quantified sentences are never checked off.)

Universal Decomposition does *not* require that the selected substitution instance be entered on every open branch passing through the universally quantified sentence being decomposed. This is appropriate because a substitution instance is often of use on one open branch passing through the sentence being decomposed but not on another. And, as universally quantified sentences are never checked off, we can always later add, to any open branch on which a universally quantified sentence occurs, any substitution instance of that sentence.

The tree started for the set {(∀x)(Fxc ⊃ Gxb), Fac & ~ Gab)} can now be completed:

1.	(∀x)(Fxc ⊃ Gxb)		SM
2.	Fac & ~ Ga✓		SM
3.	Fac		2 &D
4.	~ Gab		2 &D
5.	Fac ⊃ Gab✓		1 ∀D
6.	~ Fac	Gab	5 ⊃D
	×	×	

At line 5 we entered 'Fac ⊃ Gab' by Universal Decomposition. We could have entered any substitution instance of '(∀x)(Fxc ⊃ Gxb)', but only the one we did enter is of use in producing a closed tree.

The last tree rule is that for decomposing existentially quantified sentences:

Existential Decomposition (∃D)

(∃**x**)**P**✓

P(**a**/**x**)

where **a** is a constant foreign to the branch. A constant is foreign to a branch of a tree if and only if it does not occur in any sentence on that branch. (Existentially quantified sentences, unlike universally quantified sentences, are checked off when they are decomposed. This is because we know that if an existentially quantified sentence (∃**x**)**P** is true then there is something that is of the sort specified by **P**, but there need not be more than one such thing.) In picking an individual constant foreign to a branch, we are, so to speak, decreeing that on the current branch that individual constant designates the thing that is of the sort specified by **P**. We can do this because **a**, the selected constant, is foreign to the branch. If **a** were not foreign to the branch, it would already have a role on that branch, and quite possibly a conflicting role such as the name of something that is not of the sort specified by **P**.

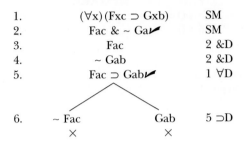

For example, the sentences 'Some cars are yellow' and 'Some cars are not yellow' are both true. Hence a set consisting of symbolizations of these sentences, {(∃x)(Cx & Yx), (∃x)(Cx & ~ Yx)}, should be quantificationally consistent and accordingly should have only open truth-trees. However, if we were to drop the restriction on Existential Decomposition just discussed, we could produce a closed tree for this set:

1.	(∃x) (Cx & Yx)✓	SM	
2.	(∃x) (Cx & ~ Yx)✓	SM	
3.	Ca & Ya✓	1 ∃D	
4.	Ca	3 &D	
5.	Ya	3 &D	
6.	Ca & ~ Ya✓	2 ∃D	**MISTAKE!**
7.	Ca	6 &D	
8.	~ Ya	6 &D	
	×		

The individual constant 'a', used in Existential Decomposition at line 6, is not, at the time 'Ca & ~ Ya' is entered, foreign to the single branch of the tree. Hence line 6 is a mistake.

The following tree contains three uses of Existential Decomposition:

1.	(∀x)Fx ⊃ (∃x) ~ Gx)✓		SM
2.	(∃x) ~ Fx✓		SM
3.	~ Fa		2 ∃D
4.	~ (∀x)Fx✓	(∃x) ~ Gx✓	1 ⊃D
5.	(∃x) ~ Fx✓		4 ~ ∀D
6.	~ Fb		5 ∃D
7.		~ Gb	4 ∃D

At line 3 Existential Decomposition is used for the first time. Since no constant occurs on the single branch that constitutes the tree at that point, 'a' is used as the instantiating constant. The next use of Existential Decomposition is at line 6 on the left-hand branch. At that point 'a' already occurs on the branch (at line 3, remember that the sentences on lines 1–3 occur on both branches of this tree). So a new instantiating constant, 'b', is used. The final use of Existential Decomposition is at line 7 on the right-hand branch. The constant 'a' cannot be used because it occurs on line 3. But 'b' can be used, for although it already occurs on the left-hand branch, it does not occur, before '~ Gb' is entered, on the right-hand branch.

The preceding tree has two open branches, each of which contains only literals and decomposed nonliterals. The complexities of predicate logic will force us to complicate the account of 'completed open branch' given in Chapter 4. However, on this revised account, as on the account of Chapter 4, an open branch that contains only literals and nonliterals that have been decomposed and checked off is a completed open branch. So both branches of the tree are completed open branches. (It will, again, turn out that from a completed open branch an interpretation is recoverable on which every member of the set being tested is true, and hence that this tree demonstrates that the set {(∀x)Fx ⊃ (∃x) ~ Gx, (∃x) ~ Fx} is quantificationally consistent.)

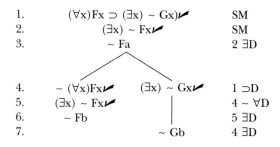

Except for Universal Decomposition, the truth-tree rules introduced in this section are like the tree rules of Chapter 4 in that the results of applying one of them must be entered on *every* open branch running through the sentence being decomposed. Also as in Chapter 4, it is generally wise to apply decomposition rules that do not produce new branches before applying those that do. In using Universal Decomposition it is a good idea to try to select a substitution instance in which the instantiating constant is a constant already occurring on the open branch in question. It is also wise to try to use Existential Decomposition before using Universal Decomposition, for the former but not the latter includes a restriction on the individual constant that can be used in forming the substitution instance to be entered on the tree. We illustrate these last two points by constructing a tree for {(∀x)(∀y) ~ Mxy, (∃x)Mxb}:

1.	(∀x)(∀y) ~ Mxy	SM
2.	(∃x)Mxb ✓	SM
3.	Mab	2 ∃D
4.	(∀y) ~ May	1 ∀D
5.	~ Mab	4 ∀D
	×	

Note that we did use Existential Decomposition before Universal Decomposition. At line 4 we entered '(∀y) ~ May' rather than, say, '(∀y) ~ Mgy', because 'a' occurs earlier on the tree. And we entered '(∀y) ~ May', rather than '(∀y) ~ Mby', because the former but *not* the latter yields, when appropriately decomposed, the negation of the sentence on line 3. Here using Universal Decomposition before Existential Decomposition—that is, decomposing the sentence on line 1 before the sentence on line 2—also produces a closed tree, but such a tree is more complex:

1.	(∀x)(∀y) ~ Mxy	SM
2.	(∃x)Mxb ✓	SM
3.	(∀y) ~ Mby	1 ∀D
4.	~ Mbb	3 ∀D
5.	Mab	2 ∃D
6.	(∀y) ~ May	1 ∀D
7.	~ Mab	6 ∀D
	×	

In this tree we had to enter 'Mab', rather than 'Mbb', at line 5 because Existential Decomposition requires that we enter a substitution instance of the sentence being decomposed in which the instantiating constant is foreign to the branch. The constant 'b' is not, at line 5, foreign to the branch. Having entered 'Mab' at line 5, we were able to close the tree only by reapplying Universal Decomposition to the sentence on line 1. Lines 3 and 4 of the tree are thus superfluous.

In Chapter 4 we developed four strategies for keeping truth-trees for sets of sentences of *PL* as concise as possible. Those strategies are also applicable here. We repeat them below, along with the two new strategies just discussed (suitably rearranged).

> *Strategies for Constructing Truth-Trees*
>
> 1. Give priority to decomposing sentences whose decomposition does not require branching.
> 2. Give priority to decomposing sentences whose decomposition results in the closing of one or more branches.
> 3. Give priority to decomposing existentially quantified sentences over universally quantified sentences.
> 4. When using Universal Decomposition, try to use a substitution instance in which the instantiating constant already occurs on the branch in question.
> 5. Stop when a tree yields an answer to the question being asked.
> 6. Where strategy 1–5 are not applicable, decompose the more complex sentences first.

Strategy 1 should be used with care when dealing with universally quantified sentences. Consider the following tree in which Universal Decomposition is used before Conditional Decomposition:

1.	$(\forall x)(Fxa \supset Fax)$		SM
2.	$(\forall y)(Hy \supset Fya)$		SM
3.	$(\exists x)(Hx \ \& \sim Fax)$ ✓		SM
4.	$Hb \ \& \sim Fab$ ✓		3 ∃D
5.	Hb		4 &D
6.	$\sim Fab$		4 &D
7.	$Faa \supset Faa$		1 ∀D
8.	$Fba \supset Fab$ ✓		1 ∀D
9.	$Ha \supset Faa$		2 ∀D
10.	$Hb \supset Fba$ ✓		2 ∀D
11.	$\sim Hb$	Fba	10 ⊃D
12.		$\sim Fba$ × Fab ×	8 ⊃D

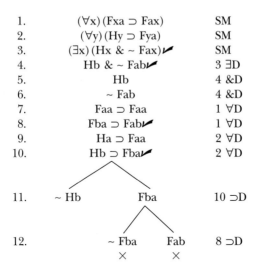

At line 7 we used Universal Decomposition and continued using it until each universally quantified sentence (there are two) had been decomposed to every substitution instance that could be formed from a constant already on the branch. The idea is that these are the substitution instances that may be useful later on. As it turns out, lines 7 and 9 are unnecessary, but this was not completely obvious at the point where we had a choice between applying Universal Decomposition and Conditional Decomposition. An alternative strategy would be to use Universal Decomposition only when no other rule can be applied. But this strategy produces the following, considerably more complex, tree:

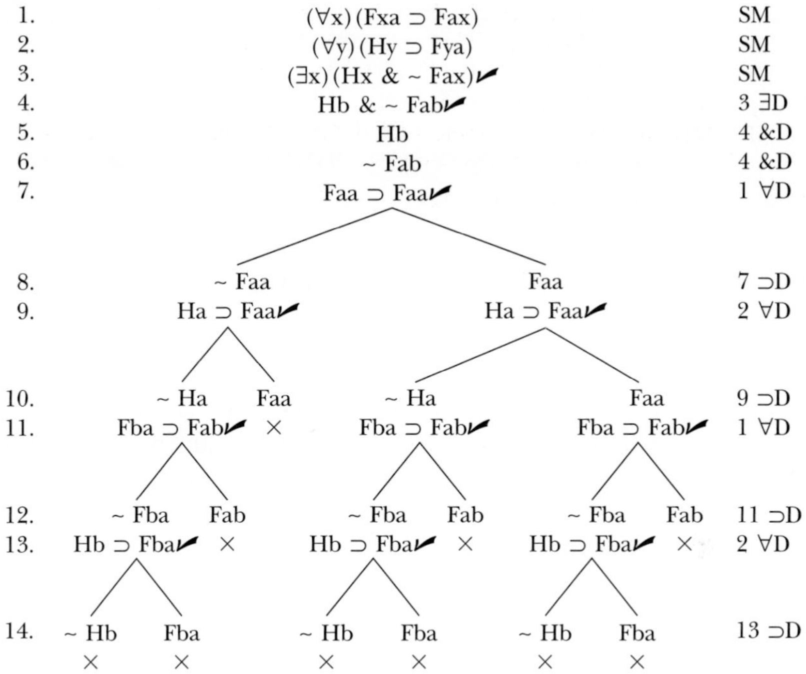

1. (∀x)(Fxa ⊃ Fax) SM
2. (∀y)(Hy ⊃ Fya) SM
3. (∃x)(Hx & ~ Fax)✔ SM
4. Hb & ~ Fab✔ 3 ∃D
5. Hb 4 &D
6. ~ Fab 4 &D
7. Faa ⊃ Faa✔ 1 ∀D
8. ~ Faa Faa 7 ⊃D
9. Ha ⊃ Faa✔ Ha ⊃ Faa✔ 2 ∀D
10. ~ Ha Faa ~ Ha Faa 9 ⊃D
11. Fba ⊃ Fab✔ × Fba ⊃ Fab✔ Fba ⊃ Fab✔ 1 ∀D
12. ~ Fba Fab ~ Fba Fab ~ Fba Fab 11 ⊃D
13. Hb ⊃ Fba✔ × Hb ⊃ Fba✔ × Hb ⊃ Fba✔ × 2 ∀D
14. ~ Hb Fba ~ Hb Fba ~ Hb Fba 13 ⊃D
× × × × × ×

The best policy appears to be to stick with strategy 1, but with the caveat that, when a shorter route to a closed tree is apparent, it should be pursued.[1]

9.1E EXERCISES

Construct truth-trees for the following sets of sentences. For each, note whether the tree you construct has a completed open branch or is closed (by the accounts of 'completed open branch' and 'closed tree' given in Chapter 4).

a. {(∃x)Fx, (∃x) ~ Fx)}
*b. {(∃x)Fx, (∀x) ~ Fx}
c. {(∃x)(Fx & ~ Gx), (∀x)(Fx ⊃ Gx)}
*d. {(∃x)(Fx & ~ Gx), (∀x)Fx ⊃ (∀x)Gx}
e. {~ (∀x)(Fx ⊃ Gx), ~ (∃x)Fx, ~ (∃x)Gx}
*f. {~ (∀x)(Fx & Gx), (∃y)(Fy & Gy)}
g. {(∃x)Fx, (∃y)Gy, (∃z)(Fz & Gz)}

---

[1] A further caveat will be required when we introduce systematic trees in Section 9.5, for the routine for constructing such trees requires abandoning strategy 1 altogether as it applies to universally quantified sentences.

*h. {(∀x)(Fx ⊃ Gx), (∀x)(Gx ⊃ Hx), (∃x)(Fx & ~ Hx)}
i. {(∀x)(∀y)(Fxy ⊃ Fyx), (∃x)(∃y)(Fxy & ~ Fyx)}
*j. {(∀x)(∃y)Lxy, Lta & ~ Lat, ~ (∃y)Lay}
k. {(∃x)Fx ⊃ (∀x)Fx, ~ (∀x)[Fx ⊃ (∀y)Fy]}
*l. {(∀x)(Fx ⊃ Gx), ~ (∀x) ~ Fx, (∀x) ~ Gx}
m. {(∀x)[Fx ⊃ (∃y)Gyx, ~ (∀x) ~ Fx, (∀x)(∀y) ~ Gxy}
*n. {(∃x)Gx ⊃ (∀x)Gx, (∃z)Gz & (∃y) ~ Gy}
o. {(∃x)Lxx, ~ (∃x)(∃y)(Lxy & Lyx)}
*p. {(∃y)(Fy ∨ Gy), ~ (∀y)Fy & ~ (∀y)Gy, ~ (∀x)(Fx & Gx)}
q. {(∃x)(Fx ∨ Gx), (∀x)(Fx ⊃ ~ Gx), (∀x)(Gx ⊃ ~ Fx), ~ (∃x)(~ Fx ∨ ~ Gx)}

9.2 TRUTH-TREES AND QUANTIFICATIONAL CONSISTENCY

So far we have seen a variety of truth-trees for sets of sentences of *PL*. Some have been closed, and others open, by the accounts of Chapter 4. The trees that are open trees by the account of Chapter 4 are so by virtue of having at least one branch such that no new sentence can be added to it (every sentence on the branch either is a literal or has been decomposed). But not all open trees for sets of sentences of *PL* are of this sort. Consider a tree for {(∃y)Gy ⊃ (∀x)Fxb, (∃z) ~ Fzb}:

1.	(∃y)Gy ⊃ (∀x)Fxb) ✓		SM
2.	(∃z) ~ Fzb ✓		SM
3.	~ Fab		2 ∃D
4.	~ (∃y)Gy ✓	(∀x)Fxb	1 ∀D
5.		Fab	4 ∀D
		×	
6.	(∀y) ~ Gy		4 ~ ∃D
7.	~ Ga		6 ∀D
8.	~ Gb		6 ∀D

This tree has one closed branch and one open branch. Further sentences could be added to the open branch, for one of the sentences on that branch, '(∀y) ~ Gy', is a universally quantified sentence, and there is no limit to the number of times a universally quantified sentence can be decomposed. (Such sentences are never checked off.) In the present example we added substitution instances of '(∀y) ~ Gy' at lines 7 and 8. While further substitution instances can be added, it is clear that, no matter what further substitution instances may be added, the branch will remain open. We have already added all the instances that can be formed from individual constants appearing earlier on the open branch. Substitution instances formed from individual constants not already on the open branch will be such that their truth or falsity does not bear on the truth of literals already on the branch, so there is no point in entering '~ Gh', for example.

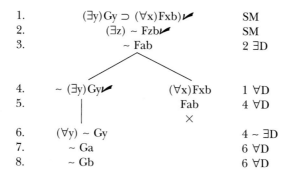

To accommodate trees such as this one, we modify our account of a completed open branch as follows:

> A branch of a truth-tree for a set of sentences of *PL* is a *completed open branch* if and only if it is a finite open branch, that is, an open branch with a finite number of entries, and each sentence occurring on that branch is one of the following:
>
> 1. A literal (an atomic sentence or the negation of an atomic sentence)
> 2. Not a universally quantified sentence, and decomposed
> 3. A universally quantified sentence $(\forall \mathbf{x})\mathbf{P}$ such that $\mathbf{P}(\mathbf{a}/\mathbf{x})$ also occurs on that branch *for each constant* **a** occurring on the branch and at least one substitution instance $\mathbf{P}(\mathbf{a}/\mathbf{x})$ occurs on the branch

By this revised account the preceding tree does contain a completed open branch.

We summarize here the important properties of truth-trees for sets of sentences of *PL*. With the exception of the notion of a completed open branch, these accounts strictly parallel those given in Chapter 4:

Closed branch:	A branch containing both an atomic sentence and the negation of that sentence
Closed truth-tree:	A tree each of whose branches is closed
Open branch:	A branch that is not closed
Completed open branch:	A finite open branch on which each sentence is of one of the sorts specified in clauses 1–3 in the preceding paragraph
Completed truth-tree:	A truth-tree each of whose branches either is closed or is a completed open branch
Open truth-tree:	A truth-tree that is not closed

Note that a tree that has a completed open branch is an open tree, as is a tree that is still under construction—one that is not a completed truth-tree. So, while some open trees may become closed trees, those with a completed open branch will always be open trees. To see why we require that a completed open branch on which a universally quantified sentence occurs contain at least one substitution instance of that sentence, consider the unit set $\{\sim (\exists x)(Fx \vee \sim Fx)\}$. The sole member of this set says that it is not the case that there is an x such that either x is F or x is not F. But each thing x either is F or is not F. So this sentence is false—and indeed is quantificationally false (since every UD is nonempty). Hence we want the trees for the unit set of this sentence to close. One tree is as follows:

1.	$\sim (\exists x)(Fx \vee \sim Fx)$ ✓	SM
2.	$(\forall x) \sim (Fx \vee \sim Fx)$	$1 \sim \exists D$
3.	$\sim (Fa \vee \sim Fa)$ ✓	$2\ \forall D$
4.	$\sim Fa$	$3 \sim \vee D$
5.	$\sim \sim Fa$ ✓	$3 \sim \vee D$
6.	Fa	$5 \sim \sim D$
	×	

At line 2 we replaced the negated existentially quantified sentence on line 1 with a universally quantified sentence by Negated Existential Decomposition. If we did not require that a completed open branch contain at least one substitution instance of every universally quantified sentence occurring on that branch, we would have, at line 2, a completed open branch, which is supposed to signal a consistent set. But the set we are testing is not consistent, and adhering to the above requirement does yield, at line 6, a closed tree. Note that this tree would close no matter what substitution instance of '$(\forall x) \sim (Fx \vee \sim Fx)$' is entered at line 3.

In *PL*, as in *SL*, a closed tree signifies inconsistency. To allow for infinite sets we make the following our official account:

> A set Γ of sentences of *PL* is *quantificationally inconsistent* if and only if at least one finite subset of Γ has a closed truth-tree.

> A set Γ of sentences of *PL* is *quantificationally consistent* if and only if Γ is not quantificationally inconsistent, that is, if and only if no finite subset of Γ has a closed tree.[2]

If a finite set Γ of sentences of *PL* has a tree with a completed open branch, then Γ is quantificationally consistent. However, in *PL*, unlike *SL*, not all consistent finite sets have trees with completed open branches. That is, some such sets have trees all of whose open branches are infinite (because all their open branches are infinite, and we require a completed open branch to be finite). We discuss such trees in detail in Section 9.5.

The following tree for the unit set {$(\exists x)Fx$} illustrates another complexity that characterizes quantificational but not sentential truth-trees:

1.	$(\exists x)Fx$ ✓	SM
2.	Fa	$1\ \exists D$

The tree for this unit set has only one open branch. But we cannot argue, as we could if it were the tree for the unit set of a sentence of *SL*, that the one member of the set in question is true *if and only if* at least one completed open branch is such that every sentence on it is true. Suppose '$(\exists x)Fx$' says, on a given interpretation, 'Someone is funny'. This sentence is true even if the person designated

[2]The proof of this result is very similar to the proof of the parallel result for sentential logic given in Chapter 6.

by 'a' on that interpretation, say, Albert, is not funny—that is, even if 'Fa' is false on that interpretation—provided some member of the UD of the interpretation is funny. Of course, we can make the weak claim that, if the sentence to which an existentially quantified sentence is decomposed is true on an interpretation, so is that existentially quantified sentence. And this weak claim does justify our taking the preceding tree as establishing the quantificational consistency of the unit set {(∃x)Fx}.

Since a sentence obtained by Existential Decomposition need not be true on an interpretation for the decomposed sentence to be true on that interpretation, how can we justify taking the following tree to show that {(∃x)(Fx & ~ Fx)} is quantificationally inconsistent?

1.	(∃x)(Fx & ~ Fx)1✓	SM
2.	Fa & ~ Fa✓	1 ∃D
3.	Fa	2 &D
4.	~ Fa	2 &D
	×	

Our reasoning is as follows: If there is indeed something that both is and is not F, then there is an interpretation that assigns that thing to 'a', and 'Fa & ~ Fa' will have to be true on that interpretation. But our tree shows that, if 'Fa & ~ Fa' is true on an interpretation, so are both 'Fa' and '~ Fa'. And we know that there is no interpretation on which an atomic sentence and its negation are both true. Hence we conclude that there is no interpretation on which '(∃x)(Fx & ~ Fx)' is true.

We shall prove in Chapter 11 that an interpretation on which every member of the set being tested is true can always be constructed from a completed open branch. Here we illustrate how interpretations are constructed from completed open branches. Consider a tree for the set {(∀x)(Gx ⊃ Hxx), ~ (∀y)Hyy, (∃z)Gz}:

1.		(∀x)(Gx ⊃ Hxx)		SM
2.		~ (∀y)Hyy✓		SM
3.		(∃z)Gz✓		SM
4.		(∃y) ~ Hyy✓		2 ~ ∀D
5.		~ Haa		4 ∃D
6.		Gb		3 ∃D
7.		Ga ⊃ Haa✓		1 ∀D
8.		Gb ⊃ Hbb✓		1 ∀D
9.	~ Gb	Hbb		8 ⊃D
	×			
10.		~ Ga	Haa	7 ⊃D
			×	

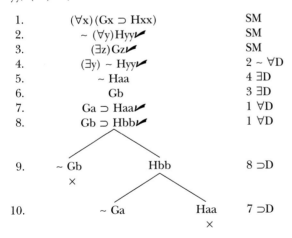

This tree has two closed branches and one completed open branch. Our strategy is to construct an interpretation on which all the literals on that open branch are true. That branch contains just two individual constants, 'a' and 'b'. So we shall take as our UD the set consisting of the positive integers 1 and 2 and assign 1 to 'a' and 2 to 'b'. We now have to interpret the predicates 'G' and 'H' in such a way that 'Gb' and 'Hbb' are true (since those literals occur on the open branch) and 'Ga' and 'Haa' are false on the resulting interpretation (since '~ Ga' and '~ Haa' occur on the open branch). One way to do this is to interpret 'Gx' as 'x is 2' and 'Hxy' as 'x is an even number equal to y'. This gives us the following interpretation:

UD:	{1, 2}
a:	1
b:	2
Gx:	x is 2
Hxy:	x is an even number equal to y

Note that, when an interpretation is constructed in this way, each individual constant on the open branch is assigned a distinct member of the UD, and each member of the UD is assigned to some constant or other. All the members of the set {(∀x)(Gx ⊃ Hxx), ~ (∀y)Hyy, (∃z)Gz} are true on this interpretation. This establishes that the set consisting of those three sentences is quantificationally consistent.

Since an interpretation on which all the members of the set being tested are true *can* always be constructed from a completed open branch, we shall take the presence of a completed open branch as itself guaranteeing that the set being tested is quantificationally consistent.

9.2E EXERCISES

Use the truth-tree method to test the following sets of sentences for quantificational consistency. State your result, and specify what it is about the tree that establishes this result.

a. {(∀x)Fx ∨ (∃y)Gy, (∃x)(Fx & Gb)}
*b. {(∀x)Fx ∨ (∃y)Gy, (∃x)(~ Fx & Gx)}
c. {(∀x)(Fx ⊃ Gxa), (∃x)Fx, (∀y) ~ Gya}
*d. {(∀x)(Fx ⊃ Gxa), (∃x)Fx}
e. {(∀x)(Fx ⊃ Gxa), (∃x)Fx, (∀y)Gya}
*f. {(∀x)(Fx ⊃ Gxa), (∃x)Fx, (∀x)(∀y)Gxy}
g. {(∀x)(Fx ∨ Gx), ~ (∃y)(Fy ∨ Gy)}
*h. {(∀x)(Fx ∨ Gx), ~ (∃y)(Fy ∨ Gy), Fa & ~ Gb}
i. {(∀z)Hz, (∃x)Hx ⊃ (∀y)Fy}
*j. {(∀z) ~ Hzb, (∃y)Fy ⊃ (∃x)Hxc}
k. {(∀x)(∀y)Lxy, (∃z) ~ Lza ⊃ (∀z) ~ Lza}
*l. {(∀x)(∀y)Lxy, (∃z) ~ Lza ⊃ (∀z) ~ Lzb}
m. {(∀x)(Rx ≡ ~ Hxa), ~ (∀y) ~ Hby, Ra}
*n. {(∀x)Fxa ≡ ~ (∀x)Gxb, (∃x)(Fxa & ~ Gxb)}

.3 TRUTH-TREES AND OTHER SEMANTIC PROPERTIES

To use truth-trees to test sentences and sets of sentences for properties other than consistency, we must specify those other properties in terms of open and closed truth-trees. We begin by so specifying quantificational falsity, quantificational truth, and quantificational indeterminacy:

> A sentence **P** of *PL* is *quantificationally true* if and only if the set {~ **P**} has a closed truth-tree.

> A sentence **P** of *PL* is *quantificationally false* if and only if the set {**P**} has a closed truth-tree.

> A sentence **P** of *PL* is *quantificationally indeterminate* if and only if neither the set {**P**} nor the set {~ **P**} has a closed truth-tree.

Quantificational equivalence, quantificational entailment, and quantificational validity are specified analogously:

> Sentences **P** and **Q** of *PL* are *quantificationally equivalent* if and only if {~ **P** ≡ **Q**} has a closed truth-tree.

> A finite set Γ of sentences of *PL* *quantificationally entails* a sentence **P** of *PL* if and only if Γ ∪ {~ **P**} has a closed truth-tree.

> An argument of *PL* is *quantificationally valid* if and only if the set consisting of the premises and the negation of the conclusion has a closed truth-tree.

We shall illustrate how truth-trees can be used to test for each of these semantic properties. We begin with quantificational truth, quantificational falsity, and quantificational indeterminacy. Consider the sentence '(∀x) (Fx & (∃y) ~ Fy)'. It says, 'Each thing is F and at least one thing is not F', a claim for which we should not hold out much hope. To verify that this sentence is quantificationally false, we construct a tree for the unit set of this sentence, expecting the tree to close, which it does:

1.	(∀x) (Fx & (∃y) ~ Fy)	SM
2.	Fa & (∃y) ~ Fy✓	1 ∀D
3.	Fa	2 &D
4.	(∃y) ~ Fy✓	2 &D
5.	~ Fb	4 ∃D
6.	Fb & (∃y) ~ Fy✓	1 ∀D
7.	Fb	6 &D
8.	(∃y) ~ Fy	6 &D
	×	

Since the tree closes, the set being tested is quantificationally inconsistent. Therefore there is no interpretation on which every member of the set is true. Since there is only one member of that set, there is no interpretation on which that sentence, '(∀x)(Fx & (∃y) ~ Fy)', is true. Hence that sentence is indeed quantificationally false. Note that we used Universal Decomposition on the sentence on line 1 twice—once to obtain the sentence on line 2 and once to obtain the sentence on line 6. This was necessary because, by the time we reached line 5, we had introduced a new constant by means of which the universally quantified sentence on line 1 had not yet been instantiated.

Now consider the sentence '(∃x) ~ Fx ⊃ ~ (∀x)Fx', which says 'If there is something that is not F, then not everything is F' and is fairly obviously quantificationally true. To verify that this sentence is quantificationally true, we construct a tree for the unit set of its negation, that is, for {~ [(∃x) ~ Fx ⊃ ~ (∀x)Fx]}. (Note that in forming the negation of this truth-functionally compound sentence we were careful to reinstate the outer brackets that had been omitted.)

1.	~ [(∃x) ~ Fx ⊃ ~ (∀x)Fx] ✓	SM
2.	(∃x) ~ Fx ✓	1 ~ ⊃D
3.	~ ~ (∀x)Fx ✓	1 ~ ⊃D
4.	(∀x)Fx	3 ~ ~ D
5.	~ Fa	2 ∃D
6.	Fa	4 ∀D
	×	

This tree is closed, so the set being tested is quantificationally inconsistent; thus there is no interpretation on which the one member of that set, '~ [(∃x) ~ Fx ⊃ ~ (∀x)Fx]', is true. Hence there is no interpretation on which the sentence of which it is the negation, '(∃x) ~ Fx ⊃ ~ (∀x)Fx', is false. So the latter sentence is quantificationally true.

One does not always have a clear intuition about a sentence's status, that is, about whether it is quantificationally true, quantificationally false, or quantificationally indeterminate. Consider, for example, '(∃x)(Fx ⊃ (∀y)Fy)'. The uninitiated at least may think that this sentence is clearly quantificationally indeterminate. It is if and only if both the tree for it and the tree for its negation are open. We begin with a tree for the sentence itself:

1.	(∃x)(Fx ⊃ (∀y)Fy) ✓		SM
2.	Fa ⊃ (∀y)Fy ✓		1 ∃D
3.	~ Fa	(∀y)Fy	2 ⊃D
4.		Fa	3 ∀D

As expected, the tree is open (it has two completed open branches), so the sentence is not quantificationally false. We next construct a tree for the negation of the sentence:

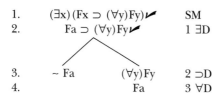

1.	~ (∃x)(Fx ⊃ (∀y)Fy)✓	SM
2.	(∀x) ~ (Fx ⊃ (∀y)Fy)	1 ~ ∃D
3.	~ (Fa ⊃ (∀y)Fy)✓	2 ∀D
4.	Fa	3 ~ ⊃D
5.	~ (∀y)Fy✓	3 ~ ⊃D
6.	(∃y) ~ Fy✓	5 ~ ∀D
7.	~ Fb	6 ∃D
8.	~ (Fb ⊃ (∀y)Fy)✓	2 ∀D
9.	Fb	8 ~ ⊃D
10.	~ (∀y)Fy	8 ~ ⊃D
	×	

Perhaps surprisingly, this tree is closed. So the negation being tested is quantificationally false, and the original sentence in which we were interested, '(∃x)(Fx ⊃ (∀y)Fy)', is, in fact, quantificationally true.

Insufficient attention to the importance of the scope of quantifiers might lead one to think that '(∃x)(Fx & Gx)' and '(∃x)Fx & (∃x)Gx' are quantificationally equivalent and hence that

(∃x)(Fx & Gx) ≡ ((∃x)Fx & (∃x)Gx)

is quantificationally true. To test this supposition, we construct a tree for the negation of the above sentence:

1.	~ ((∃x)(Fx & Gx) ≡ ((∃x)Fx & (∃x)Gx))✓					SM
2.	(∃x)(Fx & Gx)✓		~ (∃x)(Fx & Gx)✓			1 ~ ≡D
3.	~ ((∃x)Fx & (∃x)Gx)✓		(∃x)Fx & (∃x)Gx✓			1 ~ ≡D
4.	Fa & Ga✓					2 ∃D
5.	Fa					4 &D
6.	Ga					4 &D
7.	~ (∃x)Fx✓	~ (∃x)Gx✓				3 ~ &D
8.	(∀x) ~ Fx	(∀x) ~ Gx				7 ~ ∃D
9.	~ Fa	~ Ga				8 ∀D
10.	×	×	(∃x)Fx✓			3 &D
11.			(∃x)Gx✓			3 &D
12.			(∀x) ~ (Fx & Gx)			2 ~ ∃D
13.			Fa			10 ∃D
14.			Gb			11 ∃D
15.			~ (Fa & Ga)✓			12 ∀D
16.			~ (Fb & Gb)✓			12 ∀D
17.			~ Fa	~ Ga		15 ~ &D
			×			
18.				~ Fb	~ Gb	16 ~ &D
					×	

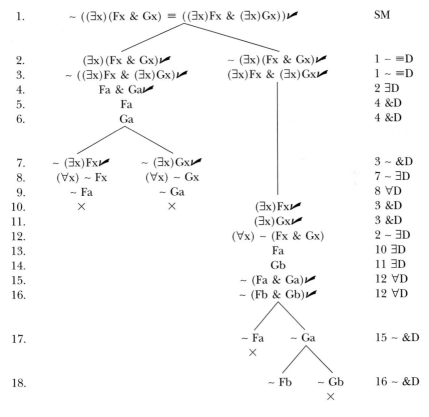

The tree has a completed open branch. So the negated biconditional we are testing is not quantificationally false, the biconditional of which it is a negation is therefore not quantificationally true, and the immediate components of that biconditional, '(∃x)(Fx & Gx)' and '(∃x)Fx & (∃x)Gx', are not quantificationally equivalent. If we are interested in establishing, by the tree method, that this biconditional is quantificationally indeterminate (and not quantificationally false), we must construct a tree for the biconditional itself:

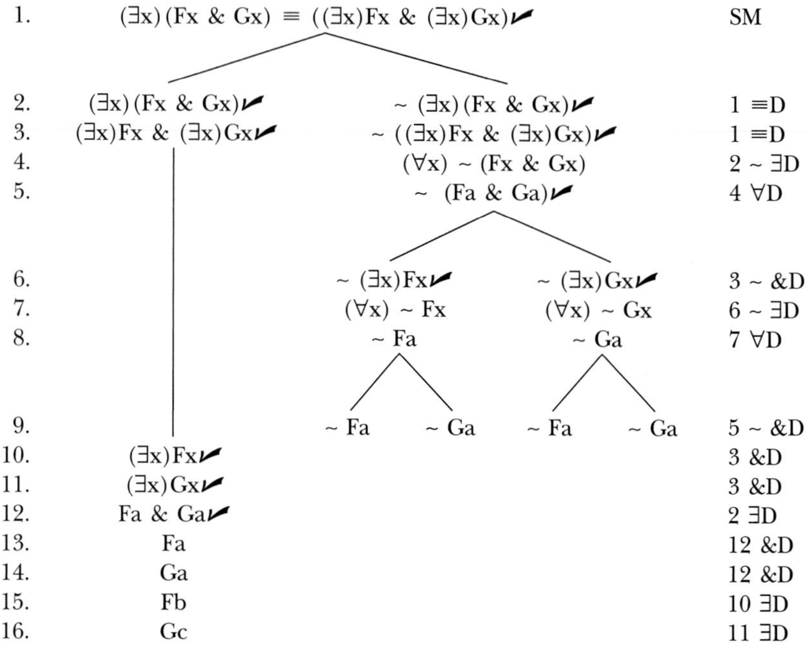

1. (∃x)(Fx & Gx) ≡ ((∃x)Fx & (∃x)Gx)✓ SM
2. (∃x)(Fx & Gx)✓ ~ (∃x)(Fx & Gx)✓ 1 ≡D
3. (∃x)Fx & (∃x)Gx✓ ~ ((∃x)Fx & (∃x)Gx)✓ 1 ≡D
4. (∀x) ~ (Fx & Gx) 2 ~ ∃D
5. ~ (Fa & Ga)✓ 4 ∀D
6. ~ (∃x)Fx✓ ~ (∃x)Gx✓ 3 ~ &D
7. (∀x) ~ Fx (∀x) ~ Gx 6 ~ ∃D
8. ~ Fa ~ Ga 7 ∀D
9. ~ Fa ~ Ga ~ Fa ~ Ga 5 ~ &D
10. (∃x)Fx✓ 3 &D
11. (∃x)Gx✓ 3 &D
12. Fa & Ga✓ 2 ∃D
13. Fa 12 &D
14. Ga 12 &D
15. Fb 10 ∃D
16. Gc 11 ∃D

It is surely not surprising that this tree has at least one completed open branch. That it does establishes that the biconditional being tested is not quantificationally false and is, given the previous open tree, quantificationally indeterminate.

The sentences '(∀x)(Fx ⊃ (∃y)Gya)' and '(∃x)Fx ⊃ (∃y)Gya' are quantificationally equivalent, as the following closed tree for the negation of their

corresponding material biconditional establishes:

1.	~ [(∀x)(Fx ⊃ (∃y)Gya) ≡ ((∃x)Fx ⊃ (∃y)Gya)] ✓				SM
2.	(∀x)(Fx ⊃ (∃y)Gya)		~ (∀x)(Fx ⊃ (∃y)Gya) ✓		1 ~ ≡D
3.	~ ((∃x)Fx ⊃ (∃y)Gya) ✓		(∃x)Fx ⊃ (∃y)Gya ✓		1 ~ ≡D
4.	(∃x)Fx ✓				3 ~ ⊃D
5.	~ (∃y)Gya ✓				3 ~ ⊃D
6.	(∀y) ~ Gya				5 ~ ∃D
7.	Fb				4 ∃D
8.	Fb ⊃ (∃y)Gya ✓				2 ∀D
9.	~ Fb	(∃y)Gya ✓			8 ⊃D
10.	×	Gca			9 ∃D
11.		~ Gca			6 ∀D
12.		×	(∃x) ~ (Fx ⊃ (∃y)Gya) ✓		2 ~ ∀D
13.			~ (Fb ⊃ (∃y)Gya) ✓		12 ∃D
14.			Fb		13 ~ ⊃D
15.			~ (∃y)Gya ✓		13 ~ ⊃D
16.			(∀y) ~ Gya		15 ~ ∃D
17.			~ (∃x)Fx ✓	(∃y)Gya ✓	3 ⊃D
18.			(∀x) ~ Fx		17 ~ ∃D
19.			~ Fb		18 ∀D
20.			×	Gca	17 ∃D
21.				~ Gca	16 ∀D
				×	

To use the tree method to test for quantificational validity, we construct a tree for the premises and the negation of the conclusion of the argument in question. Here is a tree for the argument

(∀w) ~ Gww

~ (∀x)Hx ⊃ (∃y)Gya

(∃z)(Hz & ~ Gzz)

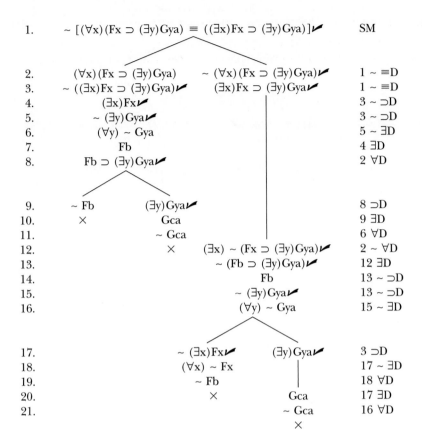

1.	(∀w) ~ Gww	SM
2.	~ (∀x)Hx ⊃ (∃y)Gya✔	SM
3.	~ (∃z)(Hz & ~ Gzz)✔	SM
4.	(∀z) ~ (Hz & ~ Gzz)	3 ~ ∃D

5.	~ ~ (∀x)Hx✔	(∃y)Gya✔	2 ⊃D
6.		Gba	5 ∃D
7.	(∀x)Hx		5 ~ ~ D
8.	~ Gaa	~ Gaa	1 ∀D
9.	~ (Ha & ~ Gaa)✔	~ (Ha & ~ Gaa)✔	4 ∀D

10.	~ Ha ~ ~ Gaa✔	~ Ha ~ ~ Gaa	9 ~ &D
11.	Ha		7 ∀D
12.	× Gaa	Gaa	10 ~ ~ D
13.	×	~ Gbb ×	1 ∀D
14.		~ (Hb & ~ Gbb)✔	4 ∀D

15.		~ Hb ~ ~ Gbb	14 ~ &D
16.		Gbb	15 ~ ~ D
		×	

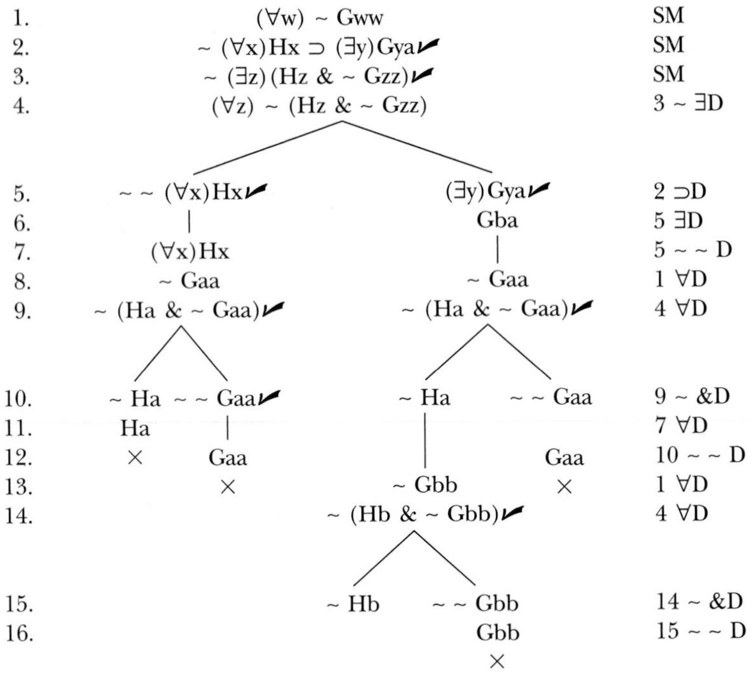

The tree has a completed open branch, so the argument is quantificationally invalid. (There is an interpretation on which the premises and the negation of the conclusion are all true, that is, on which the premises are true and the conclusion is false.)

As with truth-trees for sentential logic, the procedure for testing alleged entailments parallels that for testing for validity. Consider the claim

$$\{(\forall x)(Hx \equiv\ \sim Ix),\ \sim (\exists x)\ \sim Ix\} \vDash (\forall x)\ \sim Hx$$

If this claim is true, there is no interpretation on which the members of the above set are both true and the allegedly entailed sentence false; that is, there is no interpretation on which all the members of

$$\{(\forall x)(Hx \equiv\ \sim Ix),\ \sim (\exists x)\ \sim Ix,\ \sim (\forall x)\ \sim Hx\}$$

are true. So we shall test the latter set for quantificational consistency:

1.	$(\forall x)(Hx \equiv \sim Ix)$		SM
2.	$\sim (\exists x) \sim Ix$ ✓		SM
3.	$\sim (\forall x) \sim Hx$ ✓		SM
4.	$(\forall x) \sim \sim Ix$		$2 \sim \exists D$
5.	$(\exists x) \sim \sim Hx$ ✓		$3 \sim \forall D$
6.	$\sim \sim Ha$ ✓		$5\ \exists D$
7.	Ha		$6 \sim \sim D$
8.	$Ha \equiv \sim Ia$ ✓		$1\ \forall D$
9.	Ha	$\sim Ha$	$8 \equiv D$
10.	$\sim Ia$	$\sim \sim Ia$	$8 \equiv D$
11.	$\sim \sim Ia$ ✓	×	$4\ \forall D$
12.	Ia		$11 \sim \sim D$
	×		

The tree is closed, so the set consisting of the members of the original set and the negation of the allegedly entailed sentence is quantificationally inconsistent. Therefore there is no interpretation on which all the members of that original set are true and the allegedly entailed sentence false. So the entailment does hold.

9.3E EXERCISES

Construct truth-trees as necessary to provide the requested information. In each case state your result, and specify what it is about your tree that establishes this result.

1. Which of the following sentences are quantificationally true?

a. $(\exists x)Fx \vee \sim (\exists x)Fx$
*b. $(\exists x)Fx \vee (\exists x) \sim Fx$
c. $(\forall x)Fx \vee (\forall x) \sim Fx$
*d. $(\forall x)Fx \vee \sim (\forall x)Fx$
e. $(\forall x)Fx \vee (\exists x) \sim Fx$
*f. $(\forall x)(Fx \vee Gx) \supset [(\exists x)Fx \vee (\exists x)Gx]$
g. $(\forall x)(Fx \vee Gx) \supset [(\exists x) \sim Fx \supset (\exists x)Gx]$
*h. $(\forall x)(Fx \vee Gx) \supset [(\exists x)Fx \vee (\forall x)Gx]$
i. $[(\forall x)Fx \vee (\forall x)Gx] \supset (\forall x)(Fx \vee Gx)$
*j. $(\forall x)(Fx \vee Gx) \supset [(\forall x)Fx \vee (\forall x)Gx]$

k. $(\exists x)(Fx \,\&\, Gx) \supset [(\exists x)Fx \,\&\, (\exists x)Gx]$
*l. $[(\exists x)Fx \,\&\, (\exists x)Gx] \supset (\exists x)(Fx \,\&\, Gx)$
m. $\sim (\exists x)Fx \vee (\forall x) \sim Fx$
*n. $(\forall x)[Fx \supset (Gx \,\&\, Hx)] \supset (\forall x)[(Fx \,\&\, Gx) \supset Hx]$
o. $(\forall x)[(Fx \,\&\, Gx) \supset Hx] \supset (\forall x)[Fx \supset (Gx \,\&\, Hx)]$
*p. $(\forall x)(Fx \,\&\, \sim Gx) \vee (\exists x)(\sim Fx \vee Gx)$
q. $(\forall x)(Fx \supset Gx) \supset (\forall x)(Fx \supset (\forall y)Gy)$
*r. $(\forall x)(\forall y)Gxy \supset (\forall x)Gxx$
s. $(\forall x)Gxx \supset (\forall x)(\forall y)Gxy$
*t. $(\forall x)Fxx \supset (\forall x)(\exists y)Fxy$
u. $(\exists x)(\forall y)Gxy \supset (\forall x)(\exists y)Gyx$
*v. $(\exists x)(\exists y)(Lxy \equiv Lyx)$
w. $((\exists x)Lxx \supset (\forall y)Lyy) \supset (Laa \supset Lgg)$

2. Which of the following sentences are quantificationally false?
a. $(\forall x)Fx \,\&\, (\exists x) \sim Fx$
*b. $(\forall x)Fx \,\&\, \sim (\exists x)Fx$
c. $(\exists x)Fx \,\&\, (\exists x) \sim Fx$
*d. $(\exists x)Fx \,\&\, \sim (\forall x)Fx$
e. $(\forall x)(Fx \supset (\forall y) \sim Fy)$
*f. $(\forall x)(Fx \supset \sim Fx)$
g. $(\forall x)(Fx \equiv \sim Fx)$
*h. $(\exists x)Fx \supset (\forall x) \sim Fx$
i. $(\exists x)(\exists y)(Fxy \,\&\, \sim Fyx)$
*j. $(\exists x)Fx \,\&\, \sim (\exists y)Fy$
k. $(\forall x)(\forall y)(Fxy \supset \sim Fyx)$
*l. $(\forall x)(Gx \equiv \sim Fx) \,\&\, \sim (\forall x) \sim (Gx \equiv Fx)$
m. $(\exists x)(\forall y)Gxy \,\&\, \sim (\forall y)(\exists x)Gxy$

3. What is the quantificational status (quantificationally true, quantificationally false, or quantificationally indeterminate) of each of the following sentences?
a. $(\exists x)Fxx \supset (\exists x)(\exists y)Fxy$
*b. $(\exists x)(\exists y)Fxy \supset (\exists x)Fxx$
c. $(\exists x)(\forall y)Lxy \supset (\exists x)Lxx$
*d. $(\forall x)(Fx \supset (\exists y)Gyx) \supset ((\exists x)Fx \supset (\exists x)(\exists y)Gxy)$
e. $(\forall x)(Fx \supset (\exists y)Gya) \supset (Fb \supset (\exists y)Gya)$
*f. $((\exists x)Lxx \supset (\forall y)Lyy) \supset (Laa \supset Lgg)$
g. $(\forall x)(Fx \supset (\forall y)Gxy) \supset (\exists x)(Fx \supset \sim (\forall y)Gxy)$

4. Which of the following pairs of sentences are quantificationally equivalent?

a.	$(\forall x)Mxx$	$\sim (\exists x) \sim Mxx$
*b.	$(\exists x)(Fx \supset Ga)$	$(\exists x)Fx \supset Ga$
c.	$(\forall x)(Fa \supset Gx)$	$Fa \supset (\forall x)Gx$
*d.	$Ls \equiv (\forall x)Lx$	$(\exists x)Lx$
e.	$(\exists x)Fx \supset Ga$	$(\exists x)(Fx \supset Ga)$
*f.	$(\forall x)(Fx \vee Gx)$	$(\forall x)Fx \vee (\forall x)Gx$
g.	$(\forall x)Fx \supset Ga$	$(\exists x)(Fx \supset Ga)$
*h.	$(\exists x)(Ax \,\&\, Bx)$	$(\exists x)Ax \,\&\, (\exists x)Bx$

i.	(∀x)(∀y)(Fx ⊃ Gy)	(∀x)(Fx ⊃ (∀y)Gy)
*j.	(∀x)(Fx ≡ ~ Gx)	(∀x) ~ (Fx ≡ Gx)
k.	(∀x)(Fx ≡ Gx)	Fa ≡ (∀x)Gx
*l.	(∀x)(Fx ∨ (∃y)Gy)	(∀x)(∃y)(Fx ∨ Gy)
m.	(∀x)(Fx ⊃ (∀y)Gy)	(∀x)(∀y)(Fx ⊃ Gy)

5. Which of the following arguments are quantificationally valid?

a. (∀x)(Fx ⊃ Gx)
Ga
———
Fa

*b. (∀x)(Tx ⊃ Lx)
~ Lb
———
~ Tb

c. (∀x)(Kx ⊃ Lx)
(∀x)(Lx ⊃ Mx)
———
(∀x)(Kx ⊃ Mx)

*d. (∀x)(Fx ⊃ Gx)
(∀x)(Hx ⊃ Gx)
———
(∀x)((Fx ∨ Hx) ⊃ Gx)

e. (∀x)(Fx ⊃ Gx) ⊃ (∃x)Nx
(∀x)(Nx ⊃ Gx)
———
(∀x)(~ Fx ∨ Gx)

*f. (~ (∃y)Fy ⊃ (∃y)Fy) ∨ ~ Fa
———
(∃z)Fz

g. (∀x)(~ Ax ⊃ Kx)
(∃y) ~ Ky
———
(∃w)(Aw ∨ ~ Lwf)

*h. (∀y)(Hy & (Jyy & My))
———
(∃x)Jxb & (∀x)Mx

i. (∀x)(∀y)Cxy
———
(Caa & Cab) & (Cba & Cbb)

*j. (∃x)(Fx & Gx)
(∃x)(Fx & Hx)
———
(∃x)(Gx & Hx)

k. (∀x)(Fx ⊃ Gx)
~ (∃x)Fx
———
~ (∃x)Gx

*l. (∃z)Bzz
(∀x)(Sx ⊃ Bxx)
———
~ Sg

m. (∃x)Cx ⊃ Ch
———
(∃x)Cx ≡ Ch

*n. Fa ∨ (∃y)Gya
Fb ∨ (∃y) ~ Gyb
———
(∃y)Gya

6. Which of the following alleged entailments hold?

a. {(∀x) ~ Jx, (∃y)(Hby ∨ Ryy) ⊃ (∃x)Jx} ⊨ (∀y) ~ (Hby ∨ Ryy)
*b. {(∀x)(∀y)(Mxy ⊃ Nxy)} ⊨ (∀x)(∀y)(Mxy ⊃ (Nxy & Nyx))
c. {(∀y)((Hy & Fy) ⊃ Gy), (∀z)Fz & ~ (∀x)Kxb} ⊨ (∀x)(Hx ⊃ Gx)
*d. {(∀x)(Fx ⊃ Gx), (∀x)(Hx ⊃ Gx)} ⊨ (∀x)(Fx ∨ Hx)
e. {(∀z)(Lz ≡ Hz), (∀x) ~ (Hx ∨ ~ Bx)} ⊨ ~ Lb

To apply the tree method to the language *PLE*, we must modify the tree system developed in the preceding sections so as to accommodate the unique features of *PLE*, namely, the identity predicate and complex terms. We shall accomplish this by introducing one new decomposition rule (Identity Decomposition), by modifying the definitions of a closed branch and of a completed open branch, and by refining the Universal Decomposition rule to accommodate complex terms. The modified tree system we develop here applies to *PLE*. The system developed in earlier sections remains intact and is adequate as it now stands for the language *PL*.

We begin with the modification to Universal Decomposition, which is straightforward. The set {(∀x) ~ Bx, B*f*(c)} contains a closed complex term, '*f*(c)', and is clearly quantificationally inconsistent, so we want it to have a closed truth-tree. To make this happen, we need to allow Universal Decomposition to yield substitution instances formed, not just from constants, but from all closed terms. For example, we want the following to count as a correctly constructed closed tree:

1.	(∀x) ~ Bx	SM
2.	B*f*(c)	SM
3.	~ B*f*(c)	1 ∀D
	×	

To make this so, we need to revise Universal Decomposition as follows:

Universal Decomposition (∀D)

(∀x)P

P(t/x)

where **t** is a closed term

This change makes the use of Universal Decomposition at line 3 of the previous tree allowable. Since 'B*f*(c)' is an atomic sentence, and '~ B*f*(c)' is the negation of that sentence, the tree is closed the set being tested quantificationally inconsistent. We must also amend our definition of a completed open branch so as to require every universally quantified sentence to be decomposed to every substitution instance that can be formed from a *closed individual term* (individual constant or closed complex term) occurring on the branch in question. Previously we required only that such sentences be decomposed to every individual constant occurring on the branch in question.

Here is another set: $\{(\exists y)Gy, (\forall z) \sim Gh(z)\}$. One might be tempted to construct the following tree for this set, assuming we need to modify Existential Decomposition in the same way we did Universal Decomposition.

1.	$(\exists y)Gy$	SM
2.	$(\forall z) \sim Gh(z)$	SM
3.	$Gh(a)$	1 ∃D
	$\sim Gh(a)$	2 ∀D
	×	

Line 3 was added on the assumption that Existential Decomposition needs to be modified so as to allow decomposition to any substitution instance formed from an individual term foreign to the branch, hence allowing use of substitution instances formed from closed complex terms, as well as from individual constants. This assumption is erroneous. To see this, consider the interpretation

UD: Set of positive integers
Gx: $x = 1$
$h(x)$: the successor of x

On this interpretation '$(\exists y)Gy$' says there is a positive integer that is equal to 1, and this is, of course, true. '$(\forall z) \sim Gh(z)$' says each positive integer is such that its successor is not equal to 1. This is also true. So the set we are working with is, in fact, quantificationally consistent. Existential Decomposition cannot be modified to allow decomposition to substitution instances formed from closed complex terms.

Consider again the previous set. '$(\exists y)Gy$' does tell us there is something that is G, but it does not tell us anything further about that thing. More specifically, it does not say there is something that is G that is also the value of the function *h* for some member of the UD. In other words, the claim '$(\exists y)Gh(y)$' is substantially stronger than the claim '$(\exists y)Gy$'. The former tells us two things: that there is something that is of the sort G, and that that thing is the value of the function *h* for some member of the UD. The latter tells us only that there is something of the sort G.

We now turn to crafting the rule we need to accommodate the identity predicate.

Identity Decomposition (=D)

$$\mathbf{t}_1 = \mathbf{t}_2$$

$$\mathbf{P}$$

$$\mathbf{P}(\mathbf{t}_1//\mathbf{t}_2)$$

This rule is to be understood as follows: Where $\mathbf{t}_1$ and $\mathbf{t}_2$ are closed individual terms[3] and a branch contains both a literal **P** containing $\mathbf{t}_2$ and a sentence of the form $\mathbf{t}_1 = \mathbf{t}_2$, $\mathbf{P}(\mathbf{t}_1//\mathbf{t}_2)$ may be entered on that branch provided $\mathbf{P}(\mathbf{t}_1//\mathbf{t}_2)$ is like **P** except that it contains $\mathbf{t}_1$ *in at least one place* where **P** contains $\mathbf{t}_2$. Sentences of the form $\mathbf{t}_1 = \mathbf{t}_2$ are not checked off because they can be decomposed again and again. The idea behind this rule is that if $\mathbf{t}_1$ and $\mathbf{t}_2$ are identical (are one and the same thing) then whatever is true of one is true of the other. So whatever is claimed of $\mathbf{t}_2$ can be claimed of $\mathbf{t}_1$. Identity Decomposition is used in the following tree:

1.	$(\forall x)(Fx \supset Gx)$		SM
2.	Fc		SM
3.	~ Gd		SM
4.	c = d		SM
5.	$Fc \supset Gc$ ✓		1 ∀D
6.	~ Fc	Gc	5 ⊃D
7.	×	~ Gc	4, 3 =D
		×	

Identity Decomposition is used at line 7. Here $\mathbf{t}_1 = \mathbf{t}_2$ is 'c = d', **P** is '~ Gd', and $\mathbf{P}(\mathbf{t}_1//\mathbf{t}_2)$ is '~ Gd(c//d)', that is, '~ Gc', the sentence entered on line 7. Note that the justification column for line 7 contains two line numbers. This is because Identity Decomposition licenses the entry of a sentence on a branch based on the presence of two other sentences. In this respect it is unlike the other decomposition rules.

Consider the sentence '$(\exists y) \sim y = y$'. This sentence says 'There is something that is not identical with itself' and is clearly quantificationally false. So we want the tree for the unit set of this sentence to close:

1.	$(\exists y) \sim y = y$ ✓	SM
2.	$\sim a = a$	1 ∃D

The one branch on this tree does not contain an atomic sentence and its negation. So it is not, by our present account, a closed branch. What is perhaps worse, the one branch on this tree is, by the account given in Section 9.2, a completed open branch—the sentence on line 1 has been decomposed, and the sentence on line 2 is a literal. We cannot countenance this result. We need to find a way either of counting this branch as a closed branch or of creating a closed branch from it.

[3]Note that we are here using $\mathbf{t}_1$ and $\mathbf{t}_2$ as metavariables ranging over closed individual terms, not just over individual constants. This is required for the rule to be applicable to identity sentences containing complex terms.

The latter alternative could be accomplished by requiring that a sentence of the form $(\forall \mathbf{x})\mathbf{x} = \mathbf{x}$ be entered on every branch on which a sentence of the form $\sim \mathbf{t} = \mathbf{t}$ occurs. Since sentences of the former sort are all quantificationally true, adding them to trees never produces unwanted results. In the present case we would get the following closed tree:

1.	$(\exists y) \sim y = y$	SM
2.	$\sim a = a$	1 $\exists$D
3.	$(\forall y)y = y$	New identity rule
4.	$a = a$	3 $\forall$D
	×	

At line 3 we enter '$(\forall y)y = y$'. Universal Decomposition yields '$a = a$' at line 4, an atomic sentence whose negation appears on line 2. So the tree is closed. On this approach we retain the notion that a branch is closed if and only if it contains an atomic sentence and its negation. But the cost is that of introducing a second identity rule, one that is not remotely a "decomposition" rule.

The other approach, that of suitably revising our account of a closed branch, is more simply accomplished and is the one we choose. The rationale for declaring a branch on which an atomic sentence and its negation both occur a closed branch is that there is no interpretation on which an atomic sentence and its negation are both true. Almost as obviously, there is no interpretation on which a sentence of the form $\sim \mathbf{t} = \mathbf{t}$ is true, this by the fixed interpretation of the identity predicate. So we can modify our account of a closed branch as follows:

> *Closed branch:* A branch on which some atomic sentence and its negation both occur or on which a sentence of the form $\sim \mathbf{t} = \mathbf{t}$ occurs

Given this revised account, we need only one identity rule, Identity Decomposition.

Just as we want the tree method to yield a closed tree for $\{(\exists y) \sim y = y\}$, we want it to yield an open tree for $\{Fa \vee Ga, \sim Ff(b), a = b, \sim Fb\}$. Here is the start of such a tree:

1.	$Fa \vee Ga$ ✓		SM
2.	$\sim Ff(b)$		SM
3.	$a = b$		SM
4.	$\sim Fb$		SM
5.	Fa	Ga	1 $\vee$D

Our present account of a completed open branch is as follows: A completed open branch is a finite open branch on which every sentence is one of the following:

1. A literal
2. Not a universally quantified sentence, and decomposed
3. A universally quantified sentence $(\forall \mathbf{x})\mathbf{P}$ such that $\mathbf{P}(\mathbf{t}/\mathbf{x})$ also occurs on that branch *for each closed individual term* **t** occurring on the branch and at least one substitution instance $\mathbf{P}(\mathbf{t}/\mathbf{x})$ occurs on the branch

Both branches on the preceding tree qualify, by this account, as completed open branches. But this result is not welcome, even though the set we are testing is quantificationally consistent, for Identity Decomposition does allow further lines to be added to the tree, and doing so will produce one closed branch. Accordingly we add a fourth clause to accommodate identity sentences:

4. A sentence of the form $\mathbf{t}_1 = \mathbf{t}_2$, where $\mathbf{t}_1$ and $\mathbf{t}_2$ are closed terms, such that the branch also contains, for every literal **P** on that branch containing $\mathbf{t}_2$, every sentence $\mathbf{P}(\mathbf{t}_1//\mathbf{t}_2)$ that can be obtained from **P** by Identity Decomposition

Clause 4 requires that we continue work on our last tree. There are two literals on that tree that contain 'b': '~ F*f*(b)' and '~ Fb'. Since 'a = b' also occurs on the one open branch of the tree, we have to replace 'b' in these two literals with 'a'. Since Identity Decomposition is not a branching rule, but Disjunction Decomposition is, we choose to apply the former before the latter, yielding the following revised tree:

1.	Fa ∨ Ga		SM
2.	~ F*f*(b)		SM
3.	a = b		SM
4.	~ Fb		SM
5.	~ F*f*(a)		3, 2 =D
6.	~ Fa		3, 4 =D
7.	Fa	Ga	1 ∨D
	×		

Note that the closure of the left branch results from the presence of 'Fa' and '~ Fa' on that branch, not from 'Fa' and '~ F*f*(a)'. The latter two literals can both be true on a single interpretation. The right-hand branch may appear to be a completed open branch, but technically it is not. This is because we must, by clause 4 above, replace every occurrence of 'b' in a literal on a branch on which ‘a = b’ occurs with ‘a’. We must remember that ‘a = b’ is itself such a literal. Replacing ‘b’ with ‘a’ in this literal produces ‘a = a’.

This final application of Identity Decomposition yields the following completed tree, a tree with one closed branch and one completed open branch:

1.	Fa ∨ Ga		SM
2.	~ F*f*(b)		SM
3.	a = b		SM
4.	~ Fb		SM
5.	~ F*f*(a)		3, 2 =D
6.	~ Fa		3, 4 =D
7.	Fa	Ga	1 ∨D
8.	×	a = a	3, 3 =D

Adding a sentence of the form **t** = **t** will never, of course, bring about the closure of a branch, for if the negation of that sentence, ~ **t** = **t** were already on a branch, or later added to a branch, the presence of that sentence by itself would close all the branches on which it occurs. For this reason we shall informally allow the omission of applications of Identity Decomposition that result in adding sentences of the form **t** = **t** to a branch. However, we shall have to drop this informal practice when we develop *systematic trees* in Section 9.5, for the metatheory of Chapter 11 assumes that Identity Decomposition is rigorously applied in all systematic trees.

Given our expanded set of rules and revised notions of closed and completed open branches, the explications developed in Sections 9.2 and 9.3 of semantic properties in terms of open and closed trees also hold for *PLE*. We therefore adopt them for *PLE* without repeating them here.

The set {a = b, (∀x)(Fbx & ~ Fxa)} is quantificationally inconsistent, as the following tree shows:

1.	a = b	SM
2.	(∀x)(Fbx & ~ Fax)	SM
3.	Fbb & ~ Fab ✓	2 ∀D
4.	Fbb	3 & D
5.	~ Fab	3 & D
6.	Fab	1, 4 =D
	×	

What is interesting here is the use of Identity Decomposition at line 6. We generated ‘Fab’ from ‘a = b’ and ‘Fbb’ by replacing only the first occurrence of ‘b’ in the latter with ‘a’. (When generating $\mathbf{P}(\mathbf{t}_1//\mathbf{t}_2)$ from **P**, given $\mathbf{t}_1 = \mathbf{t}_2$, it is not required that *every* occurrence of $\mathbf{t}_2$ in **P** be replaced with $\mathbf{t}_1$ but only that at least one occurrence be so replaced.) We could also have closed the tree by entering 'Faa' at line 6 (replacing both occurrences of 'b' in 'Fbb' with 'a') and then entering '~ Faa' at line 7, both by Identity Decomposition.

Consider now a quantificationally consistent set: {c = b, (∀x)(Fxc ⊃ ~ Gxb), (∀x)Gxc}. Here is a tree for this set:

1.	c = b			SM
2.	(∀x)(Fxc ⊃ ~ Gxb)			SM
3.	(∀x)Gxc			SM
4.	Gcc			3 ∀D
5.	Gbc			3 ∀D
6.	Fcc ⊃ ~ Gcb ✓			2 ∀D
7.	Fbc ⊃ ~ Gbb ✓			2 ∀D
8.	~ Fcc		~ Gcb	6 ⊃D
9.			~ Gcc	1, 8 =D
			×	
10.	~ Fbc	~ Gbb		7 ⊃D
11.		~ Gbc		1, 10 =D
		×		

The left-hand branch of this tree is a completed open branch and hence establishes that this set is quantificationally consistent. The left-hand branch contains every required sentence that can be generated from the identity on line 1 and a literal containing 'c' (excepting the sentence 'c = c'). We could generate 'Gcc' from lines 1 and 5, but it already occurs on line 4. Similarly we could generate '~ Fcc' from lines 1 and 10, but it already occurs at line 8. Note also that, while Identity Decomposition allows, given an identity sentence $\mathbf{t}_1 = \mathbf{t}_2$, the generation of literals in which one or more occurrences of $\mathbf{t}_2$ in an existing literal have been replaced with $\mathbf{t}_1$, it does not license the generation of literals in which one or more occurrences of $\mathbf{t}_1$ have been replaced with $\mathbf{t}_2$. We could rewrite Identity Decomposition so as to allow this, but we do not need to do so. That is, if a set is inconsistent it will have a closed tree given the rules as presently written. Rewriting Identity Decomposition in the suggested way would frequently require adding more literals to trees. In the present case it would require adding 'Gbb', '~ Fbb', and '~ Fcb' to that branch.

As noted in Chapter 7, identity is a relation that is transitive, symmetric, and reflexive. Accordingly, we expect the following sentences of *PLE*, which assert, respectively, the transitivity, symmetry, and reflexivity of identity to be quantificationally true:

(∀x)(∀y)(∀z)[(x = y & y = z) ⊃ x = z]
(∀x)(∀y)(x = y ⊃ y = x)
(∀x)x = x

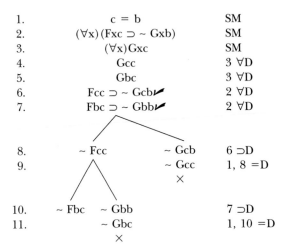

As we might expect, the truth-tree method produces closed trees for the negations of these sentences. Here is the relevant tree for the claim that identity is reflexive:

1.	$\sim (\forall x)x = x$ ✓	SM
2.	$(\exists x) \sim x = x$ ✓	$1 \sim \forall D$
3.	$\sim a = a$	$2\ \exists D$
	×	

The tree is closed, so the truth-tree method yields, as desired, the result that the sentence '$\sim (\forall x)x = x$' is quantificationally false, and '$(\forall x)x = x$' quantificationally true; that is, that identity is a reflexive relation. It should be noted that, when we earlier modified the definition of a closed branch so as to count every branch containing a sentence of the form '$\sim \mathbf{t}_1 = \mathbf{t}_1$' as a closed branch, we were, in effect, presupposing the reflexivity of identity. The present result is therefore neither a surprising one nor an independent proof of the reflexivity of identity. Symmetry is next. The relevant tree is

1.	$\sim (\forall x)(\forall y)(x = y \supset y = x)$ ✓	SM
2.	$(\exists x) \sim (\forall y)(x = y \supset y = x)$ ✓	$1 \sim \forall D$
3.	$\sim (\forall y)(a = y \supset y = a)$ ✓	$2\ \exists D$
4.	$(\exists y) \sim (a = y \supset y = a)$ ✓	$3 \sim \forall D$
5.	$\sim (a = b \supset b = a)$ ✓	$4\ \exists D$
6.	$a = b$	$5 \sim \supset D$
7.	$\sim b = a$	$5 \sim \supset D$
8.	$\sim a = a$	$6, 7 = D$
	×	

The tree is closed—also a desired result, since '$\sim (\forall x)(\forall y)(x = y \supset y = x)$' is quantificationally false and '$(\forall x)(\forall y)(x = y \supset y = x)$' is quantificationally true; that is, identity is symmetric.

Finally we consider transitivity. The relevant tree is

1.	$\sim (\forall x)(\forall y)(\forall z)[(x = y \ \&\ y = z) \supset x = z]$ ✓	SM
2.	$(\exists x) \sim (\forall y)(\forall z)[(x = y \ \&\ y = z) \supset x = z]$ ✓	$1 \sim \forall D$
3.	$\sim (\forall y)(\forall z)[(a = y \ \&\ y = z) \supset a = z]$ ✓	$2\ \exists D$
4.	$(\exists y) \sim (\forall z)[(a = y \ \&\ y = z) \supset a = z]$ ✓	$3 \sim \forall D$
5.	$\sim (\forall z)[(a = b \ \&\ b = z) \supset a = z]$ ✓	$4\ \exists D$
6.	$(\exists z) \sim [(a = b \ \&\ b = z) \supset a = z]$ ✓	$5 \sim \forall D$
7.	$\sim [(a = b \ \&\ b = c) \supset a = c]$ ✓	$6\ \exists D$
8.	$(a = b \ \&\ b = c)$ ✓	$7 \sim \supset D$
9.	$\sim a = c$	$7 \sim \supset D$
10.	$a = b$	$8\ \&D$
11.	$b = c$	$8\ \&D$
12.	$a = c$	$10, 11 = D$
	×	

This tree, as expected, is closed, reflecting the fact that the sentence on line 1 is quantificationally false and

$$(\forall x)(\forall y)(\forall z)[(x = y \;\&\; y = z) \supset x = z]$$

is quantificationally true; that is, that identity is transitive. Here we closed the tree by applying Identity Decomposition to lines 10 and 11, taking 'a = b' as $\mathbf{t}_1 = \mathbf{t}_2$ and 'b = c' as **P**, producing 'a = c' as $\mathbf{P}(\mathbf{t}_1//\mathbf{t}_2)$. Since '~ a = c' occurs on line 9, the one branch of the tree contains an atomic sentence, 'a = c', and its negation, '~ a = c', and is therefore closed.

Consider now the sentence '(∀x)(∀y)[(Fxx & ~ Fyy) ⊃ ~ x = y]'. We expect this sentence to be quantificationally true (if x but not y bears a relation F to itself, then x and y are not identical). The following truth-tree confirms this expectation:

1.	~ (∀x)(∀y)[(Fxx & ~ Fyy) ⊃ ~ x = y]✓	SM
2.	(∃x) ~ (∀y)[(Fxx & ~ Fyy) ⊃ ~ x = y]✓	1 ~ ∀D
3.	~ (∀y)[(Faa & ~ Fyy) ⊃ ~ a = y]✓	2 ∃D
4.	(∃y) ~ [(Faa & ~ Fyy) ⊃ ~ a = y]✓	3 ~ ∀D
5.	~ [(Faa & ~ Fbb) ⊃ ~ a = b]✓	4 ∃D
6.	Faa & ~ Fbb✓	5 ~ ⊃D
7.	~ ~ a = b✓	5 ~ ⊃D
8.	a = b	7 ~ ~ D
9.	Faa	6 &D
10.	~ Fbb	6 &D
11.	~ Faa	8, 10 =D
	×	

At line 11 we replaced both occurrences of 'b' in '~ Fbb' with 'a' to generate '~ Faa'. Replacing just one occurrence, while allowed, would not have produced a closed tree.

Here is another example:

(∃x)Gxa & ~ (∃x)Gax

(∀x)(Gxb ⊃ x = b)

~ a = b

To test this argument for quantificationally validity, we construct a tree for the premises and the negation of the conclusion:

1.	(∃x)Gxa & ~ (∃x)Gax✓		SM
2.	(∀x)(Gxb ⊃ x = b)		SM
3.	~ ~ a = b✓		SM
4.	a = b		3 ~ ~ D
5.	(∃x)Gxa✓		1 &D
6.	~ (∃x)Gax✓		1 &D
7.	(∀x) ~ Gax		6 ~ ∃D
8.	Gca		5 ∃D
9.	Gab ⊃ a = b		2 ∀D
10.	Gbb ⊃ b = b		2 ∀D
11.	Gcb ⊃ c = b✓		2 ∀D
12.	~ Gaa		7 ∀D
13.	~ Gab		7 ∀D
14.	~ Gac		7 ∀D
15.	~ Gcb	c = b	11 ⊃D
16.	~ Gca			4, 15 =D
17.	×	a = c	15, 4 =D
18.		Gaa	17, 8 =D
		×	

This tree is closed. Therefore the argument we are testing is quantificationally valid. The secret to keeping this tree reasonably concise is to carefully study the sentences on lines 9–11 to determine which should be decomposed first. The identity on line 4 licenses replacing 'b' with 'a' in literals, and line 11 yields '~ Gcb' on the left branch when decomposed. Replacing the 'b' with 'a' in that literal yields '~ Gca' at line 16, which closes the left branch. At line 15 the right branch is open and contains 'c = b'. This branch contains, at that point, two identity claims: 'a = b' and 'c = b'. From these and the other literals on the branch ('Gca', '~ Gaa', '~ Gab', and '~ Gac'), a host of sentences could be obtained by Identity Decomposition. Careful study reveals that any of 'Gac', 'Gab', and 'Gaa' would close the branch. But only the latter will come from 'Gca' on line 8 in one step. ('Gaa' can be obtained by replacing 'c' with 'a' in 'Gca'.) But to do so we first had to obtain 'a = c'. The latter was obtained from lines 15 and 4 by Identity Decomposition. (The sentence 'c = b' on line 15 allows us to replace one or more occurrence of 'b' with 'c' in any literal containing 'b'. The sentence 'a = b' on line 4 is such a literal. So we applied Identity Decomposition to these sentences to yield 'a = c' at line 17.) At line 18 we obtained 'Gaa', also by Identity Decomposition, and closed the branch and the tree.

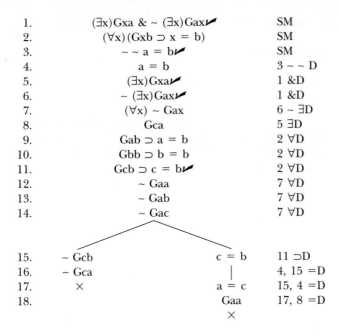

In the remainder of this section, we shall work through a number of examples involving functors and identity. Consider first the sentence '~ (∃x)x = *g*(a)'. This sentence is fairly obviously quantificationally false, for it says that there is nothing that is identical to *g*(a); but, of course, we know that something *is* identical to $g(a)$, namely, $g(a)$ itself. Here is the start of a tree:

1.	$\sim (\exists x)x = g(a)$ ✓	SM
2.	$(\forall x) \sim x = g(a)$	$1 \sim \exists D$
3.	$\sim a = g(a)$	$2\ \forall D$

As of line 3 this tree has one open branch. It might seem that this branch is a completed open branch, and hence that our intuitions about the sentence we are testing must have been misguided. The sentence on line 1 is checked off, the sentence on line 3 is a literal, and the sentence on line 2 is a universally quantified sentence that has been decomposed to a substitution instance formed from the constant 'a'. But the branch is not completed, for there is another closed individual term on the branch, '$g(a)$', and the sentence on line 2 has not been decomposed to a substitution instance formed from this term. Doing this decomposition results in the following *closed* tree:

1.	$\sim (\exists x)x = g(a)$ ✓	SM
2.	$(\forall x) \sim x = g(a)$	$1 \sim \exists D$
3.	$\sim a = g(a)$	$2\ \forall D$
4.	$\sim g(a) = g(a)$	$2\ \forall D$
	×	

It is now apparent that line 3 is unnecessary—the branch would close without that step. It is important to remember that before a branch qualifies as a completed open branch all universally quantified sentences on that branch must be decomposed to every substitution instance that can be formed from a closed individual term on that branch, and these consist of all the constants and all the closed complex terms on the branch.

Consider next '$(\forall x)f(x) = x$'. This sentence is clearly not quantificationally true (a one-place function does not always return the argument it takes as its value). For example, *successor* returns, for value x, x plus 1, not x itself. The following tree establishes that this sentence is not quantificationally true:

1.	$\sim (\forall x)f(x) = x$ ✓	SM
2.	$(\exists x) \sim f(x) = x$ ✓	$1 \sim \forall D$
3.	$\sim f(a) = a$	$2\ \exists D$

The one branch on this tree is a completed open branch. The sentences on lines 1 and 2 have been checked off, and the sentence on line 3 is a literal. The sentence on line 1 is therefore not quantificationally false, and the sentence of which it is a negation, '$(\forall x)f(x) = x$', is not quantificationally true.[4]

[4]We shall show that this sentence is not quantificationally false in Section 9.5.

The sentence '$(\forall x)(\forall y)f(x,y) = f(y,x)$' is also not quantificationally true, as the following tree shows:

1.	$\sim (\forall x)(\forall y)f(x,y) = f(y,x)$ ✓	SM
2.	$(\exists x) \sim (\forall y)f(x,y) = f(y,x)$ ✓	$1 \sim \forall D$
3.	$\sim (\forall y)f(a,y) = f(y,a)$ ✓	$2\ \exists D$
4.	$(\exists y) \sim f(a,y) = f(y,a)$ ✓	$3 \sim \exists D$
5.	$\sim f(a,b) = f(b,a)$	$4\ \exists D$

The one branch on this tree is a completed open branch. The first four sentences are checked off, and the last one is a literal. So '$\sim (\forall x)(\forall y)f(x,y) = f(y,x)$' is not quantificationally false, and '$(\forall x)(\forall y)f(x,y) = f(y,x)$' is not quantificationally true.

Next consider the sentence '$(\forall x)[Ex \supset (\exists y)(Oy \,\&\, y = f(x))]$'. We can use the truth-tree method to show that this sentence is not quantificationally true.

1.	$\sim (\forall x)[Ex \supset (\exists y)(Oy \,\&\, y = f(x))]$ ✓	SM
2.	$(\exists x) \sim [Ex \supset (\exists y)(Oy \,\&\, y = f(x))]$ ✓	$1 \sim \forall D$
3.	$\sim [Ea \supset (\exists y)(Oy \,\&\, y = f(a))]$ ✓	$2\ \exists D$
4.	Ea	$3 \sim \supset D$
5.	$\sim (\exists y)(Oy \,\&\, y = f(a))$ ✓	$3 \sim \supset D$
6.	$(\forall y) \sim (Oy \,\&\, y = f(a))$	$5 \sim \exists D$
7.	$\sim (Oa \,\&\, a = f(a))$ ✓	$6\ \forall D$
8.	$\sim (Of(a) \,\&\, f(a) = f(a))$ ✓	$6\ \forall D$
9.	$\sim Of(a)$ | $\sim f(a) = f(a)$ ×	$8 \sim \&D$
10.	(under $\sim Of(a)$:) $\sim Oa$ | $\sim a = f(a)$	$7 \sim \&D$

This tree has two completed open branches. Every sentence on each of these branches either is a literal, or has been checked off, or is a universally quantified sentence. There is only one of the latter (at line 6), and it has been decomposed to every closed term on the relevant branch (each branch contains only the closed terms 'a' and '$f(a)$'). Because this tree has at least one completed open branch, '$\sim (\forall x)[Ex \supset (\exists y)(Oy \,\&\, y = f(x))]$' is not quantificationally false, and '$(\forall x)[Ex \supset (\exists y)(Oy \,\&\, y = f(x))]$' is not quantificationally true.

By definition a one-place function returns exactly one value for each argument. So the following sentence is quantificationally true:

$$(\forall x)(\exists y)[y = f(x) \,\&\, (\forall z)(z = f(x) \supset z = y)]$$

Here is a tree that establishes this:

1.	$\sim (\forall x)(\exists y)[y = f(x) \;\&\; (\forall z)(z = f(x) \supset z = y)]$ ✓		SM
2.	$(\exists x) \sim (\exists y)[y = f(x) \;\&\; (\forall z)(z = f(x) \supset z = y)]$ ✓		$1 \sim \forall D$
3.	$\sim (\exists y)[y = f(a) \;\&\; (\forall z)(z = f(a) \supset z = y)]$ ✓		$2\ \exists D$
4.	$(\forall y) \sim [y = f(a) \;\&\; (\forall z)(z = f(a) \supset z = y)]$		$3 \sim \exists D$
5.	$\sim [f(a) = f(a) \;\&\; (\forall z)(z = f(a) \supset z = f(a))]$ ✓		$4\ \forall D$
6.	$\sim f(a) = f(a)$	$\sim (\forall z)(z = f(a) \supset z = f(a))$ ✓	$5 \sim \& D$
7.	×	$(\exists z) \sim (z = f(a) \supset z = f(a))$ ✓	$6 \sim \forall D$
8.		$\sim (b = f(a) \supset b = f(a))$ ✓	$7\ \exists D$
9.		$b = f(a)$	$8 \sim \supset D$
10.		$\sim b = f(a)$	$8 \sim \supset D$
		×	

Note that at line 5 we chose to replace 'y' with 'f(a)' rather than with 'a'. Both are individual terms already occurring on the branch, but using the former does, at line 6, generate a closed branch on the left and, a few steps later, a closed branch on the right.

Next consider the argument

$(\forall x)[Px \supset (Ex \vee x = f(a)]$
$Pc \;\&\; \sim c = f(a)$

Ec

This argument is quantificationally valid, as the following tree demonstrates:

1.	$(\forall x)[Px \supset (Ex \vee x = f(a)]$			SM
2.	$Pc \;\&\; \sim c = f(a)$ ✓			SM
3.	$\sim Ec$			SM
4.	Pc			2 &D
5.	$\sim c = f(a)$			2 &D
6.	$Pc \supset (Ec \vee c = f(a))$ ✓			$1\ \forall D$
7.	$\sim Pc$	$Ec \vee c = f(a)$ ✓		$6 \supset D$
	×			
8.		Ec	$c = f(a)$	$7 \vee D$
		×	×	

The following argument is quantificationally invalid, as our next tree shows.

$(\forall x)[Fx \supset (\exists y)x = f(y)]$

$\sim Fc$

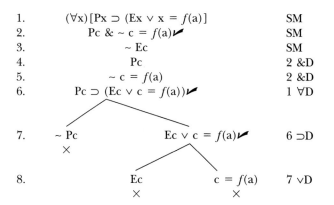

1.	$(\forall x)[Fx \supset (\exists y)x = f(y)]$				SM
2.	$\sim\sim Fc$ ✓				SM
3.	Fc				$2 \sim\sim D$
4.	$Fc \supset (\exists y)c = f(y)$ ✓				$1\ \forall D$
5.	$\sim Fc$	$(\exists y)c = f(y)$ ✓			$4 \supset D$
6.	×	$c = f(a)$			$5\ \exists D$
7.		$Fa \supset (\exists y)a = f(y)$ ✓			$1\ \forall D$
8.		$Ff(a) \supset (\exists y)f(a) = f(y)$ ✓			$1\ \forall D$
9.		$\sim Fa$		$(\exists y)a = f(y)$	$7 \supset D$
10.		$\sim Ff(a)$	$(\exists y)f(a) = f(y)$	$\sim Ff(a)$ / $(\exists y)f(a) = f(y)$	$8 \supset D$
11.		$\sim Fc$			$6, 10 = D$

At line 11 the leftmost of the four open branches, ending in '$\sim$ Fc', becomes a completed open branch, establishing that the argument is quantificationally invalid. Note that every sentence on that branch either is a literal (lines 3, 6, 9, and 11), or is checked off (lines 2, 4, 5, 7, and 8), or is a universally quantified sentence (line 1). The sentence on line 1 has been decomposed to every substitution instance that can be formed from a closed term on the branch, that is, from the terms 'c', 'a', and 'f(a)'. Finally the identity sentence at line 6 has been decomposed by replacing 'f(a)' in every literal in which it occurs with 'c', except that we have, following our informal convention, not entered 'c = c'. It is also worth noting that the right-hand branch of this tree is the beginning of an infinite branch—this because of the interplay of the existential quantifier within the scope of the universal quantifier of the sentence on line 1.

9.4E EXERCISES

Construct truth-trees as necessary to provide the requested information. In each case state your result, and specify what it is about your tree that establishes this result.

1. Determine, for each of the following sets, whether the set is quantificationally consistent.

a. $\{(\forall x)Fxx,\ (\exists x)(\exists y) \sim Fxy,\ (\forall x)x = a\}$
*b. $\{(\forall x)(Fxc \supset x = a),\ \sim c = a,\ (\exists x)Fxc\}$
c. $\{(\forall x)(x = a \supset Gxb),\ \sim (\exists x)Gxx,\ a = b\}$
*d. $\{(\exists x)(\exists y) \sim x = y,\ (\forall x)(Gxx \supset x = b),\ Gaa\}$
e. $\{(\forall x)((Fx \,\&\, \sim Gx) \supset \sim x = a),\ Fa \,\&\, \sim Ga\}$
*f. $\{(\exists y)(\forall x)Fxy,\ \sim (\forall x)(\forall y)x = y,\ Fab \,\&\, \sim Fba\}$

g. $\{(\forall x)(x = a \supset Gxf(b)), \sim (\exists x)Gxf(x), f(a) = f(b)\}$
*h. $\{(\forall x)(Gxx \supset x = f(x,b)), Gaa, (\forall x) \sim f(a,x) = a\}$
i. $\{(\exists x) \sim x = g(x), (\forall x)(\forall y)x = g(y)\}$
*j. $\{(\exists x)(\exists y)f(x,y) = f(y,x), (\forall x)\ [f(x,a) = f(a,x) \supset \sim a = x]\}$
k. $\{(\forall x)[Hx \supset (\forall y)Txy], (\exists x)Hf(x), \sim (\exists x)Txx\}$
*l. $\{Hf(a,b), (\forall x)(Hx \supset \sim Gx), (\exists y)Gy\}$
m. $\{(\forall x)[Fx \supset (\exists y)f(y) = x], (\exists x)Fx\}$
*n. $\{(\exists x)[x = f(s)\ \&\ (\forall y)(y = f(s) \supset y = x)]\}$

2. Determine, for each of the following sentences, whether it is quantificationally true, quantificationally false, or quantificationally indeterminate.
a. $a = b \equiv b = a$
*b. $(\sim a = b\ \&\ \sim b = c) \supset \sim a = c$
c. $(Gab\ \&\ \sim Gba) \supset \sim a = b$
*d. $(\forall x)(\exists y)x = y$
e. $Fa \equiv (\exists x)(Fx\ \&\ x = a)$
*f. $\sim (\exists x)x = a$
g. $(\forall x)x = a \supset [(\exists x)Fx \supset (\forall x)Fx]$
*h. $(\forall x)(\forall y)x = y$
i. $(\forall x)(\forall y) \sim x = y$
*j. $(\exists x)(\exists y)x = y$
k. $(\exists x)(\exists y) \sim x = y$
*l. $(\forall x)(\forall y)[x = y \supset (Fx \equiv Fy)]$
m. $(\forall x)(\forall y)[(Fx \equiv Fy) \supset x = y]$
*n. $(\forall x)(\forall y)[x = y \supset (\forall z)(Fxz \equiv Fyz)]$
o. $[(\exists x)Gax\ \&\ \sim (\exists x)Gxa] \supset (\forall x)(Gxa \supset \sim x = a)$

3. Determine which of the following sentences are quantificationally true.
a. $(\exists x)x = f(a)$
*b. $(\forall x)(\exists y)y = f(x)$
c. $(\exists x)(\exists y)x = y$
*d. $(\exists x)(\exists y)x = f(y)$
e. $(\forall x)[Gx \supset (\exists y)f(x) = y]$
*f. $(\forall x)(\forall y)[x = y \supset f(x) = f(y)]$
g. $(\forall y)(\exists x)[\sim y = x\ \&\ f(x) = y]$
*h. $(\forall x)(\exists y)[y = f(x)\ \&\ (\forall z)(z = f(x) \supset z = y)]$

4. Determine which of the following pairs of sentences are quantificationally equivalent.

a.	$\sim a = b$	$\sim b = a$
*b.	$(\exists x) \sim x = a$	$(\exists x) \sim x = b$
c.	$(\forall x)x = a$	$(\forall x)x = b$
*d.	$a = b\ \&\ b = c$	$a = c\ \&\ b = c$
e.	$(\forall x)(\forall y)x = y$	$(\forall x)x = a$
*f.	$(\forall x)(\exists y)x = y$	$(\forall y)(\exists x)x = y$
g.	$(\forall x)(Fx \supset x = a)$	$(\forall x)(Fa \supset x = a)$
*h.	$(\forall x)(x = a \vee x = b)$	$(\forall x)x = a \vee (\forall x)x = b$
i.	$(\forall x)Fx \vee (\forall x) \sim Fx$	$(\forall y)(Fy \supset y = b)$
*j.	$a = b$	$(\forall y)(y = a \supset y = b)$
k.	$(\exists x)(x = a\ \&\ x = b)$	$a = b$

5. Determine which of the following arguments are quantificationally valid.

a. a = b & ~ Bab
____
~ (∀x)Bxx

*b. Ge ⊃ d = e
Ge ⊃ He
____
Ge ⊃ Hd

c. (∀z)(Gz ⊃ (∀y)(Ky ⊃ Hzy))
(Ki & Gj) & i = j
____
Hii

*d. (∃x)(Hx & Mx)
Ms & ~ Hs
____
(∃x)((Hx & Mx) & ~ x = s)

e. a = b
____
Ka ∨ ~ Kb

*f. (∃x) ~ Pxx ⊃ ~ a = a
a = c
____
Pac

g. (∀x)(x = a ∨ x = b)
(∃x)(Fxa & Fbx)
____
(∃x)Fxx

*h. (∃x)Fxa
(∀y)(y = a ⊃ y = b)
____
(∃y)Fyy

i. (∀x)(∀y)(Fxy ∨ Fyx)
a = b
____
(∀x)(Fxa ∨ Fbx)

*j. (∃x)Fxa & (∃x)Fxb
~ a = b
____
(∀x)(∀y)((Fxa & Fyb) ⊃ ~ x = y)

k. (∀x)(Fx ≡ ~ Gx)
Fa
Gb
____
~ a = b

*l. ~ (∃x)Fxx
____
(∀x)(∀y)(Fxy ⊃ ~ x = y)

m. (∀x)(∀y)x = y
____
~ (∃x)(∃y)(Fx & ~ Fy)

*n. (∀x)(~ x = a ≡ (∃y)Gyx)
Gbc
____
~ c = a

o. (∀x)Hx ⊃ H*f*(x)
(∃z) ~ H*f*(z)
____
~ (∀x)Hx

*p. (∀y)(Hy ⊃ *g*(y) = y)
(∃x) ~ *g*(x) = x
____
(∃x) ~ Hx

q. (∀x)(∀y)(Hxy ≡ ~ Hyx)
(∃x)[Hx*f*(x) & ~ H*f*(x)x]
____
~ (∀x)*f*(x) = x

*r. (∃x)*h*(x) = x
(∀x)(Fx ⊃ ~ F*h*(x))
____
(∃x) ~ Fx

s. $(\forall x)[Px \supset (Ox \vee \sim x = f(b))]$
$(\exists x)[(Px \,\&\, \sim Ox) \,\&\, x = f(b)]$

Ob

*t. $(\forall x)(\forall y)(Hxy \supset f(x) = y)$
$(\exists x)Hxx$

$(\exists x)f(x) = x$

6. Determine which of the following claims are true.

a. $\{(\forall x)(Fx \supset (\exists y)(Gyx \,\&\, \sim y = x)), (\exists x)Fx)\} \vDash (\exists x)(\exists y) \sim x = y$
*b. $\{\sim (\exists x)(Fxa \vee Fxb), (\forall x)(\forall y)(Fxy \supset \sim x = y)\} \vDash \sim a = b$
c. $\{(\forall x)(Fx \supset \sim x = a), (\exists x)Fx\} \vDash (\exists x)(\exists y) \sim x = y$
*d. $\{(\forall x)(\exists y)(Fxy \,\&\, \sim x = y), a = b, Fab\} \vDash (\exists y)(Fay \,\&\, y = b)$
e. $\{(\exists w)(\exists z) \sim w = z, (\exists w)Hw\} \vDash (\exists w) \sim Hw$
*f. $\{(\exists w)(\forall y)Gwy, (\exists w)(\forall y)(\sim w = y \supset \sim Gwy)\} \vDash (\exists z) \sim Gzz$
g. $\{(\forall x)(\forall y)((Fx \equiv Fy) \equiv x = y), (\exists z)Fz\} \vDash (\exists x)(\exists y)(\sim x = y \,\&\, (Fx \,\&\, \sim Fy))$
*h. $\{(\forall x)(\exists y)y = f(x)\} \vDash (\exists z)z = f(a)$
i. $\{(\forall x)(\forall y)[\sim x = g(y) \supset Gxy], \sim (\exists x)Gax\} \vDash (\exists x)a = g(x)$

9.5 FINE-TUNING THE TREE METHOD

Neither *PL* nor *PLE* with their associated test procedures constitute a *decidable* system in this sense: There is no mechanical test procedure that always yields, in a finite number of steps, a "yes" or "no" answer to such questions as 'Is this argument of *PL/PLE* valid?' Let a *finite truth-tree* be a truth-tree that either is closed or has a completed open branch. Given the preceding caveat, it should come as no surprise that not every finite set of sentences of *PL/PLE* has a finite truth-tree.

Here is the start of a tree for $\{(\forall y)(\exists z)Fyz\}$, a set that, given the tree system we have developed, has no finite truth-tree:

1.	$(\forall y)(\exists z)Fyz$	SM
2.	$(\exists z)Faz$ ✓	1 ∀D
3.	Fab	2 ∃D
4.	$(\exists z)Fbz$ ✓	1 ∀D
5.	Fbc	4 ∃D
6.	$(\exists z)Fcz$ ✓	1 ∀D
7.	Fcd	6 ∃D
	•	
	•	
	•	

The dots indicate that the tree continues indefinitely. There is no hope of closing the one open branch on this tree. At every other step after the first, a new atomic sentence is added to the open branch, and since every atomic sentence is quantificationally consistent with every other atomic sentence, continuing to add more atomic sentences never closes the tree. This branch also never becomes a completed open branch. Every time Universal Decomposition is applied to the sentence '$(\forall y)(\exists z)Fyz$' on line 1, a new existentially quantified sentence is added to the branch. And decomposing that sentence adds a new individual constant to the branch, necessitating a further application of Universal Decomposition to '(∀y)(∃z)Fyz', resuming the cycle. We call an open branch that cannot be completed—one that never closes and will never, in a finite number of steps, become a completed open branch—a *nonterminating branch.*

The one nonterminating branch of the preceding tree is produced through the interplay of Universal and Existential Decomposition. That is, each use of Existential Decomposition produces a new constant, which, in turn, requires the use of Universal Decomposition, which introduces a new existentially quantified sentence. Another source of nonterminating branches on trees for finite sets of sentences is the inclusion of functors in *PLE.* Consider a tree for the set {(∀x)H*f*(x)}:

1.	(∀x)H*f*(x)	SM
2.	H*f*(a)	1 ∀D
3.	H*f*(*f*(a))	1 ∀D
4.	H*f*(*f*(*f*(a)))	1 ∀D
	•	
	•	
	•	

To qualify as a completed open branch, every universally quantified sentence on that branch must be decomposed at least once and must be decomposed to every closed term occurring on the branch. To satisfy the first requirement, we decompose at line 2 the universally quantified sentence on line 1, using the constant 'a'. This introduces *two* new closed terms to the one branch of the tree: 'a' and '*f*(a)'. So, we must again apply Universal Decomposition to line 1, this time using the closed term '*f*(a)'. This produces line 3, and a new closed term, '*f*(*f*(a))', and triggers another decomposition of the universally quantified sentence on line 1, producing yet a new closed term at line 4, '*f*(*f*(*f*(a)))', which triggers yet another use of Universal Decomposition, and so on. Clearly this branch will never close and will never become a completed open branch.

It is an unavoidable result that not every finite set of sentences of *PL*/*PLE* has a finite tree. There are, however, two ways in which the tree method we have developed can be improved. First, we would like assurances that when a set does have a finite tree we will eventually find it. The tree rules we have presented do not guarantee this, for they allow the construction of trees such as the following:

1.	(∀x)Fx	SM
2.	(∀x) ~ Fx	SM
3.	Fa	1 ∀D
4.	Fb	1 ∀D
5.	Fc	1 ∀D
6.	Fd	1 ∀D
	•	
	•	
	•	

Continuing in this way does not involve misusing any tree rule but never produces a closed tree or a completed open branch. A closed tree for the above set can be produced in just four lines:

1.	$(\forall x)Fx$	SM
2.	$(\forall x) \sim Fx$	SM
3.	Fa	1 $\forall$D
4.	$\sim Fa$	2 $\forall$D
	×	

What we need is a procedure for applying the decomposition rules that always yields a finite tree where one exists.

The second problem with the tree method as we have presented it is that some sets that we would like to have finite trees do not have them. To help understand this problem, we introduce the notion of a model. A model for a set of sentences of *PL/PLE* is an interpretation on which all the members of the set are true. (So all and only consistent sets have models.) A finite model is an interpretation with a finite UD, and an infinite model is an interpretation with an infinite UD. There are finite sets of sentences of *PL* and of *PLE* that have only infinite models. That is, there are finite quantificationally consistent sets such that every interpretation on which all the members of the set are true is an interpretation with an infinite UD. For example, $\{(\forall x)(\forall y)(\forall z)[(Fxy \ \& \ Fyz) \supset Fxz], \sim (\exists x)Fxx, (\forall x)(\exists y)Fxy\}$ has only infinite models. (We shall, later in this section, start a tree for this set and explain why that tree will never close and never have a completed open branch.)

We would like to have a tree system such that every finite inconsistent set has a closed tree *and* every finite set with a finite model has a finite tree with a completed open branch. The tree system we have developed *is* such that every finite inconsistent set has a closed tree, though we currently have no guarantee that we shall always find that tree. Unfortunately it is *not* such that every finite set with a finite model has a finite tree. We saw previously that the sets $\{(\forall x)(\exists y)Fxy\}$ and $\{(\forall x)Hf(x)\}$ do not have finite trees. Yet each does have a finite model. The following is a model for the first set:

UD: The set {1}
Fxy: x = y

Each thing in this restricted universe of discourse, namely, the positive integer 1, is equal to something, namely, itself. So the single member of $\{(\forall x)(\exists y)Fxy\}$ is true on this interpretation. A model for the second set is

UD: The set {2}
Hx: x is even
f(x): the product of x and 1

On this interpretation *f*(x) is just x, and the only value of x in this UD is 2, and 2 is even. So the single member of $\{(\forall x)Hf(x)\}$ is true on this interpretation.

We have, then, two tasks in this section: to devise a procedure that guarantees the construction of a finite tree where one exists[5] and to revise the tree rules so that every finite set with a finite model has a finite tree. We begin with the latter. Our strategy will be to modify the rule of Existential Decomposition and to add a rule dealing specifically with closed complex terms, so as to ensure that every finite set with a finite model has a finite tree with a completed open branch.

Recall that our Existential Decomposition rule requires that a sentence of the form (∃**x**)**P** be decomposed to a substitution instance **P**(**a**/**x**), where **a** is a constant foreign to the branch in question. To use a constant that already occurs on the branch would be to make the unwarranted assumption that the thing that is of the sort **P** is also of the sort specified by the formulas in which it occurs elsewhere on the branch.

The set {(∃x)Fx, (∃x) ~ Fx} is clearly consistent. Here is a tree for this set that misuses the current Existential Decomposition rule:

1.	(∃x)Fx	SM	
2.	(∃x) ~ Fx	SM	
3.	Fb	1 ∃D	
4.	~ Fb	2 ∃D	**MISTAKE!**
	×		

There is no interpretation on which something is of the sort F and that very same thing is of the sort not-F, and in using 'b' at line 4 as well as line 3, we are, in effect, looking for such an interpretation. It is no surprise that the search fails. So we cannot simply drop the present restriction on Existential Decomposition—doing so sometimes, as here, produces closed trees for consistent sets. But consider next a tree for {(∃x)Fx, (∃x)Gx} that similarly misuses Existential Decomposition:

1.	(∃x)Fx✓	SM	
2.	(∃x)Gx✓	SM	
3.	Fa	1 ∃D	
4.	Ga	2 ∃D	**MISTAKE!**

This tree is open, and from it we can construct an interpretation on which all the members of {(∃x)Fx, (∃x)Gx} are true, for example:

UD: The set {San Francisco}
Fx: x is a city
Gx: x is in California

[5]Up until now, in applying Identity Decomposition we have been omitting "trivial" identity sentences—that is, sentences of the form **t** = **t**, where **t** is a closed term—on the grounds that such sentences are never needed to close a branch. In this section we are working toward a process for constructing trees that will always lead, in a finite number of steps, to a completed open branch where there is one, and a closed tree where there is one. We call trees that are constructed following this process *systematic trees.* As the metatheory of Chapter 11 presupposes that such trees include trivial identity sentences wherever use of Identity Decomposition will generate one, we here abandon our practice of informally omitting trivial identity sentences.

The point is that trees are intended to give us information about the existence or nonexistence of interpretations on which all the members of the set being tested are true. In applying Existential Decomposition, it is not safe (witness the first of the preceding two trees) to use only a substitution instance formed from a constant already on the branch in question. But we also should not assume that the only viable interpretations are those we are led to by using a constant foreign to that branch; witness the second of the preceding trees. This suggests that we need a *branching* existential decomposition rule (we shall call it 'Existential Decomposition-2', abbreviated '∃D2'), for we need to consider both substitution instances formed from constants already on the branch and one formed from a new constant. Pursuing this line of reasoning, we can redo the two trees as follows:

1.	(∃x)Fx✓		SM
2.	(∃x) ~ Fx✓		SM
3.	Fa		1 ∃D2
4.	~ Fa	~ Fb	2 ∃D2
	×		

The closed left-hand branch shows that there is no interpretation on which '(∃x)Fx' and '(∃x) ~ Fx' are both true *and* some one thing is of the sort F and of the sort not-F. The right-hand branch is open and shows that there is an interpretation, whose UD need not be of a size greater than two, on which both these two sentences are true. Here is a tree for the set {(∃x)Fx, (∃x)Gx} that uses Existential Decomposition-2.

1.	(∃x)Fx✓		SM
2.	(∃x)Gx✓		SM
3.	Fa		1 ∃D2
4.	Ga	Gb	2 ∃D2

Both branches of this tree are open. The left-hand branch, on which only one constant occurs, reveals that there is an interpretation on which both '(∃x)Fx' and '(∃x)Gx' are true and whose UD need not be of a size greater than one. The right-hand branch reveals that there is such an interpretation whose UD need not be of a size greater than two.

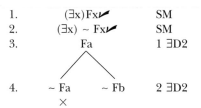

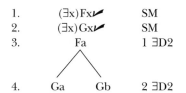

We are devising an existential decomposition rule that is a branching rule. But it is unlike other branching rules. First, it does not always produce additional branches. If there are no constants already on the branch in question, there is only one case to consider, that where a new constant is used. (See line 3 of each of the preceding two trees.) Second, if there is already more than one constant on a branch, the new Existential Decomposition rule will produce more than two branches, as a tree for the set {~ Fa, (∃x)(Fx & Gx), (∃x) ~ Gx} illustrates.

1.		~ Fa			SM
2.		(∃x)(Fx & Gx)✓			SM
3.		(∃x) ~ Gx✓			SM
4.	Fa & Ga✓		Fb & Gb✓		2 ∃D2
5.	Fa		Fb		4 &D
6.	Ga		Gb		4 &D
	×				
7.		~ Gb	~ Gc	~ Ga	3 ∃D2

The rule we are developing can be schematically presented as follows:

<u>*Existential Decomposition-2* (∃D2)</u>

$(\exists \mathbf{x})\mathbf{P}$✓

$\mathbf{P}(\mathbf{a}_1/\mathbf{x}) \quad \ldots \quad \mathbf{P}(\mathbf{a_m}/\mathbf{x}) \quad \mathbf{P}(\mathbf{a}_{\mathbf{m}+1}/\mathbf{x})$

where $\mathbf{a}_1$ through $\mathbf{a_m}$ are the constants already occurring on the branch on which Existential Decomposition-2 is being applied to decompose $(\exists \mathbf{x})\mathbf{P}$ and $\mathbf{a}_{\mathbf{m}+1}$ is a constant foreign to that branch

This rule is to be interpreted as requiring that in decomposing an existentially quantified sentence $(\exists \mathbf{x})\mathbf{P}$ appropriate substitution instances of that sentence be entered on every open branch passing through it. The schema specifies, for any such branch, which instances are to be entered on *that* branch. Specifically substitution instances formed from the constants $\mathbf{a}_1$ through $\mathbf{a_m}$ are to be entered, each on a distinct branch, **a**. And $\mathbf{P}(\mathbf{a}_{\mathbf{m}+1}/\mathbf{x})$ is to be entered on a further branch where $\mathbf{a}_{\mathbf{m}+1}$ is any constant foreign to the branch to which Existential Decomposition-2 is being applied. Existential Decomposition-2 is a branching rule, but a rule that produces a varying number of new branches.[6] As a result, if there is more than one open branch passing through $(\exists \mathbf{x})\mathbf{P}$, applying Existential Decomposition-2 to that sentence need not result in adding the same number of branches to each branch passing through $(\exists \mathbf{x})\mathbf{P}$. We shall see examples of this shortly.

[6]This Existential Decomposition rule is due to George Boolos, "Trees and Finite Satisfiability: Proof of a Conjecture of Burgess," *Notre Dame Journal of Formal Logic*, 25(3)(1984), 193–197.

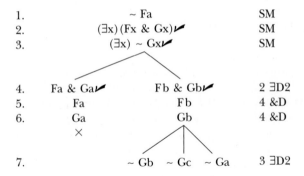

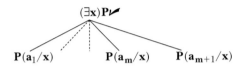

Here is a tree for $\{(\forall y)(\exists z)Fyz\}$ that uses Existential Decomposition-2 instead of Existential Decomposition:

1.	$(\forall y)(\exists z)Fyz$		SM
2.	$(\exists z)Faz$		$1\ \forall D$
3.	Faa	Fab	$2\ \exists D2$

Think of the tree this way: Line 2 says there is something to which a bears F. To find an interpretation on which this sentence is true, we consider both the case where that thing is a itself (this is the left-hand branch) and the case where it might be something else (this is the right-hand branch). If both branches close, we will know there is neither sort of interpretation. But if *either* becomes a completed open branch, we will have a finite open tree and a branch from which we can construct a finite model for the set being tested. Here the left-hand branch is completed, and from it we can recover an interpretation with a UD of size one (for there is only one constant on that branch)—for example, the interpretation given above (UD: {1}, Fxy: x = y). The right-hand branch is open but is *not* a completed open branch; the universally quantified sentence on line 1 has not been decomposed to a substitution instance formed from 'b'.

Replacing Existential Decomposition with Existential Decomposition-2 assures that the interplay of universal and existential quantifiers will not produce trees with only nonterminating open branches for sets that do have finite models. That is, this move addresses one kind of problem case noted at the beginning of this section. But there remains the case where the presence of one or more complex term produces only nonterminating open branches for finite sets that have finite models.

Before turning to the second task of this section, that of developing a tree construction procedure that yields a finite tree wherever one exists, we present two more trees using Existential Decomposition-2. Consider first a tree for the set $\{(\forall x)(Fx(\exists y)Gyx), (\forall x)Fx\}$:

1.		$(\forall x)(Fx \supset (\exists y)Gyx)$		SM
2.		$(\forall x)Fx$		SM
3.		Fa		$2\ \forall D$
4.		$Fa \supset (\exists y)Gya$ ✓		$1\ \forall D$
5.	$\sim Fa$ ×	$(\exists y)Gya$		4 D
6.		Gaa	Gba	$5\ \exists D2$

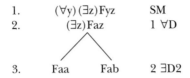

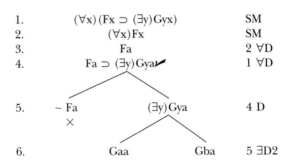

This tree has one completed open branch, the middle branch. The two universally quantified sentences on the branch have been decomposed to every constant on the branch, namely, 'a'. Every other sentence on the branch either is a literal or has been decomposed. So the set is quantificationally consistent. Had we used Existential Decomposition at line 6, the tree would have had only two branches. The one open branch would go on to yield more closed branches and a single nonterminating branch.

Consider next a tree for the set {~[(∀x)(∃y)Fxy ≡ (∀x)Fxa]}:

1.			~ [(∀x)(∃y)Fxy ≡ (∀x)Fxa] ✓			SM
2.		(∀x)(∃y)Fxy		~ (∀x)(∃y)Fxy ✓		1 ~ ≡D
3.		~ (∀x)Fxa ✓		(∀x)Fxa		1 ~ ≡D
4.				(∃x) ~ (∃y)Fxy ✓		2 ~ ∀D
5.				Faa		3 ∀D
6.			~ (∃y)Fay ✓		~ (∃y)Fby ✓	4 ∃D2
7.			(∀y) ~ Fay		(∀y) ~ Fby	6 ~ ∃D
8.			~ Faa		~ Fba	7 ∀D
9.			×		Fba	3 ∀D
10.		(∃x) ~ Fxa ✓			×	3 ~ ∀D
11.		(∃y)Fay ✓				2 ∀D
12.	~ Faa			~ Fba		10 ∃D2
13.	Faa	Fab	Faa	Fab	Fac	11 ∃D2
14.	×	(∃y)Fby ✓	(∃y)Fby	(∃y)Fby	(∃y)Fby	2 ∀D
15.	Fba	Fbb	Fbc			14 ∃D2

Note that using Existential Decomposition-2 at line 13 results in adding two new branches to the existing leftmost branch and three new branches to the other existing open branch. At line 15, Existential Decomposition-2 produces three branches from the leftmost open branch of line 14. Although the tree is not now complete, it has two completed open branches, one ending in 'Fba' and one ending in 'Fbb'. The branch ending in 'Fbc' is not complete, as '(∀x)(∃y)Fxy' has not been decomposed to '(∃y)Fcy'. The branches ending in undecomposed existentially quantified sentences are also, for that reason, not complete.

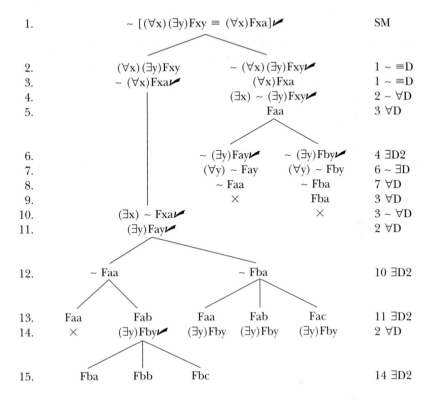

The replacement of Existential Decomposition with Existential Decomposition-2 will allow us to avoid infinite branches that are created by, for example, the interplay of universal and existential quantifiers where the latter fall within the scope of the former and the set being tested does have a finite model. But we will need another strategy for avoiding infinite branches driven by universal quantifiers whose scope extends over a complex term. We illustrated such a case at the start of this section:

1.	$(\forall x)Hf(x)$	SM
2.	$Hf(a)$	1 ∀D
3.	$Hf(f(a))$	1 ∀D
4.	$Hf(f(f(a)))$	1 ∀D
	•	
	•	
	•	

The one branch of this tree will never end because the current account of a completed open branch requires that every sentence on the branch be of one of four sorts, the third sort being this:

> A universally quantified sentence $(\forall \mathbf{x})\mathbf{P}$ such that $\mathbf{P}(\mathbf{t}/\mathbf{x})$ also occurs on that branch *for each closed individual term* **t** occurring on the branch and at least one instance $\mathbf{P}(\mathbf{t}/\mathbf{x})$ occurs on the branch

It is this requirement that drives the repeated application of Universal Decomposition on the preceding tree. Prior to the introduction of complex terms, we used the following simpler requirement:

> A universally quantified sentence $(\forall \mathbf{x})\mathbf{P}$ such that $\mathbf{P}(\mathbf{a}/\mathbf{x})$ also occurs on that branch *for each constant* **a** occurring on the branch and at least one instance $\mathbf{P}(\mathbf{a}/\mathbf{x})$ occurs on the branch

We now revert to this simpler requirement that deals only with constants. As a result, the set $\{(\forall x)Hf(x)\}$ has the following two-line tree with the single branch being a completed open branch, a desirable outcome.

1.	$(\forall x)Hf(x)$	SM
2.	$Hf(a)$	1 ∀D

Unfortunately this move also declares the following tree to have a completed open branch.

1.	$(\forall x) \sim Bx$	SM
2.	$Bf(c)$	SM
3.	$\sim Bc$	1 ∀D

This is not a desirable outcome, as we know that the set $\{(\forall x) \sim Bx, Bf(c)\}$ is inconsistent. It has the following closed tree:

1.	$(\forall x) \sim Bx$	SM
2.	$Bf(c)$	SM
3.	$\sim Bf(c)$	1 ∀D
	×	

Note that this tree is a legitimate tree. We are considering dropping the requirement that, where a branch contains a universally quantified sentence $(\forall \mathbf{x})\mathbf{P}$, that branch must also contain $\mathbf{P}(\mathbf{t}/\mathbf{x})$ for every closed term **t** on the branch, and for at least one closed term, to be a completed open branch. We are not considering disallowing using Universal Decomposition to generate substitution instances of universally quantified sentences formed from closed complex terms.

What we need, then, is some way to disqualify the single branch on the following tree as being a completed open branch:

1.	$(\forall x) \sim Bx$	SM
2.	$Bf(c)$	SM
3.	$\sim Bc$	1 ∀D

If there is a finite model for the set we are testing, then on that model the member of the UD assigned to 'c' either is or is not the same member as that 'f(c)' designates on the model. We cannot assume it is the same member, but neither should we assume it is not. We should not declare a branch a completed open branch until we have explored both possibilities. This suggests a strategy analogous to the one that motivates Existential Decomposition-2.

1.	$(\forall x) \sim Bx$		SM
2.	$Bf(c)$		SM
3.	$\sim Bc$		1 ∀D
4.	$c = f(c)$	$d = f(c)$	New rule
5.	$c = c$	$d = d$	4, 4 =D
6.	Bc	Bd	4, 2 =D
7.	×	$\sim Bd$	1 ∀D
8.		×	

On this tree we use, at line 4, an as-yet-unnamed rule to explore the possibility that, on the interpretation we are looking for, 'c' and 'f(c)' designate the same member of the UD, as well as the possibility that they do not. Having generated two identity sentences at line 4, clause 4 of our working definition of a completed open branch,

> 4. A sentence of the form $\mathbf{t}_1 = \mathbf{t}_2$ where $\mathbf{t}_1$ and $\mathbf{t}_2$ are closed terms such that the branch also contains, for every literal **P** on that branch containing $\mathbf{t}_2$, every sentence $\mathbf{P}(\mathbf{t}_1//\mathbf{t}_2)$ that can be obtained from **P** by Identity Decomposition

prevents us from declaring either of the branches that are open as of line 4 a completed open branch.

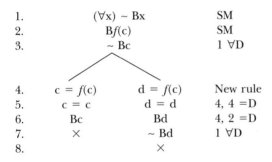

Application of Identity Decomposition to the two branches of the preceding tree produces a trivial identity sentence on each branch ('c = c' on the left and 'd = d' on the right) and two literals ('Bc' on the left and 'Bd' on the right). The left branch closes at this point. The right branch closes when the universally quantified sentence on line 1 is decomposed to '~ Bd'.

Using this same new rule in a tree for {(∀x)H*f*(x)} produces the following tree:

1.	(∀x)H*f*(x)		SM
2.	H*f*(a)		1 ∀D
3.	a = *f*(a)	b = *f*(a)	New rule
4.	a = a	b = b	3, 3 =D
5.	Ha	Hb	3, 2 =D

The left-hand branch is now a completed open branch, and this establishes that {(∀x)H*f*(x)} is quantificationally consistent. It also shows that this set has a finite model and that the size of the UD of that model need be no larger than one and that on that model the same member of the UD will be designated by 'a' and by '*f*(a)'. (We shall prove this in Chapter 11.) Note that the right-hand branch is not a completed open branch, for it contains the individual constant 'b' but not the substitution instance of '(∀x)H*f*(x)' that can be formed from 'b'. But there is no need to explore this branch further as the tree does contain one completed open branch.

We need a name for the new rule we are introducing, as well as a clear specification of what it requires, and we need a new account of what constitutes a completed open branch. We shall call the rule 'Complex Term Decomposition' because what the rule does, for every closed complex term on the branch we are working on, is yield a constant that can be used in place of that closed complex term (this is what a sentence of the form **a** = **t** tells us, where **a** is a constant and **t** a closed complex term). Here is the rule:

<u>*Complex Term Decomposition* (CTD)</u>

$$\ldots f(\mathbf{a}_1, \ldots, \mathbf{a}_n) \ldots$$

$$\mathbf{b}_1 = f(\mathbf{a}_1, \ldots, \mathbf{a}_n) \ldots \quad \mathbf{b}_m = f(\mathbf{a}_1, \ldots, \mathbf{a}_n) \quad \mathbf{b}_{m+1} = f(\mathbf{a}_1, \ldots, \mathbf{a}_n)$$

where $f(\mathbf{a}_1, \ldots, \mathbf{a}_n)$ is a closed complex term occurring within a literal on a branch, $\mathbf{a}_1$ through $\mathbf{a}_n$ are individual constants, $\mathbf{b}_1$ through $\mathbf{b}_m$ are the individual constants already occurring on that branch, and $\mathbf{b}_{m+1}$ is any constant not occurring on the branch before the current application of CTD

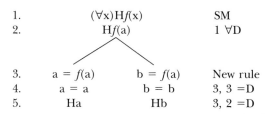

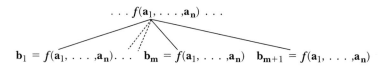

Note that Complex Term Decomposition can be used on the complex term '*g*(a,b)' as it occurs in a literal, as in 'H*g*(a,b)', but not on '*f*(a,*g*(a,b))' as it occurs in 'H*f*(a,*g*(a,b))', because '*f*(a,*g*(a,b))' contains a closed term that is not a

constant, 'g(a,b)'. Since the sentences to which Complex Term Decomposition is applied are literals, those sentences are not checked off. In the justification column we enter the line number on which the complex term occurs in a literal and the abbreviation 'CTD'. (There may be more than one such literal on a branch, in which case we arbitrarily pick one of them to cite in the justification column.)

By using Complex Term Decomposition, we can show that the sentence '(∀x)f(x) = x' is not quantificationally true:

```
1.            (∀x)f(x) = x                  SM
2.               f(a) = a                   1 ∀D
                 /      \
3.       a = f(a)        b = f(a)           2 CTD
4.        a = a           b = a             3, 3 =D
5.     f(a) = f(a)                          2, 2 =D
```

The left branch of this tree is a completed open branch. Hence '(∀x)f(x) = x' is not quantificationally false. In Section 9.4 we established that '(∀x)f(x) = x' is not quantificationally true. Therefore it is quantificationally indeterminate.

We shall illustrate the use of Complex Term Decomposition by using the tree method to show that '(∀x) [Hg(x,f(b)) ⊃ ~ Hg(f(b),x)]' is quantificationally indeterminate:

```
1.                          (∀x) [Hg(x,f(b)) ⊃ ~ Hg(f(b),x)]                      SM
2.                             Hg(b,f(b)) ⊃ ~ Hg(f(b),b) ✓                        1 ∀D
                                    /                  \
3.                   ~ Hg(b,f(b))                        ~ Hg(f(b),b)              2 ⊃D
                      /        \                          /        \
4.             b = f(b)       c = f(b)             b = f(b)       c = f(b)        3 CTD
5.              b = b          c = c                 b = b          c = c         4, 4 =D
6.            ~ Hg(b,b)      ~ Hg(b,c)            ~ Hg(b,b)      ~ Hg(b,c)        4, 3 =D
              /       \
7.  b = g(b,b)    c = g(b,b)                                                      6 CTD
8.       |          c = c                                                         7, 7 =D
9.     ~ Hb         ~ Hc                                                          7, 6 =D
```

The leftmost branch is a completed open branch. The remaining branches are incomplete, but since the tree does have at least one completed open branch there is no need to complete them. This tree establishes that '(∀x) [Hg(x,f(b)) ⊃ ~ Hg(f(b),x)]' is not quantificationally false. In constructing the tree we reached the sentences '~ Hb' and '~ Hc' through repeated applications of Complex Term Decomposition and Identity Decomposition, applying CTD first to line 3 to produce the identities on line 4, then to 'g(b,b)' as that closed term occurs in a literal on line 6. The following tree establishes that '(∀x) [Hg(x,*f*(b)) ⊃ ~ Hg(*f*(b),x)]' also is not quantificationally true, and hence that it is quantificationally indeterminate:

1.	~ (∀x) [Hg(x,*f*(b)) ⊃ ~ Hg(*f*(b),x)]✓					SM
2.	(∃x) ~ [Hg(x,*f*(b)) ⊃ ~ Hg(*f*(b),x)]✓					1 ~ ∀D
3.	~ [Hg(b,*f*(b)) ⊃ ~ Hg(*f*(b),b)]✓		~ [Hg(c,*f*(b)) ⊃ ~ Hg(*f*(b),c)]✓			2 ∃D2
4.	Hg(b,*f*(b))		Hg(c,*f*(b))			3 ~ ⊃D
5.	~ ~ Hg(*f*(b),b)✓		~ ~ Hg(*f*(b),c)✓			3 ~ ⊃D
6.	Hg(*f*(b),b)		Hg(*f*(b),c)			5 ~ ~ D
7.	b = *f*(b)	c = *f*(b)	b = *f*(b)	c = *f*(b)	d = *f*(b)	6 CTD
8.	Hg(b,b)	Hg(b,c)	Hg(c,b)	Hg(c,c)	Hg(c,d)	7, 4 =D
9.	|	Hg(c,b)	Hg(b,c)	|	Hg(d,c)	6, 5 =D
10.	b = b	c = c	b = b	c = c	d = d	7, 7 =D
11.	b = *g*(b,b) / c = *g*(b,b)					8 CTD
12.	| / c = c					10, 10 =D
13.	Hb / Hc					11, 8 =D

The left two branches of this tree are now completed open branches, so there is no point in continuing to work on the other branches. Note that the closed term '*f*(b)' occurs in literals on lines 4 and 6. Nonetheless we applied CTD to this closed term only once—at line 7, citing line 6. We could equally well have cited line 4. (There is no point to applying CTD twice to the same closed term, as the results will always be the same.) Also note that we applied Identity Decomposition at line 8 to lines 7 and 4 on all five branches. At line 9 we applied it only to the branches where a new literal is yielded. The availability of CTD justifies our relaxing the requirement in clause 3 of our definition of a completed open branch so as *not* to require that universally quantified sentences be decomposed to substitution instances formed from closed complex terms. Such decompositions are still allowed and will sometimes produce closed trees sooner than will using CTD, but they are not required for a branch to be a completed open branch. It turns out that we can similarly loosen the requirement concerning the use of Identity Decomposition. So our final, not-to-be-further-revised account of a completed open branch is this:

> A *completed open branch* is a finite open branch on which each sentence is of one of the following four sorts:
>
> 1. A literal
> 2. A sentence that has been decomposed and is neither a universally quantified sentence nor an identity sentence

3. A universally quantified sentence $(\forall \mathbf{x})\mathbf{P}$ such that $\mathbf{P}(\mathbf{a}/\mathbf{x})$ also occurs on that branch *for each constant* **a** occurring on the branch and $\mathbf{P}(\mathbf{a}/\mathbf{x})$ occurs on the branch for at least one constant **a**
4. A sentence of the form $\mathbf{a} = \mathbf{t}$, where **a** is an individual constant and **t** is a closed term and where the branch also contains, for every literal **P** on that branch containing **t**, every sentence $\mathbf{P}(\mathbf{a}//\mathbf{t})$ that can be obtained from **P** by Identity Decomposition

and on which Complex Term Decomposition has been applied to every closed complex term occurring in a literal on the branch that does not itself contain a complex term

Note that Identity Decomposition can be used on sentences of the form $\mathbf{t}_1 = \mathbf{t}_2$ when $\mathbf{t}_1$ is a complex term, but not using it will not prevent a branch from becoming a completed open branch. So, where $\mathbf{t}_1 = \mathbf{t}_2$ occurs on a branch and $\mathbf{t}_1$ is a complex term, Identity Decomposition should be used when we suspect that doing so will produce a closed branch, but not otherwise.

Before turning to the second task of this section, that of developing a tree construction procedure that yields a finite tree wherever one exists, we shall construct several more trees using one or both of Existential Decomposition-2 and Complex Term Decomposition. One might fear that, by not requiring universally quantified sentences to be decomposed to *every* substitution instance that can be formed from a closed term already occurring on the branch, we may in some cases be left with an open branch when we should have a closed one. Consider the set $\{(\forall x)(\exists y)y = g(x)\}$. The one member of this set is quantificationally true, so we want the tree for its negation to close:

1.	$\sim (\forall x)(\exists y)y = g(x)$ ✓	SM
2.	$(\exists x) \sim (\exists y)y = g(x)$ ✓	$1 \sim \forall D$
3.	$\sim (\exists y)y = g(a)$ ✓	$2\ \exists D2$
4.	$(\forall y) \sim y = g(a)$	$3 \sim \exists D$
5.	$\sim a = g(a)$	$4\ \forall D$

We can close this tree by adding '$\sim g(a) = g(a)$' on line 6, by applying Universal Decomposition to line 4. But our revised account of what constitutes a completed open branch does not require us to do this, as '$g(a)$' is a complex term.

It may seem that we now have a completed open branch, for every sentence on the one branch of our tree either is a literal, or has been checked off, or is a universally quantified sentence that has been decomposed at least once to a substitution instance formed from a constant and has been decomposed to every substitution instance that can be formed from a constant already on the branch. That is, this branch meets conditions 1–4 specified previously for being a completed open branch. But it does *not* satisfy the final requirement—namely, that Complex Term Decomposition has been applied to every closed complex term occurring in a literal on the branch. When we do so apply Complex Term Decomposition we obtain the following tree:

1.	~ (∀x) (∃y)y = *g*(x) ✓		SM
2.	(∃x) ~ (∃y)y = *g*(x) ✓		1 ~ ∀D
3.	~ (∃y)y = *g*(a) ✓		2 ∃D2
4.	(∀y) ~ y = *g*(a)		3 ~ ∃D
5.	~ a = *g*(a)		4 ∀D
6.	a = *g*(a)	b = *g*(a)	5 CTD
7.	×	b = b	6, 6 =D
8.		~ b = *g*(a)	4 ∀D
		×	

This example illustrates why it is necessary, in loosening the requirement concerning the decomposition of universally quantified sentences, to add the requirement that Complex Term Decomposition be used.

Next we shall use the tree method to determine the quantificational status of the sentence '(∀x) (∃y)P*f*(x,y)'. Here is a tree for the negation of the sentence:

1.	~ (∀x) (∃y)P*f*(x,y) ✓	SM
2.	(∃x) ~ (∃y)P*f*(x,y) ✓	1 ~ ∀D
3.	~ (∃y)P*f*(a,y) ✓	2 ∃D2
4.	(∀y) ~ P*f*(a,y)	3 ~ ∃D
5.	~ P*f*(a,a)	4 ∀D

The tree does not yet contain a completed open branch, because it does contain a literal containing a closed complex term, '~ P*f*(a,a)', and Complex Term Decomposition has not yet been applied. We continue as follows:

1.	~ (∀x) (∃y)P*f*(x,y) ✓		SM
2.	(∃x) ~ (∃y)P*f*(x,y) ✓		1 ~ ∀D
3.	~ (∃y)P*f*(a,y) ✓		2 ∃D2
4.	(∀y) ~ P*f*(a,y)		3 ~ ∃D
5.	~ P*f*(a,a)		4 ∀D
6.	a = *f*(a,a)	b = *f*(a,a)	5 CTD
7.	~ Pa	~ Pb	6, 5 =D
8.	a = a	b = b	6, 6 =D

Having entered identity sentences in which the left term is a constant at line 6, we must, to produce one or more completed open branch, use Identity Decomposition at lines 7 and 8. When this is done, the left-hand branch becomes a completed open branch. Every sentence on it either is a literal, is checked off, or is a universally quantified sentence that has been decomposed to at least one substitution instance formed from a constant and has been decomposed to every substitution instance that can be formed from a constant already on the branch. Finally, Complex Term Decomposition and Identity Decomposition have been used as specified, so the sentence we are testing is not quantificationally false.

Note that the right-hand branch of the preceding tree is not a completed open branch. It contains a constant, 'b', and the universally quantified sentence on line 4 has not been decomposed to a substitution instance formed from this constant. Work on the right-hand branch could be continued as follows (though there is no need to do so, since we already have a tree with a completed open branch).

6.	a = *f*(a,a)		b = *f*(a,a)		5 CTD
7.	~ Pa		~ Pb		6, 5 =D
8.	a = a		b = b		6, 6 =D
9.			~ P*f*(a,b)		4 ∀D
10.		a = *f*(a,b)	b = *f*(a,b)	c = *f*(a,b)	8 CTD
11.		~ Pa	~ Pb	~ Pc	9, 8 =D
12.		a = a		c = c	9, 9 =D

At this point the three leftmost branches are completed open branches but the rightmost branch is not, for it contains a constant 'c', requiring a further application of Universal Decomposition to the sentence on line 4. But there is no point in going any farther. We know, and knew as of line 8, that the sentence we are interested in is not quantificationally true.

We now construct a tree for the sentence itself, to determine whether it is quantificationally false or quantificationally indeterminate:

1.		(∀x)(∃y)P*f*(x,y)		SM
2.		(∃y)P*f*(a,y) ✓		1 ∀D
3.		P*f*(a,a)	P*f*(a,b)	2 ∃D2
4.	a = *f*(a,a)	b = *f*(a,a)		3 CTD
5.	Pa	Pb		4, 3 =D
6.	a = a	b = b		4, 4 =D

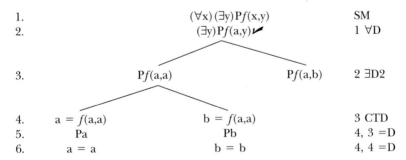

At this point the tree has one completed open branch, the leftmost branch. The other branches are not completed open branches because each contains the constant 'b', and the universally quantified sentence on line 1 has not been decomposed to substitution instances formed from 'b'. Because the tree does have at least one completed open branch, the sentence we are testing is true on at least one interpretation and is therefore not quantificationally false. This, together with the tree we constructed for the negation of the sentence, establishes that ‘$(\forall x)(\exists y)Pf(x,y)$’ is quantificationally indeterminate.

We shall next show that ‘$(\forall x)(\forall y)f(x,y) = f(y,x)$’ is quantificationally indeterminate. We start by constructing a tree for the sentence itself:

1.	$(\forall x)(\forall y)f(x,y) = f(y,x)$		SM
2.	$(\forall y)f(a,y) = f(y,a)$		1 $\forall$D
3.	$f(a,a) = f(a,a)$		2 $\forall$D
4.	$a = f(a,a)$	$b = f(a,a)$	3 CTD
5.	$a = a$	$b = b$	4, 3 =D
6.	$f(a,a) = a$	$f(a,a) = b$	4, 3 =D

The left-hand branch is, as of line 6, a completed open branch. So the sentence we are testing is not quantificationally false. The right-hand branch is not completed, as it contains a constant, ‘b’, and does not contain substitution instances of the sentences on lines 1 and 2 that can be formed from ‘b’. Here is a tree for the negation of our sentence:

1.					$\sim (\forall x)(\forall y)f(x,y) = f(y,x)$ ✓						SM
2.					$(\exists x) \sim (\forall y)f(x,y) = f(y,x)$ ✓						1 ~$\forall$D
3.					$\sim (\forall y)f(a,y) = f(y,a)$ ✓						2 $\exists$D2
4.					$(\exists y) \sim f(a,y) = f(y,a)$ ✓						3 ~$\forall$D
5.				$\sim f(a,a) = f(a,a)$			$\sim f(a,b) = f(b,a)$				
				×							
6.		$a = f(a,b)$			$b = f(a,b)$				$c = f(a,b)$		5 CTD
7.		$\sim a = f(b,a)$			$\sim b = f(a,b)$				$\sim c = f(b,a)$		6, 5 =D
8.		$a = a$			$b = b$				$c = c$		6, 6 =D
9.	$a = f(b,a)$	$b = f(b,a)$	$c = f(b,a)$	$a = f(b,a)$	$b = f(b,a)$	$c = f(b,a)$	$a = f(b,a)$	$b = f(b,a)$	$c = f(b,a)$	$d = f(b,a)$	5 CTD
10.	×	$\sim a = b$	$\sim a = c$	$\sim b = a$	×	$\sim b = c$	$\sim c = a$	$\sim c = b$	×	$\sim c = d$	9, 7 =D
11.		$b = b$	$c = c$	$a = a$		$c = c$	$a = a$	$b = b$		$d = d$	9, 9 =D
12.		$\sim f(a,b) = b$	$\sim f(a,b) = c$	$\sim f(a,b) = a$		$\sim f(a,b) = c$	$\sim f(a,b) = a$	$\sim f(a,b) = b$		$\sim f(a,b) = d$	9, 5 =D

This tree has six completed open branches, so the sentence at line 1 is not quantificationally false, and the sentence of which it is the negation is not quantificationally true. So ‘$(\forall x)(\forall y)f(x,y) = f(y,x)$’ is quantificationally indeterminate.

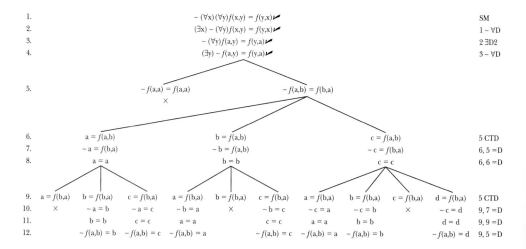

The set of tree rules we developed in Section 9.2, along with the account we there gave of a completed open branch, and the tree rules we developed in this section, and the new account of a completed open branch, are alike in this sense: Under both sets of rules a finite set of sentences of *PL/PLE*

has a closed tree if and only if it is quantificationally inconsistent, and a finite set of sentences of *PL/PLE* that has a tree with a completed open branch is quantificationally consistent. As was to be anticipated, trees constructed using the rules Existential Decomposition-2 and Complex Term Decomposition are frequently considerably more complicated than those constructed using Existential Decomposition and without using Complex Term Decomposition. It is for this reason that we did not introduce Existential Decomposition-2 as the only existential decomposition rule, and that we did not introduce Complex Term Decomposition in Section 9.4.

The preceding example should make it clear that truth-trees can become very complex. It can happen that one or more of the branches on a tree are nonterminating but that others, if pursued, will become completed open branches. In such cases, unless care is taken, one can work continuously on a branch that is, in fact, nonterminating while ignoring a branch that, if continued, will become a completed open branch. To prevent this, to guarantee that all possibilities are pursued, we introduce procedures for constructing trees in a systematic fashion, that is, in a fashion that will always, in a finite number of steps, find a completed open branch if one exists and close the tree if it can be closed.

The System for PL

List the members of the set to be tested.

Exit Conditions

Stop if

a. The tree closes.

b. An open branch becomes a completed open branch.

Construction Procedures

Stage 1: Decompose all truth-functionally compound and existentially quantified sentences and each resulting sentence that is itself either a truth-functional compound or an existentially quantified sentence.

Stage 2: For each universally quantified sentence $(\forall \mathbf{x})\mathbf{P}$ on the tree, enter $\mathbf{P}(\mathbf{a}/\mathbf{x})$ on every open branch passing through $(\forall \mathbf{x})\mathbf{P}$ for every constant **a** on the branch. On each open branch passing through $(\forall \mathbf{x})\mathbf{P}$ on which no constant occurs, enter $\mathbf{P}(a/\mathbf{x})$.

Repeat this process until every universally quantified sentence on the tree, including those added as a result of this process, has been so decomposed.

Return to Stage 1.

The System for *PLE* is somewhat more complicated.

The System for PLE

List the members of the set to be tested.

Exit Conditions

Stop if

a. The tree closes.

b. An open branch becomes a completed open branch.

Construction Procedures

Stage 1: Decompose all truth-functionally compound and existentially quantified sentences and each resulting sentence that is itself either a truth-functional compound or an existentially quantified sentence.

Stage 2: For each universally quantified sentence $(\forall \mathbf{x})\mathbf{P}$ on the tree:

1. Enter $\mathbf{P}(\mathbf{a}/\mathbf{x})$ on each open branch passing through $(\forall \mathbf{x})\mathbf{P}$ for each individual constant already occurring on that branch.
2. On each open branch passing through $(\forall \mathbf{x})\mathbf{P}$ on which no constant occurs, enter $\mathbf{P}(a/\mathbf{x})$.
3. Enter $\mathbf{P}(\mathbf{t}/\mathbf{x})$ on an open branch passing through $(\forall \mathbf{x})\mathbf{P}$ for a closed complex term $\mathbf{t}$ if and only if doing so closes the branch.

Repeat this process until every universally quantified sentence on the tree, including those added as a result of this process, has been so decomposed.

Stage 3: Apply Complex Term Decomposition to every complex term on an open branch that does not itself contain a complex term and to which Complex Term Decomposition has not already been applied.

Stage 4: For every sentence of the form $\mathbf{t}_1 = \mathbf{t}_2$ occurring on an open branch, apply Identity Decomposition as follows:

1. Where $\mathbf{t}_1$ is an individual constant, apply Identity Decomposition until every open branch passing through $\mathbf{t}_1 = \mathbf{t}_2$ also contains, for every literal $\mathbf{P}$ containing $\mathbf{t}_2$ on that branch, every sentence $\mathbf{P}(\mathbf{t}_1//\mathbf{t}_2)$ that can be obtained from $\mathbf{P}$ by Identity Decomposition.
2. Where $\mathbf{t}_1$ is a closed complex term, apply Identity Decomposition to $\mathbf{t}_1 = \mathbf{t}_2$ and a literal $\mathbf{P}$ containing $\mathbf{t}_2$ that occurs on a branch passing through $\mathbf{t}_1 = \mathbf{t}_2$ if and only if only doing so closes the branch.

Return to Stage 1.

Note that Stage 3 does not require us to apply Complex Term Decomposition to the same complex term and on the same branch more than once, even though a complex term may occur in more than one literal on an open branch.

In The System for *PLE*, Stage 4 ensures that after passing through that stage every sentence of the form **a** = **t** on every open branch meets the requirements of clause 4 of the definition of a completed open branch. That is, if the branch is not completed, it is *not* because we have failed to apply Identity Decomposition the required number of times.[7] Stages 2 and 4 both contain instructions to apply a decomposition rule in certain cases only if doing so closes a branch. This is because the decompositions in question do not need to be done to meet the requirements for having a completed open branch and because doing such decompositions where the result is not a closed branch may result in a branch becoming an infinite branch whereas not doing the decomposition and continuing application of The System may yield a completed open branch.

We could eliminate from Stage 2 of The System the clause calling for the decomposition of universally quantified sentences to substitution instances formed from complex terms if and only if doing so produces a closed branch. Similarly we could eliminate from Stage 4 the clause calling for the use of Identity Decomposition when $\mathbf{t}_1$ of $\mathbf{t}_1 = \mathbf{t}_2$ is a complex term and the result is a closed branch. That is, The System, so modified, would still guarantee that if a set has a closed tree we will find it in a finite number of steps, and if a set has a finite model we will find a completed open branch in a finite number of steps. But trees produced by following The System would, as a result, become somewhat more complex.

We call trees that have been constructed in accordance with the appropriate System (*PL* or *PLE*) *systematic trees*. In all systematic trees Existential Decomposition-2 is used rather than Existential Decomposition. To construct a systematic tree, proceed through the tree construction stages in the order specified. That is, first list the members of the set being tested; next all truth-functionally compound and all existentially quantified sentences are decomposed. When doing so it is wise to apply nonbranching rules before applying branching rules. When and only when the tree contains no undecomposed truth-functional compounds and no undecomposed existentially quantified sentences do we proceed to Stage 2. At Stage 2 each universally quantified sentence on the tree is decomposed as specified. It is important to note that work at Stage 2 is not complete until every universally quantified sentence on the tree has been decomposed in the required manner, including universally quantified sentences that are entered as a result of work at Stage 2 and those that were on the tree when we passed from Stage 1 to Stage 2. After completion of Stage 2, we either return to Stage 1 (for *PL*) or proceed to Stage 3 and 4 (for *PLE*) and then return to Stage 1.

Systematic trees differ from nonsystematic trees in several respects. In systematic trees Existential Decomposition-2 is always used to decompose existentially quantified sentences. In nonsystematic trees either Existential Decomposition, or Existential Decomposition-2 (or both) may be used. This alone frequently makes systematic trees more complex than nonsystematic trees. In systematic trees

[7] In Chapter 11 we shall establish various results about the tree system for *PL* and *PLE* where all trees are constructed in accordance with the relevant system (*PL* or *PLE*). Some of those results presuppose that Identity Decomposition is applied as required by clause 4 of our definition of a completed open branch. This is why we allow, informally but not formally, the omission of applications of Identity Decomposition that yield sentences of the form **t** = **t**.

Complex Term Decomposition and Identity Decomposition must be used wherever applicable and as specified, even where using them does not, in fact, advance the goal of either finding a completed open branch or closing the tree. Finally, The System does not allow work on one branch to be continued to the point of excluding all work on another open branch. The advantage of constructing systematic trees is, again, that doing so will always lead, in a finite number of steps, to a completed open branch when one exists, and to a closed tree when one exists. The disadvantage is that systematic trees are often much larger than are nonsystematic trees. Here is the start of a systematic tree for {(∀x) (∃y)Fxy, ~ (∃x)Fxx, (∀x) (∀y) (∀z) [(Fxy & Fyz) ⊃ Fxz]}:

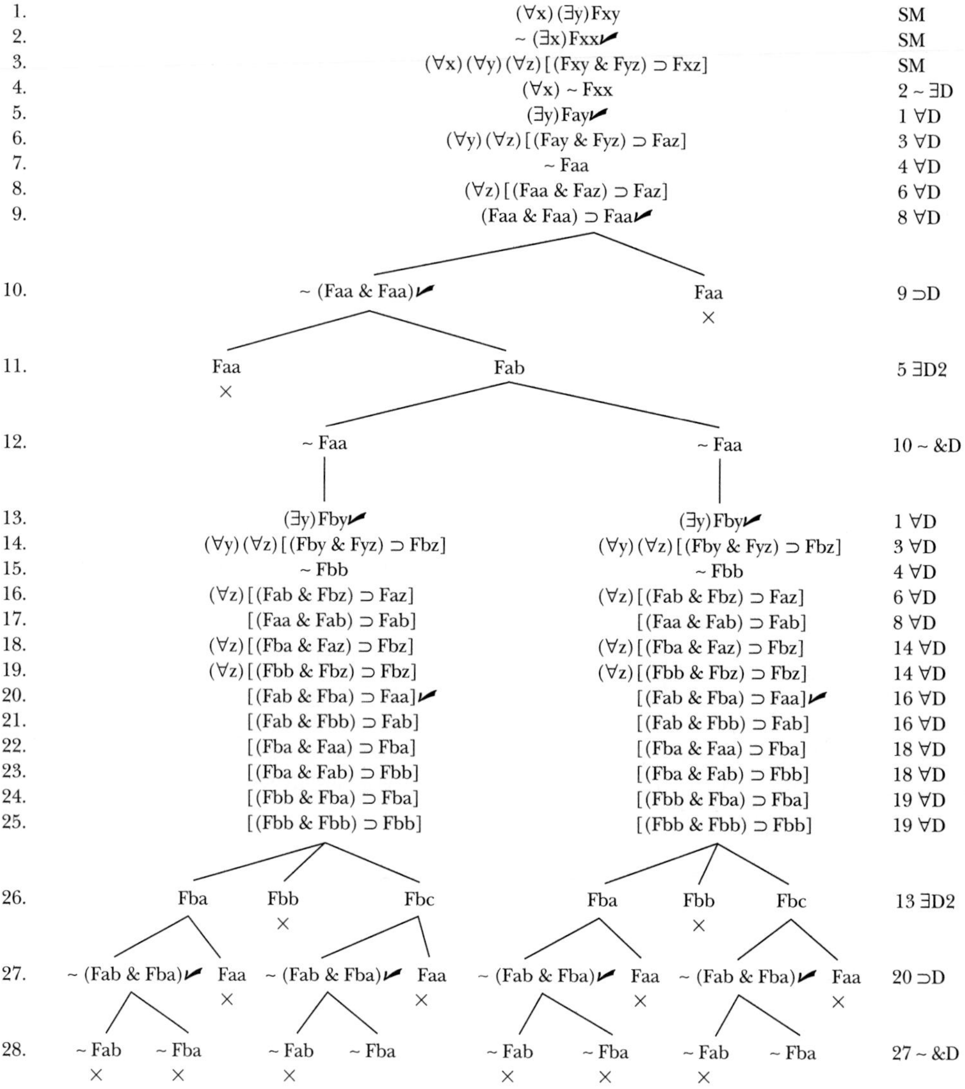

Because all the members of the set being tested are sentences of *PL*, we use The System for *PL*. After listing the members of the set, we begin work at Stage 1. After '~ (∃x)Fxx' is decomposed to '(∀x) ~ Fxx', every truth-functional compound (the sentence on line 2) and every existentially quantified sentence on the tree (there are none) have been decomposed. We proceed to Stage 2. Since there are, at this point, no constants on the tree, we decompose each universally quantified sentence on the tree to a substitution instance formed from 'a'. This takes us through line 9. We now return to Stage 1. There are two sentences to be decomposed: the existentially quantified sentence on line 5 and the truth-functional compound on line 9. The former branches when decomposed because there is already one constant, 'a', on the one branch of the tree; the latter branches because the sentence is a material conditional. We choose to decompose the latter first, as it yields one closed branch (the right branch), at line 10. Next we decompose the existentially quantified sentence on line 5. It yields one closed branch (the left branch) and one open branch.

One truth-functional compound remains to be decomposed—the negation of a conjunction on line 10. Decomposing this sentence yields two open branches. As it happens these are identical; that is, exactly the same sentences occur on each branch. Nonetheless The System requires us to pursue both branches. We do so by proceeding to Stage 2.

All the universally quantified sentences on the tree have already been decomposed to substitution instances formed from 'a'. But 'b' now also occurs on the tree, in 'Fab' at line 11, and both open branches pass through that sentence. So the universally quantified sentences must all be decomposed to substitution instances formed from 'b'. We do this on lines 13–25. At line 26 we return to Stage 1. On each branch we have seven truth-functional compounds, all material conditionals, and one existentially quantified sentence to decompose. We decompose the existentially quantified sentence on line 13 first, splitting each of the existing two branches into three branches. Two of these branches—the ones ending in 'Fbb'—close. At line 27 we decompose the material conditional occurring on line 20. Of the eight resulting branches, four close—the ones ending in 'Faa'. We next decompose '~ (Fab & Fba)', which occurs four times on line 27. Of the resulting eight branches, six close. The remaining two open branches are branches on which the constant 'c' occurs.

Were we to continue, we would next decompose the remaining truth-functional compounds. Some, but not all branches, would close. Eventually we would return to Stage 1 and decompose all universally quantified sentences to substitution instances formed from 'c'. This would produce a new existentially quantified sentence that would eventually be decomposed to substitution instances formed from 'a', 'b', 'c', and 'd', respectively. Branches containing the first three substitution instances would eventually close; not all the branches containing the latter substitution instance would do so.

We have not demonstrated that this tree will never close and will never have a completed open branch, but this is the case. The only way to demonstrate this is to show, independently of the tree method, that our set is quantificationally consistent, that it has only infinite models, and that no set with only infinite models has a finite tree. Here the point is that the tree method cannot be used to show that sets such as this one are quantificationally consistent. We abandon the tree; we do not complete it. And an abandoned tree is a failure to establish that the set being tested is consistent and a failure to establish that it is inconsistent. However, having used The System, we can be sure that we have not, as far as we have gone, missed a completed open branch or a chance to close the tree.

Although The System has not been presented as a mechanical method and will not yield any result if a set has only infinite models, it does place restrictions on how trees can be constructed and prevents us from failing to find closed trees and completed open branches, where they exist, provided we persevere long enough (a finite tree can be indefinitely large). Consider again the tree presented earlier for {(∀x)Fx, (∀x) ~ Fx}:

1.	(∀x)Fx	SM
2.	(∀x) ~ Fx	SM
3.	Fa	1 ∀D
4.	Fb	1 ∀D
5.	Fc	1 ∀D
6.	Fd	1 ∀D

As noted earlier, a tree constructed in this fashion can be continued indefinitely, for there is an infinite supply of substitution instances of '(∀x)Fx', and no tree rule is being misused. So long as '(∀x) ~ Fx' is not decomposed, the tree never closes. Clearly the above tree is, while allowed, a silly tree, for the inconsistency of the set being tested is quite obvious. The System prevents the construction of such trees and produces instead, in this case, the following tree:

1.	(∀x)Fx	SM
2.	(∀x) ~ Fx	SM
3.	Fa	1 ∀D
4.	~ Fa	2 ∀D
	×	

This tree illustrates an advantage of The System: It prevents us from endlessly and pointlessly decomposing one universally quantified sentence while ignoring other sentences on the branch. That is, Stage 2 places a restriction on how many instances of a universally quantified sentence we can enter before going on to work on other sentences. Moreover Stage 2 guarantees that we choose appropriate constants in doing Universal Decomposition. Hence Stage 2 prevents us from constructing trees such as the following:

1.	(∀x)Fx	SM
2.	(∀x) ~ Fx	SM
3.	Fa	1 ∀D
4.	~ Fb	2 ∀D
5.	Fc	1 ∀D
6.	~ Fd	2 ∀D

This tree could also be continued indefinitely without closing. But it is not a systematic tree. Were we to use The System, Stage 2 would prevent us from constructing such a tree by requiring that, at line 4, '(∀x) ~ Fx' be decomposed to a substitution instance formed from a constant already on the branch. The only such constant is 'a', and entering '~ Fa' at line 4 would close the tree.

Here is a systematic tree for the set {(∀x)(∃y)Fxy, Ga & ~ (∃y)Fay}:

1.	(∀x)(∃y)Fxy		SM
2.	Ga & ~ (∃y)Fay ✓		SM
3.	Ga		2 &D
4.	~ (∃y)Fay ✓		2 &D
5.	(∀y) ~ Fay		4 ~ ∃D
6.	(∃y)Fay ✓		1 ∀D
7.	~ Faa		5 ∀D
8.	Faa	Fab	6 ∃D2
9.	×	~ Fab	5 ∀D
		×	

The tree closes the second time we pass through Stage 2.

Though The System is not a mechanical method, it does, as these examples illustrate, yield either closed or finite completed open branches when such are forthcoming. And, since The System is reliable in the aforementioned sense, it should be used when one does not see how to close a branch or produce a completed open branch without using The System. This is usually not so in cases as simple as the ones we have just considered. It should, moreover, be remembered that The System is not as economical as it is reliable. Frequently strict adherence to it produces more complex trees than are necessary to establish the desired result.

In Section 9.4 we constructed two trees for the set {(∀x) ~ Bx, B*f*(c)}:

1.	(∀x) ~ Bx	SM
2.	B*f*(c)	SM
3.	~ B*f*(c)	1 ∀D
	×	

and

1.	(∀x) ~ Bx		SM
2.	B*f*(c)		SM
3.	~ Bc		1 ∀D
4.	c = *f*(c)	d = *f*(c)	2 CTD
5.	Bc		4, 2 =D
6.	×	Bd	4, 2 =D
7.		~ Bd	1 ∀D
		×	

Both are legitimate trees and both establish the inconsistency of the set being tested. However, only the first tree, which is the simpler of the two, is a systematic tree. This illustrates the reason we include, in Stage 2 of The System for *PLE*, the instruction that universally quantified sentences be decomposed to substitution instances formed from closed complex terms if and only if doing so produces a closed branch. Were that instruction omitted, the second of the above trees would be a systematic tree.

In Section 9.4 we constructed the following tree, which is also a systematic tree:

1.	~ (∃x)x = *g*(a)✓	SM
2.	(∀x) ~ x = *g*(a)	1 ~ ∃D
3.	~ a = *g*(a)	2 ∀D
4.	~ *g*(a) = *g*(a)	2 ∀D
	×	

Without the Stage 2 instruction concerning complex terms, The System would again yield a more complex tree:

1.	~ (∃x)x = *g*(a)✓		SM
2.	(∀x) ~ x = *g*(a)		1 ~ ∃D
3.	~ a = *g*(a)		2 ∀D
4.	a = *g*(a)	b = *g*(a)	3 CTD
5.	×	b = b	4, 4 =D
6.		~ b = *g*(a)	2 ∀D
		×	

The point we are here illustrating is that, while following The System often produces longer trees than not following it, the reverse is also sometimes true.

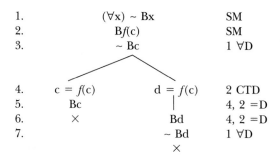

The sentence '$(\forall x)(\exists y)y = f(f(x))$' is quantificationally true. So the truth-tree for the negation of that sentence should close, and it does:

1.	$\sim (\forall x)(\exists y)y = f(f(x))$ ✓	SM
2.	$(\exists x) \sim (\exists y)y = f(f(x))$ ✓	1 $\sim \forall$D
3.	$\sim (\exists y)y = f(f(a))$ ✓	2 $\exists$D2
4.	$(\forall y) \sim y = f(f(a))$	3 $\sim \exists$D
5.	$\sim a = f(f(a))$	4 $\forall$D
6.	$\sim f(f(a)) = f(f(a))$	4 $\forall$D
	×	

This is a systematic tree. We closed the tree by taking advantage of the instruction in The System that a universally quantified sentence be decomposed to a substitution instance formed from a complex term if and only if doing so closes the branch. So we decompose the universally quantified sentence on line 4 to the substitution instance formed from '$f(f(a))$', and the one branch closes. Were we to remove the instruction dealing with decomposing universally quantified sentences to substitution instances formed from complex terms, the resulting systematic tree for '$(\forall x)(\exists y)y = f(f(x))$' would be substantially more complicated. Here it is:

1.			$\sim (\forall x)(\exists y)y = f(f(x))$ ✓		SM
2.			$(\exists x) \sim (\exists y)y = f(f(x))$ ✓		1 $\sim \forall$D
3.			$\sim (\exists y)y = f(f(a))$ ✓		2 $\exists$D2
4.			$(\forall y) \sim y = f(f(a))$		3 $\sim \exists$D
5.			$\sim a = f(f(a))$		4 $\forall$D
6.	$a = f(a)$		$b = f(a)$		5 CTD
7.	$\sim a = f(a)$		$\sim a = f(b)$		6, 5 =D
8.	×		$b = b$		6, 6 =D
9.			$\sim b = f(f(a))$		4 $\forall$D
10.		$a = f(b)$	$b = f(b)$	$c = f(b)$	7 CTD
11.		$\sim a = a$	$\sim a = b$	$\sim a = c$	10, 7 =D
12.		×	$\sim b = f(b)$	$\sim b = f(b)$	6, 9 =D
13.			$\sim b = b$	$\sim b = c$	10, 12 =D
			×	$c = c$	10, 10 =D
14.				$\sim c = f(f(a))$	4 $\forall$D
15.				$\sim c = f(b)$	6, 14 =D
16.				$\sim c = c$	10, 15 =D
				×	

As a final example we shall construct a substantially more complicated systematic tree. This tree establishes that the sentence '$(\exists x)(\exists y)Hg(x,y) \equiv (\exists x)(\exists y)Hg(y,x)$' is quantificationally true.

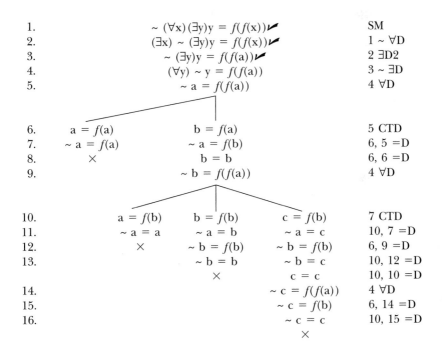

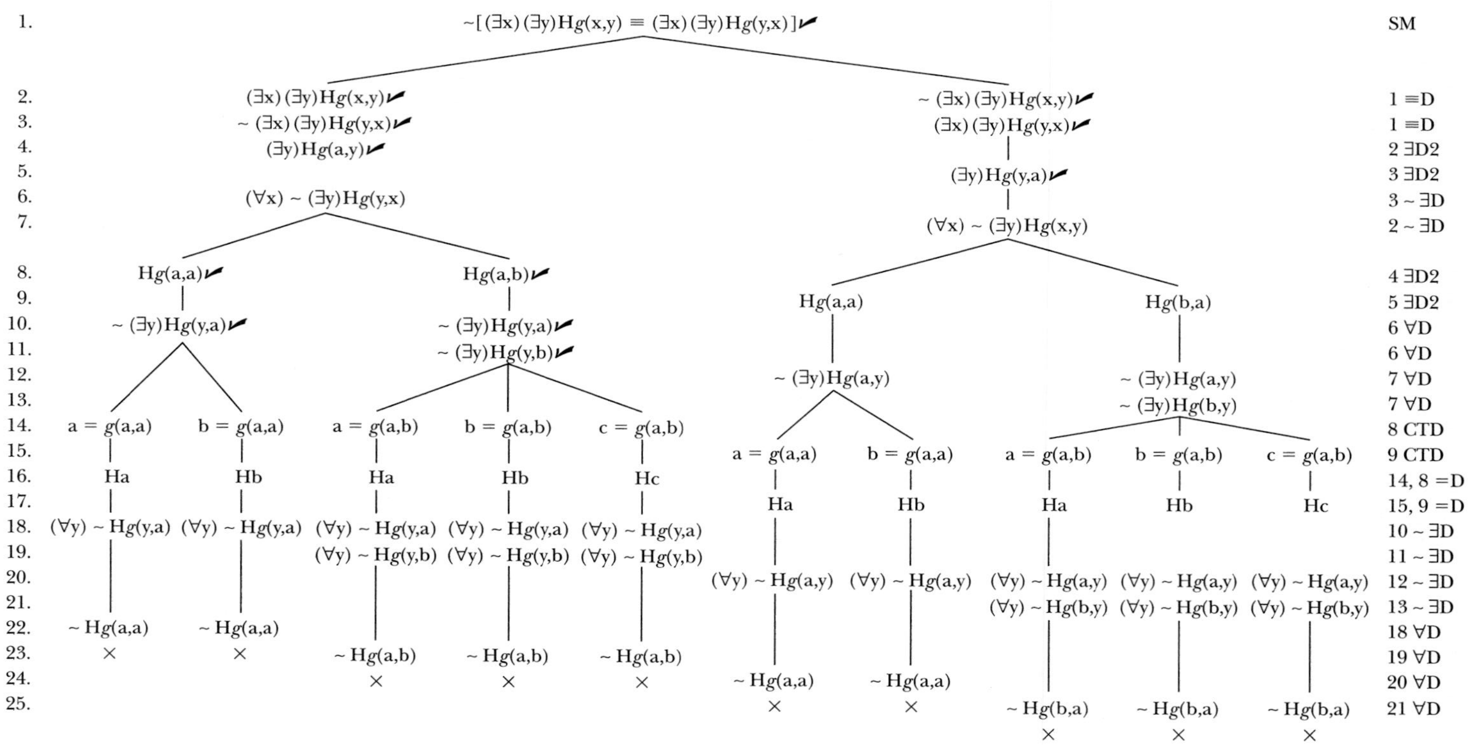
1. ~[(∃x)(∃y)Hg(x,y) ≡ (∃x)(∃y)Hg(y,x)] SM
2. (∃x)(∃y)Hg(x,y) ~ (∃x)(∃y)Hg(x,y) 1 ≡D
3. ~ (∃x)(∃y)Hg(y,x) (∃x)(∃y)Hg(y,x) 1 ≡D
4. (∃y)Hg(a,y) 2 ∃D2
5. (∃y)Hg(y,a) 3 ∃D2
6. (∀x) ~ (∃y)Hg(y,x) 3 ~ ∃D
7. (∀x) ~ (∃y)Hg(x,y) 2 ~ ∃D
8. Hg(a,a) Hg(a,b) 4 ∃D2
9. Hg(a,a) Hg(b,a) 5 ∃D2
10. ~ (∃y)Hg(y,a) ~ (∃y)Hg(y,a) 6 ∀D
11. ~ (∃y)Hg(y,b) 6 ∀D
12. ~ (∃y)Hg(a,y) ~ (∃y)Hg(a,y) 7 ∀D
13. ~ (∃y)Hg(b,y) 7 ∀D
14. a = g(a,a) b = g(a,a) a = g(a,b) b = g(a,b) c = g(a,b) 8 CTD
15. a = g(a,a) b = g(a,a) a = g(a,b) b = g(a,b) c = g(a,b) 9 CTD
16. Ha Hb Ha Hb Hc 14, 8 =D
17. Ha Hb Ha Hb Hc 15, 9 =D
18. (∀y) ~ Hg(y,a) (∀y) ~ Hg(y,a) (∀y) ~ Hg(y,a) (∀y) ~ Hg(y,a) (∀y) ~ Hg(y,a) 10 ~ ∃D
19. (∀y) ~ Hg(y,b) (∀y) ~ Hg(y,b) (∀y) ~ Hg(y,b) 11 ~ ∃D
20. (∀y) ~ Hg(a,y) (∀y) ~ Hg(a,y) (∀y) ~ Hg(a,y) (∀y) ~ Hg(a,y) (∀y) ~ Hg(a,y) 12 ~ ∃D
21. (∀y) ~ Hg(b,y) (∀y) ~ Hg(b,y) (∀y) ~ Hg(b,y) 13 ~ ∃D
22. ~ Hg(a,a) ~ Hg(a,a) 18 ∀D
23. × × ~ Hg(a,b) ~ Hg(a,b) ~ Hg(a,b) 19 ∀D
24. × × × ~ Hg(a,a) ~ Hg(a,a) 20 ∀D
25. × × ~ Hg(b,a) ~ Hg(b,a) ~ Hg(b,a) 21 ∀D
× × ×

We begin work on the tree by decomposing all the truth-functionally compound sentences and all the existentially quantified sentences on the tree, and all those that are added by doing those decompositions. This Stage-1 work takes us through line 9 of the tree. At that point we move to Stage 2 of The System and, on each branch, decompose all universally quantified sentences on that branch to substitution instances that can be formed from constants already on the branch. This takes us through line 13. We next move to Stage 3 and apply Complex Term Decomposition on each branch to every complex term occurring in a literal on that branch. We complete this stage at line 15. We move to Stage 4 and apply Identity Decomposition as directed at lines 16 and 17. At this point we have moved through The System once, but the tree has not closed and does not have a completed open branch. So we return, as instructed, to Stage 1. We apply Negated Existential Decomposition yielding lines 18–21. We then move to Stage 2 and apply Universal Decomposition, yielding lines 22–25. After these four applications of Universal Decomposition, every branch is closed, and we have a closed tree.

Note that The System specifies, at Stage 3, that we apply Complex Term Decomposition. We did so in this tree, even though the results (the introduction of the literals 'Ha', 'Hb', and 'Hc' on appropriate branches) play no role in closing any branch. It is common, with systematic trees, for a tree to contain entries that are not germane to the final result. This is the price we pay for being sure we explore all possibilities.

We have not given instructions for identifying a systematic tree that is caught in an endless cycle of decompositions and is such that it has only nonterminating branches. There are no such instructions because there is no effective test for quantificational consistency. We can only say that, if one has cycled through the stages of The System several times and there are still open branches, one should consider the possibility that the set has only infinite models and consider abandoning the tree. Abandoning a tree, again, constitutes a failure to find an answer to the question being asked. Having abandoned a tree, one can try to establish the consistency of the set in question by trying to find an interpretation on which all the members of the set are true.

9.5E EXERCISES

1. Construct systematic trees to determine, for each of the following sets, whether that set is quantificationally consistent. State your result. If you abandon a tree, explain why.

a. {(∀x)Jx, (∀x)(Jx ≡ (∃y)(Gyx ∨ Ky))}
*b. {(∀x)(Fx ⊃ Cx), ~ (∀x)(Fx & Cx)}
c. {(∃x)Fx, (∃x) ~ Fx}
*d. {~ (∀x) ~ Hx, (∀x)(Hx ⊃ Kx), ~ (∃x)(Kx & Hx)}

e. $\{(\exists x)Fx \,\&\, (\exists x) \sim Fx,\ (\exists x)Fx \supset (\forall x) \sim Fx\}$
*f. $\{(\exists x)Fx \,\&\, (\exists x) \sim Fx,\ (\forall x)Fx \supset (\forall x) \sim Fx\}$
g. $\{(\forall x)(\exists y)Fxy,\ (\exists y)(\forall x) \sim Fyx\}$
*h. $\{(\forall x)(\sim Gx \supset Fx),\ (\exists x)(Fx \,\&\, \sim Gx),\ Fa \supset \sim Ga\}$
i. $\{(\exists x)Hx,\ \sim (\forall x)Hx,\ (\forall x)(Hx \supset Kx),\ (\exists x)(Kx \,\&\, Hx)\}$
*j. $\{(\exists x)(\forall y)Lxy,\ (\exists x)(\forall y) \sim Lxy\}$
k. $\{(\forall x)(\exists y)Lxy,\ (\forall x)(\exists y) \sim Lxy\}$
*l. $\{(\forall x) \sim (\exists y)Lxy,\ (\forall w)(\forall y)(Swy \vee \sim Lwy),\ \sim (\exists x) \sim (\exists z)Sxz\}$
m. $\{(\forall x)(\exists y)Fxy,\ (\exists x)(\exists y) \sim Fxy\}$
*n. $\{(\forall x)(\forall y)(\forall z)((Hxy \,\&\, Hyz) \supset Hxz),\ (\forall x)(\forall y)(Hxy \supset Hyx),\ (\exists x) \sim Hxx\}$
o. $\{\sim (\forall x)(Kx \supset (\forall y)(Ky \vee Lxy)),\ (\forall y)(Ky \supset (\forall x)(Rx \supset Lyx)),\ (\forall x)Rx\}$
*p. $\{(\exists x)f(x) = f(a),\ (\forall x) \sim f(x) = f(b)\}$
q. $\{(\forall x)(\forall y)[\sim x = g(y) \supset Gxy],\ \sim (\exists x)Gax\}$
*r. $\{(\forall x)f(x) = f(a),\ \sim (\exists x)x = f(a)\}$
s. $\{(\exists x)(\exists y)Hf(x,y),\ \sim (\exists x)Hx\}$
*t. $\{(\exists x)(\forall y)x = f(y),\ (\exists x)(\forall y) \sim x = f(y)\}$
u. $\{(\forall x)Lxf(x),\ (\exists y) \sim Lf(y)y\}$
*v. $\{(\forall x)(Gx \supset Gh(x)),\ (\exists x)(Gx \,\&\, \sim Gh(x))\}$
w. $\{(\forall x)(Gx \supset \sim Gh(x)),\ (\exists x)(\sim Gx \,\&\, \sim Gh(x))\}$
*x. $\{(\forall x) \sim x = f(x),\ (\exists x)x = f(f(x))\}$

2. Show that the following sentences are not quantificationally true by constructing an appropriate systematic truth-tree.
a. $(\forall x)(Pf(x) \supset Px)$
*b. $(\forall x)(\forall y)(x = g(y) \vee y = g(x))$
c. $(\exists x)(\forall y)x = g(y)$
*d. $(\forall x) \sim x = f(x)$
e. $(\forall x)(\forall y)(Dh(x,y) \supset Dh(y,x))$

3. Show that the following sentences are quantificationally true by constructing an appropriate systematic tree.
a. $(\forall x)(\exists y)y = f(f(x))$
*b. $(\forall x)(\forall y)(\forall z)((y = f(x) \,\&\, z = f(x)) \supset y = z)$

4. Construct systematic trees to determine, for each of the following sentences, whether that sentence is quantificationally true, quantificationally false, or quantificationally indeterminate. In each case state your result. If you abandon a tree, explain why.
a. $(\forall x)(Fax \supset (\exists y)Fya)$
*b. $(\exists x) \sim Fx \supset (Fa \supset \sim Fb)$
c. $(\forall x)[Fx \supset (\forall y)(Hy \supset Fy)]$
*d. $(\exists y)(\forall x)Fxy \supset (\forall x)(\exists y)Fxy$
e. $(\exists x)(Fx \vee \sim Fx) \equiv ((\exists x)Fx \vee (\exists x) \sim Fx)$
*f. $(\forall x)(Fx \equiv [(\exists y)Gyx \supset H]) \supset (\forall x)[Fx \supset (\exists y)(Gyx \supset H)]$
g. $(\forall x)(Fx \supset [(\exists y)Gyx \supset H]) \supset (\forall x)[Fx \supset (\exists y)(Gyx \supset H)]$
*h. $(\forall x)Gf(x)x$
i. $(\forall x)(\exists y)y = f(f(x))$
*j. $(\forall x)(Fx \vee \sim Fg(x))$

5. Construct systematic trees to determine which of the following arguments are quantificationally valid. In each case state your result. If you abandon a tree, explain why.

a. Fa
$\underline{(\forall x)(Fx \supset Cx)}$
$(\forall x)(Fx \mathbin{\&} Cx)$

*b. $\underline{(\forall x)(Jx \lor Ixb) \lor (\forall x)(\exists y)(Hxy \supset Mx)}$
Iab

c. Fa
$\underline{(\forall x)(Fx \supset Cx)}$
$(\exists x)(Fx \mathbin{\&} Cx)$

*d. $\underline{\sim (\forall y)Kyy \lor (\forall x)Hxx}$
$(\exists x)(\sim Hxx \supset \sim Kxx)$

e. $(\forall x)(\forall y)(\forall z)[(Lxy \mathbin{\&} Lyz) \supset Lxz]$
$\underline{(\forall x)(\forall y)(Lxy \supset Lyx)}$
$(\forall x)Lxx$

*f. $(\forall x)(\forall y)(Fx \lor Gxy)$
$\underline{(\exists x)Fx}$
$(\exists x)(\exists y)Gxy$

g. $(\exists x)[(Lx \lor Sx) \lor Kx]$
$\underline{(\forall y) \sim (Ly \lor Ky)}$
$(\exists x)Sx$

*h. $(\exists x)((Lx \lor Sx) \lor Kx)$
$\underline{(\forall y) \sim (Ly \lor Ky)}$
$(\forall x)Sx$

i. $(\forall x)(Hx \supset Kcx)$
$(\forall x)(Lx \supset \sim Kcx)$
$\underline{Ld}$
$(\exists y) \sim Hy$

*j. $\underline{(\forall x)\ Pf(f(x))}$
$Pf(a)$

k. $(\exists x)(Fg(x) \mathbin{\&} \sim Hg(x))$
$\underline{(\forall x)(Fx \supset Hx)}$
$\sim Ra$

*l. $\underline{(\forall x)(Fx \lor Fg(x))}$
$(\forall x)(Fx \lor Fg(g(x)))$

m. $\underline{a = f(b) \mathbin{\&} b = f(a)}$
$(\exists x)(\exists y) \sim x = y$

*n. $(\forall x)[Fx \supset \sim (\exists y)Gxy]$
$\underline{(\exists y)Fg(y)}$
$(\exists y)Gyy$

o. $(\exists x)Hx$
$\underline{(\forall x)(Hx \supset (\exists y) \sim Hy)}$
$(\exists w) \sim Hg(w)$

6. Construct systematic trees to determine which of the following pairs of sentences are quantificationally equivalent. In each case state your result. If you abandon a tree, explain why.

a. $(\forall x)(\forall y) \sim Sxy$ $\qquad \sim (\exists x)(\exists y)Sxy$
*b. $(\forall x)(\exists y)Lxy$ $\qquad (\exists y)(\forall x)Lyx$
c. $(\exists x)(Ax \supset B)$ $\qquad (\forall x)Ax \supset B$
*d. $(\forall x)(Ax \supset B)$ $\qquad (\forall x)Ax \supset B$

e.	$(\forall x)(Ax \supset B)$	$(\exists x)Ax \supset B$
*f.	$(\exists x)(Ax \supset B)$	$(\exists x)Ax \supset B$
g.	$(\exists x)(\exists y)Hxy$	$(\exists y)(\exists x)Hxy$
*h.	$Labf(b)$	$Laf(b)b$
i.	$(\forall x)(\exists y)y = f(x)$	$(\forall x)(\exists y)x = f(y)$
*j.	$(\forall x)Bh(x)x$	$(\forall x)Bxh(x)$

7. Construct systematic trees to determine which of the following alleged entailments hold. In each case state your result. If you abandon a tree, explain why.

a. $\{(\forall x)(Fax \supset Fxa)\} \vDash Fab \vee Fba$

*b. $\{(\forall x)(\forall y)(Fx \vee Gxy), (\exists x)Fx\} \vDash (\exists x)(\exists y)Gxy$

c. $\{\sim Fa, (\forall x)(Fa \supset (\exists y)Gxy)\} \vDash \sim (\exists y)Gay$

*d. $\{(\exists x)(\forall y)Gxy\} \vDash (\forall y)(\exists x)Gxy$

e. $\{(\exists x)Gx, (\forall x)(Gx \supset Dxx)) \vDash (\exists x)(Gx \ \& \ (\forall y)Dxy)$

*f. $\{(\forall y)(\exists x)Gxy \vDash (\exists x)(\forall y)Gxy$

g. $\{(\forall x)(\forall y)x = g(x,y)\} \vDash (\forall x)x = g(x,x)$

*i. $\{(\exists x)(\forall y)x = g(y)\} \vDash h(a) = g(a)$

***8.** Show that if the members of a set Γ of sentences of *PL* contain only '~' and universal and existential quantifiers as logical operators, then Γ has no tree with more than one branch if the rule ∃D is used but may have a tree with more than one branch if ∃D2 is used.

9. Show that no closed truth-tree can have an infinite branch.

***10.** Could we replace Universal Decomposition and Existential Decomposition with the following two rules? Explain.

$(\forall \mathbf{x})\mathbf{P}$	$(\exists \mathbf{x})\mathbf{P}$
$\sim (\exists \mathbf{x}) \sim \mathbf{P}$	$\sim (\forall \mathbf{x}) \sim \mathbf{P}$

11. Let $\mathbf{P}(\mathbf{a}/\mathbf{x})$ be a substitution instance of some sentence $(\exists \mathbf{x})\mathbf{P}$ such that $\{\mathbf{P}(\mathbf{a}/\mathbf{x})\}$ has a closed tree. Does it follow that $\{(\exists \mathbf{x})\mathbf{P}\}$ has a closed tree? Explain.

***12.** Let $(\forall \mathbf{x})\mathbf{P}$ be a sentence such that, for every substitution instance $\mathbf{P}(\mathbf{a}/\mathbf{x})$, $\{\mathbf{P}(\mathbf{a}/\mathbf{x})\}$ has a closed tree. Does it follow that a systematic tree for $\{(\forall \mathbf{x})\mathbf{P}\}$ will close? Explain.

13. What would have to be done to make The System a mechanical procedure?

***14.** Suppose a tree for a set Γ of sentences of *PL* is abandoned without either closing or having a completed open branch. Suppose also that we find a model on which all the members of Γ are true. Suppose the model is an infinite model. Does it follow that all the open branches on the abandoned tree are nonterminating branches? Suppose the model is finite. Does anything follow regarding the abandoned tree?

SUMMARY

Key Semantic Properties

QUANTIFICATIONAL CONSISTENCY: A finite set Γ of sentences of *PL/PLE* is *quantificationally consistent* if and only if Γ has an open truth-tree.

QUANTIFICATIONAL INCONSISTENCY: A set Γ of sentences of *PL/PLE* is *quantificationally inconsistent* if and only if at least one finite subset of Γ has a closed truth-tree.

QUANTIFICATIONAL TRUTH: A sentence **P** of *PL/PLE* is *quantificationally true* if and only if the set {~ **P**} has a closed truth-tree.

QUANTIFICATIONAL FALSITY: A sentence **P** of *PL/PLE* is *quantificationally false* if and only if the set {**P**} has a closed truth-tree.

QUANTIFICATIONAL INDETERMINACY: A sentence **P** of *PL/PLE* is *quantificationally indeterminate* if and only if neither the set {**P**} nor the set {~ **P**} has a closed truth-tree.

QUANTIFICATIONAL EQUIVALENCE: Sentences **P** and **Q** of *PL/PLE* are *quantificationally equivalent* if and only if the set {~ **P** ≡ **Q**} has a closed truth-tree.

QUANTIFICATIONAL ENTAILMENT: A finite set Γ of sentences of *PL/PLE quantificationally entails* a sentence **P** of *PL/PLE* if and only if Γ ∪ {~ **P**} has a closed truth-tree.

QUANTIFICATIONAL VALIDITY: An argument of *PL/PLE* is *quantificationally valid* if and only if the set consisting of the premises and the negation of the conclusion has a closed truth-tree.

Key Truth-Tree Concepts

CLOSED BRANCH: A branch containing both an atomic sentence and the negation of that sentence.

CLOSED TRUTH-TREE: A tree each of whose branches is closed.

OPEN BRANCH: A branch that is not closed.

COMPLETED TRUTH-TREE: A truth-tree each of whose branches is either closed or is a completed open branch.

OPEN TRUTH-TREE: A truth-tree that is not closed.

COMPLETED OPEN BRANCH OF A TRUTH-TREE FOR A SET OF SENTENCES OF *PL*: A finite open branch on which each sentence is either

1. A literal (an atomic sentence or the negation of an atomic sentence)
2. Not a universally quantified sentence, and decomposed
3. A universally quantified sentence (∀**x**)**P** such that **P**(**a**/**x**) also occurs on that branch *for each constant* **a** occurring on the branch and at least one substitution instance **P**(**a**/**x**) occurs on the branch

(SECTION 9.4 ACCOUNT) COMPLETED OPEN BRANCH OF A TRUTH-TREE FOR A SET OF SENTENCES OF *PLE*: A finite open branch on which each sentence is either

1. A literal
2. Not a universally quantified sentence, and decomposed
3. A universally quantified sentence (∀**x**)**P** such that **P**(**t**/**x**) also occurs on that branch *for each closed individual term* **t** occurring on the branch and at least one substitution instance **P**(**t**/**x**) occurs on the branch
4. A sentence of the form $\mathbf{t}_1 = \mathbf{t}_2$, where $\mathbf{t}_1$ and $\mathbf{t}_2$ are closed terms such that the branch also contains, for every literal **P** on that branch containing $\mathbf{t}_2$, every sentence $\mathbf{P}(\mathbf{t}_1//\mathbf{t}_2)$ that can be obtained from **P** by Identity Decomposition

(SECTION 9.5 ACCOUNT) COMPLETED OPEN BRANCH OF A TRUTH-TREE FOR A SET OF SENTENCES OF *PLE*: A finite open branch on which each sentence is either

1. A literal
2. A sentence that has been decomposed and is neither a universally quantified sentence nor an identity sentence

3. A universally quantified sentence $(\forall \mathbf{x})\mathbf{P}$ such that $\mathbf{P}(\mathbf{a}/\mathbf{x})$ also occurs on that branch *for each constant* **a** occurring on the branch and $\mathbf{P}(\mathbf{a}/\mathbf{x})$ occurs on the branch for at least one constant **a**
4. A sentence of the form $\mathbf{a} = \mathbf{t}$ where **a** is an individual constant and **t** is a closed term and where the branch also contains, for every literal **P** on that branch containing **t**, every sentence $\mathbf{P}(\mathbf{a}//\mathbf{t})$ that can be obtained from **P** by Identity Decomposition

and on which Complex Term Decomposition has been applied to every closed complex term occurring in a literal on the branch that does not itself contain a complex term.

NONTERMINATING BRANCH: An open branch that never closes and will never, in a finite number of steps, become a completed open branch.

hapter

10

PREDICATE LOGIC: DERIVATIONS

).1 THE DERIVATION SYSTEM *PD*

A natural deduction system for predicate logic is developed in this chapter. The system, called *PD* (for *p*redicate *d*erivations), provides syntactic methods for evaluating sentences and sets of sentences of *PL*, just as the natural deduction system *SD* provides methods for evaluating sentences and sets of sentences of *SL*. The derivation rules of *PD* allow us to derive sentences on the basis of the *forms* of sentences. Although the derivation rules can be applied without having in mind any interpretation of the sentences in question, the derivation rules of *PD* were chosen with an eye to semantics. The derivation rules of *PD*, like the derivation rules of *SD*, are truth-preserving. Given the semantics developed for *PL*, the derivation rules of *PD* never lead us from true sentences to false ones.

The derivation rules of *PD* include all the derivation rules of *SD*, with the understanding that they apply to sentences of *PL*. For example, the following is a derivation in *PD*:

Derive: ~ (∀x)Hx

1	(∀x)Hx ⊃ ~ (∃y)Py	Assumption
2	(∃y)Py	Assumption
3	(∀x)Hx	Assumption
4	~ (∃y)Py	1, 3 ⊃E
5	(∃y)Py	2 R
6	~ (∀x)Hx	3–5 ~ I

PD has four additional derivation rules, which allow us to introduce and eliminate quantifiers.

ELIMINATION RULE FOR UNIVERSAL QUANTIFIERS

The elimination rule for universal quantifiers is *Universal Elimination* (sometimes called Universal Instantiation). To understand the basis of this rule, consider some informal reasoning showing that the conclusion of the following argument is a consequence of its premises:

All philosophers are somewhat strange.
Socrates is a philosopher.
___
Socrates is somewhat strange.

The first premise makes a universal claim: Each thing is such that if it is a philosopher then it is somewhat strange. It follows from this premise that if David Hume is a philosopher then David Hume is somewhat strange; and if Isaac Newton is a philosopher then Isaac Newton is somewhat strange; and if the Milky Way is a philosopher then the Milky Way is somewhat strange; and so forth. In this case we are interested in Socrates. It follows from the first premise that if Socrates is a philosopher then Socrates is somewhat strange. Since we have from the second premise the information that Socrates is a philosopher, we can conclude that Socrates is somewhat strange. The inference from a universal claim to a specific instance of it is captured in *PD* by the rule Universal Elimination (∀E). Here is a derivation for a symbolized version of the preceding argument in which the rule Universal Elimination is used.

Derive: Ss

1	(∀y) (Py ⊃ Sy)	Assumption
2	Ps	Assumption
3	Ps ⊃ Ss	1 ∀E
4	Ss	2, 3 ⊃E

Recall that a *substitution instance* of a quantified sentence is generated by removing the initial quantifier and replacing each occurrence of the free variable in the resulting open sentence with some one individual constant. Where

$(\forall \mathbf{x})\mathbf{P}$

is a sentence of *PL*,

$\mathbf{P}(\mathbf{a}/\mathbf{x})$

is used to designate a substitution instance of (∀**x**)**P**. The expression '**P**(**a**/**x**)' is read as '**P** with **a** (everywhere) in place of **x**'. Notice that **x** must occur in **P**, for (∀**x**)**P** is a sentence. The individual constant **a** in this case is called the *instantiating constant.* Thus the universally quantified sentence

(∀y) (Py ⊃ Sy)

has as a substitution instance

$$Ps \supset Ss$$

where 's' is the instantiating constant.

The derivation rule Universal Elimination permits us to derive a substitution instance of a universally quantified sentence from the universally quantified sentence. This rule is

Universal Elimination (∀E)

	$(\forall \mathbf{x})\mathbf{P}$
▷	$\mathbf{P}(\mathbf{a}/\mathbf{x})$

The individual constant employed in using Universal Elimination may or may not already occur in the quantified sentence. In the following case 't' does not occur in the universally quantified sentence, and it is proper to derive a substitution instance where 't' is the instantiating constant:

1	(∀x)Lxa	Assumption
2	Lta	1 ∀E

If everyone loves Alice, then it follows that Tom loves Alice. In the next case, 'a' does occur in the universally quantified sentence, and it is equally proper to derive a substitution instance where 'a' is the instantiating constant:

1	(∀x)Lxa	Assumption
2	Laa	1 ∀E

If everyone loves Alice, then it follows that Alice loves herself.

10.1.1**E** EXERCISES

1. Complete the following derivations.

a. Derive: Fa & Fb

1	(∀x)Fx	Assumption

*b. Derive: Kg

1	(∀x)(∀y)Hxy	Assumption
2	Hcf ⊃ Kg	Assumption

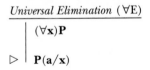

c. Derive: $\sim$ Qe

1	$(\forall z)Mz$	Assumption
2	$(\forall z) \sim Mz$	Assumption

*d. Derive: $Pi \supset Ai$

1	$(\forall z)(Px \equiv Tx)$	Assumption
2	$(\forall z)(Tz \equiv Az)$	Assumption

INTRODUCTION RULE FOR EXISTENTIAL QUANTIFIERS

The introduction rule for existential quantifiers is *Existential Introduction* (sometimes called Existential Generalization). Consider the following:

Gold is a metal that is precious.

There is a metal that is precious.

The conclusion follows from the premise, for it is a generalization from a specific instance. This kind of inference is reflected in *PL* by Existential Introduction ($\exists$I). Existential Introduction permits us to derive an existentially quantified sentence from a substitution instance of that sentence. Here is a derivation for a symbolized version of the preceding argument that uses Existential Introduction:

1	Mg & Pg	Assumption
2	$(\exists z)(Mz \& Pz)$	1 $\exists$I

More formally, where

$(\exists \mathbf{x})\mathbf{P}$

is a sentence of *PL*,

$\mathbf{P}(\mathbf{a}/\mathbf{x})$

is used to designate a substitution instance of $(\exists \mathbf{x})\mathbf{P}$. Hence the rule Existential Introduction is

Existential Introduction ($\exists$I)

	$\mathbf{P}(\mathbf{a}/\mathbf{x})$
▷	$(\exists \mathbf{x})\mathbf{P}$

This rule does not require that every occurrence of a given individual constant be generalized. For instance, the following derivations illustrate three proper uses of Existential Introduction:

1	Rmm	Assumption
2	(∃x)Rxx	1 ∃I

If Mount McKinley resembles Mount McKinley, then it follows that something resembles itself.

1	Rmm	Assumption
2	(∃x)Rxm	1 ∃I

If Mount McKinley resembles Mount McKinley, then it follows that something resembles Mount McKinley. And

1	Rmm	Assumption
2	(∃x)Rmx	1 ∃I

If Mount McKinley resembles Mount McKinley, then it follows that Mount McKinley resembles something. Notice that 'Rmm' is a substitution instance of '(∃x)Rxx', of '(∃x)Rxm', and of '(∃x)Rmx'. In each of these three cases, 'Rmm' is the result of dropping the quantifier '(∃x)' and rewriting the rest with the instantiating constant 'm' replacing every occurrence of the individual variable 'x'. Of course, the inference is not from the existentially quantified sentence to its substitution instance, but the other way around—*from* the substitution instance *to* the existentially quantified sentence.

10.1.2**E** EXERCISES

1. Complete the following derivations.

a. Derive: (∃x)(Ax & Jx)

1	Jc	Assumption
2	Ac	Assumption

*b. Derive: (∃x)Fxax

1	Faaa	Assumption

c. Derive: $(\exists y)(\exists z)Cyz$

1	$(\forall w)(\forall z)Cwz$	Assumption

*d. Derive: Wf

1	$(\forall x)Sx$	Assumption
2	$(\exists z)Sz \supset (\forall z)Wz$	Assumption

INTRODUCTION RULE FOR UNIVERSAL QUANTIFIERS

The introduction rule for universal quantifiers is *Universal Introduction* (sometimes called Universal Generalization). To understand the basis for this rule, consider the reasoning we might use to show that the conclusion of this argument follows from its premises:

> Anybody who has run the distance of a marathon has run over 20 miles.
>
> Anybody who has run over 20 miles has great stamina.
>
> ---
>
> Anybody who has run the distance of a marathon has great stamina.

Informally we can show that the conclusion of the argument follows from the premises by reasoning about a specific individual, say, Kerry. From the first premise we can infer that if Kerry has run the distance of a marathon then Kerry has run over 20 miles. From the second premise we can infer that if Kerry has run over 20 miles then Kerry has great stamina. Hence it follows that if Kerry has run the distance of a marathon then Kerry has great stamina. So far our reasoning has been about Kerry. However, Kerry was arbitrarily selected. Any other individual could have been chosen, and the reasoning carried out in an analogous manner. For example, if Chris had been selected, then our reasoning would have led to the result that if Chris has run the distance of a marathon then Chris has great stamina. If we had picked Sir Walter Raleigh, then our reasoning would have led to the result that if Sir Walter Raleigh has run the distance of a marathon then Sir Walter Raleigh has great stamina. In short, although we have reasoned about a specific individual, the result is completely general in that it holds for every individual. No special information about Kerry was used. Therefore we can generalize to the claim that each individual is such that if he or she has run the distance of a marathon then he or she has great stamina.

Universal Introduction ($\forall$I) is a rule of inference that permits the derivation of a universally quantified sentence from a substitution instance of that sentence. Here is a derivation for a symbolized version of the preceding argument that uses Universal Introduction:

Derive: $(\forall x)(Dx \supset Sx)$

1	$(\forall x)(Dx \supset Ox)$	Assumption
2	$(\forall x)(Ox \supset Sx)$	Assumption
3	$Dk \supset Ok$	1 $\forall$E
4	$Ok \supset Sk$	2 $\forall$E
5	Dk	Assumption
6	Ok	3, 5 $\supset$E
7	Sk	4, 6 $\supset$E
8	$Dk \supset Sk$	5–7 $\supset$I
9	$(\forall x)(Dx \supset Sx)$	8 $\forall$I

In this derivation 'k' is the instantiating constant on lines 3 and 4. The constant 'k' has been *arbitrarily selected,* in the sense that any other individual constant could have been selected to produce an analogous result on line 8. Since 'k' does not occur in any undischarged assumption of the derivation, we did not use any special information about any individual that 'k' may designate. So the result obtained on line 8 can be generalized. Universal Introduction allows us to derive the universally quantified sentence of which the sentence on line 8 is a substitution instance.

Now let us examine a case in which the result obtained cannot be generalized:

> Phidippides, a Greek messenger, has run the distance of a marathon and has announced the Greek victory to the Athenians.
>
> Anybody who has run the distance of a marathon has run over 20 miles.
>
> Anybody who has run over 20 miles has great stamina.

From the first sentence we infer that Phidippides has run the distance of a marathon. From the second sentence we infer that if Phidippides has run the distance of a marathon, then Phidippides has run over 20 miles. Hence it follows that Phidippides has run over 20 miles. From the third sentence we infer that if Phidippides has run over 20 miles, then Phidippides has great stamina. Hence we conclude that Phidippides has great stamina. This conclusion certainly follows from the sentences. However, suppose we now generalize from the result that Phidippides has great stamina to the claim that everyone has great stamina. This generalization is *not* justified. In this case the individual is *not* arbitrarily selected, for analogous results cannot be obtained for every other individual. For instance, we cannot infer that Kerry has great stamina because the sentences do not contain the information that Kerry is a runner who has run the distance of a marathon. We cannot use the sentences to obtain this result about Chris or Sir Walter Raleigh or any individual except Phidippides. Consequently, to generalize from this result would be a mistake. A derivation that formalizes our reasoning about Phidippides is

1	Gp & (Dp & Ap)	Assumption
2	(∀x)(Dx ⊃ Ox)	Assumption
3	(∀x)(Ox ⊃ Sx)	Assumption
4	Dp & Ap	1 &E
5	Dp	4 &E
6	Dp ⊃ Op	2 ∀E
7	Op	5, 6 ⊃E
8	Op ⊃ Sp	3 ∀E
9	Sp	7, 8 ⊃E

Because in this derivation 'p' is not an arbitrarily selected constant, Universal Introduction cannot be applied to 'Sp' on line 9 to obtain '(∀x)Sx'. The constant 'p' is not arbitrarily selected, for it occurs in the first assumption, and this information is used to derive 'Sp' on line 9. Notice that, given these assumptions, similar derivations for 'Sk', 'Sc', and 'Sr' are not possible.

The rule Universal Introduction is

Universal Introduction (∀I)

	P(**a**/**x**)
▷	(∀**x**)**P**

provided that

(i) **a** does not occur in an undischarged assumption.
(ii) **a** does not occur in (∀**x**)**P**.

The restrictions placed on the rule are important, for if followed, they ensure that the constant is arbitrarily selected. For instance, in the preceding derivation Universal Introduction cannot be applied to the sentence on line 9 because 'p' occurs in an undischarged assumption on line 1. Applying the rule in this case would violate the first restriction. Here are two simple examples of what can happen if the restrictions on Universal Introduction are not observed. The first restriction decrees that the relevant individual constant not occur in any currently undischarged assumption. The following move is therefore mistaken:

1	Et	Assumption	
2	(∀x)Ex	1 ∀I	**MISTAKE!**

It does not follow from the fact that 2 is even that all numbers are even.

The second restriction tells us that the relevant individual constant cannot occur in the resulting universally quantified sentence. Here is what can happen if it does:

1	$(\forall x)Exx$	Assumption	
2	Ess	1 $\forall$E	
3	$(\forall x)Exs$	2 $\forall$I	**MISTAKE!**

Every number is equal to itself. But it does not follow that every number is equal to 7.

For a further illustration of the use of Universal Introduction and the other derivation rules introduced so far, consider this argument:

Everyone loves a lover.

Tom loves Alice.

Everyone loves everyone.

A derivation for a symbolized version of this argument, where we restrict the universe of discourse to persons, is given here:

Derive: $(\forall x)(\forall y)Lxy$

1	$(\forall z)(\forall y)((\exists w)Lyw \supset Lzy)$	Assumption
2	Lta	Assumption
3	$(\exists w)Ltw$	2 $\exists$I
4	$(\forall y)((\exists w)Lyw \supset Ljy)$	1 $\forall$E
5	$(\exists w)Ltw \supset Ljt$	4 $\forall$E
6	Ljt	3, 5 $\supset$E
7	$(\exists w)Ljw$	6 $\exists$I
8	$(\forall y)((\exists w)Lyw \supset Lky)$	1 $\forall$E
9	$(\exists w)Ljw \supset Lkj$	8 $\forall$E
10	Lkj	7, 9 $\supset$E
11	$(\forall y)Lky$	10 $\forall$I
12	$(\forall x)(\forall y)Lxy$	11 $\forall$I

Notice that Universal Introduction cannot be applied to 'Lta' on line 2 to derive '$(\forall y)Lty$', for 'a' occurs in an undischarged assumption, namely, the one on line 2. Moreover Universal Introduction cannot be applied to 'Ljt' on line 6 to derive '$(\forall y)Ljy$' since 't' occurs in an undischarged assumption, again on line 2. To derive '$(\forall x)(\forall y)Lxy$', we first need to derive an atomic sentence with the predicate 'L' and two individual constants that do not occur in any undischarged assumption. The expression 'Lkj' is such a sentence, and it is derived on line 10. The sentence 'Lkj' can be used to derive '$(\forall y)Lky$' by Universal Introduction since 'j' does not occur in an undischarged assumption and does not occur in '$(\forall y)Lky$'. Finally Universal Introduction is applied to '$(\forall y)Lky$' to derive '$(\forall x)(\forall y)Lxy$' on line 12. This is allowed since 'k' does not occur in an undischarged assumption or in the derived sentence on line 12.

The kind of reasoning suggested by Universal Introduction occurs in mathematics. A mathematician might arbitrarily select a prime number and show that there is a larger prime number. The mathematician can then generalize this result; that is, he or she can assert that for every prime number there is a larger prime number. However, in order to generalize properly, the mathematician must be careful that the prime number is indeed arbitrarily selected in the sense that no special properties of that number other than the fact that it is prime are appealed to. If the mathematician chooses the number 5 and notes that 5 is less than 7, it would clearly be incorrect for him or her to generalize that all prime numbers are less than 7. Generalization is legitimate only if any prime number could have been chosen and an analogous result obtained for it. Similarly, in using Universal Introduction, we must be sure that the instantiating constant is arbitrarily selected. If the restrictions on the rule are not violated, we can be sure that the constant is arbitrarily chosen.

10.1.3E EXERCISES

1. Complete the following derivations.

a. Derive: (∀y)Hy

1	(∀x)Hx	Assumption

*b. Derive: (∀y)(Hyy & By)

1	(∀y)Hyy	Assumption
2	(∀z)Bz	Assumption

c. Derive: (∀x)(∃x ⊃ Kx)

1	(∀x)(Ex ⊃ Sx)	Assumption
2	(∀x)(Sx ⊃ Kx)	Assumption

*d. Derive: (∀w) ~ Bw

1	(∀z)(∀y)Lzy	Assumption
2	(∀x)(∀y)(Lxy ⊃ ~ Bx)	Assumption

ELIMINATION RULE FOR EXISTENTIAL QUANTIFIERS

The elimination rule for existential quantifiers is *Existential Elimination* (sometimes called Existential Instantiation). To introduce this rule, we consider the following argument:

> If anybody is a genius, then Einstein is.
> Somebody is a genius.
> ___
> Einstein is a genius.

The derivation for a standard symbolization of this argument is quite simple:

Derive: Ge

1	$(\exists x)Gx \supset Ge$	Assumption
2	$(\exists x)Gx$	Assumption
3	Ge	1, 2 $\supset$E

But, as we noted in Chapter 7, a sentence like

> If anybody is a genius, then Einstein is a genius

can also be symbolized as

$$(\forall x)(Gx \supset Ge)$$

The derivation for the argument using this symbolization is somewhat more difficult. To understand it, consider how we might informally reason that the English version of the argument is valid. The second premise tells us that there is somebody who is a genius but not who he or she is. Let us suppose that Matt is a genius. From the first premise we can infer that if Matt is a genius then Einstein is a genius. Since we are assuming that Matt is a genius, we can conclude that Einstein is a genius. Of course, this conclusion is reached on the basis of an assumption that Matt is a genius, which may be false. But notice that reference to Matt played only an intermediary role. Any individual would have done, and the reasoning would have gone through just as well. Since the second premise guarantees that there is some individual who is a genius, we are sure that the conclusion follows and does not depend upon the assumption that it is Matt who is a genius. In *PD* Existential Elimination is the derivation rule that captures this kind of reasoning. Here is a derivation of a symbolized version of this argument that uses Existential Elimination ($\exists$E):

Derive: Ge

1	$(\forall x)(Gx \supset Ge)$	Assumption
2	$(\exists x)Gx$	Assumption
3	Gm	Assumption
4	$Gm \supset Ge$	1 $\forall$E
5	Ge	3, 4 $\supset$E
6	Ge	2, 3–5 $\exists$E

The derivation formalizes our previous reasoning. On line 3 a substitution instance of the existentially quantified sentence on line 2 is assumed. The conclusion, 'Ge', has been reached on line 5 but only under the assumption on line 3. The instantiating constant, 'm', does not occur in 'Ge'. The instantiating constant plays only an intermediary role; that is, any individual constant could have been used in place of 'm' to reach the result on line 5. On the basis of our assumption at line 2, '(∃x)Gx', we know that some individual is G. Hence Existential Elimination can be used to derive 'Ge' on line 6 by appealing to line 2 and the subderivation from line 3 to line 5.

The rule Existential Elimination is

Existential Elimination (∃E)

	(∃**x**)**P**	
		P(**a**/**x**)
		———
		Q
▷	**Q**	

provided that

(i) **a** does not occur in an undischarged assumption.
(ii) **a** does not occur in (∃**x**)**P**.
(iii) **a** does not occur in **Q**.

Notice that the sentence **Q** can be any sentence of *PL* as long as it does not contain the instantiating constant **a**. The sentence **Q** must occur as the last sentence of the subderivation immediately next to the scope line of the subderivation.

The restrictions for the rule Existential Elimination are important because they ensure that the instantiating constant employed in the assumption plays only an intermediary role. The following illustrates a violation of the first restriction:

1	Ef		Assumption	
2	(∃x)Ox		Assumption	
3		Of	Assumption	
4		Ef & Of	1, 3, &I	
5		(∃x)(Ex & Ox)	4 ∃I	
6	(∃x)(Ex & Ox)		2, 3–5 ∃E	**MISTAKE!**

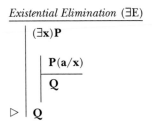

It is true that 4 is even (first assumption) and that some number is odd (second assumption). It does not follow that some number is even and odd. The mistake is in using the individual constant 'f' in the assumption on line 3 when it already occurs in an assumption on line 1. Notice that a similar derivation of the sentence on line 5 is not possible if the instantiating constant is other than ‘f’. Thus ‘f’ is playing more than an intermediary role in deriving the sentence on line 5.

Here is a violation of the second restriction:

1	$(\forall x)(\exists y)Lyx$	Assumption	
2	$(\exists y)Lyk$	1 ∀E	
3	$\quad$ Lkk	Assumption	
4	$\quad$ $(\exists x)Lxx$	3 ∃I	
5	$(\exists x)Lxx$	2, 3–4 ∃E	**MISTAKE!**

It is true that for every number there is a larger number, but it does not follow that some number is larger than itself. The existentially quantified sentence on line 2 indicates that there is a number larger than k. But the assumption on line 3 is that it is k that is larger than k. Here again the instantiating constant ‘k’ plays more than an intermediary role in deriving the sentence on line 4. A similar derivation of ‘(∃x)Lxx’ is not possible if ‘m’, for example, is used as the instantiating constant.

If the third restriction is violated, the attempted derivation can go astray as follows:

1	$(\exists x)Nx$	Assumption	
2	$\quad$ Nt	Assumption	
3	$\quad$ Nt	2 R	
4	Nt	1, 2–3 ∃E	**MISTAKE!**

It is true that some number is negative, but it does not follow that 2 is a negative number. The instantiating constant plays more than an intermediary role in deriving the sentence on line 3. A similar derivation of ‘Nt’ is not possible if any constant other than ‘t’ is used as the instantiating constant. As long as the restrictions for Existential Elimination are not violated, we can be sure that the instantiating constant plays only an intermediary role.

Consider the application of Existential Elimination in the derivation for a more complex argument:

France is a country that is bigger than Luxembourg.

Some country is bigger than France.

If one thing is bigger than a second and the second is bigger than a third, then the first is bigger than the third.

Some country is bigger than France and bigger than Luxembourg.

A symbolization and derivation for this argument are given here:

Derive: (∃z)[Cz & (Bzf & Bzl)]

1	Cf & Bfl	Assumption
2	(∃x)(Cx & Bxf)	Assumption
3	(∀x)(∀y)(∀z)[(Bxy & Byz) ⊃ Bxz]	Assumption
4	Cr & Brf	Assumption
5	Brf	4 &E
6	Bfl	1 &E
7	Brf & Bfl	5, 6 &I
8	(∀y)(∀z)[(Bry & Byz) ⊃ Brz]	3 ∀E
9	(∀z)[(Brf & Bfz) ⊃ Brz]	8 ∀E
10	(Brf & Bfl) ⊃ Brl	9 ∀E
11	Brl	7, 10 ⊃E
12	Brf & Brl	5, 11 &I
13	Cr	4 &E
14	Cr & (Brf & Brl)	13, 12 &I
15	(∃z)[Cz & (Bzf & Bzl)]	14 ∃I
16	(∃z)[Cz & (Bzf & Bzl)]	2, 4–15 ∃E

The second assumption is an existentially quantified sentence. A substitution instance of this existentially quantified sentence is assumed on line 4. The instantiating constant 'r' is new to the derivation. From this assumption the sentence on line 15, which does not contain an occurrence of 'r', is derived. Notice that 'r' plays only an intermediary role. Any other individual constant could have been used in place of 'r', and the sentence on line 15 derived. The assumption on line 4 is discharged by moving to the left at line 16, and Existential Elimination is then used to derive the sentence entered on line 16 by appeal to line 2 and the subderivation from line 4 to line 15.

10.1.4E EXERCISES

1. Complete the following derivations.

a. Derive: (∃y)(Zy ∨ Hy)

1	(∃x)Zx	Assumption

*b. Derive: (∃x)Lx

1	(∀x)(Fx ⊃ Lx)	Assumption
2	(∃x)Fx	Assumption

c. Derive: (∀x)(∃y)Bxy

1	(∃y)(∀x)Bxy	Assumption

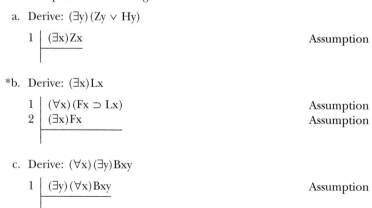

*d. Derive: (∃y)(∃x)Gxy

1	(∃x)(∃y)Gxy	Assumption

2. Given the following start of a derivation

1	(∀x)Saaxx	Assumption
2	Saabb	1 ∀E
3		

which of the following sentences could be derived on line 3 by one of the quantifier introduction or elimination rules?

a. Saacc
*b. Saaaa
c. Saaab
*d. (∃x)Saxbb
e. (∃x)Sxabb
*f. (∃y)Saayb
g. (∃w)Swwbb
*h. (∃x)Sxaxb
i. (∀x)Sxxbb
*j. (∀x)Saaxx
k. (∀x)Saxxb
*l. (∀z)Saabz

0.2 APPLYING THE DERIVATION RULES OF *PD*

Universal Introduction, Existential Introduction, Existential Elimination, and Universal Elimination are rules of inference that must be applied to entire sentences on earlier lines and, in the case of Existential Elimination, to entire subderivations as well. A common error is illustrated by the following:

1	(∀y)Cym ⊃ Em	Assumption	
2	Crm ⊃ Em	1 ∀E	**MISTAKE!**

It may be true that if everybody casts his or her ballot for Marty then Marty will be elected. But it does not follow that if Robinson casts her vote for Marty then Marty will be elected. The mistake here was in trying to apply the rule Universal Elimination to the antecedent of the sentence on line 1. Since the sentence on line 1 is not a universally quantified sentence, Universal Elimination cannot be used.

A similar error is illustrated by the following:

1	~ (∀x)Px	Assumption	
2	~ Pk	1 ∀E	**MISTAKE!**

It does not follow from the fact that not everyone has been president that John Kennedy has not been president. The sentence on line 1 is not a universally quantified sentence but the negation of a universally quantified sentence. Hence Universal Elimination cannot be applied to it.

10.2E EXERCISES

1. Complete the following derivations by entering the appropriate justification for each sentence.

a. Derive: (Mk & Gh) & Md

1 | (∀x)(Mx & Gx)
2 | Mk & Gk
3 | Mk
4 | Mh & Gh
5 | Gh
6 | Mk & Gh
7 | Md & Gd
8 | Md
9 | (Mk & Gh) & Md

*b. Derive: ~ (Jb & Qb)

1 | (∀z)(Jz ⊃ Lz)
2 | (∀w)(~ Qw ≡ Lw)
3 | | Jb & Qb
4 | | Jb
5 | | Jb ⊃ Lb
6 | | Lb
7 | | ~ Qb ≡ Lb
8 | | ~ Qb
9 | | Qb
10 | ~ (Jb & Qb)

c. Derive: (∃x)(~ Bxx ⊃ (∀z)Msz)

1 | Bnn ∨ (Kn & Lj)
2 | ~ (∀z)Msz ⊃ ~ Kn
3 | | ~ Bnn
4 | | | Bnn
5 | | | | ~ Kn
6 | | | | Bnn
7 | | | | ~ Bnn
8 | | | Kn
9 | | | Kn & Lj
10 | | | Kn
11 | | Kn
12 | | | ~ (∀z)Msz
13 | | | ~ Kn
14 | | | Kn
15 | | (∀z)Msz
16 | ~ Bnn ⊃ (∀z)Msz
17 | (∃x)(~ Bxx ⊃ (∀z)Msz)

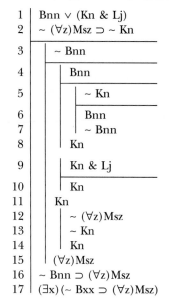

*d. Derive: Jaa

1	Kmm & ~ Cmr
2	(∃y) ~ (Kmy ⊃ Cyr) ⊃ (∀x)Jxx
3	Kmm ⊃ Cmr
4	Kmm
5	Cmr
6	~ Cmr
7	~ (Kmm ⊃ Cmr)
8	(∃y) ~ (Kmy ⊃ Cyr)
9	(∀x)Jxx
10	Jaa

e. Derive: ((∀x)Hxg ∨ Rg) ∨ Lg

1	(∀z)[(Rz ∨ (∀x)Hxz) ≡ Kzzz]
2	Kggg
3	(Rg ∨ (∀x)Hxg) ≡ Kggg
4	Rg ∨ (∀x)Hxg
5	Rg
6	(∀x)Hxg ∨ Rg
7	(∀x)Hxg
8	(∀x)Hxg ∨ Rg
9	(∀x)Hxg ∨ Rg
10	((∀x)Hxg ∨ Rg) ∨ Lg

*f. Derive: (∀w)(Lwg ∨ Jw)

1	(∀x)(Dxx ∨ Px)
2	(∀y) ~ Dyy
3	(∀z)(Pz ⊃ Jz)
4	~ Daa
5	Daa ∨ Pa
6	Pa ⊃ Ja
7	Daa
8	~ Ja
9	Daa
10	~ Daa
11	Ja
12	Pa
13	Ja
14	Ja
15	Lag ∨ Ja
16	(∀w)(Lwg ∨ Jw)

g. Derive: (∀w)(∃z) ~ (Hz & Rzw)

1 | (∀z)[Hz ⊃ (Rzz ⊃ Gz)]
2 | (∀z)(Gz ⊃ Bz) & (∀z) ~ Bz
---
3 | Ha ⊃ (Raa ⊃ Ga)
4 | (∀z)(Gz ⊃ Bz)
5 | Ga ⊃ Ba
6 | (∀z) ~ Bz
7 | | Ha & Raa
  | ---
8 | | Ha
9 | | Raa ⊃ Ga
10 | | Raa
11 | | Ga
12 | | Ba
13 | | ~ Ba
14 | ~ (Ha & Raa)
15 | (∃z) ~ (Hz & Rza)
16 | (∀w)(∃z) ~ (Hz & Rzw)

*h. Derive: (∃w) ~ Lwn

1 | (∃y)(My & Ry)
2 | (∀y)[Lyn ⊃ ~ (Ry ∨ Cy)]
---
3 | | Ma & Ra
  | ---
4 | | Lan ⊃ ~ (Ra ∨ Ca)
5 | | | Lan
  | | ---
6 | | | ~ (Ra ∨ Ca)
7 | | | Ra
8 | | | Ra ∨ Ca
9 | | ~ Lan
10 | | (∃w) ~ Lwn
11 | (∃w) ~ Lwn

i. Derive: Sc

1 | (∃x)Px ⊃ Sc
2 | (∃x)[Txx & (∃y)(Py & ~ Jy)]
---
3 | | Taa & (∃y)(Py & ~ Jy)
  | ---
4 | | (∃y)(Py & ~ Jy)
5 | | | Pb & ~ Jb
  | | ---
6 | | | Pb
7 | | | (∃x)Px
8 | | | Sc
9 | | Sc
10 | Sc

*j. Derive: (∃y) (∀w) (∃x) Hxxwyxx

1	(∀x) (∀y) (∃w) (∀z) Hwwxyzz	
2	(∀y) (∃w) (∀z) Hwwayzz	
3	(∃w) (∀z) Hwwabzz	
4	(∀z) Hccabzz	
5	Hccabcc	
6	(∃x) Hxxabxx	
7	(∃x) Hxxabxx	
8	(∀w) (∃x) Hxxwbxx	
9	(∃y) (∀w) (∃x) Hxxwyxx	

2. For each of the following find the *mistakes* in the application of the rules.

a. Derive: ~ Na

1	(∀x) Hx ⊃ ~ (∃y) Ky	Assumption
2	Ha ⊃ Na	Assumption
3	Ha	1 ∀E
4	Na	2, 3 ⊃E

*b. Derive: (∀x) (Bx & Mx)

1	Bk	Assumption
2	(∀x) Mx	Assumption
3	Mk	2 ∀E
4	Bk & Mk	1, 3 &I
5	(∀x) (Bx & Mx)	4 ∀I

c. Derive: (∃x) Zx

1	(∃x) Qx	Assumption
2	(∀x) (Zx ≡ Qx)	Assumption
3	Zd ≡ Qd	2 ∀E
4	Qd	1 ∃E
5	Zd	3, 4 ≡E
6	(∃x) Zx	5 ∃I

*d. Derive: (∃x) Gx

1	(∀x) (Fx ⊃ Gx)	Assumption
2	~ (∃x) Fx	Assumption
3	Fi	Assumption
4	Fi ⊃ Gi	1 ∀E
5	Gi	3, 4 ⊃E
6	(∃x) Gx	5 ∃I
7	(∃x) Gx	2, 3–6 ∃E

e. Derive: (∀x)(Jx & Gc) ∨ Lc

1	(∀x)(∀y)(Jx & Gy)	Assumption
2	(∀x)(Jx & Gc)	1 ∀E
3	(∀x)(Jx & Gc) ∨ Lc	2 ∨I

*f. Derive: (∃y)Sy

1	(∀x)(∃y)(Dx & Sy)	Assumption
2	(∃y)(Da & Sy)	1 ∀E
3	Da & Sz	Assumption
4	Sz	3 &E
5	(∃y)Sy	4 ∃I
6	(∃y)Sy	2, 3–5 ∃E

g. Derive: (∃x)(∃z)Azx

1	(∃w)(∃y)Awy	Assumption
2	(∃y)Aky	Assumption
3	Aka	Assumption
4	(∃z)Aza	3 ∃I
5	(∃z)Aza	2, 3–4 ∃E
6	(∃x)(∃z)Azx	5 ∃I
7	(∃x)(∃z)Azx	1, 2–6 ∃E

*h. Derive: ~ Sg

1	(∀x)Rxx	Assumption
2	(∀x)(∀y)Rxy ⊃ ~ Sg	Assumption
3	Raa	1 ∀E
4	(∀y)Ray	3 ∀I
5	(∀x)(∀y)Rxy	4 ∀I
6	~ Sg	2, 5 ⊃E

10.3 BASIC CONCEPTS OF *PD*

The basic concepts for the system *PD* are analogous to the basic concepts for the system *SD* introduced in Chapter 5. A *derivation in PD* is a finite series of sentences of *PL* in which each sentence either is taken as an assumption with an indication of its scope or is justified by one of the rules of *PD*. As illustrated in the previous sections, derivations in *PL* are constructed in the same format as derivations in *SD*, that is, with line numbers, justifications, scope lines, and so on. The concept of derivability is also defined in a similar way.

> A sentence **P** of *PL* is *derivable in PD* from a set Γ of sentences of *PL* if and only if there is a derivation in *PD* in which all the primary assumptions are members of Γ and **P** occurs in the scope of only those assumptions.

Suppose we wish to show that

$$(\exists z)Mz$$

is derivable in *PD* from the set of sentences

$$\{(\forall x)((\exists y)Lxy \supset (\exists y) \sim Jy),\ (\exists y)(\exists z)Lyz,\ (\forall x)(\sim Jx \equiv Mx)\}$$

That is, expressed in terms of the turnstile notation, we wish to show that

$$\{(\forall x)((\exists y)Lxy \supset (\exists y) \sim Jy),\ (\exists y)(\exists z)Lyz,\ (\forall x)(\sim Jx \equiv Mx)\} \vdash (\exists z)Mz$$

We begin by taking the members of the set as assumptions and proceed to derive '$(\exists z)Mz$':

Derive: $(\exists z)Mz$

1	$(\forall x)((\exists y)Lxy \supset (\exists y) \sim Jy)$	Assumption
2	$(\exists y)(\exists z)Lyz$	Assumption
3	$(\forall x)(\sim Jx \equiv Mx)$	Assumption
4	$\quad(\exists z)Lmz$	Assumption
5	$\quad\quad Lmn$	Assumption
6	$\quad\quad(\exists y)Lmy \supset (\exists y) \sim Jy$	1 $\forall$E
7	$\quad\quad(\exists y)Lmy$	5 $\exists$I
8	$\quad\quad(\exists y) \sim Jy$	6, 7 $\supset$E
9	$\quad\quad\quad \sim Ji$	Assumption
10	$\quad\quad\quad \sim Ji \equiv Mi$	3 $\forall$E
11	$\quad\quad\quad Mi$	9, 10 $\equiv$E
12	$\quad\quad\quad(\exists z)Mz$	11 $\exists$I
13	$\quad\quad(\exists z)Mz$	8, 9–12 $\exists$E
14	$\quad(\exists z)Mz$	4, 5–13 $\exists$E
15	$(\exists z)Mz$	2, 4–14 $\exists$E

Although additional assumptions have been made in the derivation, they have all been discharged by the end of the derivation so that '$(\exists z)Mz$' on line 15 lies in the scope of only the primary assumptions. Hence '$(\exists z)Mz$' is derivable in *PD* from the given set of sentences.

The definition of validity in *PL* is as follows:

> An argument of *PL* is *valid in PD* if and only if the conclusion of the argument is derivable in *PD* from the set consisting of the premises. An argument of *PL* is *invalid in PD* if and only if it is not valid in *PD*.

This definition simply formalizes a concept we have been using informally. To show that an argument is valid in *PD*, we take its premises as primary assumptions and derive its conclusion so that the only undischarged assumptions are primary assumptions. Consider the argument

Only people who are neither wealthy nor famous are logicians.
Anybody who doesn't need to ask the price of anything is wealthy.

Logicians need to ask the price of something.

This argument can be symbolized as

$$(\forall x)(Lx \supset [Px \,\&\, (\sim Wx \,\&\, \sim Fx)])$$
$$(\forall x)[(Px \,\&\, \sim (\exists y)Nxy) \supset Wx]$$

$$(\forall x)(Lx \supset (\exists y)Nxy)$$

The symbolized argument is shown to be valid in *PL* by the following derivation:

Derive: $(\forall x)(Lx \supset (\exists y)Nxy)$

1	$(\forall x)(Lx \supset [Px \,\&\, (\sim Wx \,\&\, \sim Fx)])$	Assumption
2	$(\forall x)[(Px \,\&\, \sim (\exists y)Nxy) \supset Wx]$	Assumption
3	$\quad Lb$	Assumption
4	$\quad\quad \sim (\exists y)Nby$	Assumption
5	$\quad\quad Lb \supset [Pb \,\&\, (\sim Wb \,\&\, \sim Fb)]$	1 ∀E
6	$\quad\quad Pb \,\&\, (\sim Wb \,\&\, \sim Fb)$	3, 5 ⊃E
7	$\quad\quad \sim Wb \,\&\, \sim Fb$	6 &E
8	$\quad\quad \sim Wb$	7 &E
9	$\quad\quad Pb$	6 &E
10	$\quad\quad Pb \,\&\, \sim (\exists y)Nby$	9, 4 &I
11	$\quad\quad (Pb \,\&\, \sim (\exists y)Nby) \supset Wb$	2 ∀E
12	$\quad\quad Wb$	10, 11 ⊃E
13	$\quad (\exists y)Nby$	4–12 ~ E
14	$Lb \supset (\exists y)Nby$	3–13 ⊃I
15	$(\forall x)(Lx \supset (\exists y)Nxy)$	14 ∀I

Although auxiliary assumptions are made in the derivation, they are discharged by the end of the derivation. The conclusion of the argument on the last line of the derivation lies in the scope of only primary assumptions that are the premises of the argument.

A special case of deriving a sentence from a set of sentences occurs when the set is the empty set.

> A sentence **P** of *PL* is a *theorem in PD* if and only if **P** is derivable in *PD* from the empty set.

So to demonstrate that

$$(\forall x)(Hxx \supset (\exists y)Gy) \equiv ((\exists x)Hxx \supset (\exists y)Gy)$$

is a theorem, that is, to show that

$$\vdash (\forall x)(Hxx \supset (\exists y)Gy) \equiv ((\exists x)Hxx \supset (\exists y)Gy)$$

we might construct the following derivation:

Derive: $(\forall x)(Hxx \supset (\exists y)Gy) \equiv ((\exists x)Hxx \supset (\exists y)Gy)$

1	$(\forall x)(Hxx \supset (\exists y)Gy)$	Assumption
2	$(\exists x)Hxx$	Assumption
3	Hkk	Assumption
4	$Hkk \supset (\exists y)Gy$	1 $\forall$E
5	$(\exists y)Gy$	3, 4 $\supset$E
6	$(\exists y)Gy$	2, 3–5 $\exists$E
7	$(\exists x)Hxx \supset (\exists y)Gy$	2–6 $\supset$I
8	$(\exists x)Hxx \supset (\exists y)Gy$	Assumption
9	Hkk	Assumption
10	$(\exists x)Hxx$	9 $\exists$I
11	$(\exists y)Gy$	8, 10 $\supset$E
12	$Hkk \supset (\exists y)Gy$	9–11 $\supset$I
13	$(\forall x)(Hxx \supset (\exists y)Gy)$	12 $\forall$I
14	$(\forall x)(Hxx \supset (\exists y)Gy) \equiv ((\exists x)Hxx \supset (\exists y)Gy)$	1–7, 8–13 $\equiv$I

During the derivation we made several assumptions, but by the end of the derivation the assumptions were all discharged. There are no primary assumptions in the derivation. Hence the sentence on the last line is a theorem in *PD*.

Equivalence in *PD* is defined as follows:

> Sentences **P** and **Q** of *PL* are *equivalent in PD* if and only if **Q** is derivable in *PD* from {**P**} and **P** is derivable in *PD* from {**Q**}.

To show that the two sentences

$$(\forall x)(Ax \supset Bx)$$

and

$$(\forall x)(\sim Bx \supset \sim Ax)$$

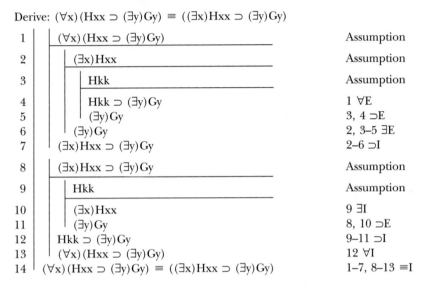

are equivalent in *PD*, we construct two derivations. We derive the second sentence from the first:

Derive: (∀x)(~ Bx ⊃ ~ Ax)

1	(∀x)(Ax ⊃ Bx)	Assumption
2	~ Ba	Assumption
3	Aa	Assumption
4	Aa ⊃ Ba	1 ∀E
5	Ba	3, 4 ⊃E
6	~ Ba	2 R
7	~ Aa	3–6 ~ I
8	~ Ba ⊃ ~ Aa	2–7 ⊃I
9	(∀x)(~ Bx ⊃ ~ Ax)	8 ∀I

so that the only undischarged assumption is the first sentence. Then we derive the first sentence from the second:

Derive: (∀x)(Ax ⊃ Bx)

1	(∀x)(~ Bx ⊃ ~ Ax)	Assumption
2	Aa	Assumption
3	~ Ba	Assumption
4	~ Ba ⊃ ~ Aa	1 ∀E
5	~ Aa	3, 4 ⊃E
6	Aa	2 R
7	Ba	3–6 ~ E
8	Aa ⊃ Ba	2–7 ⊃I
9	(∀x)(Ax ⊃ Bx)	8 ∀I

so that the only undischarged assumption is the second sentence. Hence the two sentences are equivalent in *PD*.

Inconsistency in *PD* is defined as follows:

> A set Γ of sentences of *PL* is *inconsistent in PD* if and only if both a sentence **P** of *PL* and its negation ~ **P** are derivable in *PD* from Γ. A set Γ of sentences of *PL* is *consistent in PD* if and only if it is not inconsistent in *PD*.

In Chapter 1 we claimed that the following set of sentences is inconsistent:

Anyone who takes astrology seriously is foolish.
Alice is my sister, and no sister of mine has a foolish husband.
Horace is Alice's husband, and he reads the horoscope column every morning.
Anyone who reads the horoscope column every morning takes astrology seriously.

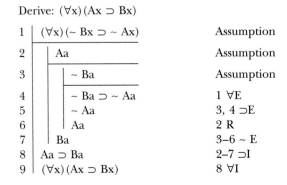

This set of sentences can be symbolized in *PL* as

$(\forall z)(Az \supset Fz)$
$Sa \,\&\, (\forall z)[Sz \supset \sim (\exists y)(Hyz \,\&\, Fy)]$
$Hha \,\&\, Rh$
$(\forall z)(Rz \supset Az)$

Now we have the techniques to show that this symbolized version of the set of sentences is inconsistent in *PD*. We take the members of the set as primary assumptions and construct a derivation like this one:

1	$(\forall z)(Az \supset Fz)$	Assumption
2	$Sa \,\&\, (\forall z)[Sz \supset \sim (\exists y)(Hyz \,\&\, Fy)]$	Assumption
3	$Hha \,\&\, Rh$	Assumption
4	$(\forall z)(Rz \supset Az)$	Assumption
5	$(\forall z)[Sz \supset \sim (\exists y)(Hyz \,\&\, Fy)]$	2 &E
6	$Sa \supset \sim (\exists y)(Hya \,\&\, Fy)$	5 ∀E
7	Sa	2 &E
8	$\sim (\exists y)(Hya \,\&\, Fy)$	6, 7 ⊃E
9	$Rh \supset Ah$	4 ∀E
10	Rh	3 &E
11	Ah	9, 10 ⊃E
12	$Ah \supset Fh$	1 ∀E
13	Fh	11, 12 ⊃E
14	Hha	3 &E
15	$Hha \,\&\, Fh$	14, 13 &I
16	$(\exists y)(Hya \,\&\, Fy)$	15 ∃I

Since we have derived a sentence '$(\exists y)(Hya \,\&\, Fy)$' on line 16 and its negation on line 8, and since both of these sentences occur in the scope of only the primary assumptions, we have shown that the set of sentences is inconsistent in *PD*.

Since *PD* is a syntactic system, it is not essential that we have any interpretation of the formulas in mind when testing for the properties just defined. Recall that the derivation rules allow us to manipulate symbols on the basis of the forms of the sentences alone rather than on the basis of their truth-conditions. Although syntax and semantics are distinct, the results of one parallel the results of the other. The following claims are proved in Chapter 11:

1. A sentence **P** is derivable in *PD* from a set Γ of sentences of *PL* if and only if **P** is quantificationally entailed by Γ.
2. An argument of *PL* is valid in *PD* if and only if the argument is quantificationally valid.
3. A sentence **P** of *PL* is a theorem of *PD* if and only if **P** is quantificationally true.

4. Sentences **P** and **Q** of *PL* are equivalent in *PD* if and only if **P** and **Q** are quantificationally equivalent.
5. A set Γ of sentences of *PL* is inconsistent in *PD* if and only if Γ is quantificationally inconsistent.

10.4 STRATEGIES FOR CONSTRUCTING DERIVATIONS IN *PD*

In principle we could (if we wanted) develop a decision procedure for constructing derivations in *SD*. However, the situation with *PD* is different. We could not (even if we wanted) develop a decision procedure for *PD*. As a result, the need for strategies in constructing derivations in *PD* is all the more important.

Once again we use goal analysis in constructing derivations. The sentence that we hope ultimately to derive is taken as the goal sentence, and we look for subgoal sentences such that if we can derive them we can, in turn, derive our goal sentence. These subgoal sentences become our new goal sentences, and the process is repeated until we are able to derive the goal sentences easily from the assumptions, if any. Consider an example of this approach. Suppose we wish to construct a derivation showing that the following argument is valid in *PD*:

(∀z) (Szz ⊃ Tz)
(∀y) [(Ty ∨ Uyy) ⊃ Wy]
―――――――――――――
(∀z) [(Szz & ~ Kz) ⊃ (Wz & ~ Kz)]

The derivation is begun by listing the premises as assumptions. Next the conclusion is entered down the page:

Derive: (∀z) [(Szz & ~ Kz) ⊃ (Wz & ~ Kz)]

1	(∀z) (Szz ⊃ Tz)	Assumption
2	(∀y) [(Ty ∨ Uyy) ⊃ Wy]	Assumption
	(∀z) [(Szz & ~ Kz) ⊃ (Wz & ~ Kz)]	

Using the goal analysis approach, we next ask ourselves what sentences, if we could derive them, would allow us to derive the goal sentence, which in this case is the conclusion. A universally quantified sentence can be derived in many ways, but one possibility is to derive it by using Universal Introduction.

Pursuing this strategy, we enter a substitution instance of the universally quantified sentence on the immediately preceding line as a subgoal. Of course, we must be careful not to violate any of the restrictions on the use of Universal Introduction. When the derivation is completed, we must be sure that the instantiating constant does not occur in any undischarged assumption on a prior line, and we must be sure that it does not occur in the derived universally quantified sentence. We choose the constant 'j' as our instantiating constant. We can also enter '∀I' in the justification column for the last sentence, although the line reference for the justification is still unknown.

Derive: (∀z)[(Szz & ~ Kz) ⊃ (Wz & ~ Kz)]

1	(∀z)(Szz ⊃ Tz)	Assumption
2	(∀y)[(Ty ∨ Uyy) ⊃ Wy]	Assumption
	(Sjj & ~ Kj) ⊃ (Wj & ~ Kj)	
	(∀z)[(Szz & ~ Kz) ⊃ (Wz & ~ Kz)]	__ ∀I

Our new goal sentence is '(Sjj & ~ Kj) ⊃ (Wj & ~ Kj)'. Since this sentence is a conditional, Conditional Introduction should be helpful. Thus we construct a subderivation that has the antecedent of the goal sentence as its assumption and the consequent of the goal sentence as its last sentence. The derivation under construction is

Derive: (∀z)[(Szz & ~ Kz) ⊃ (Wz & ~ Kz)]

1	(∀z)(Szz ⊃ Tz)	Assumption
2	(∀y)[(Ty ∨ Uyy) ⊃ Wy]	Assumption
3	Sjj & ~ Kj	Assumption
	Wj & ~ Kj	
	(Sjj & ~ Kj) ⊃ (Wj & ~ Kj)	3–__ ⊃I
	(∀z)[(Szz & ~ Kz) ⊃ (Wz & ~ Kz)]	__ ∀I

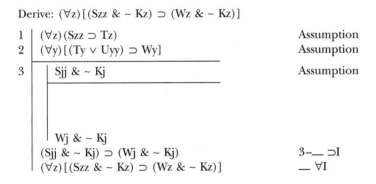

Notice that, although 'j' is the individual constant used in the assumption on line 3, the assumption is discharged before Universal Introduction is applied to derive the last sentence. Hence there will be no violation of the restrictions put on the use of Universal Introduction. Our new goal is to derive 'Wj & ~ Kj' on the basis of the two primary assumptions and the auxiliary assumption just made. This is not difficult since we can instantiate the universally quantified assumptions using 'j'. With the line references filled in, the completed derivation looks like this:

Derive: (∀z)[(Szz & ~ Kz) ⊃ (Wz & ~ Kz)]

1	(∀z)(Szz ⊃ Tz)	Assumption
2	(∀y)[(Ty ∨ Uyy) ⊃ Wy]	Assumption
3	Sjj & ~ Kj	Assumption
4	Sjj ⊃ Tj	1 ∀E
5	Sjj	3 &E
6	Tj	4, 5 ⊃E
7	(Tj ∨ Ujj) ⊃ Wj	2 ∀E
8	Tj ∨ Ujj	6 ∨I
9	Wj	7, 8 ⊃E
10	~ Kj	3 &E
11	Wj & ~ Kj	9, 10 &I
12	(Sjj & ~ Kj) ⊃ (Wj & ~ Kj)	3–11 ⊃I
13	(∀z)[(Szz & ~ Kz) ⊃ (Wz & ~ Kz)]	12 ∀I

In this example goal analysis had led us to the proper auxiliary assumption: 'Sjj & ~ Kj'. But, if the ultimate goal were ignored, then it might be tempting to assume '(∀z)(Szz & ~ Kz)' and try to derive '(∀z)(Wz & ~ Kz)'. This would be a mistake. The conditional derived by using Conditional Introduction would be

(∀z)(Szz & ~ Kz) ⊃ (∀z)(Wz & ~ Kz)

which is *not* the sentence we are seeking. With regard to making the proper assumptions, it is instructive to compare where goal analysis led us in the previous example with where it leads us in the next.

Suppose we wish to construct a derivation to show

⊢ ((∃x)Fx ∨ (∃x)Gx) ⊃ (∃x)(Fx ∨ Gx)

In contrast to our last example, in this one our ultimate goal is not to derive a quantified sentence, a sentence that begins with a quantifier whose scope extends over the entire sentence, but rather to derive a conditional. Hence we can enter the skeleton of a subderivation in the derivation under construction. The assumption of the subderivation is the antecedent of the desired conditional, and the last sentence of the subderivation is the consequent of the conditional. If the subderivation can be completed, our goal sentence can be obtained by Conditional Introduction.

Derive: ((∃x)Fx ∨ (∃x)Gx) ⊃ (∃x)(Fx ∨ Gx)

1	(∃x)Fx ∨ (∃x)Gx	Assumption
	(∃x)(Fx ∨ Gx)	
	((∃x)Fx ∨ (∃x)Gx) ⊃ (∃x)(Fx ∨ Gx)	1–__ ⊃I

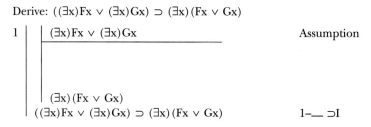

The goal now is to derive '(∃x) (Fx ∨ Gx)' from the assumption. Since the assumption is a disjunction, a promising approach is to apply Disjunction Elimination.

Derive: ((∃x)Fx ∨ (∃x)Gx) ⊃ (∃x) (Fx ∨ Gx)

1	(∃x)Fx ∨ (∃x)Gx	Assumption
2	(∃x)Fx	Assumption
	(∃x) (Fx ∨ Gx)	
	(∃x)Gx	Assumption
	(∃x) (Fx ∨ Gx)	
	(∃x) (Fx ∨ Gx)	1, 2–__, __–__ ∨E
	((∃x)Fx ∨ (∃x)Gx) ⊃ (∃x) (Fx ∨ Gx)	1–__ ⊃I

Now our goal is to derive '(∃x) (Fx ∨ Gx)' within each of the subderivations. This presents us with a very common situation in constructing derivations. Our goal sentence must be derived from an existentially quantified sentence. Whenever this situation occurs, a good procedure is to take a substitution instance of the existentially quantified sentence as an assumption, planning to derive the goal sentence by Existential Elimination.

Derive: ((∃x)Fx ∨ (∃x)Gx) ⊃ (∃x) (Fx ∨ Gx)

1	(∃x)Fx ∨ (∃x)Gx	Assumption
2	(∃x)Fx	Assumption
3	Fb	Assumption
	(∃x) (Fx ∨ Gx)	
	(∃x) (Fx ∨ Gx)	2, 3–__ ∃E
	(∃x)Gx	Assumption
	Gb	Assumption
	(∃x) (Fx ∨ Gx)	
	(∃x) (Fx ∨ Gx)	__, __–__ ∃E
	(∃x) (Fx ∨ Gx)	1, 2–__, __–__ ∨E
	((∃x)Fx ∨ (∃x)Gx) ⊃ (∃x) (Fx ∨ Gx)	1–__ ⊃I

Our new goal is to derive '(∃x) (Fx ∨ Gx)' from the most recent assumptions: 'Fb' in the upper subderivation and 'Gb' in the lower subderivation. The sentence

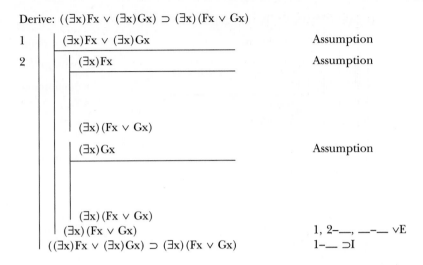

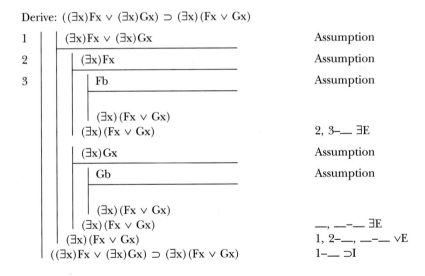

'$(\exists x)(Fx \vee Gx)$' can be obtained from '$Fb \vee Gb$' by Existential Introduction, and '$Fb \vee Gb$' is easy to derive from the given assumptions.

Derive: $((\exists x)Fx \vee (\exists x)Gx) \supset (\exists x)(Fx \vee Gx)$

1	$(\exists x)Fx \vee (\exists x)Gx$	Assumption
2	$(\exists x)Fx$	Assumption
3	Fb	Assumption
4	$Fb \vee Gb$	3 $\vee$I
5	$(\exists x)(Fx \vee Gx)$	4 $\exists$I
6	$(\exists x)(Fx \vee Gx)$	2, 3–5 $\exists$E
7	$(\exists x)Gx$	Assumption
8	Gb	Assumption
9	$Fb \vee Gb$	8 $\vee$I
10	$(\exists x)(Fx \vee Gx)$	9 $\exists$I
11	$(\exists x)(Fx \vee Gx)$	7, 8–10 $\exists$E
12	$(\exists x)(Fx \vee Gx)$	1, 2–6, 7–11 $\vee$E
13	$((\exists x)Fx \vee (\exists x)Gx) \supset (\exists x)(Fx \vee Gx)$	1–12 $\supset$I

Notice that, although the assumptions on lines 3 and 8 both contain the constant 'b', these assumptions are discharged when Existential Elimination is applied. Hence the restrictions on Existential Elimination are not violated.

Of the rules for introducing and eliminating quantifiers, Existential Elimination is probably the most difficult to apply, for this rule requires the construction of a subderivation. A good rule of thumb to follow is this: If it looks as if an existential quantifier must be eliminated in order to derive a goal sentence, set up the structure of a subderivation that has a substitution instance of the existentially quantified sentence as its assumption and the goal sentence as its last sentence. Of course, we must be careful to select a proper substitution instance of the existentially quantified sentence (that is, an instance that does not violate any of the restrictions on Existential Elimination). Once the subderivation is filled in, the goal sentence can be derived by Existential Elimination. For instance, suppose we want to construct a derivation to show that the following argument is valid:

$(\exists x)(\forall y)Nxxy$

$(\exists y)(\exists z)(Bzy \,\&\, \sim Py)$

$(\forall z)(\forall w)[(Nzzw \,\&\, \sim Pw) \supset Sz]$

$(\exists z)Sz$

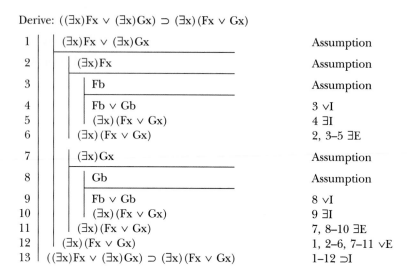

Our goal sentence is '$(\exists z)Sz$', and it is likely that we shall have to eliminate some existential quantifiers in deriving this sentence. Thus, after listing the premises as primary assumptions, we can take a substitution instance of the assumption on line 1 as an auxiliary assumption.

```
Derive: (∃z)Sz

1  | (∃x)(∀y)Nxxy                              Assumption
2  | (∃y)(∃z)(Bzy & ~ Py)                      Assumption
3  | (∀z)(∀w)[(Nzzw & ~ Pw) ⊃ Sz]              Assumption
   |------------------------------
4  |  | (∀y)Naay                                Assumption
   |  |---------------------------
   |  |
   |  |
   |  |
   |  | (∃z)Sz
   | (∃z)Sz                                    1, 4–__ ∃E
```

Ultimately we plan to derive the goal sentence by Existential Elimination, but now our objective is to derive the goal sentence within the subderivation. However, the second assumption is an existentially quantified sentence, and thus we can repeat the process by setting up the structure of another subderivation whose assumption is a substitution instance of the assumption on line 2.

```
Derive: (∃z)Sz

1  | (∃x)(∀y)Nxxy                              Assumption
2  | (∃y)(∃z)(Bzy & ~ Py)                      Assumption
3  | (∀z)(∀w)[(Nzzw & ~ Pw) ⊃ Sz]              Assumption
   |------------------------------
4  |  | (∀y)Naay                                Assumption
   |  |---------------------------
5  |  |  | (∃z)(Bzb & ~ Pb)                    Assumption
   |  |  |------------------------
   |  |  |
   |  |  |
   |  |  |
   |  |  | (∃z)Sz
   |  | (∃z)Sz                                 2, 5–__ ∃E
   | (∃z)Sz                                    1, 4–__ ∃E
```

Notice that in making the assumption on line 5 we picked an instantiating constant other than 'a'. The use of Existential Elimination on the second-to-last line of the derivation would not be legitimate if 'a' were used, for at that point 'a' would occur in the undischarged assumption on line 4. The current goal is to derive '(∃z)Sz' within the innermost subderivation. But the assumption of the innermost subderivation is an existentially quantified sentence, and consequently we can set up another subderivation and plan to obtain the goal sentence by another application of Existential Elimination.

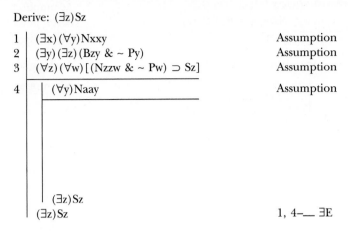

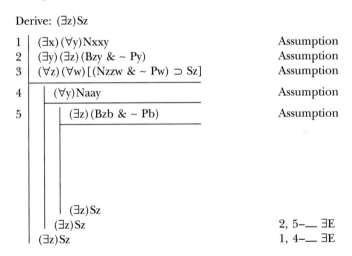

Derive: (∃z)Sz

1	(∃x)(∀y)Nxxy	Assumption
2	(∃y)(∃z)(Bzy & ~ Py)	Assumption
3	(∀z)(∀w)[(Nzzw & ~ Pw) ⊃ Sz]	Assumption
4	(∀y)Naay	Assumption
5	(∃z)(Bzb & ~ Pb)	Assumption
6	Bcb & ~ Pb	Assumption
	(∃z)Sz	
	(∃z)Sz	5, 6–___ ∃E
	(∃z)Sz	2, 5–___ ∃E
	(∃z)Sz	1, 4–___ ∃E

At line 6 an instantiating constant new to the derivation, 'c', is used. It is a good practice to pick an instantiating constant that is completely new to the derivation when making an assumption of a subderivation that will later be appealed to in using Existential Elimination. If the instantiating constant is completely new to the derivation, then there is no chance that it occurs in earlier undischarged assumptions or in the existentially quantified sentence that is appealed to in using Existential Elimination. The derivation at hand can easily be completed by deriving the goal sentence '(∃z)Sz' within the innermost subderivation.

Derive: (∃z)Sz

1	(∃x)(∀y)Nxxy	Assumption
2	(∃y)(∃z)(Bzy & ~ Py)	Assumption
3	(∀z)(∀w)[(Nzzw & ~ Pw) ⊃ Sz]	Assumption
4	(∀y)Naay	Assumption
5	(∃z)(Bzb & ~ Pb)	Assumption
6	Bcb & ~ Pb	Assumption
7	Naab	4 ∀E
8	~ Pb	6 &E
9	Naab & ~ Pb	7, 8 &I
10	(∀w)[(Naaw & ~ Pw) ⊃ Sa]	3 ∀E
11	(Naab & ~ Pb) ⊃ Sa	10 ∀E
12	Sa	9, 11 ⊃E
13	(∃z)Sz	12 ∃I
14	(∃z)Sz	5, 6–13 ∃E
15	(∃z)Sz	2, 5–14 ∃E
16	(∃z)Sz	1, 4–15 ∃E

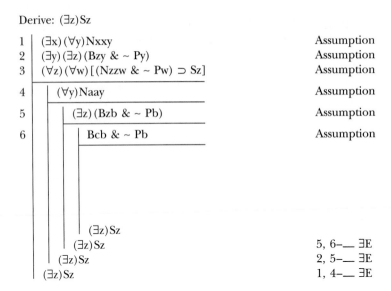

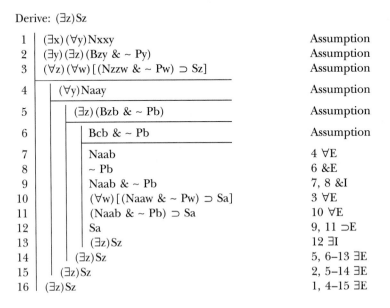

Using individual constants that already occur in a derivation to guide the application of Universal Elimination is an important technique in constructing derivations. Consider the following:

Derive: (∃x)Cx

1	(∀x)(∀y)[Gxy ≡ (Ky ⊃ Cx)]	Assumption
2	(∀w)Giw	Assumption
3	(∃z)Kz	Assumption
4	Kg	Assumption
	(∃x)Cx	
	(∃x)Cx	3, 4–__ ∃E

Our goal is to derive '(∃x)Cx'. Since it is likely that we shall need to eliminate an existential quantifier, we have followed the rule of thumb given in the last example and set up a subderivation for use with Existential Elimination. We can derive '(∃x)Cx' by Existential Introduction if we can obtain a substitution instance of that sentence. Since the predicate 'C' occurs in the first assumption, it is likely that the substitution instance we are seeking will be derived in some way from this sentence. Thus Universal Elimination must be applied to this universally quantified assumption, but which instantiating constant should we pick? The choice is important because we hope to derive sentences with similar sentential components so that the derivation rules for sentential connectives can be applied. Therefore we should allow the individual constants that already occur in the derivation to guide our choice. Since 'i' occurs in 'Giw' (line 2) where 'x' occurs in 'Gxy' (line 1), 'i' is a good choice as an instantiating constant.

Derive: (∃x)Cx

1	(∀x)(∀y)[Gxy ≡ (Ky ⊃ Cx)]	Assumption
2	(∀w)Giw	Assumption
3	(∃z)Kz	Assumption
4	Kg	Assumption
5	(∀y)[Giy ≡ (Ky ⊃ Ci)]	1 ∀E
	(∃x)Cx	
	(∃x)Cx	3, 4–__ ∃E

Now it is clear that 'Ci' is the substitution instance of '(∃x)Cx' we are seeking. It is also clear that more universal quantifiers must be eliminated in order to derive it. Since 'g' occurs in 'Kg' (line 4) where 'y' occurs in 'Ky' (line 5), it is wise to use 'g' as the instantiating constant when applying Universal Elimination to the sentence on line 5.

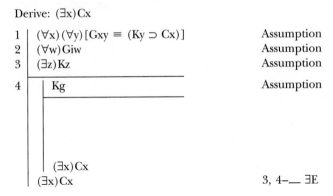

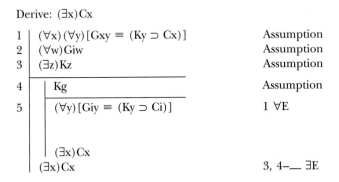

Derive: $(\exists x)Cx$

1	$(\forall x)(\forall y)[Gxy \equiv (Ky \supset Cx)]$	Assumption
2	$(\forall w)Giw$	Assumption
3	$(\exists z)Kz$	Assumption
4	Kg	Assumption
5	$(\forall y)[Giy \equiv (Ky \supset Ci)]$	1 $\forall$E
6	$Gig \equiv (Kg \supset Ci)$	5 $\forall$E
	Ci	
	$(\exists x)Cx$	— $\exists$I
	$(\exists x)Cx$	3, 4–— $\exists$E

Similarly, since 'g' occurs in 'Gig' (line 6) where 'w' occurs in 'Giw' (line 2), Universal Elimination should be applied to the sentence on line 2, with 'g' as the instantiating constant.

Derive: $(\exists x)Cx$

1	$(\forall x)(\forall y)[Gxy \equiv (Ky \supset Cx)]$	Assumption
2	$(\forall w)Giw$	Assumption
3	$(\exists z)Kz$	Assumption
4	Kg	Assumption
5	$(\forall y)[Giy \equiv (Ky \supset Ci)]$	1 $\forall$E
6	$Gig \equiv (Kg \supset Ci)$	5 $\forall$E
7	Gig	2 $\forall$E
	Ci	
	$(\exists x)Cx$	— $\exists$I
	$(\exists x)Cx$	3, 4–— $\exists$E

Since we have chosen the instantiating constants carefully, we can finish the derivation by application of the derivation rules for sentential connectives.

Derive: $(\exists x)Cx$

1	$(\forall x)(\forall y)[Gxy \equiv (Ky \supset Cx)]$	Assumption
2	$(\forall w)Giw$	Assumption
3	$(\exists z)Kz$	Assumption
4	Kg	Assumption
5	$(\forall y)[Giy \equiv (Ky \supset Ci)]$	1 $\forall$E
6	$Gig \equiv (Kg \supset Ci)$	5 $\forall$E
7	Gig	2 $\forall$E
8	$Kg \supset Ci$	6, 7 $\equiv$E
9	Ci	4, 8 $\supset$E
10	$(\exists x)Cx$	9 $\exists$I
11	$(\exists x)Cx$	3, 4–10 $\exists$E

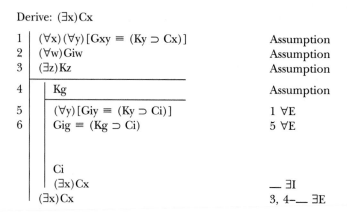

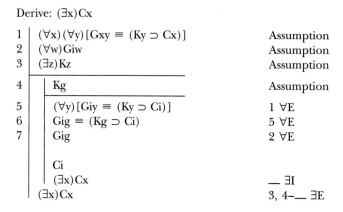

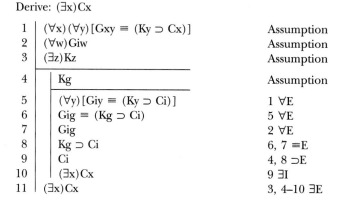

As mentioned in Section 10.2, the introduction and elimination rules for quantifiers are rules of inference that must be applied to entire sentences on single lines. Therefore sentences that are negations of quantified sentences pose special difficulties. For example, Universal Elimination cannot be applied to '~ (∀x)Fx'. In such situations the rules Negation Introduction and Negation Elimination are very useful. Consider their application in the following derivations:

```
Derive: (∃x) ~ Fx

1 | ~ (∀x)Fx                      Assumption
  |-----------
2 |  | ~ (∃x) ~ Fx                Assumption
  |  |---------
3 |  |  | ~ Fc                    Assumption
  |  |  |------
4 |  |  | (∃x) ~ Fx               3 ∃I
5 |  |  | ~ (∃x) ~ Fx             2 R
6 |  | Fc                         3–5 ~ E
7 |  | (∀x)Fx                     6 ∀I
8 |  | ~ (∀x)Fx                   1 R
9 | (∃x) ~ Fx                     2–8 ~ E
```

```
Derive: (∀x) ~ Fx

1 | ~ (∃x)Fx                      Assumption
  |-----------
2 |  | Fc                         Assumption
  |  |------
3 |  | (∃x)Fx                     2 ∃I
4 |  | ~ (∃x)Fx                   1 R
5 | ~ Fc                          2–4 ~ I
6 | (∀x) ~ Fx                     5 ∀I
```

Using goal analysis and knowing the special techniques introduced in this section facilitate the construction of derivations in *PD*. But there is no substitute for practice in learning to construct derivations.

10.4E EXERCISES

1. Using the techniques of goal analysis on each of the following, indicate the *goal* sentence at the current state of construction and specify a next plausible *subgoal* sentence or sentences. When appropriate, set up subderivation structures that will lead to the subgoal sentence(s). Remember to consider the form of the goal sentence and the content of the accessible sentences in selecting proper subgoals. Continue to use the goal analysis method and complete each of the derivations.

a. Derive: (∀x)Ax ≡ (∀x)(Ax & Ax)

```
|
|
|
| (∀x)Ax ≡ (∀x)(Ax & Ax)
```

*b. Derive: (∃z)Az ⊃ (∃z)Zz

1	(∀x)(Ax ⊃ Zx)	Assumption
2	(∃z)Az	Assumption
3		
	(∃z)Zz	
	(∃z)Az ⊃ (∃z)Zz	2–__ ⊃I

c. Derive: (∀x)(Fx ⊃ Hx)

1	(∀x)(Fx ⊃ Gx)	Assumption
2	(∀x)(Gx ⊃ Hx)	Assumption
	(∀x)(Fx ⊃ Hx)	

*d. Derive: (∀x)(∀y)((Bx & Ny) ⊃ Txy)

1	(∀x)(∀y)(Bx ⊃ Txy)	Assumption
	(∀x)(∀y)((Bx & Ny) ⊃ Txy)	

e. Derive: (∀x)(Hx ∨ ~ Sx)

1	(∀x) ~ Kx	Assumption
2	(∀x)(~ Kx ⊃ ~ Sx)	Assumption
	~ Sa	
	Ha ∨ ~ Sa	__ ∨I
	(∀x)(Hx ∨ ~ Sx)	__ ∀I

*f. Derive: (∃x)(Hx ≡ Mx)

1	Ma	Assumption
2	(∀x)(Mx ⊃ Hx)	Assumption
	(∃x)(Hx ≡ Mx)	

g. Derive: (∃x) ~ Cx

1	(∃x) ~ (Cx ∨ ~ Rx)	Assumption
	(∃x) ~ Cx	

*h. Derive: (∃y)Lyy

1	(∃x)(Nx ∨ Lxx)	Assumption
2	(∀x) ~ Nx	Assumption
3	Nh ∨ Lhh	Assumption
	(∃y)Lyy	
	(∃y)Lyy	1, 3–___ ∃E

i. Derive: (∃x)(∃y)(~ Kx & ~ Oy)

1	(∃x)(Mx & ~ Kx)	Assumption
2	(∃y)(~ Oy & Wy)	Assumption
3	Mj & ~ Kj	Assumption
	(∃x)(∃y)(~ Kx & ~ Oy)	
	(∃x)(∃y)(~ Kx & ~ Oy)	1, 3–___ ∃E

*j. Derive: (∀y)(∀x)(Cxy ⊃ Px)

1	(∀y)(∀x)(Cxy ⊃ Qx)	Assumption
2	(∀y)(Qy ≡ Py)	Assumption
3	Cmb	Assumption
	Qm	
	Qm ≡ Pm	2 ∀E
	Pm	___, ___ ≡E
	Cmb ⊃ Pm	3–___ ⊃I
	(∀x)(Cxb ⊃ Px)	___ ∀I
	(∀y)(∀x)(Cxy ⊃ Px)	___ ∀I

k. Derive: $(\forall x)(Fx \supset (\exists y)(Gxy \vee \sim Hxy))$

1	$(\forall x)(Fx \supset (\exists y)Gxy)$	Assumption
2	Fa	Assumption
	$(\exists y)(Gay \vee \sim Hay)$	
	$Fa \supset (\exists y)(Gay \vee \sim Hay)$	2–__ $\supset$I
	$(\forall x)(Fx \supset (\exists y)(Gxy \vee \sim Hxy))$	__ $\forall$I

2. Show that each of the following derivability claims holds in *PD*.

a. $\{(\forall x)Kxx\} \vdash (\forall z)Kzz$

*b. $\{(\exists x)Kxx\} \vdash (\exists z)Kzz$

c. $\{(\forall z)(Gz \supset Hz),\ Gi\} \vdash (\exists y)Hy$

*d. $\{(\forall x)Mx\} \vdash (\forall x)(\sim Mx \supset Mx)$

e. $\{(\exists y)Byyy\} \vdash (\exists x)(\exists y)(\exists z)Bxyz$

*f. $\{(\forall x)[(Hx \,\&\, \sim Kx) \supset Ix],\ (\exists y)(Hy \,\&\, Gy),\ (\forall x)(Gx \,\&\, \sim Kx)\} \vdash (\exists y)(Iy \,\&\, Gy)$

3. Show that each of the following arguments is valid in *PD*.

a. $(\forall x)(\forall y)Cxy$

$(Caa \,\&\, Cab) \,\&\, (Cba \,\&\, Cbb)$

*b. $(\forall x)(Tx \supset Lx)$

$\sim Lb$

$\sim Tb$

c. $(\forall y)[(Hy \,\&\, Fy) \supset Gy]$

$(\forall z)Fz \,\&\, \sim (\forall x)Kxb$

$(\forall x)(Hx \supset Gx)$

*d. $(\exists x)Cx \supset Ch$

$(\exists x)Cx \equiv Ch$

e. $(\forall x)(\sim Ax \supset Kx)$

$(\exists y) \sim Ky$

$(\exists w)(Aw \vee \sim Lwf)$

*f. $(\forall y)[Hy \,\&\, (Jyy \,\&\, My)]$

$(\exists x)Jxb \,\&\, (\forall x)Mx$

4. Show that each of the following is a theorem in *PD*.

a. $(\forall x)(\exists y)(Ay \supset Ax)$

*b. $(\forall x)(Ax \supset \sim \sim Ax)$

c. $(\forall x)(Ax \supset Bx) \supset ((\forall x)Ax \supset (\forall x)Bx)$

*d. $(\exists x)(Ax \,\&\, Bx) \supset ((\exists x)Ax \,\&\, (\exists x)Bx)$

e. $(\forall x)(Bi \supset Ax) \equiv (Bi \supset (\forall x)Ax)$
*f. $(\forall x)(Ax \supset Bi) \equiv ((\exists x)Ax \supset Bi)$

5. Show that the members of each of the following pairs of sentences are equivalent in *PD*.

a. $(\forall x)Ax$
$(\forall x)(Ax \,\&\, Ax)$
*b. $(\forall x)(\forall y)(Ax \,\&\, By)$
$(\forall x)Ax \,\&\, (\forall y)By$
c. $(\exists x)(Ax \vee Bx)$
$(\exists x)Ax \vee (\exists x)Bx$
*d. $(\forall x) \sim Ax$
$\sim (\exists x)Ax$
e. $\sim (\forall x)Ax$
$(\exists x) \sim Ax$
*f. $(\forall x)(\forall y)[(Axy \,\&\, Ayx) \supset Axx]$
$(\forall x)[(\exists y)(Axy \,\&\, Ayx) \supset Axx]$

6. Show that each of the following sets of sentences is inconsistent in *PD*.

a. $\{(\forall x)Hx, (\forall y) \sim (Hy \vee Byy)\}$
*b. $\{(\forall x)(Rx \equiv \sim Rx)\}$
c. $\{(\forall x)Rx, (\exists x) \sim Rx\}$
*d. $\{(\exists x)(\forall y)Fxy, \sim (\forall y)(\exists x)Fxy\}$
e. $\{(\forall w)(\forall z)(Jwz \equiv \sim Jwz)\}$
*f. $\{\sim (\exists y)Jy, \sim (\exists x) \sim Hx, (\forall z)(Jz \vee \sim Hz)\}$

7. Show that each of the following derivability claims holds in *PD*.

a. $\{(\forall x)(\sim Bx \supset \sim Wx), (\exists x)Wx\} \vdash (\exists x)Bx$
*b. $\{(\forall x)(\forall y)(\forall z)Gxyz\} \vdash (\forall x)(\forall y)(\forall z)(Gxyz \supset Gzyx)$
c. $\{(\forall x)(Hx \supset (\forall y)Rxyb), (\forall x)(\forall z)(Razx \supset Sxzz)\} \vdash Ha \supset (\exists x)Sxcc$
*d. $\{\sim (\forall x)(Fx \,\&\, Aix) \equiv \sim (\forall x)Kx, (\forall y)[(\exists x) \sim (Fx \,\&\, Aix) \,\&\, Ryy]\} \vdash \sim (\forall x)Kx$
e. $\{(\forall z)(\sim Lz \vee (\exists y)Ky)\} \vdash (\exists z)Lz \supset (\exists y)Ky$
*f. $\{(\exists x)(Jxa \,\&\, Ck), (\exists x)(Sx \,\&\, Hxx), (\forall x)[(Ck \,\&\, Sx) \supset \sim Ax]\} \vdash (\exists z)(\sim Az \,\&\, Hzz)$
g. $\{(\exists x)(Cx \vee (\forall y)(Wxy \supset Cy)), (\forall x)(Wxa \,\&\, \sim Ca)\} \vdash (\exists x)Cx$
*h. $\{(\forall x)(\forall y)(Dxy \supset Cxy), (\forall x)(\exists y)Dxy, (\forall x)(\forall y)(Cyx \supset Dxy)\} \vdash$
$(\exists x)(\exists y)(Cxy \,\&\, Cyx)$

8. Show that each of the following arguments is valid in *PD*.

a. $(\forall x)(Zx \supset (\exists y)Ky)$
————————
$(\forall x)(Zx \supset (\exists y)(Ky \vee Sy))$

*b. $(\exists x) \sim (\exists y)(Rxy \,\&\, \sim Uy) \supset (\exists x)(Px \,\&\, Jx)$
$(\exists x) \sim (\exists y)(Rxy \,\&\, \sim Uy)$
————————
$\sim (\forall x)(Px \supset \sim Jx)$

c. $(\forall x)(Hx \supset Fx)$
$(\forall x)((Fx \,\&\, Uxx) \supset Wxx)$
$(\forall z)Uzz$
————————
$(\forall x)(Hx \supset Wxx)$

*d. $(\forall x)((Fx \,\&\, Gx) \equiv (\exists y)(Axy \,\&\, Py))$

$(\exists x)(\exists y)(Fx \,\&\, (Axy \,\&\, Py))$

$(\exists x)(Fx \,\&\, Gx)$

e. $(\forall x)(Lx \supset Yx)$

$(\exists x)(Cx \,\&\, Yx) \,\&\, (\exists x)(Cx \,\&\, \sim Yx)$

$\sim (\forall x)(Cx \supset Lx)$

*f. $(\forall x)(Px \supset Qx)$

$((\exists x)Px \,\&\, (\exists x)Qx) \equiv (\exists x)(Px \,\&\, Qx)$

g. $(\forall x)(\forall y)((Ry \vee Dx) \supset \sim Ky)$

$(\forall x)(\exists y)(Ax \supset \sim Ky)$

$(\exists x)(Ax \vee Rx)$

$(\exists x) \sim Kx$

*h. $(\forall y)(My \supset Ay)$

$(\exists x)(\exists y)[(Bx \,\&\, Mx) \,\&\, (Ry \,\&\, Syx)]$

$(\exists x)Ax \supset (\forall y)(\forall z)(Syz \supset Ay)$

$(\exists x)(Rx \,\&\, Ax)$

i. $(\forall x)(\forall y)[(Hky \,\&\, Hxk) \supset Hxy]$

$(\forall z)(Bz \supset Hkz)$

$(\exists x)(Bx \,\&\, Hxk)$

$(\exists z)[Bz \,\&\, (\forall y)(By \supset Hzy)]$

*j. $(\forall x)((Fx \,\&\, \sim Kx) \supset (\exists y)[(Fy \,\&\, Hyx) \,\&\, \sim Ky])$

$(\forall x)[(Fx \,\&\, (\forall y)[(Fy \,\&\, Hyx) \supset Ky]) \supset Kx] \supset Mp$

Mp

k. $(\forall x)(\forall y)[(Gx \,\&\, Gy) \supset (Hxy \supset Hyx)]$

$(\forall x)(\forall y)(\forall z)([(Gx \,\&\, Gy) \,\&\, Gz] \supset [(Hxy \,\&\, Hyz) \supset Hxz])$

$(\forall w)[[Gw \,\&\, (\exists z)(Gz \,\&\, Hwz)] \supset Hww]$

*l. $(\forall x)(\forall y)[(Ax \,\&\, By) \supset Cxy]$

$(\exists y)[Ey \,\&\, (\forall w)(Hw \supset Cyw)]$

$(\forall x)(\forall y)(\forall z)[(Cxy \,\&\, Cyz) \supset Cxz]$

$(\forall w)(Ew \supset Bw)$

$(\forall z)(\forall w)[(Az \,\&\, Hw) \supset Czw]$

9. Show that each of the following is a theorem in *PD*.

a. $[(\forall x)(\forall y)Axy \ \& \ (\forall x)(Axx \supset Bi)] \supset Bi$

*b. $(\forall x)(\exists y)(Ax \supset By) \supset ((\forall x)Ax \supset (\exists y)By)$

c. $(\forall x)Ax \equiv \sim (\exists x) \sim Ax$

*d. $(\forall x)(Ax \vee Bi) \equiv (\forall x)(Ax \vee Bi)$

e. $(\exists x)(Bi \supset Ax) \equiv (Bi \supset (\exists x)Ax)$

*f. $(\exists x)(Ax \supset Bi) \equiv ((\forall x)Ax \supset Bi)$

10. Show that the members of the following pairs of sentences are equivalent in *PD*.

a. $(\forall x)(Ax \supset Ax)$
$(\forall x)(Bx \supset Bx)$

*b. $(\forall x)(Ax \vee Ax)$
$(\forall x)Ax$

c. $(\forall x)(\forall y)(Ax \supset By)$
$(\exists y) \sim By \supset (\forall x) \sim Ax$

*d. $(\exists x)Ax \supset ((\exists y)By \supset (\forall z)Cz)$
$(\forall x)(\forall y)(\forall z)[(Ax \ \& \ By) \supset Cz]$

e. $(\exists x)(\forall y)(Ax \supset By)$
$\sim (\forall x)Ax \vee (\forall y)By$

*f. $(\forall x)(\exists y) \sim (Axy \ \& \ Bxy)$
$(\forall x)(\sim (\forall y)Axy \vee \sim (\forall y)Bxy)$

11. Show that each of the following sets of sentences is inconsistent in *PD*.

a. $\{(\forall y)(\exists z)Byz, (\forall w) \sim Baw\}$

*b. $\{(\exists x)(Hx \ \& \ Mxc), (\forall x)(Lx \supset \sim Hx), (\exists y)(Ly \ \& \ Hy)\}$

c. $\{(\exists x)(\sim Bx \ \& \ Lxx), (\forall z)(Cz \ \& \ Bz), (\forall y)[(By \ \& \sim Cy) \equiv Lyy]\}$

*d. $\{(\forall x)(\forall y)[(Jx \ \& \ Gy) \supset Hxy], (\exists x)(\exists y)[(Jx \ \& \sim Jy) \ \& \sim Hxy], (\forall w)Gw\}$

e. $\{(\exists x)(\exists y)Fxy \vee (\forall x)(\forall y)(\forall z)Hxxyz, (\exists x)(\exists y)Fxy \supset \sim Haaab,$
$(Hbbba \vee \sim Haaab) \equiv (\forall x) \sim (Ax \vee \sim Ax)\}$

*f. $\{(\forall x)(\exists y)(Hx \supset By), \sim (\exists y)(\forall x)(Hx \supset By)\}$

12. Symbolize the following arguments in *PL* and show that the arguments are valid in *PD*.

a. Skiers are either very crazy or terrifically brave. George has a friend who is a skier but who is not terrifically brave. Thus George has a very crazy friend.

*b. Groucho Marx doesn't stay in any hotel that is willing to have him as a guest. Any hotel not willing to have Groucho Marx as a guest doesn't. Therefore Groucho Marx doesn't stay in any hotel.

c. Anybody who is loved by at least two persons is more fortunate than anyone who is loved by only one person. Hildegard and Gertrude are two people who love Norad. Since only Dora loves Manfred, Norad is more fortunate than Manfred.

*d. Everyone who knows wine prefers every red wine to every equally priced or lower-priced white wine. Geribaldi Special is a red wine, but no one prefers it to anything. It follows that either no white wine is equally priced or lower-priced than Geribaldi Special or nobody knows wines.

e. Some hunters shoot deer. Other hunters don't shoot any deer. Anybody who shoots a deer or a hunter is a lawbreaker. Hunters are people who shoot only deer or hunters. Of course, every hunter shoots something. Hence, if no hunter shoots a hunter, then some lawbreakers shoot themselves.

*f. A baby is always cared for by his or her father, mother, or babysitter. A person is a parent of a baby if and only if the person is the baby's father or mother. Some babies are sometimes cared for by babysitters, for sometimes they are not cared for by their parents.

13. Symbolize the following passages in *PL* and show that the resulting sets of sentences of *PL* are inconsistent in *PD*.

a. Some psychiatrists understand those and only those who don't understand themselves.

*b. Nobody pleads guilty unless he or she is. Anybody who is guilty deserves punishment. However, there are some who plead guilty who do not deserve punishment.

c. Nobody who practices birth control acts morally. Any person who uses the rhythm method practices birth control. People who use the rhythm method act morally. There are, indeed, people who use the rhythm method.

*d. Everyone who likes some wine likes some red wine. Mike is a person who likes wine but only sauterne. No sauterne is a red wine.

10.5 THE DERIVATION SYSTEM *PD+*

We now enlarge the set of derivation rules and create the natural deduction system *PD+*. The additional derivation rules of *PD+* will not allow us to derive any more than can be derived in *PD*. However, the additional derivation rules will often allow us to construct derivations more easily. *PD+* contains all the derivation rules of *SD+* with the understanding that they are to be applied to the sentences of *PL*. The rules of replacement, unlike the rules of inference, can be applied to subformulas of sentences, as well as to sentences, of *PL*. Thus the rules of replacement are powerful rules for manipulating the internal structure of quantified sentences. The following is a correct derivation:

1	(∀x) [Mx ∨ (Kx ∨ (∃y) (Nxy)]	Assumption
2	(∀x) [Mx ∨ ((∃y)Nxy ∨ Kx)]	1 Com
3	(∀x) [(Mx ∨ (∃y)Nxy) ∨ Kx]	2 Assoc
4	(∀x) [(~ ~ Mx ∨ (∃y)Nxy) ∨ Kx]	3 DN
5	(∀x) [(~ Mx ⊃ (∃y)Nxy) ∨ Kx]	4 Impl

In this example each of the replacement rules has been applied to a subformula. For instance, Double Negation has been applied to the subformula 'Mx' of the sentence on line 3 to generate '~ ~ Mx', which is a subformula of the sentence on line 4.

PD+ also contains the rules for introducing and eliminating quantifiers—Universal Introduction, Universal Elimination, Existential Introduction, and Existential Elimination. The only additional quantifier rule of *PD+* is *Quantifier Negation.* Quantifier Negation is a rule of replacement. Where **P** is an open sentence of *PL* in which **x** occurs free, the rule is

Quantifier Negation (QN)

~ (∀**x**)**P** ◁ ▷ (∃**x**) ~ **P**
~ (∃**x**)**P** ◁ ▷ (∀**x**) ~ **P**

Like all rules of replacement, Quantifier Negation can be applied to subformulas within a sentence, as well as to an entire sentence on a line of a derivation. Quantifier Negation is a two-way rule in that a sentence (or subformula) that has the form of the expression on the left of the '◁ ▷' can be replaced by a sentence (or subformula) that has the form of the expression on the right of the '◁ ▷', and vice versa. All these are proper uses of Quantifier Negation:

1	(∀w) ~ (∃x)Hxw ∨ (∃y) ~ (∀z)Kyz	Assumption
2	~ (∃w)(∃x)Hxw ∨ (∃y) ~ (∀z)Kyz	1 QN
3	(∀w)(∀x) ~ Hxw ∨ (∃y) ~ (∀z)Kyz	1 QN
4	(∀w) ~ (∃x)Hxw ∨ ~ (∀y)(∀z)Kyz	1 QN
5	(∀w) ~ (∃x)Hxw ∨ (∃y)(∃z) ~ Kyz	1 QN

Care must be taken when applying the rules of replacement to the internal structure of quantified sentences to be sure that only sentences or subformulas are manipulated. The following is *not* correct:

1	(∀x)[Lx ∨ (∃y)(Bxy ∨ Jxy)]	Assumption	
2	(∀x)[(Lx ∨ (∃y)Bxy) ∨ Jxy]	1 Assoc	**MISTAKE!**

In order for Association to be applicable to the sentence on line 1, the relevant subformulas must have the form **P** ∨ (**Q** ∨ **R**). But the right disjunct of 'Lx ∨ (∃y)(Bxy ∨ Jxy)' is a quantified formula, not a disjunction. Consequently Association cannot be applied to the sentence on line 1 to derive the sentence on line 2. In applying the rules of replacement, it is important to identify correctly the main logical operators of the sentences and their subformulas.

The definitions of the basic concepts of *PD+* are exactly like the definitions of the basic concepts of *PD*, except that '*PD*' is replaced by '*PD+*'. Consequently the tests for the various syntactic properties are carried out in the same way. The important difference between *PD* and *PD+* is that *PD*, with fewer rules, provides theoretical elegance and *PD+*, with more rules, provides practical ease.

10.5E EXERCISES

1. Show that each of the following derivability claims holds in *PD+*.

a. {~ (∀y)(Fy & Gy)} ⊢ (∃y)(~ Fy ∨ ~ Gy)
*b. {(∀w)(Lw ⊃ Mw), (∀y)(My ⊃ Ny)} ⊢ (∀w)(Lw ⊃ Nw)
c. {(∃z)(Gz & Az), (∀y)(Cy ⊃ ~ Gy)} ⊢ (∃z)(Az & ~ Cz)
*d. {~ (∃x)(~ Rx & Sxx), Sjj} ⊢ Rj

e. $\{(\forall x)[(\sim Cxb \vee Hx) \supset Lxx], (\exists y) \sim Lyy\} \vdash (\exists x)Cxb$
*f. $\{(\forall x)Fx, (\forall z)Hz\} \vdash \sim (\exists y)(\sim Fy \vee \sim Hy)$

2. Show that each of the following arguments is valid in *PD+*.

a. $(\forall x) \sim Jx$

$(\exists y)(Hby \vee Ryy) \supset (\exists x)Jx$

$(\forall y) \sim (Hby \vee Ryy)$

*b. $\sim (\exists x)(\forall y)(Pxy \ \& \sim Qxy)$

$(\forall x)(\exists y)(Pxy \supset Qxy)$

c. $(\forall x) \sim ((\forall y)Hyx \vee Tx)$

$\sim (\exists y)(Ty \vee (\exists x) \sim Hxy)$

$(\forall x)(\forall y)Hxy \ \& \ (\forall x) \sim Tx$

*d. $(\forall z)(Lz \equiv Hz)$

$(\forall x) \sim (Hx \vee \sim Bx)$

$\sim Lb$

e. $(\forall z)[Kzz \supset (Mz \ \& \ Nz)]$

$(\exists z) \sim Nz$

$(\exists x) \sim Kxx$

*f. $(\exists x)[\sim Bxm \ \& \ (\forall y)(Cy \supset \sim Gxy)]$

$(\forall z)[\sim (\forall y)(Wy \supset Gzy) \supset Bzm]$

$(\forall x)(Cx \supset \sim Wx)$

g. $(\exists z)Qz \supset (\forall w)(Lww \supset \sim Hw)$

$(\exists x)Bx \supset (\forall y)(Ay \supset Hy)$

$(\exists w)(Qw \ \& \ Bw) \supset (\forall y)(Lyy \supset \sim Ay)$

*h. $(\forall y)(Kby \supset \sim Hy)$

$(\forall x)[(\exists y)(Kby \ \& \ Qxy) \supset (\exists z)(\sim Hz \ \& \ Qxz)]$

i. $\sim (\forall x)(\sim Px \vee \sim Hx) \supset (\forall x)[Cx \ \& \ (\forall y)(Ly \supset Axy)]$

$(\exists x)[Hx \ \& \ (\forall y)(Ly \supset Axy)] \supset (\forall x)(Rx \ \& \ (\forall y)Bxy)$

$\sim (\forall x)(\forall y)Bxy \supset (\forall x)(\sim Px \vee \sim Hx)$

3. Show that each of the following sentences is a theorem in *PD+*.

a. $(\forall x)(Ax \supset Bx) \supset (\forall x)(Bx \vee \sim Ax)$
*b. $(\forall x)(Ax \supset (Ax \supset Bx)) \supset (\forall x)(Ax \supset Bx)$

c. $\sim (\exists x)(Ax \vee Bx) \supset (\forall x) \sim Ax$
*d. $(\forall x)(Ax \supset Bx) \vee (\exists x)Ax$
e. $((\exists x)Ax \supset (\exists x)Bx) \supset (\exists x)(Ax \supset Bx)$
*f. $(\forall x)(\exists y)(Ax \vee By) \equiv (\exists y)(\forall x)(Ax \vee By)$

4. Show that the members of each of the following pairs of sentences are equivalent in *PD+*.

a. $\sim (\forall x)(Ax \supset Bx)$
$(\exists x)(Ax \;\&\; \sim Bx)$
*b. $(\exists x)(\exists y)Axy \supset Aab$
$(\exists x)(\exists y)Axy \equiv Aab$
c. $\sim (\forall x) \sim [(Ax \;\&\; Bx) \supset Cx]$
$(\exists x)[\sim Ax \vee (\sim Cx \supset \sim Bx)]$
*d. $\sim (\forall x)(\exists y)[(Ax \;\&\; Bx) \vee Cy]$
$(\exists x)(\forall y)[\sim (Cy \vee Ax) \vee \sim (Cy \vee Bx)]$
e. $(\forall x)(Ax \equiv Bx)$
$\sim (\exists x)[(\sim Ax \vee \sim Bx) \;\&\; (Ax \vee Bx)]$
*f. $(\forall x)(Ax \;\&\; (\exists y) \sim Bxy)$
$\sim (\exists x)[\sim Ax \vee (\forall y)(Bxy \;\&\; Bxy)]$

5. Show that each of the following sets of sentences is inconsistent in *PD+*.

a. $\{[(\forall x)(Mx \equiv Jx) \;\&\; \sim Mc] \;\&\; (\forall x)Jx\}$
*b. $\{\sim Fa, \sim (\exists x)(\sim Fx \vee \sim Fx)\}$
c. $\{(\forall x)(\forall y)Lxy \supset \sim (\exists x)Tz, (\forall x)(\forall y)Lxy \supset ((\exists w)Cww \vee (\exists z)Tz),$
$(\sim (\forall x)(\forall y)Lxy \vee (\forall z)Bzzk) \;\&\; (\sim (\forall z)Bzzk \vee \sim (\exists w)Cww), (\forall x)(\forall y)Lxy\}$
*d. $\{(\exists x)(\forall y)(Hxy \supset (\forall w)Jww), (\exists x) \sim Jxx \;\&\; \sim (\exists x) \sim Hxm\}$
e. $\{(\forall x)(\forall y)(Gxy \supset Hc), (\exists x)Gix \;\&\; (\forall x)(\forall y)(\forall z)Lxyz, \sim Lcib \vee \sim (Hc \vee Hc)\}$
*f. $\{(\forall x)[(Sx \;\&\; Bxx) \supset Kax], (\forall x)(Hx \supset Bxx), (\exists x)(Sx \;\&\; Hx),$
$(\forall x) \sim (Kax \;\&\; Hx)\}$

6.a. Show that Universal Introduction and Universal Elimination are eliminable in *PD+* by developing routines that can be used in place of these rules to obtain the same results. (*Hint:* Consider using Quantifier Negation, Existential Introduction, and Existential Elimination.)
*b. Show that Existential Introduction and Existential Elimination are eliminable in *PD+* by developing routines that can be used in place of these rules to obtain the same results. (*Hint:* Consider using Quantifier Negation, Universal Introduction, and Universal Elimination.)

0.6 THE DERIVATION SYSTEM *PDE*

The symbolic language *PLE* includes sentences not found in *PL*, sentences that contain functors and/or the identity predicate. Accordingly we need to revise the derivation system we developed earlier in this chapter to allow for derivations that include these new sentences of *PLE*. We shall do so by adding an introduction rule and an elimination rule for the identity predicate, and then modifying three other rules so as to allow for sentences containing functors. The resulting *extended* predicate derivation system is called *PDE.*

IDENTITY

The introduction rule for '=' is

Identity Introduction (=I)

$\triangleright$ | $(\forall \mathbf{x})\mathbf{x} = \mathbf{x}$

Identity Introduction permits us to derive a sentence of the form $(\forall \mathbf{x})\mathbf{x} = \mathbf{x}$, where **x** is any individual variable. Hence sentences such as '$(\forall x)x = x$' and '$(\forall z)z = z$' can be entered on any new line of a derivation. These sentences claim that everything is identical with itself. Because that claim is always true, Identity Introduction is a truth-preserving derivation rule. Here is a very simple derivation of a theorem using the rule Identity Introduction:

Derive: $(\forall w)w = w$

1	$(\forall w)w = w$	=I

Identity Introduction is an axiom schema that allows us to enter any sentence of the form $(\forall \mathbf{x})\mathbf{x} = \mathbf{x}$ on any line of a derivation.

The elimination rule for '=' is

Identity Elimination (=E)

	$\mathbf{a} = \mathbf{b}$			$\mathbf{a} = \mathbf{b}$
	$\mathbf{P}$	or		$\mathbf{P}$
$\triangleright$	$\mathbf{P}(\mathbf{a}//\mathbf{b})$		$\triangleright$	$\mathbf{P}(\mathbf{b}//\mathbf{a})$

The notation

$\mathbf{P}(\mathbf{a}//\mathbf{b})$

means that at least one occurrence (but not necessarily all) of an individual constant **b** in **P** has been replaced by an individual constant **a**. Similarly $\mathbf{P}(\mathbf{b}//\mathbf{a})$ means that at least one occurrence (but not necessarily all) of **a** in **P** has been replaced by **b**. Identity Elimination is a truth-preserving rule. This rule permits the replacement of one name with another in a sentence only if both names occur in an identity sentence. Intuitively, whatever is true of something should be true of it regardless of its name. The application of this rule is illustrated by the following examples:

1	Rjjm	Assumption
2	j = m	Assumption
3	Rmjm	1, 2 =E

1	Rjjm	Assumption
2	j = m	Assumption
3	Rmmm	1, 2 =E

1	Rjjm	Assumption
2	j = m	Assumption
3	Rjjj	1, 2 =E

In constructing derivations using identity sentences, it is often useful to obtain a sentence of the form **a** = **a**, where **a** is some constant. This can be done by using the derivation rule Identity Introduction and then deriving the desired identity claim by the rule Universal Elimination, as in the following derivation:

Derive: k = k

1	(∀z)z = z	=I
2	k = k	1 ∀E

An identity claim of the form **a** = **a** also can be obtained by applying the rule of Identity Elimination to an identity sentence of the form **a** = **b**, where **a** and **b** are different constants. The rule Identity Elimination is simply applied to the sentence itself! Consider the derivation

Derive: k = k

1	i = k	Assumption
2	k = k	1, 1 =E

Because i is identical to k by line 1 the rule Identity Elimination allows us to replace 'i' with 'k' wherever 'i' occurs in a sentence. In this derivation 'i' has been replaced with 'k' in the identity sentence 'i = k' itself to derive 'k = k' on line 2.

These identity rules, along with the other rules of *PD*, are needed to establish derivability claims that depend upon identity. Consider the following argument as an example:

The Roman general who defeated Pompey conquered Gaul.
Julius Caesar was a Roman general, and he defeated Pompey.
______
Julius Caesar conquered Gaul.

We know this argument must be valid, for if Julius Caesar was a Roman general who defeated Pompey, then he must have been the same person who conquered Gaul. We can show that this argument is valid by symbolizing it in *PLE* and deriving the conclusion from the premises in *PDE*:

$(\exists x)[((Rx \& Dxp) \& (\forall y)[(Ry \& Dyp) \supset y = x]) \& Cxg]$
$Rj \& Djp$
———
Cjg

Notice that the definite description 'the Roman general who defeated Pompey' has been captured in *PLE* by using the identity predicate. Here is a derivation that shows this argument is valid in *PDE*:

Derive: Cjg

1	$(\exists x)[((Rx \& Dxp) \& (\forall y)[(Ry \& Dyp) \supset y = x]) \& Cxg]$	Assumption
2	$Rj \& Djp$	Assumption
3	$\quad((Ra \& Dap) \& (\forall y)[(Ry \& Dyp) \supset y = a]) \& Cag$	Assumption
4	$\quad(Ra \& Dap) \& (\forall y)[(Ry \& Dyp) \supset y = a]$	3 &E
5	$\quad(\forall y)[(Ry \& Dyp) \supset y = a]$	4 &E
6	$\quad(Rj \& Djp) \supset j = a$	5 ∀E
7	$\quad j = a$	2, 6 ⊃E
8	$\quad Cag$	3 &E
9	$\quad Cjg$	7, 8 =E
10	Cjg	1, 3–9 ∃E

FUNCTORS

Next we need to adjust our derivation system to accommodate sentences containing functors. Let's begin with a very simple argument that employs both identity and functions:

The sum of 1 and 8 is 9.
The sum of 2 and 2 is 4.
4 is less than the sum of 1 and 8.
———
Therefore, the sum of 2 and 2 is less than 9.

We can begin by symbolizing the premises and the sentence to be derived as follows:

Derive: L*s*(t,t)n

1	*s*(o,e) = n	Assumption
2	*s*(t,t) = f	Assumption
3	Lf*s*(o,e)	Assumption

Here we use 's(x,y)' to express the addition function, 'o' to designate 1, and 'e' to designate 8. 'Lxy' expresses 'x is less than y'. To complete our derivation, we need to adjust our original statement of the Identity Elimination rule so that it applies to both identity sentences containing complex terms and those containing individual constants. In *PDE* the generalized rule becomes

<u>*Identity Elimination* (=E)</u>

	$\mathbf{t}_1 = \mathbf{t}_2$			$\mathbf{t}_1 = \mathbf{t}_2$
	P	or		**P**
▷	$\mathbf{P}(\mathbf{t}_1//\mathbf{t}_2)$		▷	$\mathbf{P}(\mathbf{t}_2//\mathbf{t}_1)$

where $\mathbf{t}_1$ and $\mathbf{t}_2$ are closed terms

Because of the stipulation in the rule, '**t**' ranges over both individual constants and complex terms containing no variables. The notation

$\mathbf{P}(\mathbf{t}_1//\mathbf{t}_2)$

means that one or more occurrences of the closed term $\mathbf{t}_2$ in **P** have been replaced by the closed term $\mathbf{t}_1$.

Now we can return to our symbolized argument and complete the derivation easily using Identity Elimination.

Derive: Ls(t,t)n

1	s(o,e) = n	Assumption
2	s(t,t) = f	Assumption
3	Lfs(o,e)	Assumption
4	Ls(t,t)s(o,e)	2, 3 =E
5	Ls(t,t)n	1, 4 =E

The derivation rule Universal Elimination is generalized for *PDE* as well.

<u>*Universal Elimination* (∀E)</u>

	(∀**x**)**P**
▷	**P**(**t**/**x**)

where **t** is any closed term

This rule is plausibly extended to apply to closed complex terms in addition to individual constants because both kinds of terms designate individuals. The revised Universal Elimination rule is, like all the rules of *PD* and *PDE*, truth-preserving. If a claim is true of everything, then it is true of every individual including those designated by closed complex terms.

The derivation rule Existential Introduction is generalized for *PDE* as follows:

Existential Introduction (∀I)

	$\mathbf{P(t/x)}$
▷	$(\exists \mathbf{x})\mathbf{P}$

where **t** is any closed term

The rule is truth-preserving because, if a claim is true about an individual including one designated by a closed complex term, then there exists something about which the claim is true.

But the rule Universal Introduction and the rule Existential Elimination in *PDE* remain as defined in *PD*. To understand why, consider the following:

1	$(\forall x)Ed(x)$	Assumption	
2	$Ed(f)$	1 ∀E	
3	$(\forall x)Ex$	2 ∀I	**MISTAKE!**

Let's consider the positive integers, take '$d(x)$' to express multiplication by 2, and take 'Ex' to express 'x is even'. The primary assumption claims that any positive integer multiplied by 2 is even, which is true. It follows by Universal Elimination on line 2 that 5 multiplied by 2 (that is, 10) is even. But applying Universal Introduction on line 3 is a mistake. It is not true that every positive integer is even. Notice that, if we had generalized the rule Universal Introduction for closed complex terms, this derivation would have been allowed. But we do not allow it because the rule Universal Introduction depends upon picking out an *arbitrary* individual. An individual that is designated by a complex term is *not* arbitrarily selected—we do know something about it, namely, that it is a value of the function in question. In this example it would be a mistake to reason that, if an arbitrary positive integer that is a multiple of 2 is even, it follows that *every* positive integer is even.

We conclude that the rule Universal Introduction must be carried over to *PDE* as it is defined in *PD*. Only individual constants, and not closed complex terms, can occur in the relevant substitution instances when applying the rule Universal Introduction.

Similarly the rule Existential Elimination remains as defined in *PD*. Why? Here is an erroneous line of a derivation:

1	$(\exists x)Ox$	Assumption	
2	$\quad Od(i)$	Assumption	
3	$\quad (\exists x)Od(x)$	2 ∃I	
4	$(\exists x)Od(x)$	1, 2–3 ∃E	**MISTAKE!**

Again consider the positive integers, let '$d(x)$' represent multiplication by 2, and let 'Ox' represent 'x is odd'. In this case the primary assumption claims correctly that an odd positive integer exists. Line 2 says that multiplying an arbitrary integer i by 2 results in an odd number. Under this assumption the sentence on line 3, '$(\exists x)Od(x)$', follows. But the sentence on line 4 is clearly false under our interpretation. There is no positive integer that when doubled is odd. Note that, if we had generalized the rule Existential Elimination for closed complex terms, this derivation would have been allowed.

The rule Existential Elimination succeeds by ensuring that an arbitrary individual is designated in the substitution instance taken as the auxiliary assumption, and it ensures this by requiring that the individual be designated by a constant rather than as the value of a function. The rule Existential Elimination remains the same in *PDE* as it is in *PD*. Only individual constants, and not closed complex terms, can occur in the relevant substitution instance when applying the rule.

The following derivations demonstrate how the rules of *PDE* can be used. In this first derivation Universal Introduction is properly applied when the instantiating individual constant occurs within a complex term.

Derive: $(\forall x)Gg(x)$

1	$(\forall x)(Gf(x) \supset Gg(x))$	Assumption
2	$(\forall x)Gf(x)$	Assumption
3	$Gf(a) \supset Gg(a)$	1 ∀E
4	$Gf(a)$	2 ∀E
5	$Gg(a)$	3, 4 ⊃E
6	$(\forall x)Gg(x)$	5 ∀I

Again it was correct to derive '$(\forall x)Gg(x)$' by ∀I because the constant 'a' on line 5 is the instantiating term. It would *not* have been correct to derive '$(\forall x)Gx$', taking '$g(a)$' as the instantiating term on line 5.

Similarly Existential Elimination can be applied correctly when the instantiating individual constant is contained within a complex term.

Derive: $(\exists x)Gf(x)f(f(x))$

1	$(\forall x)(Ox \supset Gxf(x))$	Assumption
2	$(\exists x)Of(x)$	Assumption
3	$\quad Of(a)$	Assumption
4	$\quad Of(a) \supset Gf(a)f(f(a))$	1 ∀E
5	$\quad Gf(a)f(f(a))$	3, 4 ⊃E
6	$\quad (\exists x)Gf(x)f(f(x))$	5 ∃I
7	$(\exists x)Gf(x)f(f(x))$	2, 3–6 ∃E

The rule Identity Elimination allows for the replacement of closed complex terms, as well as individual constants. Notice in the following example that the identity sentence on line 2 serves as both the identity sentence and the sentence, **P**, in which the identity substitution occurs. We can use Identity Elimination by replacing 'a' within the complex term '*f*(a)' with '*f*(a)' itself to produce the new complex term '*f*(*f*(a))' in the sentence on line 3. Finally the use of Universal Introduction on line 4 generalizes correctly from an individual constant on line 3, and not from a complex term.

Derive: (∀x)*f*(*f*(x)) = x

1	(∀x)*f*(x) = x	Assumption
2	*f*(a) = a	1 ∀E
3	*f*(*f*(a)) = a	2, 2 =E
4	(∀x)*f*(*f*(x)) = x	3 ∀I

The syntactical properties of *PD*, such as derivability, validity, and consistency, carry over analogously to the system *PDE*. Here is an example of a derivation showing that a symbolization of the following argument is valid in *PDE*:

Every natural number greater than 2 is the sum of two primes.
A billion is a natural number greater than 2.

Some natural number and a sum of two primes are equal.

Derive: (∃x)(∃y)(∃z)(Nx & ((Py & Pz) & x = *s*(y,z)))

1	(∀x)((Nx & Gxt) ⊃ (∃y)(∃z)((Py & Pz) & x = *s*(y,z)))	Assumption
2	Nb & Gbt	Assumption
3	(Nb & Gbt) ⊃ (∃y)(∃z)((Py & Pz) & b = *s*(y,z)))	1 ∀E
4	(∃y)(∃z)((Py & Pz) & b = *s*(y,z))	2, 3 ⊃E
5	(∃z)((Pi & Pz) & b = *s*(i,z))	Assumption
6	(Pi & Pj) & b = *s*(i,j)	Assumption
7	Nb	2 &E
8	Nb & ((Pi & Pj) & b = *s*(i,j))	6, 7 &I
9	(∃z)(Nb & ((Pi & Pz) & b = *s*(i,z)))	8 ∃I
10	(∃y)(∃z)(Nb & ((Py & Pz) & b = *s*(y,z)))	9 ∃I
11	(∃x)(∃y)(∃z)(Nx & ((Py & Pz) & x = *s*(y,z)))	10 ∃I
12	(∃x)(∃y)(∃z)(Nx & ((Py & Pz) & x = *s*(y,z)))	5, 6–11 ∃E
13	(∃x)(∃y)(∃z)(Nx & ((Py & Pz) & x = *s*(y,z)))	4, 5–12 ∃E

Notice once more that the individual constants 'i' and 'j' are used in the substitution instances on lines 5 and 6 so that no violation of the Existential Elimination rule occurs.

We expect

(∀x)(∀y)(∀z)[(x = *f*(z) & y = *f*(z)) ⊃ x = y]

to be a theorem in *PDE*, since it is quantificationally true: A function produces at most one value for a given argument. The next derivation shows that this sentence is indeed a theorem in *PDE*.

Derive: $(\forall x)(\forall y)(\forall z)[(x = f(z) \,\&\, y = f(z)) \supset x = y]$

1	$\quad a = f(c) \,\&\, b = f(c)$	Assumption
2	$\quad a = f(c)$	1 &E
3	$\quad b = f(c)$	1 &E
4	$\quad a = b$	2, 3 =E
5	$(a = f(c) \,\&\, b = f(c)) \supset a = b$	1–4 ⊃I
6	$(\forall z)[(a = f(z) \,\&\, b = f(z)) \supset a = b]$	5 ∀I
7	$(\forall y)(\forall z)[(a = f(z) \,\&\, y = f(z)) \supset a = y]$	6 ∀I
8	$(\forall x)(\forall y)(\forall z)[(x = f(z) \,\&\, y = f(z)) \supset x = y]$	7 ∀I

There is an important difference between *PD+* and our latest system, *PDE*. Although both are extensions of *PD* in the sense that each adds new rules to *PD*, *PD+* is not stronger than *PD*. Everything derivable in *PD+* is derivable in *PD*. However, *PDE*, with two new identity rules and adaptations of the *PD* introduction and elimination rules for quantifiers, allows us to derive results in *PDE* that are not derivable in *PD*. The previous examples in this section involving the identity predicate and complex terms illustrate this.

However, it should be clear that we can augment the rules of *PDE* with the additional rules of *PD+* to form a derivation system *PDE+* that is equivalent to *PDE*. Here is a short derivation in *PDE+*:

Derive: $\sim (\exists x) f(x) = x$

1	$(\forall x)(\forall y)(f(x) = y \supset \sim f(y) = x)$	Assumption
2	$\quad f(a) = a$	Assumption
3	$\quad (\forall y)(f(a) = y \supset \sim f(y) = a)$	1 ∀E
4	$\quad f(a) = a \supset \sim f(a) = a$	3 ∀E
5	$\quad \sim f(a) = a$	2, 4 ⊃E
6	$\quad f(a) = a$	3 R
7	$\sim f(a) = a$	2–6 ~I
8	$(\forall x) \sim f(x) = x$	7 ∀I
9	$\sim (\exists x) f(x) = x$	8 QN

10.6E EXERCISES

1. Show that each of the following is a theorem in *PLE*.

a. $a = b \supset b = a$

*b. $(a = b \,\&\, b = c) \supset a = c$

c. $(\sim a = b \,\&\, b = c) \supset \sim a = c$

*d. $\sim a = b \equiv \sim b = a$

e. $\sim a = c \supset (\sim a = b \vee \sim b = c)$

2. Show that each of the following is valid in *PDE*.

a. $a = b \ \& \sim Bab$

$\sim (\forall x)Bxx$

*b. $Ge \supset d = e$

$Ge \supset He$

$Ge \supset Hd$

c. $(\forall z)[Gz \supset (\forall y)(Ky \supset Hzy)]$

$(Ki \ \& \ Gj) \ \& \ i = j$

Hii

*d. $(\exists x)(Hx \ \& \ Mx)$

$Ms \ \& \sim Hs$

$(\exists x)[(Hx \ \& \ Mx) \ \& \sim x = s]$

e. $a = b$

$Ka \vee \sim Kb$

3. Show that each of the following is a theorem in *PDE*.

a. $(\forall x)(x = x \vee \sim x = x)$
*b. $(\forall x)(\forall y)(x = x \ \& \ y = y)$
c. $(\forall x)(\forall y)(x = y \equiv y = x)$
*d. $(\forall x)(\forall y)(\forall z)[(x = y \ \& \ y = z) \supset x = z]$
e. $\sim (\exists x) \sim x = x$

4. Symbolize each of the following arguments in *PLE* and show that each argument is valid in *PDE*.

a. The number 2 is not identical to 4. The numbers 2 and 4 are both even numbers. Therefore there are at least two different even numbers.
*b. Hyde killed some innocent person. But Jekyll is Hyde. Jekyll is a doctor. Hence some doctor killed some innocent person.
c. Shakespeare didn't admire himself, but the queen admired Bacon. Thus Shakespeare isn't Bacon since Bacon admired everybody who was admired by somebody.
*d. Rebecca loves those and only those who love her. The brother of Charlie loves Rebecca. Sam is Charlie's brother. So Sam and Rebecca love each other.
e. Somebody robbed Peter and paid Paul. Peter didn't rob himself. Surely Paul didn't pay himself. Therefore somebody else robbed Peter and paid Paul.

5. Which of the following illustrate mistakes in *PDE*? Explain what each mistake is.

a.

1	$(\exists x)Sx$	Assumption
2	$\quad Sg(f)$	Assumption
3	$\quad (\exists x)Sg(x)$	2 $\exists$I
4	$(\exists x)Sg(x)$	1, 2–3 $\exists$E

*b.	1	$(\exists x)Sg(x,x)$	Assumption
	2	| $Sg(i,i)$	Assumption
	3	| $(\exists x)Sg(i,x)$	2 $\exists$I
	4	$(\exists x)Sg(i,x)$	1, 2–3 $\exists$E

c.	1	$(\exists x)Hxg(x)$	Assumption
	2	| $Heg(e)$	Assumption
	3	| $(\exists y)Hyg(y)$	2 $\exists$I
	4	$(\exists y)Hyg(y)$	1, 2–3 $\exists$E

*d.	1	$(\forall x)Rf(x)$	Assumption
	2	$Rf(a)$	1 $\forall$E
	3	$(\forall z)Rf(z)$	2 $\forall$I

e.	1	$(\forall x)Lxxx$	Assumption
	2	$Lf(a,a)a$	1 $\forall$E
	3	$(\forall x)Lf(x,x)x$	2 $\forall$I

*f.	1	$(\forall x)Mx$	Assumption
	2	$Mf(f(a))$	1 $\forall$E
	3	$(\exists x)Mf(x)$	2 $\exists$I

g.	1	$(\forall x)Rf(x,x)$	Assumption
	2	$Rf(c,c)$	1 $\forall$E
	3	$(\forall y)Ry$	2 $\forall$I

*h.	1	$(\forall x)Jx$	Assumption
	2	$Jf(f(a))$	1 $\forall$E
	3	$(\exists y)Jf(f(y))$	2 $\exists$I

i.	1	$(\forall x)Jx$	Assumption
	2	$Jf(g(a,b))$	1 $\forall$E
	3	$(\exists x)Jf(g(x,b))$	2 $\exists$I

*j.	1	$(\forall x)Lx$	Assumption
	2	$Lf(a,a)$	1 $\forall$E
	3	$(\forall x)Lf(a,x)$	2 $\forall$I

6. Show that each of the following is a theorem in *PDE.*

a. $(\forall x)(\exists y)f(x) = y$

*b. $(\forall x)(\forall y)(\forall z)[(f(x) = g(x,y)\ \&\ g(x,y) = h(x,y,z)) \supset f(x) = h(x,y,z)]$

c. $(\forall x)Ff(x) \supset (\forall x)Ff(g(x))$

*d. $(\forall x)[\sim f(x) = x \supset (\forall y)(f(x) = y \supset \sim x = y)]$

e. $(\forall x)(f(f(x)) = x \supset f(f(f(f(x)))) = x)$

*f. $(\forall x)(\forall y)(\forall z)[(f(g(x)) = y\ \&\ f(y) = z) \supset f(f(g(x))) = z]$

g. $(\forall x)(\forall y)[(f(x) = y\ \&\ f(y) = x) \supset x = f(f(x))]$

7. Show that each of the following is valid in *PDE.*

a. $(\forall x)(Bx \supset Gxf(x))$
$(\forall x)Bf(x)$
____
$(\forall x)Gf(x)f(f(x))$

*b. $(\forall x)(Kx \vee Hg(x))$
____
$(\forall x)(Kg(x) \vee Hg(g(x)))$

c. $(\forall x)(\forall y)(f(x) = y \supset Myxc)$
$\sim Mbac\ \&\ \sim Mabc$
____
$\sim f(a) = b$

*d. $\sim (\exists x)Rx$
____
$(\forall x) \sim Rf(x,g(x))$

e. $(\exists x)(\forall y)(\forall z)Lxyz$
____
$(\exists x)Lxf(x)g(x)$

*f. $(\forall x)[\sim Lxf(x) \vee (\exists y)Ng(y)]$
____
$(\exists x)Lf(x)f(f(x)) \supset (\exists x)Ng(y)$

g. $(\forall x)[Zx \supset (\forall y)(\sim Dxy \equiv Hf(f(y)))]$
$(\forall x)(Zx\ \&\ \sim Hx)$
____
$(\forall x)Df(x)f(x)$

*h. $(\forall x)(\forall y)(\exists z)Sf(x)yz$
$(\forall x)(\forall y)(\forall z)(Sxyz \supset \sim (Cxyz \vee Mzyx))$
____
$(\exists x)(\exists y) \sim (\forall z)Mzg(y)f(g(x))$

GLOSSARY[1]

DERIVABILITY IN *PD*: A sentence **P** of *PL* is *derivable in PD* from a set Γ of sentences of *PL* if and only if there is a derivation in *PD* in which all the primary assumptions are members of Γ and **P** occurs in the scope of only those assumptions.

VALIDITY IN *PD*: An argument of *PL* is *valid in PD* if and only if the conclusion of the argument is derivable in *PD* from the set consisting of the premises. An argument of *PL* is *invalid in PD* if and only if it is not valid in *PD*.

THEOREM IN *PD*: A sentence **P** of *PL* is a *theorem in PD* if and only if **P** is derivable in *PD* from the empty set.

EQUIVALENCE IN *PD*: Sentences **P** and **Q** of *PL* are *equivalent in PD* if and only if **Q** is derivable in *PD* from {**P**} and **P** is derivable in *PD* from {**Q**}.

INCONSISTENCY IN *PD*: A set Γ of sentences of *PL* is *inconsistent in PD* if and only if both a sentence **P** of *PL* and its negation ~ **P** are derivable in *PD* from Γ. A set Γ of sentences of *PL* is *consistent in PD* if and only if it is not inconsistent in *PD*.

[1] Similar definitions hold for the derivation systems *PD*+, *PDE*, and *PDE*+.

Chapter **11**

PREDICATE LOGIC: METATHEORY

11.1 SEMANTIC PRELIMINARIES FOR *PL*

We have been tacitly assuming that our semantic and syntactic concepts of predicate logic coincide. For example, we have assumed that a sentence **P** of *PL* is quantificationally true if and only if **P** is a theorem in *PD,* and also that **P** is quantificationally true if and only if {~ **P**} has a closed truth-tree. In this chapter we shall show that our semantic and syntactic concepts do coincide. We shall establish four major results: the soundness and completeness of the natural deduction systems *PD, PD+*, and *PDE,* and the soundness and completeness of the truth-tree method developed in Chapter 9. The results we establish are part of the *metatheory* of predicate logic.

In our proofs of the adequacy of the natural deduction systems and the tree method, we shall use some fundamental semantic results that may seem obvious but that nevertheless must be proved. The purpose of this section is to establish these results. One may skim over this section on the first reading without working through all the proofs but should keep in mind that later metatheoretic proofs depend on the results presented here.

Given any formula **P**, variable **x**, and constant **a**, let **P**(**a**/**x**) be the formula that results from replacing every free occurrence of **x** in **P** with **a**. Our first result establishes that any variable assignment **d** will treat **P**(**a**/**x**) exactly as $\mathbf{d[I(a)/x]}$ treats **P**. If **d** satisfies $\mathbf{P(a/x)}$, then the variable assignment that is just like **d** except that it assigns the denotation of **a** to **x** will satisfy **P**, and vice versa. This should not be surprising, for if **x** is used to refer to exactly the same thing as **a**, we would expect **P** and $\mathbf{P(a/x)}$ to behave the same way.

> **11.1.1:** Let **P** be a formula of *PL*, let $\mathbf{P(a/x)}$ be the formula that results from replacing every free occurrence of **x** in **P** with an individual constant **a**, let **I** be an interpretation, and let **d** be a variable assignment for **I**. Then **d** satisfies $\mathbf{P(a/x)}$ on **I** if and only if $\mathbf{d[I(a)/x]}$ satisfies **P** on **I**.

To prove the result, we shall use mathematical induction on the number of occurrences of logical operators—truth-functional connectives and quantifiers—that occur in **P**.

Basis clause: If **P** is a formula that contains zero occurrences of logical operators, then **d** satisfies $\mathbf{P(a/x)}$ if and only if $\mathbf{d[I(a)/x]}$ satisfies **P**.

Proof of basis clause: If **P** contains zero occurrences of logical operators, then **P** is either a sentence letter or a formula of the form $\mathbf{At_1 \ldots t_n}$, where **A** is a predicate and $\mathbf{t_1, \ldots, t_n}$ are individual constants or variables. If **P** is a sentence letter, then $\mathbf{P(a/x)}$ is simply **P**—a sentence letter alone does not contain any variables to be replaced. **d** satisfies $\mathbf{P(a/x)}$, then, if and only if $\mathbf{I(P) = T}$. And $\mathbf{d[I(a)/x]}$ satisfies **P** if and only if $\mathbf{I(P) = T}$. So **d** satisfies $\mathbf{P(a/x)}$ if and only if $\mathbf{d[I(a)/x]}$ satisfies **P**.

If **P** has the form $\mathbf{At_1 \ldots t_n}$, then $\mathbf{P(a/x)}$ is $\mathbf{At'_1 \ldots t'_n}$, where $\mathbf{t'_i}$ is **a** if $\mathbf{t_i}$ is **x** and $\mathbf{t'_i}$ is just $\mathbf{t_i}$ otherwise. By the definition of satisfaction,

a. **d** satisfies $\mathbf{At'_1 \ldots t'_n}$ if and only if $<\mathrm{den}_{\mathbf{I,d}}(\mathbf{t'_1}), \mathrm{den}_{\mathbf{I,d}}(\mathbf{t'_2}), \ldots, \mathrm{den}_{\mathbf{I,d}}(\mathbf{t'_n})>$ is a member of $\mathbf{I(A)}$.

b. $\mathbf{d[I(a)/x]}$ satisfies $\mathbf{At_1 \ldots t_n}$ if and only if $<\mathrm{den}_{\mathbf{I,d[I(a)/x]}}(\mathbf{t_1}), \mathrm{den}_{\mathbf{I,d[I(a)/x]}}(\mathbf{t_2}), \ldots, \mathrm{den}_{\mathbf{I,d[I(a)/x]}}(\mathbf{t_n})>$ is a member of $\mathbf{I(A)}$.

But now we note that

c. $<\mathrm{den}_{\mathbf{I,d}}(\mathbf{t'_1}), \mathrm{den}_{\mathbf{I,d}}(\mathbf{t'_2}), \ldots, \mathrm{den}_{\mathbf{I,d}}(\mathbf{t'_n})> = <\mathrm{den}_{\mathbf{I,d[I(a)/x]}}(\mathbf{t_1}), \mathrm{den}_{\mathbf{I,d[I(a)/x]}}(\mathbf{t_2}), \ldots, \mathrm{den}_{\mathbf{I,d[I(a)/x]}}(\mathbf{t_n})>$.

Consider: If $\mathbf{t_i}$ is a constant, then $\mathbf{t'_i}$ is $\mathbf{t_i}$ and so $\mathrm{den}_{\mathbf{I,d}}(\mathbf{t'_i}) = \mathbf{I(t_i)}$ and $\mathrm{den}_{\mathbf{I,d[I(a)/x]}}(\mathbf{t_i}) = \mathbf{I(t_i)}$. If $\mathbf{t_i}$ is any variable other than **x**, then $\mathbf{t'_i}$ is $\mathbf{t_i}$ and so $\mathrm{den}_{\mathbf{I,d}}(\mathbf{t'_i}) = \mathbf{d(t_i)} = \mathbf{d}_{\mathbf{[I(a)/x]}}(\mathbf{t_i}) = \mathrm{den}_{\mathbf{I,d[I(a)/x]}}(\mathbf{t_i})$—the assignment of $\mathbf{I(a)}$ to **x** in the variable assignment does not affect the value assigned to $\mathbf{t_i}$ in this case. If $\mathbf{t_i}$ is the variable **x**, then $\mathbf{t'_i}$ is **a** and $\mathrm{den}_{\mathbf{I,d}}(\mathbf{a}) = \mathbf{I(a)} = \mathbf{d[I(a)/x](x)} = \mathrm{den}_{\mathbf{I,d[I(a)/x]}}(\mathbf{x})$. (The variant ensures that the denotations of **x** and of **a** coincide.)

Because the **n**-tuples are the same **n**-tuple, we conclude from (a) and (b) that **d** satisfies $\mathbf{At'_1 \ldots t'_n}$ if and only if $\mathbf{d[I(a)/x]}$ satisfies $\mathbf{At_1 \ldots t_n}$.

The basis clause—in particular, the case where an atomic formula has the form $\mathbf{At_1 \ldots t_n}$—is the crux of our proof. Having shown that at the atomic level the thesis we are proving holds, it is straightforward to show that the addition of connectives and quantifiers to build larger formulas does not change matters. The inductive step in the proof of 11.1.1 is

Inductive step: If every formula **P** that contains **k** or fewer occurrences of logical operators is such that **d** satisfies **P(a/x)** if and only if **d[I(a)/x]** satisfies **P**, then every formula **P** that contains **k** + 1 occurrences of logical operators is such that **d** satisfies **P(a/x)** if and only if **d[I(a)/x]** satisfies **P**.

Proof of inductive step: Letting **k** be an arbitrary positive integer, we assume that the inductive hypothesis holds—that our claim is true of every formula with **k** or fewer occurrences of logical operators. We must show that it follows that the claim is also true of every formula **P** with **k** + 1 occurrences of logical operators. We consider each form that **P** may have.

Case 1: **P** has the form ~ **Q**. Then **P(a/x)** is ~ **Q(a/x)**, the negation of **Q(a/x)** (that is, any replacements of **x** that were made had to be made within **Q**). By the definition of satisfaction,

a. **d** satisfies ~ **Q(a/x)** if and only if it does not satisfy **Q(a/x)**.

Because **Q(a/x)** contains fewer than **k** + 1 occurrences of logical operators, it follows from the inductive hypothesis that

b. **d** does not satisfy **Q(a/x)** if and only if **d[I(a)/x]** does not satisfy **Q**.

And, by the definition of satisfaction,

c. **d[I(a)/x]** does not satisfy **Q** if and only if **d[I(a)/x]** does satisfy ~ **Q**.

So, by (a)–(c), **d** satisfies ~ **Q(a/x)** if and only if **d[I(a)/x]** satisfies ~ **Q**.

Case 2: **P** has the form **Q** & **R**. Then **P(a/x)** is

Q(a/x) & **R(a/x)**

—all replacements of **x** occurred within **Q** and **R**. By the definition of satisfaction,

a. **d** satisfies **Q(a/x)** & **R(a/x)** if and only if **d** satisfies **Q(a/x)** and **d** satisfies **R(a/x)**.

Both conjuncts contain fewer than $\mathbf{k} + 1$ occurrences of logical operators so, by the inductive hypothesis,

b. **d** satisfies **Q**(**a**/**x**) if and only if **d**[**I**(**a**)/**x**] satisfies **Q**.

c. **d** satisfies **R**(**a**/**x**) if and only if **d**[**I**(**a**)/**x**] satisfies **R**.

By the definition of satisfaction,

d. **d**[**I**(**a**)/**x**] satisfies both **Q** and **R** if and only if **d**[**I**(**a**)/**x**] satisfies **Q** & **R**.

By (a)–(d), then, **d** satisfies **Q**(**a**/**x**) & **R**(**a**/**x**) if and only if **d**[**I**(**a**)/**x**] satisfies **Q** & **R**.

Cases 3–5: The proofs for the case in which **P** has one of the forms **Q** ∨ **R**, **Q** ⊃ **R**, and **Q** ≡ **R** are similar to that of Case 2 and are left as exercises.

Case 6: **P** has the form (∀**y**)**Q**. We must consider two possibilities. If **y** is not the variable **x** that **a** is replacing in (∀**y**)**Q**, then **P**(**a**/**x**) is (∀**y**)**Q**(**a**/**x**)—all replacements of **x** are made within **Q**. By the definition of satisfaction,

a. **d** satisfies (∀**y**)**Q**(**a**/**x**) if and only if, for every member **u** of the UD, **d**[**u**/**y**] satisfies **Q**(**a**/**x**).

Because **Q** contains fewer than $\mathbf{k} + 1$ occurrences of logical operators, it follows from the inductive hypothesis that for every member **u** of the UD,

b. **d**[**u**/**y**] satisfies **Q**(**a**/**x**) if and only if **d**[**u**/**y**, **I**(**a**)/**x**] satisfies **Q**.

Each variant **d**[**u**/**y**, **I**(**a**)/**x**] is identical to **d**[**I**(**a**)/**x**, **u**/**y**] because **x** and **y** are not the same variable, and hence neither of the assignments within the brackets can override the other. So every member **u** of the UD is such that

c. **d**[**u**/**y**, **I**(**a**)/**x**] satisfies **Q** if and only if **d**[**I**(**a**)/**x**, **u**/**y**] satisfies **Q**.

And, by the definition of satisfaction again,

d. Every member **u** of the UD is such that **d**[**I**(**a**)/**x**, **u**/**y**] satisfies **Q** if and only if **d**[**I**(**a**)/**x**] satisfies (∀**y**)**Q**.

So, by (a)–(d), in the case where **y** is not the variable **x** that **a** is replacing, **d** satisfies (∀**y**)**Q**(**a**/**x**) if and only if **d**[**I**(**a**)/**x**] satisfies (∀**y**)**Q**.

If $\mathbf{P}$ is $(\forall \mathbf{x})\mathbf{Q}$, where $\mathbf{x}$ is the variable that $\mathbf{a}$ is replacing, then $\mathbf{P}(\mathbf{a}/\mathbf{x})$ is also $(\forall \mathbf{x})\mathbf{Q}$. Because $\mathbf{a}$ replaces only *free* occurrences of $\mathbf{x}$ in $\mathbf{P}$ and $\mathbf{x}$ does not occur free in $\mathbf{P}$, no replacements are made within $\mathbf{Q}$. By the definition of satisfaction,

a. $\mathbf{d}$ satisfies $(\forall \mathbf{x})\mathbf{Q}$ (which is our $\mathbf{P}(\mathbf{a}/\mathbf{x})$) if and only, if for every member $\mathbf{u}$ of the UD, $\mathbf{d}[\mathbf{u}/\mathbf{x}]$ satisfies $\mathbf{Q}$.

b. $\mathbf{d}[\mathbf{I}(\mathbf{a})/\mathbf{x}]$ satisfies $(\forall \mathbf{x})\mathbf{Q}$ (which is our $\mathbf{P}$) if and only if, for every member $\mathbf{u}$ of the UD, $\mathbf{d}[\mathbf{I}(\mathbf{a})/\mathbf{x}, \mathbf{u}/\mathbf{x}]$ satisfies $\mathbf{Q}$.

What is $\mathbf{d}[\mathbf{I}(\mathbf{a})/\mathbf{x}, \mathbf{u}/\mathbf{x}]$? This variable assignment is just $\mathbf{d}[\mathbf{u}/\mathbf{x}]$—the first assignment made to $\mathbf{x}$ within the brackets is overridden by the second. So

c. Every member $\mathbf{u}$ of the UD is such that $\mathbf{d}[\mathbf{I}(\mathbf{a})/\mathbf{x}, \mathbf{u}/\mathbf{x}]$ satisfies $\mathbf{Q}$ if and only if every member $\mathbf{u}$ of the UD is such that $\mathbf{d}[\mathbf{u}/\mathbf{x}]$ satisfies $\mathbf{Q}$.

Therefore, by (a)–(c), $\mathbf{d}[\mathbf{I}(\mathbf{a})/\mathbf{x}]$ satisfies $(\forall \mathbf{x})\mathbf{Q}$ if and only if $\mathbf{d}$ satisfies $(\forall \mathbf{x})\mathbf{Q}$.

Case 7: $\mathbf{P}$ has the form $(\exists \mathbf{y})\mathbf{Q}$. Again we consider two possibilities. If $\mathbf{y}$ is not the variable $\mathbf{x}$ that $\mathbf{a}$ is replacing, then $\mathbf{P}(\mathbf{a}/\mathbf{x})$ is $(\exists \mathbf{y})\mathbf{Q}(\mathbf{a}/\mathbf{x})$. By the definition of satisfaction,

a. $\mathbf{d}$ satisfies $(\exists \mathbf{y})\mathbf{Q}(\mathbf{a}/\mathbf{x})$ if and only if, for some member $\mathbf{u}$ of the UD, $\mathbf{d}[\mathbf{u}/\mathbf{y}]$ satisfies $\mathbf{Q}(\mathbf{a}/\mathbf{x})$.

By the inductive hypothesis, because $\mathbf{Q}(\mathbf{a}/\mathbf{x})$ contains fewer than $\mathbf{k} + 1$ occurrences of logical operators,

b. $\mathbf{d}[\mathbf{u}/\mathbf{y}]$ satisfies $\mathbf{Q}(\mathbf{a}/\mathbf{x})$ if and only if $\mathbf{d}[\mathbf{u}/\mathbf{y}, \mathbf{I}(\mathbf{a})/\mathbf{x}]$ satisfies $\mathbf{Q}$.

Because $\mathbf{y}$ and $\mathbf{x}$ are different variables, $\mathbf{d}[\mathbf{u}/\mathbf{y}, \mathbf{I}(\mathbf{a})/\mathbf{x}]$ is the same variable assignment as $\mathbf{d}[\mathbf{I}(\mathbf{a})/\mathbf{x}, \mathbf{u}/\mathbf{y}]$. So

c. $\mathbf{d}[\mathbf{u}/\mathbf{y}, \mathbf{I}(\mathbf{a})/\mathbf{x}]$ satisfies $\mathbf{Q}$ if and only if $\mathbf{d}[\mathbf{I}(\mathbf{a})/\mathbf{x}, \mathbf{u}/\mathbf{y}]$ satisfies $\mathbf{Q}$,

and by the definition of satisfaction,

d. $\mathbf{d}[\mathbf{I}(\mathbf{a})/\mathbf{x}, \mathbf{u}/\mathbf{y}]$ satisfies $\mathbf{Q}$ if and only if $\mathbf{d}[\mathbf{I}(\mathbf{a})/\mathbf{x}]$ satisfies $(\exists \mathbf{y})\mathbf{Q}$.

It follows from (a)–(d) that in the case where $\mathbf{y}$ and $\mathbf{x}$ are different variables, $\mathbf{d}$ satisfies $(\exists \mathbf{y})\mathbf{Q}(\mathbf{a}/\mathbf{x})$ if and only if $\mathbf{d}[\mathbf{I}(\mathbf{a})/\mathbf{x}]$ satisfies $(\exists \mathbf{y})\mathbf{Q}$.

If **P** is $(\exists \mathbf{x})\mathbf{Q}$, where **x** is the variable that **a** is replacing, then $\mathbf{P}(\mathbf{a}/\mathbf{x})$ is $(\exists \mathbf{x})\mathbf{Q}$—no replacements are made within **Q** because **x** is not free in $(\exists \mathbf{x})\mathbf{Q}$. So we must show that $\mathbf{d}[\mathbf{I}(\mathbf{a})/\mathbf{x}]$ satisfies $(\exists \mathbf{x})\mathbf{Q}$ if and only if **d** satisfies $(\exists \mathbf{x})\mathbf{Q}$. By the definition of satisfaction,

a. $\mathbf{d}[\mathbf{I}(\mathbf{a})/\mathbf{x}]$ satisfies $(\exists \mathbf{x})\mathbf{Q}$ if and only if, for some member **u** of the UD, $\mathbf{d}[\mathbf{I}(\mathbf{a})/\mathbf{x}, \mathbf{u}/\mathbf{x}]$ satisfies **Q**.

$\mathbf{d}[\mathbf{I}(\mathbf{a})/\mathbf{x}, \mathbf{u}/\mathbf{x}]$ is just $\mathbf{d}[\mathbf{u}/\mathbf{x}]$—the second assignment to **x** overrides the first—and so

b. $\mathbf{d}[\mathbf{I}(\mathbf{a})/\mathbf{x}, \mathbf{u}/\mathbf{x}]$ satisfies **Q** if and only if $\mathbf{d}[\mathbf{u}/\mathbf{x}]$ satisfies **Q**.

By the definition of satisfaction,

c. $\mathbf{d}[\mathbf{u}/\mathbf{x}]$ satisfies **Q** if and only if **d** satisfies $(\exists \mathbf{x})\mathbf{Q}$.

Therefore, by (a)–(c), $\mathbf{d}[\mathbf{I}(\mathbf{a})/\mathbf{x}]$ satisfies $(\exists \mathbf{x})\mathbf{Q}$ if and only if **d** satisfies $(\exists \mathbf{x})\mathbf{Q}$.

With the basis clause and the inductive step established, the conclusion of the argument is also established—every formula **P** is such that **d** satisfies $\mathbf{P}(\mathbf{a}/\mathbf{x})$ on **I** if and only if $\mathbf{d}[\mathbf{I}(\mathbf{a})/\mathbf{x}]$ satisfies **P** on **I**. And that completes the proof of result 11.1.1.

The second result will enable us to prove a claim that was made in Chapter 8: that for any interpretation and any sentence of *PL*, either all variable assignments satisfy the sentence or none do. We used this claim in defining truth and falsehood for sentences: A sentence is true on an interpretation if it is satisfied by all variable assignments and false if it is satisfied by none. The reason this claim turns out to be true is that there are no free variables in sentences. Result 11.1.2 assures us that only the values that a variable assignment assigns to the variables that are free in a formula play a role in determining whether the formula is satisfied:

11.1.2: Let **I** be an interpretation, **d** a variable assignment for **I**, and **P** a formula of *PL*. Then **d** satisfies **P** on **I** if and only if **P** is satisfied on **I** by every variable assignment that assigns the same values to the free variables in **P** as does **d**.

Proof: Let **I** be an interpretation, **d** a variable assignment for **I**, and **P** a formula of *PL*. We shall prove 11.1.2 by mathematical induction on the number of occurrences of logical operators in **P**.

Basis clause: If **P** is a formula that contains zero occurrences of logical operators, then **d** satisfies **P** if and only if **P** is satisfied by every variable assignment that assigns the same values to the free variables in **P** as does **d**.

Proof of basis clause: If $\mathbf{P}$ contains zero occurrences of logical operators, then $\mathbf{P}$ is either a sentence letter or a formula of the form $\mathbf{At_1 \ldots t_n}$. If $\mathbf{P}$ is a sentence letter, then any variable assignment satisfies $\mathbf{P}$ on $\mathbf{I}$ if and only if $\mathbf{I(P)} = \mathbf{T}$. Therefore $\mathbf{d}$ satisfies $\mathbf{P}$ if and only if every variable assignment that assigns the same values to the free variables in $\mathbf{P}$ as $\mathbf{d}$ satisfies $\mathbf{P}$.

If $\mathbf{P}$ has the form $\mathbf{At_1 \ldots t_n}$, then by the definition of satisfaction,

a. $\mathbf{d}$ satisfies $\mathbf{P}$ if and only if $<\text{den}_{\mathbf{I,d}}(\mathbf{t_1}), \text{den}_{\mathbf{I,d}}(\mathbf{t_2}), \ldots, \text{den}_{\mathbf{I,d}}(\mathbf{t_n})>$ is a member of $\mathbf{I(A)}$.

And where $\mathbf{d'}$ is a variable assignment that assigns the same values to the free variables in $\mathbf{P}$ as does $\mathbf{d}$,

b. $\mathbf{d'}$ satisfies $\mathbf{P}$ if and only if $<\text{den}_{\mathbf{I,d'}}(\mathbf{t_1}), \text{den}_{\mathbf{I,d'}}(\mathbf{t_2}), \ldots, \text{den}_{\mathbf{I,d'}}(\mathbf{t_n})>$ is a member of $\mathbf{I(A)}$.

But now we note that

c. $<\text{den}_{\mathbf{I,d}}(\mathbf{t_1}), \text{den}_{\mathbf{I,d}}(\mathbf{t_2}), \ldots, \text{den}_{\mathbf{I,d}}(\mathbf{t_n})> =$ $<\text{den}_{\mathbf{I,d'}}(\mathbf{t_1}), \text{den}_{\mathbf{I,d'}}(\mathbf{t_2}), \ldots, \text{den}_{\mathbf{I,d'}}(\mathbf{t_n})>$.

For if $\mathbf{t_i}$ is a constant, then $\text{den}_{\mathbf{I,d}}(\mathbf{t_i}) = \mathbf{I}(\mathbf{t_i})$ and $\text{den}_{\mathbf{I,d'}}(\mathbf{t_i}) = \mathbf{I}(\mathbf{t_i})$. If $\mathbf{t_i}$ is a variable, then $\mathbf{t_i}$ is free in $\mathbf{At_1 \ldots t_n}$ and is therefore by stipulation assigned the same value by $\mathbf{d'}$ as it is assigned by $\mathbf{d}$. So $\text{den}_{\mathbf{I,d}}(\mathbf{t_i}) = \mathbf{d}(\mathbf{t_i}) = \mathbf{d'}(\mathbf{t_i}) = \text{den}_{\mathbf{I,d'}}(\mathbf{t_i})$. Hence, by (a)–(c), we conclude that $\mathbf{d}$ satisfies $\mathbf{At_1 \ldots t_n}$ if and only if every variable assignment $\mathbf{d'}$ that assigns the same values to the free variables in $\mathbf{At_1 \ldots t_n}$ as $\mathbf{d}$ satisfies $\mathbf{At_1 \ldots t_n}$.

Inductive step: If every sentence $\mathbf{P}$ that contains $\mathbf{k}$ or fewer occurrences of logical operators is such that $\mathbf{d}$ satisfies $\mathbf{P}$ on $\mathbf{I}$ if and only if $\mathbf{P}$ is satisfied by every variable assignment that assigns the same values to the free variables in $\mathbf{P}$ as $\mathbf{d}$, then every sentence $\mathbf{P}$ that contains $\mathbf{k} + 1$ occurrences of logical operators is such that $\mathbf{d}$ satisfies $\mathbf{P}$ on $\mathbf{I}$ if and only if $\mathbf{P}$ is satisfied by every variable assignment that assigns the same values to the free variables in $\mathbf{P}$ as $\mathbf{d}$.

Proof of inductive step: Assume that, for an arbitrary positive integer $\mathbf{k}$, the inductive hypothesis is true. We shall show that on this assumption our claim must also be true of every sentence $\mathbf{P}$ that contains $\mathbf{k} + 1$ occurrences of logical operators. Let $\mathbf{I}$ be an interpretation and $\mathbf{d}$ a variable assignment for $\mathbf{I}$. We consider each form that $\mathbf{P}$ may have.

Case 1: $\mathbf{P}$ has the form $\sim \mathbf{Q}$. By the definition of satisfaction,

a. $\mathbf{d}$ satisfies $\sim \mathbf{Q}$ if and only if $\mathbf{d}$ does not satisfy $\mathbf{Q}$.

Because **Q** contains fewer than **k** + 1 occurrences of logical operators, it follows from the inductive hypothesis that

b. **d** does not satisfy **Q** if and only if every variable assignment that assigns to the free variables in **Q** the same values as **d** assigns to those variables does not satisfy **Q**.

And, by the definition of satisfaction,

c. Every variable assignment that assigns to the free variables in **Q** the same values as **d** assigns to those variables fails to satisfy **Q** if and only if every such assignment does satisfy ~ **Q**.

The variable assignments that assign the same values to the free variables of **Q** as does **d** are the variable assignments that assign the same values to the free variables of ~ **Q** as does **d** because **Q** and ~ **Q** contain the same free variables. So, by (a)–(c), **d** satisfies ~ **Q** if and only if every variable assignment that assigns the same values to the free variables in ~ **Q** as does **d** satisfies ~ **Q**.

Case 2: P has the form **Q** ∨ **R**. By the definition of satisfaction,

a. **d** satisfies **Q** ∨ **R** if and only if either **d** satisfies **Q** or **d** satisfies **R**.

Because **Q** and **R** each contain fewer than **k** + 1 occurrences of logical operators, it follows by the inductive hypothesis that

b. **d** satisfies **Q** if and only if every variable assignment that assigns to the free variables in **Q** the same values as **d** satisfies **Q**.

c. **d** satisfies **R** if and only if every variable assignment that assigns to the free variables in **R** the same values as **d** satisfies **R**.

By (a)–(c),

d. **d** satisfies **Q** ∨ **R** if and only if either every variable assignment that assigns to the free variables in **Q** the same values as **d** satisfies **Q** or every variable assignment that assigns to the free variables in **R** the same values as **d** satisfies **R**.

Because every variable that is free in **Q** is also free in **Q** ∨ **R**,

> e. Every variable assignment that assigns the same values as **d** to the free variables in **Q** ∨ **R** is a variable assignment that assigns the same values as **d** to the free variables in **Q**.

(The converse does not hold.) And, for a similar reason,

> f. Every variable assignment that assigns the same values as **d** to the free variables in **Q** ∨ **R** is a variable assignment that assigns the same values as **d** to the free variables in **R**.

Assume now that **d** satisfies **Q** ∨ **R**. By (d), either (i) every variable assignment that assigns to the free variables in **Q** the same values as **d** satisfies **Q** or (ii) every variable assignment that assigns to the free variables in **R** the same values as **d** satisfies **R**. If (i) is the case, then, by (e), we may conclude that every variable assignment that assigns the same values as **d** to the free variables in **Q** ∨ **R** satisfies **Q** and hence **Q** ∨ **R**. If (ii) is the case, then, by (f), we may conclude that every variable assignment that assigns the same values as **d** to the free variables in **Q** ∨ **R** satisfies **R** and hence **Q** ∨ **R**. Either way, then, we conclude that if **d** satisfies **Q** ∨ **R**, then every variable assignment that assigns the same values to the free variables in **Q** ∨ **R** as **d** satisfies **Q** ∨ **R**.

Conversely, if every variable assignment that assigns the same values to the free variables in **Q** ∨ **R** as does **d** satisfies **Q** ∨ **R**, then, trivially, **d** satisfies **Q** ∨ **R**.

Cases 3–5: P has one of the forms **Q** & **R**, **Q** ⊃ **R**, or **Q** ≡ **R**. These cases are left as an exercise.

Case 6: P has the form (∀**x**)**Q**. By the definition of satisfaction,

> a. **d** satisfies (∀**x**)**Q** if and only if every member **u** of the UD is such that **d**[**u**/**x**] satisfies **Q**.

Because **Q** contains fewer than **k** + 1 occurrences of connectives, it follows from the inductive hypothesis that

> b. Each member **u** of the UD is such that **d**[**u**/**x**] satisfies **Q** if and only if every variable assignment that assigns the same values to the free variables in **Q** as **d**[**u**/**x**] satisfies **Q**.

It follows from (a) and (b) that

> c. **d** satisfies (∀**x**)**Q** if and only if for each member **u** of the UD every variable assignment that assigns the same values to the free variables in **Q** as **d**[**u**/**x**] satisfies **Q**.

Because the variables other than **x** that are free in **Q** are also free in (∀**x**)**Q**, every variable assignment that assigns the same values to the free variables in **Q** as **d**[**u**/**x**] is a variant **d**′[**u**/**x**] of a variable assignment **d**′ that assigns the same values to the free variables in (∀**x**)**Q** as **d**, and vice versa. So (c) is equivalent to

d. **d** satisfies (∀**x**)**Q** if and only if for each member **u** of the UD every variable assignment **d**′ that assigns the same values to the free variables in (∀**x**)**Q** as **d** is such that **d**′[**u**/**x**] satisfies **Q**.

If follows by the definition of satisfaction that

e. **d** satisfies (∀**x**)**Q** if and only if every variable assignment that assigns the same values to the free variables in (∀**x**)**Q** as **d** satisfies (∀**x**)**Q**.

Case 7: **P** has the form (∃**x**)**Q**. This case is left as an exercise.

It follows immediately from 11.1.2 that

11.1.3: For any interpretation **I** and sentence **P** of *PL*, either every variable assignment for **I** satisfies **P** or no variable assignment for **I** satisfies **P**.

Proof: Let **d** be any variable assignment. Because **P** is a sentence and hence contains no free variables, every variable assignment for **I** assigns the same values to the free variables in **P** as does **d**. By result 11.1.2, then, **d** satisfies **P** if and only if every variable assignment satisfies **P**. Therefore either every variable assignment satisfies **P** or none does.

Each of the following results, which can be established using results 11.1.1–11.1.3, states something that we would hope to be true of quantified sentences of *PL*.

11.1.4: For any universally quantified sentence (∀**x**)**P** of *PL*, {(∀**x**)**P**} quantificationally entails every substitution instance of (∀**x**)**P**.

Proof: Let (∀**x**)**P** be any universally quantified sentence, let **P**(**a**/**x**) be a substitution instance of (∀**x**)**P**, and let **I** be an interpretation on which (∀**x**)**P** is true. Then, by 11.1.3, every variable assignment satisfies (∀**x**)**P**, and so, for every variable assignment **d** and every member **u** of the UD, **d**[**u**/**x**] satisfies **P**. In particular, for every variable assignment **d** the variant **d**[**I**(**a**)/**x**] must satisfy **P**. By 11.1.1, then, every variable assignment **d** satisfies **P**(**a**/**x**), so **P**(**a**/**x**) is also true on **I**.

11.1.5: Every substitution instance **P**(**a**/**x**) of an existentially quantified sentence (∃**x**)**P** is such that {**P**(**a**/**x**)} ⊨ (∃**x**)**P**.

Proof: See Exercise 3.

11.1.4 and 11.1.5 are results that were used to motivate informally two of the quantifier rules in Chapter 10, Universal Elimination and Existential Introduction, and they will play a role in our proof of the soundness of *PD*. We also want to ensure that the motivations for Universal Introduction and Existential Elimination were correct. Prior to showing this, we establish two further results that we shall need:

> **11.1.6:** Let **I** and **I′** be interpretations that have the same UD and that agree on the assignments made to each individual constant, predicate, and sentence letter in a formula **P** (that is, **I** and **I′** assign the same values to those symbols). Then each variable assignment **d** satisfies **P** on interpretation **I** if and only if **d** satisfies **P** on interpretation **I′**.

In stating result 11.1.6, we have made use of the fact that if two interpretations have the same UD then every variable assignment for one interpretation is a variable assignment for the other—because the collection of objects that can be assigned to the variables of *PL* is the same. The result should sound obvious: If two interpretations with identical universes of discourse treat the nonlogical symbols of **P** in the same way, and if the free variables are interpreted the same way on the two interpretations, then **P** says the same thing on both interpretations. The values that **I** and **I′** assign to other symbols of *PL* have no bearing on what **P** says; **P** must either be satisfied by the variable assignment on both interpretations or be satisfied on neither.

> **Proof of 11.1.6:** Let **P** be a formula of *PL* and let **I** and **I′** be interpretations that have the same UD and that agree on the values assigned to each nonlogical symbol in **P**. We shall now prove, by mathematical induction on the number of occurrences of logical operators in **P**, that a variable assignment satisfies **P** on interpretation **I** if and only if it satisfies **P** on interpretation **I′**.
>
> *Basis clause:* If **P** contains zero occurrences of logical operators, then a variable assignment satisfies **P** on **I** if and only if it satisfies **P** on **I′**.
>
> **Proof of basis clause:** Let **d** be a variable assignment. If **P** is a sentence letter, then **d** satisfies **P** on **I** if and only if **I(P)** = **T**, and **d** satisfies **P** on **I′** if and only if **I′(P)** = **T**. **I(P)** = **I′(P)** because we have stipulated that **I** and **I′** assign the same values to the nonlogical symbols in **P**. So **d** satisfies **P** on **I** if and only if **d** satisfies **P** on **I′**.
>
> If **P** is an atomic formula $\mathbf{At}_1 \ldots \mathbf{t_n}$ then by the definition of satisfaction,
>
> a. **d** satisfies **P** on **I** if and only if <$\text{den}_{\mathbf{I,d}}(\mathbf{t}_1)$, $\text{den}_{\mathbf{I,d}}(\mathbf{t}_2)$, . . . , $\text{den}_{\mathbf{I,d}}(\mathbf{t_n})$> is a member of **I(A)**.

b. **d** satisfies **P** on **I′** if and only if $<den_{I',d}(t_1), den_{I',d}(t_2), \ldots, den_{I',d}(t_n)>$ is a member of **I′**(**A**).

We note that

c. $<den_{I,d}(t_1), den_{I,d}(t_2), \ldots, den_{I,d}(t_n)> =$
$<den_{I',d}(t_1), den_{I',d}(t_2), \ldots, den_{I',d}(t_n)>$.

If t_i is a constant, then $den_{I,d}(t_i) = I(t_i)$, $den_{I',d}(t_i) = I'(t_i)$, and $I'(t_i) = I(t_i)$ since **I** and **I′** assign the same values to the nonlogical symbols in **P**; and if t_i is a variable, then $den_{I,d}(t_i) = d(t_i) = den_{I',d}(t_i)$. Moreover,

d. **I**(**A**) = **I′**(**A**), by our assumption about **I** and **I′**.

So, by (c) and (d),

e. $<den_{I,d}(t_1), den_{I,d}(t_2), \ldots, den_{I,d}(t_n)>$ is a member of **I**(**A**) if and only if $<den_{I',d}(t_1), den_{I',d}(t_2), \ldots, den_{I',d}(t_n)>$ is a member of **I′**(**A**).

And, by (a), (b), and (e), it follows that **d** satisfies $At_1 \ldots t_n$ on **I** if and only if it does so on **I′**.

Inductive step: If every formula **P** that contains **k** or fewer occurrences of logical operators is such that a variable assignment satisfies **P** on **I** if and only if it satisfies **P** on **I′**, then every formula **P** that contains **k** + 1 occurrences of logical operators is such that a variable assignment satisfies **P** on **I** if and only if it satisfies **P** on **I′**.

Proof of inductive step: We shall consider the forms that **P** may have.

Case 1: **P** has the form ~ **Q**. By the definition of satisfaction,

a. A variable assignment **d** satisfies ~ **Q** on **I** if and only if it does not satisfy **Q** on **I**.

Because **Q** contains fewer than **k** + 1 occurrences of logical operators, it follows from the inductive hypothesis that

b. A variable assignment fails to satisfy **Q** on **I** if and only if it fails to satisfy **Q** on **I′**.

By the definition of satisfaction again,

c. A variable assignment fails to satisfy **Q** on **I′** if and only if it does satisfy ~ **Q** on **I′**.

So, by (a)–(c), a variable assignment satisfies ~ **Q** on **I** if and only if it satisfies ~ **Q** on **I′**.

Case 2: **P** has the form **Q** & **R**. By the definition of satisfaction,

a. A variable assignment satisfies **Q** & **R** on **I** if and only if it satisfies both **Q** and **R** on **I**.

Q and **R** each contain **k** or fewer occurrences of logical operators, and so by the inductive hypothesis,

b. A variable assignment satisfies both **Q** and **R** on **I** if and only if it satisfies both **Q** and **R** on **I**′.

By the definition of satisfaction again,

c. A variable assignment satisfies both **Q** and **R** on **I**′ if and only if it satisfies **Q** & **R** on **I**′.

By (a)–(c), a variable assignment satisfies **Q** & **R** on **I** if and only if it satisfies **Q** & **R** on **I**′.

Cases 3–5: **P** has the form **Q** ∨ **R**, **Q** ⊃ **R**, or **Q** ≡ **R**. We omit proofs for these cases as they are strictly analogous to Case 2.

Case 6: **P** has the form (∀**x**)**Q**. By the definition of satisfaction,

a. A variable assignment **d** satisfies (∀**x**)**Q** on **I** if and only if for every member **u** of **I**'s UD, **d**[**u**/**x**] satisfies **Q** on **I**.
b. **d** satisfies (∀**x**)**Q** on **I**′ if and only if, for every member **u** of **I**′'s UD (which is the same as **I**'s UD), **d**[**u**/**x**] satisfies **Q** on **I**′.

Because **Q** contains fewer than **k** + 1 occurrences of logical operators, it follows from the inductive hypothesis that

c. For each member **u** of the common UD, **d**[**u**/**x**] satisfies **Q** on **I** if and only if **d**[**u**/**x**] satisfies **Q** on **I**′.

By (a)–(c), it follows that a variable assignment satisfies (∀**x**)**Q** on **I** if and only if it satisfies (∀**x**)**Q** on **I**′.

Case 7: **P** has the form (∃**x**)**Q**. This case is similar to Case 6.

That completes the proof of the inductive step, and we may now conclude that 11.1.6 is true of every formula **P** and pair of interpretations that agree on their assignments to nonlogical symbols in **P**.

Result 11.1.7 follows as an immediate consequence of 11.1.6.

11.1.7: Let **I** and **I**′ be interpretations that have the same UD and that agree on the assignments made to each individual constant, predicate, and sentence letter in a sentence **P**. Then **P** is true on **I** if and only if **P** is true on **I**′.

Proof: Let **I** and **I**′ be as specified for a sentence **P**. If **P** is true on **I**, then, by 11.1.2, **P** is satisfied by every variable assignment on **I**. By 11.1.6, this is the case if and only if **P** is satisfied by every variable assignment on **I**′, that is, if and only if **P** is true on **I**′.

With results 11.1.6 and 11.1.7 at hand, we may now show that our motivations for the rules Universal Introduction and Existential Elimination are correct.

11.1.8: Let **a** be a constant that does not occur in (∀**x**)**P** or in any member of the set Γ. Then if Γ ⊨ **P**(**a**/**x**), Γ ⊨ (∀**x**)**P**.

11.1.9: Let **a** be a constant that does not occur in the sentences (∃**x**)**P** and **Q** and that does not occur in any member of the set Γ. Then if Γ ⊨ (∃**x**)**P** and Γ ∪ {**P**(**a**/**x**)} ⊨ **Q**, Γ ⊨ **Q** as well.

Result 11.1.8 says, in effect, that if a sentence containing an individual constant is quantificationally entailed by a set of sentences, and if no sentence in the set contains that constant (no specific assumptions were made about the individual designated by that constant), then what **P** says with that constant may be said about everything. And result 11.1.9 says that if a set of sentences quantificationally entails an existentially quantified sentence, and if we can take a substitution instance of that sentence involving a new constant, add it to the set, and find that a sentence making no mention of the individual designated by the constant is quantificationally entailed, then **Q** must have been entailed by the set without the substitution instance thrown in. Intuitively this is so because **Q** does not draw any conclusion about the individual designated by the constant in the substitution instance, and so all that was really needed to entail **Q** was the existential claim that the set entails, and not a specific claim about the individual in question. We shall prove 11.1.8 here; 11.1.9 is left as an exercise.

Proof of 11.1.8: Assume that Γ ⊨ **P**(**a**/**x**), where **a** does not occur in (∀**x**)**P** or in any member of Γ. We shall assume, contrary to what we want to show, that Γ does not quantificationally entail (∀**x**)**P**—that there is at least one interpretation, call it **I**, on which every member of Γ is true and (∀**x**)**P** is false. We shall use **I** as the basis for constructing an interpretation **I**′ on which every member of Γ is true and the substitution instance **P**(**a**/**x**) is false, contradicting our original assumption. Having done so, we may conclude that if Γ does quantificationally entail **P**(**a**/**x**) it must also quantificationally entail (∀**x**)**P**.

So assume that **I** is an interpretation on which every member of Γ is true and on which (∀**x**)**P** is false. Because (∀**x**)**P** is false, there is no variable assignment for **I** that satisfies (∀**x**)**P**. That is, for every variable assignment **d**, there is at least one member **u** of the UD such that **d**[**u**/**x**] does not satisfy **P**. Choose one of these members, calling it **u**, and let **I**′ be the interpretation that is just like **I** except that it assigns **u** to **a** (all other assignments made by **I** remain the same). It is now straightforward to show that every member of Γ is true on $\mathbf{I}'$ and $\mathbf{P}(\mathbf{a}/\mathbf{x})$ is false. That every member of Γ is true on $\mathbf{I}'$ follows from 11.1.7 because $\mathbf{I}$ and $\mathbf{I}'$ assign the same values to all the nonlogical symbols of *PL* other than **a**, and, by stipulation, **a** does not occur in any member of Γ. $\mathbf{I}$ and $\mathbf{I}'$ therefore agree on the values assigned to the nonlogical symbols of each sentence in Γ, and each of these sentences must be true on $\mathbf{I}'$ because it is true on $\mathbf{I}$.

On our assumption that $\mathbf{d}[\mathbf{u}/\mathbf{x}]$ does not satisfy **P** on **I** it follows from 11.1.6 that $\mathbf{d}[\mathbf{u}/\mathbf{x}]$ does not satisfy **P** on $\mathbf{I}'$ (again $\mathbf{I}$ and $\mathbf{I}'$ assign the same values to all the nonlogical constants in **P**; **a** does not occur in **P**). By the way we have constructed $\mathbf{I}'$, **u** is $\mathbf{I}'(\mathbf{a})$ and so $\mathbf{d}[\mathbf{u}/\mathbf{x}]$ is $\mathbf{d}[\mathbf{I}'(\mathbf{a})/\mathbf{x}]$. Result 11.1.1 tells us that $\mathbf{d}[\mathbf{I}'(\mathbf{a})/\mathbf{x}]$ satisfies **P** on $\mathbf{I}'$ if and only if **d** satisfies $\mathbf{P}(\mathbf{a}/\mathbf{x})$ on $\mathbf{I}'$. So, because $\mathbf{d}[\mathbf{I}'(\mathbf{a})/\mathbf{x}]$ does not satisfy **P** on $\mathbf{I}'$, **d** does not satisfy $\mathbf{P}(\mathbf{a}/\mathbf{x})$ on $\mathbf{I}'$. By 11.1.3, then, no variable assignment satisfies $\mathbf{P}(\mathbf{a}/\mathbf{x})$ on $\mathbf{I}'$, and it is therefore false on this interpretation. But this contradicts our first assumption, that $\Gamma \models \mathbf{P}(\mathbf{a}/\mathbf{x})$, and so we conclude that if $\Gamma \models \mathbf{P}(\mathbf{a}/\mathbf{x})$, then $\Gamma \models (\forall \mathbf{x})\mathbf{P}$ as well.

As a consequence of 11.1.8, we know that the rule Universal Introduction is indeed truth-preserving.

We shall state four more semantic results that will be needed in the sections that follow and that the reader should now be able to prove. The proofs are left as exercises. The first result relies on 11.1.6 and 11.1.7, much as the proofs of 11.1.8 and 11.1.9 do.

11.1.10: If **a** does not occur in any member of the set $\Gamma \cup \{(\exists \mathbf{x})\mathbf{P}\}$ and if the set is quantificationally consistent, then the set $\Gamma \cup \{(\exists \mathbf{x})\mathbf{P}, \mathbf{P}(\mathbf{a}/\mathbf{x})\}$ is also quantificationally consistent.

Results 11.1.11 and 11.1.12 concern interpretations of a special sort: interpretations on which every member of the UD has a name.

11.1.11: Let **I** be an interpretation on which each member of the UD is assigned to at least one individual constant. Then, if every substitution instance of $(\forall \mathbf{x})\mathbf{P}$ is true on **I**, so is $(\forall \mathbf{x})\mathbf{P}$.

11.1.12: Let **I** be an interpretation on which each member of the UD is assigned to at least one individual constant. Then, if every substitution instance of $(\exists \mathbf{x})\mathbf{P}$ is false on **I**, so is $(\exists \mathbf{x})\mathbf{P}$.

Result 11.1.13 says that, if we rename the individual designated by some individual constant in a sentence **P** with a constant that does not already occur in **P**, then, for any interpretation on which **P** is true, there is a closely related interpretation (one that reflects the renaming) on which the new sentence is true.

11.1.13: Let **P** be a sentence of *PL*, let **b** be an individual constant that does not occur in **P**, and let $\mathbf{P}(\mathbf{b}/\mathbf{a})$ be the sentence that results from replacing every occurrence of the individual constant **a** in **P** with **b**. Then if **P** is true on an interpretation **I**, **P**(**b**/**a**) is true on the interpretation **I**′ that is just like **I** except that it assigns **I**(**a**) to **b** (**I**′(**b**) = **I**(**a**)).

11.1E EXERCISES

***1.** Prove Cases 3–5 in the proof of result 11.1.1.

***2.** Prove Cases 3–5 and 7 in the proof of result 11.1.2.

***3.** Prove result 11.1.5.

***4.** Prove result 11.1.9.

5. Prove result 11.1.10.

6. Prove result 11.1.11.

***7.** Prove result 11.1.12.

***8.** Prove result 11.1.13.

1.2 SEMANTIC PRELIMINARIES FOR *PLE*

When we turn to the metatheory for *PLE*, we shall need versions of Section 11.1's semantic results that apply to sentences containing the identity operator and complex terms. In this section we discuss the changes that must be made in the statement of the semantic results and in their proofs.

Starting with 11.1.1, we note that we must generalize the result to read:

> Let **P** be a formula of *PLE*, let **P**(**t**/**x**) be the formula that results from replacing every free occurrence of **x** in **P** with a closed term **t**, let **I** be an interpretation, let **d** be a variable assignment for **I**, and let **d**′ = **d**[den$_{\mathbf{I,d}}$(**t**)/**x**] (that is, **d**′ is just like **d** except that it assigns to **x** whatever **d** and **I** assign to **t**). Then **d** satisfies **P**(**t**/**x**) on **I** if and only if **d**′ satisfies **P** on **I**.

To modify the proof of 11.1.1, we first establish a result concerning complex terms:

> **11.2.1:** Let **t** be a complex term of *PLE*, let **t**(**t**$_{\mathbf{c}}$/**x**) be the term that results from replacing every occurrence of the variable **x** in **t** with a closed term **t**$_{\mathbf{c}}$, let **I** be an interpretation, let **d** be a variable assignment for **I**, and let **d**′ = **d**[den$_{\mathbf{I,d}}$(**t**$_{\mathbf{c}}$)/**x**]. Then den$_{\mathbf{I,d'}}$(**t**) = den$_{\mathbf{I,d}}$(**t**(**t**$_{\mathbf{c}}$/**x**)).

The result states that, if the sole difference between two complex terms $\mathbf{t_1}$ and $\mathbf{t_2}$ is that one contains the closed term $\mathbf{t_c}$ where the other contains the variable $\mathbf{x}$, then if $\mathbf{x}$ and $\mathbf{t_c}$ denote the same individual so do the complex terms $\mathbf{t_1}$ and $\mathbf{t_2}$. We shall prove 11.2.1 by mathematical induction on the number of occurrences of functors in the term.

Basis clause: If a complex term $\mathbf{t}$ contains one functor, then $\text{den}_{\mathbf{I,d'}}(\mathbf{t}) = \text{den}_{\mathbf{I,d}}(\mathbf{t}(\mathbf{t_c}/\mathbf{x}))$.

Proof of basis clause: If a complex term $\mathbf{t}$ contains one functor, then $\mathbf{t}$ is $f(\mathbf{t_1}, \ldots, \mathbf{t_n})$ where f is a functor, each $\mathbf{t_i}$ is either a variable or a constant, and $\mathbf{t}(\mathbf{t_c}/\mathbf{x})$ is $f(\mathbf{t'_1}, \ldots, \mathbf{t'_n})$ where $\mathbf{t'_i}$ is $\mathbf{t_i}$ if $\mathbf{t_i}$ is not $\mathbf{x}$, and $\mathbf{t'_i}$ is $\mathbf{t_c}$ if $\mathbf{t_i}$ is $\mathbf{x}$.

As in the proof of the basis clause of 11.1.1, we note that if $\mathbf{t_i}$ is a constant or variable other than $\mathbf{x}$ then $\text{den}_{\mathbf{I,d'}}(\mathbf{t_i}) = \text{den}_{\mathbf{I,d}}(\mathbf{t_i})$—since $\mathbf{d'}$ does not differ from $\mathbf{d}$ in a way that affects the denotation of these terms. If $\mathbf{t_i}$ is $\mathbf{x}$, then $\mathbf{t'_i}$ is $\mathbf{t_c}$, and by the definition of how $\mathbf{d'}$ was constructed, $\text{den}_{\mathbf{I,d'}}(\mathbf{x}) = \text{den}_{\mathbf{I,d}}(\mathbf{t_c})$. So we know that $<\text{den}_{\mathbf{I,d'}}(\mathbf{t_1}), \text{den}_{\mathbf{I,d'}}(\mathbf{t_2}), \ldots, \text{den}_{\mathbf{I,d'}}(\mathbf{t_n})> = <\text{den}_{\mathbf{I,d}}(\mathbf{t'_1})$, and $\text{den}_{\mathbf{I,d}}(\mathbf{t'_2}), \ldots, \text{den}_{\mathbf{I,d}}(\mathbf{t'_n})>$. Therefore the $\mathbf{n}$ + 1-tuple $<\text{den}_{\mathbf{I,d'}}(\mathbf{t_1}), \text{den}_{\mathbf{I,d'}}(\mathbf{t_2}), \ldots, \text{den}_{\mathbf{I,d'}}(\mathbf{t_n}), \mathbf{u}>$ is a member of $\mathbf{I}(f)$ if and only if $<\text{den}_{\mathbf{I,d}}(\mathbf{t'_1}), \text{den}_{\mathbf{I,d}}(\mathbf{t_2}), \ldots, \text{den}_{\mathbf{I,d}}(\mathbf{t'_n}), \mathbf{u}>$ is a member of $\mathbf{I}(f)$ since these are the same $\mathbf{n}$-tuple, so $\text{den}_{\mathbf{I,d'}}(f(\mathbf{t_1}, \ldots, \mathbf{t_n})) = \text{den}_{\mathbf{I,d}}(f(\mathbf{t_1}, \ldots, \mathbf{t'_n}))$.

Inductive step: If every complex term $\mathbf{t}$ that contains $\mathbf{k}$ or fewer functors is such that $\text{den}_{\mathbf{I,d}}(\mathbf{t}) = \text{den}_{\mathbf{I,d'}}(\mathbf{t}(\mathbf{t_c}/\mathbf{x}))$, then every complex term that contains $\mathbf{k} + 1$ functors is such that $\text{den}_{\mathbf{I,d}}(\mathbf{t}) = \text{den}_{\mathbf{I,d'}}(\mathbf{t}(\mathbf{t_c}/\mathbf{x}))$.

Proof of inductive step: Letting $\mathbf{k}$ be an arbitrary positive integer, we assume that the inductive hypothesis holds—that our claim is true of every complex term with that contains $\mathbf{k}$ or fewer functors. We must show that the claim is also true of every complex term that contains $\mathbf{k} + 1$ functors. If $\mathbf{t}$ contains $\mathbf{k} + 1$ functors, then $\mathbf{t}$ is $f(\mathbf{t_1}, \ldots, \mathbf{t_n})$, where each $\mathbf{t_i}$ has $\mathbf{k}$ or fewer functors, and $\mathbf{t}(\mathbf{t_c}/\mathbf{x})$ is $f(\mathbf{t'_1}, \ldots, \mathbf{t'_n})$, where each $\mathbf{t'_i}$ is $\mathbf{t_i}(\mathbf{t_c}/\mathbf{x})$. So each $\mathbf{t_i}$ falls under the inductive hypothesis; that is, $\text{den}_{\mathbf{I,d'}}(\mathbf{t_i}) = \text{den}_{\mathbf{I,d}}(\mathbf{t_i}(\mathbf{t_c}/\mathbf{x}))$, and so $<\text{den}_{\mathbf{I,d'}}(\mathbf{t_1}), \text{den}_{\mathbf{I,d'}}(\mathbf{t_2}), \ldots, \text{den}_{\mathbf{I,d'}}(\mathbf{t_n})> = <\text{den}_{\mathbf{I,d}}(\mathbf{t'_1}), \text{den}_{\mathbf{I,d}}(\mathbf{t'_2}), \ldots, \text{den}_{\mathbf{I,d}}(\mathbf{t'_n})>$. Therefore the $\mathbf{n}$ + 1-tuple $<\text{den}_{\mathbf{I,d'}}(\mathbf{t_1}), \text{den}_{\mathbf{I,d'}}(\mathbf{t_2}), \ldots, \text{den}_{\mathbf{I,d'}}(\mathbf{t_n}), \mathbf{u}>$ is a member of $\mathbf{I}(f)$ if and only if $<\text{den}_{\mathbf{I,d}}(\mathbf{t'_1}), \text{den}_{\mathbf{I,d}}(\mathbf{t'_2}), \ldots, \text{den}_{\mathbf{I,d}}(\mathbf{t'_n}), \mathbf{u}>$ is a member of $\mathbf{I}(f)$, so $\text{den}_{\mathbf{I,d'}}(f(\mathbf{t_1}, \ldots, \mathbf{t_n})) = \text{den}_{\mathbf{I,d}}(f(\mathbf{t'_1}, \ldots, \mathbf{t'_n}))$.

With result 11.2.1 in hand, we can modify the basis clause of result 11.1.1 as follows:

Basis clause: If $\mathbf{P}$ is a formula that contains zero occurrences of logical operators, then $\mathbf{d}$ satisfies $\mathbf{P}(\mathbf{t}/\mathbf{x})$ if and only if $\mathbf{d'}$ satisfies $\mathbf{P}$.

Proof of basis clause: If $\mathbf{P}$ is a formula that contains zero occurrences of logical operators, then $\mathbf{P}$ is either a sentence letter or a formula of the form $\mathbf{At_1 \ldots t_n}$, where $\mathbf{A}$ is a predicate and $\mathbf{t_1, \ldots, t_n}$ are terms. If $\mathbf{P}$ is a sentence letter, then $\mathbf{P(t/x)}$ is simply $\mathbf{P}$—a sentence letter alone does not contain any variables to be replaced. $\mathbf{d}$ satisfies $\mathbf{P(t/x)}$, then, if and only if $\mathbf{I(P)} = \mathbf{T}$. And $\mathbf{d'}$ satisfies $\mathbf{P}$ if and only if $\mathbf{I(P)} = \mathbf{T}$. So $\mathbf{d}$ satisfies $\mathbf{P(t/x)}$ if and only if $\mathbf{d'}$ satisfies $\mathbf{P}$.

If $\mathbf{P}$ has the form $\mathbf{At_1 \ldots t_n}$, then $\mathbf{P(t/x)}$ is $\mathbf{At'_1 \ldots t'_n}$, where $\mathbf{t'_i}$ is $\mathbf{t}$ if $\mathbf{t_i}$ is $\mathbf{x}$ and $\mathbf{t'_i}$ is just $\mathbf{t_i}$ otherwise. By the definition of satisfaction,

a. $\mathbf{d}$ satisfies $\mathbf{At'_1 \ldots t'_n}$ if and only if $<den_{\mathbf{I,d}}(\mathbf{t'_1}), den_{\mathbf{I,d}}(\mathbf{t'_2}), \ldots, den_{\mathbf{I,d}}(\mathbf{t'_n})>$ is a member of $\mathbf{I(A)}$.

b. $\mathbf{d'}$ satisfies $\mathbf{At_1 \ldots t_n}$ if and only if $<den_{\mathbf{I,d'}}(\mathbf{t_1}), den_{\mathbf{I,d'}}(\mathbf{t_2}), \ldots, den_{\mathbf{I,d'}}(\mathbf{t_n})>$ is a member of $\mathbf{I(A)}$.

But now we note that

c. $<den_{\mathbf{I,d}}(\mathbf{t'_1}), den_{\mathbf{I,d}}(\mathbf{t'_2}), \ldots, den_{\mathbf{I,d}}(\mathbf{t'_n})> = <den_{\mathbf{I,d'}}(\mathbf{t_1}), den_{\mathbf{I,d'}}(\mathbf{t_2}), \ldots, den_{\mathbf{I,d'}}(\mathbf{t_n})>$.

Consider: If $\mathbf{t_i}$ is a constant, then $\mathbf{t'_i}$ is $\mathbf{t_i}$ and so $den_{\mathbf{I,d}}(\mathbf{t'_i}) = \mathbf{I(t_i)}$ and $den_{\mathbf{I,d'}}(\mathbf{t_i}) = \mathbf{I(t_i)}$. If $\mathbf{t_i}$ is a variable other than $\mathbf{x}$, then $\mathbf{t'_i}$ is $\mathbf{t_i}$ and so $den_{\mathbf{I,d}}(\mathbf{t'_i}) = \mathbf{d(t_i)} = \mathbf{d'(t_i)} = den_{\mathbf{I,d'}}(\mathbf{t_i})$—the variation in the variable assignment does not affect the value assigned to $\mathbf{t_i}$ in this case. If $\mathbf{t_i}$ is the variable $\mathbf{x}$, then $\mathbf{t'_i}$ is $\mathbf{t}$ and $den_{\mathbf{I,d}}(\mathbf{t}) = den_{\mathbf{I,d'}}(\mathbf{x})$. (The variant $\mathbf{d'}$ was defined in a way that ensures that the denotations of $\mathbf{x}$ and of $\mathbf{t}$ coincide.) And if $\mathbf{t_i}$ is a complex term, it follows from 11.2.1 that $den_{\mathbf{I,d}}(\mathbf{t'_i}) = den_{\mathbf{I,d'}}(\mathbf{t_i})$.

Because the **n**-tuples are the same **n**-tuple, we conclude from (a) and (b) that $\mathbf{d}$ satisfies $\mathbf{At'_1 \ldots t'_n}$ if and only if $\mathbf{d'}$ satisfies $\mathbf{At_1 \ldots t_n}$.

We must also add a new case to the proof of the basis clause, to cover formulas of the form $\mathbf{t_1} = \mathbf{t_2}$. We leave this as an exercise. The rest of the proof of 11.1.1 remains the same, except that we replace $\mathbf{d[I(a)/x]}$ with $\mathbf{d'}$ (which is shorthand for $\mathbf{d}[den_{\mathbf{I,d}}(\mathbf{t_c})/\mathbf{x}]$) throughout.

The proof of 11.1.2 is modified in a similar way. First, we need to prove

11.2.2: Let $\mathbf{I}$ be an interpretation, $\mathbf{d}$ a variable assignment for $\mathbf{I}$, and $\mathbf{t}$ a complex term of *PLE*. Then, for any variable assignment $\mathbf{d'}$ that assigns the same values to the variables in $\mathbf{t}$ as does $\mathbf{d}$, $den_{\mathbf{I,d'}}(\mathbf{t}) = den_{\mathbf{I,d}}(\mathbf{t})$.

Proof: See Exercise 2.

With this result the basis clause in the proof of 11.1.2 must be modified to include atomic formulas containing complex terms along the same lines that we modified the basis clause in the proof of 11.1.1, and also to include formulas of the form $\mathbf{t_1} = \mathbf{t_2}$. Both modifications are left as exercises.

The proof of result 11.1.6 can be similarly modified, once we have established

11.2.3: Let **t** be a complex term of *PLE* and let **I** and **I′** be interpretations that have the same UD and that agree on the values assigned to each individual constant and functor in **t**. Then, for any variable assignment **d**, $\text{den}_{\mathbf{I},\mathbf{d}}(\mathbf{t}) = \text{den}_{\mathbf{I}',\mathbf{d}}(\mathbf{t})$.

Proof: See Exercise 3.

Result 11.1.6 must itself be changed to say:

Let **I** and **I′** be interpretations that have the same UD and that agree on the assignments made to each individual constant, functor, predicate, and sentence letter in a formula **P**. Then each variable assignment **d** satisfies **P** on interpretation **I** if and only if **d** satisfies **P** on interpretation **I′**.

The basis clause must be modified to cover formulas containing complex terms, as well as formulas of the form $\mathbf{t}_1 = \mathbf{t}_2$. This is left as an exercise.

The proofs of results 11.1.3–11.1.5 and 11.1.7–11.1.13 for *PLE* are the same as for *PL*, except for the following changes:

1. The proofs must use the modified versions of 11.1.1, 11.1.2, and 11.1.6 in order to apply to *PLE.*
2. Where '**a**' and '**P**(**a**/**x**)' are used in results 11.1.4 and 11.1.5 to refer to substitution instances of **P**, we need to use '**t**' and '**P**(**t**/**x**)' instead to allow for instantiation with arbitrary terms.
3. In 11.1.7, **I** and **I′** must also agree on the assignments made to each functor.
4. Results 1.1.11 and 1.1.12 are true for *PLE* in two senses: We can change 'every substitution instance' to 'every substitution instance in which the instantiating individual term is a constant', or we can leave the phrase as it is, to include substitution instances with instantiation by all closed terms, complex ones as well as constants.

Finally we shall need two additional semantic results for *PLE*:

11.2.4: For any closed terms $\mathbf{t}_1$ and $\mathbf{t}_2$, if **P** is a sentence that contains $\mathbf{t}_1$, then $\{\mathbf{t}_1 = \mathbf{t}_2, \mathbf{P}\} \vDash \mathbf{P}(\mathbf{t}_2//\mathbf{t}_1)$, and if **P** is a sentence that contains $\mathbf{t}_2$, then $\{\mathbf{t}_1 = \mathbf{t}_2, \mathbf{P}\} \vDash \mathbf{P}(\mathbf{t}_1//\mathbf{t}_2)$.

Proof: See Exercise 4.

11.2.5: If a quantificationally consistent set Γ contains a sentence with a complex term $f(\mathbf{a}_1, \ldots, \mathbf{a}_n)$, where $\mathbf{a}_1, \ldots, \mathbf{a}_n$ are constants, and the constant **b** does not occur in Γ, then the set $\Gamma \cup \{\mathbf{b} = f(\mathbf{a}_1, \ldots, \mathbf{a}_n)\}$ is also quantificationally consistent.

Proof: See Exercise 5.

11.2E EXERCISES

*1. Show the changes that must be made in the basis clauses of the proofs of the following results so that they cover formulas containing complex terms and formulas of the form $\mathbf{t}_1 = \mathbf{t}_2$:

a. Result 11.1.1
b. Result 11.1.2
c. Result 11.1.6

*2. Prove result 11.2.2.

*3. Prove result 11.2.3.

4. Prove result 11.2.4.

*5. Prove result 11.2.5.

11.3 THE SOUNDNESS OF *PD*, *PD+*, AND *PDE*

We shall now establish the soundness of our natural deduction systems. A natural deduction system is said to be *sound* for predicate logic if every rule in that system is truth-preserving—that is, if no derivation that uses the rules of that system can lead from true assumptions to a false conclusion. The *Soundness Metatheorem* for *PD* is

> **Metatheorem 11.3.1:** If $\Gamma \vdash \mathbf{P}$ in *PD*, then $\Gamma \models \mathbf{P}$.

(If **P** is derivable from Γ in *PD*, then **P** is quantificationally entailed by Γ.) To establish Metatheorem 11.3.1, we shall prove that each sentence in a derivation is quantificationally entailed by the set of undischarged assumptions within whose scope the sentence lies. It will then follow that the last sentence of any derivation is quantificationally entailed by the set of undischarged assumptions of that derivation—and hence that $\Gamma \models \mathbf{P}$ if $\Gamma \vdash \mathbf{P}$. (As in Chapter 6, we drop 'in *PD*' when we use the single turnstile here, and we use the double turnstile to signify *quantificational* entailment.) The proof is by mathematical induction and is, in outline, like the proof that we presented in Chapter 6 establishing the soundness of *SD* for sentential logic. In fact, we shall see that much of the proof in Chapter 6 can be used here—for in Chapter 6 we showed that the rules for the truth-functional connectives are all sound for sentential logic, and with a change from talk of truth-value assignments to talk of interpretations, those rules are established to be sound for predicate logic in the same way. The bulk of the proof will therefore concentrate on the rules for quantifier introduction and elimination.

In our proof we shall use several semantic results that were presented in Section 11.1 along with the following result:

11.3.2: If $\Gamma \models \mathbf{P}$ and Γ^* is a superset of Γ, then $\Gamma^* \models \mathbf{P}$.

Proof: If every member of Γ^* is true on an interpretation **I**, then every member of its subset Γ is true on **I**. And if $\Gamma \models \mathbf{P}$, then **P** is also true on **I**. Hence $\Gamma^* \models \mathbf{P}$.

Letting $\mathbf{P_i}$ be the sentence at position **i** in a derivation and letting $\Gamma_\mathbf{i}$ be the set of assumptions that are undischarged at position **i** (and hence within whose scope $\mathbf{P_i}$ lies), the proof of Metatheorem 11.3.1 by mathematical induction is

Basis clause: $\Gamma_1 \models \mathbf{P}_1$.

Inductive step: If $\Gamma_\mathbf{i} \models \mathbf{P_i}$ for every position **i** in a derivation such that $\mathbf{i} \leq \mathbf{k}$, then $\Gamma_{\mathbf{k}+1} \models \mathbf{P}_{\mathbf{k}+1}$.

Conclusion: Every sentence in a derivation is quantificationally entailed by the set of undischarged assumptions in whose scope it lies (for every position **k** in a derivation, $\Gamma_\mathbf{k} \models \mathbf{P_k}$).

Proof of basis clause: The first sentence in any derivation in *PD* is an assumption, and it lies in its own scope. Γ_1 is just $\{\mathbf{P}_1\}$, and it is trivial that $\{\mathbf{P}_1\} \models \mathbf{P}_1$.

Proof of inductive step: We choose an arbitrary position **k** and assume the inductive hypothesis: For every position **i** such that $\mathbf{i} \leq \mathbf{k}$, $\Gamma_\mathbf{i} \models \mathbf{P_i}$. We must now show that the same holds for position $\mathbf{k} + 1$. We shall show this by considering the justifications that might be used for the sentence at position $\mathbf{k} + 1$, establishing that the entailment claim holds no matter which justification is used.

Cases 1–12: $\mathbf{P}_{\mathbf{k}+1}$ is justified by one of the rules of *SD*. For each of these cases, use the corresponding case from the proof of the soundness of *SD* in Section 6.3, changing talk of truth-value assignments to talk of interpretations, and talk of truth-functional concepts (inconsistency and so on) to talk of quantificational concepts.

Case 13: $\mathbf{P_{k+1}}$ is justified by Universal Elimination. Then $\mathbf{P_{k+1}}$ is a sentence $\mathbf{Q(a/x)}$ derived as follows:

h	$(\forall \mathbf{x})\mathbf{Q}$	
k + 1	$\mathbf{Q(a/x)}$	**h** ∀E

where every assumption that is undischarged at position **h** is also undischarged at position **k** + 1 (because $(\forall \mathbf{x})\mathbf{Q}$ at position **h** is accessible at position **k** + 1)—so $\Gamma_{\mathbf{h}}$ is a subset of $\Gamma_{\mathbf{k}+1}$. By the inductive hypothesis, $\Gamma_{\mathbf{h}} \vDash (\forall \mathbf{x})\mathbf{Q}$. It follows, by 11.3.2, that the superset $\Gamma_{\mathbf{k}+1} \vDash (\forall \mathbf{x})\mathbf{Q}$. By 11.1.4, which says that a universally quantified sentence quantificationally entails every one of its substitution instances, $\mathbf{Q(a/x)}$ is true on every interpretation on which $(\forall \mathbf{x})\mathbf{Q}$ is true. So $\Gamma_{\mathbf{k}+1} \vDash \mathbf{Q(a/x)}$ as well.

Case 14: $\mathbf{P_{k+1}}$ is justified by Existential Introduction. Then $\mathbf{P_{k+1}}$ is a sentence $(\exists \mathbf{x})\mathbf{Q}$ derived as follows:

h	$\mathbf{Q(a/x)}$	
k + 1	$(\exists \mathbf{x})\mathbf{Q}$	**h** ∃I

where every assumption that is undischarged at position **h** is also undischarged at position **k** + 1. So $\Gamma_{\mathbf{h}}$ is a subset of $\Gamma_{\mathbf{k}+1}$. By the inductive hypothesis, $\Gamma_{\mathbf{h}} \vDash \mathbf{Q(a/x)}$ and so, by 11.3.2, $\Gamma_{\mathbf{k}+1} \vDash \mathbf{Q(a/x)}$. By 11.1.5, we know that $(\exists \mathbf{x})\mathbf{Q}$ is true on every interpretation on which $\mathbf{Q(a/x)}$ is true, so $\Gamma_{\mathbf{k}+1} \vDash (\exists \mathbf{x})\mathbf{Q}$ as well.

Case 15: $\mathbf{P_{k+1}}$ is justified by Universal Introduction. Then $\mathbf{P_{k+1}}$ is a sentence $(\forall \mathbf{x})\mathbf{Q}$ derived as follows:

h	$\mathbf{Q(a/x)}$	
k + 1	$(\forall \mathbf{x})\mathbf{Q}$	**h** ∀I

where every assumption that is undischarged at position **h** is also undischarged at position **k** + 1—so $\Gamma_{\mathbf{h}}$ is a subset of $\Gamma_{\mathbf{k}+1}$—and in addition **a** does not occur in $(\forall \mathbf{x})\mathbf{Q}$ or in any member of $\Gamma_{\mathbf{k}+1}$ because the rule ∀I stipulates this. By the inductive hypothesis, $\Gamma_{\mathbf{h}} \vDash \mathbf{Q(a/x)}$. Because $\Gamma_{\mathbf{h}}$ is a subset of $\Gamma_{\mathbf{k}+1}$, it follows from 11.3.2 that $\Gamma_{\mathbf{k}+1} \vDash \mathbf{Q(a/x)}$. And because **a** does not occur in $(\forall \mathbf{x})\mathbf{Q}$ or in any member of $\Gamma_{\mathbf{k}+1}$, it follows from 11.1.8, which we repeat here, that $\Gamma_{\mathbf{k}+1} \vDash (\forall \mathbf{x})\mathbf{Q}$ as well.

11.1.8: Let **a** be a constant that does not occur in $(\forall \mathbf{x})\mathbf{P}$ or in any member of the set Γ. Then if $\Gamma \vDash \mathbf{P(a/x)}$, $\Gamma \vDash (\forall \mathbf{x})\mathbf{P}$.

Case 16: $\mathbf{P_{k+1}}$ is justified by Existential Elimination. Then $\mathbf{P_{k+1}}$ is derived as follows:

h	$(\exists \mathbf{x})\mathbf{Q}$		
j		$\mathbf{Q(a/x)}$	
m		$\mathbf{P_{k+1}}$	
k + 1	$\mathbf{P_{k+1}}$		**h**, **j–m** ∃E

where every member of $\Gamma_{\mathbf{h}}$ is a member of $\Gamma_{\mathbf{k+1}}$ and every member of $\Gamma_{\mathbf{m}}$ except $\mathbf{Q(a/x)}$ is a member of $\Gamma_{\mathbf{k+1}}$ (if any other assumptions in $\Gamma_{\mathbf{m}}$ were discharged prior to position **k** + 1, then the subderivation **j–m** would not be accessible at position **k** + 1). Because every member of $\Gamma_{\mathbf{m}}$ except $\mathbf{Q(a/x)}$ is a member of $\Gamma_{\mathbf{k+1}}$, $\Gamma_{\mathbf{m}}$ is a subset of $\Gamma_{\mathbf{k+1}} \cup \{\mathbf{Q(a/x)}\}$. Moreover **a** does not occur in $(\exists \mathbf{x})\mathbf{Q}$, $\mathbf{P_{k+1}}$, or any member of $\Gamma_{\mathbf{k+1}}$ because the rule ∃E stipulates this. By the inductive hypothesis, $\Gamma_{\mathbf{h}} \vDash (\exists \mathbf{x})\mathbf{Q}$, and so because $\Gamma_{\mathbf{h}}$ is a subset of $\Gamma_{\mathbf{k+1}}$, it follows from 11.3.2 that $\Gamma_{\mathbf{k+1}} \vDash (\exists \mathbf{x})\mathbf{Q}$. Also by the inductive hypothesis, $\Gamma_{\mathbf{m}} \vDash \mathbf{P_{k+1}}$, and so, because $\Gamma_{\mathbf{m}}$ is a subset of $\Gamma_{\mathbf{k+1}} \cup \{\mathbf{Q(a/x)}\}$, it follows from 11.3.2 that $\Gamma_{\mathbf{k+1}} \cup \{\mathbf{Q(a/x)}\} \vDash \mathbf{P_{k+1}}$. Because **a** does not occur in $(\exists \mathbf{x})\mathbf{Q}$, $\mathbf{P_{k+1}}$, or any member of $\Gamma_{\mathbf{k+1}}$, it follows from the last two entailments noted that $\Gamma_{\mathbf{k+1}} \vDash \mathbf{P_{k+1}}$, by 11.1.9, which we repeat here.

11.1.9: Let **a** be a constant that does not occur in the sentences $(\exists \mathbf{x})\mathbf{P}$ and **Q** and that does not occur in any member of the set Γ. Then, if $\Gamma \vDash (\exists \mathbf{x})\mathbf{P}$ and $\Gamma \cup \{\mathbf{P(a/x)}\} \vDash \mathbf{Q}$, $\Gamma \vDash \mathbf{Q}$ as well.

This completes the proof of the inductive step; all of the derivation rules of *PD* are truth-preserving. Note that, in establishing that the two quantifier rules ∀I and ∃E are truth-preserving, we made essential use of the restrictions that those rules place on the instantiating constant **a**—the restrictions were included in those rules to ensure that they would be truth-preserving. Having established that the inductive step is true, we may conclude that every sentence in a derivation of *PD* is quantificationally entailed by the set of undischarged assumptions in whose scope it lies. Therefore, if $\Gamma \vdash \mathbf{P}$ in *PD*, then $\Gamma \vDash \mathbf{P}$. This establishes Metatheorem 11.1, the Soundness Metatheorem for *PD*.

The proof that *PD+* is sound for predicate logic involves the additional steps of showing that the rules of replacement of *SD+*, the three derived rules of *SD+*, and the rule Quantifier Negation are all truth-preserving. The steps in the soundness proof for *SD+*, which show that its rules are truth-preserving for sentential logic, can with appropriate adjustments to quantificational talk be converted into steps showing that the rules are truth-preserving for quantificational logic. We leave the proof that the additional rule of replacement in *PD+*, Quantifier Negation, is truth-preserving as an exercise.

Finally we can prove that *PDE* is sound for predicate logic with identity and functions by extending the inductive step of the proof for *PD* to cover the two identity rules, Identity Introduction and Identity Elimination, and by making one change in the basis clause of the soundness proof. We note that, since we have shown in Section 11.2 that all of the semantic results in Section 11.1 can be extended to predicate logic with identity and functions, a soundness proof for *PDE* can refer to all of those results. In particular, even though the rules ∀E and ∃I have been changed for *PDE*, the proof for Cases 13 and 14 in the inductive step of the soundness proof for *PD* will remain the same except that in place of the substitution instance $\mathbf{Q}(\mathbf{a}/\mathbf{x})$ we now have a substitution instance $\mathbf{Q}(\mathbf{t}/\mathbf{x})$, where $\mathbf{t}$ is any closed term.

We first discuss the change in the basis clause of the soundness proof. In the basis clause for *PD*, we said that the first sentence in a derivation is an assumption. This is not always the case in *PDE*; the first sentence *can* be an assumption, but it can also be a sentence of the form $(\forall \mathbf{x})\mathbf{x} = \mathbf{x}$, introduced by Identity Introduction. So the proof of the basis clause will look like this:

> The first sentence in a derivation in *PDE* is either an assumption or a sentence introduced by Identity Introduction. If the first sentence is an assumption, then it lies in its own scope. In this case Γ_1 is just $\{\mathbf{P}_1\}$, and it is trivial that $\{\mathbf{P}_1\} \vDash \mathbf{P}_1$.
>
> If the first sentence is introduced by Identity Introduction, then Γ_1 is empty—there are no assumptions, and hence no undischarged assumptions, at that point. So it remains to be shown that ∅ truth-functionally entails every sentence of the form $(\forall \mathbf{x})\mathbf{x} = \mathbf{x}$—that is, that every such sentence is quantificationally true. This was proved in Exercise 8.7.10a.

We add the following two cases to the proof of the inductive step for *PD*:

> **Case 17:** $\mathbf{P}_{k+1}$ is introduced by Identity Introduction. Then $\mathbf{P}_{k+1}$ is a sentence of the form $(\forall \mathbf{x})\mathbf{x} = \mathbf{x}$ derived as follows:
>
> | | | |
> |---|---|---|
> | **k** + 1 | $(\forall \mathbf{x})\mathbf{x} = \mathbf{x}$ | =I |
>
> We have already noted that the empty set quantificationally entails every sentence of the form $(\forall \mathbf{x})\mathbf{x} = \mathbf{x}$. And the empty set is a subset of Γ_{k+1}, so, by 11.3.2, $\Gamma_{k+1} \vDash (\forall \mathbf{x})\mathbf{x} = \mathbf{x}$.
>
> **Case 18:** $\mathbf{P}_{k+1}$ is introduced by Identity Elimination. Then $\mathbf{P}_{k+1}$ is derived as follows:
>
> | | | | | | | |
> |---|---|---|---|---|---|---|
> | **h** | $\mathbf{t}_1 = \mathbf{t}_2$ | | | **h** | $\mathbf{t}_1 = \mathbf{t}_2$ | |
> | **j** | $\mathbf{P}$ | | or | **j** | $\mathbf{P}$ | |
> | **k** + 1 | $\mathbf{P}(\mathbf{t}_1//\mathbf{t}_2)$ | **h**, **j** =E | | **k** + 1 | $\mathbf{P}(\mathbf{t}_2//\mathbf{t}_1)$ | **h**, **j** =E |

where both Γ_h and Γ_j are subsets of Γ_{k+1} (because the sentences at positions **h** and **j** are accessible at position **k** + 1). By the inductive hypothesis, $\Gamma_h \vDash t_1 = t_2$ and $\Gamma_j \vDash P$. Because these are both subsets of Γ_{k+1}, it follows, by 11.3.2, that $\Gamma_{k+1} \vDash t_1 = t_2$ and $\Gamma_{k+1} \vDash P$.

Let **I** be any interpretation on which all the members of Γ_{k+1} are true. Then $t_1 = t_2$ and **P** are both true because they are quantificationally entailed by Γ_{k+1}. It follows from 11.2.4, which we repeat here:

11.2.4: For any closed terms t_1 and t_2, if **P** is a sentence that contains t_1, then $\{t_1 = t_2, P\} \vDash P(t_2//t_1)$, and if **P** is a sentence that contains t_2, then $\{t_1 = t_2, P\} \vDash P(t_1//t_2)$.

that the sentence at position **k** + 1 is true as well. So $\Gamma_{k+1} \vDash P_{k+1}$.

These changes establish that *PDE* is sound for predicate logic with identity and functions; like *PD* and *PD+*, *PDE* never leads from true premises to a false conclusion.

11.3E EXERCISES

1. Using Metatheorem 11.3.1, prove the following:
a. Every argument of *PL* that is valid in *PD* is quantificationally valid.
b. Every sentence of *PL* that is a theorem in *PD* is quantificationally true.
*c. Every pair of sentences **P** and **Q** of *PD* that are equivalent in *PD* are quantificationally equivalent.

2. Prove the following (to be used in Exercise 3) by mathematical induction:

11.3.4. Let **P** be a formula of *PL* and **Q** a subformula of **P**. Let $[P](Q_1//Q)$ be a sentence that is the result of replacing one or more occurrences of **Q** in **P** with a formula Q_1. If **Q** and Q_1 contain the same nonlogical symbols and variables, and if on any interpretation **Q** and Q_1 are satisfied by exactly the same variable assignments, then on any interpretation **P** and $[P](Q_1//Q)$ are satisfied by exactly the same variable assignments.

3. Using 11.3.4, show how we can establish, as a step in an inductive proof of the soundness of *PD+*, that Quantifier Negation is truth-preserving for predicate logic.

***4.**a. Suppose that the rule ∀I did not have the restriction that the instantiating constant **a** in the sentence $P(a/x)$ to which ∀I applies must not occur in any undischarged assumption. Explain why *PD* would *not* be sound for predicate logic in this case.
b. Suppose that the rule ∃E did not have the restriction that the instantiating constant **a** in the assumption $P(a/x)$ must not occur in the sentence **Q** that is derived. Explain why *PD* would *not* be sound for predicate logic in this case.

11.4 THE COMPLETENESS OF *PD*, *PD+*, AND *PDE*

In this section we shall prove that our natural deduction systems are *complete* for predicate logic. A natural deduction system is complete for predicate logic if, whenever a sentence is quantificationally entailed by a set of sentences, there is at least one derivation of the sentence from members of that set in the natural deduction system. Metatheorem 11.4.1 is the *Completeness Metatheorem* for *PD*:

Metatheorem 11.4.1: If $\Gamma \vDash \mathbf{P}$, then $\Gamma \vdash \mathbf{P}$ in *PD*.

We shall prove the Completeness Metatheorem for *PD* in a manner analogous to that in which the completeness of *SD* for sentential logic was shown in Chapter 6. We note that the Completeness Metatheorem follows almost immediately from the Inconsistency Lemma for predicate logic:

> **11.4.2** (the *Inconsistency Lemma*): If a set Γ of sentences of *PL* is quantificationally inconsistent, then Γ is also inconsistent in *PD*.

To see how Metatheorem 11.4.1 follows, assume that, for some set Γ and sentence **P**, $\Gamma \vDash \mathbf{P}$ (this is the antecedent of the metatheorem). Then the set $\Gamma \cup \{\sim \mathbf{P}\}$ is quantificationally inconsistent (see Exercise 1). It follows, from Lemma 11.4.2, that $\Gamma \cup \{\sim \mathbf{P}\}$ is also inconsistent in *PD*. And from this it follows that $\Gamma \vdash \mathbf{P}$ in *PD* (see Exercise 2).

So the bulk of this section is devoted to proving Lemma 11.4.2. We shall do so by proving its contrapositive:

> If a set Γ of sentences of *PL* is consistent in *PD*, then Γ is quantificationally consistent.

If the contrapositive is true, then we may conclude of any set that is quantificationally *in*consistent that it is also inconsistent in *PD*. The proof of the contrapositive is in four steps:

> *Step 1 in proof of Lemma 11.4.2:* We shall prove in result 11.4.3 that, for any set Γ that is consistent in *PD*, if we double the subscript of every individual constant in Γ (so that every resulting subscript will be even), then the resulting set $\Gamma_{\mathbf{e}}$ is also consistent in *PD*. We call such a set an *evenly subscripted set.*
>
> *Step 2 in proof of Lemma 11.4.2:* We shall then show that, because there are infinitely many individual constants (namely, all the oddly subscripted constants) that do not occur in the sentences of any evenly subscripted set, every evenly subscripted set Γ that is

consistent in *PD* is a subset of a set that is *maximally consistent in PD* and that is *∃-complete.* This will be established as result 11.4.4, the Maximal Consistency Lemma for predicate logic. Maximal consistency is defined as it was for *SD*:

> A set Γ of sentences of *PL* is *maximally consistent in PD* if and only if Γ is consistent in *PD*, and for every sentence **P** of *PD* that is not a member of Γ, Γ ∪ {**P**} is inconsistent in *PD*.

If a set is maximally consistent in *PD*, then adding even one new sentence to the set makes it inconsistent in *PD*. ∃-completeness (read aloud as *existential completeness*) is a new concept, but a simple one:

> A set Γ of sentences of *PL* is *∃-complete* if and only if, for each sentence in Γ that has the form (∃**x**)**P**, at least one substitution instance of (∃**x**)**P** is also a member of Γ.

If, for example, '(∃**x**)Gx' is a member of a set that is ∃-complete, then at least one of 'Ga', 'Gb', 'Gc', . . . is also a member of the set.

Step 3 in proof of Lemma 11.4.2: We shall next show that there is a straightforward way to construct an interpretation on which every member of a set that is maximally consistent in *PD* and that is ∃-complete is true, from which it follows that any such set is quantificationally consistent and hence that all of its subsets are also quantificationally consistent. This will be established as result 11.4.8, the Consistency Lemma for predicate logic. It follows from the Consistency Lemma that the evenly subscripted set from which we built the maximally consistent set in Step 2 must be quantificationally consistent.

Step 4 in proof of Lemma 11.4.2: Finally we shall show, in result 11.4.9, that the set that we began with, whose subscripts were doubled in Step 1, must be quantificationally consistent as well.

It follows from Steps 1–4 that every set of sentences that is consistent in *PD* is also quantificationally consistent and therefore that the contrapositive of this statement, the Consistency Lemma 11.4.2, is true.

So let us turn to Result 11.4.3, which will establish *Step 1*:

11.4.3: Let Γ be a set of sentences of *PL* and let Γ_e be the set that results from doubling the subscript of every individual constant that occurs in any member of Γ. Then if Γ is consistent in *PD*, Γ_e is also consistent in *PD*.

Proof: Assume that Γ is consistent in *PD* and that, contrary to what we wish to prove, Γ_e is *in*consistent in *PD*. Then there is a derivation of the sort

1	$\mathbf{P}_1$
2	$\mathbf{P}_2$
.	.
n	$\mathbf{P}_n$
.	.
k	**Q**
.	.
p	~ **Q**

where $\mathbf{P}_1, \mathbf{P}_2, \ldots, \mathbf{P}_n$ are members of Γ_e. We shall convert this derivation into a derivation that shows that Γ is inconsistent in *PD*, contradicting our first assumption. Our strategy, not surprisingly, will be to halve the subscript of every evenly subscripted individual constant occurring in the derivation, thus converting each of $\mathbf{P}_1, \mathbf{P}_2, \ldots, \mathbf{P}_n$ back to a member of the original Γ. There is a complication, though—in so doing we may end up with a sequence in which either an $\exists$E restriction or an $\forall$I restriction is violated. If, for example, $\mathbf{P}_1$ in the derivation above is 'Ba_2', and later in the derivation the sentence '$(\forall x)Lx$' is legally derived from the sentence 'La_1' by $\forall$I (note that an odd subscript *may* occur in the above derivation *after* the primary assumptions), then in changing $\mathbf{P}_1$ to 'Ba_1' we shall have introduced an individual constant into a primary assumption that *prevents* the later use of $\forall$I. Our first step is thus to ensure that this will not happen.

When the rule $\exists$E is used to justify a sentence, let the constant **a** that is the instantiating constant in the substitution instance $\mathbf{P}(\mathbf{a}/\mathbf{x})$ that begins the subderivation cited be called the *instantiating constant for that use of* $\exists$*E*. Similarly the *instantiating constant for a use of* $\forall$*I* is the instantiating constant **a** in the sentence $\mathbf{P}(\mathbf{a}/\mathbf{x})$ cited. Let $\mathbf{a}_1, \ldots, \mathbf{a}_m$ be the distinct constants that are instantiating constants for uses of $\exists$E and $\forall$I in the above derivation. Let $\mathbf{b}_1, \ldots, \mathbf{b}_m$ be distinct constants that have odd subscripts that are larger than the subscript of any constant occurring in the derivation. (Because every derivation is a finite sequence, we know that of the constants occurring in our derivation there is one that has the largest subscript—and, whatever this largest subscript may be, there are infinitely many odd numbers that are larger.) We replace each sentence **R** in the original derivation with a sentence $\mathbf{R}^*$ that is the result of first replacing each occurrence of $\mathbf{a}_i$ in **R**, $1 \leq \mathbf{i} \leq \mathbf{m}$, with $\mathbf{b}_i$, and then halving every even subscript in a constant in the resulting sentence.

We claim that the resulting sequence is a derivation in *PD* of $\mathbf{Q}^*$ and ~ $\mathbf{Q}^*$ from members of the set Γ. First note that, for every new primary assumption $\mathbf{P}_i^*$, $\mathbf{P}_i^*$ is a member of Γ. This is because none of

$\mathbf{a}_1, \ldots, \mathbf{a}_m$ can occur in a primary assumption of the original derivation (lest an instantiating constant restriction be violated—for these are the instantiating constants for uses of ∃E and ∀I in that derivation). So $\mathbf{P}^*$ is just $\mathbf{P_i}$ with all its individual constant subscripts halved—that is, a member of the set Γ from which $\Gamma_\mathbf{e}$ was constructed by doubling subscripts. It remains to be shown that the resulting sequence counts as a derivation in *PD*—that every sentence in that sequence can be justified. This is left as an exercise.

Step 2 in our proof of Lemma 11.4.2 is contained in the Maximal Consistency Lemma for predicate logic:

> **11.4.4** (the *Maximal Consistency Lemma*): If Γ is an evenly subscripted set of sentences that is consistent in *PD*, then Γ is a subset of at least one set of sentences that is both maximally consistent in *PD* and ∃-complete.

We shall establish this lemma by showing how, beginning with Γ, to construct a superset that has the two properties. We assume that the sentences of *PL* have been enumerated, that is, that they have been placed in a one-to-one correspondence with the positive integers so that there is a first sentence, a second sentence, a third sentence, and so on. The enumeration can be done analogously to the enumeration of the sentences of *SL* in Section 6.4; we leave proof of this as an exercise (Exercise 4). We shall now build a sequence of sets Γ_1, Γ_2, Γ_3, . . . starting with an evenly subscripted set Γ that is consistent in *PD* and considering each sentence in the enumeration, adding the sentence if it can consistently be added, and, if the added sentence is existentially quantified, adding one of its substitution instances as well. The sequence is constructed as follows:

1. Γ_1 is Γ.
2. Γ_{i+1} is
   (i) $\Gamma_\mathbf{i} \cup \{\mathbf{P_i}\}$, if $\Gamma_\mathbf{i} \cup (\mathbf{P_i})$ is consistent in *PD* and $\mathbf{P_i}$ does not have the form $(\exists \mathbf{x})\mathbf{P}$, or
   (ii) $\Gamma_\mathbf{i} \cup \{\mathbf{P_i}, \mathbf{P_i}^*\}$, if $\Gamma \cup \{\mathbf{P_i}\}$ is consistent in *PD* and $\mathbf{P_i}$ has the form $(\exists \mathbf{x})\mathbf{Q}$, where $\mathbf{P_i}^*$ is a substitution instance $\mathbf{Q}(\mathbf{a}/\mathbf{x})$ of $(\exists \mathbf{x})\mathbf{Q}$ and $\mathbf{a}$ is the alphabetically earliest constant that does not occur in $\mathbf{P_i}$ or in any sentence in $\Gamma_\mathbf{i}$, or
   (iii) $\Gamma_\mathbf{i}$, if $\Gamma_\mathbf{i} \cup \{\mathbf{P_i}\}$ is inconsistent in *PD*.

As an example of (ii), if $\Gamma_\mathbf{i}$ is the set {(∀x)(Fxa ⊃ Gx), ~ Hc ∨ (∃y)Jyy] and $\mathbf{P_i}$ is '(∃z)(Kz & (∀y)Fzy)', then $\Gamma_\mathbf{i} \cup \{\mathbf{P_i}\}$ is quantificationally consistent, and so $\mathbf{P_i}$ will be added to the set—but we must add a substitution instance of $\mathbf{P_i}$ as well. The alphabetically earliest constant that does not occur in $\mathbf{P_i}$ or in any member of $\Gamma_\mathbf{i}$ is 'b', and so this will be the instantiating constant. Γ_{i+1} is therefore

$$\{(\forall x)(Fxa \supset Gx), \sim Hc \vee (\exists y)Jyy, (\exists z)(Kz \ \& \ (\forall y)Fzy), Kb \ \& \ (\forall y)Fby\}$$

The reason for using an instantiating constant that does not already occur in Γ_i will become clear shortly when we prove that each set in the sequence is consistent in *PD*. Here it is important to note that, for any set in the sequence, there is always at least one individual constant that does not already occur in that set. This is because the set that we started with is evenly subscripted, and so we know that infinitely many oddly subscripted individual constants do not occur in Γ; and each subsequent set adds at most one new individual constant, still leaving infinitely many individual constants yet to be used. Thus the requirement in condition (ii)—that **a** be a *new* constant—is a requirement that can always be satisfied.

Because the sequence $\Gamma_1, \Gamma_2, \Gamma_3, \ldots$ is infinitely long, there is no last member in the set. We want a set that contains all the sentences in these sets, so we let Γ^* be the set that contains every sentence that occurs in some set in the infinite sequence $\Gamma_1, \Gamma_2, \Gamma_3, \ldots$ We shall show that Γ^* is both maximally consistent in *PD* and $\exists$-complete. To show that Γ^* is maximally consistent in *PD*, we first prove that each set Γ_i in the sequence is consistent in *PD*, using mathematical induction.

Basis clause: Γ_1 is consistent in *PD*.

Proof of basis clause: By definition, Γ_1 is Γ, a set that is consistent in *PD*.

Inductive step: If for every $\mathbf{i} \leq \mathbf{k}$, Γ_i is consistent in *PD*, then Γ_{k+1} is consistent in *PD*.

Proof of inductive step: If Γ_{k+1} is formed in accordance with condition (i), then Γ_{k+1} is obviously consistent in *PD*. If Γ_{k+1} is formed in accordance with condition (ii), then $\Gamma_i \cup \{\mathbf{P}_i\}$ is consistent—as stipulated by condition (ii). We need to show that it follows that $\Gamma_i \cup \{\mathbf{P}_i, \mathbf{P}_i^*\}$, which is what Γ_{k+1} was defined to be in this case, is also consistent in *PD*. Because the instantiating constant in $\mathbf{P}_i^*$ does not occur in any member of $\Gamma_i \cup \{\mathbf{P}_i\}$, the consistency of Γ_{k+1} follows immediately from result 11.4.5, the proof of which is left as an exercise.

11.4.5. If **a** does not occur in any member of the set $\Gamma \cup \{(\exists \mathbf{x})\mathbf{P}\}$, and if the set is consistent in *PD*, then the set $\Gamma \cup \{(\exists \mathbf{x})\mathbf{P}, \mathbf{P}(\mathbf{a}/\mathbf{x})\}$ is also consistent in *PD*.

(This is why condition (ii) stipulated that **a** be a new constant—the fact that **a** does not occur in the set $\Gamma \cup \{(\exists \mathbf{x})\mathbf{P}\}$ is crucial to the proof of the inductive step.) Finally, if Γ_{k+1} is formed in accordance with condition (iii), then Γ_{k+1} is Γ_k, and Γ_k is, by the inductive hypothesis, consistent in *PD*. So, no matter which condition was applied in its construction, Γ_{k+1} is consistent in *PD*.

Having established both premises, we conclude that every set in the sequence $\Gamma_1, \Gamma_2, \Gamma_3, \ldots$ is consistent in *PD*.

We now need to show that the set Γ^*, which contains all the sentences that occur in any set in the sequence, is itself consistent in *PD*. We shall show this by assuming that it is not consistent in *PD* and deriving a contradiction. So assume that Γ^* is not consistent in *PD*. Then there is a finite nonempty subset Γ' of Γ^* that is inconsistent in *PD* (the proof is analogous to that in the proof of 6.4.6). Because Γ' is finite, some sentence in Γ', say, $\mathbf{P_j}$ occurs later in our enumeration of the sentences of *PL* than any other sentence in Γ'. Every member of Γ' is thus a member of $\Gamma_{\mathbf{j}+1}$, by the way we constructed the sets in the sequence. (If the **i**th sentence is added to one of the sets, it is added by the time that $\Gamma_{\mathbf{i}+1}$ is constructed.) It follows that $\Gamma_{\mathbf{j}+1}$ is also inconsistent in *PD* (the proof is analogous to the proof of 6.4.7). But we have just proved that every set in the sequence is consistent in *PD*, so we conclude that, contrary to our assumption, Γ^* is also consistent in *PD*.

That Γ^* is *maximally* consistent in *PD* is proved in exactly the manner that the parallel result in Section 6.4 was proved—for any sentence $\mathbf{P_k}$, if $\Gamma^* \cup \{\mathbf{P_k}\}$ is consistent in *PD*, then the subset $\Gamma_{\mathbf{k}}$ of Γ^* is such that $\Gamma_{\mathbf{k}} \cup \{\mathbf{P_k}\}$ is consistent in *PD*, and so by the construction of the sequence of sets, $\mathbf{P_k}$ is a member of $\Gamma_{\mathbf{k}+1}$ and hence of Γ^*.

Finally the proof that Γ^* is $\exists$-complete is left as an exercise. This completes the proof of the Maximal Consistency Lemma 11.4.4—because every member of the original set Γ is also a member of Γ^*, it follows that every evenly subscripted set Γ of sentences of *PL* that is consistent in *PD* is a subset of at least one set of sentences that is both maximally consistent in *PD* and $\exists$-complete.

We now turn to *Step 3* in our proof of the Inconsistency Lemma 11.4.2. We must prove that every set Γ that is both maximally consistent in *PD* and $\exists$-consistent is consistent in *PD*. To do this we need the following preliminary results:

11.4.6: If $\Gamma \vdash \mathbf{P}$ and Γ is a subset of a set Γ^* that is maximally consistent in *PD*, then $\mathbf{P} \in \Gamma^*$.

Proof: See Exercise 9.

11.4.7: Every set Γ^* of sentences that is both maximally consistent in *PD* and $\exists$-complete has the following properties:

a. $\mathbf{P} \in \Gamma^*$ if and only if $\sim \mathbf{P} \notin \Gamma^*$.

b. $\mathbf{P} \,\&\, \mathbf{Q} \in \Gamma^*$ if and only if $\mathbf{P} \in \Gamma^*$ and $\mathbf{Q} \in \Gamma^*$.

c. $\mathbf{P} \vee \mathbf{Q} \in \Gamma^*$ if and only if either $\mathbf{P} \in \Gamma^*$ or $\mathbf{Q} \in \Gamma^*$.

d. $\mathbf{P} \supset \mathbf{Q} \in \Gamma^*$ if and only if either $\mathbf{P} \notin \Gamma^*$ or $\mathbf{Q} \in \Gamma^*$.

e. $\mathbf{P} \equiv \mathbf{Q} \in \Gamma^*$ if and only if either $\mathbf{P} \in \Gamma^*$ and $\mathbf{Q} \in \Gamma^*$ or $\mathbf{P} \notin \Gamma^*$ and $\mathbf{Q} \notin \Gamma^*$.

f. $(\forall \mathbf{x})\mathbf{P} \in \Gamma^*$ if and only if, for every individual constant $\mathbf{a}$, $\mathbf{P}(\mathbf{a}/\mathbf{x}) \in \Gamma^*$.

g. $(\exists \mathbf{x})\mathbf{P} \in \Gamma^*$ if and only if, for at least one individual constant $\mathbf{a}$, $\mathbf{P}(\mathbf{a}/\mathbf{x}) \in \Gamma^*$.

Proof: The proofs that (a)–(e) hold for sets of sentences that are maximally consistent in *PD* and ∃-complete parallel exactly the corresponding proofs in Section 6.4, using result 11.4.6 instead of 6.4.5. (In those proofs we did not appeal to a property like ∃-completeness, and we do not need to appeal to it here in establishing (a)–(e).)

Proof of (f): Assume that $(\forall \mathbf{x})\mathbf{P} \in \Gamma^*$. For any substitution instance $\mathbf{P}(\mathbf{a}/\mathbf{x})$ of $(\forall \mathbf{x})\mathbf{P}$, $\{(\forall \mathbf{x}\})\mathbf{P}\} \vdash \mathbf{P}(\mathbf{a}/\mathbf{x})$ (by ∀E); so, by 11.4.6, every substitution instance is a member of Γ^* as well. Now assume that $(\forall \mathbf{x})\mathbf{P} \notin \Gamma^*$. Then $\sim (\forall \mathbf{x})\mathbf{P} \in \Gamma^*$, by (a). The following derivation shows that $\{\sim (\forall \mathbf{x})\mathbf{P}\} \vdash (\exists \mathbf{x}) \sim \mathbf{P}$:

1	$\sim (\forall \mathbf{x})\mathbf{P}$	Assumption
2	$\quad \sim (\exists \mathbf{x}) \sim \mathbf{P}$	Assumption
3	$\qquad \sim \mathbf{P}(\mathbf{a}/\mathbf{x})$	Assumption
4	$\qquad (\exists \mathbf{x}) \sim \mathbf{P}$	3 ∃I
5	$\qquad \sim (\exists \mathbf{x}) \sim \mathbf{P}$	2 R
6	$\quad \mathbf{P}(\mathbf{a}/\mathbf{x})$	3–5 ~ E
7	$\quad (\forall \mathbf{x})\mathbf{P}$	6 ∀I
8	$\quad \sim (\forall \mathbf{x})\mathbf{P}$	1 R
9	$(\exists \mathbf{x}) \sim \mathbf{P}$	2–8 ~ E

(We assume that the constant **a** does not occur in **P**.) Therefore, by 11.4.6, $(\exists \mathbf{x}) \sim \mathbf{P}$ is also a member of Γ^*. Because Γ^* is ∃-complete, some substitution instance $\sim \mathbf{P}(\mathbf{a}/\mathbf{x})$ of $(\exists \mathbf{x}) \sim \mathbf{P}$ is a member of Γ^* as well, and it therefore follows from (a) that $\mathbf{P}(\mathbf{a}/\mathbf{x}) \notin \Gamma^*$. So, if $(\forall \mathbf{x})\mathbf{P} \notin \Gamma^*$, then there is at least one substitution instance of $(\forall \mathbf{x})\mathbf{P}$ that is not a member of Γ^*.

Proof of (g): Assume that $(\exists \mathbf{x})\mathbf{P} \in \Gamma^*$. Then, because Γ^* is ∃-complete, at least one substitution instance of $(\exists \mathbf{x})\mathbf{P}$ is also a member of Γ^*. Now assume that $(\exists \mathbf{x})\mathbf{P} \notin \Gamma^*$. If some substitution instance $\mathbf{P}(\mathbf{a}/\mathbf{x})$ of $(\exists \mathbf{x})\mathbf{P}$ is a member of Γ^*, then because $\{\mathbf{P}(\mathbf{a}/\mathbf{x})\} \vdash (\exists \mathbf{x})\mathbf{P}$ (by ∃I), it follows from 11.4.6 that, contrary to our assumption, $(\exists \mathbf{x})\mathbf{P}$ is also a member of Γ^*. So, if $(\exists \mathbf{x})\mathbf{P} \notin \Gamma^*$, then none of its substitution instances is a member of Γ^*.

We can now complete the proof of *Step 3* by establishing the Consistency Lemma for predicate logic:

> **11.4.8** (the *Consistency Lemma*): Every set of sentences of *PL* that is both maximally consistent in *PD* and ∃-complete is quantificationally consistent.

We shall prove the Consistency Lemma by showing how to construct, for a set Γ^* that is both maximally consistent in *PD* and ∃-complete, an interpretation $\mathbf{I}^*$ on which every member of Γ^* is true. We begin by associating with each individual constant a distinct positive integer—the positive integer **i** will be associated with the alphabetically **i**th constant. The number 1 will be associated with 'a', 2 with 'b', . . . , 22 with 'v', 23 with 'a_1', and so on. **I*** is then defined as follows:

1. The UD is the set of positive integers.
2. For each sentence letter **P**, **I***(**P**) = **T** if and only if **P** ∈ Γ*.
3. For each individual constant **a**, **I***(**a**) is the positive integer associated with **a**.
4. For each **n**-place predicate **A**, **I***(**A**) includes all and only those **n**-tuples ⟨**I***($\mathbf{a}_1$), . . . , **I***($\mathbf{a}_\mathbf{n}$)⟩ such that **A**$\mathbf{a}_1$ . . . $\mathbf{a}_\mathbf{n}$ ∈ Γ*.

The major feature of this interpretation is that, for each atomic sentence **P** of *PL*, **P** will be true on **I*** if and only if **P** ∈ Γ*. That is why we defined condition 4 (as well as condition 2) as we did. And to be sure that condition 4 can be met, we must have condition 3, which ensures that each individual constant designates a different member of the UD. This is necessary because, for example, if 'Fa' is a member of Γ* and 'Fb' is not a member, then if 'a' and 'b' designated the same integer—say, 1—condition 4 would require that the 1-tuple ⟨1⟩ both be and not be in the extension of 'F'. (In addition, condition 3 ensures that every member of the UD is named by a constant, which we shall shortly see is also important when we look at the truth-values that quantified sentences receive on **I***.) With all the atomic sentences in Γ* true and all other atomic sentences false, it follows that truth-functionally compound and quantified sentences are true on **I*** if and only if they are members of Γ*.

We complete the proof of the Consistency Lemma by establishing, by mathematical induction on the number of occurrences of logical operators in sentences of *PL*, that each sentence **P** of *PL* is true on **I*** if and only if **P** ∈ Γ*.

Basis clause: Each sentence **P** that contains zero occurrences of logical operators is true on **I*** if and only if **P** ∈ Γ*.

Proof of basis clause: Either **P** is a sentence letter or **P** has the form **A**$\mathbf{a}_1$ . . . $\mathbf{a}_\mathbf{n}$. If **P** is a sentence letter, then, by part 2 of the definition of **I***, it follows that **P** is true on **I*** if and only if **P** ∈ Γ*.

If **P** has the form **A**$\mathbf{a}_1$ . . . $\mathbf{a}_\mathbf{n}$, then **P** is true on **I*** if and only if ⟨**I***($\mathbf{a}_1$), . . . , **I***($\mathbf{a}_\mathbf{n}$)⟩ ∈ **I***(**A**). Part 4 of the definition of **I*** stipulates that ⟨**I***($\mathbf{a}_1$), . . . , **I***($\mathbf{a}_\mathbf{n}$)⟩ ∈ **I***(**A**) if and only if **A**$\mathbf{a}_1$ . . . $\mathbf{a}_\mathbf{n}$ ∈ Γ*. So in this case as well, **P** is true on **I*** if and only if **P** ∈ Γ*.

Inductive step: If each sentence **P** that contains **k** or fewer occurrences of logical operators is such that **P** is true on **I*** if and only if **P** ∈ Γ*, then each sentence **P** that contains **k** + 1 occurrences of logical operators is such that **P** is true on **I*** if and only if **P** ∈ Γ*.

Proof of inductive step: We assume that, for an arbitrary positive integer **k**, the inductive hypothesis is true. We must show that on this assumption it follows that any sentence **P** that contains **k** + 1 occurrences of logical operators is such that **P** is true on **I*** if and only if **P** ∈ Γ*. We consider the forms that the sentence **P** may have.

Cases 1–5: **P** has one of the forms ~ **Q**, **Q** & **R**, **Q** ∨ **R**, **Q** ⊃ **R**, or **Q** ≡ **R**. The proofs for these five cases are analogous to the proofs for the parallel cases for *SL* in Section 6.4, so we omit them here.

Case 6: **P** has the form (∀**x**)**Q**. Assume that (∀**x**)**Q** is true on **I***. Then every substitution instance **Q**(**a**/**x**) of (∀**x**)**Q** is true on **I*** because, by 11.1.4, {(∀**x**)**Q**} quantificationally entails every one of its substitution instances. Each substitution instance contains fewer than **k** + 1 occurrences of connectives, and so, by the inductive hypothesis, each substitution instance is a member of Γ* since it is true on **I***. It follows from part (f) of 11.4.7 that (∀**x**)**Q** is also a member of Γ*.

Now assume that (∀**x**)**Q** is false on **I***. In this case we shall make use of result 11.1.11, which we repeat here:

11.1.11: Let **I** be an interpretation on which each member of the UD is assigned to at least one individual constant. Then, if every substitution instance of (∀**x**)**P** is true on **I**, so is (∀**x**)**P**.

I* is an interpretation of the type specified in 11.1.11: Every positive integer in the UD is designated by the individual constant with which we have associated that integer. It follows, then, that if every substitution instance of (∀**x**)**Q** is true on **I***, then so is (∀**x**)**Q**. Therefore, if (∀**x**)**Q** is false on **I***, at least one of its substitution instances **Q**(**a**/**x**) must also be false on **I***. Because **Q**(**a**/**x**) contains fewer than **k** + 1 occurrences of logical operators, it follows from the inductive hypothesis that **Q**(**a**/**x**) ∉ Γ*. And so, by part (f) of 11.4.7, (∀**x**)**Q** ∉ Γ*.

Case 7: **P** has the form (∃**x**)**Q**. Assume that (∃**x**)**Q** is true on **I***. Then it follows from 11.1.12, which we repeat here, that at least one substitution instance **Q**(**a**/**x**) of (∃**x**)**Q** is true on **I***, for every member of the UD is designated by an individual constant.

11.1.12: Let **I** be an interpretation on which each member of the UD is assigned to at least one individual constant. Then, if every substitution instance of (∃**x**)**P** is false on **I**, so is (∃**x**)**P**.

Because the substitution instance **Q**(**a**/**x**) contains fewer than **k** + 1 occurrences of logical operators, it follows from the inductive hypothesis that **Q**(**a**/**x**) ∈ Γ*. So, by part (g) of 11.4.7, (∃**x**)**Q** is also a member of Γ*.

Now assume that (∃**x**)**Q** is false on **I***. Because each substitution instance **Q**(**a**/**x**) is such that {**Q**(**a**/**x**)} ⊨ (∃**x**)**Q** (this is result 11.1.5), it follows that every substitution instance **Q**(**a**/**x**) is also false on **I***. Each of these substitution instances contains fewer than **k** + 1 occurrences of logical operators, and so it follows from the inductive hypothesis that no substitution instance of $(\exists\mathbf{x})\mathbf{Q}$ is a member of Γ^*. Finally, by part (g) of 11.4.7, it follows that $(\exists\mathbf{x})\mathbf{Q}$ is not a member of Γ^* either.

That completes the proof of the inductive step, and we may now conclude that every sentence **P** of *PL* is such that it is true on $\mathbf{I}^*$ if and only if it is a member of Γ^*. So all the members of Γ^* are true on $\mathbf{I}^*$, and we conclude that Γ^* is quantificationally consistent. Lemma 11.4.8 is therefore true: Every set that is both maximally consistent in *PD* and $\exists$-complete is quantificationally consistent. Lemmas 11.4.4 and 11.4.8 together establish that every evenly subscripted set of sentences of *PL* that is consistent in *PD* is also quantificationally consistent.

Step 4 of the proof of the Inconsistency Lemma 11.4.2 is contained in result 11.4.9:

11.4.9: Let Γ be a set of sentences of *PL* and let $\Gamma_\mathbf{e}$ be the set that results from doubling the subscript of every individual constant that occurs in any member of Γ. Then, if $\Gamma_\mathbf{e}$ is quantificationally consistent, Γ is quantificationally consistent as well.

Proof: See Exercise 8.

We have now completed the four steps in the proof of the Inconsistency Lemma 11.4.2, so we may conclude that, if a set Γ of sentences of *PL* is quantificationally inconsistent, then Γ is also inconsistent in *PD*. And this establishes the completeness of *PD* for predicate logic. If $\Gamma \vDash \mathbf{P}$, then $\Gamma \cup \{\sim \mathbf{P}\}$ is quantificationally inconsistent. By the Inconsistency Lemma, $\Gamma \cup \{\sim \mathbf{P}\}$ is also inconsistent in *PD*, and hence $\Gamma \vdash \mathbf{P}$ in *PD*. And that is what Metatheorem 11.4.1, the Completeness Theorem for *PD*, states.

Because *PD* is complete for predicate logic, so is *PD+*. Every rule of *PD* is a rule of *PD+*, and so every derivation in *PD* is a derivation in *PD+*. So, if $\Gamma \vDash \mathbf{P}$, then $\Gamma \vdash \mathbf{P}$ in *PD+* because we know, by Metatheorem 11.4.1, that $\Gamma \vdash \mathbf{P}$ in *PD*.

We also want to be sure that *PDE* is complete for predicate logic with identity and functions. The completeness proof for *PDE* is similar to the completeness proof for *PD*, but there are some important changes. Results 11.4.3 and 11.4.9 must now take into account sentences containing the identity predicate and complex terms; the necessary changes are left as an exercise. Maximal consistency is defined for *PDE* as it was for *PD*, while the definition of $\exists$-completeness must be modified slightly:

A set Γ of sentences of *PLE* is $\exists$-complete if and only if, for each sentence in Γ that has the form $(\exists\mathbf{x})\mathbf{P}$, at least one substitution instance of $(\exists\mathbf{x})\mathbf{P}$ in which the instantiating individual term is a constant is also a member of Γ.

The proof of the Maximal Consistency Lemma 11.4.4 for *PDE*—that every evenly subscripted set of sentences that is consistent in *PDE* is a subset of a set of sentences that is both maximally consistent in *PDE* and ∃-complete—is just like the proof for *PD* except that *PLE* and *PDE*, rather than *PL* and *PD*, are spoken of. However, the proof of the Consistency Lemma 11.4.8 is different because the interpretation **I*** that is constructed for a maximally consistent and ∃-complete set of sentences must be defined differently.

The interpretation **I*** of the maximally consistent and ∃-complete set Γ* that we constructed in the proof of the Consistency Lemma 11.4.8 stipulated that a distinct positive integer be associated with each individual constant and that

3. For each individual constant **a**, **I***(**a**) is the positive integer associated with **a**.

This will not do in the case of *PDE*, for suppose that Γ, and consequently its superset Γ*, contains a sentence **a** = **b**, where **a** and **b** are different constants. If we interpret the constants of *PLE* in accordance with condition 3, **a** and **b** will denote *different* members of the UD, and hence **a** = **b** will be false. But the interpretation is supposed to make all members of Γ*, including **a** = **b**, true. So we shall have to change condition 3 to take care of the case where a sentence like **a** = **b** is a member of the set Γ*. We shall also have to interpret the functors in the language, and to do so in a way that makes sentences containing complex terms true if and only if those sentences are members of Γ.

Before turning to the construction of an interpretation for Γ*, however, we first establish some facts about sets of sentences that are maximally consistent in *PDE* and ∃-complete. As the reader may easily verify, the properties listed in result 11.4.7 remain true for maximally consistent, ∃-complete sets of sentences of *PDE*. We add three additional properties to the list in result 11.4.7:

h. For every closed term **t**, **t** = **t** ∈ Γ*.

Proof: Let **t** be any closed term. ∅ ⊢ **t** = **t**, by =I and ∀E. Because the empty set is a subset of Γ*, it follows from 11.4.6 that **t** = **t** ∈ Γ*.

i. If a sentence $\mathbf{t_1} = \mathbf{t_2}$, where $\mathbf{t_1}$ and $\mathbf{t_2}$ are closed terms, is a member of Γ*, then

   a. If **Q** is a sentence in which $\mathbf{t_1}$ occurs, **Q** ∈ Γ* if and only if every sentence $\mathbf{Q(t_2//t_1)}$ (every sentence obtained by replacing one or more occurrences of $\mathbf{t_1}$ in **Q** with $\mathbf{t_2}$) is a member of Γ*.

   b. If **Q** is a sentence in which $\mathbf{t_2}$ occurs, **Q** ∈ Γ* if and only if every sentence $\mathbf{Q(t_1//t_2)}$ is a member of Γ*.

Proof: Let $\mathbf{t_1} = \mathbf{t_2}$ be a sentence that is a member of Γ* and let **Q** be a sentence in which $\mathbf{t_1}$ occurs. Assume that **Q** ∈ Γ*. Every sentence $\mathbf{Q(t_2//t_1)}$ is derivable from the set {$\mathbf{t_1} = \mathbf{t_2}$, **Q**} by =E. Therefore, by 11.4.6, every sentence $\mathbf{Q(t_2//t_1)}$ is a member of Γ*. Now assume that **Q** ∉ Γ*. Every sentence $\mathbf{Q(t_2//t_1)}$ is such that {$\mathbf{t_1} = \mathbf{t_2}$, $\mathbf{Q(t_2//t_1)}$} ⊢ **Q**, by =E—use $\mathbf{t}_1$ to replace every occurrence of $\mathbf{t}_2$ that replaced $\mathbf{t}_1$ in $\mathbf{Q}(\mathbf{t}_2//\mathbf{t}_1)$, and the result is $\mathbf{Q}$ once again. So, if any sentence $\mathbf{Q}(\mathbf{t}_2//\mathbf{t}_1)$ is in Γ^*, then, by 11.4.6, $\mathbf{Q}$ must be as well. Therefore, if $\mathbf{Q} \notin \Gamma^*$, then no sentence $\mathbf{Q}(\mathbf{t}_2//\mathbf{t}_1)$ is a member of Γ^*.

Similar reasoning shows that, if $\mathbf{t}_1 = \mathbf{t}_2 \in \Gamma^*$ and $\mathbf{Q}$ is a sentence in which $\mathbf{t}_2$ occurs, then $\mathbf{Q} \in \Gamma^*$ if and only if every sentence $\mathbf{Q}(\mathbf{t}_1//\mathbf{t}_2)$ is a member of Γ^*.

j. For each **n**-place functor f and **n** terms $\mathbf{t}_1, \ldots, \mathbf{t}_\mathbf{n}$, there is at least one constant **b** such that the formula $f(\mathbf{t}_1, \ldots, \mathbf{t}_\mathbf{n}) = \mathbf{b}$ is a member of Γ^*.

Proof: By property (h), $f(\mathbf{t}_1, \ldots, \mathbf{t}_\mathbf{n}) = f(\mathbf{t}_1, \ldots, \mathbf{t}_\mathbf{n}) \in \Gamma^*$. Since $f(\mathbf{t}_1, \ldots, \mathbf{t}_\mathbf{n}) = f(\mathbf{t}_1, \ldots, \mathbf{t}_\mathbf{n}) \vdash (\exists \mathbf{x})f(\mathbf{t}_1, \ldots, \mathbf{t}_\mathbf{n}) = \mathbf{x}$, the sentence $(\exists \mathbf{x})f(\mathbf{t}_1, \ldots, \mathbf{t}_\mathbf{n}) = \mathbf{x}$ must also be a member of Γ^*, by 11.4.6. And because Γ^* is $\exists$-complete, it follows (from our revised definition of $\exists$-completeness) that there is at least one constant **b** such that the formula $f(\mathbf{t}_1, \ldots, \mathbf{t}_\mathbf{n}) = \mathbf{b}$ is also a member of Γ^*.

We now turn to the proof of the Consistency Lemma 11.4.8 for *PDE*—that every set of sentences of *PLE* that is both maximally consistent in *PDE* and $\exists$-complete is also quantificationally consistent. Let Γ^* be a set of sentences that is both maximally consistent in *PLE* and $\exists$-complete. We associate positive integers with the individual constants of *PLE* as follows:

First associate the positive integer **i** with the alphabetically **i**th individual constant of *PLE*. Let **p** designate this association and let **p**(**a**) stand for the integer that has been associated with the constant **a**. Thus **p**('a') is 1, **p**('b') is 2, and so on.

Now we define a second association, which we shall designate with **q**. For each constant **a**, **q**(**a**) = **p**(**a**′), where **a**′ is the alphabetically earliest constant such that **a** = **a**′ is a member of Γ^*.

Note that for each constant **a** property (h) of maximally consistent, $\exists$-complete sets assures us that $\mathbf{a} = \mathbf{a} \in \Gamma^*$, and so we can be certain that **q** assigns a value to **a** because there is always at least one **a**′ such that $\mathbf{a} = \mathbf{a}' \in \Gamma^*$. According to the definition, **q**('a') is always 1 since property (h) assures us that 'a = a' is a member of Γ^*, and because 'a' is the alphabetically earliest constant of *PLE*, there can be no earlier constant that stands to the right of the identity predicate in a sentence containing 'a' to the left. But for any other constant, the value that it receives from **q** depends on the identity sentences that the particular set Γ^* contains. Suppose that 'b = a', 'b = b', 'b = e', and '$\mathrm{b} = \mathrm{m}_{22}$' are the only identity sentences in Γ^* that contain 'b' to the left of the identity predicate. In this case there is an alphabetically earlier constant to the right, namely, 'a', and this is the alphabetically earliest constant so occurring. So **q**('b') = **p**('a') = 1. If 'c = c', 'c = f', and '$\mathrm{c} = \mathrm{g}_3$' are the only identity sentences in Γ^* that contain 'c' to the left of the identity predicate, then 'c' is the alphabetically earliest constant occurring to the right, and so $\mathbf{q}$('c') = $\mathbf{p}$('c') = 3. The definition of $\mathbf{q}$ plays a role in ensuring that identity sentences come out true on the interpretation that we shall construct if and only if they are members of Γ^*, as a consequence of

11.4.10: For any constants **a** and **b**, $\mathbf{q}(\mathbf{a}) = \mathbf{q}(\mathbf{b})$ if and only if $\mathbf{a} = \mathbf{b} \in \Gamma^*$.

Proof: Let $\mathbf{a}'$ be the alphabetically earliest constant such that $\mathbf{a} = \mathbf{a}' \in \Gamma^*$. (Remember that property (h) guarantees that there is at least one such constant.) Then

a. $\mathbf{q}(\mathbf{a}) = \mathbf{p}(\mathbf{a}')$.

Let $\mathbf{b}'$ be the alphabetically earliest constant such that $\mathbf{b} = \mathbf{b}' \in \Gamma^*$. Then

b. $\mathbf{q}(\mathbf{b}) = \mathbf{q}(\mathbf{b}')$.

It follows from (a) and (b) that

c. $\mathbf{q}(\mathbf{a}) = \mathbf{q}(\mathbf{b})$ if and only if $\mathbf{q}(\mathbf{a}') = \mathbf{p}(\mathbf{b}')$.

And because $\mathbf{p}$ associates different values with different constants,

d. $\mathbf{p}(\mathbf{a}') = \mathbf{p}(\mathbf{b}')$ if and only if $\mathbf{a}'$ and $\mathbf{b}'$ are the same constant.

From (c) and (d) we conclude that

e. $\mathbf{q}(\mathbf{a}) = \mathbf{q}(\mathbf{b})$ if and only if $\mathbf{a}'$ and $\mathbf{b}'$ are the same constant.

Assume that $\mathbf{q}(\mathbf{a}) = \mathbf{q}(\mathbf{b})$. It follows from (e) that $\mathbf{a}'$ and $\mathbf{b}'$ are the same constant. Therefore, because $\mathbf{b} = \mathbf{b}' \in \Gamma^*$, it follows trivially that $\mathbf{b} = \mathbf{a}'$, which is the same sentence, is a member of Γ^*. And because $\mathbf{a} = \mathbf{a}' \in \Gamma^*$, it follows from property (i) of maximally consistent, ∃-complete sets that $\mathbf{a} = \mathbf{b} \in \Gamma^*$ ($\mathbf{a} = \mathbf{b}$ is a sentence $\mathbf{a} = \mathbf{a}'$ $(\mathbf{b}//\mathbf{a}')$).

Now assume that $\mathbf{a} = \mathbf{b} \in \Gamma^*$. Then, because $\mathbf{a} = \mathbf{a}' \in \Gamma^*$, it follows from property (i) that $\mathbf{b} = \mathbf{a}' \in \Gamma^*$, and because $\mathbf{b} = \mathbf{b}' \in \Gamma^*$ as well, it also follows from property (i) that $\mathbf{a} = \mathbf{b}' \in \Gamma^*$. $\mathbf{a}'$ was defined to be the alphabetically earliest constant that appears to the right of the identity predicate in an identity statement containing **a**, and so from the fact that $\mathbf{a} = \mathbf{b}' \in \Gamma^*$ we conclude that $\mathbf{b}'$ is not alphabetically earlier than $\mathbf{a}'$. $\mathbf{b}'$ was defined to be the alphabetically earliest constant that appears to the right of the identity predicate in an identity statement containing **b**, and so from the fact that $\mathbf{b} = \mathbf{a}' \in \Gamma^*$ we conclude that $\mathbf{a}'$ is not alphabetically earlier than $\mathbf{b}'$. These two observations establish that $\mathbf{a}'$ and $\mathbf{b}'$ must be the same constant. So, from (e), we may conclude that $\mathbf{q}(\mathbf{a}) = \mathbf{q}(\mathbf{b})$.

Result 11.4.10 guarantees that if there is an identity statement in Γ^* that contains the individual constants **a** and **b** then $\mathbf{q}(\mathbf{a}) = \mathbf{q}(\mathbf{b})$, and if there is no identity statement in Γ^* that contains **a** and **b** then $\mathbf{q}(\mathbf{a}) \neq \mathbf{q}(\mathbf{b})$. And this fact will be crucial in our construction of an interpretation on which every member of a set that is both maximally consistent in *PDE* and ∃-complete is true. We turn now to the construction.

Let Γ^* be a set that is both maximally consistent in *PDE* and ∃-complete, and define the interpretation $\mathbf{I}^*$ as follows:

1. The UD is the set of positive integers that **q** associates with at least one individual constant of *PLE.*
2. For each sentence letter **P**, $\mathbf{I}^*(\mathbf{P}) = \mathbf{T}$ if and only if $\mathbf{P} \in \Gamma^*$.
3. For each individual constant **a**, $\mathbf{I}^*(\mathbf{a}) = \mathbf{q}(\mathbf{a})$.
4. For each **n**-place functor *f*, $\mathbf{I}^*(f)$ is the set that includes all and only those $\mathbf{n} + 1$-tuples $<\mathbf{I}^*(\mathbf{a}_1), \ldots, \mathbf{I}^*(\mathbf{a}_\mathbf{n}), \mathbf{I}^*(\mathbf{b})>$, where $\mathbf{a}_1, \ldots, \mathbf{a}_\mathbf{n}$ and **b** are individual constants such that $f(\mathbf{a}_1, \ldots, \mathbf{a}_\mathbf{n}) = \mathbf{b} \in \Gamma^*$.
5. For each **n**-place predicate **A** other than the identity predicate, $\mathbf{I}^*(\mathbf{A})$ is the set that includes all and only those **n**-tuples $\langle \mathbf{I}^*(\mathbf{a}_1), \ldots, \mathbf{I}^*(\mathbf{a}_\mathbf{n})\rangle$ such that $\mathbf{A}\mathbf{a}_1 \ldots \mathbf{a}_\mathbf{n} \in \Gamma^*$.

We must ensure that conditions 4 and 5 can be met.

For condition 4 we must ensure that the interpretation of *f* is indeed a function on the UD: that for each **n** members $\mathbf{u}_1, \ldots, \mathbf{u}_\mathbf{n}$ of the UD there is exactly one member $\mathbf{u}_{\mathbf{n}+1}$ of the UD such that $<\mathbf{u}_1, \ldots, \mathbf{u}_\mathbf{n}, \mathbf{u}_{\mathbf{n}+1}>$ is a member of $\mathbf{I}^*(f)$. That there is *at least one* such member of the UD follows from the fact that every member of the UD is denoted by at least one individual constant (this is guaranteed by condition 1 of our definition of $\mathbf{I}^*$), and property (j) of sets that are maximally consistent in *PDE* and ∃-complete, which we repeat here:

j. For each **n**-place functor *f* and **n** constants $\mathbf{a}_1, \ldots, \mathbf{a}_\mathbf{n}$, there is at least one constant **b** such that the formula $f(\mathbf{a}_1, \ldots, \mathbf{a}_\mathbf{n}) = \mathbf{b}$ is a member of Γ^*.

Given these two facts, condition 4 ensures that for each **n** members $\mathbf{u}_1, \ldots, \mathbf{u}_\mathbf{n}$ of the UD there is at least one member $\mathbf{u}_{\mathbf{n}+1}$ of the UD such that $<\mathbf{u}_1, \ldots, \mathbf{u}_\mathbf{n}, \mathbf{u}_{\mathbf{n}+1}>$ is a member of $\mathbf{I}^*(f)$, for any functor *f*. To show that there is at most one such member $\mathbf{u}_{\mathbf{n}+1}$, let us assume, to the contrary, that there is also a member of the UD $\mathbf{u}'_{\mathbf{n}+1}$, where $\mathbf{u}'_{\mathbf{n}+1} \neq \mathbf{u}_{\mathbf{n}+1}$, such that $<\mathbf{u}_1, \ldots, \mathbf{u}_\mathbf{n}, \mathbf{u}'_{\mathbf{n}+1}>$ is a member of $\mathbf{I}(f)$. This means that, in addition to the sentence $f(\mathbf{a}_1, \ldots, \mathbf{a}_\mathbf{n}) = \mathbf{b}$, Γ includes a sentence $f(\mathbf{a}_1, \ldots, \mathbf{a}_\mathbf{n}) = \mathbf{c}$, such that $\mathbf{I}^*(\mathbf{c}) = \mathbf{u}'_{\mathbf{n}+1} \neq \mathbf{I}^*(\mathbf{b})$. Then $\mathbf{q}(\mathbf{a}) \neq \mathbf{q}(\mathbf{b})$ by virtue of clause 3 of the definition of $\mathbf{I}^*$. But this is impossible, since $\{f(\mathbf{a}_1, \ldots, \mathbf{a}_\mathbf{n}) = \mathbf{b}, f(\mathbf{a}_1, \ldots, \mathbf{a}_\mathbf{n}) = \mathbf{c}\} \vdash \mathbf{b} = \mathbf{c}$ by =E, so $\mathbf{b} = \mathbf{c} \in \Gamma^*$, by 11.4.6, and therefore $\mathbf{q}(\mathbf{c}) = \mathbf{q}(\mathbf{b})$, by 11.4.10. It follows that $\mathbf{I}^*(\mathbf{c}) = \mathbf{I}^*(\mathbf{b})$, and so there is at most one member $\mathbf{u_{n+1}}$ of the UD such that $<\mathbf{u}_1, \ldots, \mathbf{u_n}, \mathbf{u_{n+1}}>$ is a member of $\mathbf{I}^*(f)$.

We must also ensure that condition 4 can be met, that is, that there are not two atomic sentences $\mathbf{Aa}_1 \ldots \mathbf{a_n}$ and $\mathbf{Aa}_1' \ldots \mathbf{a_n'}$ such that one is in Γ^* and the other is not in Γ^*, yet $\langle \mathbf{I}^*(\mathbf{a}_1), \ldots, \mathbf{I}^*(\mathbf{a_n})\rangle = \langle \mathbf{I}^*(\mathbf{a}_1'), \ldots, \mathbf{I}^*(\mathbf{a_n'})\rangle$. In the case of *PD*, it was simple to show this, for distinct constants were interpreted to designate distinct individuals. However, $\mathbf{q}$ may assign the same positive integer to more than one constant, and as a consequence condition 3 may interpret several constants to designate the same value. Here our previous results will be useful. Suppose that the constants $\mathbf{a}_1, \ldots, \mathbf{a_n}$ and $\mathbf{a}_1', \ldots, \mathbf{a_n'}$ are such that $\langle \mathbf{I}^*(\mathbf{a}_1), \ldots, \mathbf{I}^*(\mathbf{a_n})\rangle = \langle \mathbf{I}^*(\mathbf{a}_1'), \ldots, \mathbf{I}^*(\mathbf{a_n'})\rangle$. Then, by clause 3 of the definition of $\mathbf{I}^*$, we know that for each $\mathbf{i}$, $\mathbf{q}(\mathbf{a_i}) = \mathbf{q}(\mathbf{a_i'})$. It follows from 11.4.10 that for each $\mathbf{i}$, $\mathbf{a_i} = \mathbf{a_i'} \in \Gamma^*$. Because $\mathbf{a}_1 = \mathbf{a}_1'$ is a member of Γ^*, property (i) assures us that $\mathbf{Aa}_1 \ldots \mathbf{a_n}$ is a member of Γ^* if and only if $\mathbf{Aa}_1'\mathbf{a}_2 \ldots \mathbf{a_n}$ is a member of Γ^*. And because $\mathbf{a}_2 = \mathbf{a}_2'$ is also a member of Γ^*, property (i) assures us that $\mathbf{Aa}_1'\mathbf{a}_2 \ldots \mathbf{a_n}$ is a member of Γ^* if and only if $\mathbf{Aa}_1'\mathbf{a}_2' \ldots \mathbf{a_n}$ is a member of Γ^*, and so on until we note that because $\mathbf{a_n} = \mathbf{a_n'}$ is in Γ^*, $\mathbf{Aa}_1'\mathbf{a}_2' \ldots \mathbf{a_n}$ is a member of Γ^* if and only if $\mathbf{Aa}_1'\mathbf{a}_2' \ldots \mathbf{a_n'}$ is a member of Γ^*. We conclude that, if $\langle \mathbf{I}^*(\mathbf{a}_1), \ldots, \mathbf{I}^*(\mathbf{a_n})\rangle = \langle \mathbf{I}^*(\mathbf{a}_1'), \ldots, \mathbf{I}^*(\mathbf{a_n'})\rangle$, then $\mathbf{Aa}_1 \ldots \mathbf{a_n} \in \Gamma^*$ if and only if $\mathbf{Aa}_1' \ldots \mathbf{a_n'} \in \Gamma^*$. So condition 4 can indeed be met.

To establish Lemma 11.4.8 for *PDE*—that every set Γ^* that is both maximally consistent in *PDE* and ∃-complete is also quantificationally consistent—we can prove by mathematical induction that a sentence $\mathbf{P}$ of *PDE* is true on $\mathbf{I}^*$ if and only if $\mathbf{P} \in \Gamma^*$. The proof is similar to that for *PD*, except that we must change the basis clause to consider closed complex terms as well as constants, and also to consider formulas containing the identify operator. We shall find the following result useful here:

> **11.4.11:** For any closed complex term $\mathbf{t}$ and variable assignment $\mathbf{d}$, $\text{den}_{\mathbf{I}^*,\mathbf{d}}(\mathbf{t}) = \mathbf{I}^*(\mathbf{a})$, where $\mathbf{a}$ is the alphabetically earliest individual constant such that $\mathbf{t} = \mathbf{a}$ is a member of Γ^*. (Property (j) of sets that are maximally consistent in *PDE* and ∃-complete guarantees that there *is* such a constant $\mathbf{a}$.)
>
> **Proof:** See Exercise 16.

Here is the revised proof.

> **Proof of basis clause:** Either $\mathbf{P}$ is a sentence letter or $\mathbf{P}$ has the form $\mathbf{At}_1 \ldots \mathbf{t_n}$ or $\mathbf{t}_1 = \mathbf{t}_2$. If $\mathbf{P}$ is a sentence letter, then, by clause 2 of the definition of $\mathbf{I}^*$, it follows that $\mathbf{P}$ is true on $\mathbf{I}^*$ if and only if $\mathbf{P} \in \Gamma^*$.
>
> If $\mathbf{P}$ has the form $\mathbf{At}_1 \ldots \mathbf{t_n}$ then $\mathbf{P}$ is true on $\mathbf{I}^*$ if and only if, for every $\mathbf{d}$, $<\text{den}_{\mathbf{I}^*,\mathbf{d}}(\mathbf{t}_1), \ldots, \text{den}_{\mathbf{I}^*,\mathbf{d}}(\mathbf{t_n})>$ is a member of $\mathbf{I}^*(\mathbf{A})$. Now property (j) guarantees, for each complex term $\mathbf{t_i}$, that there is an alphabetically earliest constant $\mathbf{a_i}$ such that $\mathbf{t_i} = \mathbf{a_i}$ is a member of Γ^*. Moreover, by virtue of the rule $=$ D, the set consisting of $\mathbf{P}$ and each of these identity sentences quantificationally entails $\mathbf{At}_1' \ldots \mathbf{t_n'}$, where

t'_i is t_i if t_i is a constant and t'_i is a_i otherwise. So, by 11.4.6, $P \in \Gamma^*$ if and only if the sentence $At'_1 \ldots t'_n$ is also a member of Γ^*. In addition, $den_{I^*,d}(t_i) = I^*(t'_i)$, trivially if t_i is a constant and by 11.4.11 if t_i is a complex term. So $<den_{I^*,d}(t_1), \ldots, den_{I^*,d}(t_n)>$ is a member of $I^*(A)$ if and only if $<I^*(t'_1), \ldots, I^*(t'_n)>$ is a member of $I^*(A)$; and clause 5 in the definition of I^* guarantees that $At'_1 \ldots t'_n$ is a member of Γ^* if and only if $<I^*(t'_1), \ldots, I^*(t'_n)>$ is a member of $I^*(A)$. We conclude that $At_1 \ldots t_n \in \Gamma^*$ if and only if $At_1 \ldots t_n$ is true on I^*.

If P has the form $t_1 = t_2$, then P is true on I^* if and only if, for each variable assignment d, $den_{I^*,d}(t_1) = den_{I^*,d}(t_2)$. Again, for each complex term t_i, property (j) guarantees that there is an alphabetically earliest constant a_i such that $t_i = a_i$ is a member of Γ^* and so, by virtue of =D and result 11.4.6, $t_1 = t_2 \in \Gamma^*$ if and only if the sentence $t'_1 = t'_2$ is also a member of Γ^*, where t'_i is t_i if t_i is a constant and t'_i is a_i otherwise. Moreover $den_{I^*,d}(t_i) = I^*(t'_i)$, trivially if t_i is a constant and by result 11.4.11 if t_i is a complex term. So $den_{I^*,d}(t_1) = den_{I^*,d}(t_2)$ if and only if $I^*(t'_1) = I^*(t'_2)$. By the way in which I^* was constructed, $I^*(t'_1) = I^*(t'_2)$ if and only if $q(t'_1) = q(t'_2)$. By result 11.4.10, $q(t'_1) = q(t'_2)$ if and only if $t'_1 = t'_2 \in \Gamma^*$. We may conclude that $t_1 = t_2 \in \Gamma^*$ if and only if $t_1 = t_2$ is true on I^*.

Because every member of Γ^* is true on I^*, Γ^* is quantificationally consistent. And, with Lemmas 11.4.4 and 11.4.8 established for *PDE*, along with the necessary modifications of 11.4.9 (see Exercise 11.4.15), we know that the Inconsistency Lemma 11.4.2 is also true for *PDE*. It follows that *PDE* is complete for predicate logic with identity and functions.

11.4E EXERCISES

*1. Prove that if $\Gamma \vDash P$ then $\Gamma \cup \{\sim P\}$ is quantificationally inconsistent.

2. Prove that if $\Gamma \cup \{\sim P\}$ is inconsistent in *PD* then $\Gamma \vdash P$.

3. Using Metatheorem 11.4.1, prove the following:
a. Every argument of *PL* that is quantificationally valid is valid in *PD*.
b. Every sentence of *PL* that is quantificationally true is a theorem in *PD*.
*c. Every pair of sentences P and Q of *PL* that are quantificationally equivalent are equivalent in *PD*.

4. Prove that the sentences of *PL* can be enumerated. (*Hint:* See Section 6.4.)

5. Prove the following:

If $\Gamma \vdash P$ and Γ is a subset of Γ', then $\Gamma' \vdash P$.

6.a. Prove 11.4.5.
b. Prove that any set Γ^* constructed as in our proof of Lemma 11.4.4 is $\exists$-complete.

7. Prove that the sequence of sentences constructed in the proof of 11.4.3 is a derivation in *PD* by showing (by mathematical induction) that each sentence in the new sequence can be justified with the same rule as the corresponding sentence in the original derivation.

***8.** Prove 11.4.9, using result 11.1.13.

***9.** Prove 11.4.6.

10. Explain why, in Lemmas 11.4.4 and 11.4.8, we constructed a set that was both ∃-complete and maximally consistent in *PD*, rather than a set that was just maximally consistent in *PD*.

11. Let system *PD** be just like *PD* except that the rule ∀E is replaced by the following rule:

*Universal Elimination** (∀E*)

| (∀**x**)**P**
|
| ~ (∃**x**) ~ **P**

Prove that the system *PD** is complete for predicate logic.

***12.** Let system *PD** be just like *PD* except that the rules ∃E and ∃I are replaced by the following two rules:

*Existential Elimination** (∃E*)

| (∃**x**)**P**
|
| ~ (∀**x**) ~ **P**

*Existential Introduction** (∃I*)

| ~ (∀**x**) ~ **P**
|
| (∃**x**)**P**

Prove that system *PD** is complete for predicate logic.

13. Using the results in the proof of Metatheorem 11.4.1, prove the following theorem (known as the *Löwenheim Theorem*):

If a sentence **P** of *PL* is not quantificationally false, then there is an interpretation with the set of positive integers as the UD on which **P** is true.

***14.** Prove the following metatheorem (known as the *Löwenheim-Skolem Theorem*):

If a set Γ of sentences of *PL* is quantificationally consistent, then there is an interpretation with the set of positive integers as the UD on which every member of Γ is true.

***15.** Show the changes that must be made in the proofs of 11.4.3 and 11.4.9 so that these results will hold for *PLE* and *PDE*. (*Hint:* Exercise 8 suggested that you use result 11.1.13 in proving 11.4.9; so you must check whether 11.1.13 needs to be changed.)

16. Prove result 11.4.11.

17. Show that the Löwenheim Theorem (and consequently the more general Löwenheim-Skolem Theorem) does *not* hold for *PLE*.

11.5 THE SOUNDNESS OF THE TREE METHOD

We have presented the tree method as a means of testing for semantic properties of sentences and sets of sentences in both sentential logic and predicate logic. In this section and the next we shall prove that the tree method in Chapter 9 fulfills a claim we have made: A finite set of sentences of *PL* is quantificationally inconsistent if and only if every systematic tree for that set closes. In this section we shall prove that the tree method is *sound* for predicate logic—that if a systematic tree for a set of sentences of *PL* closes, then the set is quantificationally inconsistent. We shall prove the same for predicate logic with identity and functions. In both cases we can then be assured that, if we pronounce a set of sentences inconsistent because a tree for that set closes, our pronouncement is correct. In the next section we shall prove that the tree method is *complete* for predicate logic—that if a set of sentences is quantificationally inconsistent, then every systematic tree for that set is bound to close. Knowing that the method is complete, we shall also know that open systematic trees do establish quantificational consistency. (With a simple adaptation of parts of our proofs, the soundness and completeness of the tree method for sentential logic can also be established. This will be addressed in the exercises.)

Our *Soundness Metatheorem* for the tree method is this:

Metatheorem 11.5.1: If a systematic tree for a set Γ of sentences of *PL* closes, then Γ is quantificationally inconsistent.

(As we shall see in the exercises for this section, soundness also holds for nonsystematic trees.) Our proof of Metatheorem 11.5.1 will rely heavily on the following observation about the decomposition rules used in constructing trees: Each rule is consistency-preserving in the sense that, if we have a consistent set of sentences and apply a decomposition rule to one of the sentences in that set, at least one of the sentences that results (there will be only one in the case of a nonbranching rule) can consistently be added to the set. As we build a tree for a set of sentences, we are, in effect, building supersets of the one we started with—the set of sentences occurring on a branch is a superset of the original set. Given the sense in which the decomposition rules are consistency-preserving, at least one of the supersets formed on a branch by repeated application of decomposition rules will be quantificationally consistent. This will be important in establishing Metatheorem 11.5.1, for the supersets that comprise the branches of a closed tree are all quantificationally inconsistent, each such branch containing some literal and its negation. Because the decomposition rules are consistency-preserving in the sense described, it follows that the only way we can end up with every superset being quantificationally inconsistent (with a closed tree) is by starting with a set that is quantificationally inconsistent. And that is what Metatheorem 11.5.1 says.

Our observation that the decomposition rules are consistency-preserving must be proved. To facilitate our proof, we introduce the concept of a *level* of a tree. The first (occurrence of a) sentence on any tree is at level 1. For any other sentence **P**, **P** is at level **i** + 1, where **i** is the level of the sentence occurring immediately before **P** on the same branch of the tree. The line numbers used to annotate trees in Chapters 4 and 9 do not always correspond to levels because we adopted the convention in those chapters that only one decomposition rule can be cited on each line. Consider, for example, the tree on page 464. Lines 1–3 do correspond directly to levels 1–3 of that tree. Line 4, however, displays only one of the sentences occurring at level 4. The sentence in line 10 on the left-hand branch is *also* at level 4, for the sentence that occurs immediately before it on the same branch is at level 3. Similar observations hold for sentences further down the branches of the tree.

We shall establish that our decomposition rules are consistency-preserving by showing that each level **i** of a systematic tree for a quantificationally consistent set of sentences is such that either there is at least one branch that was completed prior to that level on which the sentences form a quantificationally consistent set (a quantificationally consistent superset has resulted from applying as many rules as could be applied) or there is at least one branch that extends at least as far as level **i** such that the sentences on that branch up to and including level **i** form a quantificationally consistent set (the rules thus far have preserved consistency).

As an example of what we want to prove, here is a completed open tree for the set {$(\forall x)Fx \lor Ga$, $(\exists y) \sim Fy$}:

1.	$(\forall x)Fx \lor Ga$					SM
2.	$(\exists y) \sim Fy$					SM
3.		$\sim Fa$		$\sim Fb$		2 $\exists$D2
4.	$(\forall x)Fx$	Ga	$(\forall x)Fx$	Ga		1 $\lor$D
5.	Fa		Fb			4 $\forall$D
	$\times$		$\times$			

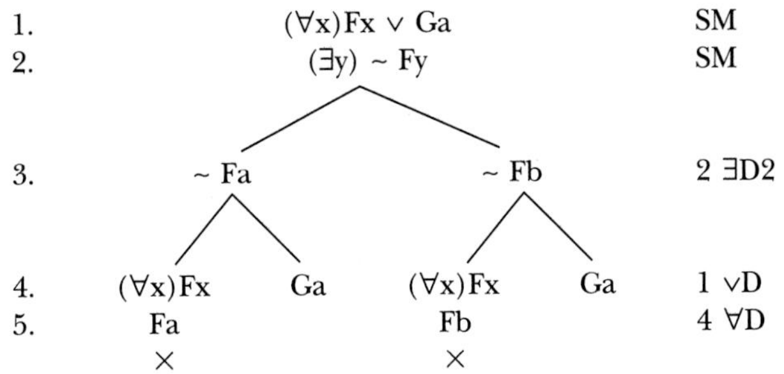

Each of the levels 1–5 is such that our claim holds. At level 1 there is at least one branch such that the set of sentences occurring on that branch through and including level 1 form a quantificationally consistent set: {(∀x)Fx ∨ Ga}. At level 2 there is at least one branch such that the set of sentences occurring on that branch form a quantificationally consistent set: {(∀x)Fx ∨ Ga, (∃y) ~ Fy}. At level 3 there are two (and so at least one) such branches: {(∀x)Fx ∨ Ga, (∃y) ~ Fy, ~ Fa} and {(∀x)Fx ∨ Ga, (∃y) ~ Fy, ~ Fb}. At level 4 there are also two such branches: {(∀x)Fx ∨ Ga, (∃y) ~ Fy, ~ Fa, Ga} and {(∀x)Fx ∨ Ga, (∃y) ~ Fy, ~ Fb, Ga}. The branches that include '(∀x)Fx' are not candidates, but we have not claimed that quantificationally consistent sets will be found on *all* branches. At level 5 there is no branch that extends to that level that contains a quantificationally consistent set of sentences, but there is at least one branch that was completed at an earlier level, level 4, on which the sentences form a quantificationally consistent set. So the claim is true of all levels of this tree.

The fact that the claim holds for every level of a systematic tree for a quantificationally consistent set allows us to conclude that if a tree for a set of sentences closes then the set must be quantificationally inconsistent. Consider: If a tree closes, then the tree has only a finite number of levels, and the longest branch ends at a finite level. In the following closed tree the longest branch ends at level 4:

1.	(∀x)Fx ∨ Fa		SM
2.	~ Fa		SM
3.	(∀x)Fx	Fa	1 ∨D
4.	Fa	×	3 ∀D
	×		

No branch that closes before the last level contains a quantificationally consistent set of sentences (each such branch containing a literal and its negation), and the branch that closes at the last level does not contain a quantificationally consistent set. So, at the last level of a closed tree, our claim about the levels of a tree for a quantificationally consistent set is not true; and we may conclude that the set for which the tree was constructed is therefore quantificationally *in*consistent.

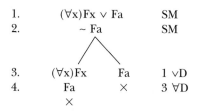

To prove our claim about the levels of any systematic tree for a quantificationally consistent set of sentences, we also introduce the concept of a path to a level of a tree. For any branch that extends to level **i** or further, we call that part of the branch that extends to level **i** a *path* to level **i**, and we say that the path *contains* the set of sentences that occur on it. In the last tree displayed, there is exactly one path to level 1, and it contains the set of sentences {(∀x)Fx ∨ Fa}. There is exactly one path to level 2, and it contains the set of sentences {(∀x)Fx ∨ Fa, ~ Fa}. There are two paths to level 3; one contains the set of sentences {(∀x)Fx ∨ Fa, ~ Fa, (∀x)Fx}, and the other contains the set {(∀x)Fx ∨ Fa, ~ Fa, Fa}. There is one path to level 4, and it contains the set $\{(\forall x)Fx \vee Fa, \sim Fa, (\forall x)Fx, Fa\}$. Finally a *completed* path to level **i** of a tree is a completed branch of that tree that ends at level **i**. We state our claim about the levels of a systematic tree for a quantificationally consistent set in terms of paths in the Consistent Branch Lemma:

> **11.5.2** (the *Consistent Branch Lemma*): Each level **i** of a tree for a quantificationally consistent set of sentences of *PL* is such that either (a) there is at least one completed path to a level earlier than **i** that contains a quantificationally consistent set of sentences or (b) there is at least one path to level **i** that contains a quantificationally consistent set of sentences.

We shall prove 11.5.2 by establishing a more specific claim (which will later be useful in proving that systematic trees for sets of sentences with finite models always have a completed open branch). Let Γ be a finite set of sentences of *PL* that is quantificationally consistent, and let **I** be an interpretation. We call interpretation **I′** a *path-variant* of **I** for path **p** of a tree for the set of sentences Γ if **I′** is just like **I** except that, for each constant **a** that occurs in some sentence on the path but not in any member of Γ, there is a member **u** of the UD such that **I′**(**a**) = **u** and such that, for every other constant **b** occurring on the path but not in Γ, **I′**(**b**) ≠ **u**. We shall show that

> **11.5.3:** If a finite set Γ of sentences of *PL* is true on an interpretation **I**, then each level **i** of a systematic tree for Γ is such that either (a) there is at least one completed path **p** to a level earlier than **i** that contains a set of sentences all of which are true on a path-variant of **I** for **p** or (b) there is at least one path **p** to level **i** that contains a set of sentences all of which are true on a path-variant of **I** for **p**.

We establish result 11.5.3 by mathematical induction on the levels of a systematic tree for a quantificationally consistent set of sentences of *PL*. Letting Γ be a finite set of sentences of *PL* and **I** an interpretation on which every member of Γ is true,

> *Basis clause:* Level 1 of a systematic tree for Γ is such that either (a) or (b) holds.
>
> *Inductive step:* If every level less than or equal to level **k** of a systematic tree for Γ is such that either (a) or (b) holds, then level **k** + 1 of a systematic tree for Γ is also such that either (a) or (b) holds.
>
> ---
>
> *Conclusion:* Every level of a systematic tree for Γ is such that either (a) or (b) holds.

Proof of basis clause: There is exactly one path to level 1 of any tree, and that path contains the unit set {**P**}, where **P** is a member of the set Γ for which the tree is being constructed. **P** is true on **I** since every member of Γ is, and **I** is in this case a path-variant of itself (since the path contains no constants that do not occur in Γ). So there is a path to level 1 that contains a set of sentences all of which are true on a path-variant of **I**, and (b) holds for level 1.

Proof of inductive step: We assume the inductive hypothesis for an arbitrary positive integer **k**: For each level **i** less than **k** + 1 of a tree for Γ, either (a) or (b) holds. We must show that on this assumption either (a) or (b) holds for level **k** + 1 of a tree for Γ as well. We first note that if (a) holds for an earlier level **i**, then (a) holds for level **k** + 1 as well. That is, if there is at least one completed path to a level earlier than **i** that contains a set of sentences all of which are true on a path-variant of **I** for that path, then that path is also a completed path to a level earlier than **k** + 1.

Now we must consider the case where (a) does not hold for any level prior to **k** + 1. In this case it follows from the inductive hypothesis that (b) holds for every level prior to **k** + 1 and, in particular, that (b) is true of level **k**. If, in addition, there is a *completed* path to level **k** that contains a set of sentences all of which are true on a path-variant of **I** for that path, then (a) is true of level **k** + 1. If there is not such a path to level **k**, we still know, because (b) is true of level **k**, that at least one (noncompleted) path to level **k** contains a set of sentences all of which are true on a path-variant of **I** for that path. Call this path $\Gamma_{\mathbf{k}}$ and the variant $\mathbf{I}_{\Gamma_{\mathbf{k}}}$. Because the path is not complete at level **k**, it is extended to level **k** + 1 by application of some tree rule. We shall now consider the rules that might be used to extend the path to level **k** + 1 and show that in each case application of the rule results in at least one path to level **k** + 1 that contains a set of sentences all of which are true on a path-variant of **I** for that path—thereby establishing that (b) holds for level **k** + 1 as well.

We divide the rules into six cases.

Case 1: The path $\Gamma_{\mathbf{k}}$ is extended to level **k** + 1 by adding a set member at that level. Because decomposition rules apply *after* all set members have been entered, the only sentences on the path $\Gamma_{\mathbf{k}}$ are members of Γ, and the sentence entered at level **k** + 1 is also a member of Γ. So there is a path to level **k** + 1 that contains a subset of Γ, all members of which are true in **I**, which in this case is a path-variant of itself.

Case 2: The path $\Gamma_{\mathbf{k}}$ is extended to level **k** + 1 as a result of applying one of the nonbranching rules ~ ~ D, &D, ~ ∨D, ~ ⊃D, ~ ∀D, or ~ ∃D to a sentence **P** on $\Gamma_{\mathbf{k}}$. In each case {**P**} quantificationally entails the sentence **Q** entered on level **k** + 1 (see Exercise 11.5.3). Therefore all the sentences on $\Gamma_{\mathbf{k}}$ and the sentence **Q** are true on $\mathbf{I}_{\Gamma_{\mathbf{k}}}$, which is a path-variant of **I** for the extended path that we are considering (because none of the rules in this case add a new individual constant to the tree and $\mathbf{I}_{\Gamma_k}$ itself was a path-variant of **I** for Γ_k). Thus there is a path to level **k** + 1—the path that extends Γ_k to include **Q**—that contains a set of sentences all of which are true on a path-variant of **I** for this path.

Case 3: The path is extended to form two paths to level **k** + 1 as a result of applying one of the branching rules ~ &D, ∨D, or ⊃D to a sentence **P** on Γ_k. Letting **Q** be one of the sentences that was entered on level **k** + 1 and **R** the other, it can be shown that on any interpretation on which **P** is true either **Q** is true or **R** is true (see Exercise 4). Therefore either all the sentences on Γ_k plus **Q** are true on $\mathbf{I}_{\Gamma_k}$, which is a path-variant of **I** for the new path containing **Q**, or all the sentences on Γ_k plus **R** are true on $\mathbf{I}_{\Gamma_k}$, which is a path-variant of **I** for the new path containing **R**. Thus there is a path to level **k** + 1—either the path that extends Γ_k to include **Q** or the path that extends Γ_k to include **R**—that contains a set of sentences all of which are true on a path-variant of **I** for that path.

Case 4: The path is extended to level **k** + 1 as a result of applying either ≡D or ~ ≡D (see Exercise 5).

Case 5: The path is extended to level **k** + 1 as a result of applying ∀D. Then Γ_k contains a sentence (∀**x**)**P** such that **P**(**a**/**x**) is entered at level **k** + 1, where **a** is either 'a' if no constants occur on Γ_k or the alphabetically earliest constant that does occur. Because (∀**x**)**Px** ⊨ **P**(**a**/**x**) (result 11.1.4), **P**(**a**/**x**) is true on $\mathbf{I}_{\Gamma_k}$. If no constant occurred on Γ_k, then $\mathbf{I}_{\Gamma_k}$ is also a path-variant of **I** for the new path to level **k** + 1 because $\mathbf{I}_{\Gamma_k}$ (**a**) ≠ $\mathbf{I}_{\Gamma_k}$ (**b**) for any other constant **b** occurring on Γ_k but not in Γ—there are no other constants **b** occurring on Γ_k. If, on the other hand, **a** is a constant that already occurs on Γ_k, then we have added no new constant to the path, and so $\mathbf{I}_{\Gamma_k}$ is in this case also a path-variant of **I** for the new path to level **k** + 1. Either way, there is a path to level **k** + 1 that contains a set of sentences all of which are true on a path-variant of **I** for that path.

Case 6: The path is extended to level **k** + 1 as a result of applying ∃D2. Then Γ_k contains a sentence (∃**x**)**P** such that **P**($\mathbf{a}_1$/**x**), . . . , **P**($\mathbf{a}_m$/**x**), **P**($\mathbf{a}_{m+1}$/**x**) are entered on distinct paths to level **k** + 1, where $\mathbf{a}_1$, . . . , $\mathbf{a}_m$ are all the individual constants that occur in sentences on Γ_k and $\mathbf{a}_{m+1}$ is the alphabetically earliest constant that does not occur on Γ_k. We consider two possibilities:

a. If any one (or more) of **P**($\mathbf{a}_1$/**x**), . . . , **P**($\mathbf{a}_m$/**x**) is true on $\mathbf{I}_{\Gamma_k}$, then the path to level **k** + 1 on which that substitution instance was entered is a path that contains a set of sentences all of which are true on a path-variant of **I** for that path ($\mathbf{I}_{\Gamma_k}$ is a path-variant of the newly formed path because the substitution instance does not introduce a new constant).

b. Now consider the case where none of $\mathbf{P}(\mathbf{a_1}/\mathbf{x}), \ldots,$ $\mathbf{P}(\mathbf{a_{m+1}}/\mathbf{x})$ is true on $\mathbf{I}_{\Gamma_\mathbf{k}}$. Because $(\exists\mathbf{x})\mathbf{P}$ is true on $\mathbf{I}_{\Gamma_\mathbf{k}}$ and because $\mathbf{a_{m+1}}$ does not occur in any sentence on $\Gamma_\mathbf{k}$, our proof of result 11.1.10 (Exercise 11.1.5) shows that $\mathbf{P}(\mathbf{a_{m+1}}/\mathbf{x})$ is true on an interpretation $\mathbf{I}'_{\Gamma_\mathbf{k}}$ that is just like $\mathbf{I}_{\Gamma_\mathbf{k}}$ except that $\mathbf{I}'_{\Gamma_\mathbf{k}}(\mathbf{a_{m+1}}) = \mathbf{u}$, where $\mathbf{u}$ is a member of the UD such that $\mathbf{d}[\mathbf{u}/\mathbf{x}]$ satisfies $\mathbf{P}$ on $\mathbf{I}_{\Gamma_\mathbf{k}}$. This member $\mathbf{u}$ is not assigned to any other individual constant $\mathbf{b_i}$ occurring on $\Gamma_\mathbf{k}$ but not in Γ (for, if it were, it would follow from result 11.1.13 that $\mathbf{P}(\mathbf{b_i}/\mathbf{x})$ is true on $\mathbf{I}_{\Gamma_\mathbf{k}}$, which contradicts our assumption here). Thus $\mathbf{I}'_{\Gamma_\mathbf{k}}$ is a path-variant of $\mathbf{I}$ for the path extended to level $\mathbf{k} + 1$ by the addition of $\mathbf{P}(\mathbf{a_{m+1}}/\mathbf{x})$, and one on which every sentence in the new path is true.

Either way, then, there is a path to level $\mathbf{k} + 1$ that contains a set of sentences all of which are true on a path-variant of **I** for that path.

We have considered each rule that might be used to extend the path $\Gamma_\mathbf{k}$ to level $\mathbf{k} + 1$ and have shown that in each case there is at least one path to level $\mathbf{k} + 1$ that contains a set of sentences all of which are true on a path-variant of **I** for that path. That completes the proof of the inductive step.

Therefore, result 11.5.3 holds for every level of a tree for a set of sentences all of which are true on interpretation **I**.

The Consistent Branch Lemma 11.5.2 follows immediately from result 11.5.3, for in establishing the existence of paths containing sentences all of which are true on some path variant of **I**, we have established that the sentences on each such path form a quantificationally consistent set.

Metatheorem 11.5.1 follows from the Consistent Branch Lemma and from the fact that the null tree, which is the single tree for the empty set of sentences of *PL*, is not closed (the null branch does not contain any sentences and therefore does not contain some atomic sentence and its negation). If a tree for a set Γ of sentences is closed, then every branch on that tree is closed and hence contains a literal and its negation. Any path to the last level of the tree is a closed branch, and hence the set of sentences on that branch is quantificationally inconsistent (because it contains some literal and its negation). So (b) does not hold for the last level of such a tree. Nor does (a); all completed paths to earlier levels are closed branches, and therefore the sets of sentences on those branches are also quantificationally inconsistent. Because the last level of any closed tree is such that neither (a) nor (b) holds, it follows, by the Consistent Branch Lemma, that the set for which the tree was constructed is quantificationally inconsistent. We conclude that the tree method is sound for predicate logic.

To establish that the tree method for predicate logic with identity and functions is also sound, we first note that the cases in the inductive proof of result 11.5.3 carry over to predicate logic with identity and functions. We must also add two more cases to the inductive step, one to cover paths that are extended by an application of =D and one to cover paths that are extended by an application of CTD.

Case 7: The path Γ_k is extended to level $\mathbf{k} + 1$ as a result of applying =D. Then Γ_k contains sentences $\mathbf{t}_1 = \mathbf{t}_2$ and $\mathbf{P}$ such that a sentence $\mathbf{P}(\mathbf{t}_1//\mathbf{t}_2)$ was entered at level $\mathbf{k} + 1$. It follows from 11.2.4, which we repeat here, that $\mathbf{P}(\mathbf{t}_1//\mathbf{t}_2)$ is true on $\mathbf{I}_{\Gamma_k}$.

11.2.4: For any closed terms $\mathbf{t}_1$ and $\mathbf{t}_2$, if $\mathbf{P}$ is a sentence that contains $\mathbf{t}_1$, then $\{\mathbf{t}_1 = \mathbf{t}_2, \mathbf{P}\} \models \mathbf{P}(\mathbf{t}_2//\mathbf{t}_1)$, and if $\mathbf{P}$ is a sentence that contains $\mathbf{t}_2$, then $\{\mathbf{t}_1 = \mathbf{t}_2, \mathbf{P}\} \models \mathbf{P}(\mathbf{t}_1//\mathbf{t}_2)$.

In addition, $\mathbf{I}_{\Gamma_k}$ is a path-variant for the new path to level $\mathbf{k} + 1$ because =D does not introduce new constants. Therefore there is a path to level $\mathbf{k} + 1$ that contains a set of sentences all of which are true on some path-variant of **I** for that path.

Case 8: The path Γ_k is extended to level $\mathbf{k} + 1$ as a result of applying CTD. Then Γ_k contains a literal sentence with a closed complex term $f(\mathbf{a}_1, \ldots, \mathbf{a}_n)$, where $\mathbf{a}_1, \ldots, \mathbf{a}_n$ are all constants, such that $\mathbf{b}_1 = f(\mathbf{a}_1, \ldots, \mathbf{a}_n), \ldots, \mathbf{b}_m = f(\mathbf{a}_1, \ldots, \mathbf{a}_n)$ $\mathbf{b}_{m+1} = f(\mathbf{a}_1, \ldots, \mathbf{a}_n)$ are entered on distinct paths to level $\mathbf{k} + 1$, where $\mathbf{b}_1, \ldots, \mathbf{b}_m$ are all the individual constants that occur in sentences on Γ_k and $\mathbf{b}_{m+1}$ is the alphabetically earliest constant that does not occur on Γ_k. We consider two possibilities:

a. If any one (or more) of $\mathbf{b}_1 = f(\mathbf{a}_1, \ldots, \mathbf{a}_n), \ldots,$ $\mathbf{b}_m = f(\mathbf{a}_1, \ldots, \mathbf{a}_n)$ is true on $\mathbf{I}_{\Gamma_k}$, then the path to level $\mathbf{k} + 1$ on which that identity sentence was entered is a path that contains a set of sentences all of which are true on a path-variant of **I** for that path. ($\mathbf{I}_{\Gamma_k}$ is a path-variant of the newly formed path because the identity sentence does not introduce a new constant.)

b. Now consider the case where none of $\mathbf{b}_1 = f(\mathbf{a}_1, \ldots, \mathbf{a}_n),$ $\ldots, \mathbf{b}_m = f(\mathbf{a}_1, \ldots, \mathbf{a}_n)$ is true on $\mathbf{I}_{\Gamma_k}$. Because $\mathbf{b}_{m+1}$ does not occur in any sentence on Γ_k, our proof of result 11.2.5 (Exercise 11.2.7) shows that $\Gamma \cup \{\mathbf{b}_{m+1} = f(\mathbf{a}_1, \ldots, \mathbf{a}_n)\}$ is true on an interpretation $\mathbf{I}'_{\Gamma_k}$ that is just like $\mathbf{I}_{\Gamma_k}$ except that $\mathbf{I}'_{\Gamma_k}(\mathbf{b}_{m+1}) = \mathbf{u}$, where $\mathbf{u}$ is the member of the UD such that $< \mathbf{I}_{\Gamma_k}(\mathbf{a}_1), \ldots, \mathbf{I}_{\Gamma_k}(\mathbf{a}_n), \mathbf{u}>$ is a member of $\mathbf{I}_{\Gamma_k}(f)$. This member $\mathbf{u}$ is not assigned to any other individual constant $\mathbf{b}_i$ occurring on Γ_k but not in Γ (for, if it were, it would follow that $\mathbf{b}_i = f(\mathbf{a}_1, \ldots, \mathbf{a}_n)$ is true on $\mathbf{I}_{\Gamma_k}$, which contradicts our assumption here). Thus $\mathbf{I}'_{\Gamma_k}$ is a path-variant of $\mathbf{I}_{\Gamma_k}$ for the path extended to level $\mathbf{k} + 1$ by the addition of $\mathbf{b}_{m+1} = f(\mathbf{a}_1, \ldots, \mathbf{a}_n)$, and one on which every sentence in the new path is true.

Finally we must note that a branch of a tree for predicate logic with identity closes in one of *two* cases: Either the branch contains some literal and its negation or the branch contains a sentence of the form ~ **t** = **t**. In showing that Metatheorem 11.5.1 for predicate logic followed from the Consistent Branch Lemma 11.5.2, we made use of the fact that each closed branch contained a literal and its negation—arguing that the set of the sentences on that branch was therefore quantificationally inconsistent. In the present case we must also be sure that the set of sentences on a branch that closes because it contains a sentence ~ **t** = **t** is quantificationally inconsistent. This is not hard to show: **t** = **t** is quantificationally true, so ~ **t** = **t** is quantificationally false, and therefore any set that contains ~ **t** = **t** is quantificationally inconsistent. This and the addition of Cases 7 and 8 in the proof of result 11.5.3 suffice to show that the tree method is sound for predicate logic with identity and functions.

Result 11.5.3 also allows us to prove another claim made in Chapter 9:

Metatheorem 11.5.4: If a finite set Γ of sentences of *PL* has a finite model, that is, an interpretation with a finite UD on which every member of Γ is true, then every systematic tree for Γ will contain a *completed* open branch.[1]

In such a case, we shall be able to conclude in a *finite* number of steps that the set is quantificationally consistent.

Proof of Metatheorem 11.5.4: Let Γ be a finite set of sentences such that there is an interpretation **I** with a finite UD on which every member of Γ is true. By result 11.5.3, every level **i** of a systematic tree for Γ is such that either (a) there is at least one completed path to a level earlier than **i** that contains a set of sentences all of which are true on a path-variant of **I** for that path or (b) there is at least one path to level **i** that contains a set of sentences all of which are true on a path-variant of **I** for that path.

Consider, for any level **i**, a path that satisfies either (a) or (b). There is a limit to the number of distinct individual constants not already occurring in Γ that can occur on this path (constants that were introduced by an application of ∀D or ∃D), namely, the size **n** of the finite UD for **I**. For if a path contains more than **n** new individual constants, it cannot meet the condition in the definition of path-variants that each of these constants be assigned a member of the UD that is *different* from the members assigned to other new constants; there would not be enough members of the UD to go around. In addition, because Γ contains only a finite number of constants, a path that satisfies either (a) or (b) can contain only a finite number of constants.

[1]This metatheorem, along with result 11.5.3, is due to George Boolos, "Trees and Finite Satisfiability: Proof of a Conjecture of Burgess," *Notre Dame Journal of Formal Logic*, 25(3) (1984), 193–197.

We now show that a path of a systematic tree that contains only a finite number of individual constants must be finitely long. Each of the decomposition rules &D, ~ &D, ∨D, ~ ∨D, ~ ⊃D, ~ ≡D, ~ ~ D, ∀D, and ∃D2 produces sentences with fewer occurrences of logical operators than the sentence being decomposed. The rules ⊃D, ≡D, ~ ∃D, and ~ ∀D produce one or two sentences with the same number of occurrences of logical operators as the sentence being decomposed, but the sentences so produced have one of the forms ~ **P** (in the case of ⊃D and ≡D), (∃**x**) ~ **P** (in the case of ~ ∀D), or (∀**x**) ~ **P** (in the case of ~ ∃D). Each of the latter sentences, if not a literal, will be decomposed by a rule that produces only sentences with fewer occurrences of logical operators. Because subsequent applications of decomposition rules produce sentences with fewer and fewer occurrences of logical operators, literals are eventually reached. The only way in which a branch of a systematic tree can continue indefinitely is through repeated instantiation of one or more universally quantified sentences by ∀D, each instantiation containing a different instantiating constant. But this cannot be the case with a branch that contains a finite number of individual constants. Therefore the paths that we are guaranteed by result 11.5.3 can be only finitely long.

In addition, the System was designed to guarantee that if a path *can* be completed (or closed) after a finite number of applications of rules, it *will* be completed. Stages 1 and 2 (and stage 3, in the case of *PLE*) each require that we decompose *all* sentences on the tree of the specified sort before going to the next stage, and at each stage there are only finitely many sentences. The System does not allow one branch to be developed indefinitely while others are ignored, and so a branch that can be completed after a finite number of steps will be completed.

We conclude that at some finite level **i** of a systematic tree for Γ, there is a path that meets condition (a) of result 11.5.3. In addition, because this path meets (a), it is a completed *open* path. This establishes Metatheorem 11.5.4.

Metatheorem 11.5.4 is also true of *PLE*; this proof is left as an exercise.

11.5E EXERCISES

***1.** Show that Metatheorem 11.5.1 holds for nonsystematic trees as well as for systematic ones. (Result 11.5.3 is not generally true of nonsystematic trees, so you should prove Lemma 11.5.2 directly by mathematical induction.)

2. Using Metatheorem 11.5.1, prove the following:

a. If a sentence **P** of *SL* is such that {**P**} has a closed truth-tree, then **P** is quantificationally false.

b. If a sentence **P** of *SL* is such that {~ **P**} has a closed truth-tree, then **P** is quantificationally true.

*c. If a set {~ (**P** ≡ **Q**)} has a closed truth-tree, then **P** and **Q** are quantificationally equivalent.
d. If a set Γ ∪ {~ **P**} has a closed truth-tree, then Γ ⊨ **P**.
*e. If the set consisting of the premises and the negation of the conclusion of an argument has a closed truth-tree, then that argument is quantificationally valid.

3. Prove that, if a sentence **Q** is obtained from a sentence **P** by application of one of the following tree rules, then {**P**} ⊨ **Q**.

a. ~ ~ D
*b. &D
*c. ~ ∨D
d. ~ ⊃D
e. ∀D
*f. ~ ∀D
*g. ~ ∃D

4. Prove that, if sentences **Q** and **R** are obtained from a sentence **P** by application of one of the following tree rules, then on any interpretation on which **P** is true, either **Q** is true or **R** is true.

a. ~ &D
*b. ∨D
*c. ⊃D

5. Prove Case 4 in the inductive step of the proof of Lemma 11.5.2.

6. If we were to drop the rule ∀D from the tree method, would the method still be sound for predicate logic? Explain.

7. Explain how we can adapt the proof of Metatheorem 11.5.1 to establish that the tree method for *SL* is sound for sentential logic.

***8.** Prove that Metatheorem 11.5.4 is true of *PLE*.

11.6 THE COMPLETENESS OF THE TREE METHOD

In the last section we established that the tree method is sound for predicate logic—if a tree for a set of sentences of *PL* closes, then that set is quantificationally inconsistent. In this section we shall prove that the tree method is also *complete* for sentential logic. The *Completeness Metatheorem* for the tree method is as follows:

> **Metatheorem 11.6.1:** If a finite set of Γ of sentences of *PL* is quantificationally inconsistent, then every systematic tree for Γ closes.

Whereas soundness ensures that we are correct in pronouncing a set inconsistent if we can construct a closed tree for that set, completeness ensures that we are correct in pronouncing a set consistent if a systematic tree for that set does not close. The requirement that the tree be systematic is important, as we shall see; and the reader should remember that a tree that is constructed in accordance with The System but is abandoned before every branch closes and before at least one branch becomes a completed open branch does not count as a systematic tree.

We shall prove that the tree method is complete by establishing that the contrapositive of Metatheorem 11.6.1 is true—that if a systematic tree for a set of sentences of *PL* does not close, then the set is quantificationally consistent. There are three parts to the proof. First, we shall prove that, if a systematic tree fails to close and does not contain a completed open branch after a finite number of steps in its construction, then it has at least one branch with infinitely many sentences. Second, we shall prove that for any completed open branch or infinite branch of a systematic truth-tree, the set of sentences occurring on that branch is a special sort of set known as a *Hintikka set.*[2] Finally we shall present a method of constructing, for any Hintikka set, an interpretation on which every member of that set is true. This will establish that every Hintikka set is quantificationally consistent and consequently that the set of sentences occurring on either a completed open branch or an infinite branch of a systematic truth-tree is quantificationally consistent. Because each sentence in the set Γ for which a tree is constructed occurs on every branch of that tree, it follows that, if a systematic tree for Γ fails to close, Γ is a subset of a Hintikka set and is therefore also quantificationally consistent. Therefore, if a finite set Γ is quantificationally *in*consistent, then every systematic tree for Γ will close—and that is what Metatheorem 11.6.1 says.

Consider a systematic tree such that at no level **i** does the tree contain a completed open branch and at no level **i** is the tree closed. Our first task is to show that such a tree must contain an infinite branch. Because the tree fails to close or to contain a completed open branch at any level **i**, the tree must contain infinitely many sentences (strictly speaking, infinitely many *occurrences* of sentences—the sentences need not be distinct). The tree contains infinitely many sentences because it takes infinitely many steps to construct a systematic tree that neither is closed nor contains a completed open branch at any level, and each step in the construction involves adding at least one new sentence. It remains to be shown that a systematic truth-tree containing infinitely many sentences has at least one branch that is infinitely long—at least one branch that contains an infinite number of sentences. The reason that this needs to be *proved* is that a tree *could* contain infinitely many sentences and yet be such that each of its branches was only finitely long, *if* it contained infinitely many branches. So we need to establish the following lemma, the Infinite Branch Lemma:

> **11.6.2** (the *Infinite Branch Lemma*): Every systematic tree that contains an infinite number of occurrences of sentences has at least one branch that is infinitely long.[3]

---

[2]These sets were first studied by J. Hintikka, in "Form and Content in Quantification Theory," *Acta Philosophica Fennica,* 8 (1955), 7–55; and "Notes on Quantification Theory," *Societas Scientiarum Fennica, Commentationes Physico-Mathematicae,* 17(12) (1955).

[3]This follows as a special case of a famous lemma known as *König's Lemma* (D. König, *Theorie der endlichen und unendlichen Graphen,* Leipzig, 1936).

Proof of Lemma 11.6.2: Some definitions will be useful for the proof. We shall say that a sentence **P** (throughout, read *occurrence of a sentence* whenever we speak of a sentence) in a tree is *above* sentence **Q** when **P** and **Q** lie on the same branch of the tree and **P** is at an earlier level of the tree. **Q** is an *immediate successor* of **P** if **P** and **Q** lie on the same branch and **P** is one level earlier than **Q**. Every sentence in a tree, except those that occur at the ends of branches, has a finite number of immediate successors—one if a nonbranching rule is applied, two if a branching rule other than ∃D2 is applied, and **m** + 1, where **m** is the number of individual constants already occurring on the sentence's branch, if ∃D2 is applied.

We shall now show that if a systematic tree contains infinitely many sentences then there is at least one infinite branch in the tree, by starting at level 1 and working down through the levels of the tree. The sentence at level 1 of such a tree—call it $\mathbf{P}_1$—is above every other sentence in the tree. Therefore this sentence is above infinitely many sentences (subtracting 1 from an infinite number leaves an infinite number). $\mathbf{P}_1$ has a finite number of successors at level 2. At least one of these immediate successors is above infinitely many sentences. Consider the possibility that each of the immediate successors—call them $\mathbf{Q}_1$, . . . , $\mathbf{Q}_\mathbf{n}$—is above only a finite number of sentences. Then **P** itself would be above only finitely many sentences: $\mathbf{Q}_1$, . . . , $\mathbf{Q}_\mathbf{n}$, $\mathbf{Q}_1$'s successors, . . . , and $\mathbf{Q}_\mathbf{n}$'s successors together would constitute only a finite number of sentences. $\mathbf{P}_1$ must therefore have at least one immediate successor $\mathbf{P}_2$ that is above an infinite number of sentences. The reasoning that we have just used can be generalized: If a sentence at any level is above infinitely many sentences, then at least one immediate successor of that sentence is above infinitely many sentences. So $\mathbf{P}_2$, being above infinitely many sentences, has an immediate successor $\mathbf{P}_3$ that is above infinitely many sentences, and $\mathbf{P}_3$ has an immediate successor $\mathbf{P}_4$ that is above infinitely many sentences, and so on, for each positive integer. The sentences $\mathbf{P}_1$, $\mathbf{P}_2$, $\mathbf{P}_3$, $\mathbf{P}_4$, . . . constitute a branch with an infinite number of sentences. Therefore, if a systematic tree contains infinitely many sentences, then it has at least one branch that is infinitely long.

We may now conclude that a systematic tree that fails to close either has a completed open branch after a finite number of steps or has at least one infinite branch. This will be important in what follows.

Turning to the second step of the proof of Metatheorem 11.6.1, we define a *Hintikka set* to be a set Γ of sentences of *PL* that has the following properties:

a. There is no atomic sentence **P** such that both **P** and ~ **P** are members of Γ.

b. If ~ ~ **P** ∈ Γ, then **P** ∈ Γ.

c. If **P** & **Q** ∈ Γ, then **P** ∈ Γ and **Q** ∈ Γ.

d. If ~ (**P** & **Q**) ∈ Γ, then either ~ **P** ∈ Γ or ~ **Q** ∈ Γ.

e. If $\mathbf{P} \vee \mathbf{Q} \in \Gamma$, then either $\mathbf{P} \in \Gamma$ or $\mathbf{Q} \in \Gamma$.
f. If $\sim (\mathbf{P} \vee \mathbf{Q}) \in \Gamma$, then $\sim \mathbf{P} \in \Gamma$ and $\sim \mathbf{Q} \in \Gamma$.
g. If $\mathbf{P} \supset \mathbf{Q} \in \Gamma$, then either $\sim \mathbf{P} \in \Gamma$ or $\mathbf{Q} \in \Gamma$.
h. If $\sim (\mathbf{P} \supset \mathbf{Q}) \in \Gamma$, then $\mathbf{P} \in \Gamma$ and $\sim \mathbf{Q} \in \Gamma$.
i. If $\mathbf{P} \equiv \mathbf{Q} \in \Gamma$, then either $\mathbf{P} \in \Gamma$ and $\mathbf{Q} \in \Gamma$ or $\sim \mathbf{P} \in \Gamma$ and $\sim \mathbf{Q} \in \Gamma$.
j. If $\sim (\mathbf{P} \equiv \mathbf{Q}) \in \Gamma$, then either $\mathbf{P} \in \Gamma$ and $\sim \mathbf{Q} \in \Gamma$ or $\sim \mathbf{P} \in \Gamma$ and $\mathbf{Q} \in \Gamma$.
k. If $(\forall \mathbf{x})\mathbf{P} \in \Gamma$, then at least one substitution instance of $(\forall \mathbf{x})\mathbf{P}$ is a member of Γ, and for every constant **a** that occurs in some sentence of Γ, $\mathbf{P}(\mathbf{a}/\mathbf{x}) \in \Gamma$.
l. If $\sim (\forall \mathbf{x})\mathbf{P} \in \Gamma$, then $(\exists \mathbf{x}) \sim \mathbf{P} \in \Gamma$.
m. If $(\exists \mathbf{x})\mathbf{P} \in \Gamma$, then for at least one constant **a**, $\mathbf{P}(\mathbf{a}/\mathbf{x}) \in \Gamma$.
n. If $\sim (\exists \mathbf{x})\mathbf{P} \in \Gamma$, then $(\forall \mathbf{x}) \sim \mathbf{P} \in \Gamma$.

We call a branch of a tree a *Hintikka branch* if and only if the sentences on that branch constitute a Hintikka set. We now prove that every completed open branch and every infinite branch of a systematic tree is a Hintikka branch, which will establish the Hintikka Branch Lemma:

11.6.3 (the *Hintikka Branch Lemma*): Every systematic tree that is not closed has at least one Hintikka branch.

Afterward we shall show that every Hintikka set is quantificationally consistent.

Proof of Lemma 11.6.3: If a systematic tree fails to close, then either the tree has a completed open branch or, by Lemma 11.6.2, the tree has an infinite branch. We shall show that each of these two types of branches is a Hintikka branch—that is, that the set of sentences occurring on such a branch has properties (a)–(n).

First consider completed open branches. By definition a completed open branch is a finite branch that is open—there is no pair of literals **P** and ~ **P** such that both **P** and ~ **P** occur on the branch—and each sentence on that branch is one of the following:

1. A literal (an atomic sentence or the negation of an atomic sentence)
2. A sentence that is not universally quantified and that has been decomposed
3. A universally quantified sentence $(\forall \mathbf{x})\mathbf{P}$ such that at least one substitution instance of $(\forall \mathbf{x})\mathbf{P}$ occurs on the branch and, for each constant **a** occurring on the branch, $\mathbf{P}(\mathbf{a}/\mathbf{x})$ occurs on the branch

The set of sentences on a completed open branch has property (a) because there is no pair of literals **P** and ~ **P** occurring on the branch. Every sentence that has one of the forms described in properties (b)–(j) and (1)–(n) has been decomposed (part 2 of the definition of a completed open branch), and so it is easily verified that the set of sentences on a completed open branch has those properties. (For example, if a sentence ~ ~ **P** occurs on a completed open branch and has been decomposed by an application of ~ ~ D, then **P** also occurs on that branch—which establishes property (b).) Finally the set of sentences on a completed open branch also has property (k), for part 3 of the definition of completed open branches stipulates that property (k) is satisfied. We conclude that the set of sentences occurring on a completed open branch has properties (a)–(n) and that the branch is therefore a Hintikka branch.

Now we turn to infinite branches. The System for tree construction was designed to guarantee that every infinite (nonterminating) branch is a Hintikka branch; we shall explain how it does so. First, a nonterminating branch is not closed (a branch that closes contains only finitely many sentences); so the set of sentences on such a branch must have property (a) of Hintikka sets. Second, the alternation of stages 1 and 2 of The System ensures that each nonliteral sentence that does not have the form $(\forall \mathbf{x})\mathbf{P}$ is decomposed a finite number of levels after the level on which it occurs, that for each universally quantified sentence $(\forall \mathbf{x})\mathbf{P}$ and constant **a** on a branch of the tree $\mathbf{P}(\mathbf{a}/\mathbf{x})$ is entered within a finite number of levels, and that at least one substitution instance $\mathbf{P}(\mathbf{a}/\mathbf{x})$ is entered. Each such addition yields only a finite number of levels, so every sentence on a branch must be decomposed if the branch is infinite. Therefore the set of sentences on a nonterminating branch satisfies properties (b)–(n) of Hintikka sets, as well as property (a). Every infinite branch of a systematic tree is therefore a Hintikka branch.

Finally we shall prove the Hintikka Set Lemma:

11.6.4 (the *Hintikka Set Lemma*): Every Hintikka set is quantificationally consistent.

From this it follows that if a systematic tree for a set Γ of sentences does not close then Γ is quantificationally consistent—for one of the branches that contains the sentences in Γ is a Hintikka branch.

Proof of Lemma 11.6.4: Let Γ be a Hintikka set of sentences of *PL*. We first associate with each individual constant of *PL* a distinct positive integer—**i** is associated with the alphabetically **i**th constant. We shall prove that every sentence of Γ is true on the interpretation **I** defined as follows:

1. The UD is the set consisting of the positive integers that are associated with the individual constants occurring in members of Γ. If no member of Γ contains an individual constant, let the UD be the set {1}.
2. For each sentence letter **P**, **I**(**P**) = **T** if and only if **P** $\in \Gamma$.
3. For each individual constant **a** that occurs in some sentence in Γ, **I**(**a**) is the positive integer associated with **a**. For each constant **a** that does not occur in any sentence of Γ, **I**(**a**) is the smallest positive integer in the UD (which, by specification 1, is nonempty).
4. For each **n**-place predicate **A**, **I**(**A**) includes all and only those **n**-tuples $\langle \mathbf{u}_1, \ldots, \mathbf{u}_n \rangle$ such that for some constants $\mathbf{a}_1, \ldots, \mathbf{a}_n$, $\mathbf{Aa}_1 \ldots \mathbf{a}_n \in \Gamma$ and $\langle \mathbf{I}(\mathbf{a}_1), \ldots, \mathbf{I}(\mathbf{a}_n) \rangle = \langle \mathbf{u}_1, \ldots, \mathbf{u}_n \rangle$.

We shall use mathematical induction to prove that every member of Γ is true on **I**. Our induction will not be on the number of occurrences of logical operators in a sentence since some of the clauses of the proof would not work in that case (see Exercise 11.6.5). Instead, we shall appeal to the *length* of a sentence. Where **P** is a formula of *PL*, let the *length* of **P** be the number of occurrences of sentence letters, predicates, and logical operators in **P**. No sentence of *PL* has length 0 since every sentence contains at least one sentence letter or predicate. So the basis clause begins with length 1.

Basis clause: Every sentence **P** of length 1 is such that if **P** $\in \Gamma$ then **I**(**P**) = **T**.

Inductive step: If every sentence **P** of length less than or equal to **k** is such that if **P** $\in \Gamma$ then **I**(**P**) = **T**, then every sentence **P** of length **k** + 1 is such that if **P** $\in \Gamma$ then **I**(**P**) = **T**.

Conclusion: Every sentence **P** is such that if **P** $\in \Gamma$, then **I**(**P**) = **T**.

Proof of basis clause: A sentence of length 1 is an atomic sentence. (If a sentence contains any logical operators, then because it also must contain at least one sentence letter or predicate it has a length that is greater than 1.) If **P** is a sentence letter, then by part 2 of the definition of **I**, **I**(**P**) = **T** if **P** $\in \Gamma$. If **P** is an atomic sentence of the form $\mathbf{Aa}_1 \ldots \mathbf{a}_n$, then, by part 4 of the definition of **I**, if $\mathbf{Aa}_1 \ldots \mathbf{a}_n \in \Gamma$ then $\langle \mathbf{I}(\mathbf{a}_1), \ldots, \mathbf{I}(\mathbf{a}_n) \rangle \in \mathbf{I}(\mathbf{A})$, and so **I**(**P**) = **T**.

Proof of inductive step: We assume that the inductive hypothesis holds for some arbitrary positive integer **k**—that every sentence of length **k** or smaller that is a member of Γ is true on **I**. We must show that any sentence **P** of length **k** + 1 is also such that if it is a member of Γ then it is true on **I**. It is easy to verify that **P**, being nonatomic, must have one of the forms specified in properties (a)–(n) of Hintikka sets; and we shall consider each of these forms that **P** may have.

Case 1: **P** has the form ~ **Q**, where **Q** is an atomic sentence. If ~ **Q** ∉ Γ then, by property (a) of Hintikka sets, **Q** ∈ Γ. If **Q** is a sentence letter then, by part 2 of the definition of **I**, **I**(**Q**) = **F** and so **I**(~ **Q**) = **T**.[4] If **Q** has the form $\mathbf{Aa_1 \ldots a_n}$ then, by part 4 of the definition of **I**, $\langle \mathbf{I(a_1)}, \ldots, \mathbf{I(a_n)} \rangle \notin \mathbf{I(A)}$. This is because each constant that occurs in some member of Γ designates a positive integer different from that designated by any other constant occurring in Γ (by part 3), and so there is no other set of constants occurring in Γ that also designate the members of the **n**-tuple $\langle \mathbf{I(a_1)}, \ldots, \mathbf{I(a_n)} \rangle$, and consequently there can be no sentence $\mathbf{Aa'_1 \ldots a'_n}$ in Γ such that $\langle \mathbf{I(a_1)}, \ldots, \mathbf{I(a_n)} \rangle = \langle \mathbf{I(a'_1)} \ldots \mathbf{I(a'_n)} \rangle$. We may therefore conclude, from the fact that $\mathbf{Aa_1 \ldots a_n} \notin \Gamma$, that the **n**-tuple $\langle \mathbf{I(a_1)}, \ldots, \mathbf{I(a_n)} \rangle$ is not in the extension of **A**. So $\mathbf{I(Aa_1 \ldots a_n)} = \mathbf{F}$ and $\mathbf{I(\sim Aa_1 \ldots a_n)} = \mathbf{T}$.

Case 2: **P** has the form ~ ~ **Q**. If ~ ~ **Q** ∈ Γ then, by property (b) of Hintikka sets, **Q** ∈ Γ. The length of **Q** is less than **k** + 1, so, by the inductive hypothesis, **I**(**Q**) = **T**. Therefore **I**(~ ~ **Q**) = **T** as well.

Case 3: **P** has the form **Q** & **R**. If **Q** & **R** ∈ Γ then, by property (c) of Hintikka sets, **Q** ∈ Γ and **R** ∈ Γ. By the inductive hypothesis (**Q** and **R** both having lengths less than **k** + 1), **I**(**Q**) = **T** and **I**(**R**) = **T**. So **I**(**Q** & **R**) = **T**.

Case 4: **P** has the form ~ (**Q** & **R**). If ~ (**Q** & **R**) ∈ Γ then, by property (d) of Hintikka sets, either ~ **Q** ∈ Γ or ~ **R** ∈ Γ. The lengths of ~ **Q** and of ~ **R** are less than the length of ~ (**Q** & **R**), so, by the inductive hypothesis, either **I**(~ **Q**) = **T** or **I**(~ **R**) = **T**. If **I**(~ **Q**) = **T**, then **I**(**Q**) = **F**, **I**(**Q** & **R**) = **F**, and **I**(~ (**Q** & **R**)) = **T**. If **I**(~ **R**) = **T**, then **I**(~ (**Q** & **R**)) = **T** as well. Either way, then, **I**(~ (**Q** & **R**)) = **T**.

Cases 5–10: **P** has one of the forms **Q** ∨ **R**, ~ (**Q** ∨ **R**), **Q** ⊃ **R**, ~ (**Q** ⊃ **R**), **Q** ≡ **R**, or ~ (**Q** ≡ **R**) (see Exercise 3).

Case 11: **P** has the form (∀**x**)**Q**. If **P** ∈ Γ then, by property (k) of Hintikka sets, for every constant **a** that occurs in Γ, **Q**(**a**/**x**) ∈ Γ (and there is at least one such constant). Each substitution instance has a length smaller than **k** + 1, so it follows from the inductive hypothesis that, for each of these sentences, **I**(**Q**(**a**/**x**)) = **T**. Moreover each member of the UD is designated by some constant occurring in Γ (by part 1 of the definition of the interpretation **I**—because at least one constant

[4]Note that we have here bypassed the intermediate step of observing that a sentence is true on an interpretation if and only if it is satisfied by every variable assignment for that interpretation. We shall continue this practice until we reach Cases 11–14; the reader who so desires may fill in the intermediate steps for Cases 1–10 without much trouble.

occurs in Γ), so for each member of the UD there is a constant **a** such that **Q**(**a**/**x**) ∈ Γ and hence is true on **I**. It therefore follows from 11.6.5 that **I**((∀**x**)**Q**) = **T**.

11.6.5: Let **I** be an interpretation on which for each member **u** of the UD there is at least one constant **a** such that **I**(**a**) = **u** and **I**(**P**(**a**/**x**)) = **T**. Then **I**((∀**x**)**P**) = **T**.

Proof: See Exercise 4.

Case 12: **P** has the form ~ (∀**x**)**Q**. If ~ (∀**x**)**Q** ∈ Γ, then, by property (l) of Hintikka sets, (∃**x**) ~ **Q** ∈ Γ, and by property (m) ~ **Q**(**a**/**x**) ∈ Γ for some constant **a**. ~ **Q**(**a**/**x**) has a length less than **k** + 1, so, by the inductive hypothesis, **I**(~ **Q**(**a**/**x**)) = **T** and therefore **I**(**Q**(**a**/**x**)) = **F**. Because {(∀**x**)**Q**} ⊨ **Q**(**a**/**x**) (result 11.1.4), it follows that **I**((∀**x**)**Q**) = **F** and so **I**(~ (∀**x**)**Q**) = **T**.

Cases 13 and 14: **P** has one of the forms (∃**x**)**Q** or ~ (∃**x**)**Q** (see Exercise 3).

That completes the proof of the inductive step. Therefore every sentence that is a member of the Hintikka set Γ is true on **I**, and this shows that Γ is quantificationally consistent.

The Hintikka Branch Lemma 11.6.3 and the Hintikka Set Lemma 11.6.4 can now be used to establish Metatheorem 11.6.1. If a systematic tree for a set Γ of sentences does not close, then the tree has at least one Hintikka branch (Lemma 11.6.3). The set of sentences on that Hintikka branch is quantificationally consistent (Lemma 11.6.4). Therefore, because every member of Γ lies on that branch (as well as on every other branch), Γ is quantificationally consistent. So if Γ is quantificationally *inconsistent,* then every systematic tree for Γ closes.

We note that the proof that we have just given is a *constructive* completeness proof. We have shown how, given a Hintikka branch of a systematic tree for a set of sentences Γ, to construct an interpretation on which every member of Γ is true. This establishes a claim made in Chapter 9: An interpretation showing the quantificational consistency of Γ can always be constructed from a completed open branch of a tree for Γ.

Finally the tree method for predicate logic with identity and functions is also complete, and this can be shown by making appropriate changes in the proofs of Lemmas 11.6.3 and 11.6.4. We define a Hintikka set for *PLE* to be a set Γ that has the properties (a)–(n) of our earlier definition and that also has these properties:

o. No sentence of the form ~ **t** = **t** is a member of Γ.

p. If **a** = **t**, where **a** is a constant, is a member of Γ, and a literal sentence **P** ∈ Γ contains **t**, then every sentence **P**(**a**//**t**) is also a member of Γ.

q. If a complex term $f(\mathbf{a}_1, \ldots, \mathbf{a}_n)$ in which $\mathbf{a}_1, \ldots, \mathbf{a}_n$ are individual constants occurs in any literal sentence in Γ, then, for at least one constant **b**, $\mathbf{b} = f(\mathbf{a}_1, \ldots, \mathbf{a}_n) \in \Gamma$.

The proof of Lemma 11.6.3—that every systematic tree that does not close *has* a Hintikka branch—runs as before, except that we replace talk of the constant **a** occurring on a branch with talk of the closed term **t** occurring on a branch. We must also add the following:

> The set of sentences on a completed open branch of a systematic tree must have property (o), because by definition a branch that does not close does not contain a sentence of the form ~ **t** = **t**. Property (p) must hold by virtue of the requirement in clause 4 of the definition of a completed open branch. Property (q) must hold by virtue of the final component of the definition of a completed open branch.
>
> Similar remarks establish that infinite branches are also Hintikka branches: The cycle of stages 1–4 in The System, and the fact that each stage adds only a finite number of sentences, guarantees that every sentence on a branch will be decomposed if the branch is infinite. Note that the requirement in stage 2 of The System, that **P(t/x)** be entered for a *complex* term **t** only if doing so will close the branch on which it is entered, plays a crucial role here. If The System allowed such substitutions for complex terms that did not close the branch, we could have a branch containing a sequence such as '(∀x)G*f*(x)', 'G*f*(a)', 'a = *f*(a)', 'G*f*(*f*(a))', 'G*f*(*f*(*f*(a)))', 'G*f*(*f*(*f*(*f*(a))))', . . . in which '*f*(a)' has been continuously substituted for 'a' at the expense of decomposing other sentences on the branch. Similarly the restriction (ii) in stage 4 guarantees that we will not have an branch containing a sequence such as 'a = *f*(a)', 'a = *f*(*f*(a))', 'a = *f*(*f*(*f*(a)))', . . . or 'a = *f*(a)', 'Ga', 'G*f*(a)', 'G*f*(*f*(a))', G*f*(*f*(*f*(a))), . . . in which '*f*(a)' has been continuously substituted for 'a' at the expense of decomposing other sentences on the branch.

To show that Lemma 11.6.4 holds for predicate logic with identity and functions, we must define the UD for the interpretation for a *PLE* Hintikka set Γ differently than it was defined for *PL*, as follows:

> Associate the positive integer **i** with the alphabetically **i**th individual constant of *PLE*. Let **p** designate this association and let **p(a)** stand for the integer that has been associated with the constant **a**. Next we define a second association, which we shall designate with **q**, as follows: $\mathbf{q}(\mathbf{a}) = \mathbf{p}(\mathbf{a}')$ if $\mathbf{a}'$ is the alphabetically earliest constant such that $\mathbf{a}' = \mathbf{a}$ is a member of Γ, and $\mathbf{q}(\mathbf{a}) = \mathbf{p}(\mathbf{a})$ otherwise.
>
> 1. The UD is the set consisting of the positive integers that **q** assigns to the individual constants occurring in members of Γ. If no

member of Γ contains an individual constant, let the UD be the set {1}.

We change clause 3 in the interpretation constructed in Lemma 11.6.4 to this:

3. For each individual constant **a** that occurs in some sentence in Γ, $\mathbf{I(a)} = \mathbf{q(a)}$. For each constant **a** that does not occur in any sentence of Γ, $\mathbf{I(a)}$ is the smallest positive integer in the UD.

We must also add a fifth clause to complete the definition of the interpretation:

5. For each **n**-place functor *f*, $\mathbf{I}(f)$ consists of all $\mathbf{n} + 1$-tuples $<\mathbf{d_1}, \ldots, \mathbf{d_n}, \mathbf{d_{n+1}}>$ of members of the UD such that either (i) there exist constants $\mathbf{a_1}, \ldots, \mathbf{a_n}, \mathbf{a_{n+1}}$ such that $\mathbf{a_{n+1}} = f(\mathbf{a_1}, \ldots, \mathbf{a_n})$ is a member of Γ and $\mathbf{d_i} = \mathbf{I(a_i)}$, $1 \leq \mathbf{i} \leq \mathbf{n} + 1$, or (ii) there are no such constants, and $\mathbf{d_{n+1}}$ is the smallest member of the UD.

We must ensure that clause 5 correctly defines the interpretation of an **n**-place functor as a function that assigns exactly one member of the UD to each **n**-tuple of members of the UD. It is clear that it assigns at least one member of the UD to each **n**-tuple, because if case (i) doesn't apply then case (ii) will. Moreover, if case (i) doesn't apply then case (ii) will assign at most one member. It remains to show that if case (i) applies it will also assign at most one member.

Now, if (i) assigned more than one member of the UD to some **n**-tuple of members of the UD, that would be because there existed constants $\mathbf{a_1}, \ldots, \mathbf{a_n}, \mathbf{a_{n+1}}$ such that $\mathbf{a_{n+1}} = f(\mathbf{a_1}, \ldots, \mathbf{a_n})$ is a member of Γ and constants $\mathbf{b_1}, \ldots, \mathbf{b_n}, \mathbf{b_{n+1}}$ such that $\mathbf{b_{n+1}} = f(\mathbf{b_1}, \ldots, \mathbf{b_n})$ is a member of Γ, where $\mathbf{I(a_i)} = \mathbf{I(b_i)}$ for $1 \leq \mathbf{i} \leq \mathbf{n}$ and $\mathbf{I(a_{n+1})} \neq \mathbf{I(b_{n+1})}$. But note that if $\mathbf{I(a_i)} = \mathbf{I(b_i)}$ then, by the way we defined **I** via the association **q**, either (a) $\mathbf{a_i} = \mathbf{b_i}$ is a member of Γ, or (b) $\mathbf{b_i} = \mathbf{a_i}$ is a member of Γ, or (c) there is a constant $\mathbf{c_i}$ such that both $\mathbf{c_i} = \mathbf{a_i}$ and $\mathbf{c_i} = \mathbf{b_i}$ are members of Γ. We now perform the following substitutions in the sentences $\mathbf{a_{n+1}} = f(\mathbf{a_1}, \ldots, \mathbf{a_n})$ and $\mathbf{b_{n+1}} = f(\mathbf{b_1}, \ldots, \mathbf{b_n})$. For each $\mathbf{a_i}$ and $\mathbf{b_i}$ occurring on the right-hand side of these identities:

If (a) holds then replace $\mathbf{b_i}$ with $\mathbf{a_i}$ in $\mathbf{b_{n+1}} = f(\mathbf{b_1}, \ldots, \mathbf{b_n})$.
Otherwise, if (b) holds then replace $\mathbf{a_i}$ with $\mathbf{b_i}$ in $\mathbf{a_{n+1}} = f(\mathbf{a_1}, \ldots, \mathbf{a_n})$.
Otherwise, if (c) holds then replace $\mathbf{a_i}$ with $\mathbf{c_i}$ in $\mathbf{a_{n+1}} = f(\mathbf{a_1}, \ldots, \mathbf{a_n})$ and replace $\mathbf{b_i}$ with $\mathbf{c_i}$ in $\mathbf{b_{n+1}} = f(\mathbf{b_1}, \ldots, \mathbf{b_n})$.

Note that each replacement generates a sentence that is also a member of Γ by property (p) of Hintikka sets, and at the end of the replacements, the right-hand sides of the final identity statements will be identical. That is, we have shown that there are constants $\mathbf{d_1}, \ldots, \mathbf{d_n}$ such that both $\mathbf{a_{n+1}} = f(\mathbf{d_1}, \ldots, \mathbf{d_n})$ and $\mathbf{b_{n+1}} = f(\mathbf{d_1}, \ldots, \mathbf{d_n})$ are also members of the Hintikka set. By virtue of property (o), it follows that $\mathbf{a_{n+1}} = \mathbf{b_{n+1}}$, which is $\mathbf{a_{n+1}} = f(\mathbf{d_1}, \ldots, \mathbf{d_n})$

$(\mathbf{b_{n+1}}//f(\mathbf{d_1}, \ldots, \mathbf{d_n}))$, is also in the Hintikka set, and so are $\mathbf{b_{n+1}} = \mathbf{a_{n+1}}$, $\mathbf{b_{n+1}} = \mathbf{b_{n+1}}$, and $\mathbf{a_{n+1}} = \mathbf{a_{n+1}}$, all by property (p). But then $\mathbf{I}(\mathbf{a_{n+1}}) = \mathbf{I}(\mathbf{b_{n+1}})$, contrary to our previous assumption. For it follows from the construction of **I** that, if no identity sentence with a constant that is alphabetically earlier than $\mathbf{a_{n+1}}$ or $\mathbf{b_{n+1}}$ occurring on the left-hand side is a member of Γ, then both constants will denote either $\mathbf{p}(\mathbf{a_{n+1}})$ or $\mathbf{p}(\mathbf{b_{n+1}})$, depending on which is alphabetically earlier. Or, if there is a constant **c** that is alphabetically earlier than both $\mathbf{a_{n+1}}$ and $\mathbf{b_{n+1}}$ such that either $\mathbf{c} = \mathbf{a_{n+1}}$ or $\mathbf{c} = \mathbf{b_{n+1}}$ is a member of Γ, then, because the identity sentences $\mathbf{a_{n+1}} = \mathbf{b_{n+1}}$ and $\mathbf{b_{n+1}} = \mathbf{a_{n+1}}$ are both members of Γ, it follows that both $\mathbf{c} = \mathbf{a_{n+1}}$ and $\mathbf{c} = \mathbf{b_{n+1}}$ must be members of Γ as well, and hence both $\mathbf{I}(\mathbf{a_{n+1}})$ and $\mathbf{I}(\mathbf{b_{n+1}})$ are defined to be $\mathbf{p}(\mathbf{c})$ for the alphabetically earliest such constant **c**. We conclude that case (i) will not assign more than one member of the UD to any given **n**-tuple of members of the UD.

We shall use the following result in the proof that every member of a Hintikka set is true on the interpretation **I** we have just defined:

> **11.6.6:** If a Hintikka set Γ contains a literal sentence **P** with a closed complex term **t**, it also contains each sentence $\mathbf{P}(\mathbf{a}//\mathbf{t})$ for some constant **a** such that $\text{den}_\mathbf{I}(\mathbf{a}) = \text{den}_\mathbf{I}(\mathbf{t})$[5], where **I** is the interpretation that has just been defined for the Hintikka set.

Proof: We shall prove this using mathematical induction on the *complexity* of **t**, which is defined recursively as follows:

> If **t** is $f(\mathbf{a_1}, \ldots, \mathbf{a_n})$, where each $\mathbf{a_i}$ is a constant, the complexity of **t** is 1.
>
> If **t** is $f(\mathbf{t_1}, \ldots, \mathbf{t_n})$, where some $\mathbf{t_i}$ is not a constant, the complexity of **t** is 1 greater than the maximum complexity of the terms $\mathbf{t_1}, \ldots, \mathbf{t_n}$.

So 'f(a, b)' has complexity 1, '$f(g(\text{a}), g(\text{b}))$' has complexity 2, and '$f(g(h(\text{a})), g(\text{b}))$' has complexity 3.

Basis clause: 11.6.6 holds for every closed complex term **t** of complexity 1.

Proof of basis clause: In this case the Hintikka set contains an identity sentence $\mathbf{a} = \mathbf{t}$, where **a** is a constant, by property (q) of Hintikka sets, and so, by property (p), it follows that each sentence $\mathbf{P}(\mathbf{a}//\mathbf{t})$ is also a member of Γ. In addition, $\text{den}_\mathbf{I}(\mathbf{t}) = \text{den}_\mathbf{I}(\mathbf{a})$ by the way that $\mathbf{I}(f)$ is defined in clause 5, since the Hintikka set contains the identity sentence $\mathbf{a} = \mathbf{t}$.

Inductive step: If 11.6.6 holds for every closed complex term **t** of complexity **k** or less, then 11.6.6 holds for every closed complex term **t** of complexity $\mathbf{k} + 1$.

[5]Because all of the terms mentioned in this proof are closed terms, we omit reference to a variable assignment **d** when referring to the denotation of a term. We do so because the denotation is independent of any particular variable assignment.

Proof of inductive step: We assume that the inductive hypothesis holds—that is, that 11.6.6 is true of every closed complex term of complexity **k** or less. We must show that it follows that 11.6.6 also holds of every closed complex term of complexity **k** + 1. Let **t** be a closed complex term of complexity **k** + 1. Then **t** is $f(\mathbf{t}_1, \ldots, \mathbf{t}_n)$, where each $\mathbf{t}_i$ is of complexity **k** or less. It follows, by the inductive hypothesis, that for some constants $\mathbf{a}_1, \ldots, \mathbf{a}_n$ such that $den_{\mathbf{I}}(\mathbf{a}_i) = den_{\mathbf{I}}(\mathbf{t}_i)$, each formula that results from replacing one or more occurrences of $f(\mathbf{t}_1, \ldots, \mathbf{t}_n)$ in **P** with $f(\mathbf{a}_1, \ldots, \mathbf{a}_n)$ is a member of Γ. By property (q) of Hintikka sets, there is some constant **a** such that $\mathbf{a} = f(\mathbf{a}_1, \ldots, \mathbf{a}_n)$ is a member of Γ, and so, by property (p), each sentence $\mathbf{P}(\mathbf{a}//\mathbf{t})$ is also a member of Γ. Moreover, because the identity sentence $\mathbf{a} = f(\mathbf{a}_1, \ldots, \mathbf{a}_n)$ is a member of Γ, it follows from the definition of $\mathbf{I}(f)$ in clause 5 that $den_{\mathbf{I}}(\mathbf{a}) = den_{\mathbf{I}}(f(\mathbf{a}_1, \ldots, \mathbf{a}_n))$, and because $den_{\mathbf{I}}(\mathbf{a}_i) = den_{\mathbf{I}}(\mathbf{t}_i)$ for each $\mathbf{a}_i$ and $\mathbf{t}_i$, it follows that $den_{\mathbf{I}}(f(\mathbf{a}_1, \ldots, \mathbf{a}_n)) = den_{\mathbf{I}}(f(\mathbf{t}_1, \ldots, \mathbf{t}_n))$; so $den_{\mathbf{I}}(\mathbf{a}) = den_{\mathbf{I}}(f(\mathbf{t}_1, \ldots, \mathbf{t}_n))$.

The proof of the basis clause of the inductive proof in 11.6.4 that every member of a Hintikka set Γ is true on the interpretation **I** that we have just defined is changed as follows:

Proof of basis clause: A sentence of length 1 is an atomic sentence. If **P** is a sentence letter, then by part 2 of the definition of **I**, $\mathbf{I}(\mathbf{P}) = \mathbf{T}$ if $\mathbf{P} \in \Gamma$.

If **P** is an atomic sentence of the form $\mathbf{At}_1 \ldots \mathbf{t}_n$, where **A** is not the identity predicate, then it follows from 11.6.6 that Γ also contains a sentence $\mathbf{Aa}_1 \ldots \mathbf{a}_n$ such that each $\mathbf{a}_i$ is a constant and $den_{\mathbf{I}}(\mathbf{t}_i) = den_{\mathbf{I}}(\mathbf{a}_i)$. By part 4 of the definition of **I**, if $\mathbf{Aa}_1 \ldots \mathbf{a}_n \in \Gamma$, then $\langle \mathbf{I}(\mathbf{a}_1), \ldots, \mathbf{I}(\mathbf{a}_n)\rangle \in \mathbf{I}(\mathbf{A})$, and so $\mathbf{I}(\mathbf{Aa}_1 \ldots \mathbf{a}_n) = \mathbf{I}(\mathbf{At}_1 \ldots \mathbf{t}_n) = \mathbf{T}$.

If **P** is a sentence of the form $\mathbf{t}_1 = \mathbf{t}_2$, then it follows from 11.6.6 that Γ also contains a sentence $\mathbf{a}_1 = \mathbf{a}_2$ such that $\mathbf{a}_1$ and $\mathbf{a}_2$ are constants and $den_{\mathbf{I}}(\mathbf{a}_1) = \mathbf{q}(\mathbf{a}_1) = den_{\mathbf{I}}(\mathbf{t}_1)$ and $den_{\mathbf{I}}(\mathbf{a}_2) = \mathbf{q}(\mathbf{a}_1) = den_{\mathbf{I}}(\mathbf{t}_2)$. Since $\mathbf{a}_1 = \mathbf{a}_2$ is a member of Γ, it follows, by property (p) of *PLE*'s Hintikka sets, that $\mathbf{a}_1 = \mathbf{a}_1$ is also a member of Γ. Now, let $\mathbf{q}(\mathbf{a}_1)$ be $\mathbf{p}(\mathbf{b})$. Because $\mathbf{a}_1 = \mathbf{a}_1$ is a member of Γ, it follows by the way that **q** was defined that $\mathbf{b} = \mathbf{a}_1$ is a member of Γ and that **b** must be alphabetically earlier than or identical to $\mathbf{a}_1$. It also follows by property (p) that $\mathbf{b} = \mathbf{a}_2$ is a member of Γ. Let $\mathbf{q}(\mathbf{a}_2)$ be $\mathbf{p}(\mathbf{c})$. Since $\mathbf{a}_1 = \mathbf{a}_2$ is a member of Γ, it follows that **c** is the alphabetically earliest constant such that $\mathbf{c} = \mathbf{a}_2$ is a member of Γ. Now, **b** cannot be alphabetically earlier than **c**, since $\mathbf{b} = \mathbf{a}_2$ is a member of Γ. Further, by property (p), $\mathbf{c} = \mathbf{b}$ is also a member of Γ. Therefore $\mathbf{c} = \mathbf{a}_1$ is also a member of Γ, and so **c** cannot be alphabetically earlier than **b** since $\mathbf{q}(\mathbf{a}_1)$ is $\mathbf{p}(\mathbf{b})$. We conclude that **b** and **c** are the same constant, so $\mathbf{q}(\mathbf{a}_1) = \mathbf{q}(\mathbf{a}_2)$. Consequently $den_{\mathbf{I}}(\mathbf{t}_1) = den_{\mathbf{I}}(\mathbf{a}_1) = \mathbf{q}(\mathbf{a}_1) = \mathbf{q}(\mathbf{a}_2) = den_{\mathbf{I}}(\mathbf{a}_2) = den_{\mathbf{I}}(\mathbf{t}_2)$, so $\mathbf{I}(\mathbf{t}_1 = \mathbf{t}_2) = \mathbf{T}$.

We must also change the proof of Case 1 in the inductive step:

Case 1: $\mathbf{P}$ has the form $\sim \mathbf{Q}$, where $\mathbf{Q}$ is an atomic sentence.

If $\mathbf{Q}$ is a sentence letter, then if $\sim \mathbf{Q} \in \Gamma$ it follows from part 2 of the definition of $\mathbf{I}$ that $\mathbf{I}(\mathbf{Q}) = \mathbf{F}$ since by property (a) of Hintikka sets $\mathbf{Q} \notin \Gamma$. Therefore $\mathbf{I}(\sim \mathbf{Q}) = \mathbf{T}$.

If $\mathbf{Q}$ has the form $\mathbf{At}_1 \ldots \mathbf{t_n}$, where $\mathbf{A}$ is not the identity predicate and $\sim \mathbf{Q} \in \Gamma$, then, by 11.6.6, there is a formula $\sim \mathbf{Aa}_1 \ldots \mathbf{a_n}$ in Γ in which every complex term $\mathbf{t_i}$ occurring in $\sim \mathbf{Q}$ has been replaced by a constant $\mathbf{a_i}$ such that $\text{den}_\mathbf{I}(\mathbf{t_i}) = \text{den}_\mathbf{I}(\mathbf{a_i})$. By property (a) of Hintikka sets, $\mathbf{Aa}_1 \ldots \mathbf{a_n} \notin \Gamma$. It follows from part 4 of the definition of $\mathbf{I}$ that $<\mathbf{I}(\mathbf{a}_1), \ldots, \mathbf{I}(\mathbf{a_n})> \notin \mathbf{I}(\mathbf{A})$. For if it were, this would be because, for some $\mathbf{a}'_1, \ldots, \mathbf{a}'_\mathbf{n}$, $\mathbf{Aa}'_1 \ldots \mathbf{a}'_\mathbf{n} \in \Gamma$ and $\mathbf{I}(\mathbf{a_i}) = \mathbf{I}(\mathbf{a}'_\mathbf{i})$ for each $\mathbf{a_i}$. Because each of these constants occurs in a member of Γ, we would have $\mathbf{I}(\mathbf{a_i}) = \mathbf{q}(\mathbf{a_i})$ and $\mathbf{I}(\mathbf{a}'_\mathbf{i}) = \mathbf{q}(\mathbf{a}'_\mathbf{i})$ and so $\mathbf{q}(\mathbf{a_i}) = \mathbf{q}(\mathbf{a}'_\mathbf{i})$. From the last equation and the way that $\mathbf{q}$ was defined, it would follow for each $\mathbf{i}$ that either (a) $\mathbf{a_i} = \mathbf{a}'_\mathbf{i}$ is a member of Γ, or (b) $\mathbf{a}'_\mathbf{i} = \mathbf{a_i}$ is a member of Γ, or (c) there is a constant $\mathbf{c_i}$ such that both $\mathbf{c_i} = \mathbf{a_i}$ and $\mathbf{c_i} = \mathbf{a}'_\mathbf{i}$ are members of Γ. We now perform the following substitutions in the sentences $\sim \mathbf{Aa}_1 \ldots \mathbf{a_n}$ and $\mathbf{Aa}'_1 \ldots \mathbf{a}'_\mathbf{n}$. For each $\mathbf{a_i}$ and $\mathbf{a}'_\mathbf{i}$:

If (a) holds then replace $\mathbf{a}'_\mathbf{i}$ with $\mathbf{a_i}$ in $\mathbf{Aa}'_1 \ldots \mathbf{a}'_\mathbf{n}$.
Otherwise, if (b) holds then replace $\mathbf{a_i}$ with $\mathbf{a}'_\mathbf{i}$ in $\sim \mathbf{Aa}_1 \ldots \mathbf{a_n}$.
Otherwise, if (c) holds then replace $\mathbf{a_i}$ with $\mathbf{c_i}$ in $\sim \mathbf{Aa}_1 \ldots \mathbf{a_n}$ and replace $\mathbf{a}'_\mathbf{i}$ with $\mathbf{c_i}$ in $\mathbf{Aa}'_1 \ldots \mathbf{a}'_\mathbf{n}$.

Note that each replacement generates a sentence that is also a member of Γ by property (p) of Hintikka sets, and at the end of the replacements, we shall have two literal sentences, one of which is the negation of the other and both of which are members of Γ. But this is impossible because of property (a) of Hintikka sets. So, since we have now established that $<\mathbf{I}(\mathbf{a}_1), \ldots, \mathbf{I}(\mathbf{a_n})> \notin \mathbf{I}(\mathbf{A})$, it follows that $\mathbf{I}(\sim \mathbf{Aa}_1 \ldots \mathbf{a_n}) = \mathbf{T}$. Consequently, because $\text{den}_\mathbf{I}(\mathbf{t_i}) = \text{den}_\mathbf{I}(\mathbf{a_i})$ for each $\mathbf{I}$, it also follows that $\mathbf{I}(\sim \mathbf{At}_1 \ldots \mathbf{t_n})$ (that is, $\mathbf{I}(\sim \mathbf{Q})$) $= \mathbf{T}$.

If $\mathbf{Q}$ has the form $\mathbf{t}_1 = \mathbf{t}_2$ and $\sim \mathbf{Q} \in \Gamma$ then, by 11.6.6, there is a formula $\sim \mathbf{a}_1 = \mathbf{a}_2$ in Γ such that $\text{den}_\mathbf{I}(\mathbf{t_i}) = \text{den}_\mathbf{I}(\mathbf{a_i})$. By property (a) of Hintikka sets, $\mathbf{a}_1 = \mathbf{a}_2 \notin \Gamma$. It follows from the definition of $\mathbf{I}$ that $\mathbf{q}(\mathbf{a}_1) \neq \mathbf{q}(\mathbf{a}_2)$. For if $\mathbf{q}(\mathbf{a}_1) = \mathbf{q}(\mathbf{a}_2)$, then either (a) $\mathbf{a}_1 = \mathbf{a}_2$ is a member of Γ, or (b) $\mathbf{a}_2 = \mathbf{a}_1$ is a member of Γ, or (c) there is a constant $\mathbf{b}$ such that $\mathbf{b} = \mathbf{a}_1$ and $\mathbf{b} = \mathbf{a}_2$ are both members of Γ. We have already shown that (a) does not hold. Case (b) does not hold, because if it did then, by property (p) of Hintikka sets, $\sim \mathbf{a}_2 = \mathbf{a}_2$ would be a member of Γ since $\sim \mathbf{a}_1 = \mathbf{a}_2$ is, but that is impossible by property (o) of Hintikka sets. Case (c) does not hold, because if did then, by property (p) of Hintikka sets, $\sim \mathbf{b} = \mathbf{b}$ would be a member of Γ since $\sim \mathbf{a_1} = \mathbf{a_2}$ is, but that is impossible by property (o) of Hintikka sets. Since $\mathbf{q}(\mathbf{a_1}) \neq \mathbf{q}(\mathbf{a_2})$, $\mathbf{I}(\mathbf{a_1} = \mathbf{a_2}) = \mathbf{F}$ and $\mathbf{I}(\sim \mathbf{a_1} = \mathbf{a_2}) = \mathbf{T}$, so, since $den_{\mathbf{I}}(\mathbf{t_i}) = den_{\mathbf{I}}(\mathbf{a_i})$ it follows that $\mathbf{I}(\sim \mathbf{t_1} = \mathbf{t_2}) = \mathbf{T}$.

11.6E EXERCISES

1. Using Metatheorem 11.6.1, prove the following:
a. If **P** is quantificationally false, then every systematic tree for {**P**} closes.
b. If **P** is quantificationally true, then every systematic tree for {~ **P**} closes.
*c. If **P** and **Q** are quantificationally equivalent, then every systematic tree for {~ (**P** ≡ **Q**)} closes.
d. If Γ ⊨ **P**, where Γ is finite, then every systematic tree for Γ ∪ {~ **P**} closes.
*e. If an argument of *PL* is quantificationally valid, then every systematic tree for the set consisting of the premises and the negation of the conclusion of that argument closes.

2.a. What is the length of each of the following sentences?

(∀y)Wy ⊃ ~ (∀y)Bya
(∃x)Sxbc
(∀x)(Mx ≡ ~ (∃y)My)

b. Show that the length of a sentence ~ (**Q** & **R**) is greater than the length of ~ **Q** and greater than the length of ~ **R**.
*c. Show that the length of a sentence **Q** ≡ **R** is greater than the length of ~ **Q** and greater than the length of ~ **R**.
d. Show that the length of a sentence ~ (∀**x**)**Q** is greater than the length of ~ **Q**(**a**/**x**).

3. Complete the following clauses in the inductive proof of the completeness of the tree method.

a. 5
*b. 6
c. 7
*d. 8
*e. 9
f. 10
g. 13
*h. 14

***4.** Prove result 11.6.5.

5. Which clauses in the inductive proof of the completeness of the tree method would have broken down if our induction had been on the number of occurrences of logical operators in the sentences of *PL*?

6. If the rule ∃D were not included in our tree rules, where would the proof of Metatheorem 11.6.1 break down?

7. Suppose that our rule ~ ∀D were replaced by the following rule:

<u>*Negated Universal Decomposition* (~ ∀D*)</u>

~ (∀**x**)**P**

~ **P**(**a**/**x**)

where **a** is a constant foreign to all preceding lines of the tree.

Would the resulting system be complete for predicate logic? Explain.

8. Explain how we can adapt the proof of Metatheorem 11.6.1 to establish that the tree method for *SL* is complete for sentential logic.

9. Prove that every set of *PL* that is both maximally consistent and ∃-complete (as defined in Section 11.4) is a Hintikka set. Prove that every Hintikka set is ∃-complete. Prove that some Hintikka sets are not maximally consistent in *PD*.

SELECTED BIBLIOGRAPHY

The following books are suggested for further reading.

INFORMAL LOGIC

Fogelin, Robert J., and Walter Sinnott-Armstrong. *Understanding Arguments,* 6th ed. Belmont, Calif.: Wadsworth/Thomson Learning, 2000.

ELEMENTARY LOGIC

Fraassen, Bas C. van, and Karel Lambert. *Derivation and Counterexample.* Encino, Calif.: Dickenson, 1972.

Jeffrey, Richard C. *Formal Logic: Its Scope and Limits,* 3rd ed. New York: McGraw-Hill, 1991.

Leblanc, Hugues, and William Wisdom. *Deductive Logic,* 3rd ed. Englewood Cliffs, N.J.: Prentice-Hall, 1993.

Quine, W. V. O. *Methods of Logic,* 4th ed. Cambridge, Mass.: Harvard University Press, 1989.

INDUCTIVE LOGIC

Skyrms, Brian. *Choice and Chance,* 4th ed. Belmont, Calif.: Wadsworth/Thomson Learning, 1999.

ADVANCED LOGIC

Hunter, Geoffrey. *Metalogic: An Introduction to the Metatheory of First-Order Logic.* Berkeley: University of California Press, 1971.

Kleene, Stephen Cole. *Introduction to Metamathematics.* New York: American Elsevier, 1971.

Mendelson, Elliot. *Introduction to Mathematical Logic,* 4th ed. Stamford, Conn.: International Thomson Publishing, 1997.

Quine, W. V. O. *Mathematical Logic,* rev. ed. Cambridge, Mass.: Harvard University Press, 1981.

Smullyan, Raymond M. *First-Order Logic.* New York: Dover, 1995.

Smullyan, Raymond M. *Gödel's Incompleteness Theorems.* New York: Oxford University Press, 1992.

ALTERNATIVE LOGICS

Chellas, B. *Modal Logic: An Introduction.* New York: Cambridge University Press, 1980.

Gottwald, Siegfried. *A Treatise on Many-Valued Logics.* Baldock, Hertfordshire, England: Research Studies Press, 2001.

Hughes, G. E., and M. J. Cresswell. *A New Introduction to Modal Logic.* London: Routledge, Chapman & Hall, 1996.

Rescher, N. *Many-Valued Logic.* Brookfield, Vt.: Ashgate, 1993.

HISTORY OF LOGIC

Bochenski, I. M. *A History of Formal Logic.* Translated and edited by Ivo Thomas. New York: Chelsea, 1970.

Kneale, William, and Martha Kneale. *The Development of Logic.* Oxford: Clarendon, 1985.

PHILOSOPHY OF LOGIC

Gabbay, D., and Guenthner, F., eds. *Handbook of Philosophical Logic,* 2nd ed. Dordrecht, Holland: Kluwer Academic, 2002.

Haack, Susan. *Philosophy of Logics.* New York: Cambridge University Press, 1978.

Quine, W. V. O. *The Philosophy of Logic.* Cambridge, Mass.: Harvard University Press, 1986.

INDEX

INDEX OF SYMBOLS